IAN CARR was born in Scotland, brought up in the north
of England and educated at Kings College, Newcastle
upon Tyne. He became a professional musician, playing trumpet, flugel-horn and keyboards, and has made
numerous recordings. He has done regular jazz broadcasts for BBC Radio 3 and has written for the *BBC Music
Magazine* since its inception in 1992. Ian Carr is the
author of *Music Outside* (1973) and *Keith Jarrett, the
Man and his Music* (1991).

By the same author

MUSIC OUTSIDE

KEITH JARRETT
THE MAN AND HIS MUSIC

Miles Davis
The Definitive Biography

IAN CARR

HarperCollins*Publishers*

For Selina

HarperCollins*Publishers*
77–85 Fulham Palace Road,
Hammersmith, London W6 8JB

www.fireandwater.com

This paperback edition 1999
4 6 8 9 7 5 3

First published in Great Britain by Quartet Books Limited, 1982
Revised edition published by HarperCollins Publishers 1998

Copyright © Ian Carr 1998
Discography 1945 to 1982 © Brian Priestley 1982

Ian Carr asserts the moral right to
be identified as the author of this work

ISBN 0 00 6530265

Set in Sabon

Printed and bound in Great Britain by
Clays Ltd, St Ives plc

Contents

Copyright Credits for Musical Examples in Appendix A

Figure 1: 'Godchild' by George Wallington from *The Birth of the Cool*. Published by the American Academy of Music Inc. Reproduced by kind permission of Belwin-Mills Music Limited, 250 Purley Way, Croydon, Surrey.

Figure 2: 'Walkin'' by Richard Carpenter from *Walkin'*. Published by Primebeat Music Company. Reproduced by kind permission of Dominion Music Company Limited, 37–41 Mortimer Street, London W1.

Figure 3: 'Bags' Groove' by Milton Jackson from *Bags' Groove*. Published by George Weiner Music Corporation. Reproduced by kind permission of George Weiner Music Corporation, 6515 Sunset Boulevard, Hollywood, California 90028.

Figure 4: 'My Funny Valentine' by Richard Rodgers from *Cookin'*. Published by Chappell and Co. Inc. Reproduced by kind permission of Chappell Music Limited, 129 Park Street, London W1.

Figure 5a: 'Florence sur les Champs Elysées' by Miles Davis from *Jazztrack*. Published by Editions Continental. Reproduced by kind permission of Mills Music Limited, 250 Purley Way, Croydon, Surrey.

Figure 5b: 'Chez le Photographe du Motel' by Miles Davis from *Jazztrack*. Published by Editions Continental. Reproduced by kind permission of Mills Music Limited, 250 Purley Way, Croydon, Surrey.

Figure 6: 'Sid's Ahead' by Miles Davis from *Milestones*. Published by Jazz Horn Music Corporation © 1978. Reproduced by kind permission of Jazz Horn Music Corporation, c/o Peter S. Shukat, 111 West 57th Street, New York, NY 10019.

Figure 7: 'My Funny Valentine' by Richard Rodgers from *My Funny Valentine*. Published by Chappell and Co. Inc. Reproduced by kind permission of Chappell Music Limited, 129 Park Street, London W1.

Figure 8: 'Country Son' by Miles Davis from *Miles in the Sky*. Published by Jazz Horn Music Corporation © 1978. Reproduced by kind permission of Jazz Horn

Music Corporation, c/o Peter S. Shukat, 111 West 57th Street, New York, NY 10019.

Figure 9: 'Petits Machins' (Little Stuff') by Miles Davis from *Filles de Kiliman-jaro*. Published by Jazz Horn Music Corporation © 1978. Reproduced by kind permission of Jazz Horn Music Corporation, c/o Peter S. Shukat, 111 West 57th Street, New York, NY 10019.

Illustrations

The second great quintet, 1960s (© David Redfern/Redferns)
Miles and Teo Macero, 1969 (Courtesy of Sony Jazz)
The Berlin Festival, 1969 (Valerie Wilmer)
Miles with Clive Davis (Courtesy of Sony Jazz)
Keith Jarrett and Miles Davis, 1970 (Photo © G. Crane/Jazz Index)
Miles in the early 1970s (Courtesy of Sony Jazz, photo: Don Hunstein)
A selection of album covers (Courtesy of Sony Jazz).

Between pages 516 and 517
Miles in 1974 (Courtesy of Sony Jazz)
Dave Liebman, c. 1975 (© J. Kilby/Jazz Index)
Miles with Marcus Miller, 1982 (© Christian Him/Jazz Index)
Bill Evans (Photo © Allan Titmuss)
Miles Davis with John Scofield, 1985 (Photo © Allan Titmuss)
Miles Davis with Bob Berg, 1986 (Photo © Allan Titmuss)
Miles Davis with Kenny Garrett, 1989 (Photo © Allan Titmuss)
Miles Davis and Herbie Hancock, 10 July 1991 (© Dany Gignoux/Redferns)
Miles Davis with Foley McCreary, 19 July 1991 (Photo © Allan Titmuss)
Miles at the Royal Festival Hall, 19 July 1991 (Photo © Allan Titmuss)

Acknowledgements

I am grateful to the following musicians for talking to me at length: Gil Coggins, Clark Terry, Dave Holland, Herbie Hancock, Jimmy Cobb, Teo Macero, Jimmy Garrison, Red Rodney, Horace Silver, Derek Wadsworth, Harry Klein, Vic Ash, Sonny and Linda Sharrock.

I am also grateful to Gil and Anita Evans for an evening I spent in their company in New York, 1975. Special thanks to Brian Priestley for compiling the discography, and for reading through and checking my previous manuscript, but I take full responsibility for any errors.

For various help and encouragement, I'm grateful to the following people: Ray Coleman – editor-in-chief of *Melody Maker*, Trevor Timmers, Charles Fox, George Foster, Valerie Wilmer, David Apps, Alun Morgan, Tony Hall, Peter Philbin of CBS New York, Hugh Attwooll, Simon Frodsham, Jonathan Morrish and Terry Lott of CBS London, Barbara Carr and Mary Lou of ABC Records, Arthur Levy and Stanley Meises of Atlantic Records, David Marsh and Chet Flippo of *Rolling Stone* magazine, Nik Cohn, Stanley Dance, Max Jones, John Chilton, Keith Winter and Jeff Pressing of La Trobe University, Australia, Vera Brandes, Frank Modica, Don Friedman, Tony Middleton of Dobell's Jazz Record Shop, London, Keith Goodwin, Michael Rusenberg.

I am also grateful for the insights of several critics, in particular: Leonard Feather, Nat Hentoff, Ralph J. Gleason, Max Harrison, Martin Williams, Michael James, LeRoi Jones, Richard Williams and Gary Giddins.

I am grateful to BBC Radio 3 producer, Derek Drescher, who

asked me to make a radio documentary about Miles Davis and eight subsequent programmes about his music. The research for these projects greatly assisted the update of this biography.

I am grateful to Keith Jarrett, Dave Holland, Dave Liebman, Joe Zawinul and Paul Buckmaster, all of whom were interviewed for the first edition but agreed to be interviewed again, and gave fresh information and further insights. I am grateful for new and invaluable interviews with John McLaughlin, Ron Carter, George Russell, George Avakian, Jan Garbarek, John Carisi, John Scofield, Jack and Lydia DeJohnette (separately), Bob Berg and saxophonist Bill Evans.

Larry Coryell spoke to me on the telephone and then faxed some crucial information. I faxed a series of questions to Palle Mikkelborg and he spoke the answers on tape for me. Tom Callaghan in London and George Cole in Peterborough, two erudite Miles Davis enthusiasts, gave an ongoing help, sending me facts, articles, information and cassettes of rare or not easily obtainable live concerts. Jan Lohmann's magnificently comprehensive Miles Davis discography helped with the chronology of events and the personnel involved, and Jan himself was a crucial source of information on many occasions.

Many other people gave me invaluable support and/or assistance, including Miles's ex-manager Gordon Meltzer, and Peter Shukat, the lawyer for the Miles Davis estate. Other helpers included Adam Sief and Sharon Kelly of Sony Music, London, John Cumming and John Elson of Serious/Speakout, Lew Soloff, Anita Evans, John Latimer Smith, John Hiseman, Mike Dibb, John L. Walters, John and Dorothy Smallwood, Clive Davis of the London *Times*, John and Maxi Marshall, Tony Remy, Chris Parker, Guy Barker, Peter Bould, Max Roach, Volker and Ev Kriegel, Eberhard Weber, Alun Morgan, Gerald Ogilvie-Laing, Kenny Wheeler, Ack Van Rooyen, Charles Alexander, Jim Delaney at PC Workshops, Kingston on Thames, Pawel Brodowski of Jazz Forum, Jan Newey of *Top* Magazine and Ray's Jazz Shop.

ONE

Miles Dewey Davis III

'I just got on to the trumpet and studied and played.'[1]
Miles Davis

Miles Davis was born in Alton, Illinois, on 26 May 1926, and a year later his family moved south to East St Louis, a small town on the east side of the Mississippi River. There was an older sister, Dorothy, born in 1924, and in 1929 his brother Vernon was born. The family was middle-class and prosperous, having established itself in just two generations since Lincoln and Congress abolished slavery in America. The men of the family were proud, intelligent and self-willed, and the name 'Miles' was passed on to the first-born son of successive generations.

In the days of slavery the Davis family had been musicians and had performed classical string music for the plantation owners. But after Emancipation this musical tradition was broken. For several decades there were only two courses open to Negro musicians: either to be an entertainer for white folks, or to play in clip-joints, brothels or bars. Neither alternative was acceptable to the aristocratic Davis men. Miles's father (Miles II) wanted to be a musician himself but was emphatically dissuaded:

My father, Miles I, was born six years after the Emancipation (i.e., in 1869) and forbade me to play music because the only place a Negro could play then was in barrel-houses. My father was the most efficient double entry column book-keeper in Arkansas before the coming of the adding machine and white

1

men came to his home under cover of night for him to fix their books.[2]

It was no illegal 'fixing', but at that time no white man wanted it known that his accounts were being done by a black book-keeper. Miles I was eventually able to buy a thousand acres of land in Arkansas and send his son, Miles II (born 1902), to North-western College to study dentistry. Miles II worked hard and when the family moved to East St Louis he had a thriving practice and became a substantial landowner, buying a 200-acre ranch on which he raised pedigree hogs and kept horses. This enabled his son, Miles III, to grow up in the open country and to enjoy the pursuits of riding, hunting and fishing. According to his father, he liked long country walks and was an excellent horseman – 'if he was ever thrown he'd remount immediately and master his mount'.[3]

The young Miles had the ingredients for a secure and happy boyhood: caring parents, a father with professional status, wealth and property, and a mother, Cleota Henry Davis (born 1900, also in Arkansas) who was dignified and beautiful. However, this meant little if you were black and lived in a city as racist as East St Louis. The Davis family moved into an all-white neighbourhood – a bold and provocative gesture typical of them. But although East St Louis was in the officially Midwest state of Illinois, it was in *southern* Illinois and racism was still prevalent (many blacks had been murdered there in the infamous and bloody riots of 1917). One of Miles's earliest memories is of being chased down a street by a white man shouting, 'Nigger! Nigger!' Miles, a sensitive boy, never forgot it. However, it was instilled into him that the Davises were special people, and he also found particular inspiration in his paternal uncle Ferdinand, who had attended Harvard University and was well-travelled, stylish, intellectual, a ladies' man, editor of a magazine called *Color*, and an authority on black history.

In physique, Miles Davis took after his father, having the same slight, though wiry, frame. He inherited his mother's good looks

– the large, luminous eyes, the straight, finely chiselled nose, and the delicate jawline – and he also felt that his artistic talent, sense of style and love of clothes came from her. His early relationship with her was deeply affected by the racial and social situation. As the wife of a dental surgeon, Miles's mother was aware that her family had an important place in local society, and she strove to uphold that position. After Emancipation, it was the professional men and ministers of the church who were the heads of the new black society, and they were at pains to get rid of any customs, habits or mannerisms that were too 'negroid' or which harked back to slavery. It often happened that leading black citizens became the most fanatical imitators of white society.

The music in the Davis household was limited to the genteel Western variety. Miles's older sister, Dorothy, played the piano, and he used to peep through the door and watch when she had her piano lessons. His mother played the violin and wanted Miles to take it up. But another side of her musical ability, which she did not reveal to Miles for many years, was always suppressed: she could play the piano and knew the blues. In 1958 he said, 'I didn't know until after I'd gone back there for a visit a few years ago, that my mother ever knew one note of the piano. But she sat down one day and played some funky blues. Turned out that my grandmother used to teach organ.'[4] So complete was the censorship that even the knowledge of his grandmother's musical proclivities had been kept secret. But his mother did at least buy him two records by Art Tatum and Duke Ellington, and also unwittingly assisted his musical development by frequently putting Miles, Vernon and Dorothy on the train to stay with their grandparents in Arkansas, which had been one of the slave states and was saturated with black music: blues, gospel and worksong, sung by men or women, accompanied by funky guitars. Miles experienced this from the age of six or seven, walking at night on country roads with his uncles and cousins, and also at Saturday-night church services, and the potent music left an indelible impression on him.

In East St Louis, as befitted their social position, the Davis family went to church, but Miles was already showing signs of that sharp intelligence and individualism which were to illuminate and shape his adult life. He had already begun asking awkward questions and expecting honest answers: 'I went to church when I was very young, but when I was about six, I asked my mother why the church kept calling me a sinner when I hadn't done anything wrong. When I didn't get a good answer, I stopped going to church.'[5] Miles's mother was also active in community life. Later on, she was to work with such organizations as the Urban League, the aims of which were: 'To eliminate racial segregation and discrimination in the US, and to help black citizens and other economically and socially disadvantaged groups to share equally in every aspect of American life.'

Although intensely conscious of his social position, Miles's father did not attempt to blot out the past with the same fanaticism as his wife, nor did he try to ape all the customs of white society; he was proud of his own father and reminisced about his forebears. He also instilled into Miles junior the necessity for self-sufficiency, insisting there was no excuse for being poor. As a result, Miles was, from an early age, money-conscious and frugal. By the time he was ten he was doing a paper round. 'I got a paper route and it got bigger than I could handle because my customers liked me so much. I just delivered papers the best I could, and minded my business . . . I saved most of what I made except for buying records.'[6]

From the age of seven or eight, Miles had also been listening regularly to a radio show called 'Harlem Rhythms' which featured great black musicians including Louis Armstrong, Count Basie, Bessie Smith and Duke Ellington, but also included a few leading white musicians like Bobby Hackett and Harry James. Then when he was nine or ten, his father's best friend, a medical doctor called Eubank, gave Miles his first trumpet and he had some private music lessons. But by the time he'd reached his teens, Miles had become aware that his mother and father were not getting along well. (They would eventually divorce.) One confrontation occurred on Miles's thirteenth birthday. His mother wanted to give him a violin as a birthday present but, Miles recalled with irony: 'My father gave me a (new) trumpet – because he loved my mother so much!'[7] The choice represented two cultural polarities: the violin was representative of Western 'serious' music, and the trumpet (after Buddy Bolden, King Oliver, Louis Armstrong and Roy Eldridge) had come to symbolize the essence of jazz – a music with non-Western roots. Miles's mother deeply resented this choice. Furthermore, his father had not only chosen the new instrument, he'd also already chosen the teacher. Elwood Buchanan, a patient of Miles senior, worked for the local education authority as a peripatetic teacher and was an excellent trumpeter. Miles had started playing the trumpet at grade school, and from Buchanan, as well as technical lessons, he learned something of the romantic myths and folklore of jazz: 'He used to tell us all about jam sessions on the Showboat, about trumpet players like Bobby Hackett and Hal Baker.'[8]

From the start, Miles began to find out things for himself. To achieve breath control, good intonation and a clear sound, it is essential for trumpet players to practise holding long notes, and when Miles first began lessons at school, once a week the class would hold long notes. There was a certain spirit of competition in this activity:

Everybody would fight to play best. Lucky for me, I learned to play the chromatic scale right away. A friend of my father's brought me a book one night and showed me how to do it so I wouldn't have to sit there and hold that note all the time ... The next day in school I was the belle of the ball![9]

When Miles went to high school, he received daily lessons from Buchanan, and also joined the school band. The teacher gave him some advice which profoundly influenced Miles's whole approach to the trumpet. He was told not to play with vibrato: 'Buchanan didn't believe in it. He said that all the white guys used it, and the best guys were the black guys who played straight sounds.'[10] He also warned Miles: 'You're gonna get old anyway and start shaking.' From that time on, the young Miles tried to play 'fast and light and no vibrato'.[11]

The high school was racially mixed, but Miles had no real friends among the white pupils. He made rapid progress on the trumpet, but came up against racial prejudice. According to his father:

> In school competitions he was always the best, but the blue-eyed boys always won first and second prizes. Miles had always to settle for third. The officials, Miles and everybody else knew he should have had first prize. You can't treat a kid like that and tell him to come out and say the water wasn't dirty.[12]

The injustice made a deep impression on Miles. Years later, he recalled: 'It made me so mad I made up my mind to outdo anybody white on my horn. If I hadn't met that prejudice, I probably wouldn't have had as much drive in my work.'[13]

The high school band rehearsed twice a week and tried to sound like Count Basie, and soon Miles was also playing at weekends with drums, piano and an alto saxophonist who 'sounded like Guy Lombardo's first alto'. He was rising steeply in the estimation of his teacher, Buchanan, who talked of him in glowing terms. The teacher was a drinking companion of trumpeter Clark Terry, who was six years older than Miles and who lived across the river in St Louis. According to Terry, Buchanan was tremendously proud of Miles and used to say: 'Man, I gotta little cat over there! You gotta come and hear him! He's playing his ass off!' He enthused so much that eventually Terry went over to hear Miles play and was deeply impressed. If Clark Terry appreciated Miles's playing, Miles had an even greater respect for the older man, and said of Terry: 'I started to play like him. I idolized him'.[14]

Shortly after this, Miles met up with his hero again, but was rebuffed. Terry was playing with a band which was hired by the Parks Commission to play at an outdoor athletic and band competition between various Illinois high schools. Miles was competing with the East St Louis high school band and tried to chat to Clark Terry, who was busy eyeing up the numerous pretty girls. Terry recalls: 'So this kid comes up to me ... and I said, "Why don't you get lost – stop bugging me! I want to look at these girls." So it turns out it was Miles and I'd forgotten.'

Some time later, when Miles was only sixteen and still at high school, he joined the musicians' union. This enabled him to work professionally, playing little engagements at social clubs, church halls and other occasional functions in the St Louis area. It was while he was working at the Elks Club, a place where all musicians used to go for after-hours jam sessions, that Miles finally became friends with Clark Terry. The latter dropped by to do some after-hours blowing, and on his way upstairs heard a trumpet player he couldn't identify, though he 'knew every horn in town'. The club was on the third floor, and Terry ran all the way upstairs:

> And I see this little cat sitting there with his legs crossed and he's smoking his ass off. So I walk up to him and I say, 'Hey man, aren't you the guy ... ?' and he says, 'Yeah, I'm the kid you fluffed off down in Carbondale!' We always had a big laugh about it afterwards.

After this, the two became firm friends, and Terry became a kind of father figure for the young Miles. Talking of his influences, Miles says:

> The main one must have been Terry. My teacher [Buchanan] played like him ... he [Terry] and I used to go out to jam and the place would be crowded in ten minutes. He'd come over to my house and ask my father could I go, you know, and he'd take me to a session. Man! We'd play from six o'clock to six the next morning.[15]

With Clark Terry as his chaperon and mentor, Miles could rapidly broaden and deepen his experience of the musical activity in the St Louis area. St Louis is the chief city and river port of the state of Missouri and acts as a gateway between South and North. Earlier in the century, it had been a centre for ragtime, and the city was a natural stopping-off point for musicians travelling downstream from Kansas City or Chicago, or upriver from New Orleans. Jam sessions by visiting and local musicians were a prominent feature of musical life around St Louis during the 1930s and 1940s. Miles recalls:

> We always played the blues in St Louis. Bands came up on the boats from New Orleans, guys came from Kansas City and Oklahoma City, all playing the blues ... When I was a kid I was fascinated by the musicians, particularly guys who used to come up from New Orleans and jam all night ... you listened to everybody and took the parts you liked. You watched how they hold the horn, how they walk ... I mean if you're fifteen![16]

Miles could hardly have had a better model than Clark Terry. Terry came from a large, poor, ghetto family and, like the other great contemporary trumpeter, Dizzy Gillespie, whose family were similarly under-privileged, he heard his first music in church. Clark Terry insisted that his superb sense of time and feeling for rhythm have their roots in this initial experience:

> The very first thing I heard in the form of pulsating beats was at the Sanctified Church on the corner. They all played tambourines and there was a certain beat that was instilled in you right from a kid. Even the kids who weren't interested in the religious calling, they would congregate on the outside and dance with tremendous respect for this rhythm ... great rapport with the rhythm. It was just around you; you couldn't miss it, y'know, and I get mad at myself even today if I ever miss a beat.

It is unlikely that Miles's early church-going in East St Louis included such unself-conscious and enjoyable rhythmic and musical experiences. His family were at the opposite end of the social scale from the Terry family, and it is almost certain that the more vital African elements were expunged from the music of their middle-class church.

The older jazz musicians tended to be secretive about their knowledge, because they feared that the rising young players would be competitors for their jobs. Miles Davis was doubly lucky because his family were able to afford an instrument and lessons, and because the newly established trumpeters such as Terry and (later) Dizzy Gillespie were generous with their help and encouragement – most probably as a direct result of their own struggle to learn.

The approach to trumpet playing and the style that emerged in that area is so individual that it is known as 'The St Louis Sound'. Its main characteristics are a beautifully clear, round and singing brass sound that really projects and hangs on the air, and an epigrammatic and witty melodic flair. In the early 1940s the most famous exponent was probably Harold (Shorty) Baker, who had played with Don Redman, Duke Ellington and Teddy Wilson, and was with Andy Kirk from 1941 to 1942. Baker was one of Buchanan's favourites, but the whole area was full of other unsung trumpeters who had these same qualities highly developed. Clark Terry says:

Just as Miles was inspired by me, I was definitely inspired by trumpet players who were older than I . . . Levi Maddison was reputedly the most beautiful sound in the area. He went completely stone crazy, but you'd go to his home, those of us who knew him, and he'd just laugh all the time. All he did was laugh, and then we'd say, 'Play something', and he'd take out his horn and play in his room and it was just like the angels singing. It was just a pure sound with all the jazz flavourings and colorations you know.

Levi Maddison used a Heim mouthpiece recommended by a trumpet teacher called Gustav, who played first trumpet with the

St Louis Symphony Orchestra. Clark Terry could not afford to have lessons from Gustav, but he used to get second-hand lessons from musicians who did study with him. Gustav prescribed the Heim mouthpiece for all his students, and many trumpeters in the area used it – including Terry himself, and Shorty Baker. Miles Davis, who also had lessons with Gustav, began using a Heim mouthpiece at that time and continued playing one throughout his career. Terry believes that this mouthpiece was at least partly responsible for the trumpet sound prominent in the St Louis area. It was made of very thin metal, with a flat rim and a deep cup. A mouthpiece with such a deep cup tends to help in the production of a full sound, but also makes it more difficult to play high notes. This may have been one of the reasons why Miles, in his early life, had difficulty with the upper register of the instrument, but his perseverance with the Heim mouthpiece was to result in perhaps the most burnished and singing trumpet sound in jazz.

By the time he was sixteen, Miles was getting the best of both worlds: regular trumpet lessons from Elwood Buchanan and/or Gustav, plus a wide experience of the thriving musical life in St Louis. He was doubly fortunate in that he was learning to read music and to improvise at the same time. The possibility of a choice of career still lay open to him: so far as his family were concerned, he might yet be eligible for symphonic work, but at the same time he was preparing himself for small-group or big-band jazz playing. He was developing at a time when the romantic idea (mostly held by whites) of the non-reading, improvising genius was dying, while the practical idea that it was really essential to be able to read music was taking a firm hold among black musicians. Before this, many black players hadn't bothered to learn to read music simply because they believed there was no point in it: they'd never get a job with a symphony orchestra or any similar organization. Such jobs were the exclusive domain of whites, and the only outlets for blacks were in either entertainment or sport – or in jazz, which has always been a kind of fusion of aesthetics and athletics. Clark Terry was typical in that he was not only deeply involved in jazz, but was also an excellent boxer, and a close friend of Archie Moore, another St Louis man and one of the greatest fighters of all time. Miles shared this interest in boxing and was to do so all his life. As an adolescent, he listened on the radio to commentaries on all Joe Louis's fights and of course, during the 1930s and 1940s, Louis was the black community's greatest hero, as important in that role then as Martin Luther King would be in the 1960s.

When he was sixteen, Miles also met his first real girlfriend, Irene Birth, who went to the same school, Lincoln High, but was three years older and two grades ahead of him. She came from a much less privileged family, but Miles knew and liked them all. When Irene's six-year-old brother, William, died suddenly of pneumonia, the tragedy brought her and Miles much closer together. The relationship was emotionally and sexually very important for him and, though they never married, it was to continue into the 1950s and produce three children.

On 7 December 1941, the Japanese destroyed most of the American fleet at Pearl Harbor. The following day Congress declared war on Japan and, three days later, Germany and Italy declared war on the USA. America had entered the Second World War. In 1942, most jazz musicians who were the right age, including Clark Terry, were called up into the forces. Miles Davis was still at school, and at sixteen too young for military service, so he became a larger fish in a smaller pool. His reputation began to grow rapidly among local musicians, and visiting musicians began to make a point of going to listen to him. The most famous local band, Eddie Randle's Blue Devils, was also called the Rhumboogie Orchestra because it had a residency at the Rhumboogie Club in East St Louis. It was a ten-or twelve-piece outfit playing hot dance music and using arrangements from the bands of Benny Goodman, Lionel Hampton and Duke Ellington, among others. Randle himself was one of the excellent St Louis trumpeters and his band had a high reputation among musicians. In late 1939, the great bassist Jimmy Blanton was sitting in with the Blue Devils when Duke Ellington heard him and hired him immediately. Elwood Buchanan, who had enthused to Clark Terry about Miles, also recommended his young protégé to Eddie Randle. This must have eased the way for Miles when he was seventeen and Irene Birth dared him to telephone Randle and ask for a job with the Blue Devils. He did so, was auditioned and got the job, staying with the band for a year from June 1943 to June 1944.

The young pianist Gil Coggins, who was to record with Miles a decade later, first heard the trumpeter in St Louis in 1943. Coggins was drafted into the army and posted to the area. He recalled:

> There was . . . a big club with big bands and a bowling alley . . . In the same building was a cocktail bar, and Miles was playing there with a piano player called St Claire Brooks. He was called Duke Brooks because he knew all Dukes's [Ellington] tunes, and there was a drummer . . . I used to go absent without leave sometimes just to listen to Miles . . . It was just a trio – no bass. They were playing Duke Ellington tunes and stuff like that . . . kind of swing music . . . So I used to go AWOL to listen to Miles. And then there was another club where he was playing with a band . . . about a ten-piece band.

This would have been Eddie Randle's Blue Devils at the Rhum-boogie.

Emmanuel 'Duke' St Claire Brooks was one of the first local musicians of whom Miles had become aware. In the late 1930s, Brooks used to play with the bass player Jimmy Blanton in a place called the Red Inn, which was across the street from Miles senior's dental surgery. Miles used to go there to hear Brooks and Blanton, both of whom were associates of Clark Terry. Like many of the musicians in St Louis, Duke Brooks had a daytime job and did his playing in the evenings and at weekends. According to Gil Coggins, Brooks was a 'natural', and Miles learned a great deal from him. Miles confirms this: 'Duke couldn't read or write any music. We used to have a trio together in St Louis. We played like the Benny Goodman Sextet. He was always showing me things

Charlie Christian played. He made a record with Red Callender, and then he died.'[17] Like all other aspiring musicians, Duke Brooks wanted to get to New York – the Big Apple – to show off his talents and try his luck. Like most other young musicians, he also had very little money and so had to hitch-hike. It was while stealing a ride in a train wagon carrying sand and gravel that he died – it buried him and he suffocated.

While the Eddie Randle band was playing for the floor shows at the Rhumboogie Club in St Louis, saxophonist Sonny Stitt came into town on tour with Tiny Bradshaw's band. After listening to Miles play, Stitt said: 'You look like a man named Charlie Parker, and you play like him too. C'mon with us.' Stitt was serious and persuaded Bradshaw to offer Miles a job. It was an exciting moment for the young trumpeter:

> The fellows in his band had their hair slicked down, they wore tuxedos, and they offered me sixty whole dollars a week to play with them. I went home and asked my mother if I could go with them. She said no, I had to finish my last year of high school. I didn't talk to her for two weeks. And I didn't go with the band either.[18]

Silent reproaches seem to have been common between Miles and his mother, and the undercurrents of unspoken feeling in the Davis household must have played a large part in creating his exceptional awareness and sensitivity to atmosphere. The growing disharmony of his parents was, no doubt, a strong contributing factor.

Miles and his family often found themselves in conflict. Although he was still a minor and a schoolboy, he was financially fairly independent, earning around $85 a week from music. The $60 offer from Tiny Bradshaw would have meant a drop in earnings but an elevation in musical status. Miles's emphasis of the salary he was offered – sixty whole dollars a week' – was thus probably ironic. He had to accept the authority of his parents, and yet had also to be involved in the break-up of their marriage and even to make some financial contribution to family concerns.

Recalling this period, he said: 'I was already making $85 a week when I was fifteen. My parents got a divorce when I was young and I helped my sister through college.'[19]

Miles was intellectually precocious and had an almost photographic memory:

> I taught my sister mathematics. See, if I had a book, I could look at it and remember the whole page. It came to me like that. I can remember anything – telephone numbers, addresses . . . I can just glance at them and remember. That's the reason I used to take care of band payrolls: I could remember all the tabs and shit.[20]

This ability, too, resulted in another paradox: although he was usually the youngest member of the groups with which he worked, he was often the guiding light, the director and the organizer. He was becoming extremely independent and self-sufficient, yet in one sense at least, he was still tied to his mother's apron strings: 'They used to come scouting for me [bandleaders such as Bradshaw, Earl Hines, Jimmie Lunceford], but I couldn't go with them because I was too young and my mother was having a fit.'[21] Yet, although Miles was still subject to parental authority and could be prevented from going off with travelling bands, in January 1944 he graduated from Lincoln High School and later that year, he and Irene had their first child, a daughter, Cheryl.

Meanwhile, Miles's musical awareness was expanding. Any good musician, white or black, was grist to his mill. He had a great admiration for Buddy Rich, the swing and big-band drummer. A local East St Louis drummer called Larry Jackson, who played with Miles, has said that the trumpeter was always telling him to 'play like Buddy'[22] and that Miles always wanted any drummer to play like Rich. Miles also loved Duke Ellington's work and respected Count Basie, and was very much aware of Benny Goodman's small-group work. He was versed in rhythm and blues, too, and at the same time he'd had regular lessons in 'legitimate' trumpet playing. By now, he'd also heard Charlie Parker's early recordings with Jay McShann, and he'd heard a little of Dizzy Gillespie on record. Parker and Gillespie were just beginning to spearhead the revolutionary music, bebop, but Miles has always insisted that parallel developments were going on simultaneously in the Midwest, and that Charlie Christian, the guitarist with the Benny Goodman Sextet, was the main influence in this area:

> I think bop branched off from Charlie Christian. There was a trumpet player named Buddy Anderson from Kansas City. He was with Billy Eckstine, and he used to play like Charlie ... There was another boy who played with us who played Kansas City blues and that kind of thing ... and he sounded like Charlie Parker. His name was Charlie Young. We all used to work together.[23]

As Miles's involvement with jazz grew, so the pressures to leave East St Louis became more intense. New York had emerged during the 1930s as the most important music centre in America, and however good a musician might seem in a provincial city, he could never feel that he had explored the ultimate reaches of his ability unless he had gone to New York and 'made the scene' there. Gil Coggins emphasized these different standards: 'Miles was very experienced before he hit New York ... not in the New York way, of course, but so far as playing with bands was concerned.'

During his last two years at high school, Miles had to turn down other offers to leave home and join bands. Among others, he was offered jobs by Illinois Jacquet, and by A. J. Suliman, the trumpet-playing manager of McKinney's Cotton Pickers. But even after he'd graduated from high school in 1944, pressure was still on Miles to take up formal studies. However, at the beginning of the summer vacation he took a job with a small band from New Orleans called Adam Lambert's Six Brown Cats. It had just finished a residency at the Club Silhouette in Chicago, and was booked for a date at the Club Belvedere in Springfield, Illinois. The band was looking for a replacement for their trumpet player, Thomas Jefferson, who had returned to New Orleans. Miles got the job and received $100 a week – for two weeks, the length of the residency. Although brief, this was a good start for Miles: his was the only horn in the band, which was a modern swing outfit.

Back at home, Miles heard that the Billy Eckstine Band was scheduled to play at the Club Riviera in St Louis. Charlie Parker and Dizzy Gillespie, the two most talked-about musicians in jazz at the time, were with Eckstine, and Miles went along to hear them. He'd just been to a rehearsal with a local group and, with his trumpet under his arm, he was the first person in the hall. For him, every young musician's dream came true: he was asked to sit in with the band.

> This guy runs up to me and says, 'Kid, do you have a union card?' It was Dizzy. I didn't even know him. I said, 'Sure.' 'We need a trumpet player. Come on.' I wanted to hear him; I could always read, so I got on the bandstand and started playing. I couldn't read a thing from listening to Diz and Bird.[24]

Not for the first time, nor for the last time in his life, Miles was exactly the right man in exactly the right place at the right time.

In fact, he was taking the place of the third trumpet, his old friend Buddy Anderson, who had become ill with tuberculosis. Anderson never played trumpet again, and Miles filled in for him around the St Louis area for about two weeks. The band's music was already known to Miles and he recalled: 'I loved the music so much, I knew the third trumpet part by heart.'[25] But the band-leader, Billy Eckstine, remembers the experience differently: 'When I first heard Miles, I let him sit in so as not to hurt his feelings, but he sounded terrible; he couldn't play at all.'[26] In the Eckstine context, with his two idols, Parker and Gillespie, in the band, Miles may well have been overawed. In such a situation, for a young player accidentally falling into the big time, two weeks is not long enough to breed confidence. The probability is that he played the written parts reasonably well, but didn't shine if, and when, he got any solos.

When the Eckstine band left St Louis to go to Chicago for a date at the Regal Theatre there, Miles had to stay behind because his parents were still anxious for him to take up some formal studies. His experience with the band, however, had made his mind up: he knew that he had to go to New York. It is also possible that Bird had mentioned to Miles that he, Parker, intended to leave the band when it got back to New York in order to concentrate on small-group playing. Miles's taste of the big time and the new concepts of Parker and Gillespie had whetted his appetite, and he was finding St Louis stultifying and frustrating. He had learned all he could from the music scene there, and even the book he had been studying so assiduously – *Georgia Gibbs Chord Analysis* – seemed inadequate and sterile in the light of the fresh musical language Bird and Diz were creating. Miles had experienced something which, years later, Gil Evans was to put into words: 'Every form, even though it becomes traditional and finally becomes academic, originally came from someone's spirit who created the form. Then it was picked up and taught in schools after that. But all form originated from spirit.'[27] In Parker and Gillespie, Miles had found that spirit, and he knew that no schools could give him the knowledge and the experience he wanted. He would have to go to the source. Music was in the melting pot, and the crucible was New York.

TWO

Bird Land

'I spent my first week in New York and my first
month's allowance looking for Charlie Parker.'[1]

Miles Davis

Miles's mother wanted him to go to Fisk University, which had a
very good music department, but he managed to get his father's
permission to enrol at the Juilliard School of Music in New York.
His father paid his tuition fees and gave him an allowance. From
the moment he arrived in New York in September 1944, Miles
Davis found himself living a 'Jekyll and Hyde' existence. Officially,
he was enrolled at Juilliard, an institution that taught established
Western musical forms and techniques. But his unofficial interests
– his real reason for being in the city – lay in the dives and seedy
clubs of 52nd Street, where the revolutionary music, bebop, was
being created. He thus had access to two very different worlds: at
Juilliard he was a protected student with a private income of fifty
dollars a week from his family; on 52nd Street, he was merely
another competitor in the disreputable and *laissez-faire* world of
jazz – a music with no real status. His attempts to reconcile these
two musical worlds were to become a dominant theme in his life
and music. He had arrived in New York in the middle of perhaps
the most turbulent decade in the history of American music, when
jazz itself was undergoing a radical transformation.

Jazz is often described as music that reconciles and blends two
musical traditions – the non-Western (African) and the Western
(European) – but this is a distortion of the truth. From its earliest

beginnings, jazz has been dominated by the constant conflict of both traditions and by compromises that are precarious and finally disintegrate. Broadly speaking, in each of its phases the music has been created by black musicians and then taken up by whites and the music industry and turned into 'easy-listening' music. During the uneasy international peace of the 1930s, the jazz impulse had been diluted in big-band swing, culminating in the polished sterility of Glenn Miller. With World War II came a renewed interest in the blues, a growing racial pride (America needed black support for the war effort), and a resurgence of the virtuoso improviser. All these factors, plus the discoveries and experiments of some remarkable musicians, resulted in the creation of a new music: bebop. There were tendencies in this musical direction in many cities throughout the United States – particularly in St Louis and Kansas City – but in the vanguard of the movement was a handful of musicians centred in New York. In the early 1940s, at a club called Minton's Playhouse in Harlem, new ideas were pioneered by the pianist Thelonious Monk, drummer Kenny Clarke, and trumpeter Dizzy Gillespie. And in 1944, the new music hit 52nd Street when first Dizzy and later Charlie Parker began working there with small groups.

In bebop, several non-Western concepts of music were brilliantly reasserted. Its most striking characteristic is an intense, polyrhythmic drive to which even the melodies are subservient. In other words, the dynamic rhythms of the melodies are organically and intricately interwoven with the pulse and multiple accents of the rhythm section, which is typical of an African way of making music. In fast performances, the written or improvised melodies, with their streams of notes, wide interval leaps, displaced accents, and asymmetrical phrases, present a rhythmic vitality so foreign to American listeners that it drew frightened and hostile comments from all sides. Even established musicians – no doubt because they felt threatened – attacked it. But it is interesting to note that, with the exception of Louis Armstrong, who called it 'this modern malice', the most gifted members of the jazz establishment, such as Duke Ellington, Count Basie, Coleman Hawkins and some others, never derided the new music or its practitioners, but instead welcomed and encouraged them. As well as revitalizing melody and re-establishing polyrhythms, bebop also offered a contemporary restatement of the basic blues impulse. At all tempos – fast, medium and slow – the blues, with its tonal expressiveness, its deeply personal statements and its roots in the history of black America, was once more made central to jazz. On 52nd Street, every night of the week it was possible to hear the new music that was splitting musicians and public into two factions: the 'hip' people who understood it (or at least claimed to), and the 'squares' who reviled and abused it.

This was the explosive musical climate Miles Davis found when he arrived in New York and spent his first week and his first month's allowance looking for Charlie Parker, initially without success. After some time, he read that Parker would be appearing at a jam session at a club in Harlem called the Heatwave. Miles turned up at the session and renewed the friendship. Typically, and no doubt to Miles's great joy, Parker 'didn't have a place to stay at the time', so he moved in with Davis, who had a room in a house at 147th Street and Broadway. When Irene and baby Cheryl arrived in December 1944, Miles found Parker another room in the house.

Miles was extremely fortunate in being able to spend his most formative period in the close company of the fountainhead of the new music, and he flung himself into a regime of study that was both exhausting and schizophrenic. By day, he would be at Juilliard, and at night hanging around Minton's Playhouse or the clubs on 52nd Street. Parker gave him a great deal of encouragement: ' "Don't be afraid," he used to tell me, "go ahead and play." Every night on matchbox covers I'd write down those chords I heard. Everybody helped me. Next day I'd play those chords all day in the practice room at Juilliard, instead of going to classes.'[2] Other key musicians helped him too. Parker introduced him to Thelonious Monk, who wrote out chords for him, as did the pianist Tadd Dameron, who had been with Billy Eckstine as an arranger when Miles had played with the band in St Louis. Dizzy

Gillespie advised Miles to study piano and use the keyboard for working out melodic shapes.

Miles was in perfect condition for learning fast. He was in control of himself – neither smoking nor drinking – and he knew exactly which people could help him most. He had a very high regard for his mentors, but the mild-mannered and industrious young trumpeter was also beginning to develop a healthy self-respect. Coming from the Midwest, he expected to be upstaged and outclassed by every musician in New York: 'When I got to New York, I thought everybody knew as much as I did, and I was surprised. Wasn't nobody playing but Dizzy and Roy [Eldridge] and Joe [Guy] – long-haired Joe. The guys who were playing, you didn't even know or hear of.'[3]

At Juilliard, he attended classes to find out if there was anything worth learning there. As far as general theory was concerned, he felt they had nothing to teach him: 'All that shit I had already learned in St Louis.'[4] He also found the pace of lessons too slow: 'I did all the homework for summer school in one day.' But he did follow Dizzy Gillespie's advice and take some piano lessons at Juilliard. He also took trumpet lessons from symphonic players, which meant that even as he steeped himself in the new jazz, he was still subject to strong Western instrumental concepts. But in 1945 Miles found another trumpet player who was to have a powerful influence: Freddie Webster. He frequently showed up at the sessions at Minton's in Harlem, and he had all the qualities of the St Louis school of trumpeters – the big, singing sound and the marmoreally sculpted phrases. He did not play a lot of notes, nor did he play at very fast tempos; he was at his best on medium-tempo pieces and on ballads. Given these qualities, it is not surprising that Miles and he became very close, and that Webster had a lasting influence on Davis. Miles says of him:

> I used to love what he did to a note. He didn't play a lot of notes; he didn't waste any. I used to try to get his sound. He had a great big tone, like Billy Butterfield, but without vibrato. Freddie was my best friend. I wanted to play like him.

I used to teach him chords, whatever I learned at Juilliard. He didn't have any money to go. And in return, I'd try to get his tone.[5]

Over one point Miles's memory may have been playing him tricks: Webster played with a fairly wide vibrato.

A block of brownstone buildings between Fifth and Sixth Avenues constituted 52nd Street. Earlier in the century each building had housed a single affluent family, but by the end of Prohibition, they were already split up into small businesses and basement clubs. By the mid-1940s the Street had reached a peak with such clubs as the Three Deuces, the Downbeat, the Famous Door, the Spotlite, Kelly's Stables, the Yacht Club and the Onyx. The warren-like basements were too small for big bands and so small combos flourished everywhere. Apart from the new generation of musicians, some of the older and more established stars worked there regularly. It was to this shabby area with its fast-living pimps, hipsters, drug-pushers and small-time operators that the reticent Miles Davis came to listen and learn at the end of 1944 and the beginning of 1945. It occupied the other end of the spectrum from Juilliard, with its elegant building, unhurried atmosphere and reverence for the past, a world in which the composer was god. The two worlds proceeded on parallel lines, but when Miles played his first ever recording session (4 May 1945), the band-leader, saxophonist Herbie Fields, was an ex-Juilliard student. The group was a quintet accompanying vocalist Rubberlegs Williams, whose singing was reminiscent of Fats Waller's. Indeed, the loose treatment of the four pieces they recorded was similar to the method of the 'Fats Waller and his Rhythm' series. Miles has said of this occasion: 'I was too nervous to play, and I only performed in the ensembles – no solos.'[6] But, in fact, his muted horn is strongly in evidence, improvising fleet and pungent obbligati behind the voice.

Later in May, Coleman Hawkins started a residency at the Downbeat Club, with Joe Guy on trumpet. Billie Holiday was the featured attraction of the evening and she and Guy had just been married. In the first flush of marital bliss, Guy often missed some of the sets with Hawkins, and Miles would sit in on those occasions. It was a golden opportunity and Miles made the most of it, checking the Downbeat every night to see if he was needed. Hawkins had met Miles when the latter first came to New York and seemed to take a fatherly interest in him; the young trumpeter worked with him a few other times that year when Thelonious Monk was the pianist. On this particular occasion, if Joe Guy did appear, then Miles would go over to the Spotlite and sit in with Lockjaw Davis and alto saxophonist Rudy Williams. Lockjaw must have been impressed by Miles, because shortly after this he hired the young trumpeter for a month at the Spotlite. Miles Davis had got his first real employment as a trumpet player in New York.

After this, he began to get regular work on the Street, and by the early autumn of 1945 he had joined Charlie Parker's group at the Three Deuces. The rest of the quintet comprised pianist Al Haig, bassist Curley Russell and drummer Stan Levey. Miles was still nervous, but Parker showed great kindness in coaxing him along:

> Bird used to make me play. He used to lead me up on the bandstand. I used to quit every night. The tempos were so fast, the challenge so great. I used to ask, 'What do you need me for?' I used to play under Bird all the time. When Bird would play a melody, I'd play just under him and let him lead the note, swing the note. The only thing that I'd add would be a larger sound.[7]

It was around this time that Miles finally left Juilliard. He'd been spending less time there and more on the Street, and his acceptance by leading musicians gave him enough confidence to burn his boats. As Miles puts it:

> Originally I went there (Juilliard) to see what was happening, but when I found out nothing was happening, I told my

father to save his money . . . I realized I wasn't going to get
in any symphony orchestra. And I had to go down the Street
at night to play with Bird or Coleman Hawkins, so I decided
to go that way – all the way.[8]

His decision was final, and with it he irrevocably turned his back
on the life his mother wanted for him. But he took the train back
to St Louis to explain to his father what he was doing and why.
His father understood the situation immediately, giving Miles his
blessing and a promise of continued financial support, and warning
him to get his own sound, to be his own man and nobody else.

After his stint at the Three Deuces, Parker went into the Spotlite,
again taking Miles with him. The rest of the group included Dexter
Gordon on tenor saxophone, Bud Powell or Sir Charles Thompson
alternating at the piano, bassist Curley Russell, Max Roach (or
sometimes Stan Levey) on drums, and tap dancer Baby Lawrence.
Dexter Gordon recalls: 'Baby was the floor show, taking fours
and eights with the band. Bird would leave Miles and me with
our mouths open every night.'[9] The residency was cut short, however, when members of the narcotics squad and vice detectives
raided the Street, rounding up 'vicious' elements and closing several clubs, including the Spotlite. Miles then went into Minton's
with Sir Charles Thompson and a drummer for a while, after
which he was hired again by Coleman Hawkins for a brief
residency.

Parker was booked for a recording session for Savoy on 26
November, and he asked Miles to do the date. The rhythm section
comprised Curley Russell, Max Roach and pianist Argonne
Thornton (later known as Sadik Hakim; the pianist should have
been Thelonious Monk, but he failed, at the last moment, to turn
up). The session became a special occasion with several other
musicians, including Dizzy Gillespie, turning up for the event, and
the usual hipsters and hangers-on drifting in and out of the studio.
There were long breaks for refreshments, and in the middle of the
proceedings, Miles Davis took a thirty-minute nap on the studio
floor. Despite all this chaos, the results were such that the record

company, Savoy, later referred to the occasion as 'the greatest recording session in modern jazz history'.

Savoy's claims may have been rather extravagant, but nevertheless, the session did produce the first definitive recordings of bebop. Parker and Gillespie had twice recorded together earlier in the year, with swing drummers Cozy Cole and Big Sid Catlett, but the November session for Savoy had, at last, the right drummer for the music: Max Roach. Only a year older than Miles, he had grown up with the new music and understood exactly the kind of rhythms that were needed: the shimmering top-cymbal pulse, the snare-drum accents, and the use of the bass drum only for emphasis and punctuation. Another reason for the success of the occasion was, paradoxically, that instead of five confident and fully rehearsed virtuosi, the basic group was a nucleus of three musicians: Parker, then at the full height of his magnificent powers, Curley Russell and Roach. For most of the pieces, Dizzy Gillespie, the leading trumpeter of that time, played piano, and the trumpet player was the nineteen-year-old and still immature Miles Davis.

The material ultimately released from the session comprised two incomplete fragments with beautiful solos by Parker ('Warming Up a Riff' and 'Meandering'), two blues in F ('Billie's Bounce' and 'Now's the Time'), one complete performance based on the chord structure of Gershwin's 'I Got Rhythm' ('Thriving on a Riff'), and 'Koko', a fast performance based on the chord sequence of Ray Noble's 'Cherokee'. Dizzy Gillespie knew enough of the keyboard to be able to 'comp' – to play the right chords in the right rhythmic manner – but he was not enough of a pianist to be able to play a solo. At that time, he and Parker were very close, and Bird obviously knew he would get the kind of accompaniment he wanted on the medium and slow pieces from Dizzy rather than from Argonne Thornton. The latter, however, played on 'Thriving on a Riff' and revealed himself as an inventive and original stylist. With Dizzy on piano, in a purely supportive role, Parker would have to play longer solos, and Miles, as the only other solo voice, would also have to shoulder more responsibility. Lack of virtuosity at the piano and on the trumpet thus became a key factor in the quality, the poise, the sheer depth of feeling of the performances. Every note, every phrase of Parker's was made to tell, given its full weight, and even at fast tempos he seemed unhurried. Miles, too, could not afford to waste a note.

The ensemble passages at the beginning and end of 'Koko' were simply too difficult at that time for Miles, and so they were played on trumpet by Gillespie. Either because of contractual difficulties, or because Savoy did not want to pay a sixth musician on the quintet date, Dizzy's contribution to the whole session – which was considerable – had to be anonymous. On the original 78 r.p.m. issues, the pianist is listed as one Hen Gates. Miles has solos only on the two blues and 'Thriving on a Riff'. On the latter, the tempo is brisk and there is no theme statement at the beginning. After Thornton's piano introduction, the first chorus is a solo by Miles with a cup mute, and it is astonishingly fluent and assured. There's no great individuality in his phrasing – indeed he sounds rather like Dizzy – but the long melodic lines and the way he rounds off his phrases are very impressive. After Parker's two choruses, and Thornton's solo, the difficult 'Anthropology' theme is played to conclude the piece, and this is a perfect example of how Miles used to 'play under' Parker at that time. The theme is played by the alto and the edge of its magnificent sound is just tinged by the muted trumpet, so that when Miles fails to make the convoluted phrases at the end of the second and the last eight bars, the omission is barely noticeable.

'Billie's Bounce' is taken at an easy tempo, with Miles playing open horn on equal terms with Parker, and the ensemble has a relaxed, funky edge. Parker's solo stretches for four choruses, and Miles takes two, playing some beautifully poised wide intervals with oblique notes to the chords, and getting a lyrical, singing quality in some of his longer notes. After his solo he goes straight into the theme, which is played twice – strongly the first time, and very quietly for the last time. During the final chorus Miles plays a 'clinker' – not a fluff, but an actual wrong note which is clearly audible, and this probably resulted simply from a failure of nerve. In the middle 1940s, recordings couldn't be edited and had to be done in complete 'takes'. If the first theme statement was good and the solos were acceptable, the worst ordeal for a nervous musician was always the final theme statement . . . would he or would he not ruin the whole take by botching it?

Apart from 'Koko', on which Miles didn't play, the other masterpiece from that day's recording was the fourth take of 'Now's the Time'. Dizzy's piano introduction, with its relaxed but insistent dissonances, sets up an eerie, contemplative mood which is sustained throughout the performance. The theme, one of Parker's many blues compositions, builds tension by the repetition of a rhythmic phrase (riff) in the middle register, punctuated by stabs from the piano and drums. In the last four bars, the tension is brilliantly released when the trumpet rises an octave and a minor 3rd to play a phrase which paraphrases and answers the initial riff. This theme has exactly the same structure and essence as the earliest and most fundamental vocal blues in which a line is sung twice, with perhaps minor variations the second time, over eight bars, and then the punchline is sung over the last four bars. Parker's innovations did not negate the past or invalidate it; instead, they contained it, reshaped it and revitalized it. This example of progressing without losing contact with the roots of the music was not to be wasted on Miles.

The overall shape of 'Now's the Time' follows the classic structure of small-group jazz performances. The theme is played at the beginning and end, and the solos take place in the middle. This again harks back to the roots of jazz: the theme is like the 'call' of the preacher or chain-gang leader, and the solos are the 'response' to that call – replies to it and variations on it. It is an extrapolation from non-Western rituals and habits of communal music-making.

After the initial theme statement, Parker plays three choruses, creating and releasing tension by the masterful way he varies the attack and the length of his phrases and by his dramatic use of pauses. The whole solo is shot through with blues feeling – all the expressive inflexions, the vocalized tone, the fluid use of grace notes as a prelude to long melodic statements. Imaginatively and technically it is a virtuoso performance, and yet it never loses contact with the black folk tradition – the direct cry from the heart is always evident. There are also several striking qualities in Miles's solo, which covers two choruses – twenty-four bars. First, its overall structure exactly mirrors the structure of the written twelve-bar theme, in that the tension is steadily built up until it reaches a peak with the phrase he plays over the seventeenth and eighteenth bars culminating in his high B flat (concert A flat). After two beats' rest in the nineteenth bar, the tension is marvellously released when he hits his top D (concert C) and descends with the most flowing and unbroken line of the solo over the following five bars. In the earlier part of the solo the tension is built by playing short phrases in the middle register and alternating them with long, singing notes which project rich tonal quality. He also stresses weak notes such as the second step of the scale (G over an F chord) and the flattened 5th, all of which further increases the tension by implying bitonality and tugging the ear away from the tonic. All this tension is resolved with the final descent from the high register, which is rhythmically symmetrical and diatonic – going, in fact, straight down the F major scale.

The emotional climate Miles's solo generates is very akin to that of Parker: a buoyant feel with an intensely melancholy edge. And yet, unlike Parker's, Miles's phrases have very little of the blues in them at this stage in his career. The long periods of formal instruction in Western instrumental techniques seem to have drained the tonal inflexions of the blues from his playing. His sound in this solo, however, is by no means a 'straight' one, because his phrases hang together very well rhythmically – in short, he swings, albeit ponderously. It is an extremely full trumpet sound, almost a massive one. In the early 1950s he was to cite this particular solo as one of his favourites because he 'sounded like Freddie Webster', and other musicians have made the same comment. As with Webster, the solo is economical; every note tells and there are none of the idiomatic grace notes with which Parker often began his phrases. Finally, the powerful inner logic of his improvisation comes out of his intense feeling and is an expression of it. But the most important point of all is that this solo revealed an original conception of trumpet playing. Trumpeter Red Rodney said later: 'The first time we really ever heard Miles was on that . . . "Now's the Time" . . . it was a new sound . . . it was a young guy that didn't play the trumpet very well, but had discovered a whole new way of treating it and playing it.'

Once a musician starts playing and recording he becomes, of course, a public figure whose work will be talked about and evaluated by sages and idiots alike. Miles got his first taste of critics and their wisdom when the 78 r.p.m. record, with 'Billie's Bounce' on one side and 'Now's the Time' on the other, was released. It was universally condemned. The *Down Beat* reviewer wrote:

> These two sides are excellent examples of the other side of
> the Gillespie craze – the bad taste and ill-advised fanaticism
> of Dizzy's uninhibited style. Only Charlie Parker, who is a
> better musician and who deserves more credit than Dizzy for
> the style anyway, saves these from a bad fate. At that he's
> far off form – a bad reed and inexcusable fluffs do not add
> up to good jazz. The trumpet man, whoever the misled kid
> is, plays Gillespie in the same manner as a majority of kids
> who copy their idol do – with most of the faults, lack of
> order and meaning, the complete adherence to technical acro-
> batics.[10]

This critique is typical of the kind of abuse with which bebop was greeted in the middle 1940s, and Miles's lifelong mistrust and dislike of critics (with a few exceptions) may well date from this period.

In that whole recording session on 26 November 1945, both Parker and Miles revealed their essential difference from everyone else in jazz. Although still embryonic, Miles's musical identity was clearly evident. Parker, on the other hand, was fully mature and gloriously expressed the two opposite poles of his artistic nature: the furious brilliance and aggression of 'Koko', and the contemplative brooding of the nocturnal and bluesy 'Now's the Time', a prophetic title. Both pieces are small masterpieces – perfect expressions of the duality which is found in all Parker's subsequent work. Miles, in his mature work, was to bring both aspects to greater peaks of expression, and on a much larger scale. The introspective and contemplative side would be sustained for whole long-playing records, reaching its fullest realization in the albums *Kind of Blue* (1959) and *In a Silent Way* (1969). The furiously aggressive side was to reach one peak in the 'live' albums of the early 1960s and another – of almost frightening power – in 1969 and the early 1970s, when Miles was using electronics and multiple rhythm sections.

Another aspect of Charlie Parker's character also revealed itself at this recording session. He had been a heroin addict for some years by then, and was always short of money. In the studio, needing ready cash, he sold the rights to his composition, 'Now's the Time', for a mere $50 dollars. In later years, Miles would guard his own compositions jealously, but before the 1940s were over he was to make many of Parker's mistakes.

The November raids on 52nd Street by detectives and members of the vice squad had been instigated by the military authorities. The war was coming to an end, but there was still concern about the numbers of servicemen rendered unfit for duty after a night or two on the Street. Several clubs were closed, and others declared out-of-bounds for military personnel. Parker and Gillespie consequently found themselves out of work in New York, and left early in December for an eight-week engagement in California. Shortly after they'd gone, Miles took Irene and daughter Cheryl back to East St Louis in time for Christmas. Irene was pregnant with their second child, Gregory, who was born in 1946. But having decided to 'go all the way' and identify totally with the new musical revolutionaries, Miles certainly didn't want to stay in East St Louis. It may have been pleasant to revisit old friends, to sit in with local groups, and perhaps to enjoy the 'local-boy-makes-good' reputation, but this was no longer enough. By a stroke of good fortune, Benny Carter's band was working locally at the Riviera, and they were about to go to the West Coast. This was too good an opportunity to miss; Miles joined the trumpet section of the band and informed Parker that he would be coming to Los Angeles.

At the beginning of February 1946, the Parker/Gillespie quintet finished its West Coast residency and a few days later the group flew back to New York – all, that is, except for Parker, who had cashed in his plane ticket. By this time Ross Russell had started his record label, Dial, which was concentrating on bebop, and some time in mid-February Parker went along to talk to him. According to Russell, Bird didn't want to record with Gillespie any more:

> It was time for new modes. The trumpet player of his choice would not be a virtuoso capable of fireworks, but a different sort of musician, someone who played a relaxed legato style, with a warm tone, in the lower and middle registers, someone like Miles Davis, who would be arriving in Los Angeles within a week or two.[11]

The Benny Carter band arrived to play at the Orpheum Theatre in Los Angeles, and Miles was already unhappy with the job. It was a big band playing mostly old-fashioned arrangements. Parker was appearing at the Finale Club in the black quarter of the city, and Miles was soon doubling up jobs by slipping down there every night when the Carter gig was over. Having two paid jobs was against the tenets of the musicians' union, and when the authorities caught up with him, Miles was fined, after which he left the Carter band and appeared with Bird until the Finale closed because of poor business. Although most of the best local musicians came along to hear Parker and the group, there was, as yet, no audience for the new music on the West Coast.

The rhythm section with Parker and Miles at the Finale comprised pianist Joe Albany, bassist Addison Farmer (brother of trumpeter Art) and drummer Chuck Thompson, and in late February and early March some of the club sessions were recorded. They showed Miles to be much more confident, but to have lost much of his individuality. The influence of Gillespie is evident in his phrases and in his use of the higher registers of the trumpet. His technique seems much improved, but he still fails to make the same phrases on the 'Anthropology' theme. These were, of course, public performances and there was, necessarily, only one take of each piece.

Parker's first studio recording session for Ross Russell's Dial label took place at Radio Recorders on Santa Monica Boulevard in Hollywood, on 28 March 1946. This was Miles's second time in the studios with Parker, and the occasion uncannily resembled the 'Now's the Time' session in its lack of preparation. On the present occasion, four months later, there had been almost no rehearsal at all, and Bird had reshuffled his personnel the night before the recording was due to take place. He went into the studio with a septet which included Miles, tenor saxophonist Lucky Thompson, pianist Dodo Marmarosa, guitarist Arvin Garrison, bassist Vic McMillan and Roy Porter on drums. Everything – melodies, harmonies, formats and solo lengths – had to be worked out in the studio in recording time. Nothing was written down: Parker simply played the melodies on his alto, taught them to the other horns, demonstrated harmonies – occasionally actually naming a chord – and talked out various routines. His whole approach was thus spontaneous, instinctual, and non-Western. It was diametrically opposed to the entire Western conception of written musical symbols, of music that can be seen even when not heard. Parker preferred this approach to recording, and, once again, the lesson was not lost on Miles Davis. In his later career, often the most brilliant and lasting of his small-group recordings would be done in the studio, on the day, with no prior rehearsal.

Miles used his cup mute throughout the session, and still sounds like Dizzy. In fact, his approach is antithetical to the persona he revealed on the 1945 session, and on various takes he is often prodigal with notes, and frequently sounds ill at ease. Furthermore, as all four of the tunes recorded that day were either medium-fast or fast, we have no opportunity to hear Miles at the tempos he favoured then: slow to medium. Uncertain though his contribution was later in the year he won an award as *Down Beat*'s New Star on Trumpet for 1946. Dodo Marmarosa and Lucky Thompson got similar awards in their respective instrumental categories. Recording with Parker was the sure way of getting noticed fast, and the critics began to be more favourable to Miles.

The Finale Club closed suddenly without any warning. The musicians turned up for work one night only to find the club in darkness, the doors locked, and themselves out of a job. Parker disappeared and could not be found, even by his closest associates, for several days. This was Miles's first real taste of the insecurity and unpredictability of the music profession. Work for modern jazz musicians was now very hard to come by in California. Things were getting desperate for Bird, who had no money to live on and who couldn't afford the fare back to New York, but Miles still had an allowance from his father.

The trumpeter Howard McGhee and his wife, who were living in Los Angeles, took care of Parker and reopened the defunct Finale Club in May. It was a co-operative venture, and the door takings were simply divided between the members of the house band, which comprised Bird, McGhee, Marmarosa, bassist Red Callender and Roy Porter. Under these circumstances, there was no place for Miles Davis in Parker's group, and perhaps Miles was content to be out of the way because it was becoming increasingly clear that the saxophonist was physically and emotionally very ill. Parker's complete breakdown occurred in late July and, suspected of being insane, he was committed to Camarillo State Hospital for a minimum period of six months.

During his time on the West Coast, Miles had become friendly with bassist Charles Mingus, another Bird devotee, who lived in Los Angeles. In the late spring, Miles had played third trumpet on a record session under Mingus's leadership, but the two tracks they made were never released. The experience left Miles with a lasting admiration and affection for Mingus and his music. In August, both Miles and Mingus played in a group led by Lucky Thompson three nights a week at Elk's Ballroom on Central Avenue in Los Angeles. An announcement in the music press stated that the key member of Thompson's small group would be 'the brilliant young trumpet player, Miles Davis, last heard here with Benny Carter'.[12] But this group soon broke up because Thompson accepted an offer to join the Boyd Raeburn orchestra. By now, Miles was anxious to leave the West Coast, and a way out presented itself when the Billy Eckstine band arrived in Los Angeles during September. Eighteen months previously, the trumpeter Fats Navarro had joined the band, replacing Dizzy Gillespie, but when Eckstine went out to California. Navarro wanted to stay in New York. Miles was hired and spent five months with the band, going east with it in late autumn. Mingus never forgave him for leaving Los Angeles when Parker was still in hospital, but Mingus's attitude arose from a misunderstanding of the situation. He was a sentimental outsider who had not spent much time in close proximity with Parker who was, in any case, now safely in medical custody. Miles was not Bird's keeper, and his duty was to look out for himself and his family. While with the Eckstine band, however, Miles began dabbling in drugs, snorting cocaine and even trying heroin, but he wasn't yet addicted. After the Eckstine band broke up in the spring of 1947, Miles spent some time in Chicago, appearing on the south side at Jumptown with saxophonists Sonny Stitt and Gene Ammons for the jam session nights.

Then he returned to New York, and after a short stint and a recording with saxophonist Illinois Jacquet in March, he joined the trumpet section of Dizzy Gillespie's big band, which included Freddie Webster, Kenny Dorham, Fats Navarro and Dizzy himself. Charlie Parker came back to New York in April, just in time to join Gillespie's band on its first gig at the McKinley Theatre in the Bronx. Parker had got out of the Camarillo State Hospital in February, free of drugs, but had stayed on in Los Angeles and started using them again. He was also consuming large quantities of alcohol, possibly in an effort to limit his heroin intake. The result was that on that first night with Dizzy's big band, Parker played solos, but wouldn't play the written parts and kept falling asleep. Dizzy fired him on the spot, and no amount of pleading by the other musicians made him change his mind. He wanted a 'clean' band with responsible and reliable musicians.

Parker realized, however, that the new music had at last made a big impact on the general public, that Dizzy Gillespie was already famous, and that it was now possible not only to work regularly, but also to earn reasonable money. He was immediately offered a contract for four weeks with a quintet at the Three Deuces. The fee for the group was $800 a week. This meant that Parker could afford to recruit the musicians he wanted and employ them on a steady basis. He chose Miles Davis and Max Roach; the bassist was Tommy Potter, who had played with the Eckstine band, and the pianist was a comparative unknown called Duke Jordan. Miles left the Gillespie band in order to work with this new quintet, which was to stay together as a unit for over eighteen months; with it, Parker reached the zenith of his career. His sidemen could have worked for better wages elsewhere, but they wanted to be with Bird. According to Ross Russell, Jordan and Potter, the two newcomers, were paid $125 a week, and Bird's old associates, Max and Miles, received $135. Parker had the difference – the best wage he had received in his entire career to date – $280 clear. The quintet opened at the Three Deuces in April, opposite the Lennie Tristano Trio, and the club was so well attended that Parker's residency was extended indefinitely.

Parker was physically and psychologically buoyant, and at the height of his creative powers. Night after night, he pushed his great ability to the limits, never playing anything the same way twice. The inexhaustible wealth of ideas and the powerful feeling with which he invested them kept the rest of the group on their mettle. Miles Davis recalls:

Bird used to play forty different styles. He was never content to remain the same. I remember how at times he used to turn the rhythm section around. Like we'd be playing the blues, and Bird would start on the eleventh bar, and as the rhythm section stayed where they were and Bird played where he was it sounded as if the rhythm section was on one and three instead of two and four. Every time that would happen, Max Roach used to scream at Duke Jordan not to follow Bird, but to stay where he was. Then, eventually it came round as Bird had planned and we were together again.[13]

Parker's continual extending of boundaries, his invasion of unexplored territory, and the element of creative surprise which he generated, made a deep impression on Miles. Over twenty years later, Davis was to say: 'That's what I tell my musicians; I tell them to be ready to play what you know and above what you know. Anything might happen above what you've been used to playing – you're ready to get into that, and above that, and take that out.'[14]

Parker also continued to inspire and direct his group by example rather than by explicit verbal instructions. Someone had to verbalize, however, and one of the chores Miles had to take on, because of Bird's default, was that of musical director. His experiences with the Eddie Randle band in St Louis had, of course, prepared him for this to some extent: 'I was nervous . . . but I had to get out of being nervous fast because he [Bird] was never there and I had to rehearse the band.'[15] And: 'He never did talk about music. I always even had to show Duke Jordan, the pianist in the band, the chords.'[16] Miles also recalls:

The only time I ever heard Bird talk about music was an argument he had with a classical musician friend of mine about the naming of chords. That was the night Bird said you could do anything with chords. And I disagreed. 'You can't play D natural in the fifth bar of a B flat blues.' 'Yes you can,' said Bird. Well one night in Birdland, I heard Lester Young do it, and it sounded good. But he bent it.[17]

On 8 May 1947, the quintet, with Bud Powell replacing Duke Jordan at the piano, recorded for the Savoy label, and the results show a major change in Miles's thinking. The Gillespie influence and the forays into the upper register are gone; the sound is smaller than on the 'Now's the Time' recording, but it is broad, rounded and beginning to project a greater lyricism. Although not yet twenty-one, Miles has achieved some wisdom, some self-knowledge:

> I asked Dizzy, 'Why can't I play high like you?' 'Because you can't hear up there,' he said. 'You hear in the middle register.' And that's true. There are times when I can't even tell what chords Dizzy is working on when he's up high; and yet he told me what he's playing is just an octave above what I do.[18]

Although Miles's solos on this session are often much shorter than Parker's, we can detect the germs of a highly individual style. The sense of strain is gone, though he does occasionally sound a little unsteady rhythmically, and his middle register work is already showing a good grasp of harmony, original melodic lines, and unusual intervals. This growing identity was to become an integral part of the group idea Parker had conceived a year previously on the West Coast. Instead of sparks being created by the competition of two virtuoso horns, as had been the case when Dizzy was with the band, Parker was looking for the dynamism of contrast. His own gargantuan abilities would be offset against the understatement and lyricism of Miles's horn. The music of the quintet was to become subtly dramatic and, perhaps paradoxically, more potent. This concept was to be a major factor in Miles's own definitive quintet recordings of the middle 1950s.

The 8 May recording session produced two blues ('Cheryl' and 'Buzzy'), a variation of the 'I Got Rhythm' sequence ('Chasin' the Bird'), and 'Donna Lee', based on the harmonies of the standard, 'Indiana'. The first three were composed by Parker, but although 'Donna Lee' was attributed to him, it was in fact written by Miles. This was the trumpeter's debut on record as a composer, and it was an impressive one. The piece is fast, difficult, and typical bebop in its rhythmic drive and the way the melodic line flows through the chord changes. Only the symmetry of the phrases suggests that Miles, and not Bird, was the composer.

It was probably the chaos of Parker's own affairs that gave Miles his next big chance. Bird was still under contract to record for Dial, and after the May session for Savoy there was much infighting behind the scenes. It was discovered that Parker was also under contract to Savoy, having signed with them at the 'Now's the Time' session. Savoy offered him another recording date on 14 August, and in order to avoid further complications, Miles was made the leader for that event. Either for further camouflage, or at Miles's instigation, Parker abandoned his alto and played tenor saxophone for the occasion. The rest of the group comprised pianist John Lewis, bassist Nelson Boyd, and Max Roach. The four tunes they recorded ('Milestones', 'Little Willie Leaps', 'Half Nelson' and 'Sippin' at Bell's') were all composed by Miles but, although they show marked originality, these themes are rather over-written. The melodic lines are long, convoluted and full of surprises, but they are so lacking in space that they sometimes create a breathless feeling. Also, the underlying harmonies are much denser than those of Parker's usual material. 'Sippin' at Bell's', for example, is a twelve-bar blues, but there are eighteen chords in each chorus.

The most striking feature of this session is the way Miles has imposed his own personality on it. The music is unlike Parker's own recordings in that the themes and the way they are played are much more relaxed and 'laid back'. The use of the tenor sax may have something to do with the smoother sound of the ensemble, but the essence of the music goes deeper than that. The liquid spirit of Lester Young hangs over it. The solos too – and for the first time, Miles shares the honours on equal terms with Parker – echo the smooth fluency of the themes. Miles is poised and assured, tending to understate and imply melodic ideas. The self-editing process is already functioning, and there is a subtle tension between the apparent simplicity of his improvised lines and the complexity of the harmonic structures. All in all, the session is not as powerful as the rest of Parker's recordings in the period, but it offers a new and refreshing dimension – a cooler urbanity – and it gives intimations of Miles's future development.

That year, 1947, proved to be a marvellous one for Miles. He was beginning to find a solid musical identity, he was working steadily, and his progress was well documented. There were three further recording sessions with Parker for Dial, each one showing increasing musicianship and greater maturity in Miles's work, and on 21 December there was another date for Savoy. On this final one, Miles is in magnificent form, playing with perfect rhythmic poise, using space with drama and delicacy, and revealing an abundance of new ideas. He plays confidently at breakneck speed on 'Bird Gets the Worm', but even in this piece his group role, as a foil for Parker, is important. Wilfrid Mellers points out: 'Parker's reedy, anguished tone is highlighted in contrast with Miles Davis's muted trumpet, which mutes the anger as well as the sonority.'[19]

It was also in 1947 that Miles, looking for further musical outlets, began to show some independence of Parker. He became established as one of the four trumpet players who dominated 52nd Street. Another of these was Red Rodney who remembers:

I worked on 52nd Street all the time . . . I went from one club to the other . . . Miles did also . . . We were sort of rivals in a way, I guess. There was Miles, and there was Fats Navarro, myself, Kenny Dorham, and the four of us were all friendly and, well, we were competitive towards each other because we were the ones who were working, and I was the only white trumpeter. But you know, back then there was no problem of being white or black – among us anyway . . . Inasmuch as we liked each other, we didn't consider colour.

Rodney also worked with the Claude Thornhill band in 1947 when Gerry Mulligan and Lee Konitz were with it, and Gil Evans was writing the arrangements. Miles's lifelong friendship with Evans dates from that year. Gil had heard the Parker recording of 'Donna Lee' and he approached Miles:

He was asking for a release on my tune 'Donna Lee'. He wanted to make an arrangement for a government electrical transcription of it. I told him he could have it and asked him to teach me some chords and let me study some of the scores he was doing for Claude Thornhill . . . I used to write and send Gil my scores for evaluation. Gil used to say they were good, but cluttered up with too many notes. I used to think you had to use a lot of notes and stuff to be writing.[20]

The improvising and the writing were developing on parallel lines. The excesses and the inessentials were being pared away. But also in 1947, in addition to snorting cocaine, Miles had started drinking alcohol and smoking cigarettes, though he wasn't using heroin.

By the beginning of 1948, Charlie Parker and his group had gained international fame and recognition. Parker had won his first poll in *Metronome*, and Miles and Max Roach had gained places in their respective instrumental categories. Miles had won the 1947 critics' poll in *Esquire*, and had tied first with Dizzy in the critics' *Down Beat* poll. But although things looked good, the quintet was not going to stay together. Throughout the year there was growing alienation between Parker and his two strongest sidemen, Miles and Max Roach. Back in the autumn of 1947, Bird had started taking drugs again, and as the addiction progressed, the old instability reappeared. He became unpredictable and unreliable. This was aggravated by the fact that he was now in great demand as a soloist, and would go off on his own to record or to tour. The rest of Parker's group, who had all made sacrifices in order to stay with him, were bitterly resentful when they found themselves out of work. The quintet's morale sank very low and when, in late 1948, Parker deliberately behaved childishly during an engagement (doing such things as expelling the air from a balloon into the microphone and firing a cap pistol at the pianist), and seemed to be trying to humiliate his musicians, it was the last straw for Miles. He walked out of the club, saying, 'Bird makes you feel one foot high.'[21] He continued with the quintet for a few more gigs, but let Parker know that he definitely wanted to leave, and after a while, both he and Max Roach did leave. Although Bird and Miles were to play together once or twice afterwards, and record together again in the early 1950s, that evening marked the end of their close association.

Charlie Parker's influence on Miles Davis is incalculable. Even Bird's behaviour on the bandstand seems to have made a deep impression. Parker, for example, hardly ever made announcements. According to one regular witness of the evenings on 52nd Street, the communications between Parker and his musicians seemed to be on a telepathic level. Time after time, he would count in and begin playing without apparently having even told the group what piece they were going to play. At the end of a set, he occasionally back-announced some of the themes, but usually he announced only the names of the musicians. When he'd finished playing his solos, he didn't look round at the band, or offer any directions, but simply walked off the stand. During the 1950s and 1960s, Miles's own behaviour was to magnify this pattern. During performances with his groups, he would make no announcements at all, and would not only walk off the stand after his solos, but would actually disappear for several minutes.

Parker was rejecting the idea of the black musician as entertainer; he wanted his music to be taken on its own merits, to speak for itself. His behaviour, always unpredictable, often acted as a short-circuit which burned out the fuses of normal thought patterns; he was readjusting the whole relationship of performing artist and audience. The listeners, onlookers, witnesses were privileged eavesdroppers on the act of creation. His music, his behaviour, his gargantuan appetites for food, drugs, sex, jolted audiences, musicians and himself into reappraisals of values. His determination to inhabit the frontiers of experience was both magnificently heroic and magnificently foolhardy.

Charlie Parker was a supremely tragic figure in that the creative and destructive sides of his nature were interdependent. His great genius was for improvisation in both music and in life. In his quest for self-renewal, he had to be unpredictable and perpetually surprising. He had to flout the tenets of the white society that dominated American life because it demanded that: to be accepted, a person had to be a known quantity. Because of his defiance, and the way he revitalized black music, Parker was a genuine cultural hero for urban black people of his generation. Artistically, he embodied an apparently massive contradiction: he was the most advanced musician of his generation, yet he never lost touch with the people – with his folk roots. He had the admiration of his peers, and he had the power of communication with the audiences. Dizzy Gillespie described one occasion when this power of Parker's was revealed in a live performance:

> I saw something remarkable one time. He didn't show up for a dance he was supposed to play in Detroit. I was in the town, and they asked me to play instead. I went up there, and we started playing. Then I heard this big roar, and Charlie Parker had come in and started playing. He'd play a phrase, and people might never have heard it before. But he'd start it, and the people would finish it with him, humming. It would be so lyrical and simple that it just seemed the most natural thing to play.[22]

When bookers, agents, managements, entrepreneurs at last realized that they could expect only the unexpected from Parker, they were reluctant to take on the responsibility of finding him work. He was doomed to despair and drugs, and to scuffling around for small-time gigs in obscure clubs. In 1946 he had described his vision of an ordered life to Ross Russell. It included a settled home with a library, paintings, a piano and a superb record collection. It was a vision of stability and permanence that implied a withdrawal from the transient world of improvisation and jazz. He wanted to listen to the works of twentieth-century European composers and to compose 'seriously' himself. But that dream was to become more and more remote.

Even in his most creative act – playing music – Parker seemed to be destroying himself, because he always pushed his abilities to the limits. During long engagements, he would become physically and emotionally exhausted, and then he would rely heavily on heroin and alcohol. Sometimes survival would depend on simply not turning up to play; but this physical and psychological self-preservation was also economic suicide. A jazz musician was once quoted as saying: 'People wonder why we get paid relatively well. Man, we take people's chances for them.'[23] Parker lived always with what Ross Russell has described as the 'sense of peril'. He took people's chances for them – musical chances for the new generation of musicians, lifestyle chances for the hipsters, racial chances for the blacks – he took them all, and paid the price for being larger than life: premature death.

Throughout his association with Bird, Miles Davis was a quiet, polite, reasonably self-controlled young man. He was also exceptionally intelligent and sensitive, and could see clearly how Parker was destroying himself. It was obvious that there was a direct relationship between the risks taken and the power of the music produced. Playing safe led to creative death. To survive, Miles would have to look for some sort of balance. But first, like Bird, he would have to experience excess – he would have to go over the edge.

THREE

The Birth of the Cool

'I always had a curiosity about trying new things in
music. A new sound, another way to do something.'[1]

Miles Davis

In 1947, Irene Birth had joined Miles in New York, bringing with
her Cheryl, now three years old, and baby Gregory. The presence
of his family may have offered some sense of stability and continuity, but April that year also brought the death of Freddie Webster from some contaminated heroin. Webster, who was just thirty
years old, had been like an elder brother to Miles, who felt the
loss deeply. The death of someone so close to him, as a result of
drug addiction, was an ominous warning. Miles, however, was
making such progress in terms of his burgeoning identity as a
player and bandleader that he was absorbed in the present rather
than looking to the future.

Throughout 1947, Miles had gradually expunged most of the
clichés of bebop from his trumpet style, and had begun to reveal
an approach which owed a debt to Lester Young. During the
1930s, Young's tenor sax style had introduced a new element into
jazz: a smaller, lighter sound, and a more delicate, introspective
quality. He brought to artistic fruition qualities he had found in
two white musicians of the 1920s – cornettist Bix Beiderbecke and
saxophonist Frank Trumbauer. When Beiderbecke came on the
scene, the trumpet was the dominant instrument of jazz, and Louis
Armstrong, a man who phrased with classic grandeur, its prime
exponent. Bix's palette was much smaller: he confined himself to

the middle register of the instrument, but compensated for this by his burnished, singing tone, and the intensity of his lyricism. There can be no doubt that when Miles Davis abandoned the Gillespie approach to the trumpet and began confining himself to the middle register and showing a more delicate melodic flair, he was being influenced – albeit indirectly, through Lester Young – by Bix Beiderbecke.

By 1948, there was a growing audience for bebop, and in New York the revolution became the new establishment and imitators abounded everywhere. Miles and other musicians at the centre of the movement were beginning to look round for some new areas to explore. At the same time, the focal point of the jazz scene was moving away from 52nd Street, which was becoming an area of strip-joints and restaurants. Instead, the music was now being heard in the more reputable area of Broadway, and in larger clubs such as the Royal Roost where patrons were not browbeaten into drinking alcohol at high prices but, for the price of admission, could simply sit and listen to the music. Just before Miles left Charlie Parker's quintet, the group made a broadcast from the Roost and were heard by a much wider audience. It was at the Roost, too, that Miles first led his own groups after leaving Parker.

Meanwhile, he had been branching out restlessly, playing on his own as a soloist and with other musicians around New York. He worked with saxophonist Sonny Rollins on several occasions, becoming firm friends with him. Miles also gigged with bassist Oscar Pettiford, and may well have played with John Coltrane around this time. But the most important event that year was his renewed association with the composer/arranger Gil Evans. This relationship between the black, academy-trained, improvising musician, and the white, self-taught composer, ripened into a friendship that was to endure for decades and that produced, in the later 1950s, some of the finest orchestral music of the century.

In 1948, Miles was still only twenty-two and unsure of himself, even though he'd achieved a certain amount of success and recognition. On the other hand, Evans was thirty-six and full of knowledge and musical wisdom acquired empirically over the years. He was the perfect father figure for Miles at the time, because he knew and understood 'straight' music but also because he had a profound understanding and appreciation of the great jazz improvisers. The apparently irreconcilable worlds of formal composition and of improvisation were united naturally and easily in Gil Evans's concept of music. Miles has said of him: 'He is as well versed in classical music in general as Leonard Bernstein. And what the classical guys don't know is what Gil knows.'[2]

Gil Evans was born in Canada of Australian parentage, and had no formal musical training at all. When he was fourteen, he heard some Louis Armstrong records that inspired him to begin playing the piano and teaching himself music. In 1941, he became the principal arranger of the Claude Thornhill Orchestra, which was a white 'society' band. Thornhill, himself an arranger, had known and worked with Evans during the 1930s, and both men had been staff arrangers for Bob Hope's radio programme. Thornhill, an excellent pianist with a beautiful touch, was the first dance band leader to use French horns and to use the tuba as part of the ensemble colour rather than as a rhythm instrument, and his orchestra's sound was, for the most part, soft, dense and static. Gil Evans described the problems it presented:

> The sound hung like a cloud. But once this stationary effect, this sound, was created, it was ready to have other things added to it. The sound itself can only hold interest for a certain length of time. Then you have to make certain changes within that sound; you have to make personal use of harmonies, rather than work with traditional ones; there has to be more movement in the melody; more dynamics, more syncopation; speeding up of the rhythms. For me, I had to make those changes ... I did not create the sound; Claude did.[3]

Evans plays down his own part in all this with typical modesty. Such honesty and generosity are rare enough anywhere, and it was probably Evans's own qualities (musical and moral), as much as anything else, that drew so many of the most gifted young white musicians towards Thornhill's band. It was Gil who persuaded baritone saxophonist Gerry Mulligan to join it and to write arrangements for it. Other notable members were trumpeters Red Rodney and John Carisi (who also arranged), and the brilliant young alto saxophonist Lee Konitz. Gerry Mulligan who, like Konitz, was a year younger than Miles, recalls: 'Lee joined Claude's band in Chicago and knocked us all out (including Bird) with his originality.'[4] Konitz had an exceptionally soft and fluid approach to the alto, with a smooth, clear, almost diaphanous sound. It was a saxophone style without vibrato and with no blues inflexions at all . . . a 'white' sound which suited the non-vibrato sound of the Thornhill band. Konitz's style was in every way the antithesis of Parker's. The pair of them had perhaps only two things in common: the instrument they played and the great originality of their improvisations. Miles liked them both: 'Thornhill had the greatest band, the one with Lee Konitz, during these modern times. The one exception was the Billy Eckstine band with Bird.'[5]

During this period, Parker was actually sharing Gil Evans's room, and dropping in for a quick nap between his club sessions. Evans had arranged two Parker compositions ('Anthropology' and 'Yardbird Suite') and one of Miles's tunes ('Donna Lee') for Thornhill's band, and he became the focal point for aspiring young musicians interested in adapting Parker's ideas to more formal musical settings. There was something spare and ascetic about Evans's lifestyle at the time, which gave the impression that everything – all intellectual and sensuous experience – was subordinated to the experience of music. He was living in a one-room basement apartment on West 55th Street, behind a Chinese laundry, and pianist/composer George Russell has described the scene and the informal seminars which took place there:

A very big bed took up a lot of the place; there was one big lamp, and a cat named Becky. The linoleum was battered, and there was a little court outside. Inside, it was always very dark. The feeling of the room was timelessness. Whenever you got there, you wouldn't care about conditions outside. You couldn't tell whether it was day or night, summer or winter, and it didn't matter. At all hours, the place was loaded with people who came in and out. Mulligan, though, was there all the time . . . Gil, who loved musical companionship, was the mother hen – the haven in the storm. He was gentle, wise, profound, and extremely perceptive, and he always seemed to have a comforting answer for any kind of problem. He appeared to have no bitterness . . . Gil was . . . one of the strong personalities in written jazz, and I'm sure he influenced all of us.[6]

By the middle and later 1940s, several big bands had already adapted and used the ideas of bebop. Perhaps the most famous were Dizzy Gillespie's big band and those of Woody Herman and Stan Kenton. For the most part, however, these had concentrated on one side of Parker's duality – the furiously rhythmic and aggressive aspect. Gil Evans and Gerry Mulligan, in their discussions during the winter of 1947, seemed more interested in exploring Parker's other side, which had links with Lester Young – a gentler and more contemplative form of expression. They were also looking for a much more organic relationship between the orchestral score and the role of the various soloists. Evans and Mulligan worked out what they thought was the smallest number of instruments which could express the harmonic and tonal range of the Thornhill outfit, and wanted to get together a good little rehearsal band. Like so many musical happenings in America, this one was modest in its aims, was born from the enthusiasm of a few little-known individuals, and moved out of the obscure rehearsal rooms to influence the thinking of musicians all over the world.

Miles Davis had been thinking along parallel lines. He too was ready for change after the frenetic excesses of bebop, and drew a characteristic analogy: 'It's just like clothes. All of a sudden you decide you don't have to wear spats and a flower up here, you know? You wear the flower and leave off the spats, and then pretty soon you leave off both of them . . .'[7] Just as Evans and Mulligan were paring down instrumentation to the minimum, so Miles was purging his own trumpet style of excess. This quality of economy he recognized and admired in Gil Evans: 'Gil can use four instruments where other arrangers need eight.' So Miles began going round to Evans's place, taking part in the discussions and meeting new faces:

> I always wanted to play with a light sound, because I could think better when I played that way . . . I wanted Sonny Stitt and those nine pieces, but Sonny was working someplace, and Gerry [Mulligan] said get Lee [Konitz] because he has a light sound too. And Gerry was playing his baritone – in fact, I didn't expect him to play. I didn't know Gerry until I went down to Gil's house and he was there. We wanted John Simmons because he wanted everything to be light, but Gil said Joe Shulman could play real light . . . But that whole thing started out as an experiment.[8]

Miles also wrote to the pianist and composer John Lewis, who was in Paris at the time, and asked him to write something for the line-up. Lewis was at home with both musical worlds. He had spent fifteen of his first twenty-two years in extensive music studies, and was deeply interested in the possibilities of integrating elements of classical music into jazz.

By mid-1948, external events hastened the genesis of this nine-piece band (trumpet, trombone, French horn, tuba, alto sax, baritone sax, piano, bass and drums). The second recording ban of the 1940s had begun on 30 December 1947 – hence Parker's spate of recording sessions done that autumn and winter to beat the ban. The first recording ban of the decade had lasted from August 1942 until some time in 1944 – depending on when the various record companies signed the agreement with the American Federation of Musicians. The second ban, which ran throughout 1948, ending on 15 December, had powerful short- and long-term effects on jazz. It gave the *coup de grâce* to big bands (even Count Basie had to use a small group after the end of 1949), and because the ban did not extend to singers, it greatly increased the public's taste for vocal music. This dealt a very hard blow to jazz and it was not until the late 1950s that the situation improved much. Meanwhile, a few small recording companies had defied the ban, which enabled Miles to record twice with Parker during the year. Miles also recorded with a septet led by Coleman Hawkins some time in 1948. Apart from these isolated exceptions, recording was not possible during the whole of that year. Claude Thornhill's band was also hit by the slump, and when it disbanded for a while, Gil Evans took the opportunity to leave it for good. This meant that by the middle of 1948, Evans and all the gifted young musicians from Thornhill's band were spoiling for something to absorb their energies.

During the summer, Miles had a fairly long residency at the Royal Roost, leading a band that included at various times Parker, trombonist Kai Winding, and tenor saxophonist Allan Eager. The promoter, Monte Kay, who along with disc jockey Symphony Sid Torin booked groups into the Roost, offered Miles a two-week engagement there with the nine-piece in September. With this prospect, rehearsals began in earnest.

It was both natural and logical that Miles should be the leader of the band, even though it had been born out of collective discussions. Miles had a 'name' and was a musician with outstanding potential; also, his organizing abilities were vital to the whole project. Mulligan comments: 'He took the initiative and put the theories to work. He called the rehearsals, hired the halls, called the players, and generally cracked the whip ... Miles dominated the band completely; the whole nature of the interpretation was his ...'[9] In a BBC Radio 3 interview, Mulligan also explained to jazz critic Charles Fox:

Left to our own devices, Gil, John Carisi and I would probably have procrastinated and maybe never gotten the rehearsals together – Miles was the prime mover. But another factor is far more important: thinking of Miles as the lead voice affected the way we all wrote for the band. Stylistically, Miles was the perfect choice. It's hard to imagine other trumpet players having the same effect on the ensemble. If we'd had a trumpet player that had a more conventional open sound, it wouldn't have had the same impact on the ensemble. Miles's melodic approach and lead voice was a particular influence on the ultimate sound of the ensemble.

During the rehearsals, which took place over a period of several weeks in the late summer of 1948, the wisdom and knowledge of Gil Evans, and his musical conceptions, were very important to Miles. Mike Zwerin, who played trombone with the band during the live engagements, points out that, at rehearsals, 'Miles was pleasant and relaxed but seemed unsure of how to be boss. It was his first time as leader. He relied quite a bit on Evans to give musical instructions to the players.'[10] By the time the band was playing in public, however, Mulligan's description of Miles's musical dominance was probably correct.

In late August and early September, the band appeared for two weeks at the Royal Roost as a relief unit during a Count Basie engagement. Miles created a precedent by billing the arrangers' names as well as his own in front of the club. His part of the evening was billed as: 'Miles Davis Band, Arrangements by Gerry Mulligan, Gil Evans, and John Lewis'. It was the first time any experimental (and virtually unknown) arrangers in jazz, with the exception perhaps of Duke Ellington, had ever received this kind of credit. The nonet recorded a broadcast from the Roost on 4 September, and the personnel of the group was Miles, plus Mike Zwerin (trombone), John 'Bill' Barber (tuba), Junior Collins (French horn), Gerry Mulligan (baritone sax), Lee Konitz (alto sax), John Lewis (piano), Al McKibbon (bass), Max Roach (drums), and Kenneth Hagood (vocals). The last named had formerly sung with Dizzy Gillespie and was probably hired as a sop to the public's penchant for vocals. Later in September, Miles brought the band back for a second residency at the Roost and a second radio broadcast was recorded. Some decades later, nine tracks from these two broadcasts were issued on record. The band failed utterly to interest audiences, however, and its stay at the Roost was not extended. The only other time it worked live occurred the following year when Miles took it into the Clique Club for a short stint. At the Roost in 1948, one or two critics and a few musicians were impressed with the band's new music. Count Basie, with his typical enthusiasm for the work of good young musicians, was full of praise and was quoted as saying: 'Those slow things sounded strange and good. I didn't always know what they were doing, but I listened and liked it.'[11]

The live recordings taken from air-shots (broadcasts) are less tightly integrated performances than the studio recordings which took place a few months later, because the solo space – particularly that of Miles – is much longer in relationship to the written passages. In a live performance it is, of course, natural for soloists to stretch out more. Although the ensemble sound is fluid and relaxed even on the faster and more boppish pieces, the rhythm section, fired by Max Roach, and with some very muscular chord work from John Lewis, really drives along in the polyrhythmic bebop manner. The relationship of horns to rhythm section is a kind of 'ice and fire' situation which creates some marvellous tension. In his solos, Miles veers towards the fire, producing some fast, rhythmically aggressive phrases. Lee Konitz stays cool in all his solos.

These air-shots give the first real indication of just how tough musically and mentally Miles was becoming, and of how complete a musician he was even at that time. For the most part, his trumpet dominates the ensemble sound, dictating the phrasing of passages which are subtle and complex. The trumpet is also exposed because only the alto is anywhere near it in pitch. In such conditions of delicate balance, the lead player must have nerves of steel, for the slightest fluff or wrong note would be clearly audible and mar the whole ensemble sound. Miles is also the main soloist, often having to play the demanding written passages and then go straight into his solo. Even then, he often gets no respite because he has to go straight from the end of his solo into some ensemble passage or bridge to the next soloist. The fact that he does all this in a live session in September 1948, with hardly a falter, is quite remarkable. These air-shots also show how completely the band was ignored at the Royal Roost. There is an audible hubbub of conversation throughout the slower arrangements, and the audience doesn't even seem to notice when a piece has ended.

With the financial failure of his nine-piece band, Miles was forced once more to work as a soloist and with occasional small 'pick-up groups. Late in the year, he worked at a club called Soldier Meyers' in Brooklyn, and then led a group which included Sonny Stitt, Wardell Gray, Bud Powell, Nelson Boyd (bass) and Roy Haynes (drums), at the Orchid Room (the old Onyx) on 52nd Street. Over the Christmas period he appeared at the Clique, which later became Birdland – with Fats Navarro, Lucky Thompson, Dexter Gordon, Kai Winding, Milt Jackson, Bud Powell, Oscar Pettiford and Kenny Clarke, in opposition to a similarly illustrious bill at the Royal Roost. In January 1949, he worked at the Audubon, a small New York jazz room, with Art Blakey and Sonny Rollins.

The recording ban ended in December, and early in 1949, Miles was once more in the studios as a sideman, recording a couple of tracks with the Metronome All Stars. He had made third place in the current *Metronome* poll which Dizzy had won, with Fats Navarro coming second. Miles also played on a couple of tunes recorded by Tadd Dameron's band in April. He had been working on and off with Dameron's band ever since he'd left Parker. But the most important event was the securing of his own personal recording contract for the first time. When the ban ended, two major recording companies. RCA Victor and Capitol, decided to go all out with bebop (or 'modern') recording programmes. Capitol signed Miles, Tadd Dameron, singers Babs Gonzales and Dave Lambert, pianist Lennie Tristano and clarinettist Buddy DeFranco. The last two had also won places in the *Metronome* poll. Miles had a contract for twelve sides at 78 r.p.m. The long-playing

record had not yet been introduced, and there was much controversy between record companies over the relative merits of the
33 r.p.m. and the 45 r.p.m. disc.

Controversy continued to rage about bebop, but it was still a
music with a minority audience, and had no obvious commercial
potential. The really popular music in 1949 was traditional jazz
– the old styles of New Orleans/Dixieland/Chicago. There had
been a revival of interest in this at the beginning of the decade,
and by the end it was sweeping America and Europe. It was played
by old, and often resuscitated, blacks, and by young, romantically
minded whites in search of some (totally imaginary) lost purity.
The other commercially viable music of the time was largely vocal
– crooners such as Bing Crosby and Frank Sinatra, and vocal
groups such as the Andrews Sisters and the Inkspots. Given this
climate, Capitol showed courage – even recklessness – in the people
they signed. Miles Davis was a young trumpeter whose virtues
were not at all easy to spot. He was not a virtuoso like Dizzy,
and he had only recently been leading a nine-piece band which
was a total financial flop. His performance in the January 1949
Metronome poll may have established him in Capitol's eyes as a
rapidly rising star – he had come only tenth in the previous year's
poll – but his signing was ultimately attributable to the chance
enthusiasm of an individual who happened to have the ear of the
record company. The arranger Pete Rugolo suggested that Capitol
should sign Miles in order to record the library of the nine-piece
band. The company agreed, and Rugolo supervised the three
sessions which took place on 21 January, 21 April 1949, and on
9 March 1950. As the band didn't exist except in the recording
studio, the personnel differs on each of the sessions. Only Miles,
Konitz, Mulligan, and the tuba player, John 'Bill' Barber, are
present on all three dates.

The discipline of the 78 r.p.m. record, with its three-minute
time span, had a salutary effect on the nonet's music. Although
many of the finest solos in jazz may have been played live, the
finest examples of total performances – the integration of soloists
with ensembles – have usually been done in the studio. The reasons

for this are simple: to impose a time limit is to impose a form, and to make the most effective use of that form, a balanced sequence of events must take place. From the time of his earliest recordings with Parker, Miles Davis seems to have been aware of this, and there is often a great difference between his live performances and his studio recordings in any one period. In the studio recordings of the nonet, the solos are shorter and the rhythm section is much more restrained. The general atmosphere and 'feel' of the band has, therefore, a greater cohesion and relaxation, what Miles calls a 'soft sound . . . not penetrating too much. To play soft you have to relax . . . you don't delay the beat, but you might play a quarter triplet against four beats and that sounds delayed. If you do it right, it won't bother the rhythm section.'[12]

Eight of the tracks were originally issued in pairings on 78s, and there was a ten-inch LP in the early 1950s, but it wasn't until 1957 that all the tracks (except for the vocal 'Darn That Dream') were reissued on one twelve-inch LP, and entitled *The Birth of the Cool*. These performances received a great deal of critical acclaim which hindsight has shown to have been well justified because they have stood the test of time, and still sound fresh and full of sparkle. They offer an extraordinary variety of ideas and concepts. Mulligan's composition and arrangement, 'Jeru', presents an asymmetry – odd numbers of bars and beats – which was new to jazz at the time. John Carisi's piece, 'Israel', contains some brilliant passages of counterpoint and polyphony, and also plays off the lower instruments against the higher ones in an intensely dramatic way. Gil Evans's arrangement of 'Moon Dreams', apart from a few bars of baritone solo, is an entirely composed (pre-composed may be a more accurate expression) piece which turns from mellow-textured 'mood' music into dissonance and jagged movement, producing a disturbing musical vision with dark undertones.

'Boplicity', composed by Miles himself under the pseudonym Cleo Henry (his mother's name), and arranged by Gil Evans, is notable for the marvellous relaxation of the whole ensemble, the written variations on the initial melody, and the fluid way the ensemble passages are interwoven with the two soloists (baritone and trumpet). In 1951, Miles cited this as his own favourite: 'That's because of the arrangement. Gil Evans did it.'[13]

Even in these more compact performances, Miles still dominates the band. His clear, non-brassy sound gives the written passages a particular flavour, and he gets – and deserves – more solo space than anyone else. He sounds more at ease and poised on these studio recordings than he did on the Roost air-shots, and his flow of ideas is excellent. He alternates long melodic lines with lovely pauses, broken rhythms and longer notes with just a hint of vibrato which enhances their swing and their emotional power. His solo on 'Godchild' (Appendix A, Fig. 1) demonstrates all these qualities.

Some black musicians were angry that Miles had whites in his band. This was to be a recurring theme at intervals throughout his subsequent career, because in every decade he would employ one or two white musicians. His response was always that he hired musicians not for their colour, but for the music that was within them. Opinions were also expressed by some musicians and critics that the Birth of the Cool music had a basically white impulse and origin, but Miles insisted that it came from Duke Ellington via Claude Thornhill, who was influenced by Duke and Fletcher Henderson. In fact, the roots of this cool, self-communing, singable music go back to the 1920s and such classics as Louis Armstrong's vocal dialogue with the clarinet in 'West End Blues', and Ellington's 'Mood Indigo' and 'Dusk'. From 1947 onwards, Miles's music tended to be a critique of bebop, which he felt was unsingable by non-musicians, and lacked certain essential emotional dimensions.

The nonet recordings, however, spawned the cool 'West Coast Jazz' school of the 1950s. This was a largely white movement which received an enormous amount of radio play, and made records that were promoted vigorously by the record companies. The fact that much of the music was sometimes sterile and ephemeral did not seem to matter; it had a surface palatability which disc jockeys found easy to accept. From Miles's own seminal band, John Lewis went off to form the Modern Jazz Quartet, Gerry

Mulligan formed his pianoless quartet with trumpeter Chet Baker (who was influenced by Davis), and Lee Konitz worked with Lennie Tristano and formed groups of his own. These musicians were all at the centre of the movement and had the essential talent and vision to create something really valid. As had been the case with bebop, it was the second-raters who absorbed the mannerisms and missed the substance. But Miles's nonet recordings had at least one deep and lasting influence: they raised the whole question of the relationship of the soloist to the ensemble. Miles and a few other leading musicians would spend the following decades finding various answers and solutions in this problematic area.

While the Birth of the Cool recordings did not win a great audience for Miles, they established him as someone separate from Charlie Parker. Before them, he had been regarded more or less as an interesting and talented acolyte, but now he began to gain more undivided critical attention, and the reviews in *Down Beat*, for example, were all appreciative. These recordings also raised Miles's stock with other musicians; he was seen to be a leader with a flair for new sounds. Tadd Dameron, who only four years previously had been teaching Miles chords, said in 1949: 'Davis is the furthest advanced musician of his day, and "Boplicity" is one of the best small-group sounds I've heard.'[14] And musicians who were more in the mainstream of American music were also favourably impressed. The bandleader, Elliot Lawrence, for example, referred to 'those great Miles Davis sides on Capitol'. Even the Chicago-style traditionalist, Eddie Condon, murmured approval. The band and its music were a critical success, but existed only on record. From the point of view of living music, which has a voluntary, paying public, the nonet was a non-starter.

It was to take Miles another five or six years before he could achieve enough know-how and financial backing to lead bands that functioned regularly both in the studio and in clubs and concert halls.

FOUR

Cold Turkey

'I got hooked after I got back from the Paris Jazz
Festival. I got bored and was around cats that were
hung. So I wound up with a habit that took me
four years to break.'[1]

Miles Davis

Early in 1949, Miles worked for a few weeks in Chicago, and
then returned to New York to spend some time with a group led
by Tadd Dameron. In May, he went to Paris with Dameron to
play at the Salle Pleyel opposite Parker's quintet. The French had
acquired a vigorous interest in bebop since Dizzy Gillespie's big
band and Howard McGhee's quintet had played there the previous
year. There were two big annual jazz events in France in the late
1940s. the Paris Jazz Fair in the spring, and the Nice Festival in
the summer. The two main stars of the 1949 Paris Fair were
Charlie Parker and Sidney Bechet, each of whom represented very
different eras of jazz. Miles and Tadd Dameron were to play with
a pick-up group which included James Moody on tenor sax, Kenny
Clarke on drums, and bassist Barney Spieler, who had worked
with Mel Powell, Benny Goodman and Claude Thornhill. During
the week, soloists and performers from other areas of the music
were also featured: Hot Lips Page, the swing-era trumpeter, was
there, and on one night, the old blues singer, Leadbelly, gave a
recital to a tiny audience at the Cité Université.

Bird and Miles were lionized in Paris, fêted everywhere,
admired, bombarded with questions, and seemed to be always

surrounded by adoring fans and musicians. Miles was asked the usual questions – what mouthpiece he used, how much he practised and so on. For both Parker and Davis, it was their first real experience of the enormous dichotomy between their acceptance in America and their following abroad. In New York, they were members of a small clique of musicians with a tiny cult following. In Paris, they were international celebrities whose every word and note carried weight. The media covered their visit thoroughly, and there were broadcasts of the music and recorded interviews with the musicians. Denis Preston recorded an interview with Miles for BBC Radio, and found the trumpeter more co-operative than Sidney Bechet. Miles also spent some time in Paris with leading artists and intellectuals such as Pablo Picasso and Jean-Paul Sartre, and the existentialist fringe as exemplified by the trumpeter and novelist Boris Vian and his wife, and the singer Juliette Greco. Miles and Juliette fell in love and their affair continued intermittently for several years.

Thirteen performances from Miles's Paris concerts were recorded for radio, and the nine or ten of them later released on record give a vivid impression of the excitement of the occasion. Unlike the nonet air-shots, the French air-shots reveal a totally partisan audience which applauds wildly – solos, performances, anything and everything. As Miles remarked a few years later: 'In Europe, they like everything you do. The mistakes and everything. That's a little bit too much.'[2] Three of the pieces played by Miles and the quintet are 'Crazy Rhythm', 'Embraceable You' (which Miles *announces* in a crisp and pleasant voice), and 'All the Things You Are'. It is difficult to believe that the trumpeter here is the same man who, only two or three weeks previously, had recorded 'Boplicity'. In Paris, Miles plays with a broad tone and powerful aggression. He makes frequent forays into the upper register, and even ends 'Crazy Rhythm' with a sustained F sharp (E concert) above his top C – a very high note indeed. He plays a lyrical and deeply felt solo on the ballad 'Embraceable You', and then with 'All the Things You Are' goes back to wild athleticism. He takes all kinds of risks, some of which don't come off, and so there are a few fluffs. This is really the result of the occasion; it is a live performance and the improviser is intent on pushing his own physical and creative resources to their limits. Although he is always supposed to be unaware of audiences, it is highly significant that during his earlier career, the orgiastic side of Miles's trumpet playing showed itself only in live performances. Not until the 1960s and 1970s does it appear in the clinical surroundings of the recording studio.

If Miles walked on air in Paris, he came back to earth with a painful thump when he returned to New York. The acclaimed international star was reduced to an out-of-work and scuffling musician. Apart from an occasional gig, he was unemployed for the rest of the year. In August, he and Tadd Dameron rehearsed an eighteen-piece band, but because of the effects of the recording ban, the time was not ripe for such a unit, and the project did not get beyond the rehearsal stage. Like his nine-piece venture, this was another bitter setback for Miles; it seemed his luck had run out.

He was just twenty-three, yet he'd already made musical history with Parker, and on his own with the nonet recordings. He was becoming *the* new influence on trumpet players, and was regarded by musicians as one of the leaders of the scene. His life had been notable for iron self-discipline, and he had remained fairly abstemious in his habits. He had gained international recognition at the Paris Jazz Fair. In terms of American ideals and aspirations, he was a total success. He had every right to expect the natural rewards: regular work, a financial situation viable enough to enable him to lead a regular group, and certainly more recognition in his own country. Instead, he found no work at all, and no prospects of any in the foreseeable future. It is hardly surprising that despair and boredom made him turn to drugs.

His addiction was a total surprise to people who thought they knew him well, because he seemed the cleanest-living musician of the bop generation. The pianist, Gil Coggins, commented: 'He was the type of man . . . with that bourgeois shit. He never wants you to catch him nodding . . . he had that control . . . he keeps people at a distance because he don't want to get hurt.' As Miles said, boredom was probably a major factor. It was several months since he'd left Parker and, on his own at last, facing an apparently bleak future, he must have craved for the 'sense of peril' he had, up to this point, experienced only vicariously through Bird. Miles may have begun taking heroin for kicks, but he soon became completely addicted to it and slid rapidly into chaos and degradation. The clean-cut, self-disciplined, bourgeois young man underwent a rapid and horrible transformation into an uncontrolled, unreliable, amoral person. For four years he worked only fitfully, his health deteriorated, and he touched rock-bottom, living off any women who liked him or took pity on him, sometimes even resorting to pimping ('When I was using dope . . . I used to take bitches' money')[3] and often prepared to do anything to get enough cash for a fix.

Inevitably, he neglected his family, eventually moving Irene and the two children to other apartments first in Jamaica, Queens, then in St Albans. Juliette Greco had been his ideal romance and she was continually on his mind and, in addition to that, his drug addiction compounded his feelings of guilt so that he could not face Irene and the children, but left them in the care of the great singer, Betty Carter. She was a pillar of strength to Irene, and for years Miles felt the weight of Betty's disapproval of his abdication.

After the last nonet studio sessions in March 1950, Miles had no immediate prospects of any further recordings. His contract with Capitol had been fulfilled and the company, discouraged by the moderate sales of the nonet tracks, was not interested in renewing it. In May, he appeared as a sideman on six tracks recorded with the vocalist, Sarah Vaughan, and said of them later: 'I like the things with Sarah . . . I like the sound I got, especially on "It Might as Well Be Spring".'[4] In June, Miles led a septet which included J. J. Johnson, Tadd Dameron and Art Blakey, opposite Parker's group at Birdland. In the late summer, Miles worked as a sideman in a small group that Billy Eckstine took on tour. It was while he was on this concert tour that he was arrested on suspicion of being a heroin addict. The charge was subsequently dismissed, but the resulting publicity had a bad effect on his career. The critic, Leonard Feather, wrote in *Down Beat*: 'News of the arrest has shocked American music circles, for Miles has frequently expressed his disapproval of the habits of so many of his fellow-boppers.'[5] After this adverse publicity, no one wanted to employ him and he simply disappeared from the New York scene, taking himself and his habit to Chicago. He also had his family there with him at least some of the time, and this year saw the birth of his third child, a son whom he named Miles (IV).

In Chicago, Miles lived in hotels and was apparently still getting some financial assistance from his father. Gil Coggins saw him there and recalled:

> He was in a marvellous hotel then. I think it cost $28 a week, and then ... $28! ... that was a pretty nice hotel! And that time he was messing around with everybody. His old man was sending him $75 ... his old man would pay for his phone bills – $35 ... that's a lot of calling ... Shit [heroin] was cheap – you could get a capsule for a dollar ... it was pure, you know, potent.

But with an increasing drug habit and very little work, Miles was often in desperate financial straits. His brother Vernon spent some time with him in Chicago, and Babs Gonzales tells a pitiful story about the pair of them being so hard up that they tried to make off with the money ($300) of a would-be drug buyer, but were themselves tricked by one of their associates, who disappeared with the ill-gotten gains.[6]

Meanwhile, new opportunities to record were about to present themselves to Miles. Immediately after the second recording ban had ended, a small, independent label called New Jazz was started by Bob Weinstock, an enthusiast whose early love for traditional jazz and the blues had expanded to include contemporary developments. Weinstock was regularly in the audience at the Royal Roost, or 'Metropolitan Bopera House' as it was dubbed, and he had been deeply impressed by Miles's nine-piece band. Weinstock had started the New Jazz label for 'kicks with a very limited distribution planned'. After his first recording in January 1949 with Lee Konitz, the initial sales were so promising that Weinstock took his own label seriously and spent the next two years personally riding buses from city to city, building his distribution. By 1950, he'd also introduced the Prestige label, and wanted Miles to record for it. He was convinced that Miles had found his true identity with the nonet recordings, and no doubt Weinstock was hoping for some kind of continuity with them. The first problem was finding Miles. Weinstock knew that the trumpeter's family lived in East St Louis, and when he was on a business trip there he went through the Davises in the phone book and eventually got through to Miles's home:

> They told me he was in Chicago. I said, 'Please, if you should hear from Miles, ask him to call me in New York. I want to record him.' Finally he got in touch with me, and he came back East. Miles, at that time, although he still dug the cool music of Mulligan and Evans, some of the primitiveness in him started to come out. I say primitiveness, because to me the music of the bop masters is primitive music, like the original New Orleans music of King Oliver and Louis. He sort of drifted back into that element, and he liked Sonny Rollins, as crude as Sonny was at that time, and John Lewis. On his first date, you can hear a very different Miles Davis than on the Capitols.[7]

Weinstock was perceptive in recognizing the connection between bebop and the New Orleans music of Oliver and Armstrong. He was more perceptive, for example, than Louis himself, who would have been outraged at the comparison. But Weinstock's analysis and terminology are wrong. In both bebop and the music of Oliver and Armstrong in the 1920s, the non-Western (African) elements are very potent, and it is this aspect which Weinstock calls 'primitive'. The music of Charlie Parker is not at all primitive; it is extremely subtle and sophisticated. According to the criteria Weinstock seems to be using, Duke Ellington would have to be regarded as more primitive than Glenn Miller . . . an obvious absurdity.

Despite his inactivity, Miles was voted into first place in the 1951 *Metronome* poll, and continued to win this category in 1952 and 1953. This must have been due to his performances on record because, according to Leonard Feather, it was doubtful if he worked more than six or seven weeks during the whole of 1951. Financially, the situation was becoming desperate, and Miles was often reduced to earning small sums of money by transcribing music from records for lead sheets. He recalled: 'I'd take the $30 for the transcribing, go uptown, and get high.'[8] But this lowly chore was one of the lesser indignities he had to suffer during the period of his addiction. According to Babs Gonzales, Miles was exploited pitilessly by club owners and entrepreneurs, and made to play for very little money; in fact, the hoods who ran one club in New York used to beat up Miles and Bud Powell and other musicians who were addicts and in debt to them. The only other way Miles could make any money was by recording, but as he was playing very little, his embouchure or 'chops' were often in poor shape. Furthermore, as a result of his drug habit he was often in very poor health, which also affected his trumpet playing. The trumpet is a most demanding instrument physically, and the player needs to be fit. But the desperate need for cash occasionally made him accept a recording session when he was in no real condition to do it. In later years, he came to regard much of his output over this period as inferior, and commented: 'When I had a habit, I didn't care.'[9]

With the knowledge that Weinstock wanted to record him, Miles went back to New York at the beginning of 1951. It was about seven months since he'd been in the studios, and he broke that long silence on 17 January with a double date, recording first as a sideman with Charlie Parker's quintet, and then as a leader with his own sextet. It was a demanding experience after such a long lay-off, but the recordings were all for 78 or 45 r.p.m. singles, and so the tracks were very short. The brief reunion with Parker was a happy occasion, with Bird in tremendous form and Miles playing some sparse, delicately poised solos which presaged his later style.

Miles's own session on 17 January was, in fact, his first as leader of a small group. The earlier nine-piece was not only halfway towards being a big band, but it was also a unit which bore collectively much of the responsibility for the music, and there was always the father figure of Gil Evans in the background. With his sextet, the onus was entirely on Miles; he had to choose the musicians and decide on the kind of music he wanted to produce. He did not choose any of the young white musicians who had been associated with the nonet, but instead used the twenty-one-year-old tenor saxophonist, Sonny Rollins, trombonist Benny Green, John Lewis (the only link with the nonet), bassist Percy Heath (who'd worked with Gillespie and Howard McGhee), and drummer Roy Haynes. It was a group of young black musicians whose musical experience had been shaped by the bebop masters.

So far as personnel was concerned, Miles had made a clear choice, but the music he chose to record showed indecision. Of the four pieces recorded, two of them ('Morpheus' composed by John Lewis, and 'Down' written by Miles) hover uneasily between the cool style and the hotter, funkier approach. 'Morpheus' is very odd. The theme, with its dissonant chords and passages of percussion, veers towards Western abstract music, but then it suddenly turns into a fast blues with altered chord changes. 'Down' starts off as a funky blues played over a deeply grooving half-feel, but after four bars it reverts to straight 4/4 with a smoother feel, and the final bars of the theme are pure 'cool' school in the tonal quality of the voicings and the legato phrasing.

The other two pieces recorded that day were the standard tune 'Whispering', and the Rodgers and Hart ballad 'Blue Room'. The rhythm section is excellent throughout all four tracks, and Benny Green improvises some impeccably conceived and executed melodic lines, but the real power of these performances lies in the contribution of the two people who make the most mistakes: Sonny Rollins and Miles. Rollins squeaks now and then, and sometimes either fails to round off his phrases or just manages to scramble through them, but his sound, the urgency of his attack and the efforts of an obviously original mind to express itself, make his contribution a telling one. Miles too, even though he fumbles a double-tempo run on 'Whispering', and falters on both takes of 'Blue Room', nevertheless makes his impact by virtue of his huge, non-brassy trumpet sound and the depth of feeling he expresses. Of his early recordings, his playing on 'Blue Room' is technically perhaps the poorest, and yet this is one of the most moving and memorable tracks of that period.

About a week after this session, Miles recorded a track with the Metronome All Stars. Of the eleven musicians in this pollwinners' band, only two – Miles and Max Roach – were black. In the early 1950s there was an outcry in the American musical press because polls conducted in Europe were dominated by black musicians. The easy association of black and white musicians that had prevailed in the 1940s was now becoming more problematic, undermined by mistrust. But on 8 March, Miles was back in the studios, this time as a sideman with Lee Konitz, who had commissioned George Russell to compose a couple of pieces. Russell arrived at the session with 'Ezz-thetic' (named after the boxer Ezzard Charles), a fast and complex piece based on the harmonies of 'Love for Sale', and 'Odjenar', a slower, atmospheric piece. Odjenar was the maiden name of Russell's then wife, Juanita, who also came along for the occasion. Apart from Max Roach on drums and Miles, Konitz and all the other members of the group – Sal Mosca on piano, Billy Bauer on guitar and Arnold Fishkin on bass – were musical associates of Lennie Tristano, so both the material and its treatment were cool and rather abstract.

Miles, still in thrall to heroin, was in such bad shape that day that he couldn't manage the tricky theme of 'Ezz-thetic', and even tried to leave the studio. Russell recalled: 'As he was going out of the door, Juanita ran over, grabbed him by his collar and dragged him back in, and she said, "You're staying here until you finish this, and I'm going to see to it!" He wasn't in condition to do battle – at that time he wasn't really functioning.' Miles stayed, and the upshot was that Lee Konitz played the theme of 'Ezz-thetic' while Miles improvised a lyrical counter-line. Konitz was on excellent form throughout the session, but apart from one solo chorus on Konitz's piece 'Hi Beck', based on the chords of 'Pennies from Heaven', Miles hardly plays at all. His sound and poise on that one chorus are good, but he seems very ill at ease in the fragments he plays on the other three pieces, which include the standard 'Yesterdays'. Not surprisingly, the reviews were mediocre.

For his next Prestige recording session, which took place on 5 October 1951, Miles was not only in better physical and mental shape, but also revealed a surer sense of identity. He had been playing at Birdland just before this record date, which must have helped improve his performance. Also, this was his first recording for a long-playing record, which meant that, for the first time in the studio, he was not forced to compress his performances into three-minute units. His unit, from now on, was to be the duration of a long-playing record, about twenty minutes a side. He could fill this time with long or short pieces according to his inclinations. This increased freedom was perfect for Miles, because his reflective approach to improvisation blossomed when it could stretch out. On five of the seven tracks recorded that day, Miles takes double solo space, playing the first solo, and then a second one when the others have had their say. He again took a sextet into the studio, with Rollins, alto saxophonist Jackie McLean, pianist Walter Bishop Jr, bassist Tommy Potter and Art Blakey.

For the first time on record, Miles plays really long solos, and gives us a glimpse of the extent of his improvising power, revealing a great variety of rhythmic and melodic ideas. His sound is now so pure, so clear, that it is almost not a trumpet sound at all, but a disembodied sound emanating directly from him. That gloriously lyrical sound is given all the inflexions from the black vocal tradition: slurs, smears, half-valve choked effects, and superbly expressive bent notes. His sound has strong 'feminine' overtones because it is so smooth and singing, but his rhythms are often aggressively 'masculine' – though they are always subtle. Miles seems to have made some progress in reconciling the warring elements of his nature, and is beginning to achieve some internal unity at last.

The results were by no means flawless, however. The ensembles are sometimes a little ragged, and in Miles's own solos there are one or two passages – particularly those attempting to use the upper register – which sound very uneasy. But several things come off superbly: a beautiful version of the song, 'It's Only a Paper Moon', a long, self-communing trumpet solo on 'My Old Flame' and Miles's second solo on 'Blueing', which is a gem. At that time recording engineers had still not learned how to record rhythm sections properly, and so the piano, drums, and particularly the bass didn't quite match up to the sound of the horns. After 'Blueing' has petered out raggedly, Miles is heard saying in injured tones to Art Blakey: 'Play the ending, man. You know the arrangement!' Considering that the main soloists were so young – Miles was twenty-five, Bishop twenty-four, Rollins twenty-two, and McLean a mere nineteen – it is remarkable that the quality of the music is so consistent. Charlie Parker was present in the studio while the tracks were being recorded, and no doubt he gave some courage to his young protégés.

After this happy session, the old problems reasserted themselves: lack of work, lack of money, and an increasing need for drugs. Miles hardly worked at all for the rest of the year, and his health fluctuated wildly. At times he became a near derelict. His old friend and mentor, Clark Terry, came across him one day on Broadway. Miles was actually sitting on the kerb in a daze. Terry asked him what was wrong, and Miles replied, 'I don't feel well.' Clark Terry took him to a restaurant and bought him some ham and eggs. Even after eating, Miles looked so ill and worn out that Terry, who was staying at the Hotel American on West 47th Street, took him back there and put him to bed. Then, Terry recalls:

I went out and purposely stayed out so that he could get some rest and of course, people who are strung out on narcotics are not responsible for things they do, and when I came back . . . to see how he was doing and bring him a cup of tea . . .

my door was open and Miles was gone and all my belongings! But I don't hold it against him because he wasn't responsible. I just love him the more because he overcame that, y'know.

Clark, however, was so worried about Miles that he phoned his wife in St Louis and asked her to tell Davis senior about his son's condition. But when she told Miles's father the news he simply said, 'The only thing that's wrong with Miles now is because of those damn musicians like your husband that he's hanging around with.'[10]

Nevertheless, once Miles's father became fully aware of the situation, he did everything he could to help, and tried to persuade Miles to go for a cure. Red Rodney, who had joined Parker in 1949, had also become a junkie, and despite several attempts, didn't manage to kick the habit until the end of the 1950s. During one of his attempts at rehabilitation, Rodney was a patient in an institution in Kentucky, and one day he got a message that Miles was in reception, having been brought there by his father. Rodney recalls: 'I ran down the hall, and by the time I got there he was gone . . . he didn't stay. They wanted him to check in and stay for four months, and he refused. He said he wouldn't stay that long, and he and his father left.' Miles was obviously not fully ready to quit the habit. Some years later he said from the wisdom of experience: 'You can't talk a man out of a habit until he really wants to stop.'[11]

During 1952, Miles spent some periods of time at home in East St Louis, and on one of these visits he played with the band of the local tenor saxophonist Jimmy Forrest for a few weeks. This, apart from a tour with a package called Jazz Inc, headed by disc jockey Symphony Sid, and including Milt Jackson (vibraphone), Zoot Sims and Jimmy Heath (tenors), seems to have been the only extended public appearance he made that year. Also, he had only one recording date. This was a session for the Blue Note label, and for it he used a sextet which included J. J. Johnson, Jackie McLean, pianist Gil Coggins, bassist Oscar Pettiford, and Kenny Clarke on drums. But apart from these isolated events, 1952 was an empty and miserable year for Miles Davis. Early in the year, Leonard Feather wrote an article for *Melody Maker*, heading it: 'Poll-topper Miles has been at a standstill since back in 1950', and in a long piece reviewing Miles's whole career to date, he said: 'One of the most influential of modern jazzmen, through his trumpet work and through the school of orchestral bop started by his Capitol records, Miles in the past year has seen his career slip away from him while his imitators have been progressing.'[12]

During both 1952 and 1953, Miles's career was in the doldrums because of his poor health and the infrequency of his work, but he did set about reviewing his musical experience to date and reinterpreting some of the music of his immediate past. In the first few months of 1953, he did three recording sessions wildly different in emotional climate and artistic achievement. In January he recorded two of his own compositions ('Compulsion' and 'The Serpent's Tooth') and Monk's ballad, ''Round Midnight', with a sextet which included Charlie Parker and Sonny Rollins on tenors, Walter Bishop (piano), Percy Heath (bass), and Philly Joe Jones (drums). This session was a very uneasy one and the music is full of flaws. In the themes, the three horns seem to suffer from sour intonation and they don't blend at all. Miles has some problems with articulation as well as intonation, though both he and Bird produce moments of powerfully emotive music. But the renewal of the old relationship with Parker did not seem to bear fruit. The two men had words on the date, because Bird had rather incapacitated himself by drinking too much gin. Miles was angry, and pointed out that he (Miles) had never failed Bird on a record date. Parker, who must always have been conscious of Miles's bourgeois origins, replied in an exaggerated British accent: 'All right Lily Pons. To produce beauty, we must suffer pain – from the oyster comes the pearl!'[13]

In February, Miles was in the studios again, this time with a septet comprising the two white saxophonists Al Cohn and Zoot Sims, trombonist Sonny Truitt, and a rhythm section of John Lewis, Kenny Clarke and bassist Leonard Gaskin. The four pieces they recorded were all written by Al Cohn, and the resulting music could hardly be more different from that of the earlier session. This septet sounds oddly like a pit orchestra in a Broadway musical; the arrangements are light, reminiscent of showbiz music, and impeccably played. The solos are all swinging and accomplished. Cohn and Sims come out of the Lester Young school, and this music is a reversion almost to a pre-1940 swing style. Considerable craftsmanship is involved, but little substance.

Then in April, craftsmanship and content came beautifully together on a second session for Blue Note, when Miles recorded some tracks which, in later years, he admitted to liking. The material consisted largely of a couple of themes associated with Dizzy Gillespie's big band, and some compositions by Jimmy Heath and J. J. Johnson, both of whom played on the date, along with Gil Coggins, Percy Heath and Art Blakey. The horns blend superbly, the themes are executed cleanly, and Blakey's powerful polyrhythms inspire some muscular trumpet solos. These Blue Note tracks were nearly all very short – around the three- or four-minute mark – despite the advent of the LP. Whereas the February recording date had seemed like a musical aberration for Miles, this April session with his close associates sounds right and natural. With the three record dates in the early months of 1953, and the sextet session in May of the previous year, Miles had reviewed his own immediate past. There was one further quartet session – just Miles and a rhythm section – in May, and after that the survey was complete.

Outside the ordered world of the recording studios, however, things were going badly and Miles was reduced to appearing as a soloist in various towns with local musicians. His great companion during this period was drummer and fellow-junkie, Philly Joe Jones, whose musical relationship with the trumpeter was to form the nucleus of the first great Miles Davis Quintet in the middle 1950s. Miles and Philly Joe had worked together off and on since 1952 and established an almost telepathic rapport. Because it was economically impossible to run a permanent group, the two of them worked as a unit, to which they added local musicians for gigs in each new town. Philly Joe recalls:

Miles and I had been barnstorming around the country. When we got to a city where we had a gig, I'd get there first and find another horn player, a piano player and a bass player. In those days we were really putting the music together. We'd get on the plane and he'd hum the arrangements we'd play. When I got the musicians together, he never had much to say to them except 'Hi'. He'd have me talk to them ... It got to be a drag, because every town we'd play, I'd try to find the musicians that were the cream of the crop, but they wouldn't be worth shit. We finally had to sit down and hash over the musicians that we both knew who could really play. We had it all in our minds what we were going to do.[14]

The ordeal of having to rely on often inferior local musicians was beginning to wear Miles down. At the same time, other trumpet players with regular groups were beginning to gain reputations which were eclipsing Miles's own fame. The young trumpeter with Gerry Mulligan's quartet was Chet Baker, and he, though strongly in debt stylistically to Miles, was rapidly overtaking Davis in terms of exposure and popularity – largely because the quartet had both identity and stability as a unit and was building up an international audience. Also, the early 1950s saw the rise of the phenomenal young trumpet star (one of Red Rodney's pupils) Clifford Brown who, with Art Farmer (another emerging talent), was featured soloist with Lionel Hampton's band. Miles was becoming a forgotten man, and the reality of his situation was brought home to him brutally when he spent several months off the scene in the backwater of Detroit, where he was eking out his existence with a local rhythm section at a club called the Bluebird Inn.

He went back yet again to his father's place in East St Louis, and he was visited there by Max Roach and Charles Mingus, who were driving from New York to Los Angeles. Roach was going there to take over Shelly Manne's drum chair with Howard Rumsey's Lighthouse All Stars, and Miles decided to join him and Mingus on the trip. In California, Miles sat in with various musicians at the Lighthouse and on 13 September he recorded three tracks with them, later released on an album called *Miles Davis and the Lighthouse All Stars*. While there he also became friendly with Chet Baker, and met for the first time the beautiful dancer Frances Davis, later to become Miles's first legal wife. But things on the California trip soured when he behaved badly and tried the patience of Max Roach and others to breaking point. Yet again, Miles telephoned his father, asking him to send the bus fare home, and once in East St Louis, Miles went straight back to his father's farm.

Clearly, addiction was rapidly destroying Miles; it was imperative that he free himself of drugs. He had tried psychoanalysis without success, and now in desperation kicked his habit 'cold turkey'. He told *Ebony* magazine:

> I made up my mind I was getting off dope. I was sick and tired of it. You know you can get tired of anything. You can even get tired of being scared. I laid down and stared at the ceiling for twelve days and I cursed everybody I didn't like. I was kicking it the hard way. It was like having a bad case of flu, only worse. I lay in a cold sweat. My nose and eyes ran. I threw up everything I tried to eat. My pores opened up and I smelled like chicken soup. Then it was over.[15]

Miles Davis was one of the very few who broke the habit by themselves, without help or treatment. Many of the others – Fats Navarro and Sonny Berman among them – died prematurely. A few others, like Gerry Mulligan, managed to kick the habit with the aid of psychoanalysis. But to do it 'cold turkey', as Miles had done, was remarkable. Years later, he was to say that two of his heroes – boxers Sugar Ray Robinson and Jack Johnson – had given him moral strength by their example: 'Sugar Ray inspired me and made me kick the habit . . . when he started training – he wouldn't make it with chicks. He disciplined himself and all that . . . and Jack Johnson too!'[16]

The addiction had left terrible scars, and the effect of this experience on Miles's subsequent life and work cannot be over-estimated. Up to 1949, he had shown iron self-discipline, and then as a junkie had revealed great weaknesses. Without the protection and insulation of his privileged family background, he was plunged into a lifestyle exactly like that of the black ghettos in big cities. Miles Davis has always been a very proud man, and he has said little about the kinds of degradation he suffered during this period, but the knowledge of his own ignominies and of the indignities he was forced to suffer must have filled him with horror. No doubt the strength he found to break the habit was inspired as much by self-loathing as by the examples of his heroes. After this whole experience, nothing would ever be the same for him again, and his vision was immeasurably deepened. His father commented: 'It had to put a hard crust on Miles. There was always somebody trying to get him back on dope again. He had an iron will that broke it and that willpower applied to everything he did as a result. I'm proud of him.'[17]

Miles had travelled to the limits both physically and psychologically during the four years of addiction, and now that he had come out of the experience intact, he had greater strength, greater identity and greater profundity – all of which were to reveal themselves in his life and art. Some years later, he said:

I don't think nothing about death. I should have been dead a long time ago. But it missed me when I was on dope. That's why I don't have any fear in my eyes. Some people accuse me of being mean and racist because I don't bow and scrape. When they look in my eyes and don't see fear they know it's a draw.[18]

FIVE

The First Great Quintet

'The thing to judge in any jazz artist is does the man
project, and does he have ideas.'[1]

Miles Davis

Miles had kicked the drug habit by the beginning of 1954, but
the four years of addiction had taken their toll and although he
was careful about what he ate, and obsessive about exercise, he
was dogged by ill-health. It seemed that his fanatical fitness campaign was not so much to promote magnificent health as to keep
sickness at bay and ensure merely that his body was functioning
normally. But from this point onwards, he was blessed with all
kinds of musical insights, and his recordings during the seven years
up to 1960 showed a sustained, radical creativity rarely equalled
in jazz or any other twentieth-century music. During this time he
was discovering his full musical identity, minting a whole new
vocabulary of phrases, finding fresh ways of making music
'breathe' and producing a profusion of small-group and orchestral
masterpieces. A hint of the riches to come occurred in 1954 when
he revealed, at the comparatively late age of twenty-seven, rising
twenty-eight, a fully mature and totally original approach to the
trumpet. In a sense, this year resembles 1947, when Miles was
recording with Parker and made tremendous strides towards finding his own distinctive voice on trumpet. At that time, of course,
he was working (and recording) regularly with Bird's group, which
enabled him to sustain his progress. In 1954, although he was still
working irregularly and had no permanent group, he managed

to achieve an important continuity of personnel in his recording sessions. There were six that year, and on all of them the bass player is Percy Heath. On the first two sessions, the drummer is Art Blakey, and on the last four sessions, Kenny Clarke. On the first five sessions, the pianist is Horace Silver. This continuity must have promoted the kind of rapport with a rhythm section that Miles needed to allow him to create most freely. Two or three of his studio performances, from April onwards, rank with the greatest small-group recordings in jazz. During this year there emerges on record, for the first time, the intangible, indefinable capacity he had for welding together disparate personalities so that by some strange alchemy the whole ensemble becomes greater than the sum of its parts. But this extra touch of magic did not appear on the first three studio sessions of 1954.

The first two dates took place on 6 and 15 March, with a quartet (Silver, Heath and Blakey). This was Miles's first time in the studio for ten months and, as is often the case after a long lay-off, the result was a profusion of ideas and a stronger sense of identity. A sure sign of an intensely creative period in a jazz musician's career is a wealth of new written themes, or new ways of treating older material. On these March sessions, Miles recorded four new compositions of his own, and an original blues ('Blue Haze') which started a fashion for beginning blues performances with a bass solo. Also, his treatment of one standard ('Old Devil Moon') was so fresh that it brought the tune to the attention of other people, and within seven months of Miles's version, it was recorded by Sarah Vaughan, J. J. Johnson and Carmen McRae.

The music throughout these two sessions shows a general movement away from bebop and towards a much sparer style in which there are no empty mannerisms. For the most part, each note of Miles's improvisations is organically related to the notes before and after it. Only in the faster pieces, such as 'Take-Off' and 'The Leap', is he at all prodigal with notes, but even here there are innovations which point to his future development. Both these compositions use pedal points – moments when the harmonic sequence is arrested and the soloist plays over one chord for a few bars. The interest at these points becomes not so much linear and harmonic as rhythmic and spatial, and they are used in these performances to create tension that is released when the chord changes are played again. This enhances the drama of the music, and the most dramatic use of the device occurs in 'The Leap' where the pedal points last a full sixteen bars, the final two bars being an instrumental break which launches the soloist into the next section of harmonic changes. As might be expected after such a long lay-off, there are occasional failures of lip and judgement in Miles's solos, but the tonal beauty of his sound had definitely increased, and on the ballad, 'It Never Entered My Mind', his sound with the cup mute is the best of his whole career up to that time – superbly rounded and glowing. On 'Blue Haze' he treats the blues as blues, and not merely as a springboard for flights of harmonic and melodic fantasy, and his five choruses are eloquent with all the bent notes, slurs and smears that Miles uses to 'put his own substance, his own flesh on a note'[2] to quote Gil Evans. Horace Silver vividly remembers the recording of 'Blue Haze':

We'd tried it and it didn't seem to work at all. Then Miles told Bob Weinstock to put out all the lights in the studio – so the only light we had was from the window of the control booth. Miles sat in a chair and pulled his cap right over his face – and he also took his shoes off. Then he beat it in at just the right tempo . . . and the whole thing happened perfectly.

On his next recording session (3 April), Miles played all four pieces using a cup mute, and the full sound he got obviously inspired him because he produced consistently incisive phrases. The cup mute sound, however, has only a limited expressivity because it is bland and has a narrow range of tonal inflexions. The group was a quintet with Kenny Clarke on drums, the alto saxophonist Dave Schildkraut, and Silver and Heath, and although the rhythm section is excellent, and Miles in good form, the music is not totally satisfactory because Schildkraut lacked authority as a soloist, because Horace Silver had not yet fully grasped his role in Miles's music, and because the cup mute sound is too one-dimensional.

But on his very next session (29 April), Miles produced his first full-scale masterpiece, and he did it in a most casual, almost accidental way. Bob Weinstock and Prestige would not pay for rehearsals, and so (as had usually been the case with Parker), everything had to be done in the studio. This spontaneous approach usually served to put Miles on his mettle, kindling his creative spark. Horace Silver comments: 'Miles has a genius for head arrangements. In the studio, he'd sit with his head in his hands while we were setting up, and then he'd show a few things – voicings he wanted, and rhythmic things. Then we'd try it over a few times and there we'd have a nice head arrangement.' On this present occasion, however, Miles had made some attempt to prepare for the date. As well as the rhythm section of Silver, Heath and Clarke, he had also booked his old associates, Lucky Thompson (tenor) and J. J. Johnson (trombone), and he'd asked Thompson to bring some arrangements to the session. The latter stayed up half the night writing music, but all to no avail. Horace Silver describes what happened: 'We tried them in the studio, but nothing came off. They didn't seem to work and neither Miles nor the producer Bob Weinstock were happy. Eventually, they were abandoned and we busked a couple of head arrangements which turned out to be classics!' These classics were the medium-paced blues, 'Walkin'', and the fast blues, 'Blue 'n' Boogie'.

Undoubtedly, the frustration caused by the group's failure to make anything of Lucky Thompson's arrangements was a major factor in these superlative performances of familiar material. It served to focus the identity of the individual musicians, and the rhythm section, Heath and Clarke, were edgy and bursting to play. Miles had at last refined his trumpet style so that there was no more decoration at all, and the improvised phrases of his solos were totally organic. From the point of view of actually meaning what you play, his example also seems to have inspired both

Johnson and Thompson, who make all their phrases tell, and who play with great urgency. Throughout the session there is a feeling that whoever is soloing is being listened to with close attention by the horns who are not playing, and that their attention is supporting the soloist, helping him to greater levels of expression. And there is a continuing dialogue of quite remarkable brilliance between the soloing horns and the rhythm section.

The solo order and the overall shape of the two performances are absolutely crucial to their artistic success, and these were both, of course, Miles's responsibility as leader. After an eight-bar horn introduction over offbeats, the theme of 'Walkin'' is played twice. This theme, with its use of flattened 5ths, and its stark call-and-response pattern, is highly evocative – a distilled essence of the traditional and the post-bop blues. The atmosphere and sense of drama are heightened by the sonorities of trumpet, trombone and tenor all in unison, and their beautifully poised timing ... an elastic, laid-back, lazy feel on a knife-edge of balance. Kenny Clarke's immensely sensitive and subtle use of the hi-hat cymbal, which he opens and closes to point up the rhythms of the theme, also intensifies the drama. After the theme is played, the rhythm section moves into a straight 4/4 feel (the bass playing four beats to the bar instead of two), and Miles takes the first solo, playing seven choruses. He is followed by J. J. Johnson, who also plays seven, then Lucky Thompson's tenor sax solo is the emotional high spot of the performance. He plays for a few choruses and then Miles and Johnson play a backing figure that is a further distillation of the main theme, and Thompson's solo increases in intensity and power. When the backing riff stops, he has a couple of choruses to wind down, after which Horace Silver plays, not exactly a solo, but an interlude of two choruses which refer back to the simplest fundamentals of the early blues. His right-hand phrases would sound almost like a parody of the blues were it not for the single-note counter-line he plays with his left, which imbues his contribution with real feeling. Miles plays a further two choruses and then leads the front line into a convulsive riff, punctuated by Kenny Clarke, after which the rhythms subside, reverting to the two-in-the-bar feel, and the main theme is repeated twice. The introduction over offbeats now becomes the coda, and the whole lengthy performance ends, the peak or apex having occurred in the middle of the saxophone solo, and everything else having led up to, and down from, that.

Miles's first solo (Appendix A, Fig. 2), which, as it were, sets the scene and the musical standards for the whole performance, has gone beyond bebop and into the realm of archetypal blues expression. His ideas are so clear, so surprisingly original and yet simple, that they strike the listener with immediate impact and linger in the memory long afterwards. The emotional climate of the solo is potent; it is buoyant and full of energy, but there are melancholy, even tragic, undertones. It is a deeply personal statement, and shows increased rhythmic sophistication when compared with his 'Now's the Time' solo, another blues in F, recorded nine years earlier. One of the most striking features of this solo is the way it swings. Gil Evans has described this combination of apparently contradictory qualities:

Underneath his lyricism, Miles swings. He'll take care of the lyricism, but the rest of the band must complement him with an intense drive. And it's not that they supply a drive he himself lacks. Actually, they have to come up to him . . . As subtle as he is in his time and phrasing and his courage to wait, to use space, he's very forceful. There is a feeling of unhurriedness in his work and yet there's intensity underneath and through it all.[3]

In his 'Walkin'' solo, Miles makes brilliant use of triplets, and it is this, particularly in his third chorus, which sets his improvision apart from bebop and takes it beyond stylistic pigeon-holes. In fact, it recalls the work of Louis Armstrong at the time of 'West End Blues'. Curiously, Louis was then almost exactly the same age (a month before his twenty-eighth birthday) and also made great use of triplets. Because Miles's solo goes right to the roots, to the heart of the jazz mainstream, this gives it a kind of mythic power. The entire performance of 'Walkin'' has this same power, which is why, even now, over forty years after it was recorded, it still sounds fresh and still offers new revelations on repeated hearings. And this is also true of the other piece recorded that day, the fast 'Blue 'n' Boogie', one of the most dynamic and exhilarating jazz performances ever recorded in a studio.

Miles's next recording in this remarkable year was with a quintet on 29 June. This time the saxophonist was his old friend, Sonny Rollins, and the rhythm section was the same marvellous unit: Silver, Heath and Clarke. During this whole period, Miles is looking for his repertoire, his library of themes on which he wishes to improvise. He had discovered the 'Walkin'' theme in 1952, and was to continue using it until the middle 1960s. Similarly, on this June date with Rollins, Miles had discovered two themes he would use for the next six or seven years. They were the Gershwin tune 'But Not for Me', and Rollins's own composition, 'Oleo', based on the chords of 'I Got Rhythm'. Two more Rollins compositions were also recorded on this session. One was the fast 'Airegin' (Nigeria spelled backwards), which Miles was to use with his later quintet, and the other was the gospel-flavoured 'Doxy', a sixteen-bar melody with a funky two-in-the-bar feel.

'Oleo' is the outstanding track of a very good day's work. Although it is based on the 'Rhythm' thirty-two-bar sequence, Miles's version, with its dramatic use of space and timbre, is so unusual as to make it a completely fresh composition. It was with this recording that Miles Davis introduced a totally new sound to jazz: the amplified sound of the metallic Harmon mute with its stem removed. The mute has to be placed very close to the microphone, and the resulting sound is full and breathy in the lower register and thin and piercing in the upper. The two registers can therefore be played off against each other in a dramatic way, and this muted sound is much more expressive than, for example, that of the bland cup mute which Miles had been using earlier in the year. The Harmon mute can be used to express the most delicate nuances of feeling, and because its timbre is round and full and has a clear tongued edge, it is rhythmically very eloquent. With such qualities – the mixture of sweet and sour tonality and the muscularity of rhythms – it was the perfect vehicle for Miles's requirements. Like so many of his innovations, it sounded so right, and was so immediately attractive, that it spawned imitators everywhere.

The first sixteen and the last eight bars of the theme of 'Oleo' are played by muted trumpet and tenor sax in unison, accompanied only by the bass. The middle eight is played by the piano with the full rhythm section. The solos echo this pattern, each horn accompanied by bass and drums only, except for the middle eights when the piano joins in. This deployment of instruments points up the drama of the performance, giving it a satisfying shape. The timbre of the Harmon mute is thrown into marvellous relief when accompanied only by bass and drums. The overall impression is stark and compelling, and Miles is clearly inspired by the new combinations of sound. His solo is elegant, exciting and radical, because virtually every last trace of bebop has been expunged from it. Instead, it is full of buoyant new rhythms and beautifully sculpted phrases, all freshly minted. There had been nothing in jazz quite like this dancing, playful new sound bouncing off the bass and drums.

In 1954, Bob Weinstock and Prestige were doing well. Although it was only a small, independent label, Prestige had some of the most important contemporary musicians under contract. As well as Miles, Thelonious Monk and the Modern Jazz Quartet (John Lewis, Milt Jackson, Percy Heath and Kenny Clarke) were also signed to the label. One of the reasons why Heath and Clarke functioned so well together was that they were a regular unit in a working band. Miles's use of them as his studio rhythm section for most of that year suited everybody: musically they were perfect for him at the time, and as they were signed to Prestige the extra exposure was good for them and for Weinstock. The growing success of the label enabled Weinstock, in April 1954, to turn over all recording to Rudy Van Gelder, one of the finest sound engineers. The excellent recorded sound of Miles's sessions from April onwards was due to the genius of Van Gelder. At last, the rhythm section was properly recorded, which gave added point to the horn solos, increasing the impact of the whole performance. The mid-1950s mono sound of Prestige (and Blue Note and Savoy, which Van Gelder also engineered) was so good that even twenty years later it did not seem dated.

Miles's last date in 1954, on Christmas Eve, was the brainchild of Weinstock, who had the idea of using three MJQ members (Jackson, Heath and Clarke), Thelonious Monk and Davis for another 'all-star' session. Ten years previously, Miles had had lessons from Thelonious, who taught him harmony and some of his tunes; now, on this session, they were reunited as equals . . . but perhaps not quite equals: Miles's star was rising, while Monk was going through a period of obscurity and unemployment, which had begun in 1945 and was to last until 1957. Monk was Weinstock's rather than Miles's choice on piano, and there was some tension in the studio. Charles Mingus recalled in *Down Beat*, some months afterwards: 'He [Miles] cursed, laid out, argued, and threatened Monk and asked Bob Weinstock why he had hired such a non-musician and would Monk lay out on his trumpet solos.'[4] Some years later, Miles explained to Nat Hentoff: 'I love the way Monk plays and writes, but I can't stand him behind me. He doesn't give you any support.'[5] There were even rumours after the event of punch-ups in the studio, but when Monk was asked whether Miles had punched him, he simply said, 'What me? He'd better not!' The massive Monk would probably have been more than a match for the diminutive Miles.

The underlying tension in the studio served to put the musicians on their mettle, adding a dimension which made the results, yet again, classic tracks. It also gave the performances more form, because after recording Monk's composition, 'Bemsha Swing', Miles asked the pianist not to play during the trumpet solos. Thus, on the other three pieces recorded that night – Miles's own 'Swing Spring', Milt Jackson's 'Bags' Groove', and Gershwin's 'The Man I Love' – the trumpet solos are accompanied only by bass and drums, which makes the atmosphere more spacious and airier. The vibraphone solos are accompanied by the entire rhythm section with Monk's idiosyncratic piano giving a dense, more angular backing.

Monk, like Miles, had converted his technical limitations into assets, creating a sinewy, economical style with no superfluities. Since the early 1940s, he'd been using the rhythm section rather as an abstract expressionist painter would use a canvas – splashing his keyboard on to it in melodic shapes and colours. His use of space – his pauses and his melodic and rhythmic interpolations – was dramatic in the extreme. Despite the clash of styles and temperaments, Miles was fully aware of Monk's virtues and of the originality of his mind: 'A main influence he has been through the years has to do with giving musicians more freedom. They feel that if Monk can do what he does, they can. Monk has been using space for a long time.'[6] Monk's solos are as powerfully emotive as Miles's are. Relief from their intensity is provided by the vibraphone of Milt Jackson, who gives free rein to his virtuosity on the session, and whose fleet improvisations are more symmetrical and less abstract than either Monk's or Miles's.

The strong individuality of the three soloists and the propulsive rhythm section of Heath and Clarke give these performances great dynamism. Even the occasional error and failure has a kind of magnificence. This is true, for example, of Monk's solo on 'The Man I Love', when the pianist gets so carried away with his variation on the theme that he loses its relationship to the chord sequence and stops playing. The bass and drums continue 'strolling' until Miles prompts Monk with a few notes on the trumpet, and the pianist suddenly fills up the yawning space with a flowing melodic line. This heightened sense of drama is echoed in Miles's own solo, which follows. He begins with open trumpet, then suddenly jams the Harmon mute into the bell and carries on playing; the whole atmosphere is changed violently, from the expansive reflections of the open sound to the claustrophobic brooding of the harmon.

The outstanding track is 'Bags' Groove', a long improvisation on the blues in the key (once more) of F, and this reveals just how far Miles Davis had refined his art. From the point of view of sound, of sheer tonal beauty, his two solos eclipse all his earlier work. Now, Chico Hamilton's description does not seem exaggerated: 'Miles Davis is a sound . . . the whole earth singing!'[7] And to this gloriously pure sound are added the expressive vocal inflexions of the blues. His two solos – a long one at the beginning and a shorter one at the end – are notable for his apparently inexhaustible flow of melodic ideas, which seem to grow organically out of each other. His first solo (Appendix A, Fig. 3) comes immediately after the theme, which means that Miles is once again setting up the whole performance – establishing the standard and the creative atmosphere for the other musicians. This solo is superior to his 'Walkin'' improvisation, though it is, in essence, the same sort of solo. All the qualities of the earlier solo are magnified and brought into sharper focus. The melodic phrases are more finely conceived, the lyricism more intense, and Miles's interpretation of the blues more personal. The rhythmic definition of his phrases – their poise and the way they relate to the basic pulse – is exquisite. The complete 'Bags' Groove' performance and the other three pieces the band recorded on that Christmas Eve were a fitting end to a remarkable twelve months.

This year, 1954, was an immensely important landmark in Miles Davis's career. At the beginning of it, he had only recently freed himself from drug addiction, and though he was a very promising trumpeter with a highly original style, the deficiencies of his self-knowledge were reflected in the uncertainties of some of his solo work. By the end of the year, he had become a master soloist, and he had acquired the knowledge and skills he needed to go on to the next stage of his development. First, he had perfected the trumpet sounds he was to use and explore for the next sixteen years or so: the singing open sound, and the muted, inward-looking timbre of the Harmon. Gil Evans has said: 'Miles . . . is aware of his complete surroundings and takes advantage of the wide range of sound possibilities that exist even in one's basic sound. He can, in other words, create a particular sound for the existing context.'[8] As well as perfecting his basic sound, Miles had also begun to collect a repertoire of themes, and had revealed that he had the vision and the inner strength to lead ensembles and inspire great performances. The format of the 'all-star blowing session' was not going to satisfy him any longer. What he needed now, more than anything else, was to form his own quintet on a regular basis. Having brought his instrumental art to a pitch of perfection, he was now free to examine Parker's legacy – the idea that the soloist is integrally related to the small-group ensemble, and that the combination of the two entities is the key to a rich and dynamic music.

Miles's reputation had risen steeply among musicians, and his records were bought by a tiny but loyal following. He was also now being noticed for the talents he encouraged and nurtured as well as for his own playing. Both Horace Silver and Sonny Rollins had made their names through recording with Miles. But although Davis had become a cult figure, he had no real financial basis for a regular band. His years of addiction and obscurity had wiped him from the mind of the majority jazz audience. He had received critical acclaim for his nine-piece band and for his trumpet playing; in the early 1950s several of his solos had been transcribed and printed in *Down Beat*. But these considerable achievements were not enough to enable him to lead a permanent quintet, because that meant having enough engagements to pay the musicians a living wage. He was also earning irregularly at this time, and in the spring of 1955, when he failed to pay support money to Irene, she had him put in gaol.

On 12 March 1955, the universal impression that an era was ending was clinched by the death of Charlie Parker at the age of thirty-four. Miles was still in gaol when he heard the news from a lawyer, Harold Lovett, who raised the money to get Miles released and soon became his manager. Parker had spent his last few months as a virtual derelict, wandering around homeless, dossing down in people's apartments, taking aimless trips on the subway, and even begging on the Bowery. Red Rodney commented: 'I do suspect that he died at the right time. I don't think that he had anything more to say. I don't think he could have improved upon anything, because he was sick. He no longer had the fire . . .

he was ill ... physically ill.' Bird's worsening health must have been partially responsible for his failing powers, but he also felt that he had come to a creative impasse. He admitted to Lennie Tristano that he had taken the blues and the ballad as far as he could. He seemed to have no way left to go musically, which is probably why, like Bix Beiderbecke, he cast longing and ineffectual glances at the world of 'straight' music. During the last two years or so of his life, he had been travelling the same musical territory which he had opened up and pioneered in the early 1940s, and he had been going round in ever diminishing circles. His actual death was caused by all, or any one, of four ailments: stomach ulcers (perforated), pneumonia, advanced cirrhosis of the liver, and a heart attack.

Parker's death shocked his old associates. It was hard to believe that the unpredictable genius, the gargantuan appetites, the huge energy and force were all snuffed out, gone for ever. It made everyone reassess Parker's achievements and take new stock of their own. Bird was less than six years older than Miles ... the trumpeter would be twenty-nine on 26 May that year. It was time he started doing something; he had already wasted four of his best years, and a jazz musician was considered old at forty. On the other hand, he was now experiencing a kind of rebirth and was brimming with ideas – new things to say and new ways of saying them. His contract with Prestige gave him a modest form of patronage; for a small advance and scale payment for each studio session, recordings of his recent work were available to the public. This, however, was not enough to enable him to launch a new band. What he needed was some kind of promotion, publicity, investment, to create an audience knowing of his existence and interested in paying to listen to his music.

Miles had been aware for some time that he needed the investment and promotion of a major record company in order to further his career. Since 1953, he had two or three times approached George Avakian, the artist and repertoire (A&R) man at Columbia Records, saying he wanted to record for that company. But Avakian knew Miles was under contract to Prestige until 1955, and so was reluctant to sign him. Miles's luck, however, which seemed to have deserted him since 1949, suddenly returned, and he found himself once again as the right man in the right place at the right time. The place was the second Newport Jazz Festival, and the time was July 1955. Miles was added to the bill almost as an afterthought, and presented as a soloist with a pick-up group assembled for the occasion. The other musicians (Gerry Mulligan, Zoot Sims, Thelonious Monk, Percy Heath and drummer Connie Kay) had all – except Kay – recorded with Miles, and so were well aware of the values he emphasized in his music. This group played two pieces by Monk ('Hackensack' and ''Round Midnight'), and finished their appearance with a version of Parker's 'Now's the Time'. Miles's solos had a great impact on audience and critics, and the reviews were all excellent, extolling the power and vitality of his contribution, and talking about his 'resurgence'. Miles commented scornfully: 'What are they talking about? I just played the way I always play.'[9] George Avakian was at Newport with his brother, the photographer Aram Avakian, who had an unerring instinct for a great musician. After Miles played ''Round Midnight', Aram turned to George and said, 'Don't hesitate. Sign him. Sign him to a contract which becomes effective when the old one expires.' George still expressed reluctance: 'It's not so easy to do because there's a lot of red tape involved, and I'm so busy with many other things that I don't want to think too much about that right now.' But Aram insisted, 'Don't be a fool. Did you hear what he played? Best thing in the whole festival!' And, not for the first time, George took his brother's advice, but it was some months before everything was settled.

By the end of 1955, the readers of *Down Beat* had voted Miles into first place in their trumpet poll. The publicity from his Newport appearance had also created so much general interest that by the late summer he was able to form a quintet on a regular basis for the first time in his life.

At this point in time, Miles had only his manager, the black lawyer Harold Lovett, taking care of his career; so far he had found no booking agent to get work for a regular group. Lovett had such an interest in jazz that he was called 'Counsellor' by many musicians, and he and Miles were so friendly that their relationship seems to have been based more on mutual liking and respect than on financial considerations. The admiration and affection Lovett felt for Miles made him defend the trumpeter's interests with fanaticism, but it was very difficult at that time for black musicians to advance their careers without the help of the white musical establishment. Virtually all the leading booking agencies were white, and Lovett was quick to take advantage of Miles's Newport success by getting him signed with the Shaw Agency, which had represented both Charlie Parker and Dizzy Gillespie. At the agency, Jack Whittemore was the man personally responsible for booking Miles's group.

Though he had not worked in public very much during the first six months of 1955, three recording sessions in June, July and August show that Miles was trying out different group sounds and contexts. The first date, on 7 June, was with a quartet – just Miles with a rhythm section. The pianist was Red Garland, the drummer Philly Joe Jones, and the bassist, Oscar Pettiford, was the only man on the session who would not become a member of the Miles Davis Quintet. Six tracks were recorded, but the results were not propitious. The actual recorded sound is very poor – one of the worst group sounds Miles ever produced on record – and it's difficult to believe that Van Gelder engineered the session. The bass is thin and barely audible, the piano is thin and tinny, and Miles's trumpet sound is rather pinched. He also seems distinctly uneasy, as if the old muscular troubles (dodgy lip) and identity doubts had returned. He plays on the whole without fire or conviction, and he also drops several 'clinkers'. To complete the dismal picture, he sounds out of tune on almost every track, and this, added to the bad recording quality, prevents piano and trumpet from blending at all comfortably. It could be that irregular work in the first six months of the year had set Miles back a little. But it could also be the fact that he was starting a new group with new people. The whole aesthetic balance of the rhythm section was the reverse of the one with which he had been recording for the last year or so. Now, instead of forceful piano and light drums, his context was giving him light piano and heavy drums. This factor may have caused him to lose his touch momentarily.

As if the June session had made him lose his nerve, the following month Miles recorded with a totally different group, which included his old associate, Charles Mingus, who played bass and wrote the arrangements. Unlike the quartet date, this was not a freewheeling blowing session, but a tightly controlled and highly organized event. As well as Miles and Mingus, the line-up included trombonist Britt Woodman, vibist Teddy Charles, and Elvin Jones on drums. This time the recorded sound is much better, and Miles makes incisive use of the Harmon mute, producing a rich, bell-like sonority. His playing on 'Nature Boy' and the ballad, 'Easy Living', is exquisite and deeply affecting.

On 5 August, he was in the studio with yet another group: a sextet this time, with Jackie McLean, Milt Jackson, Percy Heath, pianist Ray Bryant and drummer Art Taylor. Four tunes were recorded, and this was a very good session indeed. The rhythm section is excellent and Miles himself is in magnificent form. His muted and open sounds are superlative and his long solos show an extraordinary fecundity and completeness of imagination. Once again, his use of triplets during his muted solo on the blues, 'Changes', recalls the work of the young Louis Armstrong.

In September, Miles did his first *Down Beat* blindfold test with Leonard Feather. These tests consist of playing tracks from records to a musician without giving him any information about them. He then comments on the music and tries to identify the musicians involved. Feather himself devised this fascinating series, which involved musicians in the difficulties of aesthetic judgement. Miles not only identifies eight tracks out of nine, but also names many of the supporting musicians. While being generous in his praise of individuals, he is also highly critical of how they play, their relationship to the ensemble, the way the pieces are arranged and interpreted. Again and again, he says things like: 'I think they played it too fast, though. They missed the content of the tune,' or, 'You can't play that kind of song like that, with those chords.

There's another way to swing on that.'[10] He gives unreserved praise to Louis Armstrong and Bobby Hackett, awarding them five stars – the *Down Beat* maximum rating. But when Feather plays him Duke Ellington's version of 'Stormy Weather', Miles exclaims: 'I think all the musicians should get together one certain day and get down on their knees and thank Duke ... Yes, everybody should bow to Duke and Strayhorn – and Charlie Parker and Diz ... Give this all the stars you can.'[11] Miles's confident judgements are based on a knowledge and understanding of the whole jazz spectrum from traditional jazz to the music of the day, and from small-group to big-band jazz. He was, in every way now, ready to start his own group.

On drums, he naturally chose Philly Joe Jones, who had shared his dreams of a regular group. Jones had built up tremendous stamina and drive by working with rhythm and blues groups, while still absorbing the influence of new stylists such as Max Roach. Philly Joe had 'that thing', and admiration for his playing occasioned one of Miles's most quoted remarks: 'Look, I wouldn't care if he came up on the bandstand in his BVDs [underwear] and with one arm, just so long as he was there. He's got the fire I want.'[12] The bass player was Paul Chambers, a brilliant twenty-year-old musician from Detroit who had recently arrived in New York. In September, he had worked with pianist George Wallington in the Cafe Bohemia, which is where Miles probably heard him. In the recording studios, Miles's pianists had ranged from the powerfully rhythmic Horace Silver, to the flowing delicacy of Ray Bryant, whose keyboard work resembled that of the Swede, Bengt Hallberg. Both Bryant and Hallberg were, in fact, precursors of the Bill Evans style of piano playing that Miles would favour three years later. In the early autumn of 1955, Davis plumped for Red Garland, who was more rhythmic than Bryant and more delicate than Silver.

At first, Miles wanted Sonny Rollins to join the group, and was actually quoted as saying: 'I want this group to sound the way Sonny plays, the way all of the men in it play – different from anybody else in jazz today.'[13] But Rollins, who was then another heroin addict, had disappeared to Chicago in one of his attempts to kick the habit. Miles consulted the rest of his band, and they all recommended the tenor saxophonist, John Coltrane, who was living in Philadelphia, Philly Joe's home town. The drummer had worked with Coltrane there, and recommended him strongly. Miles had met Trane a few years previously and knew something of his qualities. Coltrane joined the group, but continued to live in Philadelphia.

Like Philly Joe, Coltrane had worked a great deal with rhythm and blues bands. During the 1940s, he'd played first with Eddie 'Cleanhead' Vinson, and then with Gillespie's big band, and when that broke up, with Dizzy's small group. After a period with Earl Bostic, he had joined Johnny Hodges, but had been fired for being a heroin addict. Back home in Philadelphia, he earned a living working with rhythm and blues bands such as Bull Moose Jackson, King Kolax, and Daisy Mae and the Hepcats. Coltrane was deeply frustrated and miserable. He and Rollins were close friends, and it was rumoured that Sonny deliberately stayed off the scene in order to give Coltrane a chance to get an outlet, some exposure, and some recognition. Trane was, at that time, almost completely unknown, whereas Rollins was already a cult figure with some LPs of his own, and the prospect of making more when he was ready.

So Miles Davis had formed a brand-new quintet of virtually unknown musicians, and it was difficult to see how this unit was going to develop into anything extra-special. Coltrane, although the same age as Miles, was still an immature stylist and had made no significant recordings to date; Red Garland, on the evidence of the quartet recording in June, seemed to be all surface and no depth; Philly Joe seemed to overpower everyone with his volcanic energy. The band did not fit the prevailing ideas of what a group should be, and complaints and criticism came from musicians who failed to see the potential of the group. Just as, ten years previously, musicians had failed to appreciate Thelonious Monk's qualities and had advised Coleman Hawkins to get rid of him when the pianist was with his group, so people asked Miles to get rid of

Coltrane and Philly Joe. Miles commented: 'People used to tell me Trane couldn't play and Philly Joe played too loud. But I know what I want, and if I didn't think they knew what they were doing, they wouldn't be there.'[14]

Miles himself was artistically strong enough to impose his own identity on the band. Also, he was news after his success at Newport, so the quintet got bookings; it worked and drew audiences. At the beginning of October, Miles signed a contract guaranteeing him twenty weeks a year at Birdland. The first three engagements, of two weeks each, were 13 October, 24 November, and 19 January (1956). The new group also had engagements at the Sutherland Hotel, Chicago, in the autumn, and at the Cafe Bohemia late in the year. On 27 October, Miles recorded a couple of tracks ('Budo' and 'Ah-Leu-Cha') with the group for Columbia, and then on 16 November they went into the studio to make their first album for Prestige.

This first album, called simply *The New Miles Davis Quintet*, was a clear statement of Miles's basic musical intentions at the time. Of the six pieces recorded, four were standard song tunes, and two were original compositions – 'Miles' Theme' which is based on the 'I Got Rhythm' sequence, and 'Stablemates', a theme written by saxophonist Benny Golson, a friend of Coltrane's. The only time trumpet and tenor state a theme together in unison and harmony is on 'Stablemates'. On 'Miles' Theme', they are in loosely improvised canon, and on the four standards Miles states the themes by himself, using the Harmon mute and phrasing in his own inimitable way. In other words, on the four standards, the group is essentially a quartet but features saxophone solos by a fifth member. The format is therefore very loose. It is the other end of the spectrum entirely from his 1949 nine-piece band. With the quintet, the basic material is the tempo, the chord sequence, and the melody – if there is one. Now, with a regularly working group, the ensemble techniques and different approaches could be developed by the musicians.

Clark Terry, who spent several years with Duke Ellington's orchestra, has said that Ellington always wanted his music to be in a 'state of becoming', and this is a good description of Miles Davis's attitude to music. Something Sidney Bechet once said is also pertinent: 'Those Dixieland musicianers . . . they tried to write the music down and kind of freeze it . . . that's why they lost it. You can't keep the music unless you move with it.'[15] This looseness and movement were very evident in the quintet's first album, which served notice on the jazz world that there was a new bandleader and band in existence with a fresh sound and a fresh concept. The Harmon mute – a totally new sound – dominated the album, ranging from the voluptuous tenderness of 'There Is No Greater Love', to the almost claustrophobic aggression of 'How Am I to Know' and 'S'posin''. Coltrane, too, immature though he may have been, produced some tumbling, impassioned solos which revealed a new tenor sound and the embryo of a new rhythmic feel. The rhythm section, driven along by Philly Joe, pivoting on the magnificently solid bass of the young virtuoso, Paul Chambers, and filled out by the crisp chords of Red Garland, had already been drawn into focus by Miles's own playing. To quote Cecil Taylor on Miles's relation to his rhythm sections:

His conception of time has led to greater rhythmic freedom for other players. His feeling, for another thing, is so intense that he catapults the drummer, bassist and pianist together, forcing them to play at the top of their technical ability and forcing them with his own emotional strength to be as emotional as possible.[16]

Bird was gone, but Miles had arrived. The king was dead; long live the king.

SIX

Miles Ahead

'You add to playing your instrument the running of a
band and you got plenty problems.'[1]

Miles Davis

Jazz development and history have been enormously assisted by
the chance enthusiasm of individuals and small independent record
companies. Without the tiny companies of Savoy and Dial, Charlie
Parker's greatest work in the later 1940s, which included Miles
Davis on trumpet, might not have been recorded. If Bob Weinstock
had not single-handedly started Prestige Records at the beginning
of the 1950s and actively recruited Miles to the label, the docu-
mentation of the latter's career would have been much impover-
ished, and his development much slower. The Prestige office was
situated on Eighth Avenue, near Madison Square Garden, famous
for its boxing connection, and musicians would often call in at the
office after going to a big fight, and talk business. The relationship
between Prestige and musicians was easy-going and informal.
Weinstock was definitely performing an invaluable act of patronage by recording some of the most creative musicians at a time
when no one else seemed interested in doing so.

Some musicians called Prestige the 'junkies' jazz label', because
addicted musicians who needed money for a fix could often walk
in without making prior arrangements, record some tunes, and
get ready cash as soon as the session was over. It was probably
this kind of happening which gave the 'blowing sessions' such
currency and made Prestige reluctant to pay for rehearsal time.

Before the end of 1955, Miles was feeling thwarted and frustrated by the low-key, low-budget policy of Prestige. Weinstock valued Miles and the new quintet highly, calling them 'the Louis Armstrong Hot Five of the modern era', and although he knew they were about to become economically valuable, he still either would not or could not increase his financial investment in Miles. There were meetings between the two men, at this time, during which Miles would stare expressionlessly at Weinstock and Weinstock would stare sweetly back at Miles, neither exchanging a word for twenty minutes. It was for self-preservation and self-protection that hints of the now famous Miles Davis persona began to appear – the inscrutability, the unpredictability, the refusal to be pinned down, the sudden juxtapositions of gentleness and violence. Even his favourite musicians, like John Coltrane, would never know what he was thinking or what he was going to do next. Coltrane once said: 'After I joined Miles in 1955, I found he doesn't talk much and will rarely discuss his music. He's completely unpredictable; sometimes he'd walk off stage after just playing a few notes, not even completing one chorus. If I asked him something about his music, I never knew how he was going to take it.'[2]

Miles certainly enjoyed the spectacle, in the autumn of 1955, of two record companies haggling over him. His contract with Prestige still had over a year to run and he owed the company four more albums. George Avakian had other problems:

> I said to Miles, 'What do you want in the way of an advance?' He asked for four thousand dollars advance against royalties, and that was reasonable as far as I was concerned. Then I ran into more trouble from people in the Columbia business affairs department who said: 'This is ridiculous to pay four thousand dollars to a known junkie who might be dead before he can even record, and we have to wait fourteen months, and besides, he hasn't much of a reputation.'

Avakian was able to convince them partly, perhaps, because he had already signed Dave Brubeck, whose first album on Columbia, *Jazz*

Goes to College, had become the biggest-selling LP in jazz history. Miles and Harold Lovett carried out delicate negotiations with Weinstock and Columbia, and it was ultimately agreed that the trumpeter could leave Prestige as soon as he had fulfilled his commitment for four more LPs. In addition, it was agreed that he could record for Columbia while the Prestige contract was still in force, as long as the results were not released until the expiration date of that contract. This was a highly satisfactory outcome, because no enemies were made, and while honouring his agreement with Weinstock, Miles could still pick up his advance from Columbia.

The subsequent year, 1956, was one of prodigious activity for Miles Davis. During its course, he recorded enough material for five and a half quintet albums and was also featured soloist with a nineteen-piece brass ensemble under the direction of Gunther Schuller. The reputation of the quintet also grew steadily throughout the year, and there were so many engagements that Coltrane found it impractical to continue to live in Philadelphia, and in June he and his family moved to New York. Early in the year, the quintet played on the West Coast, and from spring to late autumn appeared for much of the time at the Cafe Bohemia in New York. In November, Miles spent a few days on his own in Paris as soloist with a package show.

As Miles's popularity and fame increased with audiences and the record-buying public, evidence of critical appreciation also began to appear during the year. Two books were published, both written by Europeans, and both devoting long chapters to Miles and his nine-piece band. *Modern Jazz* was by Alun Morgan and Raymond Horricks, two Britishers; Morgan in particular had shown himself to be an extremely sensitive and perceptive critic of Miles's earlier work. The other book was by the French composer and critic, André Hodeir, and was called *Jazz: Its Evolution and Essence*. Hodeir's book was universally acclaimed when it first appeared, and has since become established as a classic of jazz criticism. This sudden elevation in critical status, coming as it did hard on the heels of Miles's success at Newport and in the *Down Beat* poll, was another piece of good fortune.

An aura of glamour was now beginning to surround Miles. His relationship with Irene was over, but he kept in touch with his three children and was now enjoying a second lease of life as the young, good-looking trumpeter-about-town with an eye for pretty girls. He kept himself in peak physical shape by working out regularly in the gymnasium, and he was also mentally buoyant. All the other members of his quintet, however, were junkies at that time. Although he'd kicked the habit, Miles didn't develop a 'holier-than-thou' attitude, but was totally realistic about addiction. He told Nat Hentoff: 'I just tell them if they work for me to regulate their habit. When they're tired of the trouble it takes to support a habit, they'll stop if they have the strength.'[3]

Once again, luck was on Miles's side, because the pressure to record enough material for five more albums that year came at exactly the right time. His new quintet was equal to the challenge, and far from there being a falling off as the recording sessions proceed during the year, there is a notable rise in the creative power of the individuals and in the collective dynamism of the group. In March, Miles recorded three tracks – two blues and Brubeck's ballad 'In Your Own Sweet Way' – with a pick-up group comprising Sonny Rollins, pianist Tommy Flanagan, Paul Chambers and drummer Art Taylor. After that event, all the other small-group sessions were done with the quintet. To fulfil his Prestige contract, Miles simply took two days – 1 May and 26 October – and on each occasion, functioning as if the quintet were doing a session in a club, he recorded enough material for two LPs.

One of the basic truths of recording improvised music, Miles had learned from Parker, was that the most creative and dynamic solos usually occurred on the first takes, and so he always tried to capture that initial magic in the studio. J. J. Johnson has said: 'I've recorded with Miles and I know how he operates. Most of the time he goes into the studio and one take is it! Goofs or not, there's no second or third take. That's his philosophy on the recording bit.'[4] This was certainly the philosophy behind the marathon sessions for Prestige, which resulted in four classic LPS: *Cookin'*, *Relaxin'*, *Workin'* and *Steamin'*. The first two were from the October session, and the last two were made up mostly of tracks from the first session in May, so the four albums, containing some three hours of music, document marvellously the essence of the quintet in the earlier and later parts of that fateful year. They also showed that Miles Davis could achieve a miraculous duality: popularity with the general public and great critical acclaim.

One of the main reasons why the quintet's music reached a wider audience was that its repertoire consisted largely of the superior songs and ballads of the day, and their themes were usually played by Miles using the distinctive Harmon mute. His muted sound was, by then, brilliantly evocative and expressive, bringing the quintet's performance very close to actual vocal music. The rest of the group's repertoire included one or two of Miles's tunes, the occasional theme by Parker or Gillespie, and a couple of Sonny Rollins compositions. For a person with Miles Davis's background and credentials, the introduction of the more popular material, and the way it was treated, was both surprising and exciting. But some of his fans were shocked at first by this development.

Gil Evans has pointed out:

Miles is a leader in jazz because he has definite confidence in what he likes and he is not afraid of what he likes. A lot of other musicians are constantly looking around to hear what the next person is doing and worry about whether they themselves are in style. Miles has confidence in his own taste, and he goes his own way.[5]

So just as Louis Armstrong had done, Miles chose to feature a high proportion of popular songs in his repertoire; and also like Louis, his interpretation of the themes, his sound and his phrasing were highly distinctive so that his own identity was always imposed on the material he used. Of all the trumpet players in jazz, Louis and Miles (the Miles of this period) are the most instantly recognizable. The way they played was very different, but their emotional power and the architectural beauty of their phrases had much in common. Miles was very aware of Louis's work and told Nat Hentoff:

> Louis has been through all kinds of styles . . . You know you can't play anything on a horn that Louis hasn't played – I mean even modern. I love his approach to the trumpet; he never sounds bad. He plays on the beat and you can't miss when you play on the beat – with feeling.[6]

But the biggest single influence on the music of Miles's quintet was the pianist Ahmad Jamal, who was four years younger than Davis. Jamal was born in Pittsburgh in 1930, and in the late 1940s and early 1950s worked with his trio at the Pershing Hotel in Chicago, where he had a big reputation and was popular locally. It was during this period that Miles frequently visited Chicago, often staying there for weeks or even months, and he liked Ahmad Jamal's trio so much that he took every available opportunity to hear them. Pittsburgh was also the birthplace of that other trio pianist, Erroll Garner, whose style fused the rhythmic directness of the older jazz tradition with the melodic and harmonic developments of modern jazz. Garner drew most of his material from popular songs and hits from musical shows, and was almost certainly an influence on Jamal. Count Basie's piano style was the other great influence on Jamal. Basie's understatement and his dramatic use of space are mirrored in Jamal's music, and it was these qualities, allied to the impeccable swing and varied pulse of the rhythm section of the latter's group, which attracted Miles. In a *Jazz Review* interview in the autumn of 1958, Davis stated: 'Listen to the way Jamal uses space. He lets it go so that you can feel the rhythm section and the rhythm section can feel you. It's not crowded . . . Ahmad is one of my favourites. I live until he makes another record.'[7] Although Miles Davis's music has changed in later years, his regard for Ahmad Jamal seems to have remained constant. Even in the early 1970s, he was still taking people to listen to the Jamal trio.

Many of the tunes in Miles's book were songs which had been

recorded by Frank Sinatra (Appendix B), and many others came straight out of Jamal's repertoire. Often only a month or two after Jamal had recorded a song, it would appear on a Miles Davis album. (See Appendix B for a list of titles and comparative recording dates.) Almost all the jaunty, medium to fast standard tunes came from Jamal's book – 'But Not for Me', 'Gal in Calico', 'Surrey with the Fringe on Top', 'All of You', 'Billy Boy', 'Squeeze Me', 'Will You Still Be Mine' – to name a few; and also the way his trio played them, his concept of performance, influenced Miles. The themes were played over a two-in-the-bar feel from the rhythm section. This means that while the bass plays two notes (minims) per bar, the drums play four beats but emphasize the second and fourth. This creates a deep, swaying pulse and tends to make the performance feel unhurried and spacious. Drama occurs when the bass switches to four notes to the bar, making the pulse shallower and more urgent. This two-beat feel has been called 'a kind of upside-down Dixieland', and it does hark back to the immediacy of earlier jazz forms. It is a 'catchy' rhythm. From Jamal also, Miles took the 'tag' endings to performances; after the theme had been played through for the final time, the rhythm section would repeat the last four bars of the harmonies over and over again until Miles, or whoever else was soloing, gave the cue for the ending. This minimized the harmonic interest and put the emphasis on rhythmic interplay.

The LP which Miles recorded with his quintet for Columbia during his Prestige period was drawn from material done in three sessions, one in October 1955, and the other two in June and September 1956. This album was given the title *Round About Midnight* at George Avakian's request, because that was the piece that had so impressed him and his brother Aram at Newport. With this and the five Prestige LPs – all six albums being recorded in the twelve-month period running from October 1955 to October 1956 – the music of this magnificent quintet was fully documented. It is extremely unlikely that any other jazz artist has made so many albums of such high quality in so short a period of time. The rapport within the group was almost telepathic. Philly

Joe Jones and Red Garland had played together a great deal in Philadelphia and had known Coltrane there. Miles's association with Philly Joe had also bred a deep mutual understanding. Ralph Gleason recounts: 'Philly Joe Jones . . . once remarked that his and Miles's minds were so attuned that he could go way out beyond easily countable time in a drum solo and come right back in with Miles, because each knew where the other was.'[8] Bassist Paul Chambers not only laid down a solid beat, but often simultaneously created counter-melodies to the lines played by the soloist.

The personalities of the three main soloists were brilliantly complementary. Miles often left audacious gaps in his spare melodic lines. Coltrane was urgent, compulsive, blowing floods of notes as if he hadn't enough time to get in everything he had to say. Red Garland, with his smooth rhythms and sprightly single-line melodies or his suave block chords, brought a welcome relief from the intensity of the two horns. And for each of these three, the rhythm section changed its character. Behind Miles, the drums were often compact and understated, the piano chords sparse, resulting in an unhurried, spacious atmosphere. When Coltrane soloed, the drums would broaden and intensify the beat, usually using the ride cymbal – the piano would intensify the rhythmic strength of the chords, and the bass would underpin the whole band with an even, flowing, unstoppable four crotchets to the bar. There would be disturbing polyrhythms under Coltrane's solo, and often a feeling of strife, as if his phrases were beating themselves into existence against the rhythm section. When Garland began his solo, suddenly the agitation would disappear and the tension would be released by the whole rhythm section playing as one man with an effortless impetus that reassured listeners and enabled them to bask in the normal joyous rhythm of jazz except that, with this group, it is supra-normal . . . a groove that bordered on ecstasy.

A perfect example of this whole process occurs in the performance of the standard, 'If I Were a Bell', on *Relaxin'*, recorded on 26 October 1956. Miles, using the Harmon mute, plays the melody over a two-beat feel from the rhythm section, after which there is a driving four-in-the-bar feel and Davis solos with great power. The Harmon sound intensifies the impact of the solos because the wild feeling seems bottled-in, which produces a claustrophobic, furiously contained effect. The tight rhythm section also contributes to this. Then, Coltrane enters and the whole climate changes; we are suddenly out in the open with his broad and bubbling sound and a looser feel from the rhythm section with plenty of polyrhythms. Trane's solo grips and disturbs with its pell-mell phrases and the vocal 'cry' in his sound. Then, abruptly, it stops, and after a piano break, Red Garland plays his solo over a smoothly riding pulse, with Philly Joe ticking off each bar with a snare drum rimshot on the fourth beat. Garland plays single-note lines first, with flow and invention, and then his solo ends with some block chords. The very stylized nature of many of Garland's solos helps to provide the reassurance that makes these group performances so satisfying and memorable.

Like Louis Armstrong's classic small-group recordings of the later 1920s, these performances of the Miles Davis Quintet are full of moments of genuine inspiration, full of surprises, full of collective and individual magic. The basic strength of the group comes from the dialogue between the powerfully active and extrovert rhythm section and the violent introversion of the two horns, which results in a profusion of ways of creating and releasing tension. From this latter point of view, the quintet's music vastly enriched the jazz vocabulary. The emotional range of the group is also extremely wide – probably wider than that of any other small group in jazz before or since – ranging as it does from the unbounded joy of Red Garland's contributions (and some of Miles's on the up-tempo popular songs) to the complex sorrow of the trumpeter's ballad interpretations with the Harmon mute. This aspect of Davis's work introduced a totally new element into jazz: the quality of profound, and sometimes almost painful, introspection.

These ballad performances were usually done by Miles with the rhythm section working as a quartet, and a perfect example of this is the October 1956 version of Richard Rodgers's ballad 'My Funny Valentine' on *Cookin'*. After Garland's four-bar piano introduction, Miles plays one chorus, referring only briefly to the original melody, and creating tremendous tension by his tonal inflexions and his use of space – the pauses he leaves, the way he varies the length of his phrases, his use of long notes and his juxtaposition of upper and lower registers. Throughout, the bass improvises a brilliant counter-line to the trumpet, though perhaps it would be more accurate to call this part of the performance a dialogue between trumpet and bass. The piano lays down the chords, and Philly Joe, using brushes, creates an unobtrusive background rhythm. The trumpet and bass dialogue builds to such intensity over the thirty-six-bar chorus that Miles's solo spills over into the first two bars of the next chorus as the rhythm section, apparently responding to internal pressure, gathers itself and moves into a double-tempo feel. This time-change dramatically releases the almost unbearable tension, and Red Garland's piano solo which follows is bright and jaunty all the way. Beneath it all, Paul Chambers's bass plays two beats to the bar, thus preserving the slow ballad pulse, while occasionally varying the line superbly to imply the double tempo. At the end of the piano solo the performance reverts to its slower, darker atmosphere and Miles plays out the last twenty-four bars with taut phrases, cliff-hanging pauses, and an impassioned coda. Once again, Garland's piano solo is essential to the shape and meaning of the piece as a whole. It not only eases the tension, but also throws into even greater relief the starkly brooding quality of Miles's muted trumpet (Appendix A, Fig. 4).

Although the five quintet albums on Prestige were to have a huge, world-wide influence on jazz, inspiring musicians of all nationalities, Miles's own fame was then much greater than that of his group. It was as a star soloist, and not as a bandleader, that he went to Europe one week after that last Prestige session. He was reluctant to leave his group behind, but had to accept the work that his burgeoning international reputation was bringing in. At the same time, the package tour reunited him with several friends and associates: the Modern Jazz Quartet (MJQ), Bud Powell and Lester Young. The tour was a short one, comprising a couple of nights at the Salle Pleyel in Paris and one or two concerts in Amsterdam and Stockholm. In Paris, the MJQ played its own set, and then Miles, Lester Young and Bud Powell appeared with a French rhythm section. Accompanying Miles were pianist René Urtreger, bassist Pierre Michelot, and drummer Christian Garros. Musicians on package tours rarely listen to one another's sets, but some observers in Paris noted that Miles stood in the wings listening attentively to Bud Powell and Lester Young. In Paris, Miles again spent some time with Juliette Greco and Jean-Paul Sartre.

After the first Paris concert, all the musicians went to the Club St Germain to relax, and there one or two English writers and critics, including Alun Morgan, managed to talk to Miles Davis. He was affable and ready to talk about his past, his own music and that of other people, but he was abrupt, tending to finish a sentence and, having decided that that was the end of the conversation, to disappear without saying goodbye. He talked enthusiastically about the October session for Prestige and said that the band had behaved in the studio exactly as if it had been in a club with an audience, and that all the tracks were first takes. When he was pressed to extend his stay in Europe and visit England, he told Alun Morgan: 'I've got to get home after this tour. I've got four guys depending on me back there. I've got the best rhythm section in the world right now. Philly Joe Jones is just great and you know that Coltrane is the best since Bird.'[9]

And yet, back in New York later that month, Miles had both Coltrane and Sonny Rollins with his group at the Cafe Bohemia, and before the end of November Coltrane had left the band. One Michael Harper has speculated:

Miles is more paradoxical than any musician I ever knew, even Coltrane. I heard he gave Trane an ultimatum to stop drinking and taking drugs or get out of the band. I think that for some unknown reason, Coltrane was really bored with the music and in effect engineered his own discharge. I also think Miles let him go in the hope that Trane would straighten himself out and come back after he was clean.[10]

Coltrane was not bored, he was anaesthetized by drugs. By the time he left the Miles Davis Quintet in 1956, Coltrane's addictions were so far advanced that he was tending to fall asleep when he was not actually playing, and he was also becoming inefficient and unreliable. Miles may have tried to jolt the saxophonist from time to time to sting him into revolting against the inexorable progress of his destructive habit. Thelonious Monk, who went backstage at the Bohemia to say hello to the group, witnessed Miles slap Coltrane's face and punch him in the stomach. The saxophonist was so meek and humble that there was no glimmer of revolt or anger. Monk is reported to have said to Trane: 'As much saxophone as you play, you don't have to take that. Why don't you come to work for me?'[11] In December 1956, however, Miles reinstated Coltrane in the quintet and started a two-month tour that included Philadelphia, Chicago, St Louis, Los Angeles and San Francisco, where they played the Blackhawk Club for two weeks. During this tour, Philly Joe Jones was a bad influence on Coltrane, and in March 1957, Miles fired both of them. So Coltrane went back to his mother's home in Philadelphia where, in the spring of 1957, he too managed to kick the habit cold turkey. He was out of Miles's band for about nine months, rejoining it in late 1957 on a rather more equal basis with the trumpeter.

After Coltrane left the group, Miles continued working for some time with Sonny Rollins on saxophone, but in the spring of 1957, the quintet disbanded altogether. Miles's recorded output had been prolific, and the development of his group from its shaky origins in the quartet recordings of June 1955 to the classic quintet albums of 1956 had been extraordinary. It was time to step back and put some kind of perspective on the situation. In March 1957, Leonard Feather wrote in the *Melody Maker*:

Miles Davis said in Chicago that he will pack away his horn as an active performer in the jazz world at the end of his current engagement in the Windy City's Modern Jazz Room. Now thirty years old, Miles started playing professionally when he was thirteen for $3 a week, and his combo now earns $700 a night. 'I've had it,' he told reporters. 'This is no sudden decision. I've been thinking about it for a long time, and after I close here I'm calling it quits.' He said he had no immediate plans but revealed that he had a record company offer for $200 a week as musical director, and another offer of a teaching post.[12]

The intense pace of the previous eighteen months had exhausted Miles, making him yearn for repose, change and fresh musical areas to explore. George Avakian, too, felt that there were so many Miles Davis Quintet albums on the market that it was time to do a special project, and his mind went back to the Birth of the Cool nine-piece band. Also, one event in the previous year had made a deep impression on Miles: the October recording sessions with the nineteen-piece Brass Ensemble of the Jazz and Classical Music Society. Gunther Schuller, who had played French horn on the Birth of the Cool sessions, was the director of this ensemble, which recorded pieces composed and arranged by J. J. Johnson, John Lewis, and the reed player Jimmy Giuffre. The album, which Schuller had conducted, was done for Columbia, Miles's new record company. Playing the flugelhorn solos with this brass ensemble had revived Miles's interest in working with orchestral scores, and his thoughts turned once more to his old friend, Gil Evans. Prestige could not have borne the financial burden of such an ambitious project, but Columbia could afford such things. It was time to establish the kind of relationship he wanted with his new company, and history was about to repeat, and improve, itself in a way that was almost uncanny.

During the 1940s, after spending about eighteen months with Parker's quintet playing regularly in clubs and recording frequently, Miles had signed with Capitol, a major record company, and produced the formally composed nonet performances. Now, after about eighteen months of intense recording and gigging with his own quintet, he had signed with Columbia, another major company, and was about to produce more formally conceived and composed music. Miles's quintet, of course, functioned in a largely intuitive way, and like Parker, Davis was reluctant to verbalize or talk about his music with the members of his group. Jazz musicians' most precious gift is their intuition, and however conscious and verbalized their ideas become, the essential non-verbal faculty must be preserved.

The aspirations of the Western intellectual have rarely been expressed more succinctly than in André Malraux's phrase: 'converting as wide a range of experience as possible . . . into conscious thought'.[13] In music this would mean, of course, to write it down, to 'kind of freeze it', to quote Bechet again, and that is why in Western music the composer, rather than the player or the improvising composer, is regarded so highly. This process of analysis and committal to paper of ideas has become so entrenched, that sometimes the score or blueprint or contemporary 'straight' works seems to be valued more highly than the music it represents. The instincts of most jazz musicians are opposed to this trend and John Lewis, who understands both cultures, has said: 'We have to keep going back to the goldmine. I mean the folk music, the blues and things that are related to it. Even things that may not have been folk to start with but have become kind of folk-like . . . Like some of Gershwin's music and James P. Johnson's.'[14] And Miles Davis, who was also aware of this, but who felt the need for some more formal musical setting than that of his freely improvising quintet, had found his ideal associate in Gil Evans. Talking of their relationship Miles said, some years later:

Now I've learned enough about writing not to write. I just let Gil write. I give him an outline of what I want and he finishes it. I can even call him on the phone and just tell him what I've got in mind, and when I see the score, it's exactly what I wanted. Nobody but Gil could think for me in that way . . . Gil is always listening to gypsy, South American and African things. Every time he comes to my house he's got some new record for me.[15]

Miles Davis and Gil Evans could, therefore, talk about and analyse music on an intellectual level without in any way destroying their intuitive faculties, which is one reason why their collaboration has resulted in such powerful and lasting music. During the seven years which lay between the Birth of the Cool recordings and his 1957 collaboration with Miles Davis on *Miles Ahead*, Evans had worked fitfully as a freelance arranger in New York, but he had, in addition, spent much time reading musical history, biographies of composers and music criticism. He had also listened to a great deal of recorded music. He was filling in 'the gaps in my musical development',[16] as he termed it, because as an auto-didact he had missed out on certain things. Like Miles, he was a late developer, and at that time, in his middle forties, he was at last arriving at his first real maturity. His relationship with Miles, renewed in early 1957, was to become symbiotic. He was to give Miles context, structures, new sounds; Miles provided Evans with the motive, the incentive he needed to emerge from his state of almost mystical contemplation leavened now and then with journeyman musical writing. In Miles, too, Evans had a solo-ist of great stature with a mind which complemented his own. He also had the support of Columbia Records, who were rich enough to finance the recording of a large ensemble.

The orchestral album, *Miles Ahead*, was in every way a total collaboration between Miles Davis and Gil Evans and its sustained quality is a direct result of this. The soloist not only understood the score, but had helped it to arrive at its shape and atmosphere; the composer not only understood the soloist, but knew intuitively how to create contexts which enhanced the elements of his style. For this recording, Miles used the flugelhorn, which increased the lyrical, singing characteristics of his playing, but expunged the bite and attack which gave his trumpet solos an extra dimension. His approach on *Miles Ahead* is softer and more delicate, and the album is pervaded by Miles's intimate self-communing, generating an atmosphere of urbane melancholy. Even the perky lines he improvises on Ahmad Jamal's tune, 'New Rhumba', and the cheeky humour of his playing on 'I Don't Wanna Be Kissed', have a wistful edge.

The orchestra, scored and conducted by Evans, was an expanded version of the earlier nonet. Apart from Miles's flugelhorn, the instrumentation included five trumpets, three tenor trombones, bass trombone, three French horns, tuba, alto saxophone, bass clarinet, three flutes doubling clarinets, bass and drums. The way Evans doubled up and strengthened highly mobile bass lines was to have a deep influence on Miles's later small-group work. On 'Blues for Pablo', there is a marvellous integration of lower and higher instruments, and the bass line is doubled up in some passages by bass clarinet and bass trombone, while the performance alternates fluidly between the slow pulse and the double-tempo feel. The whole context, with its incessant movement and shifting textures, inspires Miles to play with an intensity that matches his small-group work. Evans's superb recomposition of the Delibes piece, 'The Maids of Cadiz', also results in a Davis solo of exceptional quality. Miles's great sensitivity is noticeable in the different ways he responds to the various contexts Evans creates for him. Gil Evans's extra studies in the early 1950s had brought spectacular results, and Max Harrison, the extremely perceptive British critic, pointed out that Evans could now handle the orchestra with a freedom and plasticity that have been surpassed only in a very few works such as Stockhausen's 'Gruppen für drei Orchester'. Other critics, too, noted the variety and originality of the instrumental combinations Evans discovered. Max Harrison also pointed out that Evans's 'endless mixtures of sound ... are new not only to jazz writing but to all orchestral music'.[17] One of the reasons for this is that Evans was using and balancing in the studio instrumental combinations which were not self-balancing acoustically.

Columbia were aware that the music was unique – innovatory, yet accessible, full of new and attractive sonorities, with a score that mirrored and magnified Miles's own moving lyricism. The head of Columbia's publicity department, Debbie Ishlom, pulled out all the stops to publicize Miles; Avakian recalled:

We really had something to talk about, because here was a spectacularly different album. So that's when Debbie was able to do a great job and he was covered in all the national magazines. She got just about everything anybody could get for a trumpet player who was relatively unknown to the public . . . Miles, I think, was a very clever person who realized that he should take advantage of the exposure and develop some idiosyncrasies, and the Miles myth began to emerge with the publicity that accrued from the *Miles Ahead* album.

The album received a flood of enthusiastic reviews. Even the *New York Times* critic, John S. Wilson, who had been so impervious to Miles's small-group work ('the limp whimpering and fumbling uncertainty that have marked much of his work with small groups have smacked more of inarticulateness than of art'),[18] was pleasantly surprised: 'a promising but hitherto diffused talent suddenly takes a turn that brings it sharply into focus . . . There are times when Mr Evans seems to move out of the proper realm of jazz but, in or out, he has created an album that bubbles with fresh imaginative music.'[19] Even Max Harrison did not seem to grasp the fact that, so far as Miles's small-group work was concerned, a very different aesthetic was involved. He wrote:

The bulk of the Prestige solos are but faulty images of the thing perfectly realized in collaboration with Gil Evans, yet so much praise was given to them that when Davis did make a great record there was nothing new left to be said . . . this unprecedented work on *Miles Ahead*, an expression of everything towards which he had been working for so long.[20]

But the mainspring of the small-group performances is the improvisation and interplay between the musicians. The form is created as a by-product of the very different character of the three main soloists, and the performances are not inferior to, nor better than, *Miles Ahead*. They are simply different.

Since Miles Davis had begun his 'comeback' in 1954, his albums had astonished musicians and enthusiasts alike with their fresh sound and the new aesthetic criteria they posited. Each new release came as a shock, and to date, *Miles Ahead* had certainly produced the biggest ripple of interest. Dizzy Gillespie was so taken with it that he wore out his copy in two weeks and then went round to Miles and asked for another one. Columbia got so excited about it that they released 'Blues for Pablo' and 'The Maids of Cadiz' as a single on 45 r.p.m. But it was the album as a whole which provided the sort of revelatory shock which people began to expect from new Miles Davis releases. It was conceived as a unity, and the ten performances were linked together by organic bridge passages so that they seemed to be umbilically connected. These passages were also edited skilfully to create continuity between tracks from different recording dates. And on *Miles Ahead* the technique of splicing from different takes of the same piece was used for the first time in Miles Davis's recording career. Apart from these technical and structural innovations, the whole concept of a concerto setting for one improvising soloist, sustained and developed throughout a long-playing record, was a completely fresh one. It was also the first time that the flugelhorn had been played with this kind of expressivity and gentle lyricism. Once again, Miles had introduced a new instrumental sound to jazz, and once again, a host of imitators began playing the flugelhorn; from the relative obscurity of brass bands, it suddenly became one of the most fashionable instruments in studios, in concert halls and in jazz groups. While it was the perfect instrument for *Miles Ahead*, its smooth urbanity was not entirely satisfying to Miles, and he was never again to use it exclusively on an LP. He needed that other dimension: the unbridled bite of his open trumpet, and the intense timbre of the Harmon mute.

Miles Ahead was recorded in May 1957, and released the following autumn. It established Miles's talent and position in jazz; his small group was the pace-setter with a rapidly growing world audience, and his orchestral collaboration with Gil Evans had indeed taken him (and Gil) 'miles ahead' of everyone. New standards of excellence had been established in both categories. The question was, where to go after that? Meanwhile the Miles Davis legend was growing. Everything he touched seemed to turn to musical gold. He was living in a West-side apartment in New York which seemed to be always buzzing with visitors – friends and sidemen – with a TV set perpetually on. He was pursuing his non-musical interests: sparring in the gym, photography and fast cars. He was buying more clothes, dressing more sharply, and acquiring expensive furniture for his apartment. He was, at thirty-one, perhaps one of the most eligible men in New York.

With the orchestral album under his belt and the small group disbanded, Miles took the opportunity, in the summer of 1957, to undergo minor surgery. The previous year, he had started to suffer from nodes (a benign corn or polyp) on the vocal cords. This made his voice very hoarse, and his eerie, husky whisper can be heard between some of the tracks on the Prestige albums. It was quite unlike the ringing Ivy League tones in which he had introduced 'Embraceable You' at the Paris Jazz Fair in 1949, and this present Armstrong-like 'gravel' voice was an embarrassment to Miles. The operation to remove the nodes from his vocal cords resulted in one of the most often-quoted anecdotes about him. He was told not to raise his voice for at least ten days after the operation, but the second day after he'd left hospital, he met an entrepreneur who 'tried to convince me to go into a deal that I didn't want', to quote Miles's own words. The fiery Miles Davis temperament showed itself and he shouted in exasperation, permanently damaging his vocal cords – or so it seemed. The hoarseness remained, and in April 1975, according to Clark Terry, Miles had thirteen more nodes removed from his vocal cords.

SEVEN

The First Great Sextet

'I don't buy polish ... Polished Negroes are acting the
way they think white people want them to act, so
they can be accepted.'[1]

Miles Davis

From the autumn of 1957, there began for Miles Davis a period
of popularity in America and Europe that was accompanied by
universal critical acclaim and even greater artistic achievements.
After winning the *Down Beat* readers' poll in 1955, Miles had
come second to Dizzy Gillespie in 1956. But in 1957, he was back
in first place, and in the following two or three years he also
captured every coveted award in the USA and Europe: in America,
the *Metronome* and *Playboy* polls; and in Europe, polls in Holland's *Muziek Espress*, Hamburg's *Jazz Echo*, Paris's *Jazz Hot*,
and London's *Melody Maker*. Also, *Miles Ahead* was awarded
France's 'L'Oscar du Disque de l'Académie du Jazz', which was
the equivalent of the American Grammy award. Although all this
recognition must have been gratifying for Miles, he kept a fairly
clear perspective, commenting drily: 'I love wood. That's why I
hang up those *Down Beat* plaques I win. Otherwise, winning a
poll doesn't mean anything to me. Look at who some of the other
poll winners are.'[2] It became impossible to ignore Miles Davis. Up
to this point he had been written about mostly in jazz magazines,
with occasional reviews in the music columns of one or two dailies.
In January 1958, however, he emerged from the underground cult
level when there was a photograph and a feature on him in *Time*

magazine. This gave a potted history of his career, contained the usual romantic ideas about artists ('often lies awake nights rehearsing new arrangements in his head'), and let everyone know about his international reputation ('In Europe he is perhaps the most widely imitated modern US jazzman').[3]

Equally suddenly, Miles was elevated from being merely a great trumpet player and jazz musician, to being a representative of the black race. Seven months after the *Time* article, he was listed in *Life International* as one of the fourteen black people who 'have contributed significantly to the fields of science, law, business, sports, entertainment, art, literature and the preservation of peace among men',[4] including Miles Davis in this group of people whom they termed: 'Outstanding men of the Negro race [who] have in many areas of human achievement reached a stature that can only be defined as greatness'. Miles's typically truculent comment was: 'Why didn't they put me in the domestic edition if they believed it?' And it does seem that it was his prestige abroad which lay behind this recognition in his mother-country. *Life International* included a photograph of Miles with the caption:

> The man of the moment in US jazz is a 'cool' trumpet player, Miles Davis, who has been foremost in creating the craze for the small band and more melodic 'chamber' jazz. Although trained in the 'bop' tradition, Davis moved musically to a muted horn style that has made him widely imitated at home and abroad.

Miles's popularity and prestige coincided with, and of course contributed to, a general increased awareness of jazz on the national and international level. By 1957, there were glimmerings of academic recognition for jazz in the USA, and Brandeis University inaugurated a programme of commissioning jazz and jazz-oriented compositions. The first commissions, each of $350, were awarded to Jimmy Giuffre, Charles Mingus, George Russell, Milton Babbitt, Gunther Schuller and Harold Shapero. Also, Schuller and John Lewis collaborated to promote the idea of third-stream music, which purported to fuse European compositional techniques with jazz elements. But Miles Davis's experiences with the Brass Ensemble, run by Lewis and Schuller, had merely prompted him to look for other solutions to the problem of musical development and to work with Gil Evans. Some time later he commented: 'Somebody came to me . . . and asked me to play with that orchestra that Gunther and John have been working with. What do they call it? Orchestra USA? Anyway, I just told him, "Get outa here!" '[5] And at the other end of the spectrum from third-stream was the 'funk' trend, in which non-Western elements were exploited, often uncreatively, by musicians who reduced vocalized tone sometimes to the level of caricature, and concentrated on a kind of ethnic cliché and the indiscriminate use of blues 'licks'. The really creative exponents of this approach were Miles's old associates Horace Silver and the drummer, Art Blakey. Miles himself, whose 1954 recording of 'Walkin', had triggered off the renewed interest in black folk roots which resulted in funky jazz, was always too vital to be identified with the mere mannerisms of any trend. And finally, by 1957, while most jazz musicians were still eking out a precarious existence, for a few there were rich rewards: Brubeck and Garner could earn $3,000 per week in clubs, and up to $2,500 for a concert, and even a sideman could earn up to $20,000 a year. While the average jazz album sold fewer than 5,000 copies, the best sellers sold from 30,000 to 50,000. Jazz had become big business in America for the first time since the 1930s.

In this burgeoning economic climate, when Miles Davis was able to command the highest fees of his career to date, he chose not to work for over three months in the summer of 1957. This hiatus seems to have happened because he was artistically in limbo. When he disbanded his quintet in March, it was certainly in order to concentrate on preparing *Miles Ahead*. He and Gil Evans finished the recording sessions (but not the mixing and editing) for it by the end of May, and Miles then had a fallow period lasting until September. During this time he had throat surgery, and took stock of his general situation. There can be no doubt that he was somehow unsure of what to do next. When he did decide that he wanted to form a quintet again in the autumn of 1957, none of the original members was available.

At first, Miles used the drummer Art Taylor, who had played on *Miles Ahead*, pianist Tommy Flanagan, and the Belgian tenor saxophonist, Bobby Jaspar, who had immigrated to the States the previous year. Jaspar soon left, and Miles, looking once again for the kind of group balance he'd had with Parker and Coltrane – powerful, multi-noted saxophone and understated trumpet – managed to persuade alto saxophonist Julian 'Cannonball' Adderley to join him. Adderley had been leading a quintet with his brother Nat on trumpet, but had found the economics of running a group daunting. He said:

> Nobody was really making it except for Miles, Chico [Hamilton] and Brubeck. I had gotten an offer from Dizzy to go with his small band. I was opposite Miles at the Bohemia, told him I was going to join Dizzy, and Miles asked me why I didn't join him. I told him he'd never asked me ... Well, Miles kept talking to me for two or three months to come with him, and when I finally decided to cut loose in October 1957, I joined Miles. I figured I could learn more than with Dizzy. Not that Dizzy isn't a good teacher, but he played more commercially than Miles. Thank goodness I made the move I did.[6]

Cannonball was to stay with Miles until September 1959, and also helped with the organization of the group, collecting money and paying the musicians. The saxophonist had iron self-control and a genial disposition. He never, for example, touched drugs, and his reliability gave Miles solid moral (as well as musical) support. The relationship blossomed into a friendship that ended only with Cannonball's untimely death in 1975.

Miles's visits to Paris in 1949, and in 1956 with the package tour, had brought him a fairly big following in France. In 1957, he was still much more famous than the other members of his group, and so when he got an offer to go on his own to Paris towards the end of November, he accepted it. The plan was for him to work with a group comprising Kenny Clarke, now resident in Paris, and the French musicians Pierre Michelot (bass), René Urtreger (piano) and Barney Wilen (tenor sax). They were booked to play a concert at the Olympia Theatre followed by three weeks at the Club St Germain. At this time, the trombonist and ex-associate of Miles's, Mike Zwerin, was staying in Paris, and he describes the atmosphere of that first theatre concert:

It was 1957, and Miles was the big man – his clothes, his girls, his new loose rhythm section, his fresh open playing. So all of us who hung out at the Old Navy (cafe) were excited about Miles's arrival in Paris ... The Olympia Theatre was sold out that night, but by curtain time Miles's whereabouts were still a mystery. Finally, the curtain went up, revealing Barney Wilen, René Urtreger, Pierre Michelot and Kenny Clarke all set up. They started playing 'Walkin'' and sounded fine. But no Miles Davis. Barney took a tenor solo, and as he was finishing, backing away from the microphone, Miles appeared from the wings and arrived at the mike without breaking his stride, just in time to start playing – strong. It was an entrance worthy of Nijinsky. If his choreography was good, his playing was perfect that night. He had recently made his 'comeback' and was really putting the pots on. He was serious, and he was trying hard instead of just catting ... For the first week of his stay at the Club, as we called the St Germain, I was down there almost every night.[7]

Miles Davis's only other recording that year took place in Paris and was the opposite in every way of *Miles Ahead*. The latter was scored, premeditated, exquisitely realized. But his background music for Louis Malle's film *L'Ascenseur pour L'Echafaud*, recorded in December 1957, happened almost by accident, and was totally improvised by a small group. The results, far from being a finished masterpiece, were in fact like sketches and notes for some bigger work. And in a sense, that is exactly what they were, because they pointed to a completely new direction, opening up avenues of exploration which seemed to offer inexhaustible possibilities for improvisation.

Louis Malle was an avid Miles Davis fan, and when he heard Miles was coming to Paris to play at the Club St Germain, he met the trumpeter at the airport and asked him to play the background music for the film. Miles agreed to try. *Lift to the Scaffold* (American title: *Elevator to the Gallows*) was a thriller with Jeanne Moreau as the main star, and although the story line was fairly banal – a murder is committed and the killer gets stuck in a lift on the way out of the building where he committed the crime – the atmosphere is heightened by the brilliant use of contemporary locations: buildings, motels, lifts, limousines, powerful mechanisms created by man but which end up suffocating him.

Using the group working with him at the Club St Germain, Miles improvised the music in a studio, watching shots from the film and conferring with Malle. The entire music was realized one December night between midnight and morning, and although the resulting ten short pieces are really no more than fragments, they afford several insights into Miles's development. For perhaps the first time, it became clear to him that it was possible to create absorbing music with neither formally written themes nor any real harmonic movement. The tracks were at first released in France on a ten-inch LP, and later in America on one side of a twelve-inch LP, and this was the first time that Miles's own composing had filled up so much space on an album. The music had grown out of minimal predetermined material, each track having a tempo, a tonal centre, and perhaps one or two other factors, and yet it had a complete identity; it was very much Miles's music, and quite different from anyone else's. Several of the tracks have a strong modal flavour, hovering ambiguously around D minor and F. Miles probably felt free to experiment so audaciously because he was producing applied music intended to point the action and atmosphere of a film.

The music also threw into new relief the two polarities which were noticed first in Charlie Parker, and which gradually became more obvious in Miles's work: the quiet, brooding aspect on the one hand, and the furious aggression on the other. The only two fast pieces, ('Sur L'Autoroute' and 'Diner au Motel'), feature his aggressive playing, and for both he uses the Harmon mute, which buzzes furiously up and down like a fly on a window pane, producing the claustrophobic, bottled-in rage which mirrors brilliantly the action of the film. On the medium and slow tracks, the tonal beauty of the open horn and the extreme spareness of the phrases give an unearthly resonance to this reflective music. On the final piece, 'Chez le Photographe du Motel', Miles plays the first half with open horn, and then towards the end puts in the Harmon mute and the music concludes with a magnificent repeated and sustained high A (G concert) with the legato phrases leading to it also being repeated, until the legato figures at last descend and the sustained note is played down the octave (Appendix A, Fig. 5b). Louis Malle commented: 'I must say that in the last sequence of *Scaffold* Miles's commentary – which is of extreme simplicity – gives a really extraordinary dimension to the visual image.'[8] And Jean-Louis Ginibre, writing in *Jazz Magazine*, commented:

> *Ascenseur pour L'Echafaud* would have remained a relatively minor film without the music of Miles Davis ... [he] knew how to give tragic dimensions to this banal enough drama, and I think that Miles, in helping Louis Malle's film, also raised himself to greater heights, and became aware of the tragic character of his music which, until then, had been only dimly expressed. In this sense, *Scaffold* ... marks a decisive turning point in the work of Miles Davis.[9]

A year or two later, Miles told Louis Malle that the experience of making the music for the film *had* enriched him.

Back in New York at the end of the year, Miles found himself once more without a band, but with some new musical ideas, and he began trying to coax back Coltrane, Red Garland and Philly Joe Jones. If the year had been crucial for Miles, it had been even more important for Coltrane. During it, he had freed himself from drug addiction, and finished his musical apprenticeship by spending several months with Thelonious Monk at the Five Spot, learning and playing Monk's pieces. Coltrane describes this process:

> I'd go by his house and get him out of bed. He'd get up and go over to the piano and start playing. He'd play one of his tunes and he'd look at me. So I'd get my horn out and start trying to find what he was playing. We'd go over and over the thing until we had most of it worked out. If there were any parts that I had a lot of difficulty with he'd get his portfolio out and show me the thing written out. He would rather a guy would learn without reading because you feel it better and quicker that way. Sometimes we'd get just one tune a day.[10]

Twelve years previously, Monk had used the same methods when he was giving lessons to the nineteen-year-old Miles Davis.

The quartet which Monk led at the Five Spot throughout the summer of 1957 became a legendary unit, and among the many visitors was Miles Davis, who could witness everything he'd suspected about Trane coming true – 'the best since Bird' – so he asked Coltrane to rejoin him, and the saxophonist accepted immediately. By this time, Miles's groups were the most prestigious in jazz, and Coltrane could be sure of wide exposure and good money. He would also have plenty of freedom to develop his ideas. From his short-lived group of the previous autumn, Miles kept on Cannonball Adderley, and from the original quintet, he succeeded in persuading Paul Chambers, Red Garland and Philly Joe Jones to rejoin him. The group was now a sextet, and with the bigger line-up came a very different musical climate. Coltrane has said:

> On returning . . . I found Miles in the midst of another stage of his musical development. There was one time in his past that he devoted to multi-chorded structures. He was interested in chords for their own sake. But now it seemed that he was moving in the opposite direction, to the use of fewer

and fewer chord changes in songs. He used tunes with free-flowing lines and chordal directions. This approach allowed the soloist the choice of playing chordally [vertically] or melodically [horizontally]. In fact, due to the direct and free-flowing lines in his music, I found it easy to apply the harmonic ideas that I had. I could stack up chords – say, on a C7, I sometimes superimposed an E flat 7, up to an F sharp 7, down to an F. That way I could play three chords on one. Miles's music gave me plenty of freedom. It's a beautiful approach.[11]

Cannonball Adderley's alto saxophone sound was full, his techniques – his speed – was brilliant, and his phrases were shot through with the inflexions of the blues. Like Coltrane, he learned a great deal from observing and listening to Miles:

I was with Miles from October 1957 to September 1959. Musically, I learned a lot while with him. About spacing, for one thing, when playing solos. Also, he's a master of understatement. And he taught me more about the chords, as Coltrane did too. Coltrane knows more about chords than anyone . . . From a leader's viewpoint, I learned by watching Miles, how to bring new material into a band without changing the style of the band. And when it was necessary at times to change the style somewhat, Miles did it so subtly so that no one knew it. As for rehearsals, we had maybe five in the two years I was there, two of them when I first joined the band. And the rehearsals were quite direct, like, 'Coltrane, show Cannonball how you do this. All right, now let's do it.' Occasionally, Miles would tell us something on the stand. 'Cannonball, you don't have to play all those notes. Just stay close to the sound of the melody. Those substitute chords sound funny.' . . . I certainly picked up much advantage as a potential leader from the exposure of being with Miles . . . He would tell us to leave the stand if we had nothing to do up there.[12]

Musically, and in human terms, this period with the sextet seems to have been an exceptionally happy one for Miles Davis. He obviously loved the two saxophonists, both as musicians and as people. In March 1958, he paid Cannonball a great compliment by agreeing to appear as a sideman on the saxophonist's own album, *Somethin' Else*. Not surprisingly, Miles dominates the album musically, soloing with more aggression and power than was usual at that time. Also, the general method of Adderley's quintet, which included Hank Jones (piano), Sam Jones (bass) and Art Blakey (drums), was exactly like that of Miles's middle-1950s quintet. And in June that same year, Miles appeared for the last time as a sideman on someone else's album. *Legrand Jazz* was made by a ten-piece group which included Miles and Trane, and featured arrangements by the French composer Michel Legrand. Miles soloed on Fats Waller's 'Jitterbug Waltz', 'Wild Man Blues' (composed by Louis Armstrong and Jelly Roll Morton), ''Round Midnight' (Monk) and John Lewis's 'Django'. Coltrane, despite the acclaim he was getting from musicians, had still not acquired the same kind of confidence as Miles, and when his turn came to play a solo, he asked Legrand how he wanted the solo played. He was told, naturally, to play it the way he felt it. It was this lack of confidence which kept Coltrane a sideman in Miles's band, and it would take him another eighteen months to build up enough self-assurance to leave and form his own groups.

After *Legrand Jazz*, Miles's days as a sideman were over. People were beginning to realize that his attitude to music was unlike that of anyone else in jazz. He told Nat Hentoff: 'I never work steady. I work enough to do what I want to do. I play music more for pleasure than for work.'[13] This method of working, with frequent rest periods, served two main purposes. Firstly, the music was always fresh and rarely suffered from the staleness induced by uninterrupted strings of dates; and secondly, it enabled him to avoid the over-exposure that may well have accompanied the group's popularity. He was well aware of the importance of scarcity-value.

As he became more successful both artistically and financially,

Miles was concerned to maintain control over his own affairs. In particular, he wanted to be free of the usual pressures of the music business. Hentoff tells one typical story:

When a powerful entrepreneur once asked Miles to let a protégé sit in with his combo while Miles was working at his club, Miles refused. The potentate, paternalistically amiable only so long as his demands were being met, threatened Davis: 'You want to work here?' Miles said with literally obscene gusto that he didn't care and told the man he was going home. The club owner tried to smooth over the hassle, and asked Miles to return to the stand. Later that night, however, the protégé nevertheless was sent up to the band. Miles and his men walked off.[14]

By now, however, Miles Davis had surrounded himself with a team of people whom he coached to look after his interests. There was his personal manager, Harold Lovett, there was Jack Whittemore of the Shaw Artists' Corporation who booked his work, and there was Columbia Records. Whittemore tried to arrange a work schedule that gave Miles long periods at home to recharge his batteries. He also tried to get the maximum fees for Miles's dates, and the trumpeter took a hand in the negotiations if things were difficult. At this time, Miles was doing one-show concerts for $1,000, and he was offered a Town Hall contract for two performances on the same night. Whittemore told Davis that he might be able to get the price up to $1,500 for the two shows. Miles then said: 'I'll take $1,000 for the first show and $500 for the second, but you tell the promoter to rope off half the house for the second show and sell tickets for just the half that's left.'[15] Miles received $2,000 for the two performances.

On some occasions, Miles even had to resort to fisticuffs to protect himself. One night during a package tour run by jazz promoter Don Friedman, Davis arrived late for a concert in Chicago – although still long before he was scheduled to perform. Friedman came up to him announcing that he was going to fine

Miles $100 for being late. It was at that point that Friedman, to coin Sinatra's phrase, 'became punched'. When a reporter asked Davis why he'd done it, Miles said only, 'I should have hit him in Detroit yet.'[16] Don Friedman tells a slightly different story:

> I once went two rounds with Miles Davis in 1959. We fought, and it was about even, then Cannonball Adderley pulled us apart. I turned away and Miles hit me – knocked me out. I couldn't go home for a week because I didn't want my wife to see what my face looked like. But Miles couldn't play for a week either!

The novelist James Baldwin's description of Miles as a 'miraculously tough and tender man' begins to make sense when examined in the light of his survival in this artistic, social and economic climate. Miles Davis was well aware that his reputation for fireworks, his unpredictable behaviour, allied to the trappings of success – flashy cars, expensive clothes, etc. – made him seem a mysterious and glamorous figure. In the late 1950s, he once remarked innocently: 'They say people come to see me just because they've heard I'm so bad. Ain't that a bitch!'[17] He had never forgotten that many people went to see Charlie Parker for the same reason. This is not to say that the whole of Miles Davis's behaviour was a calculated pose culled from Parker; it was a much deeper phenomenon than that. Harold Lovett, for example, who must have been closer to Miles than most people were, was totally fascinated by him, even to the extent of aping his dress and mannerisms. The bonds that made Lovett a fanatical protector of Miles's interests were far stronger than those between a mere manager and his star. Lovett was playing John the Baptist to Miles's Jesus. He expounded, preached, cajoled and fought for Miles and his music. He even attempted to describe the Davis charisma:

> Miles is just a brand-new Negro in his thinking. He knows what he wants and is getting it. He has prepared himself for

it. He can direct his group from off-stage with his presence. He can go to the dressing-room and they know he's listening. He's as much a composer as he is a bandleader and he doesn't write anything down. His group rehearses on the date and musically it's as well organized as the Modern Jazz Quartet. It isn't luck with Miles, it's training.[18]

As if to prove the potency of his presence even *in absentia*, on the first album with the new sextet, Miles didn't play at all on one track, and on a second track he played no solo. The album was called *Milestones*, and it showed several changes in Miles's thinking. It was recorded on two consecutive days in April 1958, and this was the first small-group album he'd made for some sixteen months. The first striking change is that there are no standard tunes on it. In fact, the nearest thing to a standard is the old folk song, 'Billy Boy', which is a feature for the rhythm section only. It had been recorded by Ahmad Jamal a few years previously, and Red Garland's version faithfully follows Jamal's. The other pieces on the album are all composed by Miles or by friends of his. There are three blues in the key of F: a fast one, 'Dr Jekyll', composed by altoist Jackie McLean, and first recorded by Miles in 1955; a slow one, 'Sid's Ahead', which is a variation on Miles's own early blues, 'Weirdo'; and the medium-paced 'Straight No Chaser', by Monk. The two other tunes on the album are 'Two Bass Hit', by John Lewis, and a new piece by Davis called 'Miles' on the album label, but 'Milestones' everywhere else.

Milestones takes the art of small-group jazz to a very high level indeed. In the context of Miles's career, it is very much a transitional album. With three horns in the front-line, the old loose Davis quintet method, as exemplified on Cannonball's *Somethin' Else* the previous month, had to be modified. All the themes on *Milestones* (except, of course, for the trio track) are played by all three, or by two of the horns in unison and harmony. Miles is particularly concerned to show off and contrast his two saxophonists, and so there are only two piano solos on the whole album; one on 'Straight No Chaser', and the one on the trio track. In fact, on the second day of recording, Red Garland, furious with Miles for telling him how to play, stormed out of the session before they had recorded 'Sid's Ahead', the longest track on the album. The pianist playing the rich, harmonically ambiguous chords behind Coltrane and Adderley is Miles Davis himself. The theme is stated by the three horns in harmony over a rhythm section of bass and drums, and Miles plays his own solo with just those two instruments backing him.

Three of Miles's solos on this album are classics, and each is totally different in character. They occur on 'Sid's Ahead', 'Straight No Chaser' and 'Milestones'. They are all open horn solos, because on this album, as on *Miles Ahead*, Davis does not use the Harmon mute at all. His open sound is particularly sonorous, and its glowing, luminous quality is accompanied by an apparently effortless plasticity of inflexion which imbues every phrase, every idea with intense life. So soft and full is his sound on the title track, 'Milestones', that it suggests he may be playing flugelhorn rather than trumpet. These three horn solos are the expressions of a powerfully original mind, and Miles's self-editing process functions relentlessly.

His solo on the slow blues, 'Sid's Ahead', has an emotional depth that is almost unbearable. Here, Miles develops and expands ideas that had their germ in the *Scaffold* music. The solo (Appendix A, Fig. 6) is seven choruses long, and apart from its sparseness and severity, there are also quite specific references back to the film music. For example, the skeletal repetitions of some of that music are echoed in the last eight bars of his third chorus and culminate in a phrase in the last bar which closely mirrors the leap from F (concert) to D above the stave and down to A flat, which Miles played at the beginning of 'Florence sur les Champs-Élysées' (Appendix A, Fig. 5a). And the solo rises remorselessly to the repetitions, for the first seven bars of the final chorus, of high A flat (concert) which is, of course, the flattened 3rd of the blues scale, and the descent in bar eight leading to the stoic conclusion. This also harks back to the final section of the film music, 'Chez le Photographe du Motel' (Appendix A, Fig. 5b) where Miles repeats high G (concert) for several bars before descending. This was the passage which drew ecstatic murmurs from Louis Malle: 'A really extraordinary dimension to the visual image.' On 'Sid's Ahead', the music is not applied, but pure, and the extraordinary dimension is given, not to a visual image, but to the emotional power of the solo. After the initial theme statement, Coltrane plays the first solo, accompanied by bass, drums and Miles's moody piano chords. Trane's solo has a similar emotional depth and he sustains the atmosphere of brooding set up by the elemental blues theme. Miles then follows, supported only by bass and drums, so that even the instrumentation is pared down to the three basics: drums, bass and horn.

Cannonball Adderley, magnificent saxophonist though he was, seems to have realized that he couldn't hope to match the power of the two solos he had to follow. He simply could not sustain the mood set up by Coltrane and Miles, and he meanders aimlessly, quoting phrases from standard tunes and producing a few bluesy licks. This particular area was just not his bag, but the medium-paced blues, 'Straight No Chaser', was, and on this Cannonball solos first. At this bright and bouncy tempo he is in his element, and plays an excellent solo, bubbling along joyfully. He is followed by Miles, who plays a very different blues solo. This time, although the underlying sadness is always present, his phrases dance and sing along with a kind of impish delight. As is usual with Miles Davis, the past is ever-present, and in one chorus he actually quotes the first phrase of the old traditional tune, 'When the Saints Go Marching in', repeating it and then putting it in a minor key to fit the chord changes. But this quote is organic to his racy reinterpretation of the past, and is brilliantly woven into the fabric of the solo. After Miles, Coltrane roars in with wild verbosity. Under his onslaught it seems that the blues/jazz tradition is creaking at the seams. He piles chord on chord, plays across, through, against, alongside the pulse. Then suddenly he finishes and the rhythm section creams out in a simple groove with Red Garland's piano solo. Philly Joe ticks off the bars with a rimshot on every fourth beat – 1-2-3-tick – reassuring everyone, and Garland plays the first half of his solo with single-note lines, and the second half with block chords, but with this tremendous surprise in store: the melody which he underpins with the block chords is none other than the trumpet solo Miles played in November 1945 on Parker's historic recording of 'Now's the Time'. Garland had paid a similar tribute to Miles in November 1957 when he recorded with his own quintet, but his own album was not issued until two years later.

The piece which most obviously opens up new territory, and points to future developments, is the title track, 'Milestones'. Once more, this explores areas touched on in the *Scaffold* film music. The structure, which is forty bars long, is based on only two scales and they are closely related. The first sixteen bars are based on the G minor 7th chord which implies the scale (once again) of F major, or the Dorian mode; the second sixteen bars are based on the chord of A minor 7th and the implied scale is that of C major (Aeolian mode). The final eight bars go back to the first scale. The whole piece is thus built on only two separate scales, with harmony now becoming decorative rather than functional. In other words, when each scale is used, different chords can be picked out from the notes of that scale; the chords may thus change while the scale (and key) remains constant. This is similar to the harmonic ambiguity which was a strong feature of one or two of the film tracks. The second sixteen bars of 'Milestones', for example, have E and A roots played by the bass, but they sound like suspensions on D minor.

But even more important than this reduction of harmonic movement are the rhythms of the piece and the way the structure builds and releases tension. The written theme and its structure (which is rigorously preserved for each soloist) are a brilliant refashioning of the old call-and-response idea. The first sixteen bars are the 'call', and they set up a superbly springy rhythmic pulse. Here Miles the composer, by using extremely simple devices with immense subtlety, has created an entirely fresh feel, a new rhythmic dynamism and springboard. The three horns play, in simple triads, a three-note riff which moves up and down the scale. The notes are short, played with great precision, and don't fall on the fourth beat of any bar. The rhythm section plays a bright 4/4 and Philly Joe once more ticks off the last beat of every bar with a rimshot, thus providing a kind of punctuation for the horn riff. During the second sixteen bars, this buoyant pulse is interrupted and held back with great artistry, thus producing a feeling of slowing up, though the actual tempo remains the same. This impression is created because the bass, instead of 'walking' purposefully up and down the scale playing crotchets, is silent on the first beat of each bar then simply repeats pedal notes E and A over the last three beats, while Philly Joe's rimshot falls on different beats, thus stopping the regularity of rhythm. The two saxophonists continue playing up and down the scale in harmony, but this time with longer notes (minims), while Miles plays the same kind of thing slightly out of phase with the saxes; his rising and falling notes are played against theirs, dragging the phrases back. The tension rises as all these factors pull against the memory of that first springy rhythm, and then suddenly the last eight bars arrive, the original beat is back, and the tension is released magnificently. Miles is, once again, using very simple devices to say extremely complex things. This composition has deservedly become a standard tune in the repertoire of jazz musicians all over the world. The structure – the way the piece 'breathes' – is preserved for the three horn solos, and they match the quality of the conception of the composition. Wilfrid Mellers comments on Miles's own solo:

> Bird was a composing improviser, and Miles is an improvising composer ... When the trumpet [flugelhorn?] emerges from the beat of time ... the soft, suave tone veils tremendous passion: which gradually breaks through until the line swirls with almost Parker-like agitation. The effect of the piece depends on the contrast between the passion the line generates and the immensely ancient, modal quietude of its first statement.[19]

I have dwelt on the album *Milestones* because it is one of the great classics of jazz and occurs at a key point in Miles Davis's career. The music on it glows in the memory. It is profound, delightful, full of confidence and immense optimism. Throughout, there is the feeling that the past is rich, the present enjoyable, and the future full of promise.

EIGHT

Porgy and Bess

'Porgy and Bess was the hardest record I ever made.'[1]
Miles Davis

By 1958, Miles Davis's fame, coupled with his method of working, were beginning to cause some problems. The long rest periods he liked were not appreciated by the rest of the group, who were not paid when they were not working. Also, being with Miles meant sharing some of his fame and the aura of glamour that surrounded him, so the musicians in his group invariably got offered other jobs. Sometimes their engagements would clash with Miles's own concerts and he would have to employ a deputy drummer or pianist for the evening. For a time, Miles tried paying his musicians a retainer, but it was not enough to stop them working with other bands, and when the desired object was not achieved he stopped this expensive practice. Philly Joe Jones was very much in demand, and by 1958 was often missing Miles's jobs. Because of this it became imperative to find another drummer. Cannonball recommended Jimmy Cobb, who had worked in Adderley's quintet, and as there was even doubt as to whether Philly Joe would turn up for the recording sessions of *Milestones*, Cobb was asked to stand by in the studio. Jimmy Cobb was, naturally, overjoyed at the prospect of joining Miles's group. He recalled:

That was the best job you could have ... it was the best-paying jazz gig at the time that black people could have ... that was about as high as you could get playing jazz music,

Above: Paris Jazz Fair 1949. *Left to right* Sidney Bechet, Big Chief Russell Moore, an unknown woman and Miles.

Below: Paris Jazz Fair, 1949. *Left to right* Hot Lips Page, Miles Davis and Kenny Dorham.

A publicity photo of Miles from the 1940s.

Miles and John Coltrane in the recording studio, mid 1950s.

Miles and Red Garland, mid 1950s.

Miles with Bud Powell, 1956.

Miles and Gil Evans, 1957.

Miles and Gil Evans recording *Miles Ahead*, 1957. Lee Konitz is sitting at far right.

Miles Davis with Jeanne Moreau, who starred in *L'Ascenseur pour l'Echafaud*, a film for which Miles created and recorded the music, 1957.

Miles and Gil Evans recording *Porgy and Bess*, 1958.

Miles at the piano, with Bill Evans looking on, late 1950s.

Left to right John Coltrane, Cannonball Adderley, Miles Davis and Bill Evans, late 1950s.

so I was feeling pretty good about it. So I sat through the record date, and right soon after that he (Cannonball) told me that Joe had gone, and come down and play. Most of the things they played, I knew them, because of course they were very popular things, and I heard Joe play them, so it really wasn't that hard.

There were factors other than conflicting bookings which had made Philly Joe and Red Garland miss some of Miles's gigs. Both of them, and bassist Paul Chambers, were still drug addicts, and their condition made them unreliable. Jimmy Cobb said: 'We went to Washington once with the band and we opened on a Friday, and I think Red got there Saturday midnight. Miles liked the way he played so he put up with that sort of thing a long time.' Very soon after Philly Joe left, Red Garland did so too. To replace him, Miles hired the young white pianist, Bill Evans, who had been recommended by George Russell, Miles's old friend and associate. Evans had been playing in Russell's Smalltet which, in 1956, made one of the finest albums of the decade, and he'd also been a featured soloist in Russell's 1957 orchestral work, 'All About Rosie', composed for the Brandeis University commission. Evans's star was rising, but he was still hardly known at all. Jimmy Cobb was to stay with the group for five years, but Evans was with it for a few months only, from spring to autumn in 1958. In this short time, however, he made a great impact on the music and on Miles himself. Also, the following year Evans was temporarily reassociated with Miles Davis when the sextet made the historic album *Kind of Blue*.

By mid-1958, Miles Davis was becoming recognized as a discoverer of major talents, or at least as a catalyst enabling major talents to realize themselves. At the beginning of that year, each member of his group was the leading exponent, *the* influence, on his particular instrument: Miles on trumpet, Coltrane on tenor sax, Cannonball on alto, Paul Chambers on the bass, Philly Joe on drums and, perhaps to a slightly lesser extent, Red Garland on piano. Bill Evans was, even at this early stage of his career, an original, a major keyboard stylist, and his exposure with Miles was probably a key factor in his winning the *Down Beat* critics' New Star award in late 1958 which, perhaps ironically, was partially responsible for the brevity of his stay with Miles Davis. The sensitive Evans did not feel entirely comfortable with Miles's sextet. He said later: 'I felt the group to be composed of superhumans.' Also, he was the only white man in the group and Miles would tease him about that. Jimmy Cobb said:

> They were close, but Miles used to bug him, you know. He would just fool with him. It was good-hearted . . . Like, we'd be talking and Bill would say something and Miles would tell him, 'Man, cool it. We don't want no white opinions.' That kind of shook him because he didn't know how to take that, and Miles would be giggling behind him . . . and piano players, when they first got with the band they were always confused because he would tell them when to play and when not to play, so they got so they wouldn't know when to play.

Bill Evans had studied the piano music of the French impressionist composers, and he brought Debussian chord voicings to support his supple and flowing melodic lines. His work has quite remarkable sensitivity and depth, and in the late 1950s his sound was startlingly fresh. Miles commented: 'Another reason I like Red Garland and Bill Evans is that when they play a chord, they play a sound more than a chord.'[2] This sound in Evans's case is created by the inner voicings of his chords, and this quality made him the perfect man for Miles's musical needs at the time. Evans's creative ability with inner voicings was exactly what was necessary for exploring the decorative, as opposed to the functional, aspect of harmony.

By May 1958, both Jimmy Cobb and Bill Evans were with the sextet, and there were subtle changes in the approach and emphasis of the music. Cannonball Adderley noted some of them:

> Especially when he started to use Bill Evans, Miles changed his style from very hard to a softer approach. Bill was brilliant

in other areas, but he couldn't make the real hard things come off. Then Miles started writing new things ... Miles at first thought Jimmy Cobb wasn't as exciting [as Philly Joe] on fast tempos, and so we did less of those. And although he loves Bill's work, Miles felt Bill didn't swing enough on things that weren't subdued. When Bill left, Miles hired Red again and got used to swinging so much that he later found Wynton Kelly, who does both the subdued things and the swingers very well.[3]

Later that year, Miles told Nat Hentoff:

Boy I've sure learned a lot from Bill Evans. He plays the piano the way it should be played. He plays all kind of scales; can play 5/4 and all kinds of fantastic things. There's such a difference between him and Red Garland whom I also like a lot. Red carries the rhythm, but Bill underplays, and I like that better.[4]

In Bill Evans, Miles had with his group a pianist with the same inward-looking and self-examining approach as himself. A remark Wilfrid Mellers made about Evans is also an accurate description of Miles: 'Evans's ability to make melodic lines "speak" is of extraordinary subtlety; and always the sensuousness leads not to passivity but to growth.'[5] But it was to take about a year before Miles found the perfect fusion of his own talents and those of Bill Evans. This occurred on the album *Kind of Blue*, recorded in early 1959, several months after Evans had officially left the band. But the first intimations of the exquisite music Miles would produce in this new setting occurred when he took the group into the studios in late May 1958, to record a couple of movie theme tunes, 'On Green Dolphin Street', from the 1946 film of that name, and 'Stella by Starlight', from a film called *The Uninvited* (1943), and a piece he had written himself, 'Fran Dance' based on a dance tune, 'Put Your Little Foot Right Out'.

From Bill Evans's solo piano at the beginning of 'Green Dolphin

Street', when he plays the melody *colla voce*, to the coda with the sad, descending harmonies of the two saxes over which Miles's trumpet with Harmon mute improvises, the whole performance is flawless. It has an atmosphere of sumptuous brooding, a kind of sadness of the ages allied to a rather more Western European sensibility. The rhythm section, with Jimmy Cobb sounding relaxed and confident on drums, alternates pedal points and free-wheeling time with chord changes in the usual Davis manner of building and releasing tension. The four solos – by Miles, Coltrane, Adderley and Evans – are superb, and their order brilliantly devised: the two masters of understatement, Miles and Evans, play before and after the two prolific soloists. It is a long performance, lasting almost ten minutes, and it is totally absorbing.

'Stella by Starlight' is half that length, and Cannonball does not play on the track. Although it does not quite have the power of 'Dolphin Street', it is a hauntingly beautiful performance with one magnificent dramatic moment. This occurs after Miles has interpreted the theme, using the Harmon once more, and with Jimmy Cobb using brushes to create a gentle pulse. Then, instead of playing a solo, Davis projects a strident sustained high note while Cobb changes to sticks, and the rhythm section drives along massively as Coltrane enters. This suddenly raises the intensity, and Trane sustains this atmosphere of sobriety and swing by also, like Miles, simply playing the melody and embellishing it. This is another surprise, and a delightful one, because Coltrane's beautiful sound with its expressive long notes gives new dimensions to the tune.

There may have been very personal reasons for the romantic eloquence of these performances, because it seems that Miles had fallen deeply in love again. He had renewed his acquaintance with Frances Taylor who, with Chita Rivera, was one of the dancers in Leonard Bernstein's *West Side Story* when it opened at the Wintergarden Theatre on 26 September 1957. Miles had gone many times to see the show during the eight months that Frances was in it, and by the early summer of 1958, she had moved into his Tenth Avenue apartment. His enormously tender composition

'Fran Dance' was inspired by Frances Taylor. Frances and Miles were ultimately married in 1960 after what she described as 'four years of rehearsal'. Not all the musicians on this session, however, were entirely happy about the exquisite restraint of the music. According to Bill Evans, Paul Chambers and Jimmy Cobb were 'getting edgy having to hold back and wanted to cook on something. Miles just turned and said, "Love for Sale", and kicked it off.'[6] The result was a classic performance of great drive. This track was not released for many years, probably because during the late 1950s it did not fit in with Miles's prevailing ideas, and during the 1960s it seems to have been simply overlooked.

Despite the fact that it has often been suggested (usually by whites) that Miles Davis is prejudiced against whites, many of his deepest friendships and closest associations have been with white people. His attitude has probably always been something like that of Jonathan Swift, who said: 'I love Tom, Dick and Harry, but I hate that animal Man.' Miles's association with whites at key points in his career has often resulted in greater insights that led to fresh musical ideas. Gil Evans had been a constant friend and colleague since 1947. Other influential and fruitful friendships were with Lee Konitz and Gerry Mulligan in the late 1940s and early 1950s, with Bill Evans in the late 1950s; and in the late 1960s and the 1970s, with Joe Zawinul, Dave Holland, John McLaughlin and Dave Liebman. Certainly, Miles has always been scrupulously fair in recognizing genuine talent when he sees it, whether in blacks or whites, and when asked if he thought the ability to swing was exclusive to black musicians, he is alleged to have said: 'I once nearly gave myself a hernia trying to get two black cats to swing!'

To survive, Miles Davis had to be extremely tough, and he demanded a certain toughness from the musicians who worked with him. Black or white, he kept them alert by his unpredictable and often mystifying behaviour. Not only did he tease Bill Evans about being the only white man in the group, but he also frequently had the other musicians guessing what he would do next. During club engagements, which usually lasted a few days or a week, he would sometimes, in the middle of someone's solo, disappear from the scene for the rest of the evening. Jimmy Cobb described how confusing this was:

> From time to time he would start a tune . . . and he would play on it, and then while the band was playing on it, he would leave . . . but most of the time it would be pretty close to the end of the night, where I guess he figured the proprietor wouldn't be mad any more and wouldn't dock him, or something like that. But he used to do that quite often.

Miles also tended to needle new sidemen by comparing them with their predecessors. Lena Horne once said: 'Miles is a potentate. He's also a puritan, and the combination can be pretty sadistic.'[7] When Jimmy Cobb replaced Philly Joe, Miles said to his new sideman: 'My favourite drummer is Philly Joe.' For some time after Cobb joined, Miles would stand behind him counting the bars or beats, as if calling in question Jimmy Cobb's time-playing – the most sacrosanct part of a drummer's craft. Some years later, when Coltrane had left the band and Hank Mobley was the saxophonist, Miles is alleged to have said quite audibly while Mobley was playing: 'Any time Sonny Rollins shows up with his horn, he's got the job.' And sometimes, when someone fell below his own standards, Miles could be rude and unkind, as he was to Barney Wilen in 1956. The French saxophonist was playing with Miles at the Club St Germain, and during an intermission he told Mike Zwerin: 'You wouldn't believe what Miles said to me in the middle of my solo on the last tune. He said, "Man, why don't you stop playing those awful notes." '[8] Despite this sometimes cruel behaviour, Miles Davis had a great affection and respect for his musicians, and usually treated them with thoughtfulness and generosity. When Bill Evans left the sextet in the autumn of 1958 in order to try his luck with his own trio, Miles went out of his way to help him by phoning agents and talking to them about the pianist.

When Bill Evans was in the band, the Western European

elements in the music had intensified, but at the same time Miles was also going more deeply into his own ethnic roots. Paradoxically, he did so by collaborating once more with his friend Gil Evans. Their next project was to record excerpts from Gershwin's opera, *Porgy and Bess*, with the aim of transferring the full flavour of the vocal score into music for orchestra only. Again, this idea had come to him after he'd gone many times to see Frances in a stage production of the opera. Miles, on flugelhorn and muted (Harmon) trumpet, was to be the 'singer'. At this period, he was still living in his mid-town apartment, a relatively new building on Tenth Avenue, near 57th Street. In it he had a good piano and an adequate mono record player, and during the first six months of the year, whenever Miles was at home 'resting', Gil Evans went there to talk about the project, and to try out the various musical ideas.

Their version of *Porgy and Bess* was recorded in four three-hour sessions, which took place in July and August 1958, and the orchestra was similar to the *Miles Ahead* unit: four trumpets, four trombones, two saxophones, three French horns, two flutes, tuba, bass and drums. But the way this ensemble is used, and its relationship with Miles's flugelhorn and trumpet, differ subtly from *Miles Ahead*. There is much more of Miles on *Porgy*, and he assumes very much the role of preacher, while the orchestra plays that of congregation. It is a wonderful reinterpretation of the call-and-response pattern, with sections of the orchestra responding to one another, and all of them responding to Miles. Two pieces, 'Summertime' and 'It Ain't Necessarily So', are simply solos by Davis, and the ensemble plays the same role as the gospel choir backing a singer – replying to his phrases with hypnotically repetitive riffs. Gil Evans and Miles devised this kind of mutual incitement: Miles responding to the written orchestral responses. A perfect example is the deeply moving 'Gone, Gone, Gone', which is an instrumental version of the old, antiphonal black funeral service.

This communication between Miles Davis and the orchestra under Evans's direction attains an ominous, terrifying grandeur on 'Prayer', a remarkable piece that makes the hair rise on the back of one's neck. It has no real harmonic movement at all, staying in B flat minor throughout, without any modulations. The first part is out of tempo, with a brass tremolo over which Miles does some magnificent calls, using all the tonal inflexions of which he is now master – slurs, bent notes, stabs, long singing notes which cry out powerfully. In his pauses, the orchestra screams out ragged responses, the more affecting because of their very raggedness. Evans's writing for brass instruments is superb on *Porgy* – far more dynamic than on *Miles Ahead* – and it is this which helps give the dialogue between Miles and the orchestra such potency. Eventually, 'Prayer' changes from the out-of-time tremolo to a repeated figure (ostinato) played by the lower instruments in slow 12/8 time – the most typical church rhythm. This starts very quietly, repeating its dark incantations with gradually increasing insistence. Over this ritualistic, hypnotic figure, Miles continues his calls, at first plaintively but, as the other instruments take up the ostinato, Davis's calls climb to the upper registers of the trumpet, becoming more insistent, more passionate, until it seems that the total ensemble has ignited. At that point he sustains a blazing E flat concert above his top C, and descends with a long swooping phrase. This is a magnificent climax, and the cumulative grandeur of the gradually increasing choir of instruments is heightened simply because, even under the pressure of the dynamic incitement of the orchestra, Miles keeps his grip on the prayerful aspect of the occasion; he plays no fast or glib phrases, but picks his notes at eloquent intervals, with a nobility of phrasing that is extraordinary. After this peak, there is a slow dispersal of voices from the ostinato, which subsides to the lower instruments and stops on a long note. In this performance, Miles seems to have cut his way back through layers of experience, through bebop, through early jazz, through Western orchestral music, through and beyond the whole Western tradition, to the archetypal expression of the black race where the 'field holler' began, and where the spokesman (soloist) is expressing the aspirations of a complete and homogeneous society.

The level of inspiration throughout *Porgy and Bess* is exceptionally high: Miles plays as one possessed and Evans writes with the same intensity. They do more than justice to Gershwin's great opera, transforming it, deepening it, and uncovering roots of which even Gershwin was probably unaware. The album is full of musical felicities because the music conforms with Gil Evans's own basic criterion: it is alive – the 'form originates from the spirit'. It also encompasses a wide range of expression, from the gentle lyricism of 'Bess, You Is My Woman Now' and 'Bess, Oh Where's My Bess', to the ominous grandeur of 'The Buzzard Song' and 'Prayer'. There are two wonderful resting points, one either side of the album, in the long solos by Miles on 'Summertime' and 'It Ain't Necessarily So'. Once again, his playing – muted on the first and open horn on the second – reveals a deeper level of artistry because on each track he plays the entire solo from within the tune, developing the inner logic of each of the pieces.

Miles handles the responsibility of the whole album quite brilliantly, playing the written parts, in which he is often leading the whole ensemble, with great feeling and accuracy, and playing solos which are more than equal to their context. He said afterwards that it was 'the hardest record I ever made'. The strains of the previous decade or so had made him suffer occasionally from ulcerous pains, and he said later that when he was recording *Porgy*, 'I felt like I'd been eating nails'.[9] But he was very pleased with the results and said, 'I like this record. I'd buy this record myself.'[10] Also, talking of their version of the cries of the vendors on Catfish Row, Miles said: 'You listen, and you *know* what's going on. You *hear* that old strawberry-seller yellin' out strawberries ... *straw*-berries.'[11]

The whole Davis/Evans version of *Porgy and Bess* was, as *Miles Ahead* had been the previous year, recorded in only four three-hour sessions, not enough time for an album of such complex music. On one track at least, 'Gone', there are clearly audible errors from some of the instruments, and some scrappy ensemble playing in general. Years later, Gil Evans said: 'On most of those records, one more session would have cleared up most of the clinkers. Looking back on it, I'm outraged at myself for not sticking up for my rights.'[12] Despite the inadequate recording time, however, *Porgy and Bess* is a major contribution to twentieth-century music. It is outstanding in the way that a sustained dialogue is created between a great improvising soloist and a great orchestrator.

Columbia were now doing everything in their power to promote Miles Davis and his music. They had, the previous year, distributed an excellent potted biography which consisted mainly of Miles talking about himself, and which starts in his typically offhand way: 'You want me to tell you where I was born – that old story? It was in good old Alton, Illinois. In 1926. And I had to call my mother a week before my last birthday and ask her how old I would be.' This biography was published in its entirety in *Down Beat* in the spring of 1958, and provided a basis for articles in several other publications, including the feature in *Time* magazine mentioned at the beginning of Chapter 7.

Since 1956, Columbia had also signed Duke Ellington and Billie Holiday, and the company were feeling so enthusiastic about their jazz stars in the summer of 1958 that they threw a party in the Edwardian Room of the Plaza in New York. At this party, Miles's sextet and Duke's orchestra played, and Billie Holiday and Jimmy Rushing sang. Columbia also began some systematic image-building, projecting Miles Davis as the Byronic black man, the 'mean, moody, and magnificent' jazz musician. The cover of the first CBS album, *Round About Midnight*, showed a brooding Miles in sepia tints, his eyes masked with dark glasses, his down-turned head in his hands and his trumpet slung across his chest. The cover of *Milestones* was to have a magnificent portrait of him in open-necked green shirt, sitting down and staring impassively straight at the camera. Years later, this would inspire one of Joe Zawinul's compositions, 'The Man in the Green Shirt'. The two albums with Gil Evans, on the other hand, heightened the enigmatic, mysterious aspect of his image by having no picture of him on the front covers at all. *Porgy* was particularly enigmatic in that the front cover picture showed a man and woman from the waist down only. The two half-bodies are sitting and the woman's hand is reaching out to touch a trumpet which is lying across the man's lap. The symbolism must have been obvious even in the naïve 1950s.

The rest of this year was spent in concerts and tours and, in Miles's rest periods, preparing for the next recording project, to take place the following year. As 1958 ended, it must have seemed that his career was on a never-ending upward spiral. He had reached another pinnacle of artistic and financial success, he was in love again, he was a national and international celebrity, and he was acknowledged as a leading representative of his race. The following year was to bring yet further musical masterpieces, but it would also bring some rude shocks that were to have a profound effect on him.

NINE

Is It Jazz?

'An artist's first responsibility is to himself.'[1]

Miles Davis

For some years now, every new record release by Miles Davis had astonished musicians and fans alike with the freshness of its sound, and by 1958, his music had established itself as, in critic Whitney Balliett's phrase, the 'sound of surprise'. And now, at the beginning of 1959, after the brilliant small-group album, *Milestones*, and the magnificent orchestral album, *Porgy and Bess*, most people thought that Miles's music had reached its peak of expression. Early that year, however, he recorded an album that brought to even greater heights the brooding, meditative side of his music that had revealed itself for the first time at Parker's 'Now's the Time' session in November 1945. This was called *Kind of Blue*, and it was to be perhaps the most influential single album in jazz history.

Miles Davis thought that his sextet was the finest small group in jazz up to that time, and his aesthetic ideas for the group were clearly formulated, which accounts for the confidence and potency of his current musical vision. He was steadily expanding his knowledge of earlier jazz forms and performances and the interview he did with Nat Hentoff in *Jazz Review* (December 1958), shows just how perceptive and clearly thought-out were his criticisms of other musicians. He talks lovingly of Billie Holiday, the old blues singer Leadbelly, Bessie Smith and Louis Armstrong. Hentoff plays him Louis's 'Potato Head Blues', and Miles comments: 'There's form there, and you take some of those early forms, play it today, and they'd sound good. I also like all those little stops in his solo. We stop, but we often let the drums lay out altogether. If I had this record, I'd play it.'[2] At the same time, Miles was expanding his interests in other areas of music. He told Hentoff: 'I've been listening to Khachaturian carefully for six months now and the thing that intrigues me are all those different scales he uses . . . they're different from the usual Western scales.'[3] By now, too, very few of Miles's contemporaries held any interest for him. Of the leading pianist, Oscar Peterson, who was popular with musicians as well as with the general public, Miles said: 'Nearly everything he plays, he plays with the same degree of force. He leaves no holes for the rhythm section.'[4] And talking of music in general and his own group in particular, Davis comments:

> I usually don't buy jazz records. They make me tired and depressed. I'll buy Ahmad Jamal, John Lewis, Sonny Rollins. Coltrane I hear every night . . . He's been working on those arpeggios and playing chords that lead into chords, playing them fifty different ways and playing them all at once. He's beginning to leave more space except when he gets nervous . . . I never have anybody write up anything too difficult for us, because the musicians tighten up.[5]

Ironically, it was becoming more difficult to keep the group together. Bill Evans had left in November 1958, and Red Garland filled in on piano for three months. Coltrane and Adderley were now leading their own groups as well as working with Miles, and so there were three bandleaders in the sextet. The two saxophonists were also thinking of leaving the group, but Miles managed to solve that problem temporarily by asking Harold Lovett to represent Trane and get him a record contract with Atlantic. Miles also asked Jack Whittemore to get bookings for Coltrane's group whenever the sextet wasn't playing. Things improved somewhat in February 1959, when pianist Wynton Kelly replaced Garland. Kelly combined the virtues of Red Garland *and* Bill Evans, and

Miles loved his playing, as did both Coltrane and Adderley.

After an incubation period of some ten months, Miles Davis went into the recording studios again on 2 March 1959, but when Wynton Kelly arrived, he was perturbed and mystified to find Bill Evans there. Nothing had been said to Kelly about the occasion, and as he'd only recently joined the sextet, he was still unsure as to whether he was or wasn't the regular pianist. Jimmy Cobb explained: 'That's what Miles used to do sometimes. He used to bring two players down for certain ideas he had . . . He had that thing for the blues and he knew how Wynton played, and he had that thing for the pretty things, and he knew how Bill played . . .' In fact, on that first day, three pieces were recorded, and although Kelly played on only one of them, he was paid for the whole day's work. The album was finished on another session that took place in late April, during which two more pieces were recorded.

The opening track, 'So What', immediately established the mood and atmosphere of the album *Kind of Blue*. Bill Evans plays a quiet introduction with impressionist chord voicings, and then a melodic riff is played by the bass, while the rest of the sextet reply to each of his repeated phrases with a mournful two-note riff in three-part harmony. It is yet another variation on the call-and-response technique, with the bass calling (preaching) and the horns and piano saying 'amen' (or 'so what') to each of his statements. The bass riff and the 'amens' of the ensemble go on for sixteen bars, and are then raised a semitone for eight bars before going back to the original tonality for the final eight bars. Thus, in this thirty-two-bar structure, Miles has reduced the harmonic movement to two broad areas; the first sixteen bars are based on the scale of C major but harmonized with the chord of D minor 7th (the Dorian mode); the middle eight is based on the scale of D flat major, but harmonized with the chord of E flat minor (also Dorian); and the final eight goes back to the first tonality. Here, Miles was following up lines of thought first hinted at in the *Scaffold* film music, and first brought to fruition in his composition 'Milestones', also based on just two scales.

Miles Davis's use of one or two scales or modes, instead of a harmonic structure, as a basis for themes, resulted in what became known as modal jazz, and a whole series of experiences and events had led to this late-1950s phenomenon. Since they met a decade earlier, Miles and George Russell had spent some time together, and Russell's great theoretical (and profoundly practical) work *The Lydian Chromatic Concept of Tonal Organization* had, among other things, examined the scales appropriate to certain chords. The translation of chords into scales paved the way for this later modal thinking. Miles had also, with Frances Taylor, seen a performance in New York of the Ballet Africaine from Guinea, which of course featured very rhythmic modal ethnic music. The instruments had included the highly evocative and emotive African thumb piano, which is held in the hand while the several metal rods set in its sound box are flicked with thumb or finger. The dance troupe's rhythms, modes and the thumb piano had made a powerful impression on Miles. But there were other sources of inspiration nearer home. Working with Gil Evans on *Porgy and Bess* had also helped to define these modal ideas. Miles said:

> When Gil wrote the arrangement of 'I Loves You, Porgy', he only wrote a scale for me to play. No chords ... And in 'Summertime', there is a long space where we don't change the chord at all. It just doesn't have to be cluttered up ... All chords, after all, are relative to scales and certain chords make certain scales ... You go this way, you can go on for ever. You don't have to worry about [chord] changes and you can do more with the [melodic] line ... I think a movement in jazz is beginning away from the conventional string of chords, and a return to emphasis on melodic rather than harmonic variations. There will be fewer chords but infinite possibilities as to what to do with them.[6]

The tensions set up by the theme of 'So What' – the unusual role of the bass, the mournful 'amens' which are really sardonic 'so whats', the decorative function of harmony with its sudden organic use when the theme shifts up a semitone – combine to inspire the soloists. Miles plays two superbly sculpted choruses and is followed by Coltrane. With the latter, Bill Evans's accompaniment changes from the graceful ebb and flow he used for Miles, to more insistent and ominous chords. With Cannonball there is a more cheerful and relaxed feeling and finally, Evans himself plays a solo with riff backing from the horns that is a subtle variation on the original 'amen' response, giving the performance tremendous lift. George Russell has called Miles's two choruses on 'So What' 'one of the great lyrical solos of the century', and he later made it the theme for his own Living Time Orchestra's version of 'So What'. It has been transcribed and played by many other musicians, and is one of the best-known and -loved improvised solos in jazz.

The second track, 'Freddie Freeloader', has Wynton Kelly on piano and is a blues in B flat. Like 'So What', it is taken at a medium strolling tempo, and this traditional form, too, Miles has reduced to its starkest, most elemental basis. It is built on the three traditional chords of the blues – the tonic, sub-dominant and dominant – with only one tiny variation when a different harmony is used for the last two bars. This time, a harmonized, two-note 'amen' is the main thematic motif, a falling phrase like a gentle sigh, creating an atmosphere of sophisticated melancholia. It is quite remarkable how the blues has been reduced to its simplest form while the feeling which infuses it has become more subtle, more refined, more evocative. Once again, the solo order is brilliantly organized. Wynton Kelly plays first, and suddenly, after the introversion of 'So What', and the melancholy theme of this blues, Kelly's solo sparkles with unrestrained joy. He plays single-note triplets and some block chords which swing mightily, and the muscularity of his phrases, his pulse, his effervescent ideas, throw the whole of the album into relief, enhancing the impact of all the rest of the music. He is followed by Miles, who builds to a magnificent climax in his sixth and final chorus, when he is followed by Coltrane, and then by Adderley, whose irrepressible spirits burst out in fluid, bluesy phrases.

Bill Evans, who wrote the original sleeve note for *Kind of Blue*, commented: 'Miles conceived these settings only hours before the recording date, and arrived with sketches which indicated to the group what was to be played. Therefore you will hear something close to spontaneity in these performances. The group had never played these pieces before the recordings.'[7] Also, according to Evans, each piece was done in just one take. But one piece on the album was definitely worked on consciously, over a period of six months. This was 'All Blues', which opened side two. Miles worked at it on his piano at home, and took his ideas round to Gil Evans for his opinions and suggestions, but even then the piece found its ultimate form only in the studio on the actual day of the recording. Miles told Ralph Gleason: 'I wrote it in 4/4, but when we got to the studio, it hit me that it should be in 3/4. I hadn't thought of it like that before, but it was exactly right.'[8]

The striking feature of 'All Blues' is a plaintive, repeated three-note riff played in harmony by the two saxophones throughout the beginning and ending of the piece, and intermittently by the piano during the solos. This riff is yet another variation on the three-note theme of 'Milestones', and there is something of the same way in which the tension ebbs and flows according to whether the notes are played short or long. Miles knew exactly what he was doing here, and said of this riff: 'You can get a lot of tension by repetition . . . I didn't write anything for me to play; I just play what I feel like at the time.'[9] Over this hypnotic riff, Miles plays a series of haunting calls using his Harmon mute. The unhurried nature of the piece gives him time to remove his mute (while the saxes are playing the riff) and play the first solo. His use of the open trumpet sound here gives an added textural richness. Indeed, the whole piece is remarkable for the original and subtle way Davis creates the textures he wants. 'All Blues' is built up of layers of sound: the drums play straight, unobtrusive 3/4; the bass states the pulse by repeating a two-bar slow, lilting boogie-woogie figure reminiscent of Jimmy Yancey; over this Bill Evans plays a long, sustained trill in the middle register of the piano; to this is added the hypnotic saxophone riff. Over this rich texture, Miles calls with the astringent sound of the Harmon mute. Just as he plays his solo with open trumpet, so the other textures change and loosen up as the musicians start reacting to the soloists. As is usual with Miles, the formal elements of 'All Blues' are deceptively simple, and the whole is infinitely greater than the sum of its parts.

There are no fast pieces on *Kind of Blue*: 'So What', 'Freddie Freeloader' and 'All Blues' are medium-tempo performances, and 'Blue in Green' and 'Flamenco Sketches' are skeletal ballads. Miles Davis's titles are usually just methods of identifying particular pieces; they are rarely descriptive of the music. Often, he names compositions after things, people or phrases from his everyday environment. 'So What' is one of the expressions he has used a great deal, particularly to people who come up and tell him how much they like his music. And 'Freddie Freeloader' was the nickname of an ex-bartender in Philadelphia, a hipster who just hung around the jazz spots and ran errands for musicians.

The homogeneity of mood on *Kind of Blue*, and the superlative response of the musicians to the contexts Miles devised, combined to make this one of the seminal albums, and one of the most enduring classics, of jazz. It has been bought, loved and learned by non-musicians as well as by musicians, and it has influenced world-famous musicians as well as obscure performers. The more it is listened to, the more it reveals new delights and fresh depths. Typically, at the time, the musicians in the studio didn't realize that they had just made a historic recording. Jimmy Cobb recalled the playback in the studio:

After it was over and we heard it, we went through the things ... and it sounded so nice in the studio ... and it came out so good on the record ... I said 'Damn! – it sounded good!' But since then it got to be something special in the music ... a lot of people started listening to the music with that record, and a lot of guys started to play jazz from behind that record ... and I had a few people tell me that they had worn out three to four copies of that record.

The restrained elegance of *Kind of Blue*, however, could be achieved only in the cloister-like atmosphere of the recording studio, working with unfamiliar material. In live performances, Miles's groups were too irrepressibly dynamic to function in so restrained a way. With this album, Miles had taken the Western aspects of his music to their limits. 'Blue in Green', for example, takes civilized melancholia, and the introverted, self-regarding sensibilities which are European in origin, about as far as they will go without turning into mawkishness. The piece is so sad and nostalgic that it is almost painful. The qualities of Bill Evans are of crucial importance to the music of *Kind of Blue*, and it is significant that on this piece Evans claimed his contribution was more organic than on the other pieces. All the compositions on the album were attributed to Miles Davis, but some years later, Bill Evans said:

> Actually it's my tune, even though Miles is credited as co-writer for reasons only he understands. One day at Miles's apartment, he wrote on some manuscript paper the symbols for G minor and A augmented, and he said, 'What would you do with that?' I didn't really know, but I went home and wrote 'Blue in Green'.[10]

This begs the question of in what, precisely, the act of jazz composition consists. The cause of Evans's writing 'Blue in Green' (if indeed he did), as he points out, was Miles Davis's defining the area of interest: the relationship of two particular chords. In a Zen pupil-and-master sense, by pointing Evans in a particular direction, Miles was certainly 'composing' himself. Miles himself has stated that he composed everything on the album and that Evans was given the same sketches in the studio as everyone else.

This vexed problem of composition, by composing improvisers and improvising composers, had begun with the early confusion about the composer of 'Donna Lee' (it was attributed to Bird, but had been written by Miles), and would continue to be a recurrent theme throughout the rest of Miles's career. There is, of course, money in composing: composers gets a royalty every time their music is played, and if it is recorded, they can expect a steady income so long as the records either sell or get played in public on radio or television. Because of the financial advantages, some bandleaders throughout the history of jazz have exercised what might be called a sort of *droit du seigneur* so far as their sidemen's compositions were concerned, either taking over the rights completely or at least sharing them. In some cases, the problem was far simpler and less abstract than the question of the authorship of 'Blue in Green'. For example, two of Miles's most famous tunes of the early 1950s, 'Four' and 'Tune Up', have been claimed by the saxophonist and blues singer, Eddie 'Cleanhead' Vinson, who said:

> He [Miles] was in Kansas City and he needed some tunes. He said, 'Well, man, can I take these?' I said, 'Yeah, just put my name on it.' I hadn't bothered to copyright it at the time ... I've seen him since, we're still friends! Oh, he's tried to pay me, but I just enjoy his playing anyway.[11]

There is an authentic note in this claim, because of the lack of rancour. Miles himself has made the following remarks about the relationship of improvising and composing: 'Do I like composing better than playing? I can't answer that. There's a certain feeling you get from playing that you can't get from composing. And when you play, it's like a composition anyway. You make the outline.'[12] The irony and the difficulty lie in the fact that themes and structures are accepted as compositions and can be registered as such, but the improvisations on them, often where the most potent music is created, cannot usually be registered as compositions.

In 1959 Miles Davis's reputation was blossoming and the scope of his activities widening. Although the specialist magazines still wrote about all aspects of his music, he was featuring more often in the non-specialist, national press. By now his fans were often people who were not jazz enthusiasts, but Miles Davis fans. In

March, a long feature written by Nat Hentoff was published in the sophisticated, up-market magazine *Esquire*. In April, between the two recording sessions which produced *Kind of Blue*, Miles was recorded and filmed for a major TV programme, a thirty-minute show in a prestige series produced for CBS by a Welshman called Robert Herridge. The show was called 'The Sound of Miles Davis', and it immediately broke all the rules. Cannonball Adderley was ill and couldn't make the programme, so the first item was a nine-minute quintet version of 'So What', which took the show right up to the middle commercial – the show was sponsored, though CBS didn't network it. Miles's solo on 'So What' rivalled his original masterpiece recorded the previous month, but was very different from it. The second half featured Miles with Gil Evans and the orchestra (which had already played some riffs behind the solos on 'So What') playing three pieces from *Miles Ahead*: 'The Duke', 'Blues for Pablo', and 'New Rhumba'. The programme was not shown until July 1960, when it caused quite a stir because of its uncompromising emphasis on the music, and the casual, relaxed appearance of the musicians. Instead of the usual formal black suits, for example, Miles wore a tweed jacket and a sports shirt with a silk, Ascot-knotted kerchief, and Gil Evans wore a 'sloppy' sweater, though one reviewer hastened to mention that 'the effect wasn't pretentiously messy, beatnik-slobbism; only comfortable'.[13] Between the recording and the transmission, Davis watched the film at least five times.

Shortly after the TV recording, Coltrane also fell ill, and although Miles had signed a contract to play a Milwaukee night club, he cancelled the booking, thus risking legal proceedings and a fine. This gives some indication of how highly he rated his two saxophonists; if either of them had been fit, he would certainly have fulfilled his part of the contract and played at the club. But there were already signs that Adderley and Coltrane might not stay with the sextet much longer. Miles's growing fame was reflecting on all his musicians, and Adderley with his direct, blues-based style, and Coltrane with his passionate innovations, were both building up a substantial following. Cannonball was already getting inquiries from club owners about when he would start his own band, because they noticed the tremendous audience response when Cannonball's name was announced. But for the moment, there were strong inducements to stay with Miles. Adderley stated clearly why he wanted to stay:

> Jazz has no place for stagnation. I know one thing for sure. You can't repeat yourself night after night when you're working with Miles Davis. Miles and Coltrane are creating all the time and the challenge is tremendous . . . Miles's group is as it should be. It's a laboratory. New and exciting music is played each night. I learn so much being around him.[14]

But despite all the critical acclaim, the recognition, the prestige both in the USA and abroad, Miles Davis was still experiencing racial discrimination. In the early summer of 1959, for example, he drove to Chicago for an engagement, and rolled his imported Ferrari (a sure badge of money and status) into a motel on the shores of Lake Michigan, only to be told that there had been a mix-up with the reservations. But back in New York in August, Miles was to suffer an indignity so gross that it made the Chicago incident seem negligible.

One hot night, when the Davis sextet was working at Birdland on Broadway, Miles escorted a girl out of the club and hailed a cab for her. Afterwards, he speculated that it may have been this which sparked off the whole incident, because the girl was white. After her cab drove off, Miles took a breather on the pavement outside the club. As he stood there, a police patrolman came up and told him to move along. Miles replied, 'I work here', and added that he just wanted a breath of fresh air and would soon be returning to the club. The patrolman asked Miles if he was a 'wise guy', and said: 'If you don't move, I'll have to lock you up.' Miles replied, 'Go ahead, lock me up.'

As Miles's attention was fixed on the first patrolman, a second one came up behind him and beat him savagely on the head with a blackjack. Covered in blood from his head wounds, Miles was taken to gaol and his temporary cabaret card confiscated. Musicians could not work in New York without such a card. During the fracas, an angry crowd of onlookers jammed the sidewalks, blocking the traffic, and later a crowd gathered outside the 54th Precinct where Miles was being held. He was kept in gaol overnight and released on $1,000 bail the following day. He needed five stitches in his scalp, and said later, 'They beat me on the head like a tom-tom.' One eye-witness commented: 'It was the most horrible, brutal thing I'd ever seen. People were crying out to the man not to kill Miles.'[15]

The incident was given a great deal of publicity in the New York press, with indignant headlines everywhere and strong sympathy for Miles. The black paper, *Amsterdam News*, gave Miles's story prominence, and said that he had suffered from a 'Georgia head-whipping'. And press around the world covered the story, the London *Melody Maker*, for example, printing a photograph of the blood-spattered Miles standing with Frances in the police precinct. Ironically, it was Miles Davis who was charged with disorderly conduct and assault. The two policemen claimed that Miles had made the first violent move: 'Davis grabbed the stick and was going to hit the officer,' claimed the second patrolman, 'so I hit him with a billy on the head.' Miles's contention was that he was trying to protect his mouth from being battered, or his lip damaged, which is why he may have seemed to be trying to 'grab the stick'. The day after the affair, the Local 802 of the American Federation of Musicians sent the Police Commissioner a telegram requesting a complete investigation because of the conflicting accounts, and a few days later, the police said Miles could have his cabaret card back any time he wanted to collect it.

Repercussions from the affair rumbled on for months, finally stopping in the spring of 1960. In October, Miles was cleared of the charges of disorderly conduct, which still left the simple assault charge. His manager, Harold Lovett, threatened to file a million-dollar damage suit against the City of New York. But after Miles was also cleared of the other charge (the judge commented: 'It would be a travesty of justice to adjudge the victim of an illegal arrest guilty of the crime of assaulting the one who made the arrest')[16] he was not anxious for Lovett to proceed with the filing of his suit for false arrest, assault and battery, and malicious prosecution. Jack Whittemore, his booking agent, explained:

> Miles feels that if he pushes the City too far, even though he might win his damage suit, he would then be the target for the police, who would be looking to nail him on any little charge they could think of. He feels he has proved his point if he is found innocent on all charges.[17]

As the decade drew to an end, there was a feeling of change in the air. At the end of September, Cannonball Adderley finally left the sextet, even though Miles offered to guarantee him an annual salary of $20,000. Also, the new technique of stereo recording had just been introduced, and *Porgy and Bess* had been Miles's first album in stereo. When Gil Evans was editing and mixing the tapes for that LP, he was assisted by a Columbia employee called Teo Macero who, in 1959, was officially made the CBS A&R (artist and repertoire) man for Miles Davis. He became the key man in Miles Davis's recording career and retained that role until 1975. This was a significant change for Miles because, from the late 1950s onwards, actual recording techniques were to play an increasing role in music generally, and in Miles's music in particular. His orchestral albums, especially, needed great technical expertise for their realization, because the ensemble led by Gil Evans was not self-balancing like a symphony orchestra.

Teo Macero was a master craftsman of recording techniques, and one of the pioneers of stereo recording, but he was also much more than this. He had a Master's degree from Juilliard, and had also played tenor saxophone with Charles Mingus's Composers' Workshop. Between 1953 and 1955, Macero had played on several of Mingus's albums, and had also appeared in 1956 at the Newport Festival with him. It was Teo Macero who produced Mingus's album *Mingus Ah Um*, which had such a seminal influence on jazz (and rock) thinking in the 1960s. His experiences with Mingus must have stood Teo Macero in good stead when he began working with Miles. His expertise was not only technical and electronic; he also knew the problems of playing an instrument, and was still composing music himself – something he continued to do all the years he was with Columbia. In the middle 1950s he'd had a Guggenheim award to write a composition. Columbia, in their laudable efforts to promote understanding of jazz, assigned Macero to work with Leonard Bernstein on an album called *What is Jazz?* Teo recalls:

> I wrote a lot of the little examples for that album. Then I wrote an arrangement of 'Sweet Sue' which never came out. According to Lenny, it was too lugubrious . . . Lenny said he wanted something to swing, and I said, 'Then don't ask me, get somebody like Miles.' He said, 'That's a good idea,' so we got Miles . . . Miles wrote the chords himself.

The Miles Davis Quintet version of 'Sweet Sue' on *What is Jazz?* is still a most lugubrious rendering of a normally bright tune. But that marked the first time that Macero and Miles worked together in the studio. After assisting Gil Evans with *Porgy*, Teo was the producer, the man in the studio control booth, for *Kind of Blue* (where he had little to do) and for all subsequent albums, except for a brief period in the early 1960s when he and Miles fell out and were not on speaking terms. George Avakian, the man who had signed Miles for Columbia, and who had produced the first orchestral album, *Miles Ahead*, had left CBS, and it was his role in the company that Teo Macero was assuming. So far as Miles Davis was concerned, Teo was going to expand this role: he was not there merely to help the artist realize his music and record it, but also to become an intermediary between Miles and the CBS bosses. This became clear on the very first major project he did with Miles and Gil Evans: the recording of *Sketches of Spain*, the album with which Davis closed the old decade and opened up the new one.

It was while he was on the West Coast with his sextet early in

1959, that a friend played Miles a recording of 'Concierto de Aranjuez' for guitar and orchestra by the contemporary Spanish composer, Joaquín Rodrigo. 'After listening to it for a couple of weeks,' Miles said later, 'I couldn't get it out of my mind. Then when Gil and I decided to do this album, I played him the record and he liked it. As we usually do, we planned the programme first by ourselves for about two months.'[18] For the album, Evans rewrote and extended the middle section of the Concierto, which takes up most of side one, and for the rest of the music he went to the library and did some detailed research into Spanish music, flamenco, and the life of the Spanish gypsy. The other piece on side one is a version of an excerpt from Manuel de Falla's 1915 ballet, *El Amor Brujo*, and the second side of the album has three compositions ('The Pan Piper', 'Saeta', 'Solea') which are credited to Gil Evans himself.

More time was spent on recording and editing *Sketches of Spain* than was spent on any of the other orchestral albums, and it was Teo Macero's proselytizing on behalf of Miles and Gil which won the extra time. It was unheard of then to do ten or fifteen sessions in the studio with a big orchestra for one album, particularly with a jazz artist, but the first four studio sessions for *Sketches* were completely unproductive because Miles had flu. The president of CBS, Goddard Lieberson, expressed some concern to Macero, who said: 'Miles is sick ... We've had four sessions where we've received absolutely nothing from him – they were like giant rehearsals, and we were over time with the sessions too. It doesn't look like we'll finish it in five or six sessions.' Lieberson said, 'Well, do you think it will be worth it?' Macero replied, 'Absolutely. When we're finished we're going to have something of gigantic proportions!' Lieberson said simply, 'Stay there until you finish it.'

It took fifteen three-hour sessions with the orchestra to record the album. But Macero's enthusiasm and Columbia's faith and daring were fully justified and amply repaid. The finished results were ultimately hailed as a masterpiece, and the album has sold steadily over the years since it was first released. In 1976, for example, sixteen years after its release, it sold 463 copies in Great Britain, and three years later, in Germany, 4,000 were sold. By 1980 it had 'gone gold'.

Apart from the forty-five hours of recording, just to get the basic tracks on tape, Teo Macero also spent about six months editing the tapes and putting the album together. Here, for the first time, stereo recording techniques were fully exploited. Teo says:

> There were a lot of new tricks which we tried at the time. We had the bands going off the side and one band going in the middle and then coming back and splitting it and going to the sides again. Then the whole band going out – there's a little march [on 'Saeta'] . . . if you listen carefully, you'll hear all these things – movement . . .

Sketches of Spain reveals a further step away from the Western concept of orchestral function, which insists that the ensemble has to play together with machine-like precision, and that individual musicians should merge anonymously into the ensemble, which exists to express the will of a composer. *Sketches* moves even further away from this idea than *Porgy* had done, inclining more towards the non-Western idea that the individuality of the musicians should be a clearly evident part of the whole, and that the music's power is heightened by a slight raggedness. What had been perhaps a deeply subconscious idea on the two previous orchestral albums now became formulated as a conscious thought. Miles said: 'It was hard to get the musicians to *realize that they didn't have to play perfect* [my italics]. It was the *feeling that counted*.'[19] He was referring specifically to 'Saeta', but the remark stands in its general application to his whole approach. The great gap between the two musical cultures was becoming more and more apparent. The composer, Bill Russo, once said: 'The melodic curve, the organic structure, and the continuity of a Miles Davis solo . . . cannot be perceived very easily by a classically trained musician.'[20] And at this stage of his career, Miles Davis seemed to be turning his back on much of the Western musical tradition, and concentrating more on ethnic elements. With *Sketches of Spain*, he knew exactly what he was doing, and stated at a press conference in 1960: 'Flamenco is the Spanish counterpart of our blues.'[21] When asked what he and Gil Evans were going to do next, he replied: 'Gil and I are interested in doing an African ballet album. I think that will be the next direction.'[22] But something he put into words in 1964 clarifies his thinking on this whole matter of the two cultural standpoints:

> As for Gunther Schuller, I can see why [Leonard] Bernstein would get along with him. It's like the difference between talking to a Spanish nobleman and talking to a gypsy. Bernstein can talk to Schuller, who's a classical musician and doesn't really play jazz; but he can't talk to Tony Williams, my drummer – they'd have nothing in common.[23]

Miles Davis is plumping for the values of the gypsy.

Although the three great orchestral albums are always discussed as if they are virtually the same sort of thing, each one has a distinct and separate identity. *Sketches* in particular differs strongly from the first two in several important ways. Here, for the first time, there is an extensive use of percussion (tambourines, maracas, castanets etc.) for colour and texture as well as for rhythmic purposes. Throughout the album there are frequent long periods based on a single scale where the interest is textural and spatial rather than harmonic, and where Miles solos over this mobile (but harmonically static) backcloth. There is also frequent use of ostinati – repeated rhythmic figures – several of which often go on simultaneously and are sustained for long periods, thus creating a hypnotic, 'possessed' effect. There are passages where Miles solos – 'calls' – out-of-time against a rich tapestry of sounds.

The trumpeter's inward-looking self is exquisitely expressed on the 'Concierto', but a wilder, more primeval meditation is given voice on 'Saeta' and 'Solea'. Here his vocalized tone is developed and expressed to its fullest extent. On 'Saeta', which occupies the same sort of role on *Sketches* as 'Prayer' did on *Porgy*, the passionate muezzin calls which Miles utters over a droning tremolo again make the neckhair bristle. 'Solea' is a tour de force. It is a long piece presenting a continuous dialogue between Miles and the ensemble that lasts for ten minutes, and yet the interest, the movement, the efficacy of Miles's phrases – often very 'Eastern' in their intervals – are all sustained throughout.

All the conceptual implications of *Sketches of Spain* were not to be more fully explored until Miles recorded *Bitches Brew* in 1969. Meanwhile, when *Sketches* was released in 1960, it was so different that many critics simply didn't know what to make of it. At the same 1960 press conference, Miles was asked: 'Mr Davis, do you feel this new work of yours is jazz?' Miles replied: 'It's music, and I like it. I'll play anything I take a fancy to, if I feel it's possible for me to do it.'[24] Asked the same question in Great Britain, Miles replied: 'I think so ... what do you think?[25] John S. Wilson, the *New York Times* reviewer, failed to see anything of merit in the album at all, and wrote:

This is the third album that Mr Evans has written and conducted for and with Mr Davis, and one is struck by the continued exploitation of a similarity of sound on all three as Mr Evans creates a rich, exotic, hanging background through which emerges the languid, pained sound that Mr Davis squeezes from his trumpet ... For the listener in search of jazz, there is mighty little of that commodity evident in any of these selections except for a portion of the 'Concierto'.[26]

Sketches of Spain brought to a fitting climax the period of intense creativity that had begun in 1954. These six productive years seem to divide naturally into two parts: the classic small-group recordings of 1954–6 plus the *Scaffold* film music and the orchestral album, *Miles Ahead*, of 1957, are all like preparations for the tremendous achievements in the years 1958–60: *Milestones*, *Porgy and Bess*, *Kind of Blue* and *Sketches of Spain*. And there is an almost uncanny parallel with Miles Davis's second great creative period, 1964–7, when he is once more producing conceptually fresh small-group music that is a preparation for the huge achievements of the years 1968–70: *Miles in the Sky, Filles de Kilimanjaro, In a Silent Way, Bitches Brew, Live-Evil, Jack Johnson.*

By the beginning of the 1960s, Miles had won both the *Down Beat* international critics' poll and the readers' poll. As a kind of bonus, the *Down Beat* readers also voted him jazz personality of 1959. As one club owner remarked: 'The trouble with you is that everybody likes you, you little son of a bitch!'[27] With his popularity and prestige at their highest points, and with controversy about his work raging more violently than ever, Miles Davis was about to start a period of intense travel abroad, where interest in his music and his mystique had mushroomed from Europe to Japan.

TEN

After Coltrane

'I pay my sidemen the highest prices because they're
worth it and I've got the best rhythm section in jazz.
I'm retired now because I don't do nothing
unless I want to.'[1]

Miles Davis in 1960

By the beginning of 1960, the London *Melody Maker* readers'
poll had voted Miles Davis top trumpeter. For the first time in the
history of that poll, Louis Armstrong had lost the title; the honour
now belonged to the thirty-three-year-old Miles, whose whole
view of himself and his function was totally opposite to that of
Armstrong. Miles said: 'I ain't no entertainer, and ain't trying to
be one . . . My troubles started when I learned to play the trumpet
and hadn't learned to dance . . . they want you to not only play
your instrument, but to entertain them too, with grinning and
dancing.'[2] Nevertheless, Miles was the contemporary trumpeter
nearest to Armstrong in terms of beautifully sculpted phrases and
the 'singing' quality of his solos. In the same *Melody Maker* poll,
Gil Evans had ousted Duke Ellington for first place in the big-band
composer/arranger category.

By this time, Miles's super-stardom had reached such a pitch
that often, when he was announced on stage or in clubs in America,
there would be moans and screams from girls in the audience,
rather like the reception by teenagers of a popular singer such as
Sinatra. At this point in his career he was, in fact, well served by
critics. Three of the most professional and most perceptive critics

in the USA – Leonard Feather, Nat Hentoff and Ralph J. Gleason – analysed, assessed, expounded and explained Miles brilliantly. Hentoff published a long and graphic account (*Hi-Fi Review*, February 1960) of one of the recording sessions for *Sketches of Spain*. This had a kind of documentary realism and included dialogue as it was spoken in the studio, giving a vivid impression of the occasion. Later in the year, Feather was to intercede on Miles's behalf with the British public, and at regular intervals, Gleason peppered local papers from coast to coast in the USA with articles and explanations about Davis.

It was at this time that people were beginning to notice Miles's apparent obliviousness regarding audiences: his unwillingness to make announcements either of tunes or of the names of his musicians, and his persistent refusal to acknowledge applause. He had been behaving this way for years, of course, but now that so many people were aware of him, many having only recently discovered his music, his stage demeanour became the subject of comment. Ralph Gleason tried to make sense of this:

He eschews the spotlight; never smiles, makes no announcements. Many people are annoyed when, at the close of his solo, Davis walks off the stage. The Davis syndrome in performance is free individual creation, always a major part of jazz, carried to the ultimate . . . Davis's music is as uncompromising as any in history. Sociologically, he has become a symbol of the contemporary Negro as well, winning his success solely on his merits with no bending to public taste, no concession to entertainment and absolutely no cultivation of 'contacts' or of anyone likely to do him any good. In other words, no 'Uncle Tomming'.[3]

There were also in-depth articles in French jazz magazines that same year, and one of them, in a long piece entitled, 'Why So Mean, Miles?', commented: 'The behaviour of Miles Davis is not that of an ordinary star. It is that of a strong man who has decided to live without hypocrisy.'[4]

Where the bebop movement had failed to get the status of the musician elevated to that of artist rather than entertainer, Miles Davis was succeeding. Gleason's analysis, though illuminating and perceptive, nevertheless errs on the side of romanticism. Gleason (more so than Leonard Feather, who probed deeply into the Davis psyche over the years) was fascinated by the trumpeter almost to the point of adulation. Quite clearly, Miles knew how to 'impose himself', to make his presence felt and to shape events as he wanted them, because he was aware of all the salient factors in any situation.

In February 1960, the winter weather was so bad that, instead of flying to Chicago where they had an engagement at the Sutherland Lounge, the quintet had to go by train. Despite sub-zero temperatures, when the musicians arrived at the hotel, there were queues of people standing in the snow – which was six feet deep in places – waiting to get into the place. The audience was not deterred by the threat of fire either. Jimmy Cobb recalls:

And then another peculiar thing happened while we were working there . . . on the first floor of the hotel there was the reception desk, and right across from the reception desk was a little travel agency. Some time that day they had a short in the wires in the ceiling and it started smoking . . . it caught fire. The room where we were working was right on the first floor – you could walk directly from the reception desk into the club. And the club was packed! And the firemen were outside the door putting out this fire, and nobody left! Smoke was all in the joint and nobody left . . . and the place was packed . . . Yeah, Miles was very popular.

The previous autumn, the jazz world had been shaken by the appearance at the Five Spot in New York of the alto saxophonist Ornette Coleman. He had dispensed with chord sequences and traditional scales altogether and was playing 'free' jazz. But Coleman had not, as Miles, Mingus and Coltrane had, got to his present position by working through and mastering all the known techniques of jazz: he had got there by rejecting everything except the old format of theme – solos – reprise of theme, and by expressing a kind of naked emotion – the blues and roots of the music. For those who remembered Bird and bebop, it seemed like a second coming, and many musicians not in Miles Davis's impregnable position feared they would be made stylistically redundant overnight. Coleman was hailed by Leonard Bernstein, John Lewis, Gunther Schuller and others as the new Messiah. He was lionized, given a huge amount of press and publicity, and found it relatively easy to get well-paid work. By September 1960, his two albums for Atlantic were selling 25,000 at a time when 6,000 was a good average sale for a jazz record. Miles Davis believed that many of Coleman's detractors were simply jealous, and commented: 'I like Ornette, because he doesn't play clichés.'[5] And Jimmy Cobb said later: 'At the time I don't think anybody was really worried about being dated with what Miles was playing.' But it must have seemed ironical to Coltrane that he was getting so little recognition, whereas Ornette, five years younger, was getting so much. One of Trane's disadvantages was that he was always in the shadow of Miles Davis's fame and prestige. His liking and admiration for Miles were very great indeed, and the two of them had been through much together. Teo Macero said of Trane: 'He'd smile like a little boy when Miles would play something he liked.'[6]

Everywhere Miles's group went, there was controversy – sometimes bitter controversy – about Coltrane, and his impact was intensified by his stamina (both physical and mental), which was formidable and, in fact, without precedent in jazz. He was taking the whole art of improvisation into another realm of values entirely. No longer was it simply a pretty variation on an easily digested melodic theme; now, with Coltrane, it was becoming a vast and incessant flow of original ideas all conceived and expressed at white heat and with what Ralph Gleason called 'the urgency of his almost primeval cry'.[7] So it must have become clear to Coltrane at the beginning of 1960 that, in order to realize his own potential and get the kind of recognition he needed, he would have to leave Miles and go out on his own. Jimmy Cobb describes the situation in those last hectic months Coltrane spent with Miles's quintet:

> Coltrane would play all night, and come off in the inter-
> mission and go somewhere and play . . . stand in a corner or
> something . . . You know, Miles had to make him stop,
> because he would play an hour solo himself, and we were
> only supposed to be on the stand for forty minutes or some-
> thing. He had incredible chops – he couldn't stop. Miles used
> to say, 'Man, look, why don't you play twenty-seven choruses
> instead of twenty-eight?' . . . Coltrane would say, 'I get
> involved in this thing and I don't know how to stop.'

On one occasion when Coltrane said he didn't know how to stop, Miles said: 'Try taking the saxophone out of your mouth!'[8]

In March and April, the Miles Davis Quintet became part of a JATP (Jazz at the Philharmonic) package tour organized by Norman Granz. The itinerary took in Scandinavia, France and Germany, and this was the first time Miles had been abroad with his full group. Although Coltrane wanted to leave, Miles managed to persuade him to do the tour. Jimmy Cobb recalled: 'All he had with him were his horns, an airline bag, and a toilet kit. He didn't really want to make the gig, but Miles talked him into it. He sat next to me on the bus, looking like he was ready to split any time.'[9] There was savage controversy over Coltrane in Germany and France. It was rumoured that at one major concert in Ger-many, when Coltrane was booed, Miles had angrily stopped the music and taken his group offstage. In France, apart from bewil-derment at Miles's stage behaviour, there was considerable dismay about Coltrane, and many members of audiences walked out. The furore reverberated in the French jazz papers for months afterwards. But Coltrane and Miles were a new breed of musicians whom even the experienced Norman Granz failed to understand. He was mystified and furiously angry when he tried to set up a jam session involving Coltrane and Stan Getz for a television programme, and Trane had the audacity to refuse to do it. But given the direction and development of Coltrane and Miles since 1955, it should have been obvious that neither of them would want to indulge in this kind of activity. Their battle was not an external one with other instrumentalists, but an internal affair against old, received ideas and old habits of thought. It was on that final tour that Miles bought a soprano saxophone and gave it to Coltrane, which resulted in the reinstatement of that instrument as a major force in jazz.

Back in the USA, after a few more engagements with Miles, Coltrane left the quintet in order to lead his own group. Cannonball Adderley's departure had been a blow, but Coltrane's departure was a devastating loss to Miles, who almost broke down and wept during their last gig together, in Philadelphia. So strongly did he feel that he even went to the microphone and made a brief announcement about the saxophonist's imminent departure from the group. And, as Jimmy Cobb commented: 'He never talks with nobody about nothing, so you know, he really must have felt something for Coltrane.' The saxophonist's departure left a gap that, in some ways, Miles was never able to fill again. Trane had been interested in artistic growth, and his incessant exploration of the unknown had sparked off ideas in Miles, giving the trumpeter the kind of challenge he needed. Also, Coltrane's 'sheets of sound' had been a superb contrast to Miles's own spare phrasing. From now on, Miles was going to have to produce the contrasts – spare brooding and multi-noted aggression – himself. There was simply no other saxophonist of Coltrane's calibre in jazz at the time. The only other one who might have matched his power was Sonny Rollins, and he was in semi-retirement. When Trane left, Miles must have felt quite naked and insecure, and to fill the saxophone vacancy he turned to an old friend and an established star, Sonny Stitt, the man he had met in St Louis around 1943. But despite the personnel change, the popularity of Miles Davis and his group continued to grow. During the year, Miles himself was chosen favourite jazz instrumentalist by a poll of America's leading disc jockeys in *Billboard* (trade paper of the music industry). And in *Down Beat*'s first disc jockey poll in May, six of

Miles's albums were placed, *Porgy and Bess* being voted first, and *Kind of Blue* third. In August, the quintet with Sonny Stitt had a residency at the Village Vanguard in New York, playing to packed houses and ecstatic audiences. One critic wrote: 'The room was literally jammed . . . Many of the audience were obviously in protoplasmic harmony with the proceedings; that is, their neurons were jumping.'[10] And after this engagement, the group went off again to Europe for a British tour, followed by dates in Paris and Stockholm. This time the French gave Miles and the group a tremendously warm reception, cheering them at the end of the first piece, 'Walkin'', and never ceasing to acclaim them for the rest of the night. Both houses at L'Olympia were packed – 2,000 people attended each performance.

Charlie Parker had never played in Britain, and this tour was to be Miles Davis's first visit. A build-up in the musical press started some weeks before he arrived in an attempt to make up for some fifteen years of ignorance on the part of the British public. This publicity campaign culminated in a long feature article in *Melody Maker* by Leonard Feather, who emphasized the glamour surrounding Miles and attempted to reconcile the apparently paradoxical qualities of the trumpeter. Feather insisted that Miles was not anti-white, pointed out that 'the more sensitive an artist is, the more difficult he may find it to deal with insensitive people', and tabulated Miles's trappings of success:

Miles has found out the hard way, that money is power, even in race relations. He may tend to work a gig for less money if the promoter is a Negro. His fee for a single job nowadays ranges from $2,500 to $4,000, out of which his four sidemen only cost him a total of two or three hundred a night. Miles today is a wealthy man, owning some $50,000 worth of stock. He just bought an entire building in a good section of Manhattan, where he lives on the first two floors, renting out the rest of the building as apartments. He drives a Ferrari that cost $12,500 and he likes to drive fast. He has a substantial five-figure annual income from Columbia Records. Miles's apparent aloofness on the stand has a devastating effect on women, who often find his good looks more irresistible than his most lyrical solo. Recently he was married to a lovely, petite girl named Frances Taylor, who teaches dancing. He has remained close to his daughter and two sons (seventeen, fourteen and ten) by an early marriage.[11]

Despite all the column inches and the comforting presence of Sonny Stitt, who was already known to the British public via JATP, there were terrific outcries from critics, who should have known better, about Miles Davis's stage behaviour. However, one or two writers rose to the occasion, and that most perceptive of critics, Max Harrison, wrote:

The concerts revealed – again as no record has – the force with which high notes were attacked and sustained, and the controlled vehemence of some of the up-tempo phrasing showed that Davis's music has expanded its scope to the point where his mode of expression can now be as violent as it is intense . . . in his best moments . . . he extemporised solos of sometimes fierce, often acutely concentrated lyricism that were so moving as to be almost disquieting. One can analyse such improvisations in terms of their unusual melodic style, tone, personal dynamics and nuance, but the mystery of their strange power to move us remains unexplained.[12]

A few other British critics made intelligent and honourable attempts to say something pertinent about the music, but for the most part, the Miles Davis tour of Britain revealed a sadly parochial press. The *New York Post* commented acidly:

Miles Davis packed his trumpet and took off for Paris, Stockholm and home, where the citizenry is less likely to be fuddled by his sophisticated approach to jazz . . . Londoners were bothered by the fact that he seldom acknowledged applause. Jazz in this city is back in the New Orleans era. Boisterous

Dixieland is the favourite. Davis dropped into this wasteland late in September.[13]

For economic reasons, these foreign tours had to consist of concerts in big halls, but Miles did not feel really comfortable under such circumstances. He explained:

Nobody can relax at concerts, the musicians or the people, either. You can't do nothing but sit down, you can't move around, you can't have a drink. A musician has to be able to let loose everything in him to reach the people. If the musician can't relax, how's he going to make the people feel what he feels? The whole scene of jazz is feeling.[14]

Miles certainly preferred the intimate atmosphere of a club for making his music, and of course, under such conditions, when the audience are almost touching the star of the evening, the fact that he is not announcing titles or acknowledging applause becomes insignificant.

After the European trip, Miles returned to New York and in November 1960 took a two-week residency at the Village Vanguard, a tiny club (capacity perhaps two hundred) in Greenwich Village. The evenings were shared with the Bill Evans Trio with legendary bassist, Scott La Faro, and drummer Paul Motian. It was after hearing the Evans version of 'Some Day My Prince Will Come' during this engagement that Miles began playing that unlikely song himself. At the Vanguard, Miles and the group were in their element, and reviews mentioned the active responses of audiences to the music. It was also noted that Miles went about his business in an amiable way, chatting with members of the group and nodding politely when applauded.

There were two probably intentional errors of fact in Leonard Feather's account of Miles Davis for the British press: the description 'an earlier marriage' refers to Irene Birth, Miles's *common-law* wife who had borne him three children; and although Frances Taylor was with Miles during the British tour in October, they were not married until December that year. Miles and Frances were very much in love and getting on well, and in preparation for the marriage, Miles had recently bought a five-storey building at 312 West 77th Street. It was a converted Russian Orthodox church, and after it had been renovated in 1961, Miles and Frances moved into the first three storeys and rented out the two top storeys. All the children were now living with them – Miles's three, Cheryl Anne, Miles IV and Gregory, and Frances's son Jean-Pierre. Miles's parents and brother and sister also visited them. Thus began perhaps the only period of conventional family life Miles would enjoy as a husband and father.

In January 1961, a long feature article entitled 'Miles Davis: Evil Genius of Jazz', was published in the American black magazine, *Ebony*. The writer, Marc Crawford, was black and the piece, which took up seven pages of the magazine and was liberally illustrated with photographs, presented a detailed account of Miles as a successful and independent member of his race. There were photos of Miles playing, of Miles and his wife, his mother, his father, on the farm, in restaurants, and finally a whole sequence of pictures of him working out in the gym. But even in the heat of resentment at racial prejudice, Miles retained his balance and fairness:

> I don't like to stress race because I have friends of all colours. But everything I see around me stresses it. People say, 'Would you want your sister to marry a Negro?' That's jive even to ask the question. I might not want to marry your sister. It makes me sick. It makes me prejudiced. All I want for my kids is a simple thing. To be free. To not have to think about colour or anything. Just think about what it is they want to do and do it. And Negroes who try to act the way they think other people want them to act bug me worse than Uncle Toms.

Later in the year, Marc Crawford also looked Miles up in Chicago, where the trumpeter was staying at his in-laws' home.

Crawford wanted to write another feature, this time on Miles's relationship with Gil Evans. He found Davis in relaxed and expansive mood, clad in a dressing-gown and slippers, sipping Dutch beer and listening to Ravel's piano concerto in G major. Miles had just cooked himself a late breakfast of eggs, hamburger and tomatoes, garnished with salts of garlic and celery. Perhaps it was the pleasant change of actually having a *black* writer who wanted to interview him that made the trumpeter so co-operative. Eventually, in the middle of the proceedings, Miles phoned Evans, who flew from New York to 'hang out' with Davis for a few days. Evans said that he worked only for Miles and himself, that he could not do anything he did not want to do, and that he considered himself a 'commercial arranger', but only in the sense that 'what I write is popular'. And he rejected Miles's contention that he (Evans) was just beginning to receive the acclaim his talents had long deserved. Evans said: 'I haven't been around music for twenty years just waiting to be discovered. Nor am I a recent discovery. I am just now able to do the things I couldn't do before. My product just wasn't ready.'[15]

Shortly after this, Miles was back in New York and he allowed his house to be used for a confrontation between musicians of his own generation and various jazz writers. For this event, Miles laid on a bar with a barman and a plentiful supply of food. He and Frances acted as hosts, but did not take a leading part in the discussions. The man in charge of operations was Cannonball Adderley, and the other main participants were musicians Gerry Mulligan, J. J. Johnson, Horace Silver, Billy Taylor, Gil Evans and Philly Joe Jones. The critics and writers present were Nat Hentoff, Ira Gitler, John S. Wilson, Dave Solomon, Martin Williams and Stanley Dance, and they were grilled about why they labelled everything – 'East Coast', 'West Coast', 'hard bop' etc. – after which they were asked to define the qualities that made a real critic, and to say who fell into this category. As is usual in this kind of confrontation, the replies and the arguments were inconclusive, but once everyone had let off steam the evening subsided into chat and more drinking until all took their leave.

After the engagement at the Village Vanguard in November 1960, Sonny Stitt had left the quintet, and there were two candidates for the saxophone vacancy: Jimmy Heath and Hank Mobley. Heath would have been a good choice: he had already recorded with Miles, and his style would have suited the quintet. Unfortunately, however, he had had some trouble with the authorities and was on parole. Although he played a few engagements with Miles, he ultimately lost the job because his parole board refused to allow him to travel beyond a ninety-mile radius of Philadelphia. Hank Mobley, although four years younger than Miles and Jimmy Heath, was basically from the same generation. He had worked with Max Roach, Dizzy Gillespie, Horace Silver, Art Blakey and Thelonious Monk, among others, and had established himself as one of the most important of the younger tenor players of the 1950s. When Jimmy Heath became ineligible for the job, Mobley joined the Davis quintet, but stayed with the group for barely a year, because his style was so unsuited to Miles's music. Mobley's laid-back way of playing – a kind of legato approach which phrases over the rhythm section and almost never cuts into it – was antithetical to the whole approach of Miles and Coltrane.

In March 1961, when Miles Davis went into the studios to make another album, John Coltrane was working with his quartet at the Apollo Theatre, and Miles asked him to come to the studio in the intervals between the sessions at the Apollo, and play on some of the album tracks. The group was in the middle of recording the title track, 'Some Day My Prince Will Come', when Trane walked in with his horn. Hank Mobley had the chords written on a sheet of manuscript, and Coltrane, who had never played this tune before, simply looked at the chord symbols and played a solo alive with expression and tonal beauty. Coltrane played on one other track, a modal piece in 3/4 called 'Teo'. It was based on four scales played for unspecified duration by each soloist (cf. 'Flamenco Sketches'), and had a Spanish feel. On this track, Trane's playing is superlative, with a magnificent entry and a flow of ideas which bubbles into a climax of 'sheets of sound' – phrases that double back on one another and are both continuous and circular. Miles was clearly inspired by this, and played a second solo on the piece, achieving greater intensity than he had in his first one. For Hank Mobley, it must have been depressing to hear such a contrast to his own playing on the album. *Some Day My Prince Will Come*, although it contains these two gems by Coltrane, some fine playing by Miles, and some excellent work from Wynton Kelly, is nevertheless uneven in quality, and lacking in that group identity that always characterizes the best Miles Davis albums. Not surprisingly at this stage in his career, the trumpeter's musical vision was faltering. He was also in a lot of pain at the time, and was diagnosed as having sickle-cell anaemia, which was causing arthritis in his joints, particularly his left hip.

There had always been a difference between Miles's live performances and his studio recordings. In the studio, the duration of the music is circumscribed and therefore form becomes more important. Also, in the studio, every nuance, every tiny inflexion is captured, and in a very real sense, many of Miles's studio recordings were exquisite. But in live performance the idea of form became less important; the pieces began, offered a string of solos, and then ended. The interest lay in how much each player could say in his solo, how inventive his musical language was, and how much he could communicate his feeling to the audience. So in live performance, one would expect a soloist to take tremendous risks, revealing not only superb phrases and ideas, but also muffed lines, occasional mistakes and failures. As Miles's quintet was producing only uncertain results in the studio, it was an obvious step to try to capture on shellac the dynamism of the group's live performances. In April 1961, the quintet had a booking at the Blackhawk, a club in San Francisco, and two of the nights there were recorded for a live album.

The Blackhawk was a small and shabby jazz club of which its owner, Guido Caccienti, once said, 'I've worked and slaved for years to keep this place a sewer.'[16] But it had good acoustics, and was renowned for the quality of the music to be heard there. Most of the leading jazz musicians, including Charlie Parker, had played there and had found the relaxed atmosphere conducive to good music. The very shabbiness of the place deterred the expense-account type of (white) businessmen of whom Miles once said:

> They ain't come to hear good music . . . They drink too much, they get loud . . . I can't stand dumb-ass people not respecting the other customers that have come to hear the music. Sometimes one table like that has bugged me so that when I get home or to my hotel, I walk the floor because I can't sleep.[17]

Guido Caccienti had a rare respect for music and musicians. He said, 'You gotta dig music, you come in here.'[18] And he never complained when Miles didn't bother to play the last set of the evening – which happened most nights.

The Blackhawk sessions were Miles's first premeditated attempt to make a live album. Two nights (the Friday and Saturday) were recorded, and Miles and Teo Macero later edited the tapes down to make two albums out of enough material for perhaps four. This is why the tempos of various pieces go up and down: different versions of the same piece were spliced together. Jimmy Cobb commented with some feeling, because drummers are always blamed for fluctuating tempos:

> They'd take the same tunes and Miles would find solos he liked better on one version than another, and if it was close enough he'd just . . . splice . . . They spliced that album to pieces . . . But it was close because Teo was doing it and he's a musician, and Miles was probably telling him where to do it . . . But you can hear the splices.

The Blackhawk sessions are notable for the exceptionally dynamic playing of the rhythm section and their interplay with Miles. It is not just a dialogue of trumpet and drums, but a three-way affair with Wynton Kelly's piano incessantly responding to and interacting with the trumpeter's phrases. Kelly shows exceptional imagination in all his performances with Miles from this point on. In contrast to the previous month's studio session, at the Blackhawk the group feeling is phenomenal, and Kelly's inspired piano accompaniment makes Miles push his abilities to the limits. His playing is now shot through and through with the funky phrases of the old blues tradition, and his sustained use of the highest registers is thrilling. Wynton Kelly has attempted to describe something of his relationship with Miles Davis:

He's a pretty cat. If you really knew him, you couldn't knock him. He's more like a sideman than a leader. And he's always creating, playing outside the chords and me and the rhythm section finding him. When he gasses himself you can feel it all over the bandstand and sometimes I'll look up and catch that little smirk on his face and then I know for sure.[19]

A few weeks later, Miles was 'Fashion Personality for the Month of May' in the *Gentleman's Quarterly*, and on the nineteenth of that same month he allowed himself to be persuaded to play a concert at New York's Carnegie Hall. This was to be a benefit concert for an organization called the African Research Foundation, and the proceeds were to go to buy a mobile medical unit to be sent to Tanganyika (now Tanzania). Before this, no one had ever been able to persuade Davis to appear on a New York concert stage, and on this occasion it was only his interest in the African Research Foundation that prompted him to agree to do so. Miles was to appear with his own quintet, and also with the orchestra led by Gil Evans – the first time Davis had ever appeared in public with the Evans unit.

The concert was a sell-out, and Miles, showing devastating form, dominated the whole evening. It was almost as if he was demonstrating to himself and to the world that he was self-sufficient, that he could carry any event of any magnitude by himself – without the aid of John Coltrane. It was an evening of inspired music, recorded by CBS. All the critics wrote ecstatic reviews, and even the old sceptic, John S. Wilson, was captivated, admitting:

The evening was a triumph for Mr Davis. He played brilliantly . . . And although he has often been charged with treating his audiences disdainfully, he not only smiled on a couple of occasions but acknowledged applause with a quick glance over the footlights and a slight nod of the head . . . Last night [he] seemed intent on proving his all-round capabilities on the trumpet. He played with tremendous fire and spirit, soaring off into high-note runs with confidence and precision, building lines bristling with searing emotion and yet retaining all the warmest, singing elements of his gentler side. He was in the spotlight almost throughout the evening, yet he never faltered, never seemed to tire and poured out a stunning series of magnificent trumpet solos.[20]

All the other reviews were equally superlative, and justifiably so, because the two-CD Columbia Legacy album *Miles Davis at the Carnegie Hall – The Legendary Performances of May 19, 1961*, which documents the evening's music, shows that, in the words of another reviewer, 'Few jazz performances have touched the heights of that evening. It was jazz at its finest.'[21] With the Evans orchestra, Miles performed the 'Concierto de Aranjuez', but this was not issued at the time because *Sketches of Spain* had only just been released. The orchestra also joins Davis for 'So What', 'Spring Is Here', 'The Meaning of the Blues'/'Lament' and 'The New Rhumba', and he is backed by his quintet on six other pieces, including 'Teo', 'Oleo' and 'Walkin''.

This hugely successful concert was almost spoiled and cut short by a political incident. When Miles was in the middle of 'Some Day My Prince Will Come', Max Roach, dressed in a white jacket and carrying a placard on which was painted: AFRICA FOR THE AFRICANS! FREEDOM NOW!, walked up and sat down on the stage apron, while Davis and the crowd looked on in amazement. A moment later Roach was joined by another demonstrator. Miles waved his trumpet at Roach in dismay and then stopped the music and walked off-stage. Security guards carried off Max Roach and his companion, and backstage people talked Miles into going back

on, which he eventually did to prolonged applause. The anger
Davis felt expressed itself in the even greater intensity of the music.
One critic noted: 'He returned to the stage . . . a different musician,
swinging with what Gerry Mulligan has termed "controlled
violence".'[22]

Later, Miles said, 'I don't know what Max was doing. Ask
him.'[23] Roach said: 'I was told some things about the Foundation
that I thought Miles should know. Some people tried to contact
him, but they couldn't get to him. I went on stage because I
wanted Miles to be aware of these things.'[24] Roach was referring
to accusations by a group of African nationalists, who picketed
outside the hall before the concert, that the Foundation was in
league with South African diamond interests seeking to 'enslave'
Africans instead of helping them. But these reasons seem lame and
unconvincing. After the concert Roach shouted through the stage
door: 'Tell Miles I'm sorry. Tell him he was so great I was crying
during the first half. Tell Miles I love him.'[25] Inadvertently, however, by riling Miles Max Roach had made some contribution to
one of the great performances in jazz history, and 1961 had seen
the emergence of a new Miles, a player who was now going to
explore the resources of the trumpet, and of himself, to their
utmost limits. But this hugely successful recorded concert was
really only a moment of respite. Miles was unhappy because he
felt in limbo musically, and the continual pain in his joints led to
his greater dependence on pain-killing drugs and an increasing
consumption of alcohol and cocaine.

ELEVEN

In and Out of the Doldrums

'When it comes to human rights, these prejudiced
white people keep on acting like they own the
damn franchise!'[1]

Miles Davis

Throughout the rest of 1961 and the following year, and well into
1963, although Miles Davis seemed to be at the pinnacle of his
career and in a virtually impregnable economic and artistic position, he was nevertheless beset with anxieties and problems. These
were to do with the personnel of his group, with the race question,
with his own position in American society, and with his artistic
direction. But to an outsider, it must have seemed hardly conceiv-
able that Miles Davis could have any doubts about his direction,
or that he might feel, from time to time, rather insecure. His track
record, his achievements, the number of classic albums he had
produced, were already legendary. From the end of the 1950s
onwards, each new record release was often accompanied by the
issue or reissue of his early recordings. In 1959, his previous record
company, Prestige, had reissued one album and promoted six
others, and taken a full-page advertisement for them in *Down
Beat*. In the summer of 1961, Prestige also released, for the very
first time, the last of the famous 1956 quintet sessions: *Steamin'
with the Miles Davis Quintet*. By cleverly timing the release dates
of the stockpile of albums Miles had done for them in order to
terminate his contract, Prestige had cashed in on every increase in
Miles's popularity.

To an outsider also, Miles Davis seemed to have all the trappings of security and success: his expensive cars, and his brownstone house in Manhattan with its marble-tile floors, leopard-skin rugs, white brick walls, abstract paintings and electronic gadgets. Apart from Miles and Frances there were the aforementioned four children, an Italian greyhound named Milo, and some turtles. None of the children was particularly musical, although Cheryl Anne enjoyed singing, and Gregory had played the drums.

Certain things were disquieting for Miles Davis, however, and one bugbear in particular was that he'd never been approached to do a tour sponsored by the US State Department. During the 1950s, America had begun sponsoring tours abroad by jazz groups. Dizzy Gillespie's big band tour of the Middle East had taken place in the 1950s, and with its personnel of twelve black and four white musicians had shown the world, as the State Department intended it to, that racial harmony was possible in America. By 1961, these tours were frequent occurrences, and yet Miles Davis had still not been asked to do one. Travelling abroad with a group was such an expensive operation that it made government subsidy very important. There was also prestige attached to being a representative of the USA in foreign parts. Miles's brief campaign to get himself noticed by the State Department began with a typically oblique move. He made an announcement to the press that he would not do any overseas tours for the State Department until conditions improved for blacks in the USA. Miles said: 'Why should I go, the way they treat Negroes in this country? I don't want to go as a second-class citizen.'[2] But nobody paid much attention to his remarks, and by mid-summer he felt so slighted that he complained bitterly to Leonard Feather:

I'd rather have somebody curse me out than ignore me. Anyhow, I don't want them to send me over just because I'm a Negro and they want to woo Africa ... If I ever went on one of those tours, they'd have to give me a badge to wear over there. A platinum badge. It would have to say on it that this man did such and such a thing for his country and

181

government ... If Charlie Parker had been French, they'd have had a monument built for him over there, but millions of people in this country never heard of him, or just read about him when he died and then forgot him ... Come to think about it, I hope the State Department does ask me to make one of those tours – just so I can have the pleasure of saying no.[3]

But later in 1961, Miles managed to make a racial breakthrough in an area that had defeated both Ray Charles and Nat Cole. The National Association for the Advancement of Colored People (NAACP) asked Miles to play a benefit for them at San Francisco's Masonic Temple in October. The manager of the 3,200-capacity hall at first refused to allow it to be used for this purpose, giving the same reasons as he had done in the cases of Charles and Cole: 'Not because of race or colour, but because we had been advised the kind of audiences these artists draw could be destructive to our $7,000,000 auditorium.'[4] In Miles's case, however, the decision was reversed and the concert went ahead.

In September 1962, *Playboy* published a long interview with Miles dealing exclusively with the question of racial prejudice. This two-day interview at Miles's home was by the black journalist, Marc Crawford, who had written the article in *Ebony* the previous year. On this present occasion, Crawford set the scene as follows:

... his rather unusual five-storey home, a converted Russian Orthodox church on West 77th Street near the Hudson River in New York City. Miles was between gigs at the time and we accompanied him on his restless daily home routine, asking questions at propitious moments while he worked out in his basement gymnasium, made veal chops Italian style for his family, took telephone calls from fellow musicians, his lawyer and stockbroker, gave boxing lessons to his three sons, watched TV, plucked out beginner's chords on a guitar and, of course, blew one of his two Martin trumpets.

This was Miles's most comprehensive discourse on race, and it showed that the sense of injury was both deep and far-ranging. There was still the feeling that his music was not at all valued by the American cultural establishment, and that jazz musicians were regarded as inferior to their classical counterparts: 'The average jazz musician today, if he's making it, is just as trained as classical musicians. You ever see anybody go up bugging classical musicians when they are on the job and trying to work?'

Similarly, the general social humiliations were distressing. Miles gave several devastating examples, of which two are as follows:

I sent for an electrician to fix something in the house. When he rang the bell, I answered and he looked at me like I was dirt, and said, 'I want to see the owner, Mr Davis.' When I said, 'You looking at him,' the cat turned beet red. He had me figured as the porter. Now he's mad and embarrassed. What had I done but called to give him work? That same week I had seen a lot of them West Point cadets, and in a bar I asked why there was so many of them in town. Man, I just asked the cat a question and he moved up the bar and didn't speak! But then somebody recognized me and he got red as that electrician. He came trying to apologize and saying he had my records. I told him I had just paid enough taxes to cover his free ride at West Point, and walked out. I guess he's somewhere now with the others saying I'm such a bastard. It bugged me so, man, I wasn't worth a damn for two or three days. It wasn't just him ignoring me I was thinking about, but in two or three years, Gregory, my oldest boy, may be doing some Army time. How am I supposed to feel about him maybe serving under this cat?

In 1962, Miles's group, which was now a sextet with J. J. Johnson on trombone, won first place in the *Down Beat* critics' poll, unseating the Modern Jazz Quartet (MJQ), which had held the position ever since 1954. This must have seemed ironic to Miles; good though his current sextet was, it could not be compared with the great quintet and sextet with Coltrane and Adderley. During 1962, Miles and the group worked off and on at the Village Vanguard, and had a nine-day engagement, supported by black satirist and comic, Oscar Brown, at the Music Box Theatre, Los Angeles. But the run of consecutive great recordings, each one a masterpiece, was over for the time being. Indeed, Miles seemed reluctant to go into the recording studios at all at this time, largely because he felt he had nothing to say.

The declining health and death of his father that year also shook him. Two years previously his father had been driving across an unguarded country level crossing when his car had been hit by a train. The apparently minor injuries had wrecked his health – his hands shook, he seemed punch-drunk, and he could no longer work as a dentist. Miles tried to get him good medical attention, but no one seemed able to help, and his father was, in any case, too proud to accept much help or sympathy. He died suddenly at the age of sixty. Miles was working in Kansas City with his sextet at the time and J. J. Johnson broke the news to him. Before that trip, Miles's father had handed him a letter, which he hadn't bothered to open. Now he read it and his grief and guilt were multiplied because his father had written that he had only a few days to live and he wanted Miles to know that he truly loved him and was proud of him. The funeral, which took place in May 1962, was one of the biggest ever held for a black man in East St Louis. Miles regretted most of all, perhaps, not having noticed that his father was dying and therefore having missed the opportunity to express his own love, gratitude and respect. The guilt and grief persisted that year.

So far as recording was concerned, it was his poorest year for a decade. It was rumoured he planned an album of Tadd Dameron tunes, but nothing materialized. In fact, the year yielded only three undistinguished studio tracks with a septet which included bongos and vocalist Bob Dorough, and one or two South American bossa nova-style pieces with Gil Evans and the orchestra. Wayne Shorter was on the septet session, however, and Miles found that he really enjoyed Shorter's playing. That was one positive result of the sessions, but there was not enough material for even one album. Nevertheless, the backlog of albums still poured steadily on to the market, and Miles's financial situation was very good. By the early 1960s, when a jazz musician 'made it', he could earn as much money as the leading conductors and soloists on the 'serious' music scene. But of the few really high earners in jazz, Miles Davis was the only one still playing small clubs.

Miles's sextet carried within it the seeds of its own disintegration. There had been fluctuations in the rhythm section as early as autumn 1961, when Philly Joe Jones briefly replaced Jimmy Cobb at Birdhouse Club, Chicago. Red Garland had also replaced Wynton Kelly for a while, and early in 1962, when Cobb and Kelly were back, Sonny Rollins had joined for a time. J. J. Johnson, who had a strong musical life of his own, left the group permanently at the beginning of 1963 in order to fulfil some writing/composing assignments. By this time, Hank Mobley had also gone, and the rhythm section of Kelly, Chambers and Cobb were thinking of striking out on their own as a trio. External events then precipitated a complete change of personnel.

In the last week of December, Miles and the group had a five-night engagement at Philadelphia's Uptown Theatre, but they simply failed to appear for the last two nights. The promoter, a disc jockey called Woods, sued Miles for the $25,000 he claimed the cancellation had cost him, and the matter was eventually settled by Miles paying $8,000 in instalments. Shortly after this, Miles had to cancel a gig in Detroit in order to protect bassist Paul Chambers from possible arrest in connection with a marital legal action. This cancellation resulted in another legal action against Miles for compensation. Finally, a few weeks later, neither Paul Chambers nor Wynton Kelly turned up for an engagement in St Louis, so Miles had to cancel yet again. This brought yet another lawsuit against him. This final disaster was too much for Miles, and when he was booked for a three-week residency at the Black Hawk, he decided not to take Chambers and Kelly with him. He commented: 'They both wanted to come out to San Francisco with me, but even though they're both excellent musicians,

I had to say "No".'⁵ One reason for these problems was that Paul Chambers and Wynton Kelly were tired of playing only Miles's music. They wanted to play their own music, and while they were with Miles, their reputations had soared so that they were in great demand.

Either events caught Miles napping, or he couldn't find the musicians he wanted, because he telephoned the Blackhawk a few nights before his scheduled opening and obtained a week's delay. He said that the left side of his face was still swollen from a root canal operation on a lower molar; but the real problem seems to have been personnel, because he ultimately arrived without a pianist, and British-born Victor Feldman, who was living in Los Angeles, had to take over the piano stool for a few days. The group for the booking turned out to be a sextet with Frank Strozier on alto sax, George Coleman on tenor, Harold Mabern piano, Ron Carter bass, and Jimmy Cobb still on drums. As usual, when Miles was not sure he could rely on his new and unproven group, he played even more powerfully himself.

During the engagement at the Blackhawk, Jimmy Cobb left to join Chambers and Kelly, and the drum chair was filled temporarily by another Los Angeles musician, Frank Butler. While he was on the West Coast, Miles went into the studio and recorded some tracks with the Feldman–Carter–Butler rhythm section, but must have been dissatisfied with the up-tempo performances, because he went back to New York and re-recorded them with different musicians. The resulting album, *Seven Steps to Heaven*, is schizophrenic (half from the West Coast and half from the East Coast sessions) and shows graphically the difference between Miles at his most mannered and self-indulgent and Miles at his most vital.

The West Coast sessions featured a quartet – Miles with Harmon mute and the rhythm section – playing three very slow pieces: the ballad, 'I Fall in Love Too Easily', and two lugubrious reinterpretations of material from the traditional jazz of the 1920s, 'Basin Street Blues', and 'Baby Won't You Please Come Home'. When a jazz musician's vision is faltering and he is losing his direction, the only way out of this impasse is to go back to the music's roots and regroup, and this is probably what lay behind Miles's thinking, but the choice of those two old tunes astonished the jazz world at the time and no doubt helped to take everyone's mind off the shortcomings of their treatment. It is difficult to pinpoint exactly why these two performances are so unsatisfactory. There is an almost imperceptible slackness, a kind of self-indulgence; it is Miles doing his ballad formula to death, and without the necessary interplay between himself and the group. The muted trumpet is too far forward in the mix, and the piano and rhythm section very distant. Victor Feldman was a marvellous musician, but in this case his accompaniment seems ordinary, and the overall atmosphere is one of bland, easy-listening music. In fact, a similar atmosphere had pervaded some tracks Miles had recorded the previous year with Gil Evans. They were ultimately issued on a very unsatisfactory album (which neither Miles nor Gil wanted released) called *Quiet Nights*, and the meagre big-band material which made up the bulk of the album was eked out with another small-group track from the West Coast session, 'Summer Night'.

However, a return to Miles's customary creative standards occurs in the three New York performances on *Seven Steps to Heaven*. In recruiting his new rhythm section Davis had, for the first time in his career, chosen musicians from the younger generation. His new drummer, Tony Williams, was just seventeen, bassist Ron Carter was twenty-six, and pianist Herbie Hancock was twenty-three. So far as saxophonists were concerned, Strozier had left the group after the Blackhawk residency, and George Coleman was to stay with Miles for just over a year. For Herbie Hancock, being asked to join the Miles Davis Quintet was something of which he'd hardly dared dream. Later, he recalled the experience:

I got a call from Tony Williams, and he told me that Miles was going to call and ask me to come over to his house to play ... Miles called me up. He asked me if I was busy, if I was working. I was at the time, but I told him no; so he asked me if I would come over to his house the next day . . . Next day I went over. Tony was there with Ron and George Coleman. We ran over some things while Miles walked around and listened. Philly Joe Jones stopped by too. Then Miles called up Gil Evans. He said, 'Hey, Gil, I want you to hear my new drummer.' Because Tony really knocked him out. After we rehearsed the next day, he told us we were going to do a record in two days. I was wondering what was going on; he hadn't even told me whether I was in the group or not. So I didn't say anything, and we did the record – *Seven Steps*. Then we had another rehearsal, and he mentioned a job at Bowdoin College. I said, 'Wait a minute, Miles. You haven't told me if I'm in the group or what,' and he said, 'You made the record didn't you?' so I said, 'Yeah, okay.' That was fine. I was jumping through hoops.[6]

In the studio, the new young rhythm section immediately proved itself; the brash, unstoppable pulse of Tony Williams's drums, and the broad foundation of Ron Carter's 'singing' bass notes, spurred Miles into pushing himself, yet again, to the limits. On the title track, 'Seven Steps' and on 'Joshua', his use of chromaticism, which had begun to appear on the Blackhawk and Carnegie Hall live albums, was now substantially in evidence. On *Kind of Blue* with such modal pieces as 'So What' and 'All Blues', Miles had stuck to the basic scale or mode for his notes. But with the live albums, it was noticeable that on the same pieces he tended to alternate funky rhythmic phrases with more abstract ones that used any of the twelve notes in any octave – also, of course, using the microtones in his inflexions. There is a kind of paradox here: on the live albums there is a tendency towards greater 'concrete' phasing in his use of bluesy and funky phrases, which is accompanied by an opposite tendency towards more abstract chromaticism. It is often the tension between these two approaches that creates the drama of the solos. After 1960, the focal point of his solo work becomes less harmonic and gradually more rhythmic and linear. In the three New York tracks of *Seven Steps*, this abstract chromaticism is already much more prominent.

Although the young rhythm section showed tremendous confidence and panache on their first recording with the great trumpeter, the difficulties of trying to live with a legend were keenly felt by all of them. At first, on live gigs Hancock tried to adopt a sort of Wynton Kelly approach, and Tony Williams played some Jimmy Cobb patterns which often derived from Philly Joe Jones. But when George Coleman took his saxophone solo, the rhythm section would abandon its self-imposed roles and open up, playing around with the pulse much more freely. Again, a kind of schizophrenia resulted, and Hancock recalled:

And then one day Miles said, 'Why don't you play like that behind me?' I remember when that happened, we were in Detroit ... some club there, and we were playing all kinds of crazy things behind George and behind Miles we played really straight. Anyway, that's when Tony and I started playing our little musical games behind Miles in a way, because we were developing this thing ... After four days it turned around and he was leading it. Not only was he in it, but he really established that thing. And his playing was different after that. It was a most uncannily rapid adaptation to this other sound that I could ever imagine ... That's what Miles does. He feeds off everybody else and kind of puts it together.

If Miles Davis's previous rhythm sections had been superb – the best in jazz at their time with Garland, Chambers and Philly Joe in the middle 1950s, and Kelly, Chambers and Jimmy Cobb in the later 1950s and early 1960s – this rhythm section in 1963 was yet again superior. So far as straight 4/4 time-playing was concerned, it was to prove itself to be possibly the greatest rhythm section of all time, and Hancock, Carter and Williams seemed to have an inexhaustible variety of ways of creating and releasing tension, expanding and contracting space. This interaction between the members of the rhythm section was also a continual dialogue with whoever was soloing. In fact, there was no longer the idea of a soloist and rhythm section. When a horn was playing, it was a quartet functioning on equal terms. Only the bass spent most of its time in a supportive role. Piano and drums commented, spurred and generally conversed with the leading voice. But, in many ways, Ron Carter was the key new member of the group, both musically and morally. Musically he was the anchor man who gave the band stability and who never faltered, and he was also Miles's trusted right-hand man: 'I was the guy who was allowed to pay the band off, to collect money every night from the club owner, to confirm travel reservations, talking to the lawyer about publishing rights, and kind of business manager of the band.'

Miles also made Carter guardian to Tony Williams who, at seventeen, was under age. In California a person had to be eighteen and sometimes twenty-one years old to be legally entitled to enter certain clubs. So if Carter didn't go to the night club to play, Williams couldn't go in, and he had to enter always in the company of the bassist. The quintet's meteoric development may have been aided by this enforced association of the oldest and youngest men in the rhythm section. The group had come together for the recording in May 1963, and soon after that Miles took them out to Los Angeles, where they played two engagements per night, working from 10 p.m. until 2 a.m. at the Jazz Workshop, followed by a two-hour set at Basin Street West on Sunset Strip. Carter recalled,

So we were playing there almost seven hours a day as a group, and I remember us [Carter, Williams and Hancock] going to one of those all-night cafeterias and just sitting for hours after each gig, just trying to figure out what took place ... what happened on this tune and what is this chord, what is this rhythm, what is this note, trying to understand and analyse as best we could what took place and to have a clearer view of it to work on this item for tomorrow night. People think that jazz players just play off the top of their heads all the time, but quality players are aware of what goes on. They catalogue in their mind what doesn't work and should be discarded temporarily, and what seems like a real gem of an idea to be worked on the next night. And we had hundreds of these conversations.

Miles Davis did not take part in these discussions – he didn't need to because he had always had an intense curiosity about music and a tremendous awareness of the rhythm section. But George Coleman, who was only two years older than Carter, didn't take part either. Carter commented: 'I love George, he always plays great. But he was a little less curious than we were about what we were doing. I think horn players, Miles and Wayne [Shorter] excepted, are in general less curious about what rhythm sections do.' These informal seminars, plus the long hours of putting things to the test, bore fruit rapidly, and Miles was so thrilled with his new group that he asked Jack Whittemore to get as many playing engagements as possible for the rest of the summer, with the result that the quintet was booked solid. When the group appeared at the Antibes Festival in France on 27 July, it had already found its unique identity. To followers of Miles's music, the new approach was once more shocking and exhilarating. With a completely new band to introduce to the public at large, Davis wisely stuck to his old repertoire of a sprinkling of ballads and songs, some blues and some modal pieces. The performance at Antibes was recorded, and live albums were also issued of the group's performances the following year at the New York Philharmonic Hall (February), in Tokyo (July), and at the Berlin Festival (September). So five live albums (the New York Philharmonic Hall concert yielded two) documented the way Miles's new band dealt with the old material. He was not to make a studio album with the band until the beginning of 1965.

There had always been interaction in the way Miles's previous groups functioned, but there had never been anything as fundamentally wild and extreme as the performance at Antibes. Even the more conventional songs for which he used the Harmon mute ('Autumn Leaves' and 'All of You') were full of internal movement.

Miles's own playing now encompassed an awesome range of expression, veering from tenderness to ferocity and from sparseness to prodigality. The whole group's use of space was now intensely dramatic; pauses and almost empty bars juxtaposed with bars crammed with multiple activity. On these songs, however, Miles's solos were generally more diatonic and funky/lyrical; but the fast and more modal pieces were now taken at breakneck speed, and his open horn work was extremely abstract and chromatic. His dialogue with the drums is wild as the rhythm section boils along. The concentration and inspiration of Davis and the whole group is at white heat in these performances, and the self-indulgence of some of his recent performances in the studio has been completely banished; the enervating, self-regarding sadness has been obliterated by an outgoing and blistering creative onslaught. Miles had done it again – found the key musicians of the next generation, found new ways of expressing himself, and fresh avenues of exploration. According to Ralph J. Gleason, Miles was so delighted by the test pressings of the Antibes concert that he played them until they were almost worn out. Gleason commented: 'It was not a happy time for him in many ways, but these test pressings made it better.'[7]

During the autumn, Miles and Gil Evans collaborated on the music for a play called *The Time of the Barracudas*, which starred Laurence Harvey, and had a brief run in California. The music was recorded in Hollywood, and the tape recording was used for the play. Evans conducted and Miles played on the tape. The play was supposed to open on Broadway in New York in November, but for some reason it never did. The collaborations between Miles and Gil seemed doomed at this point in time. Columbia despaired of getting the two of them back in the recording studio, and at the end of the year issued *Quiet Nights*, which contained only twenty minutes of the orchestra and Miles, and a further six minutes of the small-group performance. Gil Evans said, 'They never should have released it; it was just half an album. But I guess they had to.'[8] Miles himself was furious that the album was issued, and blamed Teo Macero for the whole affair. His relationship with Macero was sometimes stormy and this was one of their first real rows. Teo recalled:

> He didn't talk to me for two-and-a-half to three years ... when we released *Quiet Nights*! He thought I was an insane person ... I was crazy. But I said, 'Look, call me what you want. I don't care. It doesn't make any difference. But one thing you must remember – for three years you've had records spilling out, and all that period I always put together the records and they always came out.' He was, I think, in a very bad period of creativity. I think that that might have been one of the things that upset him.

Seven Steps to Heaven was released in the late summer, receiving mixed reviews, but at the end of the year, *Miles Davis in Europe* (the Antibes concert) came out to universal acclaim. In January 1964, it won the *Jazz* magazine Jazz Album of the Year award, thus giving a good start to what was going to be a crucial year for Miles and the band. It had become obvious that the renewed vitality of the trumpeter and his group, the fresh treatment of old thematic material, was merely a reprieve from the real problem: the need to find new musical concepts that expressed the identity of this young band, totally different from Miles's earlier groups. With the spate of live concert recordings, it was noticeable that the music was getting rather repetitive. In an effort to keep things exciting for musicians and audiences, the old modal pieces ('So What' and 'Milestones') and the blues 'Walkin'' were played at ever increasing tempos until they were sometimes simply too fast for comfort or coherence. By late 1964, there were several versions of live performances of these pieces, as well as of Miles's favourite songs and ballads: 'All of You', 'Autumn Leaves', 'My Funny Valentine'. They all, of course, have some wonderful moments and produced some excellent music, but two of them stand out as something more than that: classic performances. The Antibes concert is the most sustained in terms of quality of inspiration in all areas – fast, medium, or slow pieces – and this is probably because the concept and the material were completely fresh to the young band at the time.

The other classic album from this period comes from the concert the group played at the New York Philharmonic Hall on 12 February 1964. During this performance, nearly all the up-tempo pieces were taken too fast and played rather scrappily, whereas the slow and medium-tempo tunes were played with more depth and brilliance than Miles had achieved before. The fast performances were issued on an album called *Four and More*, and the magnificent slower pieces were released under the title *My Funny Valentine*. It may have been the very importance of the occasion at the Philharmonic Hall which caused both the greatness of the slower things and the scrappiness of the fast ones, but there was also much tension in the quintet when they were told that, as it was a benefit concert, they would not be paid. For Miles, the concerts were a benefit for voter registration in Mississippi and Louisiana, and the co-sponsors were the NAACP (National Association for the Advancement of Colored People), the Congress of Racial Equality and the Student Non-Violent Co-ordinating Committee. Miles also told *Melody Maker*, however, that one of the concerts was to be in memory of President Kennedy. The latter had been assassinated the previous year, and his death crushed a lot of hopes for the more speedy attainment of racial equality. Miles had expressed a certain confidence in Kennedy in 1962: 'I like them Kennedy brothers; they're swinging people.'[9] So, for Miles Davis, the concerts were for his own people and also in memory of a president he had admired.

For his young rhythm section, their anger at not being paid and the importance of the occasion may have accounted for the slight desperation of some of the fast pieces. Herbie Hancock described the psychological pressure:

That was my first time playing at the Philharmonic Hall and that was, like, a big deal, because the new Carnegie Hall was the Philharmonic Hall. Just from the prestige standpoint I really wanted to play good – the whole band really wanted to play good because that was the whole band's first time playing there . . . although Miles had played at Carnegie Hall before . . . but it was really a special concert. Only the New York Philharmonic plays there . . . and I tell you something . . . it was really funny . . . When we walked away from that concert, we were all dejected and disappointed. We thought we had really bombed . . . but then we listened to the record – it sounded fantastic!

The *My Funny Valentine* album from that concert is one of the very greatest recordings of a live concert. The rapport between the large audience and the quintet is as close and immediate as if the event were taking place in a small club, and the charged atmosphere enhances the inspired creative act. There is here a kind of complicity between audience and musicians, a unity which is quite rare. In the first chorus of 'Stella by Starlight', for example, when Miles plays a particularly incisive phrase, there is a clearly audible yell of ecstasy, and other good moments are greeted with immediate delighted applause. Even the theme of 'All Blues' draws an instant response.

The playing throughout the album is inspired, and Miles in particular reaches tremendous heights. Anyone who wanted to get a vivid idea of the trumpeter's development over the previous eight years or so should compare the October 1956 version of 'Funny Valentine' and the 1958 version of 'Stella by Starlight' with the versions on this 1964 live recording. The earlier performances are romantic, melancholic, and their emotional range is narrow though deep. On the later versions, there is a strong movement away from romanticism and towards abstraction, and the emotional range is very much greater.

In the later 'Funny Valentine', for example, Miles probes more deeply into both the song's structure and his own emotional and technical resources. Despite the occasional oblique references to the original melody, and the free harmonic approach (Miles once said: 'We play "Funny Valentine" like with a scale all the way through'), the thirty-six-bar structure of the song is always there.

Miles plays open trumpet on this version (he used Harmon mute on the earlier one), and even in the extreme upper register, where most trumpeters sound strained and brash, he is still able to project his unique, lyrical sound and to bend his notes expressively. He plays the first eight bars *colla voce* with Hancock's piano accompaniment, then the bass and drums pick up the pulse. The whole ensuing trumpet solo is a dialogue with the piano and rhythm section, and the internal movement is realized with great subtlety. Alternations between the slow pulse and the double-tempo feel enhance the dramatic inner logic of Miles's solo, which moves to a blistering climax in his second chorus when he suddenly rises on the last quaver of the twenty-ninth bar, ascends for three more bars above trumpet top C to F, G, G sharp and A, and then descends, bending his high F superbly on the way down (Appendix A, Fig. 7). After the dazzling power of this solo, the listener needs the relief, the simple romanticism of George Coleman's tenor solo, which follows. The rhythm section also reassures us by playing a steady double-tempo feel. This familiarity and continuity, this everyday grooving done supremely well, is necessary after the disquieting areas into which Miles's solo took us. In the performances on this album, Miles Davis had taken the technical and emotional exploration of standard song structures as far as was possible before they disintegrated completely and metamorphosed into something else.

On the last day of February, Miles's brother Vernon called in the middle of the night and told Frances that Miles's mother had died. Frances broke the news when Miles got home in the small hours of the morning. Once again he had not had the opportunity to say goodbye. He knew she had gone into Barnes Hospital, St Louis, but hadn't realized how serious it was. He and Frances were booked on a flight to St Louis for the funeral, but when the plane aborted the take-off because of engine trouble, Miles's superstition made him get off the plane and go back home, leaving Frances to attend the funeral on her own. Once again, he was consumed by guilt and grief because his remaining parent had died unseen and uncomforted by him. It also seemed that the sunny heyday of his family life – the handsome and successful couple with their four children (albeit all from previous relationships) – was coming to an end. His relationship with Frances was starting to deteriorate, partly because she wanted another child and Miles didn't, but also because he was away touring much of the time, and he was still continually in pain, drinking too much and snorting coke. He began going to after-hours places frequented by other coke users, and he would disappear and be incommunicado for two days at a time. When he was at home, his moods would fluctuate and paranoia would be lurking around every corner. The façade of stability and patrician solidarity could still be conjured up on occasion, as when Miles and Frances threw a party for Robert Kennedy, who was running for senator of New York, and the guests included Leonard Bernstein, Bob Dylan, Lena Horne and Quincy Jones. Miles also began a friendship with the author James Baldwin, which lasted until the latter's untimely death. But the decline in Miles's behaviour went on and he and Frances had violent arguments that upset the children, until one day Frances walked out and went to California. That was the end of their relationship – another thing that Miles lived to regret.

In late spring, George Coleman left the quintet. He gave his reasons in a *Down Beat* interview in March 1980:

Miles was ill during that time – a lot of times he wouldn't make the gigs and it was frustrating . . . His hip was bothering him – and so there was a lot of pressure on me, and sometimes the money would be late and I'd get it in a cheque and have to try and get it cashed, so I really got tired of it; so I just decided to leave.

In his stead, tenor saxophonist Sam Rivers joined Miles for a couple of months, during which time the group played in Tokyo at Japan's World Jazz Festival. Miles Davis was the star of this six-day festival, and he was paid well over $20,000 for his six concerts. Leonard Feather reported on Miles's popularity in Japan:

It was Davis who drew the crowds; his photo adorned the cover of the current *Swing Journal*; he got the full VIP treatment, with first-class air transportation, a private air-conditioned limousine from hotel to concert hall, the right to refuse to be photographed during his set (even without flashbulbs), and the privilege of being the first American group on the show, so he could get out fast instead of having to wait around backstage . . . His status as the cynosure and chief attraction of the festival was the source of discomfort and obvious envy on the part of a couple of the older musicians . . . Miles Davis achieved an immediate rapport. The opening bass figure of 'So What', the first cadenza of 'Stella by Starlight', brought immediate applause, the result of strong record associations.[10]

When Sam Rivers left the band, Miles managed to persuade tenor saxophonist Wayne Shorter to join. The latter had been playing with Art Blakey's Jazz Messengers, and was strongly influenced by John Coltrane. Shorter also wrote excellent small-group compositions. Miles had been trying for some time to get Shorter to join his band, and had even gone as far as telephoning Art Blakey's backstage dressing areas to speak to the saxophonist. More pressure had been put on by Harold Lovett, who also phoned Shorter and said: 'What's the matter with you, man, don't you dig Miles?'[11] During all these communications, Blakey is said to have walked around angrily muttering, 'He's trying to steal my tenor player.'[12] At last, after Sam Rivers had gone, both Tony Williams and Herbie Hancock phoned Wayne Shorter and talked him into joining Miles's group. Shorter had no reason to regret the move:

It wasn't the bish-bash, sock-'em-dead routine we had with Blakey, with every solo a climax. With Miles, I felt like a cello, I felt viola, I felt liquid, dot-dash . . . and colours started really coming. And then a lot of people started calling me – 'Can you be on my record date?' It was six years of that.[13]

Shorter was with Miles when he played the Berlin Festival in September, and the occasion revealed that this was the best saxophonist Miles had so far found for the band. Tonally, there were definite resemblances to Coltrane, and Shorter also showed great variation in the length of his phrases and in his attack. At last, after some four years of trial and error, Miles had achieved a stable personnel.

But things were in a state of flux on the jazz scene in general. By 1964, the avant-garde movement spearheaded by Ornette Coleman and John Coltrane had gathered many more adherents, and there was much controversy about it in the specialist jazz press. The second wave of New Wavers included saxophonists Archie Shepp and Albert Ayler, and many white musicians such as Roswell Rudd, Mike Mantler and Paul Bley. The phrase 'free music' was bandied about a great deal and it seemed to denote a music 'freed' from the 'restrictions' of set structures and harmonies. Miles Davis must have observed this movement with some interest and even concern. Earlier in the year, he had used almost the same terms to describe some of his own aspirations:

> I intend recording some 'freedom' music . . . I get away from the normal bar structure. You know, away from the straight thirty-two bars. For example, we'll have maybe eleven bars written, and then I'll play. Then maybe twelve bars written, and then I'll play again. We did something like this on the *Time of the Barracudas* score.[14]

Miles's concern with high standards in all kinds of jazz was boldly expressed for all to see in the third blindfold test he did for Leonard Feather. This took place in June 1964, and the only record he liked out of the eight he listened to was 'Desafinado' by Stan Getz and João Gilberto. For the rest of the test, he severely castigates old friends like Clark Terry, his idol Duke Ellington and a couple of representatives of the avant-garde. In the case of Terry and Duke, Miles blames the record companies for the ill-conceived tracks. Feather plays him a piece by Eric Dolphy and Miles explodes: 'That's got to be Eric Dolphy – nobody else could sound that bad! . . . You have to think when you play; you have to help each other – you can't just play for yourself.'[15] And finally, when Feather plays him a Cecil Taylor piece, Davis says: 'Is that what the critics are digging? Them critics better stop having coffee. If there ain't nothing to listen to, they might as well admit it.'[16] Miles is generally disgusted with his contemporaries, and also totally disaffected by the avant-garde. At the same time, there is no doubt that during this period he was equally dissatisfied with himself. The re-examination of his own immediate past, and the glance even further back at old tunes like 'Basin Street Blues' and 'Baby Won't You Please Come Home' had not yet resulted in any new vision. Meanwhile, retrospective views of him were starting to classify him as a man of the 1950s. The thirtieth anniversary of *Down Beat* fell in 1964, and in their birthday issue (2 July 1964) there was a long feature on Miles by Leonard Feather, reviewing his whole career and bringing it up to date with recent interviews. It was entitled 'Miles and the Fifties', and it was comprehensive. In it, Miles reveals that he is still irritated by the gulf between the Western musical establishment and the jazz world, and still upset about the unequal status of musicians. He concludes with a prediction that seems more rooted in wishful thinking than in actuality:

Nowadays some of the teachers don't teach the way they used to, with that same old dry legit tone, because in the first place you can't get a job with it. The old symphonic repertorial music is going to go out. They're going to concentrate on the guys that write more or less modern music. Pretty soon all the schools of music will be together and understand one another and learn from each other's approaches, and you won't hear Beethoven's Fifth any more as a standard on a concert.

Of the future of jazz all he could say was: 'There is no next trend. If there's another trend, then we're going backwards; because, look, you had Duke, and you had Charlie Parker and Dizzy, and you had Lennie Tristano, right? And they're all just levelling off. There's not going to be another trend unless it's the walking-off-the-stage trend.' But nevertheless, it was becoming essential for Miles to find a fresh concept to suit his brand-new regular band, and in January 1965 he recorded his best studio album since *Kind of Blue*. This new one was called (perhaps ironically, because it was the name of the record label on which most of the avant-garde music was being released) *ESP*. Probably because of Miles's estrangement from Teo Macero over the release of *Quiet Nights*, the live albums of 1963–4 had been put out without the usual Davis–Macero consultation. And now, Miles chose to do his first studio album for eighteen months in Los Angeles, not New York, and the man who supervised the whole project was not Macero, but Columbia's West Coast A&R man, Irving Townsend. The freshness and absence of cliché on *ESP* came as a revelation. The germ of the idea could be seen in the greater abstraction and chromaticism of the live albums. Although Miles did not discuss music much with his group, one day he stated to Herbie Hancock that he wanted to abandon completely formal chord constructions in his solos:

> By the time we got to *ESP*, Miles said, 'I don't want to play chords any more' ... I guess what he wanted to go for was the core of the music ... Here's how I look at it ... now I don't know if this is the way Miles looks at it, but a composition is an example of a conception, so Miles, rather than play the composition, he wants to play the conception that the composition came from ... That's why you hear melody fragments and you kind of hear the momentum and the sound of the tune somewhere — something that distinguishes that tune from another one ... but maybe the chords are not there. Even when we were playing 'Walkin'' or any of those other [familiar] things, he didn't want to play the chords after we played the melody.

ESP comprises three up-tempo pieces in 4/4, three slow pieces in 3/4, and one variation of the blues in F with a rock feel. The fast pieces are characterized by skeletal, angular themes, abstract and chromatic improvisation, considerable group interplay, and a pulse which is sometimes implied rather than actually stated by the drums. The slow 3/4 performances are loose and lifting with a kind of abstract lyricism, and the solos are austere, understated and mournfully reflective. The underlying melancholy, however, also tinges the greater activity of the fast performances.

Standing out from this atmosphere of abstract severity is the blues 'Eighty-One', jointly composed by Miles and Ron Carter. This is the only piece on the album with some funk built into its theme, and its use of rock rhythms jolted the jazz world which, at the time, was snobbish about anything which smacked of 'popular' music. But there had been hints of spontaneous rock rhythms in the improvisations of his new group the previous year. During the Philharmonic Hall concert, for example, there had been a passage of spontaneous rock during Herbie Hancock's solo on 'All of You'; and a few months later, in Tokyo, the same thing had happened during Miles's solo on 'Funny Valentine'. In the studio, 'Eighty-One' was characterized by a lovely bass ostinato, a crisp and even drum rhythm, and a theme which brilliantly juxtaposed legato triplets, long notes and stab notes. The feel and the bass riff were maintained for the first part of each solo, after which the rhythm section played a straight 4/4 feel. All the musicians seemed to respond to the clear disciplines of this piece, and Miles in particular played a magnificent solo. Davis had a hand in the composition of three other pieces on the album, and was the sole composer of 'Agitation', a fast and abstract performance. *ESP* is also something of a landmark in Miles Davis's recorded work because it was the first album on which he used the 'open bars' technique in which there is no set chorus-length for the solos, and events happen on cue.

Shortly after this recording, Miles Davis went into hospital for surgery and spent most of the rest of the year out of action. His health had gradually declined as the pain in his hip increased and in Japan the previous July, it had been so severe that a doctor had had to be summoned before Miles could play the first concert. He had delayed the operation as long as possible, but he underwent major surgery on 14 April, and the hip bone was replaced with bone from his shin. This was a failure and in August a second operation gave him a plastic hip joint. Ten years later, this repair job itself was to start disintegrating, necessitating more surgery and the insertion of another artificial (plastic) hip joint.

The first operation was so serious that Miles Davis was in hospital from April until July (1965), by which time he was so bored that he got hold of a pair of crutches and discharged himself. He had hoped to be well enough to start playing again in July, but that was out of the question, and to keep Tony Williams and Herbie Hancock in work (Carter and Shorter had other outlets), he asked Sonny Rollins to play the dates that had been booked. Miles managed to get out and about a little, however, and visited the Five Spot to hear Roland Kirk, whom he applauded rather ghoulishly by banging on the floor with his crutches. He paid for his impatience to leave hospital, because on 4 August he fell down at his home, causing damage that led to the second operation, considerably delaying his recovery. Meanwhile, rumours went around that he was suffering from sickle-cell anaemia – a kind of cancer of the bone marrow common among blacks.

It was a particularly galling time to be laid up; he had just got his new personnel stabilized, and there was a feeling that Miles's own position in the jazz world might not be so impregnable. By the end of the year, the *Down Beat* readers' poll had voted John Coltrane into first place in the Hall of Fame category, Jazzman of the Year, Record of the Year (*A Love Supreme*) and first on tenor saxophone. Miles Davis was still first on trumpet, his group was second to Dave Brubeck's, and he had three albums placed in the Record of the Year category. But generally, it was Coltrane's year, and many vigorous and vociferous new musicians were coming up in his wake.

It would be foolish to suggest that Miles Davis's health problems have been psychosomatic; they are too serious, too real, for that. Nevertheless, there seems to have been a strong link in each decade of his mature career between, on the one hand, his problem of creativity and the deep inner necessity to change his music and his life-style, and on the other hand, his physical well-being. In the early 1950s he was a heroin addict, and managed to kick the habit only by a supreme effort, after which he went on to a period of gloriously creative music. Similarly, in the early 1960s, when that first brilliant phase had spent itself, his health declined and he began to suffer from the bone malady, after which he was to have another resurgence of creativity. Perhaps one simple explanation might be that periods of enforced convalescence gave him the breathing space he needed to review his past and consider the future.

It was not until November that Miles began playing again with his quintet; it had been an eight-month lay-off. He opened in mid-November at Philadelphia's Showboat Lounge, then went to Detroit for a one-week stand at the Grand Bar. After that, he went to New York's Village Vanguard for a Thanksgiving Week engagement, followed by a stint at the Bohemian Caverns in Washington D.C., Ron Carter was not available for these engagements, and the bass position was filled in Philadelphia and New York by Gary Peacock, and in Detroit by Reggie Workman. Miles finished off the year with a booking at the Plugged Nickel in Chicago, with Carter back on bass. Two nights at the Plugged Nickel were recorded, but nothing was released at the time. One album was eventually released in 1987, and a seven-CD box-set of the music of both evenings was released in 1995. It is an exciting and moving document, but Miles had clearly not fully got his strength back after the surgery and the long lay-off. His spirit is heroically willing, but the flesh is weak. There are glimpses of his greatness, but his solos are often full of long pauses, his sound is thinner and less burnished than usual, and his technique a little ragged. As Gerry Mulligan remarked at the time, however, a weak Miles is more eloquent than many a stronger trumpeter. The band plays mostly his old repertoire, taking it sometimes to the verge of disintegration. Wayne Shorter is on brilliant form, virtually reinventing the vocabulary of the tenor sax. If this music had been released at the time, Shorter would possibly have had an even greater influence on other saxophonists.

Miles Davis's return to the New York scene, in particular, was welcomed by many musicians and friends who turned up at the Vanguard to greet him. His fans also arrived in strength and there were long lines of people waiting outside the club. But there was one discordant note during the Vanguard engagement. During one intermission, the saxophonist Archie Shepp, who was strongly identified with the rising avant-garde movement, went to the dressing room and asked if he could 'sit in' with the band. Outside, in the club, people near the dressing room door could hear an argument. The dispute seemed to have been settled, however, and Miles and the band started their next set by playing the old tune, 'Four'. But when Wayne Shorter finished his solo, Archie Shepp walked out of the shadows playing his tenor and sat in with the band. Miles Davis simply melted away and was not seen again that evening. Accounts of the occasion said that Shepp's playing sparked Miles's group into new vitality, but Miles himself must have had a most unpleasant shock. Up to this point, musicians of most styles and persuasions had always shown the utmost respect for his musical standards, and his ability, and the idea of sitting in with the band was unthinkable – especially if the leader had expressly objected to it. Now, it seemed that there was a new generation of musicians who were not in awe of Miles Davis.

There was at this period an even greater discrepancy between Miles's live performances and his studio recordings. On gigs, he was still playing the old tunes, but in the studio, beginning with *ESP*, he was recording much fresh material. During the next two years, he released only three albums: *Miles Smiles* in 1966, and *The Sorcerer* and *Nefertiti* in 1967, and these three albums, with *ESP*, defined an area of abstraction which many jazz musicians are still exploring to this day. The essence of this way of playing is as follows. A melodic fragment sets up the theme of the performance: a pulse (usually 4/4 or 3/4), a tempo, and a series of phrases is played against that pulse. The improvisations are explorations of these factors posited by the theme, and so the soloist tends to refer back to thematic fragments. Paradoxically, this 'advance' in concept is a return to roots, because it is a movement away from the harmonic improvisations of bebop and post-bop jazz, and towards the melodic (and rhythmic) improvisation that was characteristic of the swing era and earlier jazz forms. The approach to improvisation set up by Miles's mid-1960s group came to be referred to as 'time – no changes', because there was a pulse but no set harmonic sequence. In fact, the soloist was free to play any kind of melodic shapes he wished because the bass and piano players were using their ears to follow wherever his inspiration took him.

Miles Smiles carries on the exploration of abstraction, but the music is fleshed out by powerfully surging rhythms. Again, there is a harking back to roots with the physical pulse of the multiple rhythms. 'Footprints', a Wayne Shorter composition, is another reworking of the blues, this time in the tonality of C, and an ostinato bass line gives the piece coherence. Another powerful performance is 'Freedom Jazz Dance', a composition by saxophonist Eddie Harris. The theme is a sort of abstraction from the blues in that an angular phrase is played and then echoed with a slight variation (the 'call'), and then the 'response' is a brilliant melodic line that weaves its angular and chromatic way up to a high stab note. For many people, 'Footprints' and 'Freedom Jazz Dance' expressed the musical essence of a period; they created reference points, standards against which other performances were judged.

It is difficult to say exactly why Miles's next two albums, *The Sorcerer* and *Nefertiti*, were not so satisfying. The playing is remarkably fresh and free from cliché, and an extremely high level of invention is sustained by everyone. Most of the themes are written by Wayne Shorter, and his highly original melodic shapes obviously inspired the players. There are also one or two fine themes written by Hancock and Tony Williams, but Miles is credited with no compositions on either album. The causes of dissatisfaction lie in the atmosphere and feeling of the music in general. There's a curious lack of abandon, a kind of self-consciousness, as if the musicians were all outside the music watching themselves playing. There's an almost wilful avoidance of cliché, a kind of 'creativity at all costs' atmosphere, and the music seems to be veering more towards cerebral Western concepts. On the fast pieces, tension is continually created and rarely released, because the pulse is perpetually 'creatively' disturbed, and the soloists resolutely avoid repetition or any harmonic resolution of phrases. And on the slower pieces there is sometimes a monotony of mood, an oppressively effete melancholia. The most memorable performances are the ones which experiment with structure: Shorter's 'Nefertiti' and 'Fall', both of which feature the whole quintet throughout, with no solos as such. The former is striking in that Shorter's superb melody is repeated by the horns throughout, and the dynamism of the performance consists in the continual reaction of the rhythm section to the phrases of the tune. Both this piece and 'Fall' are considerably less abstract than the other pieces on the two albums, and feature strong tonalities and repetitions or ostinati which enhance the improvised movement.

This whole period was one in which Miles Davis was absorbing the influences and ideas of his sidemen. Shorter's unusually imaginative melodic themes were both evocative and inspiring, and Miles was also feeding off the improvising of his fertile young musicians. This must have been one of the reasons why he wrote nothing for these two albums. Yet, according to Herbie Hancock, Davis was entirely responsible for the concept of the music. Hancock said:

I don't know why he didn't write so much, but on the other hand, his influence on the compositions was as though he'd written them. I didn't know Miles before 1963, but he's a master at being able to conceptualize a composition – someone else's composition – understand the heart of it and reshape it to get the most value out of it – musically and from a musician's standpoint, because we have to play it, so it has to be interesting enough for us to want to play it and be stimulated by it ... in a composition there are certain things you can do that reach outwards towards the audience ... in the dynamics, in the contrasts ... and Miles knows how to do that ... how to leave things out ... because they're provocative, not only for us, but also for the audience.

But in 1967, Miles Davis was again at a crossroads, and this may explain why the two albums of that year seem somehow incomplete, as if they are preparations for something else. Earlier in the year, Gil Evans had said that Miles was even toying with the idea of leading a big band, but this venture was never to materialize in the way in which Evans imagined. By the end of the year, not only Miles, but the whole American jazz scene was at a kind of crossroads because the USA had been gripped by rock and roll fever. On 16 July 1967, the jazz scene had also lost one of its most vital leaders; John Coltrane, Miles's old friend, died of cancer of the liver at the height of his powers and his fame. This left Miles Davis as the most eligible man to provide some kind of leadership for an ailing, unconfident jazz scene.

TWELVE

Miles in the Sky

'I have to change. It's like a curse.'[1]

Miles Davis

In 1966, Miles Davis became forty years old, and he became a grandfather. Although Miles's prestige was still high, his popularity had begun to decline. Also, his consistently excellent music was beginning to be taken for granted, and the press notices and reviews of albums tended to be more perfunctory. Furthermore, his record sales were falling off. Clive Davis, president of Columbia Records at the time, has said that Miles's sales dropped to around 40,000 or 50,000 per album, whereas a few years previously he'd always sold more than 100,000 and sometimes more than 150,000. There were also rumours that he was not so well off financially. In *Music Maker*, September 1966, one Pat Sanchez wrote: 'For the past two or three years he has worked so irregularly that much of his fortune is said to have evaporated. Sometimes the unemployment has been a matter of choice ... At other times illness has been the genuine cause of his problems.' In fact, Miles had been again laid up for the first two months of that year with a liver infection and was unable to work until March.

Leonard Feather's *Encyclopedia of Jazz in the Sixties* was published in 1966, and in a fairly long entry on Miles, Feather summed up his present position: 'Davis's major contributions as soloist and as orchestral innovator were made in the 1950s ... Although his combos in recent years have rarely produced any significant new group music, the solo contributions of leader and sideman alike have assured their lasting importance.' This was the general view of Miles Davis at the time, and musicians were beginning to mutter – as they had done at other stages of his career – that he was finished, that he'd reached the end of the road and would have to spend the rest of his life repeating himself and reworking the ground he had already covered. But Miles had brought a whole new dimension to the jazz life: the idea of sustained conceptual development. Up to this point, nearly all jazz instrumentalists who were innovators had developed their enlargement of the language in their youth as the natural outcome of their animal spirits and buoyancy. After ten years, or fewer, in music, they became prisoners bounded by the walls of their self-made creative compounds. Perhaps the only other musician who had shrugged off this pattern and sought for greater conceptual freedom was John Coltrane. Significantly, he had begun his first really creative phase at the late age of twenty-nine, when he joined Miles's quintet in 1955. After finally leaving Miles Davis, he had pursued an intense programme of exploration, development and change, terminated by his death in 1967. But towards the end of his life he had confessed to a fellow saxophonist, 'I can't find anything new to play,' echoing the dilemma of Charlie Parker. Coltrane's truly creative life had spanned only about twelve years, whereas Miles already had behind him some twenty-two years of constant change and search.

So by the end of 1967, Coltrane was dead, and Miles was still king – if perhaps a jaded and precarious one – of the jazz world. But that world itself was losing currency, and one of the reasons for this was the momentous rise of rock music. And the leading force in this new movement was none other than Miles Davis's own record company: Columbia. When Clive Davis joined Columbia Records in 1960 as one of the company's two corporate lawyers, Miles was already one of their biggest stars. In particular, three of his albums – *Porgy and Bess*, *Kind of Blue* and *Sketches of Spain* – had established him as one of the best-selling jazz artists of all time, and therefore one of the company's mainstays. And this was remarkable, because Columbia's general policy at the time, under the guidance of Mitch Miller, was to promote and produce middle-of-the-road (MOR) music. Their steady large profits came from such things as albums of Broadway musicals by entertainers who were heavily exposed to the general public. Their two biggest artists, for example, were Barbra Streisand and Andy Williams. But this comfortable situation was destroyed in the early 1960s when the Beatles burst on the scene and, with their clean-cut, boys-next-door image, made pop (later rock) respectable as well as exciting.

Radio play is, of course, the life-blood of record sales, and by 1965, Top Forty air time had given way to the Beatles, to Peter, Paul and Mary, to Joan Baez, and to Bob Dylan. MOR music was getting hardly any exposure at all, and the effect of this was immediately apparent in Columbia's sales. In the early part of the decade, they had had eleven gold discs virtually in succession, each album having earned over $1,000,000. But in the mid-1960s their sales slumped to a mere 75,000 per album. Faced with this crisis, even the most reactionary elements in Columbia were forced to capitulate to rock music.

In 1966, Clive Davis was made vice-president and general manager, and he began systematically signing up rock stars for Columbia. His first acquisition was the British artist, Donovan. A year later, the Monterey Pop Festival gave even more impetus to the rock scene, and Columbia were now signing groups for advances of up to $15,000. Laura Nyro and Janis Joplin also went to Columbia, and the company, by the end of 1968, was clearly established as the leader of the record industry. Record sales were once more being measured in millions and their stars were playing to huge audiences right across the country. Clive Davis had acquired Blood, Sweat and Tears for an advance of $25,000, but in 1969 the financial stakes escalated dramatically when he signed Johnny Winter for an advance of $300,000 for six albums over a three-year period.

The huge sums of money and the general atmosphere of frantic excitement at Columbia were relegating Miles Davis to the status of fringe artist so far as his record company was concerned. To make matters worse, the relegation was not merely financial. Part of Columbia's excitement was not just monetary; it was the thrill of trail-blazing, of creating and opening up new areas of musical exploitation. Rock music, with its massive amplification, its use of electronics, its thrusting rhythms, and its flamboyant stars with their colourful clothes and rebellious images, had become central to the whole era – the music of the 1960s – just as jazz had been the music of the previous decade, though its popularity had never reached the enormous proportions that rock was now enjoying. And at the end of the 1950s, Columbia, with its easy-listening music policy, had had only one great trail-blazer with a world-wide influence and audience: Miles Davis.

Miles had been their man with his finger on the pulse of the age, but this was no longer the case, and he was being shunted into the sidings of 'art' music and mentally bracketed with the company's 'serious' catalogue. Columbia were loyal to him, of course; they could not forget his great past, but they didn't seem to think he had much of a future. He was a prized possession, a trophy almost, but not exactly a prime asset. This was probably the reason Columbia had made an attempt to change their marketing image of Miles. The Byronic and brooding black man was exchanged for *Miles Smiles*, and on the cover of that album there was a photograph of Davis doing exactly that. The cover of *Nefertiti* had an exotic close-up of Miles on the front with bare torso and a kerchief knotted round his neck, and on the back another photo of him in elegant, casual clothes, sitting on his enormous fur-covered bed. The soberly suited successful-American-businessman image had been kicked out along with the Byronic brooding – but only from record sleeves at this time: in public performances Miles was, sartorially speaking, still his old conservative, though sharp self.

Clive Davis described the Miles–Colombia relationship as he saw it:

In the process of becoming the star of the jazz world, he'd acquired some expensive habits: exotic cars, beautiful women, high fashion clothes, unusual homes. He'd also gotten in the habit of calling Columbia regularly for advances. I decided to subsidize him. I felt that he contributed to Columbia's jazz and progressive music roster just as Vladimir Horowitz contributed to our classical list. It eventually got to be our problem, however. Fifty thousand albums barely takes you out of red ink. We began to give Miles additional money each time he recorded an album; we weren't making any money at all.[2]

Elsewhere in the jazz world, a certain disquiet was becoming apparent, and a few of the more perceptive observers of the scene were beginning to look around for new directions. *Down Beat* was still the leading music magazine in 1966 – *Rolling Stone* began a year later – and in the 15 December issue, Mike Zwerin, the old associate of Miles's who had played on the first Birth of the Cool sessions, wrote:

Jazz is going to have to make some adjustments, I think, with the electronic world of rock and roll if it is to retain its validity as a reflection of contemporary life . . . Increasingly sophisticated electronic devices are being introduced by a few groups that sometimes can swing very hard as well as improvise around a free and dissonant form of the blues. They swing and they improvise, and that – according to my definition – is jazz.

Twelve months later, an article under the headline 'Death of an American Art?' appeared in the *Louisville Times*. The writer, Jim Morrissey, said of *Sorcerer*: 'This is the first Miles Davis record that left me cold.' And he comments on the jazz scene in general:

My complaint is that too many of the jazz greats are producing non-communicating music. They get deeper and deeper in their own bag where fewer and fewer of their fans hang out. There must be some kind of wedding between jazz and some of the solid contemporary sounds that are evolving out of the early rock and roll garbage. Twenty years ago jazz was pop music. Today it has only a small proportion of the public on its side.[3]

This impassioned plea in a regional paper came shortly after the 1967 Monterey Pop Festival had clinched the arrival of progressive rock on the national scene, and introduced a gawping world to the brand-new concepts of Peace and Love, flower-power, and hippiedom.

The jazz scene itself was in disarray, and thus was not facing these potent new developments with a united front. It was split, broadly speaking, into two factions: on the one hand the avant-garde, and on the other, the majority of musicians making a living working veins which had been pioneered years previously. The situation was further complicated by a strong racist element. The newer faces in the avant-garde – notably Archie Shepp and Albert Aylen – in an attempt to expose white exploitation of jazz musicians, and possibly also to dislocate conventional thinking on the matter, were identifying themselves with the oppressed black population. They disassociated themselves from the word 'jazz' and called their music 'black music'.

Miles Davis, as usual, stood alone in this controversy and openly criticized both factions. As Leonard Feather put it, he had taken small-group improvisation to such a peak of brilliance that he had nowhere to look except down. He was disaffected with the more conventional scene because he rarely saw evidence of real direction and imagination in it; and he deeply disliked much of the avant-garde music he heard, for the same reasons. His attitude to both sides is clearly expressed in another blindfold test in 1968. As he had done in the similar test four years earlier, he severely criticized every piece played to him, except one; in this case, by the pop group Fifth Dimension. His comments are interesting because they show the kind of criteria he applied to his own work at this time. Of the track 'On the Que-Tee' from Freddie Hubbard's album, *Backlash*, Miles commented:

No kind of sound, straight sound, no imagination. Freddie's a great trumpet player, but if he had some kind of other direction to go . . . if you place a guy in a spot where he has to do something else, other than what he can do, so he can do that. He's got to have something that challenges his imagination, far above what he thinks he's going to play, and what it might lead into, then above that, so he won't be fighting when things change. That's what I tell all musicians; I tell them to be ready to play what you know and play above what you know. Anything might happen above what you've been used to playing – you're ready to get into that, and above that, and take that out.[4]

In this same blindfold test, Miles also dismissed a track by the Thad Jones/Mel Lewis band, though he did have a few kind words to say about Thad. Two groups, therefore, one small and one a big band, from the younger (Hubbard) and the older generation, both highly regarded by most of the jazz community, held little interest for Miles Davis. He was disgusted with contemporary/mainstream jazz; but his dislike of the so-called 'avant-garde' was even stronger and his condemnation more vitriolic. Feather played him 'The Funeral' from *Archie Shepp in Europe*, and Miles commented:

People are so gullible – they go for that – they go for something they don't know about . . . because they feel it's not hip not to go for it. But if something sounds terrible, man, a person should have enough respect for his own mind to say it doesn't sound good. It doesn't to me, and I'm not going to listen to it. No matter how long you listen to it, it doesn't sound any good. . . . and people will go for it – especially white people. They go for anything ridiculous like that.[5]

In the above diatribe, Miles was making two clear points: first, he didn't see any value in the music; second, he didn't rate it as 'black' music because it seemed to get the bulk of its response from white audiences. Such audiences are, of course, steeped in the Western notion of artistic progress, which extrapolates its values from industrial technology in which the latest model is not only the best (of engines, machines etc.), but also makes previous models redundant. Gil Evans, discussing the same problem in 1967, said: 'There's an old saying, I think it was George Bernard Shaw who said it, "I am better than you are, because I was born after you." I see this happening all the time.'[6] But the values of technology simply do not work in art. Shaw's plays did not invalidate Shakespeare's; Miles's great sextet recordings of 1958 and 1959 did not invalidate his quintet albums of 1956; the advent of Dizzy Gillespie in no way diminished the greatness of Louis Armstrong's recordings of the late 1920s. By 1968, the movement started by Ornette Coleman had been in existence for nine years – long enough for anyone, including Miles, to make up his mind about it. Davis had always believed in progress and development, but he had always been aware of his roots. He did not jettison; he added to what he already knew, and each stage of his development contained the essence of his previous stages. He seemed to view truly creative activity as a recurrent three-stage process: first, you start with what you know (and his criticism of many musicians would probably be that they stay with what they know); then you get into new and less familiar areas; in the third stage, the new area is absorbed and becomes familiar. Then the process starts all over again. This is the way Miles had proceeded throughout his career to date.

He had always had wide musical interests, ranging from the classics and 'serious' music to ethnic music of various kinds. He was deeply interested in Spanish music and he knew something of pre-jazz American music such as the rural and urban blues, gospel and worksongs. He had often expressed his distaste for the word 'jazz' and his dislike of the limitations theorists put upon it. His albums had enlarged the whole idea of what an improvising musician could do and of the contexts he could use, and several times, particularly towards the end of the 1950s with *Sketches of Spain*, his music had forced some critics to ask, 'Is it jazz?' There can be no doubt that he enjoyed the confusion he caused in inflexible minds. Even in the late 1960s, jazz criticism was still largely the preserve of whites, and now Miles was moving yet further away from any white critical standpoint, and into some area of which he seemed to be the sole inhabitant. He was moving away from his old musical associates and away from the younger generation of musicians – except, of course, for those in his own group.

During the 1968 blindfold test, Leonard Feather must have felt quite confused when they came to the only track which Davis liked and which he deemed worthy of a proper critique. This was 'Prologue, the Magic Garden' by Fifth Dimension. Miles commented:

> That record is planned, you know. It's like when I do things, it's planned and you lead into other things. It makes sense. It had different sounds in the voicing, and they're using the stereo ... coming out from different sides and different people making statements ... That's the way you should record! ... I liked the composition and the arrangement. It's Jim Webb and the Fifth Dimension. It could be a little smoother – they push it too hard for the singers. You don't have to push that hard. When you push, you get a raggedy edge, and the edge gives another vibration. I liked the instrumental introduction too. We did things like that on *Porgy and Bess* – just played parts of things.[7]

During the later 1960s, Herbie Hancock was probably closer musically to Miles than anyone else except Gil Evans. Hancock had already written his popular hit, a rhythm and blues piece called 'Watermelon Man', and his musical interests were wide, ranging from Stockhausen, Bartók and Stravinsky to pop music. He was, for a jazz musician, remarkably unprejudiced and never made a generic condemnation of music of any kind, preferring to listen to and judge any piece on its own merits. Talking of rock and pop music, he said:

I think it's become very artful ... the Beatles, for example: some of their songs are very artful. And Dionne Warwick, James Brown, Mary Wells, Smokey and the Miracles, the Supremes ... I like all kinds of music, and there are certain types that are directly related to me. Rhythm and blues is part of my own personal background, not just from being a teenager during the time rhythm and blues first started, but because I'm a Negro; and so far as pop music is concerned, it is probably basic to everybody's listening.[8]

Rhythm and blues was still providing a link between black musicians of all generations; Miles himself had started out with such a group. This experience and his general musical interests coincided almost exactly with those of Hancock.

But an even greater shock awaited Leonard Feather when he visited Miles Davis in a Hollywood hotel in 1968. He wrote: 'I found strewn around the room records or tape cartridges by James Brown, Dionne Warwick, Tony Bennett, the Byrds, Aretha Franklin, and Fifth Dimension. Not a single jazz instrumental.'[9] The names all have two things in common: the artists were very popular, and they were all noted for musical quality of one kind or another. James Brown was the king of soul music, Aretha Franklin the queen, and Fifth Dimension leading exponents of rock music. The Byrds were an extremely musical white group who came out of Los Angeles and made their reputation by 'covering' Bob Dylan hits. Dionne Warwick was a superb singer who showed a Billie Holiday influence, but with strong soul overtones. Her repertoire consisted mainly of songs and arrangements written by Burt Bacharach, probably one of the most gifted songwriters of the century. Tony Bennett sang in the Sinatra vein, and to that extent was the odd man out on the list. The popularity, the musical quality were there, but he was much closer to the night club type of intimate 'torch' singing than the others, and his audience was most probably predominantly white. As Miles had done in the previous decade, these artists were all proving that it was possible to make excellent music and still be successful commercially. The difference was that Miles had done it with purely instrumental music, whereas now, in the middle and later 1960s, the emphasis was heavily on vocal music. The basic problem facing Miles Davis and all other jazz musicians was how to reinstate instrumental music as a major force on equal terms with the ubiquitous vocal groups.

Meanwhile, the internal dilemma of jazz – a kind of tribal warfare between reactionary and avant-garde elements – seemed to be taking everyone's mind off this central problem. The split, and the wider problem of the relationship of artist and audience, had been starkly revealed in October 1967, when the Miles Davis Quintet and the Archie Shepp Quintet shared the same bill at the Jazz Expo concert in London. Miles elected to play first because, so the story went, he said that he didn't want to play to an audience of sick people – the implication being that they would be sick after listening to the Shepp group. The Hammersmith Odeon has a capacity of 3,500, and both houses were packed. The mystique surrounding Miles was still strong, and this was only his second visit to the UK; it was seven years since he had last played there. A large proportion of the audience was there to see the Miles they knew – the Miles of the live albums, and of the famous quintets and sextets of the 1950s. At the same time, much space in the musical press had been devoted to the avant-garde movement, and many of the audience had come because they wanted to hear Archie Shepp.

The curtain rose to reveal Miles Davis wearing an impeccably tailored russet-coloured suit and a neat collar and tie. The rest of the quintet – Shorter, Hancock, Carter and Williams – were wearing dinner jackets and black bow-ties. This reassured the audience; it was what everyone expected, because the image and presentation had been exactly the same during Miles's previous visit. There was that same statuesque quality about the group, a kind of rapt intensity that created the impression that their external stillness, their apparent obliviousness to the audience, were symptomatic of violent internal (imaginative) activity. The audience were expecting a series of fairly short pieces, probably including 'So

What', 'Walkin'', and some famous ballad such as 'My Funny Valentine' or 'Stella by Starlight', all of which would be given the usual jazz formula of 'theme–solos–reprise of theme'. The atmosphere was pregnant with anticipation of the familiar.

But the audience was doomed to a certain disappointment. Miles had moved on musically, and both his subject matter and his method were foreign to the majority of his listeners. He played one long, continuous set lasting about an hour, and during its course, one or two familiar themes appeared and disappeared. There was a wisp of ''Round Midnight' and some themes from *Miles Smiles*; there were obvious tonal centres; there were solos; but the drums boiled and bubbled, keeping up a continuous dialogue with whatever else was happening, and the group played brilliant collective improvisations without ever getting into the really tight rhythmic grooves for which Miles was, and is, justly famous. In other words, there was never any proper release of the immense tension that was generated, and because of this, the audience were denied the satisfaction of complicity in the performance. Instead, they were kept on the outside – respectful, attentive, but not really involved. When the curtain fell, the applause was warm, but somewhat mystified.

The second half of the concert was a very different affair. Everything about Archie Shepp's group was the antithesis of Miles's quintet. They wore casual, colourful, flamboyant clothes, and Shepp capped his anarchic regalia with a brightly-hued fez. They bobbed, weaved and moved vigorously as they played, giving an impression of great physical effort. From the first notes of Shepp's tenor, they plunged into a total, non-tonal freak-out with raving horns and rolling drums, which lasted all of twenty minutes. For the first five minutes it was a tremendously dramatic experience, but soon numerous sections of the audience became very restless, and many people walked out. It was 'energy' music with a vengeance, and it was totally iconoclastic: a complete rejection of the whole jazz/bourgeois/white/Western tradition. The audience reactions were extreme. As opposed to the numbers (and they were a minority) who walked out in angry disgust, there were those who stayed either out of curiosity or to cheer. From the first half of the evening, when the audience had been excluded from the performance and given the role of mystified outsiders watching a sacred and barely comprehensible ritual, the situation had changed radically: the audience were now being forced to commit themselves to either total rejection or to some kind of acceptance of the event.

The one musical element which Archie Shepp's and Miles Davis's concerts had in common was that they both played continuous sets with much internal movement. In other words, the structure of their performance was organic, arising largely out of group interplay, and the time continuum was non-Western in the sense that there were no real beginnings and endings, but a soundstream giving the impression of an eternal ebb and flow. There were, however, several extra-musical elements in Shepp's concert which helped to account for the fact that a substantial section of the audience was able to identify with his group. First of all, his performance was essentially a theatrical event (Shepp was actually a dramatist of some repute), which was heightened by its context – appearing after Miles's group, which seemed to be setting up most of the values Shepp was about to knock down. The clothes and mannerisms of Shepp's group were those of the younger generation, and his musicians' physical involvement with the music was nearer to the extrovert atmosphere of the rock scene. Also, the younger generation in the latter half of the 1960s worshipped iconoclasm – the smashing of traditional attitudes and old cultural mores. It was a case of *épater les vieux*. Many of Shepp's supporters enjoyed the discomfort of the members of the audience who walked out. The shattering of dreams, illusions and expectations was made concrete by the visual appearance of the group on stage and by the reactions of outraged listeners.

By the end of 1968, rock hysteria had reached a peak in America, and jazz was experiencing an all-time low. In August of that year, Dave Holland, the young English bass player, joined the Miles Davis Quintet in place of Ron Carter, and was astonished by what he found:

When I joined the band, it was on a sort of decline in America. We played a lot of clubs where there were sort of thirty or forty people in the audience in a night. We played gigs out in San Francisco in, I think it was September of that year . . . and I was amazed that so few people would come. I thought that, working with Miles, it would be a packed house every time. We played Basie's – the first gig I did – well, that was full. There were always places that were like that. We played places that were packed. But . . . I thought that Miles felt it necessary to make another move. There was definitely that period where Miles said to himself, 'I've got to make a change. There's got to be a change in the music.'

The situation was rapidly becoming like that of the 1930s, when big bands had dominated the scene and small groups found themselves out of context and without prospects. It was in the 1930s, for example, that King Oliver ended his days as janitor of a pool room, and clarinettist Johnny Dodds had to work as a taxi driver and play only in his spare time. In that decade, jazz musicians were faced with the choice of either joining some orchestra, if they were flexible enough and good enough sight-readers, or taking some other kind of employment. But in the later 1960s, the problem was much more serious, because the whole financial basis of instrumental music was being undermined. During the 1930s, the big names such as Louis Armstrong, Duke Ellington, Benny Goodman and the Dorsey brothers managed to survive and stay in the limelight by leading big bands. But thirty years later, it looked as if even the big names – and Miles's was one of the very biggest – might find themselves scuffling for work. There was, of course, no chance at all of jazz receiving the kind of massive state subsidy that so-called 'serious' music enjoys and without which it would cease to be performed.

Although the outlook was bleak, one jazz group in particular was doing very well: a quartet led by saxophonist Charles Lloyd. Miles Davis shared the bill at the Village Gate with Lloyd's quartet in early 1968 and said of it: 'Charles Lloyd . . . has a good group.'[10]

Both Tony Williams and Ron Carter had recorded with Lloyd during their period with Miles, and Lloyd's current group included pianist Keith Jarrett and drummer Jack DeJohnette, both of whom were to play and record with Davis a few years later. The Charles Lloyd Quartet was an acoustic unit, but its performance covered a wide area of expression, ranging from freely improvised passages to wildly swinging jazz pieces reminiscent of the Adderley group, rock-based blues and pieces with a strong soul or gospel tinge. Lloyd and Jarrett wrote most of the themes, but their repertoire also included an occasional rock/pop song such as the Lennon and McCartney tune, 'Here, There and Everywhere'. George Avakian, the man who had signed Miles for Columbia in the 1950s and produced *Miles Ahead*, signed up Lloyd for Atlantic Records, and made sure that the quartet was promoted as vigorously as if it had been a rock group. He persuaded Atlantic to invest money in buying advertising space, giving press conferences, and making sure that anyone who could or would write reviews was able to attend the concerts. Avakian also ensured that the group appeared at prestige concerts of all kinds, and after a resounding success at the Monterey Jazz Festival in 1966, he engineered an event the following spring that was to win over rock audiences for the quartet. Avakian tells the story:

A friend suggested to Bill Graham, operator of the Fillmore Auditorium (San Francisco), that the Charles Lloyd Quartet play a set on a Sunday afternoon to see what would happen. Graham put the quartet on with no special announcement about its music; the audience for the most part had no idea that it was listening to jazz. 'There were some kids who started to walk away,' Graham recalled ... 'but once the group's strong rhythmic sound began to penetrate, the uninitiated audience became fixed. They really dug Lloyd.' A wild ovation at the end of the first number underlined the quartet's instant success; what was to have been a half-hour fill-in set wound up with forty minutes of encores.[11]

Coming virtually from nowhere, as Lloyd had done, he was a man without a past and with all the future before him. For Miles Davis, with his credentials as one of the leading musicians of the previous twenty years, a precipitate move was out of the question; nor was it his style. Despite his reputation for impulsive, self-willed behaviour, when it came to music, he never moved until he was absolutely sure of his ground. Each step had always to be carefully tested and secured. Things were becoming pressing, however, because of poor record sales and the dwindling jazz club scene. Clark Terry said of Miles at this time: 'I happen to know that there was a period when in spite of all his many possessions – investments, home, car – there was a period when he needed to bolster these; he really needed to get into a higher financial bracket.'[12] And this was corroborated by Clive Davis when he stated that Columbia began to give Miles additional money each time he recorded an album, and went on to say:

> Miles nevertheless called constantly to ask for more. He has a raspy, low voice – a fiery whisper that conveys heat over the telephone while you are straining to find out how much money he wants. He is spellbinding, and he can talk. After a while, the money business got to be a sort of joke. For Miles called often – sometimes urgently – and I had to figure out each time if he was serious. Walter Dean got some of his calls too . . . sometimes he spent hours on the phone listening to that hoarse, almost demonic voice and dodging its monetary thrusts.[13]

Miles Davis knew one fundamental truth about the record industry: companies will promote only after they have invested money in their artists. Also, the amount of promotion is proportionate to the amount of investment. Artists' quality means little; it is their price that calls the tune. By demanding more money, Miles was simply raising the stakes. But he did not confine his attack to the internal machinery of his own record company; he began making himself accessible to journalists of all kinds, so that at the end of the 1960s he was talking in print even more than he had done at the beginning of the decade. He attacked and criticized the status quo, the record companies, and the rising white rock groups whose success was diminishing the status of black artists. It was bitterly ironical that rock music, which came from rhythm and blues roots, was beginning to undermine black soul music. *Billboard*, on 6 December 1969, reported:

> A few months ago, soul records made up as much as forty per cent or more of the playlists of some top forty stations. Today, George Wilson, a Vice President of Bartell Broadcasting and program director of WOKY in Milwaukee, has only five records in his top thirty-six that are by black artists. A couple of these are the Supremes and the Fifth Dimension, who are considered pop artists rather than soul artists ... The college kids a few months ago used to dig soul because they thought it was hip. But I think the growth in popularity of progressive rock on the campuses has hurt soul.

At this time, the civil rights movement was rapidly gaining momentum. The decade had begun with 'Negroes' asking for their rights, with sit-ins, boycotts and marches; it ended with 'blacks' demanding their rights, with riots, demonstrations and a series of assassinations. As a leading black citizen, Miles Davis couldn't possibly allow himself to be shunted into a cultural backwater by Columbia. Furthermore, he was now in search of a black audience. Until now, his audience and his record-buying public had been largely white. Only a tiny minority of blacks knew anything about him at all, and he felt this keenly. A few years later, he said: 'I don't care who buys the records as long as they get to the black people, so I will be remembered when I die.'[14] If Columbia regarded him as they did their classical music roster, Miles Davis would never get to the black audience at all.

As early as 1966, Miles was complaining in the black magazine *Jet*: 'I get awards all over the world. What I need now is some rewards.'[15] And a year or two later, he is complaining bitterly to Clive Davis about his treatment at the hands of Columbia:

Then one day Miles called me to complain about his record sales. He was tired of low sales, and angry about it. Blood, Sweat and Tears and Chicago had borrowed enormously from him – and sold millions. These young white artists – he was in a rather militant frame of mind – were cashing in while he was struggling from advance to advance. If you stop calling me a jazz man, he said at one point, and just sell me alongside these other people, I'll sell more. In part, I agreed with him.[16]

By the beginning of 1969, Miles had formed a relationship with a black-owned marketing and public relations firm called New Wave Communications, and was ready to launch a full-blooded campaign. Its immediate aim was to suggest that Columbia should set up a special marketing programme with several black promotion and talent agencies. The idea was to promote black Columbia artists in the black community through records, concerts and night clubs. As one of the New Wave officials put it: 'The trouble with a company like Columbia is that when they get a good black artist they don't promote him. And they spend very little money with the black media.'[17]

Miles took these steps because he was faced with only two alternatives: to be on top, or to be very much the underdog. His position in American society was not static; you do not stand still, you move up or down. In the middle and later 1960s he was moving down, and he was doing everything in his power to reverse that movement. The key to that was to increase his white audience and to create for the first time a substantial black audience for his music. Dave Holland put it in the following way:

He wants to be rich, he wants to be powerful, and the only way to do that is to be on top in the profession. He wasn't prepared to be a memory – somebody to go and see because you used to dig him. He wanted to be somebody who appealed to the generation that's happening now. And he's always done this, I've noticed. He always makes music which goes right to the next generation.

Two things always seemed to presage a major change in Miles Davis's music: a tendency to write much more of the music himself, and a closer association with Gil Evans. On his last two albums, none of the compositions had been attributed to him, and even if he had reshaped all the pieces written by his sidemen, the fact remains that the germ of all the pieces came from them and not from Miles. But suddenly, with *Miles in the Sky*, he is writing again, Gil Evans is once more involved in, as he called it, 'mid-wifing' pieces, and Miles's two compositions, 'Stuff' and 'Country Son', take up well over half the playing time of the album. Dave Holland comments on Miles's renewed writing activity, which began with this album and was to increase in intensity over the next two or three years: 'I think he started writing more then, because only he knew what he wanted to do at that point. I don't think anybody else really understood.' And Teo Macero recalled the following pep-talk:

For a long time he didn't write any music, and I said, 'Look, you're one son-of-a-bitch that I know can write better than anybody else – I don't care who it is – you wanna get off your ass, get a piece of paper and a couple of pencils, and get home and write some goddam music. Why get somebody else to write your music? You've got the talent; you're a very creative artist.' He didn't know quite how to take this. I said, 'You've got more talent than anybody I know. You can create better than anybody I know, but you're too goddam lazy!' Well, I tell you, he went home, and then there was a period when every record that came out was written by Miles Davis.

Throughout his career to date, the instrumentation of Miles's small groups had remained more or less the same. It had usually been the classic post-war line-up of trumpet, tenor or alto sax, piano, double bass, drums, and occasionally an extra saxophone or trombone. But for *Miles in the Sky*, he now began introducing other instrumental sounds. For the first time, he used electric guitar, electric piano, and electric bass guitar – the last instrument hitherto associated only with rock and pop music and rhythm and blues. But this new departure is done with his customary caution; the guitar is used only on 'Paraphernalia', and the electric piano and bass guitar only on 'Stuff'. Miles had been thinking of the electric keyboard for some time, and when Joe Zawinul had started using one with Cannonball's group, Davis had flown all the way to Mexico City to hear the sound of this new instrument in context. Zawinul tells the story:

> We played Mexico City and he wanted to hear that because 'Mercy Mercy' [Adderley's hit record] had just come out on the radio, and he just wanted to hear it. Funny, man, that night the electricity broke down in Mexico City and there was no electric piano! And Miles said, 'Hey, man, I come here washed and clean, and then the goddam piano ain't working!'

Miles in the Sky is a transitional album referring back to the concepts of the previous two, but looking forward in that it set up new criteria and changed the role of the instruments. One piece, 'Black Comedy', composed by Tony Williams, is very much in the manner of the preceding two albums with a scheme so skeletal as to be little more than a fragmentary riff, and a series of highly abstract solos. It is familiar territory to the musicians and they play it with confidence and panache. Miles's solo is especially potent, and Tony Williams keeps up an unfailing dialogue with the rest of the action. But 'Black Comedy' is the only track that looks back in this way. Wayne Shorter's composition, 'Paraphernalia', is in brisk 4/4 with a section in 3/4. During the solos, the 4/4 section is of indeterminate length (open bars), and the 3/4 section, which has a set length, is cued in when the soloist plays certain phrases. On this piece, George Benson's guitar is used to add texture and colouring to the rhythmic feel, and for most of the performance, which is in the tonality of D, Benson simply repeats a rhythmic figure using single strings and working on octaves of the root. To circumscribe the role of an instrument so severely shows a great change in Miles's thinking. The guitar's role is entirely supportive, and there is a similar change in the role of the drums. For the most part, Tony Williams is confined to a steady ostinato on hi-hat and cymbals, and though he does depart from this at intervals, using the rest of the drumkit to create multiple rhythms in reaction to the soloists, it is his straight time-playing which gives the track identity and life.

It was commonly believed, in contemporary jazz circles in the 1960s, that if all members of a group were outstanding impro-visers, then everyone should be seen and heard to be creating on an equal basis; no one should be 'relegated' to a supportive role. It was this attitude which lay behind Tony Williams's drum dialogues with the rest of the group, which was what usually happened in live performances right up until he left Miles in the spring of 1969. In the recording studio, however, from now on things were never going to be quite the same again. Miles Davis seemed to be turning away from the idea that creativity manifests itself in a perpetually inventive way of disturbing (and disguising) the pulse of a piece of music. Instead, he was turning towards the non-Western prac-tice of a very clear, unambiguous pulse, and rhythmic repetition, which creates a continuum in which all kinds of musical events, including rhythmic variations, can take place. Tension can then be created and released by the superimposition of one rhythm on another, by changes in rhythm, and by moving out of a regular time-feel altogether. Drama would occur when the listener sud-denly became more aware of the pulse, or of its absence, or of a new pulse.

With Miles's composition, 'Stuff', this becomes much more obvious because the whole piece is based on a rock beat. This direction had been indicated by the track 'Eighty-One' on *ESP*, but Miles had chosen to ignore it while he explored the more abstract areas that album had opened up. 'Stuff' is a long piece, occupying well over half a side of the album – and Tony Williams lays down a funky eight-to-the-bar cymbal beat all the way, spicing it now and then with some rapid fill-ins. Only occasionally do his convoluted rhythms become oblique to the basic pulse, and when they do, they are made much more dramatic simply because they are juxtaposed with his long stretches of straight time-playing. Hancock's electric piano chording is spare and very funky; he understands this idiom completely. The theme, which is full of melodic fragments, displaced accents, slurs, smears and trills, is some 164 bars long and takes almost six minutes to play. This nicely sets up that hypnotic, repetitive, non-Western time-feel, and the continuity of rhythm is superbly contrasted by the dislocated theme. Miles takes the first solo, and his phrases echo the asymmetry of the theme. He does not sound as magnificently confident as he does on 'Black Comedy', but somehow, the very tentativeness of his playing gives it more weight; we can sense his groping for a way into a new musical area. After solos by the saxophone and keyboard, Tony Williams plays a brief drum solo over the rock feel laid down by bass guitar and piano, and the horns play the piece out with a shortened version of the theme. 'Stuff' was the first Miles Davis composition for a very long time, of which the most memorable part was the rhythmic feel and the theme; the solos were important, but the indelible memory was of the piece as a whole.

'Stuff' opens the album, and the final piece on side two is Miles's other composition, 'Country Son'. This has no written theme for the horns at all, and thus presages Davis's future methods. It is a three-part structure in D minor. The first part has a swinging 4/4 feel, the second section is an out-of-time interlude and the third section is a slow rock pulse. The drama arises from the juxtaposition of these three sections. The performance begins with Miles launching into a wild improvisation on the 4/4 section. He's using a straight mute; another departure, and further evidence of his search for fresh sounds. The extremes of his playing are highlighted on this track because he moves from aggression on the swinging section to an exquisite tenderness on the free interludes. After solos by Shorter and Hancock, Miles winds up the album with a solo starting on the free section and moving into the slow rock feel. Here, some of his phrases (Appendix A, Fig. 8) are to be played again and developed a year later on *In a Silent Way*.

The two Miles Davis compositions that point to new directions open and close *Miles in the Sky*. It is clear that they were put in key positions on the album intentionally. There is change in the air; later in the year there would be changes in his group . . . and a completely new rhythm section by the spring of 1969. But first, after more musical conferences with Gil Evans, Miles was to go into the studios to try out yet more new ideas on an album to be called *Filles de Kilimanjaro*.

THIRTEEN

Play What's *Not* There!

'For me, a group has to be mixed. To get swing, you
have to have some black guys in there.'[1]

Miles Davis

The year 1968 not only saw a crisis point in the American jazz
scene; it was a year of great turbulence and instability in American
society as a whole. The anti-Vietnam War demonstrations were
at their height; Richard Nixon was elected to the office of president
for the first time; Bobby Kennedy and Martin Luther King were
both assassinated. It was a year when radical change was in the
atmosphere and, like an epidemic, the feeling spread abroad so
that even in Europe there were repercussions. In the summer of
that year, student riots took place in Paris, disrupting the city and
embarrassing General de Gaulle.

Another powerfully creative phase in Miles Davis's career also
began in 1968, one which mirrored in almost uncanny detail the
magnificently productive period which had begun ten years earlier
(1958–61). In the earlier and the later phase, the personnel of
Miles's group was in a state of flux after a period of relative
stability. And in each period, Miles uses some white musicians:
Bill Evans and Gil Evans in the earlier one, and in the later one,
Gil again plus Dave Holland, Joe Zawinul and John McLaughlin.
Also, in both periods, Miles fell in love again and remarried. Even
the nature and the order of the albums produced in each phase is
almost exactly paralleled: *Milestones* in 1958 and *Filles de Kilimanjaro* in 1968 – both albums with a wide range of expression;

232

then two exquisite expressions of Miles's reflective side – *Kind of Blue* in 1959 and *In A Silent Way* in 1969; then a reassertion of non-Western roots with *Sketches of Spain* in 1959 and *Bitches Brew* ten years later; and the faltering concept and schizophrenia of *Some Day My Prince Will Come* (1961) are both mirrored and magnified in *Black Beauty* and *Miles Davis at Fillmore* (1970); and the great live albums of 1961, *Blackhawk* and *Carnegie Hall*, are echoed in the swashbuckling power of *Jack Johnson* and *Live-Evil* of 1970.

Throughout his life, personal relationships meant a great deal to Miles Davis; that is, relationships in his public life with his musical associates, and also relationships in his private life with his women companions. Dave Holland commented: 'When he goes into something, he really goes all the way; if it's drugs, he goes all the way (as he had in the early 1950s); if it's women, he goes all the way; if it's music, he goes all the way. And he's a very inspiring man to be around, because of that.' During the earlier creative phase, Miles had married Frances Taylor, and her face had adorned the covers of some of his albums. Miles explained:

> I got this album, *Some Day My Prince Will Come*, and you know who's on the jacket cover? My wife – Frances. I just got to thinking that as many record albums as Negroes buy, I hadn't ever seen a Negro girl on a major cover unless she was the artist. There wasn't any harm meant – they just automatically thought about a white model and ordered one. It was my album and I'm Frances's prince, so I suggested they use her for a model, and they did.[2]

Frances also appeared, with Miles, on the covers of *Blackhawk* and *ESP*, but a week after the photo session for the latter album, she had finally walked out of Miles's life. Since then, he had met the actress Cicely Tyson, and they became first good friends and then lovers. A huge close-up of her right profile filled the whole front cover of *Sorcerer*. Of this, Miles said:

I have this thing about helping black women, you know.
Because when I was using dope it was costing me a couple
of grand a day and I used to take bitches' money. So when
I stopped to clean up, I got mad at *Playboy* and I wouldn't
accept their poll because they didn't have no black women
in their magazine, you know. So I started putting them on
my covers. So I put Cicely's picture on my record. It went
all round the world![3]

Nefertiti had a companion shot of Miles's left profile, so that the
two albums, when placed alongside each other, presented a highly
romantic picture of Miles and Cicely Tyson quite literally 'tête-à-
tête'. Miles and Cicely later drifted apart but remained good
friends, and reunited in 1978.

In February 1968, Miles and Frances were at last divorced, and
a few weeks later, Davis formed a relationship with a beautiful
twenty-three-year-old girl called Betty Mabry. She and Miles were
eventually married in Gary, Indiana on the last day of September
after Davis had completed an engagement at the Plugged Nickel
in Chicago. Observers noted that Miles was in excellent spirits
during that engagement, though the wedding was kept secret from
everyone except his most intimate friends. Betty Mabry said: 'He
called me from Chicago and said, "Sweetcakes, get your stuff
together and come to Chicago, we're getting married" . . . one of
the sexiest men alive is Miles Dewey Davis. We're going to be
married for ever, because I'm in love, and Mr Davis can do no
wrong as far as I'm concerned.'[4] The photograph on the front of
Filles de Kilimanjaro was of Miles's new wife, and the longest
piece, 'Mademoiselle Mabry', is named after her. Betty Mabry
was a singer tuned into the current rock and soul generations of
musicians and was particularly interested in Jimi Hendrix. It was
through her that Miles and Hendrix met and became good and
mutually inspirational friends. Betty also persuaded Miles to abandon his superbly tailored conservative suits, and to dress in the
flamboyant manner of the rising rock stars. Betty's passion for
Hendrix was not merely musical, however, and Miles's new mar-

riage lasted only one year, after which time he and Betty split up.

By mid-1968, both Herbie Hancock and Tony Williams were thinking of leaving Miles and forming their own groups. They had already made albums under their own names, and the exposure with the Davis quintet had earned them an international reputation. Ron Carter, too, was tired of the constant travelling and wanted to be based more in New York. The result was that there were frequent deputies on the bass with Miles and so he was looking out for a regular bassist. Early in July, he spent a couple of days on holiday in London and visited Ronnie Scott's Club. There the young British bass player, Dave Holland, was working with singer Elaine Delmar. Although he was only twenty-one, Holland was already a magnificent musician, but he was still flabbergasted when, just before the last set, Philly Joe Jones, who had been in the club with Miles, came over and said, 'Miles wants you to join his band. Talk to him about it after the set.' At the end of the evening, however, Miles had disappeared and gone back to his hotel. The following day, Holland got a message to call Miles at his hotel, but on phoning was told that Davis had checked out and gone back to America. This was extremely confusing, and Holland asked Philly Joe if he thought it was a genuine offer. The drummer replied in the affirmative and told Holland to write to Miles. But for another two weeks, Holland thought things over and did nothing. Then he was telephoned on Tuesday by Jack Whittemore, Miles's booking agent, who said, 'Miles has been talking about you. He wants you to come over tomorrow. There's a gig starting at Count Basie's on Friday and he wants you in there.'

Dave Holland said, 'Look, I haven't had any notice and I've got to get my things together.'

'Can you make it?' Whittemore asked tersely.

'OK. I'll make it,' Holland replied.

He managed to take a plane on the Thursday, arriving in New York that evening. He was staying with drummer Jack DeJohnette, whom he already knew, and on arrival at his place, received a message to go and see Herbie Hancock straight away. Dave

Holland has indelible memories of the events of the next twenty-four hours:

> So I went over to Herbie's house . . . It was one of those hot summer nights in August that they get in New York, where humidity is like a hundred per cent, and where you sit and you just sweat, and I remember there was a thunderstorm over the Hudson with this incredible lightning . . . New York hit me with everything it had the first day. So I went over to Herbie's house that night and went over a few pieces – some of them I knew and some I didn't – and the next night I turned up at Basie's for the gig . . . I was the only white person in the club, which is in the middle of Harlem . . . So I was sitting there waiting for the musicians to arrive; and one by one, everybody arrived. Miles arrived, and Tony arrived last. And Tony got up on the stand straight away and started getting his drums ready, and then everybody else got up on the stand – so I got up on the stand. One said hello to me, and I'd met Herbie already. I didn't speak to Tony, and Miles just said hello and didn't say anything else. And the next thing I knew, the music was started. Miles did something that said, 'Everybody go,' and it just started up. And it was like trying to keep up with a tidal wave. There was this great rush of sound and energy and I was on the crest of it, trying to hold on, and I knew that if I fell off it would go on without me. And for four or five months, that's the way it was.

But that week at Count Basie's Club was to be the last gig Herbie Hancock did as a regular member of Miles's group, though nobody knew it at the time. After it was over, Hancock got married and went to Brazil for his honeymoon. On the very first night he suffered from food poisoning. A doctor told him his liver was swollen, and throughout his time there, Hancock was under treatment. Meanwhile, Jack Whittemore phoned to say that a gig had come in for the band, and could Herbie get back to do it. The doctor, however, insisted that Hancock should stay in his hotel for a few more days until he was completely better. When he phoned Miles and his agent to tell them this, he felt that they simply did not believe that he was ill, but thought that he wanted to prolong his honeymoon. At the same time, Miles, knowing that both Herbie and Tony wanted to leave the band, and having just got a new bass player, was worried by the possibility of finding himself, as he had done in 1963, with an entirely new rhythm section on his hands. So when Herbie failed to make the engagement, Miles used Chick Corea on piano, and when he found that Corea could do the job well, he asked him to do it permanently. That way, the new pianist and bass player could work themselves into the band before Tony Williams eventually left.

Filles de Kilimanjaro straddles the period of these personnel changes, three tracks ('Petits Machins', 'Tout de Suite' and 'Filles de Kilimanjaro') being recorded in June with Ron Carter (bass guitar) and Hancock (electric piano), and two tracks ('Frelon Brun' and 'Mademoiselle Mabry') being recorded with Holland (double bass) and Corea (electric piano) in the last week of September, just before Miles's marriage to Betty Mabry. 'Kilimanjaro', incidentally, was the name of a coffee company in Tanzania that Miles owned jointly with the black actor, Jim Brown. He and Brown also owned an animated cartoon business at this time.

All the pieces on *Filles* are attributed to Miles Davis, but it is certain that Gil Evans helped to compose at least one ('Petits Machins'). Years later, recalling his work on albums of Miles's, Evans said, 'The last one I really worked on was *Filles de Kilimanjaro* – I really should have had a credit on that one.'[5] There are an extraordinary number of fresh ideas and devices on this album. Although the acoustic piano is featured from time to time, the emphasis is on the electric keyboard, which is prominent throughout. Tonally, it colours the ensemble sound, and it is also used to point up the bass figures; the bass notes of the electric keyboard are very percussive and blend well with bass guitar or string bass. Miles understood this perfectly, saying later: 'Standard [i.e. acoustic] piano is what it says – it's standard. You can't blend any notes or double up with the bass on certain figures, or get those clusters.'[6] And on live gigs, when there was a Steinway grand piano available, Chick Corea would try to sneak it in somewhere, but Miles would stop him, saying, 'The piano is over. It's an old-fashioned instrument. I don't want to hear it any more. It belongs to Beethoven. It's not a contemporary instrument.'

On *Filles*, not only is the role of the bass circumscribed like that of the drums, but Miles also writes much more for the bass than he had done at any other time. But, just as the earliest rock rhythms the band used had occurred spontaneously in the middle of performances, so, according to Herbie Hancock, did the circumscription of the drums (and presumably of the bass also) have its germ in live performances:

> Tony was real sensitive. If something didn't go right, or if he was upset about something, sometimes he wouldn't play anything. He would just play the cymbal all night. I would be thinking, 'Oh, shit!' ... but maybe out of that, because we would compensate in some way for it ... maybe out of that he kind of *purposely* started doing that at a certain point ... it just changes your roles.

Throughout this album, the bass lines are rhythmically varied and vital, and at no point does either bass player ever revert to the time-honoured jazz habit of playing four straight crotchets to the bar. In other words, there is nothing at all of the conventional jazz time-feel that had characterized nearly all of Miles's work to date, except for some parts of *Miles in the Sky* and *ESP*. Even in a piece like 'Petits Machins', which implies a brisk 4/4 pulse, the bass sticks to the half (or two-in-the-bar) feel, thus creating a deeper trough for the pulse, a greater rhythmic pivot.

The opening piece on side one, 'Frelon Brun', starts with a strong rock beat and a spacey, biting riff played by bass and keyboard. After a brief theme with a slight tinge of African kwela, Miles plays a solo which is a wild dialogue with the drums. This violent interplay is given point and coherence because the bass riff and fairly static chording on the piano are sustained throughout. Thus the atmosphere and the creation and release of tension are done in a fresh and exhilarating way; the trumpet/drum dialogue can either inhabit the continuum set up by bass and piano, reinforcing its rhythms, or play over it or against it.

The second piece, 'Tout de Suite', has a central structural idea which harks back to 'Saeta' on *Sketches of Spain*, where a sort of rough street marching band plays and then stops, and over a droning tremolo, Miles makes his haunting muezzin calls. Here, on 'Tout de Suite', the theme is used literally as an introduction and ending, but the improvised section in the middle has very little relationship to it. The actual tune is in 3/4, and is superbly melodic, developing all the time, unlike the usual jazz piece, which is based on the popular song and tends to repeat sections. The horn line is sinuous, floating and evocative (much of it is in harmony), and the atmosphere is charged with the romantic but funky chording of the electric piano. But as soon as the theme has been played, the rhythm section shifts into 8/8 time with a steady cymbal beat from the drums and some syncopated figures on tom-toms and snare. The bass and keyboard play broken rhythmic figures, given point by the steady continuity of the cymbal beat. It is this feel, with drum ostinato and broken figures from the other instruments, that Miles was to explore so brilliantly the following February on *In a Silent Way*. Miles's rhythmically biting solo on 'Tout de Suite' is followed by a Wayne Shorter solo that has an urgency and muscularity worlds away from the effete melancholy pervading some of his work on *Sorcerer* and *Nefertiti*.

'Petits Machins' has a fragmentary theme with evocative ascending bass figures. Miles takes the first solo, and this is a beauty – his best on the album (Appendix A, Fig. 9). It is a brilliant example of thematic and chromatic improvisation, and a kind of abstraction of the old blues in F. The main motif of the solo is a phrase (see the first four bars) that alternates the major and minor 3rd in a three-note figure going down to the tonic. This insinuates the whole blues tradition, and Miles returns constantly to this motif, approaching it from all angles and playing it many ways with greatly varying inflexions. Tension is created by chromatic runs and convoluted phrases, and it is released by references back to that simple, bluesy motif. The solo is superbly constructed, rising to one climax (bars 60–69) and then to an even greater one (bars 94–98) before concluding with an almost exact restatement of the opening motif.

The title track, 'Filles de Kilimanjaro', has another developing melody, and again a slight feeling of kwela in its rhythms. The tune is so strong that the horns repeat it three times with little interludes from the rhythm section in between each one. This long theme statement harks back to 'Stuff' on *Miles in the Sky*, and to 'Nefertiti' before that, and it implies many different harmonies, but is played over a bass riff on pedal G (the tonic) throughout, thus presaging what Miles was to do with the title track of *Silent Way* eight months later. On 'Filles', Miles and Wayne Shorter improvise very thematically, constantly referring back to the melodic and rhythmic shapes of the main theme, which is not restated after the solos.

The last piece, 'Mademoiselle Mabry', has no written theme at all for the horns, but is a completely composed eighteen-bar structure. Not only the voicing of the chords, but the way they were to be played rhythmically, and the actual rhythmic value of the bass notes, were all written out. It was thus a totally composed piece with a little freedom within the structure. The drums did not really play time so much as colour the movement of bass and keyboard. This is a complete reversal of the usual jazz procedure, wherein most of the writing is for the horns, and only chord symbols are given to the rhythm section. The structure of 'Mabry' is a marvellous fusion of elements from the ballad and soul music traditions; it is laid-back, unhurried, full of tenderness and yet extremely funky. It is also full of internal (written) movement, and the structure itself is so interesting that it is repeated three times before Miles starts the first solo.

This was Dave Holland's first time in the recording studio with Miles, and he described both Miles Davis's method of recording and the way the music was organized:

The pieces were very spontaneous. We'd rehearse a pile of music the day before and not do any of it in the studio – and have a set of new things. And I realize that a lot of reason for the approach that comes across on those things is just because everybody is holding back a lot more, and a lot of space is happening and we're working with the simple elements of the piece . . . His charts were like sketches. You'd often get a piece of paper with a thing written up here then another thing written halfway down the page . . . a little bit of a vamp figure, or a bass line, or a set of three-note chords that might be written in a rhythmic figure. And he might say, 'OK Dave, you play this bass line here. Chick, that's your figure up there. You play that against that.' And at the end of the session Miles might have taken an extract from this take and put it together with this one and then added this one . . . All the recording I did with him was very edited.

In 1968, Miles's concert and club performances were still based on the jazz/swing idea, and there were, as yet, no implications of rock. For six months after Dave Holland joined the band, they were still mainly using material from *Miles Smiles* and *Nefertiti*, but that may have been because Holland and Chick Corea were new to the group. In public, the band were playing sets of continuous music, and Tony Williams, eternally dialoguing with the soloists, was so loud that Dave Holland, who was still playing acoustic bass, often couldn't hear himself. Also, at this time, the musicians were wearing black suits, and Miles was still wearing sharp, but relatively conservative clothes such as striped suits. Throughout that year, Miles and the group were praised lavishly by critics, with ecstatic reviews of live performances from Ralph J. Gleason and Leonard Feather. But despite all the critical recognition, audiences were dwindling and Miles's popularity declining.

There were some signs of change; Columbia had gone further in their attempts to alter Miles's image, and *Miles in the Sky*, which was beginning to get excellent reviews, was packaged in the more flamboyant rock manner. The title came straight from the Beatles' 'Lucy in the Sky with Diamonds', and the front cover was a psychedelic abstract design using all the colours of the rainbow. On the back was a large photograph of Miles in striped pants, high leather boots and a casual jacket. He is looking directly at the camera with a slightly wrinkled brow and a rather sardonic expression as if to say, 'OK! If this is how you want it!' He is sitting astride the stuffed head of a lion with gaping jaws and a clear glass eye, which both seem to be emanating from Miles's crutch. In addition, the album was beginning to receive some radio play on rock programmes; this was a real breakthrough.

During this whole period, Miles's friendship with Jimi Hendrix flourished. Hendrix's image was flamboyant and wild, and he went in for such excesses as playing guitar solos with his teeth. The two spent much time together, and Dave Holland is convinced that Hendrix influenced Miles in many ways – even in the way he created his music. They were both very tense, charismatic people who had a way of focusing the energy around them through themselves. Holland had recorded with Hendrix and said that he worked just like Miles – setting up a figure and playing on it for a while, and then moving on to another figure. It is possible, however, that Hendrix was influenced both musically and in other ways by Miles, though not in so far as electronics were concerned; in that field, Hendrix was the trail-blazer.

In November 1968, Miles was once more in the recording studio trying out some new ideas. This time, he was experimenting with the instrumentation of his group. His thoughts were now obviously turning more to textural matters, and on this occasion he augmented his quintet (Shorter, Corea, Holland, Williams) with two ex-members, Herbie Hancock and Ron Carter. Years later, the two tracks from this session ('Two-Faced' and 'Dual Mr Tiliman Anthony') were released on an album called *Water Babies*. The use of the two keyboards is strongly in evidence on 'Dual', a fourteen-bar structure with a bluesy/gospel flavour. But although the musicians are clearly having fun, the experiment was a failure. One reason is that if superimposed textural layers are to be effective, they require minimal vertical harmonic movement, and 'Dual' had a chord sequence and at one point a rising bass line that sounds like a parody of gospel music. The pianos muddle along cheerfully, while Tony Williams plays an eight-to-the-bar cymbal beat, and the resulting sound smacks of early Charles Lloyd – embryonic rock and roll grafted somewhat arbitrarily on to a structure. But this ensemble, though with only one bass player (Holland), was to be the nucleus of the group which made *In a Silent Way* the following February.

From *Miles in the Sky* to *Filles de Kilimanjaro* was a fairly logical progression. Although there is a homogeneity of vision on *Filles* which gives it a unity the more transitional *In The Sky* lacks, nevertheless, the music of both LPs was, broadly speaking, still based on the old jazz format of theme–solos–theme. Only the pieces 'Country Son' on the earlier album and 'Mademoiselle Mabry' on the later one had veered from this, in that neither had a written theme for horns. In each case, the underlying structure was all that was posited as a basis for improvisation. The old relationship with popular or standard songs – no matter how tangential – had disappeared. It was out of the trumpet phrases on 'Country Son' (Appendix A, Fig. 8) and out of the broken keyboard figures and steady cymbal ostinato on 'Tout de Suite' (*Filles de Kilimanjaro*) that the conception of *In a Silent Way* arose. It took insight of real genius to conceive *Silent Way*, and an examination of the way it differs from Miles's previous recording methods will throw much light on the way his imagination works.

Miles's recording ideas now began to mirror the way his group functioned in concerts. The concept of continuous sets that were not tied down to Western ideas of form began to emerge. In his recordings from now on, Miles wouldn't start with the idea of set pieces; instead he would simply explore some fragmentary elements and edit them into a cohesive piece of music afterwards. Teo Macero, who collaborated closely with Miles, described the new procedure:

> The earlier things were pretty much set . . . but now there's no 'take one' etc. The recording machine doesn't stop at the

sessions, they never stop, except only to make the playback. As soon as he gets in there, we start the machines rolling. Everything that's done in the studio is recorded, so you've got a fantastic collection of everything done in the studio. There isn't one thing missed. Probably, he's the only artist in this whole world, since I've handled him, where everything is intact. Normally we used to make master reels, but then I stopped with the advent of three-track and four-track and so forth. We don't do that any more; I just pull out what I want and copy what I want, and then the original goes back into the vaults untouched. So whoever doesn't like what I did, twenty years from now they can go back and redo it.

Miles seems to have gone about the organization of the recording of *Silent Way* in his usual casual manner. Once again, he seemed to be delaying all final decisions until the last possible moment. The session was arranged for 18 February 1969, and Miles's current group plus Herbie Hancock were booked for it. At this time Tony Williams was getting ready to leave Miles Davis and start his own group, Lifetime. He had heard a tape of the British guitarist, John McLaughlin, and was so impressed that he asked McLaughlin to come over to the USA to join his group. The guitarist arrived in New York early in February 1969, and after some rehearsals with Williams they had an audition at Columbia Records – which, ironically, they failed. The day after, Tony Williams took him round to Miles's house, and though Miles had never heard the guitarist, he said, 'We're doing a date tomorrow. Bring your guitar.' It was a momentous occasion for them both; for McLaughlin, because the exposure with Miles made him world-famous; and for Miles, because the guitarist was exactly the right musician for him at this time. McLaughlin had a superb harmonic sense and melodic flair, and his playing was notable for both sensitivity and power; also, he was steeped in the jazz and the rhythm and blues traditions.

If the addition of McLaughlin to the ensemble was an afterthought, the recruiting of Joe Zawinul was almost an oversight.

Miles telephoned him early in the morning on the actual day of the recording, and said, 'Hey, man, I have a record date today at one o'clock. Why don't you come over?' Zawinul said he would come to the session. A little while later, the phone rang again, and Miles added. 'And bring some music.'

Zawinul took the music of 'In a Silent Way' with him. On the session, Zawinul played both electric piano and organ and so the ensemble with its three electric keyboards and guitar was a completely new sound in jazz. Miles's deployment of the instruments was crucial to this fresh sound. In general, the drums were confined to a steady repetition of figures, and the bass was similarly circumscribed, though Dave Holland was allowed a little more freedom. The centre of the ensemble – the three keyboards and the guitar – was where most of the dynamism and interplay occurred, and over this backcloth the solos were played.

When the session was over, Miles and Teo had about two hours of music, which Macero cut down to eighty minutes, forty minutes per album side. At that point Miles joined him in the editing room and they cut each side down to about nine minutes. Then, Teo recalled Miles saying, 'This is an album.' But Macero knew that this was only half or less of the normal playing time on an album side. They ultimately solved the problem of duration by repeating certain sections on each side of the album, and although this may have begun as a makeshift attempt to lengthen the music, it ended as an artistic triumph.

The first side is one long piece entitled, 'Shhh/Peaceful'. This stays in the tonality of D throughout, and the tonic is always being played by the bass, while the drums play an insistent semi-quaver rhythm on hi-hat cymbals – four beats to each crotchet, sixteen beats to the bar. Over this, organ, keyboards and guitar play little rhythmic and melodic figures. So fresh and interesting was this sound that the whole piece starts off with just that: rhythm and textures. After a while, the ensemble pauses, then starts again and Miles plays an open horn solo. This is followed by more pauses and solos by John McLaughlin and by Wayne Shorter on soprano sax.

After another pause, the early section with Miles's solo is edited in to end the side, which makes it a sort of theme for the piece. There is great delicacy and finesse in the solos, great subtlety in the keyboards (everybody is listening to everyone else), and the music is pervaded by Miles Davis's unique atmosphere of buoyant though melancholy reflection. Perhaps paradoxically, the total impression is powerful and seductive because the steady time with its occasional pauses (as if the music were actually breathing) creates the non-Western climate of timelessness – and in a sense, it is music that should be inhabited rather than merely listened to.

The second side begins with a rendition of Joe Zawinul's tune 'In a Silent Way' – the title-piece of the album. John McLaughlin recalled how this version came about:

> It was really fancy with a lot of chords – you know, a really heavy tune. We played it and Miles didn't like it. He wanted me to play it solo . . . Finally he said the first of his many cryptic statements to me, and that was, 'Play it like you don't know how to play the guitar.' I didn't know what he was talking about, I was nervous, anyway, shaking . . . here was this guy I'd idolized for I don't know how many years – a lot of years . . . Anyway, so I started playing the melody and I looked at him and he was like . . . yeah, right . . . so I carried on doing it. I didn't know they actually recorded it. That was the take. I played the melody twice, then Wayne played it, then Miles and Wayne together . . . I couldn't believe Miles's version . . . We played it on *one chord*, which is how I started it – E chord, the tune is in E – one simple, really simple chord, open strings, and he really dug it . . . He transformed it into something that was really special.[7]

This seems to be the first time that anyone has mentioned Miles Davis's 'cryptic comments', and it is significant that it was someone from a different cultural background who noticed and named them. Americans, and particularly black Americans, would perhaps be more used to the non-verbal tradition. And yet, some of the younger American musicians seemed to have difficulty relating to Davis's working methods. Chick Corea, for example, appears to have found no inspiration in the 'cryptic comments', and said:

> After I left him I had a whole reflection about my time in the band, and I told him I really wished he'd told me when it was good and when it was bad, what he wanted and didn't want, getting better, getting worse ... I think that's what real leadership is. Miles never even got close to doing that.[8]

Miles, however, knew how to inspire and direct his musicians, as these comments from the two Britishers, McLaughlin and Holland, show. First McLaughlin:

> Miles always spoke very cryptically, but at the same time you knew what he was saying was really it ... He plays and you just know, and that's what he likes. He makes you creative. He puts your creativity on the line. He'll make you do something that's you, but also in tune with what he wants. That's hard, but it's an incredible challenge that everyone should have because it makes you aware of areas you can go that you wouldn't normally get into.[9]

And Dave Holland:

> What he means is ... he's saying, 'Don't play what's there. Play what's not there' ... He's saying, 'Don't play what your fingers fall into. Don't play what you would play on an E minor 7th. Don't play that. Play something else. Don't play what you go for. Play the next thing.' He was always trying to put you in a new space where you weren't approaching the music from the same point of view all the time, or from a preconceived point of view. Usually, he would say those things just to put you in that space. It was almost like a haiku thing – or a Zen thing where the master says a couple of words and the student gets enlightened.

For the whole of the second side of *Silent Way*, Miles Davis expands the concept of 'Saeta' and 'Tout de Suite'. A theme (Zawinul's tune) is played at the beginning of the side, then the solos take place in a basically unrelated context, after which the original theme is repeated. There are no solos on Zawinul's tune 'In a Silent Way'. Miles reduced the performance to stark essentials and explained later that he had the *Kind of Blue* recording session in mind when he simplified this title track so that the melody is simply played four times over an arco bass pedal note, and shimmering sounds from the keyboards. It is all done *colla voce* – with no set pulse – and this with the droning bass and ruminative keyboards creates a hypnotic, spellbound atmosphere. This same performance is edited on to end the side after the central event, which is called 'It's About That Time'.

'It's About That Time' has a tightly controlled formal structure. Again, there is no written melody for the horns; the writing is all in the figures played by bass, drums and keyboards. The drums are confined to a steady eight quavers per bar on closed hi-hat cymbal and four crotchets per bar on snare-drum rim. This creates a clear, short, percussive beat. Over this, three sections are repeated for each soloist: the first section builds up tension with broken bass and keyboard figures (cf. 'Tout de Suite'). The bass plays three consecutive semi-quavers per bar, the third one falling on any one of the crotchets in the bar, and the keyboards play either with this figure or against it. In the next section the tension is slightly eased by the keyboards playing repeated legato descending chords in a three-bar cycle. The third section provides further release of tension with a flowing, unbroken, two-bar bass riff. There are three solos over this structure – by guitarist John McLaughlin, by Wayne Shorter on soprano, and finally by Miles himself.

In fact, the piece starts with a brief, almost perfunctory solo by Miles which sets up the atmosphere. The rest of the performance is a gradual build-up to Miles's main solo, which occurs at the end. The ensemble is held back on a tight rein during the delicate and thoughtful guitar solo. The more active soprano increases the tension, but even during the marvellously buoyant third section of the structure with the flowing, two-bar riff, the drums do not respond but stick to the mechanical, skeletal beat. Our expectations are aroused, but remain unsatisfied. Then, Miles's solo begins over the broken bass figure, and at last, when the two-bar bass riff is played, the drums break out and play a wild accompaniment to the trumpet. This is a totally satisfying climax to the piece, and adds another dimension to the album, which has been controlled and understated up to this point.

Though the various elements of the piece are simple, they are used to create extremely subtle and sophisticated music. Once again, Miles Davis has reduced his ideas to the bare essentials and then extracted the maximum amount of music from them. 'It's About That Time' is in the tonality of F, and once again, it is like a gigantic abstraction from the old blues in F, even to the extent of having a three-part structure; the 'call', then the repeat of the 'call', and then (the two-bar bass riff) the response. Although the piece is in F, there is always the suggestion of polytonality, and the soloist is free to use any notes he wishes. Although the bass and drums have fairly static roles, in fact, as one reviewer noted, the mere time-keeping of Tony Williams on this piece and on the first side of the album, is so fine and subtle as to make his cymbal work a star part of the whole performance. And the steady pulse set up by bass and drums contrasts brilliantly with the restless movement of the keyboards.

The homogeneity of the imagination of the eight men involved in this music is extraordinary. The economy is sustained, no one over-plays, and every note is made to tell. Once again, Miles Davis had come up with something fresh, and he had done so not by turning his back on the jazz tradition, but by finding new ways of expressing some of its basic elements. By confining the role of the drums, he had rescued the pulse from abstraction, and by having three keyboards and guitar all improvising figures, he had reworked the traditional New Orleans jazz idea of collective improvisation behind a leading solo/melody voice. Miles was also finding new ways of reconciling several of the contrary elements in his musical experience: precomposition with improvisation; freedom with control; the static and the dynamic; the blues vocabulary with harmonic abstraction; the small group with the larger ensemble. At the age of forty-two, he was once more in the middle of a brilliantly creative period. And only six months after recording this landmark, Miles would again go into the studio to invade yet more new territory on a double-album called *Bitches Brew*.

Miles knew exactly how important an achievement *Silent Way* was. He rarely enthused about his own albums, but almost as soon as the sessions for *Silent Way* were over, he was excitedly telling people about the album. He even telephoned Joe Zawinul to say how marvellous he thought it was. And he was so pleased with the multiple keyboard sound that he tried, unsuccessfully, to persuade Herbie Hancock to return permanently to team up with Corea. To one journalist, in March, Miles enthused about the album and the three keyboard players, saying, 'They sound like a full orchestra, and we wrote some things with a rock beat.'[10] And another journalist who interviewed Davis at the end of February – only a few days after the recording session – reported: 'He's high on a new record album the group cut for Columbia.'[11]

FOURTEEN

Miles Runs the Voodoo Down

'Hell, if you understand everything I said,
you'd be me.'[1]

Miles Davis

Filles de Kilimanjaro was the last album on which Gil Evans worked with Miles, and the two men were not to attempt to collaborate again until the late 1970s. Although it introduced many new ideas, *Filles* still harked back in some ways to the quintet music of the earlier 1960s – largely because the group was a five-piece unit. *Silent Way*, with its three keyboards and varied textures, presented a new sound, and immediately after recording it Miles Davis seemed exhilarated. From this point on, he was very much on his own and didn't appear to need the consultations with Gil Evans. It is significant that, on the sleeves of *Filles, Silent Way* and the following album, *Bitches Brew*, was printed in small letters: *Directions in Music by Miles Davis*. He had found new musical perspectives, and acquired a clearer idea of his own position in the music scene. He criticized certain aspects of rock music, saying, for example: 'Those cats haven't done much yet. It's very easy to take a riff and vamp for three minutes, but when they get out there to solo, they ain't got nothing to say.'[2] But at the same time, he saw vital connections between rock and jazz, and expressed the opinion that rock wouldn't fade away, 'because, like jazz, it's folk music'.[3]

Miles also fell in love with the trumpet all over again at this time, and his need to play was very great. To one journalist he stated that it would be enough, financially, for him to play only six months a year, because anything over that went entirely in taxes to the government, but nevertheless, he kept on performing because, 'I just dig playing the trumpet . . . The trumpet is a sacred instrument.'[4] And even in this, the pattern of the earlier great period (1958–61) was repeating itself in that, after the exquisite expression of the understated, reflective side of his nature (*Kind of Blue* and *Silent Way*) there was to be a period of phenomenal trumpet playing. Even the way Miles described his ideas in the earlier period is mirrored closely in the later one. In 1958 (Chapter 9), when he discovered the subtleties of modal/scalar improvisation, he said: 'There will be fewer chords but infinite possibilities as to what to do with them . . . You go this way, you can go on for ever.'[5] And in 1970, he says: 'With a C going on in the bass, you can play anything against it . . . Then we can go on for hours.'[6]

His renewed vision had had its germ in *Miles in the Sky*, and had been steadily increasing in intensity since then. It resulted in great energy and optimism. Dave Holland said that his time with the band (1968–70) seems to have been a special period in many ways. Miles was always in a positive frame of mind and did not miss a single engagement; also, he put out warm feelings to all the musicians who worked with him during that period. Holland added: 'It seemed like he was very healthy . . . There were no drugs. He ate no meat. He kept off the booze. We were all very much into health things . . . It was, like, the cleanest band in America.'

Always obsessive about exercise, Miles was now becoming equally fanatical about what he ate. As well as his personal manager, Harold Lovett, who usually accompanied him on tours, Miles now also had a trainer called Bobby Allah who always travelled with him. Allah was an ex-boxer who, according to Miles, had shown Muhammad Ali the punch with which he had knocked out Sonny Liston. Davis was still deeply interested in boxing, and was proud of his son Gregory, who had won four boxing titles when he was in the army during the 1960s. In March 1970, Bobby Allah told *Newsweek*:

I'd like to have had Miles as a fighter when he was twenty. Even at forty-three he acts like twenty-five. He's quick, he's got the reflexes – and the imagination, like a chess player seeing the moves ahead. People come in here who don't recognize him and ask me who my new fighter is.[7]

Allah, a Muslim, was a very gentle person who persuaded Miles to be more careful about his diet. The two men seem to have met during the period of recuperation after Miles's illness of the mid-1960s, and Allah not only managed to stop the trumpeter eating chilli and spaghetti and drinking things like tequila, but also went to the gym almost every day and worked out with him. In 1968, when the quintet was in West Germany, Miles said that because they couldn't find an accessible gym, the Olympic stadium was opened so that he and Allah could work out.

In February 1969, Miles Davis weighed one hundred and thirty-five pounds and was eating only one meal a day. In July of the same year, he described his eating habits as follows:

I just got through eating a soybean salad and vegetable broth. But I don't call it a dict. I just don't eat any meat. I don't even eat fish. I've been off meat for about four months, but even before that I didn't eat meat very much; I used to fix all kinds of Mexican dishes and Italian dishes – chilli and stuff. Sometimes I eat all fruit. When I go to the gym I drink some vegetable broth and have fruit salad with wheat germ on it, and that's enough for me. If I can go all night without eating, that's great, because I feel light in the morning and I can do more. And actually, it makes you stronger. I figure if horses can eat green shit and be strong and run like mother-fuckers, why shouldn't I?[8]

During that year, Miles gave many interviews to the press, and in all of them he seems to be bubbling over with high spirits. Several of the interviews concentrate on his boxing and its relationship to his trumpet playing; and 1969 culminated in a massive feature article on him in *Rolling Stone*. His photograph was on the front cover of the magazine, and of the four photos of him inside, three were of him sparring or working out in vest and shorts. One journalist reported:

> Miles Davis danced lightly on the balls of his feet, his lithe body swaying rhythmically to and fro as he shot punches in rapid-fire combinations – 'Uhn, uhn, uhn, uhn, uhn. You see, man, he comes in here and I shift this way and get him there, uhn, and there, uhn, uhn. When I'm sharp I can just drop a guy ... like this!! Uhn, uhn ... I do ten rounds a day ... like today. I did four rounds in the ring ... just moving all round the ring. Then I boxed two rounds with a friend. Then I worked with the floor bag. Forty sit-ups, five of these, five of these, five of these and ten of these ... !'[9]

Miles also described the direct relationship between physical fitness and trumpet playing:

> Playing trumpet is hard work. You have to feel strong. I play a lot of notes and sometimes have to hold a note for eighteen bars on one breath, which is tough on the lungs, stomach and legs. But my workouts help my breath control and I can play in spots that no one else can. It's not the note you play, it's what you do with it. And it takes strength to bend notes and to keep from breaking phrases in fast tempos. If you breathe in between, you lose what you're trying to do.[10]

After the recording of *In a Silent Way*, there began a period of trumpet playing in which Miles revealed more breath control, more power, more sustained use of the highest register, longer melodic lines and more audacious rhythms than ever before. His playing in some of the live sessions of the following two years or so borders on the superhuman. In 1969, there were still no implications of rock in the live performances; the pulse was still jazz-based, and the continuous sets still featured harmonic abstraction though the polyrhythms were often very powerful. The sets had definite changes of mood and thematic material, but the over-all control was centred in Miles's trumpet playing. It was this that directed the music. Only musicians of exceptional talent and sensitivity could function under such demanding conditions. Miles said: 'The trick is to surround yourself with musicians who don't play the regular run-of-the-mill clichés. I don't have trouble getting them, but I don't think it's me who attracts them. They just like playing together'.[11] But even to his outstanding musicians, Miles's control seemed magical and inexplicable. Dave Holland said:

> He would always come in and change direction at a certain point – take it into a new place – just by a few notes, and everybody would respond because everybody was waiting for that. It's that kind of alertness that he creates in his musicians that I think makes the music so exciting. As soon as he walks into a room, everybody sits up straight . . . Each tune, there'd be a characteristic phrase Miles would play and we would all know immediately that it would go to that area. So it was this edge that he put you on all the time . . . As soon as you heard him play – What's happening? Where's it going? And the music changes straight away. And it seemed like magic to a lot of people. It seemed like magic to me.

This presence, which is felt by all musicians working with Miles Davis, and which communicates intuitive musical directions, is inexplicable. It seems unlikely that he even understood it himself. During 1969 and 1970, he made great efforts to describe to curious journalists how he achieved his music, but nothing is really explained. The cellist and composer, Paul Buckmaster, has said that a mere glance from Miles Davis makes a musician play in a certain way: 'I noticed that he would just look at somebody and something would happen. The mastery that he has is that he is aware all the time of every note and every beat . . . every minute thing that's happening.'

It was only after the move towards greater abstraction that

Miles's telepathic control of the music came into full play. Within the more formal structures of his pre-1967 music it was less necessary and therefore less obvious. After the old structures (harmonies and chorus-lengths) were abandoned, an almost extrasensory perception was needed to hold the music together and give it direction. Although there is much editing on *Bitches Brew*, the music arose largely from this telepathic playing situation with the fairly large ensemble functioning, under Miles's direction, with the flexibility of a small group. *Bitches Brew* starts, as it were, where *Silent Way* left off, and is altogether more complex, more abstract, freer and yet funkier, than the earlier album. It comes out of the fundamental paradox of Miles's aspirations at this time, which were described by Tony Williams: 'He's trying to get further out (more abstract) and yet more basic (funkier) at the same time.'[12]

Once again, the choice of instruments for this recording is absolutely crucial to the music. With most jazz musicians, no matter how many instruments they add to or subtract from their groups, the music remains similar. With Miles Davis, the number and the kind of musicians have a profound effect on the identity of the music. By July 1969, Tony Williams had left, and Jack DeJohnette had joined the group on drums. One reviewer commented: 'Holland and DeJohnette don't often set up the stop-and-go interludes of Carter and Williams. Instead, they burn straight ahead, creating a deep, luxurious groove for the soloists.'[13] Dave Holland felt a greater affinity with DeJohnette than he had with Tony Williams. He said:

I had a very frustrating time with Tony, because I hadn't been able to make the kind of musical contact that I would like to make with a drummer when I play with him. Tony was a sort of immovable object to me: he had his place where he played and I was either to play with him, or on my own. But . . . I never felt that he came over to my space too much. When Jack came in the band, a whole new feeling happened for me because I had played with Jack before and I'd felt this affinity with him; so when he came into the band, the whole feeling of the music changed for me.

For *Bitches Brew*, Miles added to his quintet two more drummers, a percussionist, bass guitar, bass clarinet, guitar, and two electric keyboards. Again, Wayne Shorter played only soprano sax. With this huge textural palette, Miles was at last following up some of the ideas first touched on in *Sketches of Spain*, and indeed, one of the pieces on the August 1969 sessions was actually called 'Spanish Key'. The strength of this large ensemble lay in the fact that at least one drummer and the bass guitarist would always be stating a basic pulse when that was necessary – some of the sections are *colla voce* – which left the other drummers and the percussionist free to create polyrhythms and textures. The keyboards and guitar could function much as they had done on *Silent Way*, but here they have much greater freedom of activity and expression. The most brilliant touch of all, and the ingredient that gives the album much of its particular flavour, is the deployment of the bass clarinet, which spends much of the time playing along with the keyboards – not soloing, but creating dark, brooding textures. With so many musicians in the studio and so many electronic instruments, it was essential for Miles to be able to hear himself clearly without having to over-blow, so Teo Macero amplified the trumpet, putting a speaker directly in front of Miles.

It is not only in the denser textures that *Bitches Brew* differs from *Silent Way*. The latter album had been tightly controlled, and pervaded by the more urbane side of Miles's introspective self. There had been just one moment of dynamic explosion on the whole album, and this was fitting: *Silent Way*, within the limits of its rather narrow emotional range, is artistically flawless. But the emotional and artistic scope of *Bitches Brew* is altogether broader than that of the earlier album, and there is a perceptible deepening of the vision. There are dark undertones in many parts of the music, which is full of dynamically exploding passages. It was in 1967 that the idea of Miles as the 'Prince of Darkness' had first arisen. That was the title of a piece on *Sorcerer*, and the sleeve note made a direct connection between Miles and the album title. This idea and this feeling were not at all present in the music of *Silent Way*, but now with *Bitches Brew* a more ominous note enters the music. At times, it seems to relate to certain elements in ethnic music; there is a strong feeling of invocation, of seeking for the state of possession – which is closely connected with the rapt state of inspired improvisation. But the actual intensity of the performances on these sessions, the almost demonic power of the group's improvisations, were perhaps sparked off by some happenings in the studio.

The first session for the album was prefaced by an almighty row between Miles and Teo Macero, and the latter said:

I think *Bitches Brew* came out of a bitter battle that Miles and I had in the studio over my secretary. He wanted me to fire her, and I said absolutely under no condition would I do so. I told him, 'You're not my boss and I'm not going to take your bullshit any longer. I don't give a goddam whether you like her or not. If you can't get along with her, you don't have to talk to her, you have to talk to me.' And he kept on and on and on and on, until the point where he and I almost had a fistfight in the studio. And told him, I says, 'Take you and your fucking trumpet' (these were my exact words) 'and your fucking musicians, and get outa here! I want you out of this building! Get your ass outa here!' . . . I turned black and he turned white! And he was, like, coming at me, and I said, 'You sonofabitch, I'm coming over there!' And they were hauling him back . . . It was like something out of a movie. There were several people sitting around and everybody was dumbfounded. Then finally, Miles came over [they were in the control room] and he pushed the key down [intercom to the studio] and says, 'I want you to know what the fuck Teo said about you motherfucker musicians – Get the fuck outa here . . . He doesn't want you.' I says, 'Well, take your goddam trumpet and go!' He took his trumpet, and as he started to go out of the door he made a left turn. He went into the studio, took out his trumpet, and I said, 'Put the machines on.' At that point I could have said. 'Everybody out! – Home!' Right? But I wasn't about to be that stupid, because . . . you know, it was like having a good fight with your wife . . . but you didn't really mean it . . . you'd probably been tired and he just edged you up . . . He went out there . . . and from then on during that whole session, he kept saying, 'Come on out! Come on out! I'm going to get you! I'm going to kill you!' So I pushed the key [intercom] and I says, 'You make me sick! If I come out, I'm going to throw up all over you! You're a miserable bastard, that's what you are!' He made another take in there, then finally he kept motioning to me, right? With his hand, like, 'Come out motherfucker!' So I said, 'I'll go out.' I went out, stood right next to him, and didn't move. And he made all those fantastic tracks. This is not the first time I've done this . . . just about the whole album in two sessions . . . it was just one thing after another . . . bam, bam, bam, bam. I said, 'You sonofabitch, you should be this way all the time – mean and miserable!'

This elaborate charade may well have been Miles Davis's way of getting the adrenaline flowing. (But this interchange was not merely a charade; Miles was, perhaps, wilfully stirring things up in order to invoke the dynamism necessary for his best performances.) In a way, it was yet another variation on the old Charlie Parker trick of doing the unexpected and the outrageous, which shocks everyone else and oneself, dislocating habitual thought patterns and releasing a lot of creative energy. In the clinical environment of the recording studio such ploys are often necessary. At the same time, certain aspects of Miles's relationship with Teo Macero seem to have been almost ritualistic. Herbie Hancock said of Teo: 'He's a really nice guy. But when we're recording, sometimes Miles calls him all kinds of names . . . all these racial slurs and things. That was Miles's way – he doesn't mean any of that stuff . . . he just kind of says it – 'cause it's dynamic and strong.' But clearly, Macero understands Davis very well, because he too pushed the charade to the limit – to the point where Miles might very well have walked out of the studio and gone home. It was a legitimate risk and a fruitful one: Miles stayed and played, and the music is often very powerful indeed.

Despite their ups and downs over the years, Miles Davis certainly trusts Teo Macero. The latter once said of their relationship, 'It's like a marriage!' And the stormy beginning to *Bitches Brew* was something of a freak event. Normally things were much quieter and calmer in the studio, and hardly a word would be exchanged during the sessions. From time to time, Miles might call Macero to one side, because, as Macero said, 'He never talks in front of anybody.' The two might sit together for ten minutes without a word being exchanged, then Miles would ask Macero what he thought of the take. After a brief discussion, they'd sit on in silence for a few more minutes, then Miles would go back into the studio and probably produce some definitive music.

Bitches Brew is a double-album with a total playing time of just over ninety-three minutes. In general, the music is abstract and chromatic, but there is often a powerful rock beat. The old idea of a string of solos has been completely jettisoned now and the basic elements are Miles's trumpet and the whole of the rest of the ensemble. The main drama and interest lie in how these two factors (Miles and the ensemble) interact. If there is another solo by, say, soprano or bass clarinet, it is usually more a colour on the ensemble texture than a solo per se. Miles dominates the proceedings throughout.

The first track, 'Pharaoh's Dance', provides some continuity with *Silent Way*, because it opens with a brisk, shallow beat and some textures from keyboards and guitar. Only the low doodling of the bass clarinet hints at more ominous areas of experience. The ensemble pauses, then starts again, and Miles plays a few phrases and then stops. The ensemble plays on. Miles enters again, producing insistent little phrases using the same few notes. The ensemble responds. The roots hover around B and E, but there is strong chromaticism and polytonality; Miles uses other keys and scales. Once more, he stops while the ensemble plays on with the bass clarinet acting as a sort of leader of the responses. After an interlude in which the keyboards dominate, Miles plays some sparse phrases with pronounced echo, and the ensemble activates much more. Miles is again tacit while the bass clarinet and the ensemble interact. The soprano enters, taking over the role of leader of the responses (to Miles). The ensemble activity subsides a little, while drums and percussion play a more solid rock feel. Miles plays again, with a huge sound and much echo (reverb), slow phrases over a boiling and bubbling ensemble that threatens to engulf him. Then it simmers down and he repeats the sparse phrases he'd played at the beginning, only this time over a deeply rocking groove. This pattern is typical of most of the double-album. It is yet another variant on the old 'call-and-response' ritual, with Miles doing the calling and the entire ensemble responding. He plays a lot of trumpet, both in terms of actual duration, and in terms of how much he says. He is bursting with fresh ideas, and in each piece he plays several times, developing and extending his phrases, and inciting the ensemble into new areas of exploration.

Only two pieces on the album are not composed by Miles. 'Pharaoh's Dance' by Joe Zawinul, and 'Sanctuary' by Wayne Shorter. But in fact, both of these were virtually recomposed by Davis to fit in with his new conceptions. Dave Holland said that, in his experience, Miles never played anyone's tune the way it was written, but always moulded the material towards his musical concept. 'Sanctuary' was originally a very straight piece in 3/4 with a definite tempo and specific chord changes, but it ended up being mostly out-of-time and over a drone (sustained pedal note).

The title piece, 'Bitches Brew', harks back to 'Saeta' on *Sketches of Spain* in that it begins with some out-of-time 'muezzin' calls by Miles. After each powerful trumpet 'call' the keyboards, basses and percussion improvise *colla voce* responses. Either Davis is using an Echoplex in the studio, or else his sound is being treated with flutter echo, because his phrases re-echo, seeming to ricochet round the room. His 'chops' are obviously in magnificent shape, because not only does he bend and squeeze notes upwards, but he also plays some sustained and strong high Fs. This whole section, with its soaring and 'preaching' trumpet and raggedly rolling responses, has an eerie, hypnotic atmosphere. It is wilder and deeper than 'Saeta', and its trancelike quality takes it nearer to the archetypal priest/congregation relationship. After this, Miles snaps his fingers to bring in the bass riff, and is clearly cuing in the rest of the instruments. At one point during the rest of the performance, he can be heard calling to John McLaughlin to play, and at times one gets the impression that the musicians are not sure what is expected of them. But this track is a good example of Miles at work, creating music on the spot, and he himself plays magnificently throughout.

With the second record of this double-album, the rock beat becomes much more pronounced. 'Spanish Key' has a fairly heavy offbeat (or backbeat) on the drums, and the rhythm section produces an inspired 'boogaloo', gaining impetus as the piece progresses. Here again, there is much trumpet work, and a continually shifting point of view and emphasis. Also, there is a series of tonal centres, which occur on cue – D-G-E-A – but the harmonic freedom in each area is very great indeed.

With 'Miles Runs the Voodoo Down', we have, once more, the key of F and an abstraction from the blues, so this can be compared with 'It's About That Time' on *Silent Way*. The basic material on 'Voodoo' is even more skeletal than that of the earlier piece. Now the tonality, a simple bass riff and a slow pulse are enough for Miles and the ensemble to create fourteen minutes of compelling music. The slow, totally coherent beat is filled out and broadened by congas, and the bass clarinet's sinister brooding is deployed to greatest effect. The atmosphere of invocation, of ritual dances and of possession, is sustained brilliantly throughout. 'It's About That Time' is memorable as much for the pre-composed sections as for the solos, but in 'Voodoo', the music is virtually all created by the ebb and flow of the improvising ensemble under the spell of Miles's phenomenal trumpet playing. Form and content are one and the same thing.

Once the slow, ominous pulse is set up, Miles plays some phrases in the middle register that yet again alternate major and minor 3rds, thus implying the whole blues tradition. His tone is more vocalized than ever – a human, crying sound. After this quiet start, he develops his ideas with swooping phrases that alternately use the blues scale and then chromaticism. He makes some death-defying forays into the upper register, and his playing is alive with slurs, smears, spaces, screams, long lines, short tense phrases. It is trumpet playing at a fantastic level, not least for the blazing feeling he seems barely able to control. After his first solo, the ensemble bubbles along relieving the tension a little, and then the soprano plays a hot, hoarse-toned, bluesy solo with the bass clarinet noodling darkly underneath. After some time, the trumpet plays again with falling broad and bent phrases in the middle register. Then suddenly, Miles digs in rhythmically, the ensemble responds immediately with a harder drive and more activity, and the trumpet screams and trills. Then Miles goes back to brooding with more space, quiet phrases, and long, low notes. The ensemble winds down and almost stops, but Miles raises it up again by whipping up the tension with repeated short stabbing notes and displaced accents, until he finally releases the tension with a long, loping phrase to the lower register. The ensemble then simmers down and halts. It is the end of the brew. 'Miles Runs the Voodoo Down' is the most accomplished performance on the album. The following year, it was put out by CBS as a double-sided single, and actually got played on jukeboxes around New York.

Not all the musicians on those sessions understood immediately what was happening musically, and several made sense of the experience only sometime afterwards. John McLaughlin said years later:

The moment where I began to feel that something really extraordinary was happening – that something was really breaking open, was *Bitches Brew*. But the thing about Miles is that everybody loves him, and so everybody had this very powerful motivation to do something to make him happy. Everybody would be in a big circle in the studio, but nobody really knew what he was looking for. I don't think even Miles knew what he was looking for, but he had an idea, as he always has had, and he, like everybody else, was just experimenting with other ways of perceiving music, which of course is his unique approach – this knack of pulling things out of musicians that they might not normally be aware of. He certainly did that to me, pulled out things that I was unaware of in my own self, and that takes quite a perception. His uncanny knack of making cryptic requests would confuse us, and I think he did that intentionally, only to find something that was going on underneath the surface.

Joe Zawinul had a slightly different view of the proceedings:

When we left the studio after [recording] *Bitches Brew*, I said, 'I don't like that stuff at all, Miles.' And he was very disappointed. 'I just don't like it,' I said, 'it's too much noodling around, you know.' And then, much later on, I go to CBS and the lady working there was playing this incredible music in her office. I said, 'What the hell is this?' She said, 'What do you mean, what the hell is this? This is you and Miles and John and everybody on *Bitches Brew*.' And the way it was put together then, it was really, really nice, you know.

FIFTEEN

Jazz into Rock Will Go

'Now you can get black people who've been
conditioned by white teachers so that they can't think
and they just know straight music – they don't know
anything about no freedom in music.'[1]

Miles Davis

Even after the recording of *Bitches Brew*, there were still no real
implications of rock in the live performances by Miles Davis's
working group, which was a quintet comprising Wayne Shorter,
Chick Corea, Dave Holland and Jack DeJohnette. In September,
Miles was top of the bill at the Monterey Jazz Festival, but drew
only mild applause and some booing after a superb performance.
The greatest ovations of the weekend went to the French violinist,
Jean-Luc Ponty and the Buddy Rich Orchestra; two artists who
were still playing jazz rooted in diatonic harmony, with clearly
recognizable melodic lines and obvious rhythms. Leonard Feather
remarked:

All this, ironically, took place among an audience that was
anywhere from fifty per cent to seventy-five per cent black
. . . The thrust at every festival until recently was toward the
presentation of music as music. If the events of 1969 can be
taken as a yardstick, that era is now ended . . . the audience
have been radically changed by the inclusion of rock acts in
what were purportedly jazz concerts. The crowds at Monterey last month were representative of the trend. Music per

se has become gradually less relevant year by year while the being there, the act of making a scene, has taken precedence. During the last three or four years at Monterey a tradition has arisen for the audience to become the show.[2]

Despite its clear rhythmic grooves, *Bitches Brew* was not by any means an 'easy-listening' album; the music is demanding and abstract. But in live performances during the latter half of 1969, the group's music was even less accessible to listeners because there were no rock rhythms to offset the harmonic and linear abstraction. Although they were still working with some of the musical areas from both *Filles de Kilimanjaro* and *Bitches Brew*, these were treated so radically as to lose all relationship with the original recorded performances. The energy level of the band was high, everyone was bursting to play, and when Miles had finished his solo, the rhythm section as an entity usually ignored the piece completely, playing an open improvisation until Miles brought everything back under control. The trumpeter was giving his musicians as much freedom as possible within the confines of his conception. Dave Holland described how this happened:

> He would sometimes come on in the middle of something that I felt shouldn't have been interrupted. Sometimes he'd come in at a peak of some kind and, with a couple of notes, would bring it right down again. But the drama in that kind of thing was something else which I might not have understood in the heat of the moment; but he did, and I heard that later. His understanding of the music was often very much more objective than mine . . . The harmony we were dealing with was chromatic harmony where there were no notes which didn't work with any other notes . . . Miles was able to set the music up so that there was complete space harmonically, and you could go in whatever way you wanted.

But the trouble was that Miles's music was too far out for the old jazz audience, who were, as usual, extremely conservative and reactionary in their tastes; and at the same time, his live perform-ances did not have the rhythmic coherence that would gain him an audience among rock enthusiasts. He was thus losing the old jazz audience, but not yet gaining a new one. In particular, he was not gaining one among blacks. The band's image had changed radically by mid-1969, and everyone was wearing the casual and colourful gear associated with the rock scene. Miles had forsaken his sober suits and was now sporting leather or snakeskin pants, elaborate belts, brightly coloured scarves and shirts, and leather waistcoats with trailing thongs.

Just as in 1955 and 1963, when Miles and his groups were full of fresh ideas and creative vitality, he had wanted as many book-ings as possible, so now, having mapped out whole new areas of interest with *Silent Way* and *Bitches Brew*, he wanted his band to play as many gigs as possible. At his request, Jack Whittemore booked a whole tour of the West Coast, which included the Mon-terey Jazz Festival mentioned above, and Shelly Manne's Manne Hole in Los Angeles. Although he played festivals and occasionally concert halls, Miles was still playing mostly in jazz clubs. At Shelly's Manne Hole, in September 1969, another bizarre charade (far more elaborate than the one over Teo Macero's secretary during the recording of *Bitches Brew*) played itself out in more or less full view of the audience. Miles never liked his musicians to bring their wives or girlfriends on tour because he felt their women distracted them from the job of playing his music. But he often brought his own girlfriends with him, and this caused some bad feeling in the group. Jack DeJohnette's English wife, Lydia, was heavily pregnant with their first child and the birth was due in October. She was just twenty-three years old, knew no one in New York and she was nervous about being left there alone. DeJohnette decided that Lydia must go on the tour with him, and after protracted arguments and threats from DeJohnette not to come on the tour, Miles finally said, 'Well, bring her with you and I'll pay her fare, if it makes you happy. And if she has the baby on the road, you can at least be with her.' Lydia DeJohnette takes up the story:

It wasn't done out of generosity, it was done because he wanted Jack there. He was a game player. We decided to do that because we needed the money and we didn't want to be apart. So I went on the tour and the first gig was somewhere in the Midwest. I was very pregnant and I knew that bothered Miles, too; the whole pregnancy thing made him uncomfortable. He had one of his girlfriends, Jackie Battle, with him, one of his more serious ladies and very strong. On the plane, Miles was irritable. I was with Jack and the other musicians in the economy section of the plane, and when they started playing some rhythms and some music, Miles sent a message back saying, 'Stop that shit!' We arrived at the hotel and Jack got a phone call from Whittemore saying that Miles didn't want Lydia to come to the gig. The irony was that I hadn't intended going to the gig. Jack exploded because it was the same bullshit of game playing and said, 'I quit!' (his usual response). 'Leave my personal life out of it! It has nothing to do with you.' The phone calls flew back and forth. But I never made a habit of going to the gigs – I could sense Miles's vibrations and I wouldn't go near him unless he came to me. I felt he was competing with the women for these musicians. The musicians were *his* first, and their wives and girlfriends were secondary.

The tour ended up in California at Shelly's Manne Hole, and I went to the club on one of the nights. Because it was so crowded, I sat, not in the audience, but by the bar in the neutral area where the waitresses were. Miles came over and sat with me and talked to me, brought me some tea, talked about my taking care of myself – a very comfortable conversation, quite pleasant. And then he went into his bandroom and a couple of women went along that he didn't like – he was very intuitive and knew if someone was coming for the wrong reasons. Then these women came and sat next to me because I knew them and they were friends of the band, and suddenly we got a message from Shelly Manne saying that the band wasn't going to play if Lydia was sitting where she

was sitting. Jack exploded, 'You are *not* moving. You're not
in anybody's way, you're not in his way, you're not in the
band's way! Fuck him! I'm sick of this shit!' The rest of the
band were laughing. Shelly Manne was dying – he had a club
full of people and lines of people round the block outside
and Miles was refusing to play. Next thing is that Miles goes
and sits himself in the audience . . . 'The band doesn't go on
until my drummer's wife moves.' And I am not in the audience or the dressing room, I'm in this totally neutral area.
Jack is now saying to me, 'I've had it! You're not moving!
The hell with him!'

But Shelly was begging me to move, and he's such a nice
man and I felt so sorry for him. So I got up and went and
Shelly actually cleared a table for me in the audience and the
two women came and sat with me and I stayed there. And
anything I wanted Shelly brought me – champagne, anything
. . . and the band went on and played. Miles used to love to
fire up the drummers, so the concert at Shelly's place was
great because Jack was furious with him. The next day Miles
is calling up Jack saying, 'Oh man, don't take it seriously, you
know how fucked up I am! You know I've got shit with
women!' What we learned later was that Jackie Battle had left.
She and Miles had been fighting over this whole incident, and
she was so angry with him that she went back to New York.

At Shelly's Manne Hole, the band was playing three or four
sets and, according to another witness, they played a coherent
rhythm for Miles, but went wildly free after he'd finished his
solos. When one of his musicians was asked about this curious
dichotomy, he said, 'Miles hasn't found his freedom yet.' Which
suggests that there was a certain amount of internal tension in the
group; a disagreement about its direction. Miles himself made an
attempt to describe his own interests and intentions at this time:

In my group we play a lot of polyrhythms and everything,
you know, a lot of different keys off keys and scales off scales

... A lot of what we have in the group has been developed in clubs. I love the possibility of just freaking off on your horn in a night club. In Shelly's I really found out something. Actually it was a learning period in there, when I played everything and made the band play everything they could possibly play. That's what's good about working in clubs. You play a first set, OK; a second set, OK; third set, OK – and they're playing what they know, right? Then the last set they start playing what they don't know; which is out of sight! They start thinking, which is worth all the money in the world to me. Thrills me.[3]

But despite the poor reception at some concerts, there were signs in the latter part of 1969 that Miles was going to break through to a new audience. *In a Silent Way* was released in September and received a huge amount of press coverage, all of it favourable, most of it ecstatic. The album seemed to point in an alternative direction to the two-horned dilemma: back to conventional jazz on the one hand, or far-out with the avant-garde on the other. There was a general sigh of relief that Miles Davis had found a fresh approach that was neither a retrograde step nor anything like the established avant-garde.

Silent Way also received much acclaim from rock journalists and was hailed as something that, while being full of subtlety and art, could appeal directly to rock audiences. One writer pointed out that it had a double function in that it could be listened to intently and repaid repeated hearings, or on the other hand, like much rock music, it could be used as pleasant background music. After some years of declining press interest, Miles Davis was now regularly making headlines again, and at the end of 1969, he swept the board in the *Down Beat* readers' poll, winning first place on trumpet, first for small group, Jazz Album of the Year (*Filles de Kilimanjaro*; *Silent Way* was third), and being voted Jazzman of the Year. He was 2,000 votes ahead of Dizzy Gillespie in the trumpet poll, and 1,200 votes ahead of Elvin Jones in the small-group category. But even these victories and their huge margins were most probably insignificant when set beside the coverage *Rolling Stone* gave him in December. This enormous feature article, reviewing his whole career and quoting his views on the current American scene at length, combined with his photograph on the front cover, established Miles once again as a member of the contemporary American music scene.

In October 1969, Miles and the group went to Europe and appeared on the British Jazz Expo bill in London. They created music at an extraordinarily brilliant level of intensity, but the rhythmic feeling was the freely rolling wash of sound more associated with the 1960s jazz avant-garde than with rock, and they offered long sets of continuous music. The musical transitions seemed magically achieved, and some people wondered if there were visual signals, such as when Miles rested his trumpet on his shoulder, or raised it above his head, but this was not the case. The cues were all musical and Miles's playing was awesome (in the full sense of the word) that night, but the Hammersmith Odeon was only at seventy-five per cent capacity, and the audience gave him only a lukewarm reception. Many people were seen to walk out.

Early in 1970, Miles and the group played at a Columbia business convention in the Bahamas, and Clive Davis, announcing the group, made a speech describing how he had invited Miles to his office one day to discuss the trumpeter's career. The gist of it was that, in looking at the record sales and so on, they decided the music needed to reach a younger audience and a larger one, and that Miles had come up with these new musical ideas. Clive Davis was glad to say that the campaign had proved successful. The implication was that the president of Columbia Records had initiated the change in the music. Clive Davis, of course, had no musical influence on Miles whatsoever, but had been instrumental in getting the record company to promote the trumpeter as strongly as they did their rock groups. He was also responsible for persuading Miles to appear at big rock concert stadia that exposed his music to thousands instead of only hundreds per night. Both Clive Davis and Columbia promoted Miles brilliantly in

1970, and it is to the record company's great credit that they succeeded in widening the audience for the trumpeter's difficult music.

Teo Macero flatly denies that Clive Davis had any influence on the actual music.

> Clive was talking about *Bitches Brew*, which was recorded in 1969. Well, there were other things that were done long before that: 1965, 1967, 1968 . . . which all preceded *Bitches Brew*. There was a whole lot in there of which I never released anything. And that was because we were groping ourselves. This was the introduction of the electric piano. Clive, I think, takes credit for it . . . but go back and you'll see the source, and you'll see it in the music.

It had been Macero's job, as producer of Miles's albums, to make sure that all the latest recording techniques were at his disposal. In addition, he kept Miles informed about any new equipment or electronic gear. The motives and forces which lay behind Miles's many musical changes had always been multiple and complex, but at the centre there was always a basic logic that was essentially to do with music. His consistency had been unique; all the strands and themes postulated in his early period up to about 1950, and the later ones up to, say, 1960, had been explored, developed, taken to their ultimate conclusion – and some had even been taken to the point of disintegration.

The year 1970 was a momentous and turbulent one for Miles. By the end of it, only Jack DeJohnette remained from the old group. Around the beginning of the year Miles and Betty were divorced but stayed on friendly terms. There were always several girls in Miles's life, though usually he seemed to have an extra-close relationship with one in particular. Jackie Battle was one of his favourites, but in the autumn of 1969, he had another young regular companion, Marguerite Eskridge, who even travelled to Europe with him. Dave Holland said of her:

There was a very special lady who was having a baby of his, but I don't know if it was born or not. She was a very beautiful lady. She was like the Mona Lisa; she had a smile on her face the whole time ... she was sort of Indian-looking ... very beautiful and very peaceful, and Miles, I know, got a lot of peace from this lady because he told me that a couple of times.

Marguerite Eskridge was to give birth to Miles's youngest son, Erin, and would stay with Miles for about four years.

Throughout 1970, Miles Davis revealed an incredible appetite for work, not only by playing concerts and doing exhaustingly long evenings in clubs, but also by filling his leisure hours with activity. He was constantly thinking about music and working out new ideas, and constantly giving interviews to the press talking about everything from race, politics and sex, to music, sport and food. His image appeared in one publication after another. And one magazine, *ZygoteIIZygote*, which was read on the college circuit, devoted a whole issue (12 August 1970) to Miles Davis. The reporter spent, literally, days with Miles: in the gym, in restaurants, at concerts, in his house, at Columbia listening to his own tapes, and had mammoth conversations, which he quoted at length. So keen was Miles to co-operate with the writer (who does not sign his article), that when the latter failed to turn up one day, he phoned him and said: 'This is Miles. What are you doing? You were supposed to meet me today ... Meet me at Columbia at 2 p.m.'[4]

Obviously, Miles's old habits and attitudes of the 1960s had been discarded. Formerly a patrician of few words, he now wished to hog the limelight and dominate the musical press. Also, instead of being a rather anonymous part of the successful American establishment, he was now beginning to be identified with the younger generation as someone beyond the pale of normal bourgeois society. His outlandish clothes, flashy cars and flamboyant lifestyle were making him a more prominent figure than ever before; and he was once more being harassed by the police – a sure sign that he was on the younger, rocky road, a rebel and an outsider.

The first intimation of new troubles with the law came with a bizarre happening in late 1969. Miles and his band were playing a club engagement at the Blue Coronet, Brooklyn, New York, and for four days Davis received telephone calls threatening that 'something would happen to him' if he appeared at the club, unless he paid the caller part of his earnings. It was an attempt by some small-time gangsters to extort some protection money. Miles continued working at the club, and after one session he drove Marguerite Eskridge to her home. The two of them were sitting in Miles's parked Ferrari outside her house when they were fired on. The car was holed and Miles's left hip was grazed by one of the bullets but Marguerite Eskridge was not injured. One paper recounted: 'Reportedly, during the police examination of the auto, a small quantity of marijuana was found. Miss Eskridge and Davis were booked for possession. Later, the Manhattan D.A.'s office refused to press charges and a criminal court judge dismissed them.'[5] Miles put up $10,000 reward for information leading to the capture and conviction of the assailants, but it was never claimed, though he reported in January 1970 that the two gangsters had both been killed. When he was asked how bad the flesh wound was, he replied: 'It wasn't as bad as getting hit over the head by a white cop.' He was referring to the beating up he'd experienced outside Birdland ten years previously, and he added, 'Funny thing: the cop was killed, too, in a subway.'[6]

Then, early in March 1970, he was arrested again. On this occasion, he was wearing a turban, a white sheepskin coat, and snakeskin pants, and was sitting in his red Ferrari, which was parked in a 'no-waiting' area on Central Park South near Fifth Avenue in New York City. A policeman went to the car to ask him to move, noticed that the car had no inspection sticker, and asked to see Miles's driving licence and registration documents. Davis searched for the papers in his shoulder bag and a set of metal knuckledusters fell out of it. In New York State law, these were classified as a deadly weapon. Miles insisted he was carrying them for self-protection, but the policeman booked him on a weapons charge and for driving an unlicensed, unregistered and uninspected vehicle. Miles spent the night in gaol, and the next day had to pay a fine of $100 and a further $200 in legal fees to his lawyer. The fine was for being an unlicensed driver; he was cleared of the other charges.

This experience brought home to him, yet again, the futility of the black's plight in American society, though he was beginning to realize that the younger, non-conformist rock generation were experiencing similar treatment at the hands of the American establishment. After recounting the story of his own arrest to *Zygote*, Miles added:

> It's just the whole attitude of the police force . . . It's not so much the way black people are treated any more. It's the way they treat all the young people that think the same way, so no matter what colour you are, you get the same shit. That's what the black people have been trying to say for years . . . The country is so far gone that you can't change it, you can just fuck with it 'til they change certain laws in the city. First thing they should do is legalize marijuana and all drugs. Then you go from there. There's so much graft and shit, like, you wouldn't believe the shit going down with dope. The dope goes in and the judges know about the dope, so subsequently the dope comes up to Harlem and the Spanish people. Both of my sons are hooked because there's nothing else for them to do. There's nothing for them to go to school for 'cause they're gonna get fucked over by the system. The system is so fucked up that by the time they get out of school, they'll be in their late twenties. The whole system is fucked up and the board of education doesn't want to change it.

Miles Davis was identifying with the younger generation of Americans who were rejecting and questioning many of the values of their society, who demonstrated against the continuation of the Vietnam War, and among whom drugs such as marijuana and LSD were very popular. So far as drugs in general are concerned,

Miles seems to be drawing a parallel with the Prohibition era and suggesting that the enormous profits of under-cover dealing ensure the continuation of the traffic and, at the same time, prevent any kind of control. He knew, as the younger generation was finding out, that governments that refuse to concede anything to reason can be made to concede by force if the collective will is strong enough. A few months previously he had stated baldly:

> Man, you know whites are going to hold on to the power and the money. The white man leaning back smoking his cigar, he's not going to move. He wants everything just the same. That's what makes our music different. It comes from people who have had to learn how to make the white man move.[7]

For blacks in America at the end of the 1960s, it was clear that where reasoned requests for civil rights had failed, the urban riots and the resolution of the Black Panther movement were resulting in concessions. Wars had always resulted in an improvement in the black man's status, and the Vietnam War was no exception. Young blacks and whites alike fought in it; and black and white alike demonstrated against it. And it was not only politics which provided new links between young blacks and whites; it was also the rock music that had grown out of rhythm and blues. During the 1960s, a whole generation of young white people came to know and love the blues – the music of the rural and urban black.

This idea of black and white fusion pervades the packaging of *Bitches Brew*, which was released around the beginning of April 1970. The outside cover has a sort of psychedelic painting of black figures in a hallucinatory landscape of sea and sky and a large pink flower exuding yellow flames. The centrepiece, which hinges on the spine of the double-album jacket, has a black hand and a white hand with long, intertwined fingers, and two fingers growing into a Janus-like pair of black and white heads. The white head stares across the back of the jacket; the black one stares across the front. Inside the cover on the left there is a large colour photograph of Miles who is, once again, smiling; and on the right side, there is a smaller black-and-white photograph of Miles and Teo Macero standing together during the actual recording of the album. The sleeve note is by the ever-faithful Ralph J. Gleason, who wrote it in the fashionable 'stream-of-consciousness' style.

As packaging, it was superlative. Everything about the artwork of the album spoke to the current generation: the psychedelic front cover with black and white fusions; the inside portrait of a new and smiling Miles; the long, rambling sleeve note that struck exactly the conversational style of the age. And Columbia backed up this superb packaging with an energetic promotional campaign right across the country, with such success that, by May, the album had sold 70,000 copies and was the fastest-selling record Miles had ever released. It was getting top radio play in key cities, and this was a particular triumph for Columbia's campaign, since the actual music is not even remotely 'easy-listening'.

Just how difficult the music seemed at the time can be judged from the reactions of one of Miles's early associates, Dizzy Gillespie. The latter, one of the most powerful talents in jazz and himself an innovator at the time of the bebop movement, had great difficulty in understanding the basis of Miles's music in the late 1960s and early 1970s. Dizzy did not seem to grasp how the music was put together or how it worked, and yet he had such respect for Miles that he persevered. During a blindfold test, Leonard Feather played the Miles 1954 recording of 'It Never Entered My Mind', and Gillespie said:

As for his music, Miles has a deep, deep, deep, spiritual value to it. It's far deeper than mine ... But this album is very different to how Miles is playing today [1970] and I personally prefer it, because I can understand better what he's doing. Miles and I played several times together at the Village Gate, and a place in Harlem, and the last time he came up to me afterwards and said, 'How'd you like it?' So I said, 'What is it? Explain it to me.' Well, it seems they have a basic melody and they work around that. I guess you have to know the basic tune.

Feather commented: 'It's not so much a tune as a mode, isn't it?' Dizzy replied: 'I don't know; whatever it is. But I'd really like to spend some time having him explain it to me, because I'd like to know what it is he's doing.'[8]

Leonard Feather, one of the most intelligent critics, and an excellent musician and composer himself, shows by his comment, that he too, at that time, had not grasped the essence of the music Miles Davis was making. It was not modal music; it was chromatic improvisation and the basis was a skeletal theme or bass figure. Dizzy Gillespie commented at even greater length:

I have listened to those recent albums time after time, until I started getting cohesions. The guy is such a fantastic musician that I know he has something in mind, whatever it is. I know he knows what he's doing, so he must be doing something that I can't get to yet. He played some of it for me, and he said, 'How do you like that shit?' I said, 'What is it?' and he said, 'You know what it is; same shit you've been playing all the time,' and I said, 'Have I?' I said, 'Look, I'm going to come by your house and spend several hours and you're going to explain to me what it is.' But we never did get together. I'm sure he could explain it to me musically, though of course you can't explain anything emotionally.[9]

The music on *Bitches Brew*, which was giving such trouble to highly literate musicians, could nevertheless make an impact on several levels. First, there was the general sound of the group, which was fairly electronic with the keyboards and guitar. Also, the clear rock pulses created a continuum familiar to young audiences.

Columbia also increased Miles's exposure to audiences by putting him on the same bill as their various successful rock acts. During the year, Miles and his group were the supporting attraction on concerts with Blood, Sweat and Tears, singer Laura Nyro, and other rock stars not on the label, like the Band. This kind of exposure is so valuable that, often, supporting groups are paid only a minimal fee and, in some cases, the support group has to *pay* in order to appear on the same bill as the stars. In order to comply with this, Miles had to go against his short-term financial principles, and instead of getting as much money as he could for each concert, he had to accept much-reduced fees. This harsh reality became apparent when he did his first big concert to a rock audience. This took place at the Fillmore East in New York City, during March 1970. Miles said later:

> The only reason I played Fillmore, was because Clive Davis, president of Columbia Records, asked me to. He bends backwards for me. All I have to do at Columbia is produce and they try and sell me like they would a white idol with a head of blond hair. That means the next black man that comes up will get the same treatment.[10]

It was, therefore, more than a mere concern for record sales that made Miles play at the Fillmore. The predominantly white rock movement had tended to isolate black music and musicians and, as one observer put it, Miles was at the Fillmore to 'prove that black artists could speak to whites again and not just to themselves',[11] as they had been doing.

The Fillmore East and the Fillmore West (San Francisco) were run by a man called Bill Graham, who had put on the Charles Lloyd Quartet in 1967. Graham was a fan of Miles Davis's, but he was first and foremost a promoter of rock concerts, and possibly the most successful such promoter in America at that time. The two Fillmores were the key rock establishments, and to put Miles and his group on at either of them required some courage on Graham's part. It took courage, also, for Miles to agree to play there, and to refuse to change his music in any way, despite considerable pressure.

Miles's usual fee for a big concert performance was around $5,000, and he had to accept a huge cut because Bill Graham refused to pay him more than $1,500. As a result, the two men were barely on speaking terms during Miles Davis's two-night appearance (6 and 7 March) at the Fillmore East. The trumpeter was billed as an 'extra added attraction' on a programme that included the Steve Miller Blues Band, and Neil Young with Crazy Horse, and the young audience was totally attuned to vocal music. Some of Miles's white friends had advised him to reproduce some parts of *In a Silent Way*, and to finish his set with a strong backbeat – the heavy offbeat so familiar to rock audiences. But Miles ignored this advice. His group was now a sextet; the percussionist, Airto Moreira, had joined, but the music was still uncompromisingly abstract – exactly the same sort of thing Miles would have done at Shelly's Manne Hole.

By Fillmore standards, Miles's first set there 'bombed out' completely. There was only a smattering of applause and no calls for an encore. His second set that same Friday night was even more severe musically, and the audience reaction was similar: mystified silence leavened by sparse claps. On the Saturday night, there were again no calls for an encore after the first set, and Miles's friends once more pleaded with him to make the music more accessible. He said he would, but didn't. One observer wrote:

> If Miles was going to be accepted by this audience, he was going to be accepted on his own terms. He weaved in front of the microphone. He crouched and he blew from above, from below, from the side. He lifted the bell of his trumpet high in the air to cut off each bent, wailing note at just the perfect time. He blew so hard, he split his lip. And the audience roared. It stood on its feet. It called for more. Miles sauntered offstage with his eyes straight ahead and his chin cocked at a tilt. 'It was an easy gig,' he said afterwards. Of course, he didn't play an encore.[12]

In the spring of 1970, Wayne Shorter left the band, and the white saxophonist Steve Grossman joined. Once again, Miles had stalked his man. Grossman had just turned eighteen when Miles first heard him the previous year with a group that opened for Sonny Rollins at a Town Hall concert. Grossman said,

And I started seeing him after that in the audience at places where we were playing. Then I met him again after his Ferrari had bullet holes in it. That was at a concert and Dave Holland was on that. It was like a double quartet ... In 1969 everybody was trying crazy things. It was me and Dave Liebman, Holland and Lennie Fields on basses and one pianist – George Cables. During the break, Miles showed me the bullet holes in the car, and asked me to watch his bag while he went to the toilet. He was very nice; he started saying how great I was. Then I started going to Juilliard and I got a phone call saying Miles wanted me to show up at Columbia studios for a record date. After the recording date he said, 'We're going up to Boston, why don't you come?' So I said 'OK.' Wayne Shorter was still in the band and we played a little soprano duet. Wayne was very nice and Miles was exceptionally nice to me. I did a lot of recordings in the daytime while Wayne was still in the band. I think Miles was recording every day at that time, at ten o'clock in the morning. It was a great time for him.

Miles, aware of Shorter's imminent departure, was carefully preparing the youthful Grossman for his role in the band. In April, they played one long set at the Fillmore West in San Francisco, and this was well received by an attentive audience which included the 'Beat' poet, Allen Ginsberg. Bill Graham said, 'That one set was better than all four at the Fillmore East.' Miles smiled and said, 'I know it.'[13] The two men had obviously patched up their financial quarrel, and after the engagement, Miles sent Graham a telegram saying that he had always wanted to play a club or place where the audience could relax while the musician did his thing and that Graham had made it possible. Miles hoped that he and his band had added something to match the contribution Bill Graham had made to the music scene, and hoped that this event would be a pattern for the future. He finished by saying that he liked the apple juice and sound system but was most unhappy with the air conditioning!

The Fillmore West set was recorded and later released under the title *Black Beauty*. The band was again relentlessly abstract, except when Miles was soloing, and his almost superhuman adventures – brilliant high notes, audacious risks, and fantastic stamina – redeem the performance again and again. Miles's next engagement at the Fillmore East, four nights in June supporting Laura Nyro, was also recorded. This time he had further augmented the band with Keith Jarrett on organ and keyboards, so the group was now a septet, and more heavily electronic than ever. The money was again too low for Miles's liking, and he made a great deal of fuss about it. Having done it once, he felt that for subsequent concerts his fee should be increased. He said:

I mean they're gonna make a lot of money for those four nights. What are they gonna do, give me a set of clothes, a water-melon? They'll be kissing me and bringing me coke and offering me a reefer and all that shit. What do I get out of this? Miles is a good nigger. Miles is all right. Right on Miles. What is it with that shit? And then, when you mention it to them, they say we are all in it for the art.[14]

The sheer complexity of Miles Davis's position in American society and the various psychological pressures with which he had to deal were described in a perceptive paragraph written by the *ZygoteIIZygote* author:

Miles Davis doesn't step aside for or pander to anyone. The old house nigger sickens him. It is part of his heritage that he has been fighting against all his life. His house, his car, his women, his clothes, all his possessions state, 'I'm not as good as you are, I am better.' It is almost as if Miles would be emasculated if he accepted the past. He rebels against it, and it has not been an easy thing. He comes from middle-class parents, and cannot claim the poor, street upbringing copout. He is educated and literate, and rather than making it easier for him, these things have made it harder. More than anything, Miles wants to relate to the brother in the ghetto. He does mentally, but because of his past, he can't fully because he hasn't lived it. Miles, beyond all things, is black and he is proud of it. He doesn't want to be anything else.

During the year, Miles improved his personal possessions. He got rid of his red, bullet-holed Ferrari and bought a new battleship-grey Lamborghini. It was priced at $20,000, but he paid cash and got it for only $14,000. He also had his house completely redecorated. He had always been extremely houseproud, but even this seems to have increased to epic proportions. Whenever a journalist went to his home to do an interview, the visitor would be subjected to the same ritual: he or she would be left alone listening to tapes of Miles's latest recordings, then Davis would appear and at some point there would be a tour of the house. But, like Miles's music, the house redecoration was a spontaneous rather than a premeditated event.

A set designer called Lance Hay, who lived in Los Angeles and was a fan of Miles's, just happened to be around New York when Miles's bathroom ceiling began to crumble and fall down. Miles recalled: 'Lance said to me, "Let me do something. I'll fix you a bathroom that'll be out of sight."'[15] Hay made the bathroom a three-level affair with half-circle steps, a porthole-shaped window and a ceiling, also in three levels, where lighting was concealed between each layer. The large sunken bathtub was circular and had a frame of ersatz marble done in reverse curves. It was separated from the toilet by a curved half-wall. Miles was so pleased with this room that he asked Lance Hay to carry on and do the whole place: 'I wanted everything round. I said, "Lance, you know who I am. I don't like corners. I don't like furniture. And you don't either."'[16]

Each room (and the entrance hall) was given a floor with two or three different levels, and every visible inch of floor space was covered with blue carpet. There were more porthole windows, and a trapezoid bed with rounded corners. In a floor-to-ceiling cylinder near the bedroom, Hay installed a kitchenette, and there was also a full-sized kitchen on the main floor directly below.

There were built-in spaces for books, records and hi-fi equipment, and the living-room wall was faced with wood cut into three arches where the windows were. The only standing furniture was one round table in the living room, one round ottoman in the foyer and one curvaceous Charles Eames lounge chair in the bedroom. The decor on the lower floor had been done earlier in the year by a Valencian-born craftsman called Manuel Mauri, and there were white plaster walls and arches and wood beams across the ceiling. The façade of the house was Moorish, with wood, tiles and plaster. Miles particularly wanted the North African effect. He said: 'I got tired of living in a George Washington kind of house.'[17] The only photograph in Miles's living room was a colour shot of a pensive John Coltrane, taken during his time with Davis's group.

With all the promotion and publicity, and his exposure to large rock audiences in big auditoria, Miles was, by mid-1970, beginning to make a strong impact on the jazz and rock scenes, not only in America, but also globally. In a sense, the two main releases of the period worked like a boxer's knock-out combination; *Silent Way* was the blow which set up the public for the KO delivered by *Bitches Brew*. At the same time, albums from other periods of Miles's career were still being released. A composite album, *Miles Davis's Greatest Hits*, came out fairly early in the year, followed a few months later by the release of the 1964 Tokyo concert with Sam Rivers on sax. Superficial observers of the scene, however, accused Miles of 'selling out' to the younger generation. One or two of the more perceptive jazz critics made great efforts to understand what he was doing and why. As usual, Leonard Feather looked more deeply than most:

> Casual listeners might assume that he had been taken over by the youth movement rock, stock and barrel. The diagnosis would be dangerously over-simplistic. As can be deduced from his current album (*Bitches Brew*), he is creating a new and more complex form, drawing from the avant-garde, atonalism, modality, rock, jazz and the universe. It has no name, but some listeners have called it 'Space Music'.[18]

And Miles himself commented:

> We play music for you to learn and listen. The kids, they are
> so great they can dig what we're giving them. The rest of the
> people give them shit. They give them the same old fucking
> thing to be comfortable. That's the reason we are playing,
> not to be pop stars. What does it mean to sell out to the
> kids? I haven't sold out to the fucking kids. I don't sell out
> to nobody.[19]

But Miles was also attacked by the black press for playing
'second fiddle' to white rock groups, and for employing white
musicians as well as his black associates. In July 1970, *Jet* magazine stated: 'Not only is the Great One listed in small print as an
"extra added attraction", but he comes on first instead of holding
down the star's spot.' And the saxophonist, Eddie Harris, whose
tune 'Freedom Jazz Dance' Miles had recorded some four years
previously, gave a press conference and attacked Miles bitterly for
having a 'new white image', and added that the same non-black
musicians currently playing with Miles would soon be cutting
black brothers out of gigs they should have. Joe Zawinul – a white
man, of course – commented:

> They used to attack him for using John McLaughlin. I just
> talked to him about that and he said, 'OK, man, I'd hire one
> of them brothers if he can play as good as John McLaughlin
> – I'd hire them both!' They used to say, 'Why you got that
> white boy playing on the guitar?' And he'd say, 'Shit! Nobody
> can play as good as him. You give me one of them niggers
> and I'll hire him *and* McLaughlin.' You see, Miles is very
> racial, but he is fair. He has the greatest sense of humour.

Miles Davis was, almost single-handedly, putting jazz back on
the map in America. After he had proved it was possible to get
through to audiences at the Fillmores, other jazz musicians, including Dizzy Gillespie and his group, were booked to play there. And

Miles was also showing that it was possible for jazz musicians to achieve big record sales without diluting their music or trying to 'play down' to the public. John Hammond, of Columbia Records, asked what things revived interest in jazz at the beginning of the 1970s, replied: 'One is *Bitches Brew* by Miles Davis, which has had fantastic sales for a jazz LP – unprecedented for Miles as well.'[20]

Along with the new decor in his home and his fresh sartorial style, Miles was also experimenting with the colour of his trumpets. He had, at various times, a green one, a blue one, a black one, and a two-toned russet and black one. He explained somewhat obscurely: 'I don't want to play a gold horn ... You look at a brass horn and all you see is the horn. When you play a green horn, it sort of disappears and all you are aware of is the music.'[21] He was also experimenting at home with an electronic bug fixed into his mouthpiece and fed through a wah-wah pedal, but it was a month or two before he felt confident enough to use it with the band in public. In fact, his black trumpet lay plugged in and on top of an amplifier on several gigs before he eventually plucked up courage to use it.

In July, a performance at the Schaefer concerts in Central Park showed just how difficult it was to control this new electronic environment. The small stage was already two-thirds full of a second group's equipment when Miles and the band had to go on and play. There was nowhere for Miles to stand except in front of the group, and when he turned to move away after playing his opening statement, he tripped over the mass of wires and leads, almost falling off the bandstand. Keith Jarrett, who'd arrived and plugged in five minutes after the group started its set, was having difficulty with the modulation and fuzz of the organ. Miles had no monitor speaker with which to hear himself or check the sound balance of the group, and the amplifier from the electric piano was too close – which meant that he heard nothing except the electric piano. During the interval, he tried to get these problems sorted out, and his road manager said that he would try to do something about it if the interval was long enough; but he didn't offer much hope and told Davis that these things happen with electrical instruments at outdoor concerts, and that Miles would just have to learn to live with it.

The music on the live albums from Fillmore West (April) and Fillmore East (June) is full of extraordinary invention, but shows a schizophrenia that threatened to tear the band apart – and which ultimately did. The music seesawed between the rhythmic grooves for Miles and the completely abstract interplay of the rhythm section when it was functioning on its own. On the earlier album, the actual time-playing of the section is often so busy that it fails to provide an adequate contrast with the totally abstract interludes. The tension is built up but rarely satisfactorily released because the pulse is continually disturbed. This facet of improvisation harks back to the European 'free' jazz of the 1960s, which in turn has a certain relationship to the avant-garde 'straight' music syndrome. John McLaughlin once remarked that it's only in Europe that musicians are afraid of, or embarrassed by, funk; and it is precisely funk which differentiates the whole jazz tradition from European music. Chick Corea, however, particularly in the abstract passages, is brilliantly inventive, coming up again and again with fresh lines and figures. The new saxophonist, Steve Grossman, though much maligned by reviewers, was an excellent choice for this music, playing at white heat and creating a flow of interesting melodic lines. Although he regarded himself primarily as a tenor saxophonist, all of Grossman's tenor solos were edited out, because Miles wanted only the soprano solos. Dave Holland and Chick Corea were the main instigators of the free, abstract music, and Grossman recalled one revealing incident:

I remember one night at the Both And [club], at the end of a tune I was playing free and Miles started playing free, and Chick and Dave were very happy, but Miles cut it off very fast. And Chick asked him, 'Why did you cut it off?' And Miles said, 'So that we could do it again!' There was a lot of wisdom in that reply. When I was with him, he was in really peak condition, he was really beautiful.

On the *Fillmore West* album, Miles brings in at various times some pieces from recent albums – 'It's About That Time', 'Sanctuary', 'Spanish Key', 'Bitches Brew' – but they rarely ever settle into satisfying rhythmic coherence.

The *Fillmore East* music is much superior, largely because the rhythm section does occasionally settle so that tension is built up and released in a more satisfactory way. By this time, Keith Jarrett had joined the group on organ, and his profoundly funky feeling and pulse helped the rhythm section to cohere. Miles had been trying for some time to persuade Jarrett to work with him, but the pianist had always refused because he was running his own band and wanted to give that priority. Jarrett recalled:

> He would show up at places we were playing and he'd be sitting in a corner, and he'd say, 'You want to play with the band?' And I said, 'No'. And it kept going like that, and finally I had an open period of time with no work, and I said, 'I'll play with the band if I can leave whenever . . .' It wasn't really joining the band, it was just playing with it.

Jarrett did not really want to play electric keyboard because he much preferred the acoustic piano, but he understood perfectly the requirements of Miles's music and thought he could make a contribution to it:

> The music that he had wouldn't have worked with acoustic piano. You couldn't play chords (functional harmony) – it wasn't chordal at all. It was just . . . sounds . . . I thought the band was the most egocentric organization I had heard musically . . . except for Miles. Miles was still playing nice, beautiful things, but it sounded to me like the rest of the band was made up of people who were all in closets, playing their own ego trips and that it never had this wholeness except when Miles was playing. And the only reason it did then, is because Miles's playing was so beyond this kind of closet thing. Just the sound of his horn brought out a different

feeling. And I felt like he was restricted by that [closet thing]. So in a way ... I just wanted to do something a little bit to change the feeling. And I knew Jack DeJohnette was there, so we play well together.

Throughout the Fillmore East double-album, Miles Davis plays with tremendous intensity, but the absolute high spot was the Friday-night session. Here everyone seems to have been inspired and the music reached great heights. Miles not only utilizes the whole range of the trumpet from the lowest notes to sustained screams, but he also produces series after series of completely fresh melodic lines. The band's reception was also much better than it had been in April on the West Coast. In June, the audience was now responding to many events in the music and there was liberal applause. But in general, although Keith Jarrett's presence improves the music, it is still characterized by the same schizo-phrenia – a seesawing between the abstract and the concrete.

Miles himself was delighted with his band's music on all the Fillmore sessions. He went to Columbia to listen to the tapes, and the *Zygote* writer observed:

Miles listened to tapes for about three hours, discussing the merits of one tape, the lack of clarity on another, where a cut should be made, what changes should take place. He was extremely satisfied with his and his group's performances, and joked, bobbed to some of the music, raised his eyebrows in disbelief at some of the intricacies of passages, and rocked back on his heels, his face uplifted, at some of his dynamic trumpet solos ... Miles was so excited about the music that he wanted every set, every note made available to the public ... Miles had been so productive that Teo [Macero] has one gigantic headache. He has six months' worth of editing and enough material to produce albums for the next three years. No one quite knows what to do with all the material at hand.[22]

In fact, Miles's fecundity was becoming a bugbear for Columbia. As well as the live albums, he was also recording in the studio, and a backlog was piling up. He would phone Clive Davis or someone else at Columbia such as Bob Altshuler, and play long passages over the phone. He would say that this was the album to release. If there had been a release in December, he would record in January and want the results released immediately. Columbia would protest, talk about marketing, about time needed for sales and promotion. Then Miles would call again a month or two later and tell them to forget about the January album because he'd just made another which was the one. From August 1969 to August 1970, Miles had recorded enough material for two live double-albums (the Fillmores), a studio double-album (*Bitches Brew*), a studio single album (*Jack Johnson*), three sides of another studio double-album (*Big Fun*), and four tracks from another double-album (*Live-Evil*). It had been the most productive year of his career.

In August, Steve Grossman left the band and Gary Bartz, the (black) saxophonist joined. In October, both Dave Holland and Chick Corea left. In Dave Holland's case, the reason for leaving was not the usual one of 'join Miles Davis . . . become a star . . . leave and lead your own band'. The reason was primarily that Holland had come from one strong music scene in Europe, and his present role with Miles did not fit in with the musical ideals he had at that time. Miles was forty-four years old and had been through many, many musical experiences of all kinds. Holland was twenty-three, and there were very many musical areas he had not yet explored. The crunch came when he took round to Miles's house a tape he'd made with some of the leading British avant-garde musicians of the 1960s. Holland recalled:

> I played it to him and he listened to it and said he dug it, you know. He liked the way it sounded, but said: 'If you want to play that, well, get your own band . . . I'm not going to play that. That's not what I want to do.' That's the point where I realized that I was hitting my head against a wall. I

was either going to go along with Miles's music, or leave the band.

Years later, Holland had a clearer idea of what was going on in Miles's band at the time:

I wanted the band to go free, you know, and just take this music into another space, and I couldn't understand why Miles insisted on controlling it into this area. And we had a lot of talks about this, and a lot of discussions, and he was very patient with me. I realize now, how patient he was, you know. Oh, he was *very* patient. He took all kinds of time – I remember sitting at his house many times talking about it. I realize now, anyway, that Miles was very clear in his direction but very tolerant of a lot of things we did. Jack, Chick and myself would take all kinds of liberties with the music and Miles would be checking it out. Then he'd come up to Jack and say, 'Bring it back in.' But at the same time he wouldn't say, 'I don't want you to do that.' He really believed in letting the musicians explore. He liked to have the relationship of rhythm section to soloist and we were for much of the time going outside of that relationship. In fact, one of the great things he once came over and said to me was, 'Hey, Dave, remember you are a *bass* player.' And that was a time when I was absolutely ignoring the fundamental role of the bass, and he just put me back on track, and I've thought about that thing many, many, many times. I realized that there was a very beautiful role that I was ignoring.

When Holland told Miles that he wanted to leave, Davis asked, 'Why? Why are you leaving?'

Holland said, 'Miles, I can't function in this role any more. I need to have more space.'

Miles replied, 'But you can do anything you want. I'm not stopping you from doing anything you want. You can play any way you want.'

But Dave Holland felt, quite rightly, that the music did demand certain things, and that certain prescribed roles – particularly for the bass and drums – were necessary for it.

So by October 1970, the phase that had begun in 1968 with *Filles de Kilimanjaro* was over. Miles had to find new musicians, and his choice would be crucial to the direction of the music. He had rejected the European, Western, approach to improvisation; now he would strengthen the non-Western elements in his work.

SIXTEEN

Live-Evil

'Jazz today is closer to classical music than it
is to folklore music, and I'd rather stay closer
to folklore music.'[1]

Miles Davis

To replace Dave Holland, Miles chose nineteen-year-old Michael
Henderson, who had played with Aretha Franklin and Stevie
Wonder. This was a significant choice; Henderson played with
superb feeling and rhythmic drive, and was happy to produce
hypnotically repeating ostinati. His role was to be exactly the one
Dave Holland had not wanted: that of creating the 'drone' and
solid rhythmic foundation for the music. Henderson also had a
marvellous flair for creating bass figures – something at which Joe
Zawinul also excelled. This faculty was extremely important to
Miles in the late 1960s and the 1970s. He actually told Zawinul,
'You're the greatest bass line writer there is.' In Michael Henderson, Miles had found a similar playing, as opposed to writing,
talent. He said of Henderson: 'He's incredible. He can play lines
when there's nothing there but air.'[2] But Henderson had difficulty
at first in hearing how the oblique notes Miles played related to
the bass lines. In 1973 Miles described some of the delicate aspects
of this relationship:

I never look down or talk down to any musician because he's
nineteen or something. I don't sell nobody short. I'm always
listening. Yesterday's dead . . . Michael's got a funky sound,

293

you know, and I been teaching him for a while. Like if he's in E flat and I play an A chord or maybe a C or D, he doesn't get ruffled any more like he used to. He sticks where he is. He's used to all my stuff by now.[3]

Miles did not bother to replace Chick Corea, because by this time Keith Jarrett was playing enough for two men, and often using two keyboards simultaneously – one with either hand. With the departure of Corea and Holland, and the arrival of Henderson, all the chittering European 'free jazz' elements disappeared, and even when Miles soloed out of time with free accompaniment, the feeling was quite different from that of the two *Fillmore* albums. This tremendous change in the music, from a disruptive schizophrenia to a homogeneity with a new solidity at the core, had been presaged by some studio recordings in April, May and June of 1970 that resulted in the album *Jack Johnson*, and included some tracks released later on *Live-Evil*.

In 1970, Miles was asked to make the background music for a long documentary on the great heavyweight boxer Jack Johnson. This superbly made film also contains footage of Johnson's key fights early in the century. Jack Johnson was the first black heavyweight champion of the world, and a magnificent man in every sense, showing supreme moral and physical courage. He was also a flamboyant character with many women – several of them white – and a love for fast cars. Miraculously, Johnson lived through all the violent scenes he stirred up, only dying, at the age of sixty-eight in 1946, when he crashed the fast car he was driving. Miles not only created the music, but also wrote the album sleeve note himself. The music was edited by Teo Macero from tapes recorded in April 1970, and some earlier tapes including excerpts from the *Silent Way* session. In fact, Miles wanted to use the title track from that album, and phoned Zawinul saying, 'I'm going to do the score for *Jack Johnson* and we'd like to use "In a Silent Way"; can I put my name to it as joint composer?' Zawinul flatly refused, and so the piece was never used on this album.

The music on *Jack Johnson* is worthy of the great champion

and consists of two long pieces. 'Right Off' and 'Yesternow'. 'Right Off' has a sardonic grandeur and happened spontaneously and without premeditation, which perhaps helps to explain its extraordinary focus and dynamism. The group was Steve Grossman, Herbie Hancock on organ, John McLaughlin, Mike Henderson and Billy Cobham on drums, and they had set up in the studio and were ready to play, but Miles was in the control room talking to Teo Macero. Then McLaughlin initiated the whole thing:

> Twenty minutes had gone by, and we were just sitting there wondering what's going to happen. As far as I knew, Miles and Teo were just talking, and no mikes were on or anything, and I got fed up and I just started to play a boogie. I'm from R&B, too, and I love to boogie. And I started to do this shuffle in E, and Michael picked it up, and Billy picked it up, and in a minute things sort of started to happen. Next thing we saw was the control room door open and Miles ran in with his trumpet, and the red light was on, and he started to play, and that was it. It was really just a boogie and we played free, and that's his personal favourite record!

'Right Off' starts in the key of E, but eventually modulates to B flat. Miles plays acoustic trumpet with a massive sound, biting attack, screaming high notes and some breathtaking chromatic lines that are, at times, oblique to the key. McLaughlin and the rhythm section keep up a hypnotically rocking pulse that because it is a kind of variation on the 12/8 feel, is nearer to rhythm and blues than to rock and roll. McLaughlin, in particular, handles a confined space and a heavy beat with grace and subtlety. His 'comping' always arises organically out of the basic pulse, enhancing the rhythmic power and the emotional intensity of the piece, and he cunningly varies the colour and the harmonic implications of his chords. Herbie Hancock creates a massive, barbaric sound on the organ. He said of this session: 'By that time we weren't into playing instruments as instrumentalists – we were more into just getting a kind of sound out ... I'm not an organ player at all, but there was a sound that maybe I could fit in in some kind of way. So that's why I did it.' At the end of the first side, McLaughlin plays guitar lines with plenty of fuzz, which is a real rock sound, nothing like the polite sound of the traditional jazz guitar. Billy Cobham tried to explain why this session was such a good one:

> He would tell me what he wanted. He would even sit down and try to play. And it was not in an obnoxious way. It was not meant to degrade. I always felt that he always got the most out of the cats that worked with him because everybody loved him, if only for the musician that he is and what he stands for. He said, like in *Jack Johnson*, 'I want this and I want that,' and I said, 'Oh yeah? OK.' And I didn't do it the way he wanted me to do it, and then he just let me alone ... It was really a relaxed session ... It's just that on a Miles Davis session, everybody's very reserved. Sort of a cloud-cover comes over, and business gets taken care of![4]

The other track, 'Yesternow', is remarkable for its economy and the brilliant use of space. The first third or so is sparse but held together and given unity by an intermittent yet insistent bass figure and Miles's spare, brooding trumpet solo. All kinds of events take place within this eerily empty framework, until eventually the spaces, the holes in the music, close up, and a tight continuous groove is created while a soprano sax solo by Steve Grossman bites deeply. McLaughlin solos on guitar, after which sections from 'Shhh/Peaceful' (*Silent Way*) are edited into the track. There is some cross-fading on this side, and also some abstract electronic sounds by the guitarist, Sonny Sharrock, towards the end. Finally, the album concludes with actor Brock Peters reciting Jack Johnson's words: 'I'm black. They never let me forget it. I'm black all right. I'll never let *them* forget it.'

In the summer of 1970, Miles's group toured opening concerts at rock halls for the latin-rock guitarist, Carlos Santana, whom he liked. Then in August, he played at the Isle of Wight Festival in the UK, taking Jackie Battle with him. Jimi Hendrix and Sly and the Family Stone were also on the bill there, as well as a number of white rock groups. Miles and Gil Evans were planning to record an album with Hendrix, but on 18 September, Hendrix died after mixing sleeping pills and alcohol and choking on his own vomit. Miles was so upset by this premature death that he attended Hendrix's funeral in Seattle, but hated the event so much that he vowed never to attend another funeral. Miles was also becoming estranged from his sons, Gregory, who had returned, after two years in Vietnam, soured and disaffected, and Miles IV, who was also worrying and disappointing his father. Miles, however, took pleasure and comfort in the fact that his daughter Cheryl had graduated from Columbia University and returned to St Louis to become a school teacher. She had also made Miles a grandfather.

Live-Evil is a double-album that comprises four studio tracks from earlier in the year and four live tracks – 'Inamorata', 'What I Say', 'Sivad' and 'Funky Tonk' – recorded in a club during December 1970. Miles phoned John McLaughlin and asked him to play on the live session, so the group was once more a septet with guitar and keyboard, drums and percussion, bass guitar, saxophone and trumpet. The sounds and the atmosphere are quite unlike the previous albums; the whooping, barking percussion, the persistent bass ostinati, the raving keyboard and wailing guitar, the insistent drum rhythms, the wild saxophone sound, and the acoustic and amplified trumpet with its wah-wah and extreme tonal distortion, all give the impression of total possession ... the inspired state of rapt improvisation in which the individual and the ensemble are one, and the player becomes his instrument. The whole atmosphere on these tracks is unlike anything else in jazz, although it relates perhaps to some of Ellington's jungle music. The music on these live tracks is, nevertheless, quite varied, ranging from the ruminative feel of the slow section of 'Sivad' to the ferocity of 'What I Say'. The former passage is based on a slow, spacy riff with a cunningly displaced accent which makes it seem asymmetrical, though it is not. Over this lopsided figure, Miles improvises with wah-wah, while Airto Moreira adds some wordless singing. Then McLaughlin plays a powerful solo. There is all the time a sense of dark contemplation.

'What I Say' is the most extreme track of all. Once again it is in B flat, and the rhythm is a furiously fast rock beat. The piece actually did come out of 'what Miles said' to Jack DeJohnette:

> We were playing in California and Miles said, 'Listen to this Jimi Hendrix track.' The drummer was Buddy Miles and I said. 'Yeah, yeah, it's a nice groove' . . . Miles was trying to tell me something that he wanted, but he didn't know how. He sang the beat to me, 'dum-dum-daahh, dum-dum-daahh, dum-dum-daahh, dum-dum-daahh.' I said, 'I get the picture – you want Buddy Miles's groove with my technique.' He said, 'Right'.'

The bass guitar anchors the piece by sticking to a repetitive figure, and the drums are purely supportive, playing motor rhythms. The groove is phenomenal. Jarrett, playing electric piano, matches the energy and momentum of bass and drums, and after setting up the whole demonic atmosphere, he prepares the way for Miles's entry, which is exceptionally dramatic. The latter stabs out some high trumpet Es, giving yet more momentum to the already headlong rhythm, and then hits some notes so high that they approach bat frequencies. Everything is taken to its ultimate extremity: the sheer physical range of the trumpet, the speed of the phrases, the intensity of the rhythms. Miles seems to be beating almost despairingly at the limits of his abilities in his shrieking notes and his chromatic scurrying around. He swings madly along, however, and the whole ensemble reacts wildly to his phrases, because he is pushing the other musicians to the limits of their own abilities. There is an extraordinary collective violence in this music. After Miles, Gary Bartz plays an excellent soprano solo, and is followed by John McLaughlin, after which Keith Jarrett solos at length. This exhilarating keyboard solo metamorphoses into a long drum solo by Jack DeJohnette, which changes the pulse into a looser, rolling, triple feel. This relaxation of the tension is logical and necessary, but it doesn't occur until the original ferocious pulse has been sustained for almost fifteen minutes. This is one great difference between the present group and the one which made the two *Fillmore* albums: the earlier group would never have sustained the groove for more than two or three minutes.

The music on *Live-Evil* is the antithesis of the highly arranged, understated pieces on the 1949/50 recordings of the Birth of the Cool band. It is also the opposite end of the spectrum from the 1959 *Kind of Blue* album. 'What I Say' relates more to the live albums of the early 1960s; they swung perhaps more viciously than any previous jazz music. 'What I Say' swings in a different way and even more viciously, but in essence it is the same kind of performance. According to Keith Jarrett, however, the *Live-Evil* tracks were not entirely representative of the band at that time. He said: 'Unfortunately with *Live-Evil*, John McLaughlin just happened to be in town, and he wasn't playing (regularly) with the band. He just sat in, and the band sound wasn't the same because there was now . . . a different voice.' In Jarrett's opinion, the band (without the guitar) had been at its best some time earlier, during a week-long engagement in Boston. The Norwegian saxophonist Jan Garbarek had been in the audience, and he verified Jarrett's opinion. Keith Jarrett recalled:

> I talked to Miles the second night and said, 'Can we record here? Can you call CBS and have them send' . . . And he said he already had. You know, everyone knew how good it was. He'd already talked to them [Columbia] and they couldn't do it that quickly . . . maybe next week! And I said, 'It's not going to be next week, it's going to be these six days.' Anyway, Jan was there and he has the same opinion about the music then.

The following year, 1971, Jack DeJohnette left the group, and when Miles played the Berlin Festival and the London Festival

Hall in November, he had Leon Chancler on drums, and two percussionists, Don Alias and James Foreman; one reinforced the pulse with congas and the other produced colours and textures. Jarrett, Bartz and Henderson were still with the group, and the Berlin Festival concert in particular has some of the most deeply satisfying music of the post-*Fillmore* period. The music is not as frenetic as that of *Live-Evil*; the long stretches of beautifully rocking rhythm are a sheer delight; the *colla voce* passages are full of colour and feeling; and the key soloists – Miles, Jarrett and Bartz – are in peak form. This session was a joy throughout. Although the non-Western elements had been intensified, there was still a delicate balance and the music was not marred by an over-emphasis on physical pulse to the exclusion of other musical factors.

Miles's was the first jazz group to top the bill at the Fillmore West, which they did for three nights in May. Miles was also on the bill with Nina Simone at the Shrine Auditorium, Los Angeles, in April. Voluminous review space was given to *Live at Fillmore* and *Jack Johnson* when they were released, and although the former received some indifferent notices from mystified writers, *Jack Johnson* was given many ecstatic reviews. At the same time, the fascination with Miles continued in the general press, and he was again mentioned in *Time* magazine. There were other articles, too, such as the one in *Essence* in March, about his legendary wardrobe, his flair for clothes designing, and his own private hairdresser, James Finney the Scorpio, who had taken care of the hair of many rock stars, including Jimi Hendrix, and who is described as,

a far-out, free spirit who gave up his private hairdressing practice to travel with Miles. And as Finney says, 'It's a trip.' ... While we sipped Galliano and listened to Gladys Knight and the Pips, Miles would become concerned with his hair and summon Finney to touch up his curls. Miles sometimes wears his hair in tight, hot curls which give the effect of an extremely full, kinky Afro.[5]

It was Finney who named 'Yesternow', on the *Jack Johnson* album. At the end of the day with the journalists, Miles amazed them by preparing a meal from ancient French recipes – fish, potatoes and salad.

In January 1971, Miles received a letter from Chick Corea saying that working with Miles Davis for the previous two years had been 'one of the most beautiful experiences of my whole life'. The trumpeter was so gratified that he showed the letter to a complete stranger who had come to interview him, saying, 'Here, I got this letter from Chick the other day. It's one of the nicest letters I've ever received.'[6] Perhaps the departure from his group of Holland and Corea had disturbed Miles more deeply than he liked to admit. After leaving, they had formed a group together, Circle, which included Anthony Braxton on alto saxophone and Barry Altschul on drums, to create the kind of free/abstract music they felt was missing in Miles's band. That is clearly why it was such a relief when Corea's letter arrived and reaffirmed that it had been good working with Davis. But by the end of 1971, Circle ceased to exist when Corea left it suddenly to form the latin-rock group Return to Forever.

Also in 1971, Miles was voted Jazzman of the Year and top trumpeter in *Down Beat* magazine, but a catalogue of disasters, some minor and some fairly weighty, really upset him. The great status symbol, his Lamborghini sports car, which he now claimed was worth $30,000, had been damaged and was off the road. The rear end had been dented in one accident, and then a couple of weeks later, someone had forced Miles up on the pavement and into a brick wall on 79th Street, denting a headlamp and the grille. He took the car to a body repair shop, expecting his insurance company to pay for the repairs, but the bill came to $11,000, and Miles reported: 'They fixed the car, sent me the bill, then the insurance company was supposed to pay, but it went out of business. And I'm not going to pay.'[7] Meanwhile, he was spending a fortune on hired cars. Also, a Philadelphia deejay had sued Davis for $13,000, alleging that he failed to show up for a concert with Aretha Franklin a year previously. Miles pleaded illness as the reason for his default, but the man continued to press his suit for compensation. And in July, Davis played four concerts at the Beaco Theatre in New York as a favour to a friend but, as one journalist pointed out:

> Miles doesn't get the kind of airplay in New York that he needs to fill a 2,600-seat house for four shows in two nights. He would have done better booking himself for one concert and enough ticket buyers would have knocked on the box office window for him to turn away a couple of thousand.'[8]

In fact, the theatre was never more than forty per cent full on any night, and only 4,000 in all attended the concerts. It must have been a shock to Miles to realize that, despite all his recent publicity, acclaim and record sales, his drawing-power was still fallible; a modicum of advertising plus the word-of-mouth grapevine were not enough to get him full houses.

In addition, rumours began to fly around that Miles Davis was thinking of quitting jazz because he was being harassed by the United States Bureau of Internal Revenue. Miles was quoted as saying:

> The hell with it . . . I'm not going to work for 'the man' or anyone else. The Internal Revenue people have been messing with my bank account so often that the bank finally got sick and tired of it and closed out my account. Imagine them bothering me after I paid $40,000 in taxes last year alone. To hell with them all – they can kiss my ass. I'm through.[9]

But by the end of the year, Davis had re-signed with Columbia, and this time it was a three-year, $300,000 contract: *Live-Evil* had been released to astonished and delighted notices, and Miles and the group had had a resounding success at the Berlin Festival. Also by the end of the year, Keith Jarrett and Gary Bartz had left, and Miles was looking to funk groups (i.e. non-jazz groups) for his new musicians.

The following year, 1972, saw another decisive change in his music, and this came about in a curious way. It crystallized in the album *On the Corner*, which was recorded at a time when Miles was listening intently to some European avant-garde music (Stockhausen in particular), and having long musical discussions with a young, academy-educated British musician, Paul Buckmaster. The latter had studied the cello both privately and at the Royal Academy of Music, but his interests ranged from the classics and twentieth-century composers such as Roberto Gerhard and Humphrey Scarle to Indian classical music and jazz. As well as being able to compose for large ensembles, Buckmaster also had a remarkable feeling for rhythm, and was completely at home improvising with small jazz or rock groups. He also had an awed regard for Miles Davis's work from the 1950s on.

Paul Buckmaster was managed by Tony Hall, who had been an ardent Miles Davis fan since the late 1940s, and who had become friendly with the trumpeter during one of his trips to Europe in the 1950s. In 1969, when Miles had come to Britain to play at the Hammersmith Odeon, he had met Paul Buckmaster at Tony Hall's house. Buckmaster recalled:

> He'd heard a tape that I'd got together. It consisted of a twenty-five-minute jam [session]. All I'd supplied was a drum rhythm and a bass figure which could mutate from one form to another shape. And the thing went through a lot of mood changes – light, heavy, dark, intense – definitely space music. He liked this.

The following day, Buckmaster had accompanied Miles on a shopping spree, taking in some of the most fashionable clothes designers in London.

But it wasn't until 1972 that Paul Buckmaster received a telephone call from Miles asking him to fly over to New York and work on some music at Davis's house. Buckmaster stayed with the trumpeter for about six weeks in May and June of that year. Every morning, Miles and his protégé, who was exactly twenty years younger and also a Gemini, would talk about various aspects of music, and sometimes Davis would simply listen to Buckmaster practising the cello. At other times, Miles would sit down at the piano and play something, then he would ask Buckmaster to sit down and play. The latter recalled: 'And I would play a phrase that was maybe based on a chord or scale that he'd used and he'd say, "Right! Hold it there. Write that down." So I'd jot it down.'

At the time, Buckmaster was practising some of Bach's unaccompanied suites for cello; every morning he would read through and study them, and Miles would listen and discuss them. Sometimes he singled out particular phrases or passages and said, 'Why don't you write a piece around that?' He became very enthusiastic about Bach. But Buckmaster also introduced Miles to Stockhausen's work. He'd brought with him a record of 'Mixtur' and 'Telemusik' – music for acoustic orchestra that was also mixed up through ring modulators and transformed in that way. Miles sat upstairs for a whole day listening to this record, and had it blaring through the whole house. Subsequently, he bought a number of cassettes of Stockhausen, which he played in his car. But although Miles found the German composer's music interesting, it is unlikely that he would have willingly moved his own music towards Stockhausen's conception, because he was groping for a fresh direction that would take him nearer to the black audience in America – an audience to whom the sounds of Stockhausen were foreign.

Some four days after Paul Buckmaster arrived at Miles's house, in May 1972, he learned that there was to be a recording session in two or three weeks' time. When Miles asked him what ideas he had about the music they were going to record, Buckmaster said he would like to see what would happen if they utilized the non-regular temporal music (out-of-time passages), already indicated in some of Miles's recent work, that was typical of certain pieces of Stockhausen. The idea would be to try and combine that approach with some sort of street-music concept (city street), at the same time combining it with the space concept. As the recording date drew nearer, Buckmaster felt less sure of what Miles wanted, and more nervous about the occasion. It was not until they actually arrived at the studio that it became certain what the exact personnel for the session was going to be. Miles had phoned around and booked musicians, but a couple of the people he'd booked brought along other musicians who were then introduced to Davis. According to Buckmaster, that seemed to be how Harold Williamson, who played keyboard on one track, got on the session ... and how the drummer, Al Foster, did too; it was the first time Miles had met Foster. The total personnel comprised two drummers, bass guitar, three keyboard players, two percussionists and a tabla player, sitar, guitar, two reed players and Miles himself.

Paul Buckmaster described how Miles extracted what he needed from the material they had prepared, and how the music was created in the studio:

> There would be a bass figure, a drum rhythm that was notated, tabla and conga rhythm and a couple of keyboard phrases which fitted. In fact, I would write out a whole tune, but what actually happened in the studio was that the keyboard players related to these phrases and transformed them. They played them more or less accurately to begin with and transformed them in the Stockhausian sense – making them more unrecognizable until they became something else. I had written places where changes would occur, but these changes weren't rehearsed and they didn't occur. I made photostat copies of these parts and gave them to the musicians, and Miles asked me to sing the bass part and sing the drum part and check the keyboard phrases with the players. And I'd barely done this when he said, 'OK. That's enough of that!' and started clicking his fingers, beating time, and the thing would start and go on for half an hour until he'd say, 'OK. That's enough of that. Let's go and hear it.' ... If he wanted it to be more bouncing or raunchy rhythmically, he would signify by a characteristic shrugging of the shoulders. He

would also indicate coming down with body movements . . .
arm gestures.

It is ironic that after his discussions with Paul Buckmaster, and
after his immersion in the music of Stockhausen, Miles should
have produced an album (*On the Corner*) so alien to the European
tradition. Although the instrumentation is related to that on
Bitches Brew, the music is very different. There is some vital interplay, particularly between the chordal instruments (Herbie Hancock and John McLaughlin were on this session) and the horns,
but the rhythm section roles are very much proscribed. The sitar
provides the perpetual drone, and the brilliantly conceived
intermeshing of the two drums, the congas and tabla, the bass
line, and various other riffs, owes more to Africa and India than the
music on *Bitches Brew*. The German critic and musician, Manfred
Miller, described it as: 'Music based on the principles of West
African ritual dances, with a multi-woven rhythmical line (drum-
choir) as a basis for a "soundstream" and a collective choir which,
instead of fragmented solos, takes the place of the lead singer.'[10]
Miles plays amplified trumpet with wah-wah – never acoustic
trumpet – and he is the leading voice of the ensemble, which
interweaves with flashing rhythms and rich textures. His trumpet
is well down in the mix, and most of the time is more like a
dominant texture than a solo voice. Indeed, for long sections of the
album, Miles does not play at all, but simply directs the ensemble.

There can be no doubt that Miles Davis was radically reassessing
his own work at this time; in a *Playboy* interview, he dismissed
all of his work before 1970. He may, of course, have been trying
to shock the readers into re-evaluating his recent work, but nevertheless there must have been a deep-seated unease behind his out-
burst. The white audience who loved his earlier music of the 1950s
and 1960s had probably been attuned to it by exposure to the
French impressionists and to the Spanish influences which lay
behind the Miles Davis/Gil Evans orchestral music and much of
the Davis small-group music of that time. Many ghetto blacks, of
course, did not have this conditioning, and therefore Miles's earlier

music had largely escaped them. Perhaps the realization of this lay behind Miles's assertion in that interview that he wanted to be accepted by black audiences on the same terms as the Temptations. And from this point onwards, his music showed a much greater emphasis on rhythm – on a steadily incessant 'soundstream' in which audiences could find familiarity and reassurance. Later, his thoughts were to crystallize on this subject:

> I like when a black boy says, 'Oohh! Man, there's Miles Davis.' Like they did with Joe Louis. Some cats did me like that in Greensboro. They said, 'Man, we sure glad you came down here.' That thrilled me more than anything that happened to me that year . . . I don't feel like I'm doing anything. I mean, so what, so I play music but my race don't get it. You know what I mean, it's 'cause they can't afford it, man.[11]

During 1972, Miles attacked the record industry's 'Grammy' awards because, he said, they usually went to white artists who had made their careers out of copying black artists. Miles wanted to initiate some awards for blacks only, and to call them 'Mammy' awards. He said:

> The Mammys are going to be different. I got the idea watching this programme on TV: *Soultrain*. It's an all-black show and it's better . . . than all other shows on the stage. Kids are dancing and moving, taking off, you know. And it's no African boonga, bonga, boonga; just black Americans doing their thing . . . That is what Mammys are going to be like: fun . . . What we could do . . . is give them an award and then have them tear it up right on TV, and then give them a film clip of that as the real award. Hell, it's just going to be fun; like it should be. None of this Grammy shit of being prim and proper so the President can see it.[12]

Miles also refused, at the last moment, to play the Newport Festival because he thought his fee of $7,500 was for one show only, but discovered that he had to play twice for that money. He claimed that he once previously worked for George Wein (organizer of Newport) for a reduced fee in order to help the promoter out, and then found that other promoters wanted to pay him the same low price. Davis said:

We're past that stage of a Newport jazz artist, which is like an Uncle Tom version of a slave musician working for his master, George Wein ... He'll pay me what I want ... but I just don't want to do it. I can't cheapen myself by being one of the Newport boys. He keeps sending me telegrams saying, 'You can't do this to me', but look what he's doing to me.[13]

There had been another brush with the law in July, when Miles was charged with unlawfully imprisoning and menacing a woman in his own house. One of his former tenants, Mrs Lita Merker, charged that on 9 July Miles verbally abused her, slapped her and prevented her from leaving his apartment. A detective who examined her said he found no signs of injuries at all, but described her as being 'emotionally upset'. Miles, wearing a blue-striped shirt, flared blue pants and red shoes, pleaded innocent before the judge. The case was adjourned until 22 August, with Davis put on parole in his own custody. Miles had told this woman: 'You respect my name ... Look at these trophies and awards. Don't you ever scream at a black man. You don't know what your ancestors have done to him.'[14] The papers were full of headlines alleging that Miles Davis had molested a white woman etc., but Miles later recalled:

They neglected to say that she lived upstairs, that my woman was standing right there when it all went down, and that the white woman had got caught smuggling hashish into this country. She was upset about that and apologized for trying to take her frustrations out on me. No, the news media didn't pick that up and run with it.[15]

Miles's health was not quite so good this year. In April he had been rushed to hospital with gallstone trouble. He was also having trouble with his breathing, although he was still working out in the gym two or three times a week and usually in three-hour stints. Paul Buckmaster noted that when Miles was asleep the rasping breath of the trumpeter could be heard all over the house. And almost as if Miles were courting disaster, he crashed his car into a traffic island on Manhattan's West Side Highway at 8 a.m. on 9 October. He had felt restless and decided to take a morning drive. It was a costly whim; both his legs were broken, and he suffered facial cuts requiring twelve stitches. This effectively stopped him from working for the rest of the year. When a reporter asked him about the accident, he said: 'I'm all right ... I'll just have to stop buying those little cars.'[16]

After recording *On the Corner*, Miles had got together a band to play that music in live performance. It included drummer Al Foster, and conga player M'tume who was, in fact, the son of Miles's old associate, saxophonist Jimmy Heath. The instrumentation also included tablas (Badal Roy), sitar, guitar and saxophone. Miles rehearsed them at his home for some days before they went out on the road. After some five or six concerts, they played the Philharmonic Hall, New York, on 29 September, and this was recorded by Columbia (*Miles Davis in Concert*). The music has the rhythmic 'soundstream' of *On the Corner* but it also refers back to some of the bass figures of *Jack Johnson* and *Live-Evil*. Davis plays with wah-wah throughout and seems to be in good lip for the occasion. Although there are some excellent moments, the performance as a whole is too diffuse to bear comparison with his best work.

On the Corner was released in the autumn, and Miles wanted to tour with his new band to promote the album. They were scheduled to open at Harlem's Apollo Theatre on 24 October, but his car accident put a stop to that. This was bad luck, because *On the Corner* received excellent reviews and sold more than 50,000 in the first week, so there was every chance of it achieving really big sales if Miles promoted it properly. The artwork marked a departure, in that it consisted of caricature drawings of blacks in platform shoes, hotpants (the girls) and flared pants, all standing in various postures on the street. There are one or two token whites in the scene, but the general impression is that Columbia were attempting to make a folk hero of Miles. This was certainly what he wanted. And there was another new departure with this album: the names of the musicians were not credited on the sleeve. One reason was certainly because Miles felt that the new direction would incur the misapprehension and wrath of the usual jazz critics. He said: 'There's no critic in that world that knows as much about my music as I do. There's no but, period . . . I didn't put those names on *On the Corner* specially for that reason, so now the critics have to say, "What's that instrument, and what's that?" . . . the critics have to listen.'[17] But it also seemed that Miles might be phasing out the period when musicians climbed to stardom on his back. He was very pleased with *On the Corner* and said: 'People have to respect me, I know they respect me, there's no doubt about it because they can't do it themselves. Otherwise there'd be five *On the Corners*.'[18]

SEVENTEEN

Manhattan Jungle Symphony

'I don't care who buys the records as long as they
get to the black people, so I will be remembered
when I die.'[1]

Miles Davis

Miles Davis began 1973 on crutches and with one of his legs still
in plaster, but despite his injuries, he was determined to work and
did so throughout that year. On stage, he sat on a tall stool in
front of the band and exercised much more control than he had
done over his previous ensembles. Despite the large salaries he
had paid his musicians since 1970, most of the jazz virtuosi had
left, and Miles was now producing an essentially collective music
with multiple rhythms and textures. Early in 1973, saxophonist
Dave Liebman, who had played on the first side of *On the Corner*,
joined Miles's touring band, but even though Liebman was a virtuoso soloist, his talents were used collectively; he was not a solo
star supported by an ensemble, but a part of the colour and texture
of that ensemble. The rest of the line-up comprised Michael
Henderson, Al Foster (drums), Badal Roy (tabla), James M'tume
(percussion), Balakrishna (sitar), Reggie Lucas (guitar) and Cedric
Lawson (organ).

From this period on, Miles usually rehearsed his musicians individually at his home, showing each man the kind of rhythmic
patterns he would create for different pulses and at various tempos.
Miles now directed his ensemble both by playing and by using
bodily signals; with a flick of his wrist the whole ensemble would

slide smoothly from one complex rhythmic pattern to another. It was done so perfectly, and was such a dramatic change, that one critic, who had heard it only on record, thought that it was an edited tape-splice. On attending a concert, he was astonished to witness it happening on stage. Attempting to explain his new approach, Miles said:

It's just about three bands in one, just feeling out different rhythms. We have African drums, an Eastern section and melodies, although the melodies are shorter and most times the things I play are based on rhythm because most of the melodies you can possibly hear have been recorded by the record companies and exploited. In melody you have usually heard it somewhere before, so I use polyrhythms, and things I write might be in the bass or drums.[2]

Dave Liebman, who had previously worked with Elvin Jones and Pete LaRoca among others, learned a great deal from Miles during the eighteen months he spent with the band. Recalling this period, Liebman said:

You can play lines ... that flow over the time and rhythm. But if you point off your lines by stopping and going with a particular kind of rhythmic figure, maybe a staccato figure, you tie in the rhythm section in a very quick way. You make them come together very quickly. Miles is a master at this. He plays one note and everybody gathers to that note, or he plays something and lets the band take it from there. He said, 'Don't finish your idea; let them finish it'; and 'End your solo before you're done.' ... Before, I would always take it through a cycle, up and down like Coltrane. But Miles creates an overall mood where each solo is just a little part of a larger picture ... So the thing is to give the essence to the musicians without creating their parts for them ... Even with electronic instruments, Miles still used colour to differentiate one note from another. Even playing E flat for four hours, which is what we did most of the time, even within the context of that very limited area and beat, and four guitars and an amazing amount of sound – even within that I was able to discern the subtleties of Miles's playing.[3]

From Liebman's description, it can be seen that even though Miles's music had apparently changed radically, many of the old criteria still applied. Areas of subtlety and lyricism did exist, though now they took on rather different forms. Miles's new band and its music, however, presented great problems for some critics, particularly jazz critics, one of whom was seen openly weeping at one of Davis's concerts. Many critics who had made Herculean efforts to understand Miles's previous changes of direction now began dismissing the music.

If many jazz critics gave up at this point, many other critics were stimulated and excited by the music, using terms such as 'sonic jungle' and 'Manhattan jungle symphony' to describe their impressions. One reviewer wrote excitedly:

Miles, still suffering the after-effects of an abrupt meeting between his car and a wall, hobbled in a walking cast, and was in a genuinely good mood. Swinging about on a stool, he conducted the band, altering the texture with brief signals, guiding soloists in and out and often changing the beat completely with a single wave of his hand. And he soloed beautifully, dominating the music with a lot of open horn, some amazing wah-wah pedal trumpet, and brief patches of mute. Sometimes his sudden leaps into the upper register would leave me gasping for breath. He used sharp phrases that tugged at the rhythm, and as always his improvisation suggested and hinted much more than it actually came right out and said . . . Miles began hushing the band up at intervals and dropping poignant *Kind of Blue* lines, his trumpet pointed downward toward the floor of the stage, as if raising the spirits of his past. The dialogues with Liebman's sax were fascinating. The two men would spit lines back and forth at each other, blend them together in unison, blare them out like a wild fanfare, and then team up together on some shrieking high note until it disappeared into the heavens.[4]

This was the first time Miles had regularly utilized the dialogue technique with his saxophonist, though there had been at least one isolated example in the past (a version of 'The Theme' on *Live at the Plugged Nickel Vol. 2*, December 1965). Miles and Liebman were working on yet another variation of the call-and-response device and it was natural that the instrumental sounds were extremely vocalized. Since 1969, Miles's groups had been creating music veering further and further away from the orthodox notational system of Western music. At the time of *Bitches Brew*, only a fraction of the music was conventional enough to make transcription a possibility; by 1973, his music was almost totally beyond transcription. It was not just that the subtle rhythms and inflexions were outside the scope of Western notation, but that there were no precise symbols for the kinds of sounds Davis was using. The non-Western elements (African and Oriental) in his music were becoming ever more dominant. Reviewing a 1974 concert in the *Washington Post*, writer Gene Williams compared Miles with someone who was

leading his exploring party through a dense electronic rain forest. Sensing a clearing, Davis extends his fingers in a signal and his group halts motionless as a soprano sax or electric guitar or even the leader's trumpet slips ahead alone, reporting what he sees. The leader listens, choosing a path. He arches his body, nodding his head to the desired pulse, beckoning the rhythm guitar, and his group falls in, resuming their journey. Echoing, reverberating, electronically shaped notes and phrases form the strange beautiful foliage and strong life rhythms of Davis's musical world.[5]

This new phase of Miles's music seemed even more alien to some of his old associates. Bassist Percy Heath, for example, who had starred in all those wonderful 1954 sessions, said in 1975, 'Miles isn't playing music any more, he's only playing rhythm.' This is a curious statement that deserves a brief examination. Rhythm and pulse are, of course, the basis of all music, because they mark the passing of time – without which there can be no music. Keith Jarrett has said that for classical musicians pulse is only pulse – i.e. merely the tempo of the music, not the music itself. But his answer to that is, 'It's not just the tempo if you're *in* the tempo when you're playing it. Then it's music.' Miles Davis was always *in the tempo* when he was playing it, and he and his musicians in the mid-1970s were definitely creating music.

There were also upheavals in Miles's private life at this time. The previous year, Marguerite Eskridge had finally left him, because she was tired of being treated like a chattel and of Miles's infidelities. She continued to live in one of the upstairs apartments for a while, but eventually moved out, taking their son Erin with her. Jackie Battle then became very close to Miles, but his addiction to cocaine upset her, and when he seemed incapable of giving it up, she left him. After that there were occasional girlfriends, but Miles was mostly on his own and his cocaine consumption was unrestrained.

Miles also terminated the long business relationship with Harold Lovett, his black lawyer/manager. His new manager was white and Jewish, a man called Neil Reshin who specialized in representing 'difficult' artists. Lovett had idolized Miles, but Reshin's strength was his ability at his job, his hard-headedness and his unsentimental approach to the business of protecting the interests of his clients. In February 1973, Reshin managed to rescue Miles from a very awkward situation. Once again, the trumpeter had a brush with the law, and this time it could have become a serious matter. Davis was arrested at his own address on 23 February on charges of possession of cocaine and of possessing a dangerous weapon (a .25 calibre automatic pistol).

According to Reshin, Miles and a girlfriend got back to Miles's house around 1 a.m. and the trumpeter couldn't find his keys and began banging on his own front door. One of his tenants upstairs heard someone trying to break down the door, and phoned the police. A sergeant and a patrolman arrived on the scene, and as soon as she saw them, Miles's girlfriend threw her handbag into a corner. The two policeman saw the bag on the ground and asked to whom it belonged. Miles and his girlfriend said they didn't know, so the policeman opened it and found some cocaine and a loaded pistol, whereupon they arrested Miles and the girl. At 3 a.m., Reshin got a phone call from the police precinct saying, 'We have Miles Davis here and he's using you as his one phone call.' Miles got on the phone and said, 'Neil, get me outa here, they're treating me like a nigger.'[6] Reshin called a lawyer and then went back to sleep. But at 5 a.m., there was another phone call, and Miles said, 'Neil, get me outa here, wake up a fucking judge or something.'[7] In the morning, Reshin talked to the district attorney, who said that it was impossible to drop a gun charge on a black man in New York when policemen were getting shot on the streets every day. On 1 March Miles was fined $1,000 on the weapons charge and was given two months to pay, but the judge said that there was insufficient evidence to convict him of charges of possessing three small packages of cocaine.

Police harassment had become so familiar to Miles that he soon got over this incident, but there were other problems which struck home deeply. Despite his apparent self-sufficiency ('I don't live for my family, I live for myself')[8] his family problems continued to sadden and trouble him. He was proud of his eldest son, Gregory, who had been an army boxing champion, and kept Gregory's three trophies – each of a little gold fighter leading with his right – by his bed. But Gregory was still alienated by his army experiences in Vietnam and in trouble. Miles, pointing to the boxing trophies, told a reporter:

See these trophies? They're my son's. He was a champion boxer in the army in Germany. He comes back, a white guy pokes fun at him because of his colour, and the first thing my son does is try to break his neck, you know? And I tried to tell him about this shit . . . But he's a Black Muslim, and he says, 'What do you think I'm supposed to do, father, let the guy stand up and say that to me? They send me into the army to kill somebody I don't even know, then they won't give me a job, they make fun of me.' He's in jail now . . . in St Louis. I got to get him out fast.[9]

By 1973, several of Miles's recent ex-sidemen were world-famous superstars in their own right. Chick Corea's Return to Forever was extremely popular and successful, and his records came out on the Polydor label. But three groups were recording for Miles's own company, Columbia, and outselling their former boss: John McLaughlin's Mahavishnu Orchestra, Zawinul and Wayne Shorter's Weather Report, and Herbie Hancock and his group. The last two were already beginning to make a big impact on black audiences – the very thing that Miles wanted so much to do. In 1973, Hancock's *Head Hunters* was released and became the biggest- and fastest-selling album in jazz history. Miles actually felt in danger of being overshadowed by his ex-musicians, and phoned Neil Reshin demanding that he get him a publicity agent. Reshin called the publicity department at Columbia and told them how unhappy Miles Davis was. So Columbia began contacting writers and setting up a series of interviews.

Miles's alarm – or actual jealousy, as some writers called it – must be seen in perspective. First of all, his ex-associates were all making accessible music for which there seemed to be ready-made markets. In the case of the Mahavishnu Orchestra, there was the white, Eastward-looking rock audience that had been built up in the 1960s by the cult of the guru and the interest in Indian religion started mainly by the Beatles; in the case of Herbie Hancock and Weather Report, their secular, intensely funky sounds were acceptable to rock fans, but also appealed to the black market, whose ears were attuned to Sly Stone and Stevie Wonder. Although Miles Davis was exploring rhythms accessible to these audiences, the extremely African elements in his current music were as foreign to American blacks as they were to whites. In particular, the absence of organic harmony (chord sequences) and of diatonic melody made his music forbidding, even alien, to ears attuned to the European tradition. Furthermore, to quote the German writer, Manfred Miller, Miles was no longer sharing 'the tonal system of any "white" middle-class tradition'.[10] Also, he had never really tried to create music for a particular market. On this subject, Miles said:

> I tell the guitar player that if he likes Hendrix or Sly, to play something like that, just to open it up. It can't sound exactly like them because it'll have a little more music . . . in it. What we play on top wouldn't be like what Hendrix'll play on top; what Sly and them need is a good soloist . . . I ain't thinking about no fucking market . . . Hendrix had no knowledge of modal music; he was just a natural musician, you know, he wasn't studied, he wasn't into no market, and neither am I. Columbia tries to get me into that shit but I won't let them do it.[11]

Columbia's three 'acolyte' groups all functioned in the usual way, releasing albums only at fairly wide intervals, and promoting each album by touring and playing pieces from it. Miles, on the other hand, was prodigal with his record releases; there were usually at least two new albums a year, either or both of which, after 1970, might be double-albums. And every year saw the reissue of some gem or other from his past, or of a composite LP of some of his most famous pieces. Even when he agreed to make a 'single' (a 45 r.p.m. disc that might get top forty airplay), the one he made in 1969 was in no sense tailored for any market; even the musicians on the session didn't know what to make of the music. It was called 'Little Blue Frog' and it lasted two minutes and thirty-seven seconds – the only concession Miles made to the industry's requirements. The instrumentation for this brief piece included tabla, tambour, electric bass, acoustic bass, guitar, three keyboards, three saxophones, three drummers. Herbie Hancock, who played one of the keyboards, recalled: 'We must have come out of the studio and scratched our heads wondering what the heck was that about?

It was interesting, but we had no idea whether it was good or bad. It was just so different.'

There was always a great difference between Miles's music and that of almost all his ex-associates. Teo Macero commented:

> Of all the people that have played with him . . . sooner or later, they start out being a little aggressive and all of a sudden they revert back and they establish themselves in a groove, and there they stay. But unlike those, Miles has transposed himself from here to here, and has moved constantly. And all the other people are moving backwards . . . and you can go back and listen to any of them . . . You can listen to Bill Evans, and Cannonball when he was alive, they didn't do anything experimental . . . Coltrane was the only one. I think Coltrane had more sense of Miles in direction . . . But all the players . . . you listen to them and you say, 'What are they doing? I heard all that before.' But Miles . . . you never heard it before . . . The source was Miles Davis. Herbie, Wayne Shorter, Joe Zawinul, Chick Corea, Bill Evans – all these people, they all come from one group – McLaughlin too – he developed into something unique with Miles. With Miles, they play at their very best all of the time.

The music created by Miles's bands from 1973 onwards was much more forbidding and severe than that of his ex-associates. His habit of staying on one root for very long periods of time ('E flat for four hours' as Dave Liebman put it) was rather like taking, say, one bar or one chord of a tune and putting it under a microscope: examining in extreme close-up its melodic, rhythmic, textural, spatial implications. At the same time, this process could also contain the essence of other eras, styles and themes, hence Miles's (cryptic) comment: 'All the clichés are so condensed that you can play "Body and Soul" in two bars.'[12] The result of such austerity was that people often went to his concerts more because of the mystique surrounding Miles than because of their interest in his music. Rock fans could relate to his rhythms, but were often baffled by and complained about the 'disorganization' of the music. At the Berlin Festival, Miles and the group played a wildly exciting set and his trumpet playing (with wah-wah) was extraordinarily powerful. The feeling of invocation, of possession, was enhanced by the ritualistic way Miles bobbed up and down and sweated, a hypnotic, demonic figure in dark glasses that curved round his face like the huge eyes of an insect. He was also wearing robes that looked African, and seemed to be exulting in the 'Prince of Darkness' image. Before going on stage, he snarled at a young fan standing in the wings, and flipped his cigarette end contemptuously over her head. When a female journalist went to his hotel to interview him, he opened the door and was brutally rude to her, whereupon she retired in confusion. In 1975, when he was asked why he wasn't playing so much trumpet, Miles said:

> I play my trumpet long enough, but some people don't notice it because they are busy looking to see what I have on, how tight my pants are in the crotch, how much I'm sweating, and all that. Then there are those who just look, how you are taking care of yourself, how you are using the money you make, what kind of girls you like. But all the serious listeners in the audience want for me to do is to play. And I just give it all I got, and that's it.[13]

Miles gained some recognition at the end of 1973, however, and during the following year, which he must have found gratifying and reassuring. The Japanese quarterly magazine, *Ad Lib*, devoted its entire autumn (1973) edition to Miles Davis. In this glossy and expensive issue, there were 318 pages, hundreds of photographs, critical analyses, and discographies. It was a unique act of homage. In America, the 18 July 1974 issue of *Down Beat* (the magazine's fortieth anniversary issue) contained a long interview with Miles, and a tribute to him complete with framed adulatory quotes from people representing all aspects of the music industry. And there were particularly generous quotes from Miles's recent ex-associates: Herbie Hancock, Joe Zawinul, John McLaughlin and Chick Corea.

When Miles and his band played a concert at the Avery Fisher Hall in September, he surprised everyone by starting exactly on time, waving a fist at the audience as he walked on stage, flashing smiles at everyone, and actually fooling around with M'tume playing on the congas and then offering his horn for M'tume to play. The latter seemed taken aback and was reluctant to respond, but Miles insisted and even seemed disappointed when the percussionist blew only a few notes and tried to hand it back. At the end of the set, Miles picked up a black cane and strolled off stage, waving to the audience as he did so. During the interval, he actually reappeared on stage to touch hands with the crowd milling round the apron, and even allowed an MC to read out the personnel. One critic noted, however: 'Significantly, his present audience has a higher percentage of blacks than the white-dominated clubs he used to work ... for the first time in more than a decade, his music seems static ... Davis seems locked in a cul de sac: he has become predictable.'[14]

At this time, Miles seemed suddenly to miss his older friends – contemporaries who appeared to be alienated from him by his new music and new lifestyle. When Paul Buckmaster was staying with him, Miles had gone out to see only one musical event; he had taken Buckmaster to hear Ahmad Jamal, and had still enthused about the pianist. But, apart from this isolated example, Miles rarely saw any of the old associates to whom he had once been so close. It was after hearing that Thad Jones had walked out of one of his concerts that Miles felt pangs of rejection and a certain loneliness. He said:

You know, Thad's always around, and he doesn't come to see me. All the young musicians do, but Thad and all the friends that I like never do. Dizzy asks me to teach him. I say, 'Yeah, come by. I'll show you everything we're doing. It'll be my pleasure. You tell me when.' And he don't come by. Herbie Hancock always comes by when he's in town.

Chick does . . . No, Chick doesn't come to hear me . . . Chick wouldn't be interested in my band . . . Damn it, I'm gonna throw a party. Do you think they'll come? Max, Mingus, Gil, Dizzy, Thad? . . . That's what I'm gonna do, I'm gonna throw a party.[15]

Around the middle of the year the double-album, *Big Fun*, was released, and most of the tracks were performances from the 1969/ 70 period. Only one, 'Ife', came from the later *On the Corner* sessions. Of *Big Fun*, Miles commented: 'I'll be tired of this music before today is over. That's four years old!'[16] But the end of the year saw the release of *Get Up with It*, which was more representative of Miles's current work. On 24 May, two days before Miles's forty-eighth birthday, Duke Ellington had died of lung cancer. *Get Up with It* was dedicated to Ellington, who had done so much for jazz and for twentieth-century music in general. Miles said: 'I loved and respected Duke. He was one of my idols. He sent me a letter before he died, to say goodbye.'[17] Side one of this double-album is Miles Davis's tribute to Duke – his elegy for him. It is a long (thirty-minute) piece called 'He Loved Him Madly', and begins out-of-time with sparse, lamenting electronic sounds and broken phrases from one of the guitars. It moves imperceptibly into C minor and a time-feel, finishing with a long grooving pulse that transforms all the grieving into something positive and even optimistic. Dave Liebman plays some lyrical flute, and Miles with wah-wah shows all the glory of his acoustic tone even though he is amplified and using repeated echo. It is a superb tribute, and one Ellington would have deeply appreciated.

The rest of the album is uneven in quality, and some pieces are simply dull. The first part of 'Maiysha' for example, with its claves, its smooth latin rhythm and comfortable chord sequence, gets very near to 'easy listening' night club music, rather in the way that some pieces on *Quiet Nights* had done twelve years previously. 'Red China Blues' is also a very ordinary bit of 12/8 soul music. The fantastic spate of creative activity that started in 1968 and cut a large wedge into the 1970s was now dwindling, and encroaching illness may have had something to do with this. A decade earlier, Miles had been hospitalized with calcium deposits in his hip joints, and in 1974 the ailment returned in a much worse form. The hip joint seemed to be disintegrating, and apart from the pain this caused, Miles also complained that he could not exercise properly because his leg simply went out of its socket if he tried. By mid-1974 he was having to take about eight pain-killing pills a day. He had suffered from insomnia for years and, for example, in the late 1950s when he was on tour and couldn't sleep, he often used to wake up drummer Jimmy Cobb and talk to him. Now the pain from his hip joint was making it even more difficult for him to sleep. Late in 1974, while doing his first tour of Brazil, he drank vodka, took pills and cocaine, then collapsed and had to be rushed to hospital. The next day, however, he was perfectly fit again and played superbly. But that brush with the grim reaper made him consider, for the first time, the possibility of retiring from music. In February 1975, while touring Japan, his health worsened. He said: 'I kept throwing up in every city. I had to have pills for my leg, codeine and morphine. But you have to work, you have to make the date.'[18] Then back in the States in March, his ulcer flared up again, but he forced himself to appear at concerts that had already been booked. Herbie Hancock was now a big star after the success of his album *Head Hunters*, and Miles was chafing at the indignity of touring as support group for his ex-sideman. His road manager, Chris Murphy, said:

Miles hates to cancel gigs. I've seen him play – like the gig he did in March with Herbie Hancock in St Louis, Miles came off the stage and was sick to his stomach, violently sick. And I said, 'Come on, go lie down in the dressing room.' And he said, 'Fuck that shit,' and went back on stage and finished the set, played beautifully.[19]

There was a party after the concert in his home town, and Irene Birth, the mother of his three adult children, turned up and made a big scene in front of Miles's family, friends and musicians, accusing him of dereliction of his duties as a father, and expressing her hurt and anger at the way she had been treated over the years. Miles wept, because he knew that he bore much of the blame for the failure of their two sons, and of his relationship with Irene. After the party he collapsed with a bleeding ulcer and had to be rushed to hospital and, while there, he also had thirty polyps or nodules removed from his vocal cords. He was visited there by an old friend who always stayed faithful – Clark Terry, who was in St Louis at the time with George Wein's mini-Newport package tour. Terry said:

> I saw him in an East St Louis hospital ... Gerry Mulligan and I were doing a radio show, with my small group, Gerry's group and Gary Burton's group. Mulligan and I were sitting around talking after the show and I had a phone call from Miles's doctor who says, 'I'm Miles's doctor and I know he's a good friend of yours and he thinks a lot of you and I just thought you'd like to know that he's in hospital.' So we, my nephew and I, went right over there.

When he got out of hospital, Miles carried on playing concerts with his band. His live performances had always been variable in quality, but from the spring to the summer of 1975, there were times when, musically, the band seemed to reach an absolute nadir. This occurred when the theatrical side of a performance – the physical, non-musical, events on stage – took precedence over the actual music. One such performance was witnessed by the British trombonist and arranger, Derek Wadsworth, in San Francisco. Miles and the band were appearing in a fairly shabby, smoky cellar-club that held about three hundred people. The place was packed and the audience was mainly black.

On this occasion, Miles was wearing a superbly-cut chamois leather suit with cowboy tassels and thongs hanging from it, a Dior silk neckerchief, and a shirt with sequins. The usual huge sunglasses completely masked his eyes. He strode out on stage first, and the band followed him, scuffling subserviently to their

The Birdland beating. Miles being escorted to gaol after he was beaten and arrested by New York police outside Birdland, 1959.

The rhythm section in London, 1961. *Left to right* Jimmy Cobb, Wynton Kelly and Paul Chambers.

The Miles Davis Quintet and Gil Evans Orchestra at Carnegie Hall, 19 May 1961.

Miles at the Hammersmith Odeon, London, 1967.

Miles and his producer, Teo Macero, in the studio, 1969. The image below was used on the inside of the sleeve for *Bitches Brew*.

Above: The second great quintet, 1960s. *Left to right* Herbie Hancock, Miles, Ron Carter, Wayne Shorter and Tony Williams.

Below: The Berlin Festival, 1969. *Left to right* Dave Holland, Jack DeJohnette and Miles Davis.

Miles with Clive Davis, vice-president of CBS Records.

Keith Jarrett and Miles Davis, Isle of Wight, 1970.

Miles in the early 1970s.

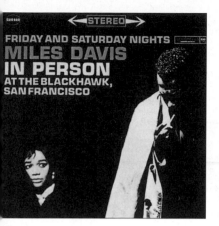

A selection of key album covers

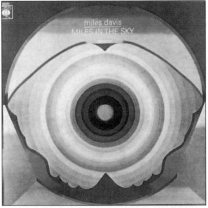

places. Almost at once, a heavy rhythm began on one chord. The whole audience was waiting for Miles to play his trumpet, but in front of him was an organ, and after the rhythm had been building up for a good ten minutes, he leaned over to play this organ. He didn't deign to use his fingers, however, or to make any coherent chord or phrase on it; he simply leaned his elbow on the keyboard and produced a violent, dissonant sound. Then he leaned back and glared at the audience. And so it went on for what seemed like a very long time: elbow on organ, then leaning back and glowering at the audience. Then he wandered over and stood in front of the conga player, staring at him, and with his back to the audience began to wiggle his bottom to the rhythm.

After a while he blew a couple of notes on his trumpet, then put it down again and went back to elbowing the organ keyboard. Almost an hour had gone by, and the key and the pulse had remained constant. The interest had been entirely visual, entirely theatrical. It was reminiscent of the Archie Shepp concert at the British Expo in 1967; in each case, the artist seemed to be attempting to rile the audience to get a reaction. By now, even the black people in the San Francisco audience were becoming disenchanted with their hero. One shouted out: 'Sketches of Spain!' Another one yelled: 'Give us a song!' And then, Miles started taking off his chamois leather jacket in a very deliberate manner, and the audience began shouting and jeering as if he were a strip-tease artist. In fact, he had made a sort of ritual of taking off his jacket at concerts for some years now. At the 1971 Festival Hall concert in Britain, he had held the entire audience riveted as he slowly removed his black velvet jacket. But on that occasion, he had also played superb trumpet. At the 1975 concert, all his mannerisms and rituals and the non-musical aspects of his performance (which he knew had drawn audiences to his concerts for years, and had thus helped to finance his whole operation) had reached macabre proportions. It was as if he were saying by his actions: 'OK. If this is what brings you to my music, then this is what I'm going to give you!' Whatever the reasons, the ritual of removing his coat, as his bottom-wiggling had done, took on grotesque comic dimensions because, when the jacket was half off, the thongs and tassels became tangled in the sequins of his shirt, and Miles was stuck with it. He could not get it back on; nor could he take it off. His four white, long-haired road managers scuttled on stage and, two at either side of Davis, began disentangling the sequins and thongs. It was a ludicrous sight; a kind of black comedy. And after almost two hours, Miles had still not played any trumpet. At that point, Derek Wadsworth and the British contingent left the club in disgust.

The only recordings of the Miles Davis band during this period were two live double-albums made during their Japanese tour earlier in the year. On 1 February, their afternoon and evening concerts were recorded and later released on Japanese CBS under the respective titles of *Agharta* and *Pangaea*. Both albums offer long stretches of powerful rhythm, plenty of trumpet playing, and some excellent saxophone from Sonny Fortune. But they are diffuse, and would have been improved by rigorous editing. Also, *Agharta* in particular suffers from a monotony of sound caused mainly by the perpetual 'freaking-out' of the lead guitarists, Pete Cosey and Reggie Lucas. Even so, the album is almost redeemed by the indomitable jazz virtuosity of Sonny Fortune, whose playing is full of vitality. But the most telling factor in both albums is the emotional climate of Miles's own trumpet playing. Although he is in good lip, and often creates strong rhythms, his sound is intensely mournful – almost weary. It is characterized by sadness which seems all-pervasive, and even the bursts of energy seem to have a certain desperation. There is nothing of his old buoyancy, that 'joy with a melancholy edge' which typified his best work. And his lamenting sound is at strange odds with the band's heavy and driving rhythms.

Miles Davis played the Newport Festival in July, and a concert in Central Park, New York City, in August, and then disbanded because he needed to sort out his health problems. With typically ghoulish humour, he organized what he called a 'doctor party'. By this time, he had a hernia as well as his other ailments, as did his old friend Gil Evans, and Gil's wife, Anita. So Miles laid on some French salads at his house and invited all his friends who had physical ailments. The guest of honour was Muhammad Ali's doctor, and after partaking of the refreshments, he examined each of the guests. This was, perhaps, Miles's way of helping his less affluent friends. Gil Evans said, recalling this event: 'Don't believe all the things you read about Miles: he's one of the nicest, gentlest men.'

In September, however, Miles's operation was delayed because he again contracted pneumonia and had to be rushed to hospital by ambulance. His general health in 1975 was so bad that it gave cause for concern to everyone. There was a general feeling of mortality in the jazz world after the many premature deaths in recent years. In 1975 Miles's old friend, Cannonball Adderley, died at the age of only forty-six. Thirteen years previously, Cannonball had been told that he had only ten years more to live because he had sugar diabetes and was overweight. So when Miles left hospital after being cured of pneumonia and went home to recuperate and gather his strength for the major hip surgery, he was at last visited by some of the friends who had been shunning him. In the late summer, Percy Heath, with his brothers Jimmy and Tootie, bulldozed their way in to visit Miles. When they were asked at the door what they wanted, they said, 'We've come to see him because we know he's sick and lonely, and we know he wants to see us.' And in they went.

In December 1975, Miles was at last strong enough to undergo surgery, and a prosthetic ball-and-socket was implanted in the hip. He spent the whole of 1976 recuperating, and during this time renewed his association with Gil Evans. The two men, after a gap of eight years or so, began to consider another collaboration, and it was rumoured that they might record excerpts from the opera *Tosca*. Miles said:

> I would just play a couple of arias on my trumpet. Some very emotional arias in *Tosca*. I wouldn't know if I could equalize it or not, I wouldn't want to drag it, you know cut it short or play under it. I like the nothing parts, the parts that ramble

. . . I can think of a lot of things to do, man, that'd be great. I can do a nine-piece brass section that plays like we play now, and it'd be a motherfucker. I'd write ten or twelve arrangements. You see, the thing about an arrangement is not to stretch it out so that it gets to be a bore.[20]

But these plans came to nothing. Miles would not touch the trumpet again until 1980, and this empty period would be a dark and desperate time.

EIGHTEEN

The Silent Years, 1976–1980

'Sex and drugs took the place that music had
occupied in my life until then and I did both of them
round the clock.'[1]

Miles Davis

It is clear that, in 1976, Miles Davis had not yet realized the extent
of his physical infirmities or his spiritual malaise, and had no idea
that it would be some years before he would be able to function
normally again. In June, his record contract with Columbia came
up for renewal, but the company did not want to pay Miles the
advance he was asking as part of the re-signing deal. His lawyer
then began negotiations with United Artists and, just as Miles was
about to sign with them, Columbia matched United Artists' offer.
So early in December 1976, Miles Davis renewed his contract with
CBS. At this point, his account was 'in the black' with Columbia,
his record sales having paid off the large advances he'd had. After
the re-signing, Columbia seemed to regard him as a permanent
affiliate and they eventually created the 'Miles Davis Fund', which
paid him on a regular basis. Only one other Columbia artist had
this status: the concert pianist, Vladimir Horowitz. Miles, however, was still in his early fifties (Horowitz was in his seventies),
and Columbia felt, not unreasonably, that they could expect some
fresh recordings. The following year, it was rumoured that Miles
was thinking of forming a group with Gil Evans on keyboards,
but again nothing transpired – 1977 remained empty and silent
on the musical front.

Miles's pride was such that he hated to be thought of as a victim, and his account of this period in his autobiography (published in 1989), has an air of bravado. The hordes of women he had, the 'rich white ladies' who gave him money, his massive consumption of cocaine, plus the wonderful state of his investments and his good financial arrangements with Columbia, all seemed like acts of will and power that put a gloss on his admissions of squalor and dereliction. But, this time, Miles seemed to be driven by forces beyond his control and his descent into darkness and disintegration plumbed the spiritual depths. It was almost as if he needed to rub himself out, erase himself and become a non-entity in order (perhaps) to start afresh. He stayed inside his house for much of the time, with the curtains drawn, the place in darkness lit only by a flickering TV screen. His companion and helper during much of this time was a young black fellow called Eric Engles. The drugs, alcohol and cigarettes continued being consumed, and the house became a shambles, neglected and filthy. Drummer Al Foster and Gil Evans visited him and other musicians also came to see him, but eventually, most people stopped coming, because they saw his disintegration and thought he was going to die. John McLaughlin, one of Miles's most trusted friends, said:

It was very disquieting. I was very worried about him – whether he would live or die – and a lot of people were also. Herbie [Hancock] would be round there . . . We're all fragile to some extent physically, spiritually, emotionally, and we're all subject to the whims of whatever karma is going to fly unexpectedly into the face. And nobody can escape, including Miles Davis. He's a man, you know, he's a great man, but he's a man.

Jack DeJohnette's wife Lydia recalled:

I saw him a couple of times during that reclusive period and Jack saw him more than I did. We thought he was going to die during that period – that he was not going to live. He kept saying, 'I can come back any time I want. How long does it take Jack to get his chops back? Three or four days? I can do it in three or four days.' And of course that wasn't true. But he used to lie on his couch most of the time watching bad television. He used to have this enormous TV screen with a horrible picture and a very bad reception. It was on twenty-four hours a day and he'd just sit there watching it with the blinds drawn. He was also doing a lot of bad drugs too. Jack said he felt the 1960s and 1970s saw a transition in Miles, because he stopped being very healthy and caring about himself when the new designer drugs came in. Miles treated them in the same way as other drugs and they're much more powerful than the other drugs. In 1971, they were going to a gig somewhere and Miles just took a handful of pills and popped them and he couldn't play. He literally could not stand on stage and Jack and the others had to walk him off stage and tell the audience he was sick. Anything Miles did in that area, he took in massive doses.

Although his drug-taking may have helped him to continue when he was working and in pain, it was always a destructive habit that ultimately stopped him functioning. In this reclusive period it seems to have served to relieve the emptiness within him as much as any physical discomfort.

A pattern had emerged over the years in the way Miles's creative vitality curved upwards and downwards, matched by similar fluctuations in his general health. In two decades, the pattern was almost identical. For about four years in the early 1950s, he was seriously ill with drug addiction. After kicking the habit and making himself fit again, there was an extraordinary spate of creativity over the years 1954–61. In the 1960s, Miles again became seriously ill and was out of action for most of 1965, after which he slowly began another exceptionally creative phase. This started with his second great quintet (Williams, Carter, Hancock, Shorter) and went on into 1968, then reached another even more radical change with electronics and the new concepts of instrumentation and procedure that resulted in his jazz-rock fusion. This last stage (1968–75) saw many personnel changes in Miles's various groups and was a period of turbulence and stress in his private life. In 1975, he once again became seriously ill and was forced into retirement. He reached his fiftieth birthday in 1976, fairly old for a jazz musician (average life-span was then about forty-two), but young for a practitioner in most of the other arts. The renewed creative activity that had characterized the previous two decades, however, was not to happen in the 1970s. He had already opened up so much new ground that it was becoming progressively more difficult each decade to find fresh sounds and modes of procedure.

Furthermore, his physical condition seemed much more serious than in the previous decades. In the later 1970s, although his new hip was functioning, his legs and feet were still paining him, and he was still suffering from bursitis (inflammation of the joints) in his shoulders and wrists. It was a recurrence of the same problem he'd had in 1965, and may perhaps have been caused by over-exercise – all those three-hour work-outs when he was well into his forties. Gil Evans suggested that it was the bursitis and the hip complaint that explained Miles's behaviour on stage just before his last total incapacitation. With painful wrists and shoulders it was agonizing to hold the trumpet to his lips, and it was because of this that he began playing organ. The complaint also made it difficult for him to practise the trumpet when he was recovering from hip surgery. In March 1976, *Rolling Stone* reported:

Rumours have spread that Miles Davis's health has drastically deteriorated – that, at 49, he may even be dying. His alleged ailments include a bad heart, blood and kidney problems, brittle bones, calcified joints, throat difficulties and an ulcer. All of which is half true. Six months ago Miles had to cancel a live recording date at San Francisco's Keystone Korner because of painful calcification in his left hip caused by progressive osteoarthritis. Miles had been barely able to walk and had difficulty sleeping. His doctor's answer was an operation to implant a prosthetic ball-and-socket in the hip, a newly developed process which so far has met with better than 95% success.[2]

The physical ailments were considerable, and must have been a severe drain on Miles's mental and emotional resources, but they were not the sole, or even the main, cause of his malaise of the spirit. To understand that, it is necessary to examine the nature of the music and Miles's role in it. At this point, he was certainly exhausted and barren artistically, and had to abdicate – to disappear from the scene and opt out of the creative struggle. The demands and pressures on the professional improvising music-maker are still little understood. Shortly before his death, Charlie Parker had said to trumpeter Red Rodney, 'I can't find anything new to do with a blues or a ballad,' and Rodney later commented, 'I suspect that he died at the right time,' meaning, when Parker had said all he had to say. John Coltrane, similarly, told saxophonist Charlie Mariano that he could find nothing new to play and had come to the end of his road, and he, too, died during this impasse. Miles Davis in the later 1970s had come to a similar impasse, having previously emerged reborn, phoenix-like, several times from the ashes of his spent phases. His present long silence was like dying, but doing so without departing from this earth.

Some, possibly most, professional improvising musicians are comfortable with familiar musical territory and can live with themselves and prosper even when not breaking radical new ground. After all, a jazz musician's life is often financially precarious and hard enough without even considering the possibility of permanent fundamental creativity and change. Permanent artistic creativity, on a daily basis, goes against the grain of average human nature. Most people's lives are fairly routine, even if shaken up at intervals by change or remarkable events or emotional upheavals, but Miles always tried to avoid the long stretches of routine that give memories of tranquillity and stability at times of change and stress. He played with fire all his life and courted the flame.

All art is, among other things, a process of self-discovery for the artist, and most jazz musicians, once they have found their own personal style of playing, are content to spend the rest of their lives exploring the area they have mapped out. Dizzy Gillespie, like Parker, had one vast burst of explosive creativity when he created bebop with Bird and reinvented the trumpet in the process. After that superhuman effort, he relaxed and spent the rest of his long life working within the parameters he had already created, rather than struggling to discover new ones. In other words, he survived his radical creativity by making do with what it once was. But perhaps the single most formative influence on Miles Davis the musician was the powerful excitement he felt when, as an eighteen-year-old, he had deputized in the trumpet section of the Billy Eckstine band for two weeks and heard Parker and Gillespie playing every night, creating a radically new strain of the jazz language: bebop. For the rest of his life, Miles was to pursue that same intensity of exploration and radical innovation in music, which is the ultimate and most testing path, particularly in the performing arts, because the exploration of new territory has always to be reconciled with the necessity for communication with immediate audiences, a problem he solved over and over again – but at a cost.

Keith Jarrett, recalling his time in the Davis band, said:

He's got so misread so often, about his intentions. But especially in so-called weak moments, he would very quickly show me that his intentions were so pure in terms of what he wanted to do with the band. It's just making some more music . . . He was, if anything, questioning everything about his image, so he enjoyed playing games with the audience and with the press and all that. But it was about the music. I don't think I can say that about any other leader . . . It taught me that that's possible, you know, on a *grand scale*. . . One day when he was very sick, he said, 'Do you know why I don't play ballads any more? . . . Because I like to play ballads so much.' And that was one of the most important statements that anybody with whom I've worked has ever made. You have to want to struggle. And what most leaders are a victim of, is the freedom not to struggle.

It was Miles's sustained effort to address the struggle of making music anew that set him apart and made him become one of the greatest of all bandleaders (if not *the* greatest), and a dominant inspiration over four or five decades. From 1947 onwards, virtually all of his music was a critique of bebop, and a quest to find other modes of expression; the fine pianist Kenny Barron remarked in 1995, 'We all used to wait for the new Miles Davis records to find out what to do next.' Miles's ear for rare talent in little-known, often very young musicians, and his own unique sensibilities, sensitivities and vision, were the bedrock of his genius. Time after time, he put his own creativity on the line in the company of young talents he had gathered together, and broke through to fresh self-discoveries and new musical modes. In the 1940s it was his Birth of the Cool band with Gil Evans, Gerry Mulligan and Lee Konitz – all three little-known at that time. In the mid-1950s, it was his quintet with the nineteen-year-old bassist, Paul Chambers, Red Garland and John Coltrane, none of whom had made any mark before they joined that group. Only Philly Joe Jones had had some reputation at the group's inception. The same pattern occurred in the early 1960s with his second great quintet – only Wayne Shorter had any kind of musical pedigree or reputation – and later in the decade, two little-known young Britishers, Dave Holland and John McLaughlin, became crucial ingredients in yet another radical musical brew. Miles Davis's great strength was that he was not looking for followers, but for co-creators, and he was providing the space and atmosphere in which he and his musicians could grow collectively.

But as well as the supremely testing musical demands of his own self-determined role, there was also the burden of leading his band, dealing with the record company, managers, agents and the logistics of tours, while at the same time, he was a touchstone and figurehead for the majority of the global jazz world. And he had to carry these responsibilities on his own shoulders, because Miles was always the 'cat that walked alone' – he was on his own with no real back-up infrastructure on which he could rely. Being so constantly in the public eye can be extremely burdensome and exhausting, especially to a person with such sensitivity, and whose health is poor, and especially when the waiting world always expects the unexpected from him. The long period of inaction happened because he was emptied, wiped out after several decades of superb and seminal innovation. Now utterly exhausted by all these factors in his life, he hadn't enough energy or desire for the necessary struggle with music. According to his own lights, he could not come back without conceiving a new musical direction, yet his previous new directions had always grown out of his relationships with his regular working associates. It was a 'Catch 22' problem that he would resolve later only by finding a new group, but during this reclusive period, he made intermittent efforts, alone at the piano and in the occasional company of other musicians, to work his way back into music.

Chance events led to a real attempt at recording again for Columbia early in 1978, though Miles had still not touched his trumpet during his lay-off. Guitarist Larry Coryell's first wife Julie had interviewed Miles for the book she was writing with Laura Friedman, *Jazz-Rock Fusion: The People, the Music* (New York: Delta Books), and had become friendly with him in the process. His physical state was pitiable at the time – he could hardly walk across a room without assistance – and Julie Coryell arranged for him to spend some time convalescing at the house of her best friend Elena Steinberg in Norwalk, Connecticut, where she and Elena took care of him. While there, he was working on a musical idea and asked Larry Coryell, with whom he'd also become friendly, to come over and assist. Coryell already had a strong international reputation as one of the leading guitarists since the 1960s, and his interests were as broad as those of Miles, encompassing jazz, rock, classical, ethnic and folk music. He was also a passionate and compelling soloist with a superb technique. He explained:

The opus itself was originally about a series of chords, and maybe a melody fragment here and there, that was initially an adagio movement . . . like a ballad. Miles had me come around the house during the late winter of early 1978 (I remember it was still cold enough for Miles to refrigerate his Heineken bottles out on the porch nestled in snow) and we'd sit at the piano while he messed around with this idea. The 'song' [second part of the piece] was basically a shuffle [rhythm] with two ninth chords a half-step [semi-tone] apart [played by Miles on guitar when he composed the part] over a rolling bass figure in F, with a couple of 'jungle' fragments as melody to be played by myself. After it took shape in a form satisfactory enough for Miles to want to record it, he connected with the other cats and organized a session at CBS [studio] in New York City, with Teo Macero present.

The session happened on 2 March 1978, and featured Miles on organ or synthesizer. Elena Steinberg had given Miles's trumpet to Coryell and told him to hand it to Miles at the beginning of the session, but he refused to take it. The rest of the group comprised Coryell on guitar, two other keyboardists – the Japanese Masabumi Kikuchi and, from Connecticut, George Paulis – and the drummer was Al Foster, Miles's trusted friend and associate, who also recruited the young bassist T. M. Stevens for the occasion. Only the one piece lasting perhaps six or seven minutes was recorded. Larry Coryell commented:

Miles was very clever, the way he arranged it, however, because when we went in there we were all thinking we were going to play the adagio movement; it was only when we were in the studio that Miles came up with doing the thing with a strong rhythm and extending that with no forays into a ballad, or non-tempo feel. When we were all standing there, getting instructions from Miles about this final encoding of the performance, complete with steady rhythm all the way through, I asked Miles, 'Miles, what about the adagio?' His reply was: 'Fuck the adagio.' It was the funniest thing I ever heard. Looking back, he was great that way; providing surprises for the musicians so they wouldn't get programmed as to what to play. I remember asking Miles how I was supposed to improvise over this piece and he said, 'Don't finish your phrases.' This was very helpful, a lesson I try to use to this day when improvising, catching myself in mid-phrase, stopping and using that little gap to go somewhere else ... it works every time ... Anyway, we did two 'rehearsal' takes, not knowing each time that Miles had recorded us – that was his technique of keeping the players fresh, because we didn't think we were recording, at least I didn't, until Miles said, 'Playback', then they played the takes back and he said to Teo, 'That's it, we're finished.'

T. M. Stevens, the bass player, also had an illuminating exchange with Miles after the session:

I was scared to death. We recorded all day long and Miles didn't say a word to me the whole time. Afterwards, he started play-boxing with me, so I felt brave enough to ask what he thought about my playing. He said simply, 'It was cool.' My pride kicked momentarily and I said. 'Cool? I played everything perfectly.' And he said: 'That's the problem. The brilliance comes in your mistakes – that's how you discover new things. And the only way to make mistakes is to stretch and take chances. If you play it safe, you'll never progress.' He also told me: 'Music is like a conversation. When you play the bass, make a question – then wait a minute and answer it.'[3]

Larry Coryell said that the whole saga had been more a great experience of working with Miles than a great musical event, because the music consisted of only one piece, with Miles on keyboards, not on trumpet. Miles was still staying in Connecticut at the time, and he took a cassette of the recording back there and played it over and over to himself. Coryell added,

He loved it! He called friends and played it over the phone for them. Then he said he had done it for me, that I could have the piece and the performance[s]. He wanted Columbia to sign me – I was overjoyed at his concern for me and my career and I saw what a compassionate man he was . . . he was like a Duke Ellington or Dizzy Gillespie in the sense that most great players I've met are also great people!

At the time, Miles also said he was thinking of forming a group, and asked Coryell to join it, but the latter declined gracefully – he was pleased and touched by the offer, but knew that Miles was in no shape to work or play the trumpet yet. Also, of course, Larry Coryell was one of the biggest names in jazz internationally, and he was then fully employed touring in duo with the Belgian-based guitarist Philip Catherine.

After this failure to conceive and create some music that satisfied him, Miles Davis seemed to lose heart again and, once back in his own house in New York City, he relapsed into silence and unbridled substance abuse. His life disintegrated again and, later in the year (1978), his erstwhile lover, Marguerite Eskridge, had him put in gaol because he was not giving her any support money for their son Erin. Miles had to pay $10,000 to get out of gaol. Also, his relationship with his two grown-up sons, Gregory and Miles IV, had reached an all-time low. He was particularly disgusted that Gregory had taken the Muslim name Rahman. But perhaps the two sons were as disappointed in their father as he was in them, and tended to behave as badly as he sometimes did. Through the rest of 1978 and much of the following year, Miles seemed to have gone to pieces, lurking in the solitary confinement of his darkened house, or occasionally making (drug-induced) hallucinatory forays into the nocturnal world outside, where he behaved crazily. Hardly any old friends visited him now, and he began to feel so lonely that one day he put up photographs all over his house of Charlie Parker, John Coltrane, Dizzy Gillespie and Max Roach. Miles's own various awards and plaques were also on display. Jack and Lydia DeJohnette visited him and Lydia recalled:

When we went to visit him during that period, I compared it to seeing a bad B movie of a has-been movie star. That sort of lost star living in their dreams and memories. It was weird because, when I first met him, his house didn't have all these sort of awards and stuff around, but during this period his stuff [memorabilia] was all around. It was as if he'd started to live in his dream and that was disconcerting because this was not the Miles I had known – I'm glad he didn't go out [die] in that state. At that time, Miles actually wanted company, which surprised me because I was still reacting from my experience of the early days of him. But Jack said Miles wanted me to come by. He genuinely wanted company and he talked a lot about the old days – he got nostalgic. He wished that some of the older guys like Dizzy would come and see him. And he did say that Cicely [Tyson] was in touch with him during that time, and he said, 'I need someone to take care of me, but who would want to live with me?' And I can understand that, but Cicely took him on.

Cicely Tyson, the actress, was seven years younger than Miles and had been his friend and lover in the later 1960s. In 1967, when he recorded *Sorcerer*, the cover bore a large photograph in colour of Cicely's right profile. By 1970, they had ceased to be lovers, but remained friendly, and during the interim years had remained in touch intermittently. She seemed to have a kind of sixth sense that always told her when Miles was ill or in some trouble, and in 1978 she began visiting him now and then. Also around this time, George Butler, who had replaced Clive Davis as vice-president at Columbia, began regular visits to Miles in an effort to coax him back into the recording studio. Miles's contract with Columbia was coming up for renewal in October 1979, and he had recorded nothing for the company during the period of his present contract, 1976–9. It became imperative to try and do something, so Miles telephoned Paul Buckmaster in London, asking him to come over to New York and work on some music with him.

Paul Buckmaster spent three months – June, July and August, 1979 – staying in a hotel in New York and going to work with Miles at his house every day. It was dark and filthy and got progressively more messy all the time, and their collaboration was generally fruitless and abortive. Gil Evans was involved in some of these co-operations, but when after several weeks he had received no money for his involvement, he left in disgust. George Butler, however, asked Buckmaster to prepare for a recording session and a date was fixed. Buckmaster told Miles about the session and then asked his friend, the fixer Gene Bianco, to book the musicians for the date. Bianco recommended a brilliant young fretless bass guitarist whose twentieth birthday had been on 14 June – this was Marcus Miller, who was to play such an important part in Miles Davis's music in the following decade. The other musicians were a young drummer called Buddy Williams, Onaje Allen Gumbs on keyboards, percussionist George Devens, guitarist Lou Volpe and Buckmaster (who had prepared some material – a couple of themes and some 'mood grooves') on organ. Miles failed to turn up for the recording, and when confronted later, said he hadn't been told about it. This group, however, recorded three or four pieces – about twenty-five minutes of music. When Miles heard a cassette of it, he liked it, though he wasn't happy with the band, and telephoned his old associate, guitarist Pete Cosey in Chicago, asking him to come to New York and form a band. A few weeks later, Buckmaster and Pete Cosey did two or three rehearsals with a group in New York. Buckmaster commented: 'Pete had two good tunes and one of them, "Electric Circle", was very memorable, and he also took one of my pieces and improved it. But Miles didn't show up, and he eventually dismissed this group too.' At this point, Columbia cut their losses and abandoned the project, but Buckmaster stayed on in New York, still attempting to help Miles kick-start his musical life.

At the beginning of July the New York radio station WKCR FM, which transmitted twenty-four hours every day, had played the whole of Miles Davis's recorded work in chronological order. The programme began at 3 p.m. on Sunday 1 July and went on continuously through the week, ending on Friday the sixth at 10 p.m. This amounted to over one hundred hours of music. Buckmaster was with Miles during much of that time and noted how he raised his eyebrows and showed pleasure on hearing his own magnificent solos. Events seemed to be conspiring to remind him of his greatness.

By now it was August, the daily temperature was ninety degrees Fahrenheit, the humidity ninety per cent, and New York City was airless and intensely oppressive. Miles's house had got even more chaotic and filthy since Buckmaster had arrived in the city, and it was now also infested with huge cockroaches five inches long. The murky, airless house, plus the general heat and humidity, were overwhelming and one Sunday, Paul Buckmaster felt so stifled that he had to get out of the city in order to breathe freely, so he told Miles that he would not be coming to work with him until 6.30 p.m. Then he went to enjoy the bracing air of the Catskill Mountains, some sixty miles north west of New York. He returned to Miles's brownstone house on West 77th Street at 6.30 to find that the electricity had been turned off (because the bill hadn't been paid) and Miles, in pain and very sick, taking huge amounts of cocaine. He occupied the first two floors of the house and there were three self-contained apartments on the upper floors, only one of which was occupied, because Miles hated to be disturbed by neighbours. The solitary occupant, a young black lawyer, returned from his Sunday outing and Buckmaster, who did not want to leave Miles alone in his present state, asked the lawyer to try and procure some candles. He managed to get only a dozen Jewish funeral candles, so Buckmaster, who had decided to stay and watch over Miles, lit only three at a time to make them last out the night. The two of them sat up talking in the candle-lit, uncared-for, cockroach-ridden house, until Miles passed out. The situation now became nightmarish for Buckmaster. Miles seemed so frail, so on the edge of life, that he could die at any time. The question was, what to do? Buckmaster sat on keeping watch until, with enormous relief, he saw Miles eventually reviving. When he could stand up, Buckmaster saw him to bed, then realizing something radical had to be done, returned to the sitting room and, although it was 3 a.m., telephoned Miles's sister Dorothy Wilburn in Chicago. He told her that the situation was very serious, that Miles was *in extremis* and could easily die, and that something had to be done immediately.

Dorothy agreed wholeheartedly, but said, 'A relative has died and I have to go to her funeral tomorrow, but I can come after that.'

Buckmaster replied, 'The dead can take care of themselves, but what about the living?'

Dorothy agreed, saying, 'You're quite right, I'll come first thing in the morning.'

Dorothy arrived at 8.30 a.m. and immediately took charge. She flung the curtains open and Buckmaster said it was like a bombshell – light flooding in for the first time for years and exposing the utter squalor. Then she called a number of people, Cicely Tyson first, pest exterminators to get rid of the cockroaches, professional house cleaners to tackle the filth and dust. The singer Chaka Khan, who lived nearby, came round and made Miles clean himself up and took him out of the house while this whirlwind of activity was going on. When Cicely Tyson arrived, she was cold towards Paul Buckmaster because she was unsure of his role there and thought he might be one of the destructive influences on Miles, such as a drug-pusher. She was now determined to take Miles firmly in hand, and this whole twenty-four-hour period, with Buckmaster's timely intervention, proved to be the turning point. Miles's impetus towards disintegration and death was arrested and slowly reversed. He was at first furious that Paul had called Dorothy and caused all these people to become involved, but later on he was very grateful.

Lydia DeJohnette said later, 'Cicely Tyson probably saved his life, and he needed somebody to do that – he said so himself.' Miles seemed relieved to be under the loving but firm care of Cicely:

She just started coming around and I stopped seeing all those other women. She helped run all those people out of my house; she kind of protected me and started seeing that I ate the right things, and didn't drink as much. She helped get me off cocaine. She would feed me health foods, a lot of vegetables, and a whole lot of juices. She turned me on to acupuncture to help get my hip back in shape. All of a sudden I started thinking clearer, and that's when I really started thinking about music again ... Cicely even got me off cigarettes ... She told me she didn't like kissing me with all that cigarette smell on my breath. She said she would stop kissing me if I didn't stop, so I did.[4]

Cicely Tyson commented:

People are saying that I did it; but he had to want to do it. There comes a time in one's life when you begin to realize certain facts about yourself, and it becomes a matter of wanting to continue or letting it end ... During the time that we were apart [i.e. after 1969], at the end of each year I would call him on New Year's Eve and I marvelled that he was still here. I used to say, 'Hey, look, you may think it's time for you to go, but The Man Upstairs is not ready for you. You have not completed your job on this earth.' Often he'd just hang up the phone, and I'd call back and say it again. Despite his anger and resistance, this always stayed in his mind. You know, the mind of this man is ... It is unlike that of any other being I have ever met, and I could not stand to watch it go to waste.[5]

It would be a long, slow haul back into music for Miles, and it would take him two years to get back the full glory of his open trumpet sound. The jazz world, however, was feverishly longing for his return, because during his four years of silence no one had replaced him. In fact his absence rather resembled the death of Julius Caesar in Shakespeare's play in that, once he was out of sight, people became much more aware of him. He and his music were sorely missed, and there had been many rumours and much speculation in the media about his health and his intentions; while the many tributes and surveys of his career in the world press, plus the FM Radio transmission of his entire opus on record, must have seemed to him like reading or hearing his own obituaries.

This groundswell of public interest in Miles Davis had also been fuelled by Columbia's promotional efforts, including the release of previously unissued material on a double-album, *Circle in the Round*, in 1979. So it was not surprising that Miles appeared in the *Down Beat* readers' poll at the end of that year. He was positioned tenth in the trumpet category, while several of his previous sidemen – Tony Williams, Jack DeJohnette, Ron Carter, Dave Holland, Chick Corea, Joe Zawinul, Herbie Hancock and Wayne Shorter – swept the board in their various categories.

There is one unquestionable masterpiece on *Circle in the Round*, and that is the May 1958 sextet version of 'Love for Sale'. Miles, using Harmon mute, plays an exquisitely laconic solo, and the other soloists, Adderley, Coltrane and Bill Evans, all sparkle, egged on by the rhythm section (Chambers and Cobb) in full cry. But the other two early takes, 'Two Bass Hit' (October 1955) featuring Coltrane, and 'Blues No. 2' (March 1961) with Philly Joe Jones on drums and tenor saxophonist Hank Mobley, are pleasant enough, but add little or nothing of importance to the Davis canon. The other pieces are from the crucial period 1967–70, and most of them are unfinished, experimental essays in structure and texture, preparing the way for *In a Silent Way* and *Bitches Brew*. But even in these unpolished efforts, Miles, who also conceived five of them, plays very adventurously. His piece 'Splash', from 1968, is in 5/4 time with a rocky rhythm, and an asymmetrical structure of six bars of 5/4 and one bar of 6/4. This was his first piece in 5/4 on record, and yet the confidence of his trumpet playing is remarkable. The title track, 'Circle in the Round' (from December 1967) is a roughly edited workout lasting a monstrous twenty-six minutes. For this, guitarist Joe Beck was added to the quintet, and given the role of repeating a short rhythmic figure throughout the entire performance. In essence, however, this piece is a new and strange departure for Miles – the feel is a kind of brisk 12/8 shuffle, with hypnotically repeating, insistent elements, a melancholy theme played by Miles and Shorter, and strong solos by both. Herbie Hancock plays celeste instead of piano throughout, and there are also other new textures and sonorities such as bell chimes. Tony Williams treats much of the piece as a drum concerto, dropping 'bombs' and ribald percussive comments through much of it. Given the scarcity of new Miles Davis releases, it is not surprising that this sometimes sketchy, but always dynamic composite album made a strong impact on the jazz public.

Although Miles Davis had, after this turning point in 1979, made his first steps on the way back to health and music, he was still frail, vulnerable and in need of constant encouragement and companionship. Cicely Tyson, now much in demand as an actress, had to be away some of the time and so couldn't be always at his side. She had instilled some self-discipline into Miles, got him to drop many of his bad habits, but had not entirely broken his dependence on drugs, and when Cicely was away, a relapse was always possible. Crucial help, however, came from Miles's nephew, Vincent Wilburn, sister Dorothy's son. When Vincent was seven years old, Miles had bought him a set of drums, and Vincent took them up seriously, eventually studying at the Chicago Conservatory of Music, and his commitment had earned him the respect and affection of his Uncle Miles. In the latter part of 1979, Vincent came to New York frequently to spend some time with Miles. Dorothy must have encouraged these visits as a way of making Miles turn his eyes outwards to a relative, a nephew whom he loved and for whom he was responsible when Vincent was staying at the house on West 77th Street. But Vincent, in his youthful enthusiasm for music, kept on talking about it to Miles, asking him questions, and urging him to play something. Music soon loomed so strongly that Miles eventually began practising the trumpet again, and early in 1980 was ready to start seriously working at music once more.

NINETEEN

A Tentative New Beginning

'I can't play like anyone else, I can't fight like
anyone else, I can't do *anything* like anyone else.
I'm just myself.'[1]

Miles Davis

Another factor helped to galvanize Miles Davis into activity in 1980: he needed money. Columbia, however, refused to renew his contract until he had shown up at the recording studio. History was repeating itself – when George Avakian had initially tried to sign Miles to Columbia in 1955, the company were reluctant to do so because he had been a drug addict with a reputation for unreliability. Now, twenty-five years later, there were real grounds for doubt, because Miles had already made at least three attempts at forming groups to record, and on the last two occasions had not even shown up at the rehearsals. The 1950s signing had occurred after his four years of heroin addiction, during which time he had diced with death. But then he had been a young man with all the resilience that implies, and he had kept up his trumpet playing. Now, he was in middle age, out of touch with the trumpet and music-making, and slowly emerging from a period of much more profound physical and spiritual malaise, when the grim reaper seemed ever present in the shadows. Early in 1980, he began practising the trumpet again, but he had to feel his way back to music in the way young people start in jazz – by playing with relatives and friends – and his twenty-two-year-old nephew, Vincent Wilburn, was the key to Miles's new beginning. He needed

347

to become a kind of beginner again and surround himself with young people in the first flush of their enthusiasm for music. The great German poet Rainer Maria Rilke believed all artists should seek this ideal state of being a beginner and explained: 'Always at the commencement of work, that first innocence must be re-achieved, you must return to that unsophisticated spot where the angel discovered you when he brought you the first binding message.'[2] This kind of beginning had happened every time Miles had formed a new band of young or little-known musicians and put his own creativity on the line, but now, in 1980, he needed to return to an even earlier state of beginning in order to find himself again.

Since the turning point in his life the previous year, he had kept in regular touch with his sister Dorothy, telephoning her in Chicago virtually every day, and during one of their conversations she played him some demo tracks recorded by Vincent and three of his friends: Randy Hall, Robert Irving and Felton Crews. They were all steeped in the music of the day – reggae, funk, soul, jazz, rock – and told *Down Beat* writer Howard Mandel: 'Miles liked what he heard, so we went to New York to cut one tune. But Miles liked it so much, and Columbia liked that Miles liked it, so we just kept working.'[3] They were all in their early or middle twenties, all unknown, but keyboardist Irving, who had studied at the University of North Carolina, would eventually spend several years with Miles Davis. Guitarist and singer Hall had studied at Berklee and Crews played bass. Of the four young musicians, only Vincent Wilburn and Hall had a reasonable knowledge of Davis's musical legacy. It was in April that the four of them came to New York to rehearse intensively with Miles, who also wanted a young saxophonist in the group, so he asked Dave Liebman to recommend someone. Liebman suggested an ex-private pupil of his, a twenty-two-year-old white saxophonist called Bill Evans, who recalled, 'I had just graduated from college two months previously, and Miles called me up and I went over to his house, and he heard me play a little bit and he said, "You know, if I played saxophone, I'd want to play it like you. I love that style." But we didn't play a concert for another year.' Miles also wanted a percussionist, and Teo Macero recommended Sammy Figueroa, whom Miles had heard on a Chaka Khan album.

On 1 May, the band, now a septet, went into the studio and began recording, but after only one day, Miles was hospitalized with a serious leg infection, a kind of blood poisoning, and was out of action for the rest of the month. Many musicians visited him there, and he even had a big party for his fifty-fourth birthday in hospital on 26 May. Gerry Mulligan telephoned him at the hospital, saying he'd heard Miles was preparing to perform again, and adding, 'I hope you're going to play pretty this time for us cats that love you.' The reply was emphatic: 'No, man – I'm gonna get a funky-ass band, go out and make some money.'[4] This may have been his true or half-true intention, but that categorical statement also served to absolve him from the now intolerable burden of perpetual trail-blazing. It was a warning not to expect anything new . . . or old. Dave Liebman also visited Miles in hospital and found the trumpeter in good spirits, enthusiastic about his new recording project and keen to get on the road and play some concerts. He was planning five or six concerts in major cities in America, Europe and the Far East.

The septet was back in the studio in June and several pieces, mostly composed by Robert Irving and Randy Hall, were recorded. There would be further studio sessions in July, but first Miles and the band took a break. He played some of the music over the phone to friends to get their opinion. Miles never moved precipitately when he was starting a fresh musical phase. He played it to Dave Liebman, who said the music was 'black disco funk and much more commercial than anything I heard him do even after I left his band'. So far, the band had recorded seven or eight pieces, but Miles had played only a little trumpet on one of them (Liebman added) and, for all his enthusiasm, Davis seemed a little concerned about how the public would react to the music. Liebman concluded: 'It's definitely air-play material . . . There's a definite effort by him and Teo and Columbia to get the stuff happening, because the record business in the States is not so good, and they want something heavy from him for commercial use . . . But after Miles puts his touches to it, I'm sure it'll come out being really special.'

Jack Chambers in his biography of Miles Davis[5] writes that this break in the recording sessions with his young band occurred because Miles did some recording with Karlheinz Stockhausen, Paul Buckmaster and others. This is contradicted by Stockhausen's trumpet-playing son, Markus, who says his father never ever met Miles Davis. Paul Buckmaster was also not there, *and* nor were the others. If there is any similarity between the music of Davis and that of Stockhausen, it is simply coincidental – their developments were parallel, and either man might well have said, like the poet Gerard Manley Hopkins, 'The influence of genius is to make me admire . . . and do otherwise.'

Miles and the band were back in the studio in June and after a total of sixty hours they had recorded more than ten pieces, but Miles had played trumpet on very few of them, and only two of their performances would appear on his first come-back album: the Hall/Irving title track 'The Man with the Horn', and their disco number 'Shout', which was not recorded until May 1981. This was because Miles had serious doubts about such popular music that did not contain enough of himself. In a *Down Beat* interview with Howard Mandel, Randy Hall described the music they had recorded with Miles:

Well, there's something for everybody . . . vocals, electronics, to appeal to young people. It's commercial enough that people who never heard Miles before will get it. Older fans of his will dig it, too. Some tunes are, like, pop, it's into a wide spectrum. The music is mostly ballads, but there's up-tempo funk, fusion, and open hi-hat sound with lots of drive that Miles instructed Vince to play, hip melodies on the top, lots of melodic changes. Miles plays trumpet and Fender Rhodes. The tracks average five minutes each.[6]

Such a hotchpotch of music must have set alarm bells ringing in Miles's head, and even 'Shout', which did get on the album, has a sound reminiscent of Herb Alpert with a heavy disco beat, a banal melody and a tight arrangement with no real freedom of movement. But Miles plays beautiful open trumpet, sounding quite incongruous in this context, and Bill Evans's passionate soprano solo continues to the fade-out. 'The Man with the Horn', again composed by Hall/Irving, is a slow soul/rock ballad, unexceptional, but well performed by the band, with a pleasant vocal by Randy Hall, and backing vocals by Angela Bofill. The lyrics in praise of Davis, however, are mediocre, and the whole thing seems soft-centred except for Miles's contribution. He plays trumpet with electric wah-wah, a thin, nasal, sardonic sound with good control and range, and his sour, keening phrases are incisive and moving. In those early sessions he was using the wah-wah because his embouchure was still weak and it masked any inadequacies of tone or articulation, but in this title track it redeems the music to some extent. It was only after one of the young musicians hid his wah-wah that Miles was forced to play without it, and soon he had no need of it.

The young group of Chicagoans had done Miles one great service: they had provided the supportive, friendly enthusiasm over several months that drew him back into music. 'After being in the studio with those guys,' he said, 'I started hearing melodies again, and that made me feel good.'[7] But the irony for the young musicians was that once Miles was back on course musically, his instincts told him that he could perhaps use only Bill Evans, Robert Irving and Vincent in his working group. He did, however, express his gratitude to the quartet from Chicago, explaining, 'It wasn't that they weren't good musicians; they were. It's just that I needed something else to satisfy what *I* wanted to do.'[8] And late in 1981, he told Cheryl McCall, 'Randy Hall and my nephew and little Bobby [Irving], they all write great music for me. I need a bubble-gum song, I just call up Randy and say, Randy send me a bubble-gum song. Like "Shout".'[9] When he later went into the studio to finish tracks for the album *The Man with the Horn*, however, only Bill Evans and percussionist Sammy Figueroa remained from the original group.

But for the rest of 1980 Miles remained out of action, with saxophonist Bill Evans taking over and expanding the role Vincent Wilburn had played as the young and enthusiastic companion. Evans said:

We became really good friends, and I hung out with him for the whole year, and at the time he was not playing the trumpet, he was just existing. I was basically trying to keep him from getting into trouble. And I was kind of the mediator between him and a lot of the hoodlums around New York, because here's this young white kid from the Midwest who just graduated school, who does no drugs, who keeps in shape, lifts weights and this kind of thing, and here's Miles Davis who does (still) do drugs at the time, and who's completely reckless, and who drives round in his Ferrari like a maniac, so I'm like his counter-type, you know. I'm this guy that he could rely on. If he was given a large sum of money for anything, he would give it to me, and I'd hold it for him, and he could count on the fact that I would give it back. It was like I was the first person at the time he could trust. Musically, I was kind of his liaison between the outside world and himself. We just hit it off really well, and we'd eat dinner all the time, and I'd go to the store for him, and stuff like that, and when he decided he wanted to go and play, he would ask me to organize it – I was like his right-hand man at the time. We would talk. I would ask him questions all the time. I wanted to know about John Coltrane and Charlie Parker. I wanted to know about *all* these different people, and when he was in the right mood, when he was laid-back and he was just kind of hanging out, he would go on for hours, talking about Bird and everything else. And I was thinking to myself – if I had a tape recorder, just to tape him talking about this would be great.

Meanwhile, news that Miles Davis was stirring musically again began to seep out across the world. The 21 June 1980 issue of the British *Melody Maker* featured a Max Jones in-depth interview with Teo Macero, Miles's friend and producer since the mid-1950s, and the bulk of it was about the state of Davis's health, the fact that he was practising again and wanted to play in public and had been recording with a group of young unknown musicians. The September issue of *Down Beat* devoted four and a half pages to him – a long and perceptive résumé of his career, 'Miles Resting on Laurels? Changing His Silent Ways?' by Charles Mitchell, and 'Miles Davis's New Direction is a Family Affair', a feature on the May/June recording sessions with quotes from Miles's nephew Vincent Wilburn and the other young unknowns.

Miles's name also cropped up in the obituaries of pianist Bill Evans, who died on 15 September 1980, at the age of fifty-one. Evans had made a crucial contribution to *Kind of Blue*, Miles's most influential and best-loved album, and Davis felt his loss keenly. He remarked to Cheryl McCall, 'It's too painful for me to think of Bill Evans and his piano. He's one of my favourite pianists. Or he was. But . . . that's the way it goes.'[10] In his 1989 autobiography, Miles also commented, 'His death made me real sad, because he had turned into a junkie, and I think he died from complications of that.'[11] And it turned Davis's thoughts to his own mortality and continuing drug abuse. He was still drinking champagne, beer and cognac, and taking cocaine, but the writing was on the wall because, as well as his other ailments, he now had diabetes. He would eventually have to stop all excesses – but it would take a violent shock and a more shattering reminder of his own physical vulnerability to bring that about. Charles Mingus, another old friend and sparring partner of Davis's, had also died prematurely, on 5 January 1979, four months before his fifty-seventh birthday. But at that time Miles was in the depths of his own disintegration, and he was probably barely aware of Mingus's demise. Now the loss of Evans brought Mingus to mind, and made Miles focus more strongly on the life ahead of him.

Towards the end of 1980, feeling the urge to record and perform again, Miles Davis at last began composing once more. He had already found his saxophonist in young Bill Evans, but was looking for a regular working band. Evans said that a few old boxing friends came to visit Miles occasionally during this period, and the great drummer Al Foster, Miles's old associate and friend, was coming round more often. After playing drums for Davis's *On the Corner* recording in 1972, Foster (born 1944) had stayed with the band until 1975, when health problems were the initial cause of Miles's long absence from music, during which time Foster had been a regular visitor and mainstay. He had worked earlier in his career with many of the jazz greats, but because of his reluctance to leave his family for long periods, he had stayed in New York between 1975 and 1980, leading his own group and working with others. Miles called Foster and asked him to play drums on his new compositions, and for other recommendations he consulted Bill Evans, who recalled:

> It was a great period for me. I hadn't done any other band of any stature before, really. I had never been on the road before. I was going from college, where I was playing with a lot of college groups or friends of mine, or sitting in with different musicians around New York. So you have this college kid joining Miles Davis's band immediately, but it didn't seem that big of a jump to me, because I wasn't able to relate it to anything else. So in essence, I helped him put the band together. Al Foster was also a great friend of mine, and I recommended bass guitarist Marcus Miller and guitarist Mike Stern, and later on, guitarist John Scofield.

Teo Macero had suggested guitarist Barry Finnerty, who did the initial rehearsals and played on the first recordings, and Miles retained Sammy Figueroa on percussion. This sextet began rehearsing in Davis's house, in readiness to record the remaining four tracks, all composed by Miles, for *The Man with the Horn*. In January 1981, Miles took this group into the Columbia recording studio, and three of his compositions were recorded – 'Back Seat Betty', 'Aida' and 'Ursula' – but he had become displeased with guitarist Finnerty, who was stubborn and did not like being told what and how to play. Bill Evans recommended Mike Stern as a replacement on guitar, and he came in for the penultimate recording in March of the fourth Davis composition, 'Fat Time' (Stern's nickname). Then in May Miles took the original band – Evans, Robert Irving III, Randy Hall, Barry Finnerty, Felton Crews, Vincent Wilburn and Sammy Figueroa – back into the studio to record different versions of 'Shout', most probably with a view to issuing it as a single as well as on LP. After this, Miles felt he needed another kind of percussionist, and came across Mino Cinelu, a percussionist from Martinique who was playing in a New York after-hours club called Mikell's. He replaced Sammy Figueroa in the band, and Miles commented,

> Mino was a prima donna-like guy, light-skinned, curly hair, thought he was a ladies' man. But I liked the way he played, so I put up with the rest of his silly shit . . . When Mino came into the group, everything was starting to fall into place. I could see where we could have a hell of a group.[12]

So, in the process of recording his first album of the 1980s, Miles had once again recruited a young band of largely unknown musicians. Only Al Foster had any kind of profile or track record, but Davis's extraordinary vision had brought to the band Bill Evans, Marcus Miller and Mike Stern, all of whom would make a big mark musically, and Mino Cinelu, also destined to become an international star. Once again, Miles Davis's new band, like most of his first great 1950s quintet, and the majority of his second in the 1960s, seemed to have arrived mysteriously from nowhere. Saxophonist Bill Evans, who had hardly any past at all when he became Miles's trusted saxophonist and associate, commented:

> He likes to find people, because he gets to shape you to his band and his ideas, and he doesn't get any preconceived attitude from anybody . . . like he found Mino in this after-hours club playing percussion . . . He could have called great percussionists where they already had names, or had them

recommend somebody that's already on the scene, but he likes to find them in his own little way and put his band together, and so it's really his thing.

Marcus Miller had, of course, been the bass guitarist at the 1979 recording session organized by Columbia and Paul Buckmaster, for which Miles had simply failed to turn up. Miller, born in June 1959, had begun as a funk and soul bassist and by the end of the 1970s was a highly regarded studio musician. Miller had been on a country and western session when he received a note with a telephone number on it and the message, 'Call Miles'. He recalled:

I didn't know who Miles was. Buddy Miles? Gil Evans's son Miles? So I called the number and The Rasp answered: 'Hey man, what's happenin'? Can you be at CBS in an hour?' And I said, 'Yeah, this thing ends in half an hour. You gonna be there?' He said, 'Yeah, if you'll be there.' I walked into the studio, said, 'Hi, I'm Marcus Miller.' He said, 'I'm Miles.' Then he walked out. When he came back in, I said, 'I'm Wynton Kelly's cousin.' He didn't say anything. So I thought, First wrong thing I said. We played for a while; at the first break, Miles came to me and said, 'Did you ever play with your genius cousin?' I said, 'No, he died when I was still young.' He said, 'He was a genius. His touch, his touch.' And after that, Miles asked me to be in his band.[13]

In rehearsals, however, Miller had to get used to Miles's manner and methods:

Miller recalled:

He showed me two notes, F sharp and G, and said, 'That's it: you got it.' I said, 'If that's what you want ... ?' So I played with the band F sharp and G, and he stopped the band after a while and said, 'Is that all you gonna play? F sharp and G?' And I said, 'No, no, I can play some other notes if you want.' So we played again, F sharp and G, and every other note I played different notes. He stopped the band again and said, 'What the fuck you doin'? Just play F sharp and G!' So I thought, Ah, shit, I'm just gonna ignore this guy. I'm not gonna let him drive me nuts. So I just played, and he let us play the whole tune through this time, so I was feeling kind of good by the end of the song ... at which point he said, 'You all playing like a bunch of faggots,' and walked out of the studio. He did give me a wink on the way out, though. We ended up pretty tight.[14]

For Miller, the first recordings with Davis were a powerfully formative experience. He told Gene Santoro:

At that time I still didn't feel like I had an identity. Miles was the one who made me nail something down as far as style. See, the music he was playing really didn't have any predetermined bass style to it – I had to come up with something, and that forced me to come up with something of my own. The tape would just be rolling all the time, so sometimes it wouldn't be so hip, but sometimes it would be *serious*. I learned to feel good about what I do, because it's a basic representation of myself; your playing is gonna get criticized or praised, so you better make sure it's *you*. If you start playing stuff you think people will like and then nobody likes it, you'll *really* feel like a jerk.[15]

Mike Stern, born in January 1953, was inspired by rock guitarists Eric Clapton and Jimi Hendrix, and after studying at the Berklee School of Music with Pat Metheny and Mick Goodrick, had worked with Blood, Sweat and Tears, then with Billy Cobham's band. But he too was virtually unknown when he joined Miles Davis.

The album *The Man with the Horn* was released in the autumn of 1981 and received, for the most part, indifferent or poor reviews. But, given the spiritual and physical depths from which Miles Davis was surfacing, the album was something of a triumph and, like the emergence of his new band, echoed other phases in his career. In particular, it had the kind of schizophrenia seen in *Seven Steps to Heaven* (1963), when Miles had been making the transition from the band with Coltrane to his second great quintet. On that occasion, there had also been two sets of musicians – the three Los Angeles tracks were recorded by a quartet comprising Miles, pianist Victor Feldman, bassist Ron Carter and drummer Frank Butler, and the three pieces recorded in New York were played by a quintet consisting of Miles, Carter, saxophonist George Coleman and the young unknowns, Herbie Hancock and Tony Williams. The atmosphere and essence of the music of the two sessions was and is very different. Now, in 1981, the schizophrenic aspect of *The Man with the Horn* was much more extreme: the slow soul/rock title track and the disco number 'Shout', by the young band from Chicago, were totally out of character with Davis's four pieces, which were played by the New York band. The order of pieces on the album is also significant. It begins and ends with two of Miles's compositions, which give a clear indication of his intent, and the two more 'commercial' tracks are tucked away in the middle.

Except for percussionist Sammy Figueroa, who played throughout *The Man with the Horn*, the first track, 'Fat Time' featured the band Miles was intending to take on tour – Evans, Stern, Miller and Foster – and all their personalities come through strongly. As in Miles's music of the early 1970s, the material is skeletal, a mere framework for making music, and 'Fat Time' has a rhythmic feel, a tempo and an atmosphere all its own. It is modal/chromatic music with the improvised structures based largely on two tonal centres, B flat (with a C minor feel) alternating with B7, but Marcus Miller creates attractive skipping bass lines that Al Foster points up with a buoyant 'dancey-dancey' drum rhythm working off a slow pulse but implying the double tempo. The structure, the dynamics and the textures are all improvised, and the whole thing breathes beautifully. Miles, using the Harmon mute, duets with Stern, Bill Evans (who plays soprano throughout the album) creates a finely considered solo, then Miles playing open trumpet whips up the ensemble with some powerful high Fs and attacking phrases over the whole range of the instrument, paving the way for Stern's guitar solo with its rocky sound and fluent lines. The piece then simmers quietly before building up again and ending with an open trumpet scream. Miles's singing acoustic trumpet sound was now slowly returning, his Harmon sound was already in place, and this track served notice that he was seriously back in the art of music-making.

The guitarist throughout the rest of the album is Barry Finnerty, who functions mostly as the creator of textures, alternating single-string riffs with rocky chords. The second piece, 'Back Seat Betty', also by Miles, is named after his ex-wife, Betty Mabry, and harks back to 'Miles Runs the Voodoo Down' on *Bitches Brew*. It is in the same key (F), has a similarly eerie, slow rock beat, the same dramatic use of space and dynamics, and a similar opening in which Miles plays major and minor thirds, implying the whole blues tradition. But in this performance there are pauses with heavy rock guitar chords, while in the slowly grooving stretches, Finnerty plays single-string riffs with the soft, pleasing sound of a balafon, the African xylophone. Miles and Evans share the solos and both project tremendous feeling. Again this is a telling performance in which Miles is reviewing his past – something he had always done when starting a new phase – and that process went on in his other two pieces, the brisk and rocky 'Aida' (later retitled 'Fast Track') with its repeated three-note motif, and 'Ursula', which ends the album and glances even further back to his 1957 music for the Louis Malle film *L'Ascenseur pour L'Echafaud* (*Lift to the Scaffold*). 'Ursula' begins with a jazz swing rhythm played only by bass drums and percussion, the tonality hovering around F and D minor, and over this, Miles solos using the Harmon mute. Eventually, Finnerty's guitar is added, and after changes of atmosphere and pacing, with powerful solos from Evans and Miles, it ends and we hear the familiar hoarse voice saying, 'Let's hear that, Teo' to Teo Macero in the control room. Since the

1950s, Davis's ghostly voice had often been heard on albums asking for a playback.

Miles Davis's four tracks on *The Man with the Horn* revealed that his young band had tremendous potential – the rhythm section of Marcus Miller and Al Foster was a truly superlative unit, and the quality of listening, concentration and creative response of the musicians was already formidable. He was very pleased with the results and played the tapes to friends, who enthused about the band and his new musicians. Miles himself was slowly recovering the glory of his playing, and his upper-register work was already sounding strong. But he also knew that once the quality of his young musicians was recognized, they would be much sought after, and later on in the year told Cheryl McCall: 'Everybody in my band could have a [i.e. his own] band right now.'[16] The same had been true of the quintet with Coltrane, and the 1960s quintet, yet Coltrane had stayed with Miles for almost five years and the later group had been together for about the same length of time. Perhaps it was a mark of his greatness that Davis could keep such powerful personalities with him for so long because they felt that they were constantly growing and developing under his leadership. But now, with the burgeoning rapprochement of jazz and rock, it might be harder to keep a band together – musicians versed in both disciplines were much in demand. Even his old friend, Gil Evans, had an eye on saxophonist Bill Evans as a possible candidate for his band.

In May 1981, Miles Davis felt ready to play in public again, and acted with characteristic decisiveness. His old sparring partner, promoter George Wein, had kept in touch with him intermittently during his reclusive years and now wanted to book his band for the Newport Festival, which had been transferred from Newport to New York City and renamed the Kool Jazz Festival. Miles agreed to play two concerts at the Avery Fisher Hall on 5 July, for that festival, and said his fee was about $90,000 for the two shows, though Wein later disputed that figure without stating the alternative, actual one. During his retirement, Davis had acquired a new manager, Mark Rothbaum, and now asked him to book the band into a small club called Kix, in the Cambridge area of Boston, for four days at the end of June. This would give the band an opportunity to play itself in, well away from New York and in front of small enthusiastic audiences. Miles now needed a road crew and managed to contact the two key people of his old team, Jim Rose and Chris Murphy, both of whom had been driving cabs during his long lay-off. Both were glad to hear from Miles, and he said: 'When I saw those guys – both with long hair – I just hugged them, I was so glad they had come back.'[17] And as if to steady himself for live performance, early in June he went to New York's Village Vanguard and sat in with the Mel Lewis big band, playing a blues with the rhythm section for almost nine minutes.

Columbia were so uncertain that Miles would be able to sustain his comeback that they decided to record any public concerts he played with his band. With Mino Cinelu now on percussion, Davis rehearsed the sextet at his house. He was still using his looser, improvisatory approach to making music (which would change radically when he eventually got into his full stride) and in these early stages it unnerved the younger musicians, though Al Foster must have been well used to it. Bill Evans recalled:

The band was finally put together and we were rehearsing at Miles's house, but there was no [written] music. I mean we never really went over tunes from beginning to end. We were just having a barbecue and hanging out in his back yard, and there was no real rehearsal, and he says, 'OK, well that's good enough . . . we'll go to the gig.' We were petrified. We were all on the phone saying, 'It's all over. His career's over, our careers are over. It's never going to work.' So from then on, we realized that the music was going to be what everybody puts into it, which is, I guess, what he'd done in the past. He trusted everybody's musicianship to create a record. And when it kicked off, it was all right. We could tell that it was happening then, that Al Foster and Marcus Miller were sounding great together, that Stern fitted in well, and that everything worked. We were excited about it, you know.

We didn't realize that we could actually put it into a record on the first gig.

The whole saga of Miles Davis's long absence from the scene, with its rumours about his motives, his state of health, his intentions, and the various abortive attempts at recording, followed by his slow, halting efforts, over eighteen months, at re-emergence in the public arena, was one of the longest and most potent public relations events in the history of jazz. But no public relations firm could ever have artificially created such an event, because it came out of the very real spiritual and physical suffering of the central figure. When Miles was in full creative flow, he knew his own worth, but often had doubts and insecurities about what he was doing. These apparent weaknesses were his great strength and help to account for the sustained quality of his work. When his creative flow was spent, however, he seemed to feel empty and of little worth. Recalling his reclusive period, Cicely Tyson said:

> I remember when he was in the hospital one time with a leg problem. I spent every day there, and we talked about whether he would play again. He said. 'Well, I don't know if there's anything there.' ... Miles is a man who produces from his gut; if there's nothing to give, he can't fake it ... like many people categorized as geniuses [he] never even knew his own true worth.[18]

Yet, possibly more than any other jazz musician's, Miles's music had touched the hearts of people all over the world, and his absence was a great deprivation for many of them.

Few people knew how physically ill he had been, or had much idea about his psychological condition, and speculation about his return had reached fever pitch months before it became a reality. The letters page of *Down Beat* magazine had communications from several continents, some pleading for his return, others accusing him of wilfully staying off the scene or suggesting it was his duty to come back, and these views were echoed in music papers and jazz magazines world-wide. When it was clear that he really was returning to public performance and had agreed to play at Avery Fisher Hall on 5 July, the trickle of publicity became a flood, graduating to major newspapers and the media in general the world over, and both his Avery Fisher Hall concerts were consequently sold out within two hours, which pleased Miles and his band greatly.

In readiness for the four preliminary concerts in Boston, he bought himself a brand-new canary yellow Ferrari sports coupé, because he wanted to be seen arriving at the club in it. His earlier Ferraris had always been important stylistic appendages for him, and this one, apart from making him feel good, would also create the impression that his return was ongoing. As he said: 'A little showbiz don't hurt sometimes.'[19] The rest of the band had flown up to Boston, but he drove there with Jim Rose in the passenger seat, while Chris Murphy drove the truck with the equipment. Although he was staying across the street from the club, he intended to drive his car to the entrance of Kix each night. He was apprehensive about his comeback, and would remain nervous before concerts for some time yet, which is why he needed all the psychological props and supports he could find. He told Leonard Feather: 'Every time I get ready to play a concert, I get butterflies in my stomach; I can't eat the day before, and everything seems like it aches. Once I'm on stage the nervousness disappears, and I gather strength while I'm playing.'[20]

Miles and the band played two sets for each of their four nights (26–9 June) at Kix. The club, which held about 425 people, was full throughout, and he and his musicians were astonished by the intensity of excitement and the open display of emotion of the audiences. Bill Evans said:

It was when we did the first concert in Boston, when I realized that this guy, this Miles Davis, who was a friend of mine I know real well, whom I'd been helping through this whole time of year, was actually the *great* Miles Davis, the trumpet player of the fascinating Prince of Darkness kind of thing that everybody envisioned him as being. He was a little bit nervous. He'd say, 'Well, let's go to the club now.' We'd walk in, and people went crazy! Jesus!

People wept with joy at seeing him and as his playing moved them. And Miles, too, recalled one of those nights when a small black man in his mid-thirties who had cerebral palsy was sitting in front of the audience in a wheelchair, and Miles played a blues to him:

Halfway through my solo, I looked into this guy's eyes, and he was crying. He reached up his withered arm, which was trembling, and with his shaking hand he touched my trumpet as though he was blessing it – and me. Man, I almost lost it right then and there, almost broke down myself and cried ... It was almost like he was telling me everything was all right and that my playing was as beautiful and strong as ever. I needed that, needed it right at that moment to go on.[21]

All four nights at Kix were recorded by Columbia, but only three tracks from the second night, 'My Man's Gone Now', 'Fast Track' ('Aida'), and 'Kix', were included on the album of live performances, We Want Miles, which was completed by 'Back Seat Betty' from the Avery Fisher Hall concert, and long and short versions of 'Jean Pierre' from a performance in Tokyo on 4 October 1981. The three Kix tracks are a revelation, because although the musicians had had very little rehearsal, and two of the pieces were new and not on the album The Man with the Horn, the band sounds as assured as a regularly working group. In particular, the twenty-minute version of 'My Man's Gone Now' is a tour de force. With this piece from Gershwin's Porgy and Bess, which Miles had recorded with Gil Evans in 1958, he was again reviewing his past and looking into it for musical clues to the present. In his arrangement of it, 'My Man's Gone Now' has three sections, a harmonically static first part with a rocky bass riff and a slow pulse, a ballad section, and a double-tempo section with a swing rhythm. Bill Evans explained how it was organized:

'He would just say, "Let's go into swing on this other section – I'll just cue it." He would just go into it da, da, da, da, da. He could do it at any point, so the rhythm section would have to keep alert, because they might be in the ballad part, and then Miles would also go da, da, da, and they'd have to come in right there.'

It is an intensely dramatic performance with dynamics ranging from a whisper in the quietly grooving passages to a roar at the climaxes, and again, the quality of listening, not only of the musicians, but also of the audience – who are transfixed by the music – is a powerful factor. Miles's brief electric keyboard introduction leads into Miller's bass riff and Foster's slow, spare drum rhythm, and then the Harmon muted trumpet sound evokes from the audience little cries of recognition and pleasure. From then on, the music ebbs and flows like a living thing, with Miles alternating open trumpet with the Harmon mute, Bill Evans solo-ing on soprano with a gentle, poetic beginning and, as the rhythm section digs in, hoarsely passionate peaks, and Mike Stern's always apt accompaniment, plus the great presence and fleet lines of his solos. Miles joins in on open trumpet during the climax of Stern's solo, bringing the band to a slow, sparser area, and again the audience's approving voices are heard.

'Fast Track', with its skeletal, three-note motif, is given an unin-hibited, ferocious performance, yet even in the heat of the moment, a few 'signifying' trumpet notes from Miles can change the whole feel of the band from frenetic to calm and considered. Stern, using various rocky sound effects, matches the unbridled energy of the rhythm section, and Miles is in astonishingly good lip. He plays with great passion and powerful rhythmic thrust and more than once, at high points, gets into the stratospheric range of the instru-ment, screaming trumpet G sharps and even As above top C – an extraordinary feat for a man whose health was still doubtful. The whole performance climaxes with Mino Cinelu's percussion solo, which is punctuated by urgent band interpolations; the audience responds wildly to this dialogue and the whole thing ends with a trumpet scream from Miles, followed by a storm of applause.

The other new piece, 'Kix', composed by Miles, is a two-part structure. The first part has a reggae rhythm and is in E flat minor, while the second section moves to F, with walking bass and a swing rhythm. Miles begins with the Harmon mute and even manages a scream with that suppressed, inward-looking sound, then plays open trumpet, producing lines of triplets that recall his 1954 solos on 'Walkin'' and 'Bags' Groove'. After strong solos by Bill Evans playing tenor saxophone (his preferred instrument), and Stern, Miles re-enters on open trumpet and, during the swing section, doubles the tempo, playing a long, dramatic solo with flowing, urgent lines, rhythmically violent single notes and a fluid chromaticism which harks back to his mid-1960s work. Evans on tenor takes over in this fast section, also playing superbly, and when the rhythm section returns to the slow tempo and reggae beat, Miles joins in with Evans to bring the proceedings to an end.

All three recorded performances from Kix show that this new group was already a working band with enormous potential, and Miles Davis was not only coming back to form, but also pushing himself to the limit. He had been paid $15,000 per night for the Kix engagement – a total of $60,000, and the club had made a profit as well. He was so pleased with his band's performance there that he decided to get more dates booked after the Avery Fisher Hall concert on 5 July. This created a problem for Bill Evans:

I had played at Town Hall [for the Kool concert on 3 July] with Gil Evans, and Gil had asked me to go to Europe with his band, and I asked Miles if I could go, and he said, 'No, I want you around, we're going to be doing some concerts and recording.' And I had to tell Gil the night before they left for Europe that I couldn't go.

Gil Evans understood the situation perfectly, knowing that Miles had first claim on the saxophonist, and so he was philosophical about this mini-crisis, which he must have experienced many times. He was also keenly interested in Miles's return to music-making because the two men were close friends, each the alter-ego of the other. Miles had always been the mover and shaker, the great player who understood orchestration and music-making with large or small ensembles, while Gil was a more contemplative master of orchestration who had complete understanding of and respect for improvising musicians in general and Miles Davis in particular. Gil was also currently glancing back at their joint venture *Porgy and Bess*, and his band's repertoire included a new arrangement of 'Here Comes de Honey Man'. In the mid-1980s, when Gil was about to tour with a British band, the drummer John Marshall asked in advance what kind of rhythmic feel he wanted and Gil said, 'Listen to *We Want Miles*.' For his European tour in the summer of 1981, he was able to get Steve Grossman, another ex-Miles Davis musician, as a last-minute replacement for Bill Evans.

Although still not in the best of health, Miles had decided to continue working after his two Kool concerts at Avery Fisher Hall on 5 July, and he had, quite literally, been forced to 'gird up his loins' in order to function. He told Richard Williams: '"When I play, I wear a truss and a rubber corset. Here": he grabbed my hand, put it to his abdomen and made me push against it. "The muscles there are important if you play from the stomach, like I do."'[22]

Extremely high notes can also put extra strain on the abdomen and, even at this early stage of his comeback, Miles was making frequent dramatic forays into the stratosphere, as if testing out his ability to do so. Later in the decade, these forays would be achieved with majesty and grandeur. He explained to Richard Williams that early on he couldn't 'hear' in that register: 'When I first started playing, it was low – middle to low register. I couldn't hear above that. Just lately, though, I've been able to hear up to octavissimo F, G. A sometimes.'[23] By 'hear' in this context, Miles is referring to the necessity for a trumpet player to be able to hear in his imagination the exact pitch, particularly of a high note, before playing it. If he cannot hear that, the attempt will be hit or miss, because with only three valves, the exact compression of the embouchure is essential for accurate pitching. Another change in his comeback style was his use of a small radio microphone clipped to the trumpet and positioned in front of the bell. This enabled him to move about on stage while playing instead of, as in the old days, standing still to play into a fixed microphone. And sometimes, when his health was poor, the only way he could hold himself together sufficiently to perform was by keeping on the move.

Miles was even more nervous about the Avery Hall concerts than he had been at Kix, and it is not hard to see why. This was a major occasion – all the critics would be there, expecting some kind of major musical statement – whereas he was still feeling his way back into the whole process of music-making. Bill Evans said:

> I could see when we played in the Avery Fisher Hall in New York that it was a huge event, that he was coming out and playing. He was talking about it and I walked out with him towards George Wein's office, and he got this big, *huge* cheque as an advance and he gave it to me. He said, 'Don't lose it.'

During this whole period, the camaraderie between Miles and his musicians was remarkable, and their support and commitment were essential to his well-being. Of Bill Evans he said: 'Bill's my right-hand man ... Without him I don't know what I'd do.'[24] Evans commented: 'A lot of the times he'd be staying in bed after the concerts and saying, "Thanks for pulling me through, guys," because sometimes he was really weaker, with pneumonia or whatever ... but he knew he could always rely on the band.' His young band, however, may have been somewhat overwhelmed by the occasion of the Kool concerts, because only an edited version of 'Back Seat Betty' from the second concert that night was deemed worthy of inclusion on the double-LP *We Want Miles*.

The prejudices and comments of the critics were depressingly predictable. They ought to have realized by then that Davis always started off a new phase by reviewing his past, but though it was generally recognized that his sound and technique were in good shape, he was accused of making music in his pre-retirement manner. All publicly performed music of any genre is a theatrical as well as a musical experience, but Miles was also accused of theatricality. The mindless prejudice against jazz-rock fusion was also much in evidence. Like any of the other jazz movements – traditional, swing, bebop, cool, modal, free – for a while it held centre stage, and then became part of the mainstream, its influence permeating the musical spectrum. The idea that it would simply go away could occur only to someone with no inkling about the relationship between tradition and innovation in art. Fusion was as radical and serious a movement as bebop – now also part of the mainstream. The young musicians in Miles's band, particularly Mike Stern (whom critics identified as a rock musician), also took a bashing and were much upset by it. At the time, their promise seemed quite obvious to anyone with ears, and in retrospect, with the evidence of the recordings, the lack of the reviewers' percipience seems downright reprehensible. Often it was not an argued criticism but a casual dismissal – guitar, bass, percussion no good. It must have taken Miles's mind back to when he was nineteen and received his first review in *Down Beat* of his solos on Charlie Parker's 'Billie's Bounce' and 'Now's the Time': 'The trumpet man, whoever the misled kid is, plays Gillespie in the same manner as a majority of kids who copy their idol do – with most of the faults, lack of order and meaning, the complete adherence to technical acrobatics.'[25]

Both of those solos have stood the test of time, and his 'Now's the Time' solo, in particular, is so admired that it has been played and recorded by musicians on other instruments over the years. Miles had been younger, when he received that put-down, than even the young musicians in his current band, and throughout his career he had received much critical flak, often from people who simply didn't understand what he was doing. In the 1950s, he had been accused of going pop when he played songs associated with Sinatra, and the initial critical impression of the quintet with Coltrane was that it consisted of a trumpeter who could play only in the middle register and fluffed half his notes, an out-of-tune tenor player, a cocktail pianist, a drummer who played so loudly that no one else could be heard, and a teenaged bassist. The critical attacks went on in the 1960s and 1970s, and it was probably this experience that made Miles realize that undeserved bad reviews are much less harmful to a musician than undeserved good ones. When good work gets bad notices, this fires musicians up and strengthens their self-criticism and resolve. But everyone loves and wants to believe praise, and time after time, undeserved praise or over-praise has tended to dull the self-critical faculties of musicians and lend to complacency. The critics knew – or ought to have known – that Miles had a nonpareil ear for unknown but brilliantly talented musicians, and that should have made them pause for thought; he had made it plain how much he loved his band. When Cheryl McCall asked him if he was happy to be touring again, he replied: 'Not really. It's just playing with Bill and those guys. It turns me on. It makes the adrenaline start flowing. It's such a great bunch of guys, they play so well, it's a pity to let them down, you know.'[26] Miles also told her that bad reviews didn't bother him because he didn't read them, since he could anticipate what they were going to say. She persisted: 'And when they knock your band for no reason?' and he replied:

One guy did it 'cause I wouldn't do an interview with him. He kind of upset my guitar player. I said [to Mike Stern], 'Man, look at me, I've been called a black motherfucker, and black this and that, some of this here and that there . . . Man, you just ignore it. The thing is not to say anything at all' . . . I love music. That takes up ninety per cent of my life. The other part is Cicely [Tyson] and some more people I know, Mark [Rothbaum], Bill, all of my guys, Fat Time [Stern], Al Foster. I stay in constant touch with Al no matter where he is.[27]

Miles also tried to reassure his young musicians when they were critically abused in the press. He said to Marcus Miller, 'Who you gonna believe, me or some guy who writes for a newspaper?' and once in mid-concert, he walked past Miller saying, 'Man, you swing better than them old motherfuckers.'[28] Miller commented:

> The Miles the band knows, no one else has ever known. This person is closer, I think, to the real person behind the stories. Once on the phone, I was telling Miles I was feeling uptight about my playing, feeling a little insecure. Miles said, 'I felt the same way when I was your age.' And I said, 'But you were playing with Bird and those guys.' He said, 'Man, Bird and them would leave me up on the bandstand, go downstairs to do their thing [fix]. The tempo would be goin' by, and I played one chorus, two choruses. By the third chorus, I didn't care what I played. Wasn't my band.' It meant so much, just to see everybody, even Miles, goes through those insecurities. And if Miles likes the way I play, I don't need to hear anything else.[29]

There was also the fatuous criticism that Miles had not been listening to the jazz being played during his retirement, and that he showed no knowledge of contemporary trends. The fact was, he also hadn't listened to much contemporary jazz in the 1960s or 1970s, his interest having been in other areas, but this hadn't inhibited the dynamism and radical innovation in his music. It was also ironic that, after the derided jazz rock fusion movement became history, no other jazz movement would hold centre stage again, and in Miles's silent years, there had been no universally recognized, fundamental new direction. Perhaps the most significant events during that period had been, in 1977, the advent of VSOP, the reconstitution of the 1960s Miles Davis Quintet with Freddie Hubbard on trumpet, and the presence of a teenage Wynton Marsalis, first in Art Blakey's Jazz Messengers, and then on a national and international tour with Davis's old rhythm section – Hancock, Carter and Tony Williams. When asked about VSOP by Richard Williams in a 1983 interview, Miles said: 'I only heard of VSOP three weeks ago. They wouldn't be able to get the same kind of intensity. I wouldn't get the same thing now either.'[30] The intensity came from the 1960s quintet's continual attempts to invade the unknown, to break new musical ground. Miles also said, during the same interview, that he listened to Prince and Michael Jackson, and asked if he drew ideas from them, replied: 'It's useful. But mainly to see what you don't want to do, as always. It's nice to see someone else fall off the ladder! You can hear things that you wouldn't do yourself, without having to go through trying them out.' When Leonard Feather interviewed Miles in his hotel room late in 1982, he noticed cassettes of Stevie Wonder and Paul McCartney and commented: 'The only recordings in sight were by pop groups.' Miles filled out the picture for him:

I like Journey. I like the Who. I know the new Weather Report must be good, because Joe Zawinul and Wayne [Shorter] are two helluva musicians. But I listen to Stockhausen and Ravel. And singers: they get the most out of a melody. You know I learned to phrase years ago from Frank Sinatra. I still go to see him, still go backstage and talk to him. And I like Al Jarreau.[31]

Sinatra often said that Billie Holiday had had the greatest influence on his phrasing, and Billie, asked what inspired her to start singing, insisted on many occasions that it had been Louis Armstrong's vocal chorus on the original version of 'West End Blues' (28 June 1928). This reveals something of the fundamental jazz inspirations behind Miles's music – no matter how he chose to express them.

Twelve days after the Avery Fisher Hall concert, Miles and his band began a seventeen-concert tour in the USA, Japan and Canada, taking over three and a half months and ending on 31 December. The first two dates were in New York City at the Savoy on 17 and 18 July, and were attended by the journalist Cheryl McCall, who had been persuaded by Mark Rothbaum to interview Miles in depth and write an article about him. She decided to meet him at the Savoy and arranged to travel around with the band on the subsequent American leg of the tour. Because she brought very few prejudices or preconceptions to her meetings with Miles, and admitted frankly to him that she was relatively unschooled in jazz, afraid of him and worried about incurring his anger, he seems to have instantly liked and trusted her. As a result, the eventual interview is one of the most friendly and eloquent Miles ever gave, and McCall's comments about him are extraordinarily perceptive.

The singer/songwriter Rickie Lee Jones, and rock stars Mick Jagger and Charlie Watts were in the audience at the Savoy. The excitement ran high, and McCall commented:

The concert was sensational. Miles took more chances than he had a couple of weeks earlier at the Kool Jazz Festival. He pushed his reviving chops to their limit, freely mixing tunes like 'All of You' with his contemporary material and even, during a long exploration of 'My Man's Gone Now' ... took an extended solo on Fender piano that had a wealth of imagination in it and more than enough technique ... Saxophonist Bill Evans soloed more comfortably than he had either at Avery Fisher Hall or on record, and the much-maligned guitarist, 'Fat Time' Stern, finally had a chance to show how much he loved bebop.[32]

During this touring period Miles was, essentially, trying to explore the potential of his musicians and experiment with repertoire – hence the surprising momentary reappearance of 'All of You' in the Savoy programme. It was one of the many standards recorded in the 1950s by pianist Ahmad Jamal, who was then such an inspiration to Miles. The latter recorded several versions of it with his 1960s quintet and now, in 1981, he was glancing back again to his past. At the Savoy also, for the first time in a public performance, he persuaded saxophonist Bill Evans to play some electric piano in 'Kix' during the first concert, and in 'My Man's Gone Now' during the concert on the second night. Cheryl McCall, noting that Evans seemed reluctant and had to be escorted over to the piano, asked about the incident and Miles said:

Bill Evans plays great piano, he used to play classical piano and give concerts of Rachmaninoff and stuff like that when he was sixteen. People don't know that. I wouldn't ask him to sit down if he couldn't play. He's one of the greatest musicians I've ever come upon. He and Gil Evans. There must be something with those Evanses. Must be a *breed*.[33]

This leading of Bill Evans over to the piano also happened on subsequent occasions. During the last six months of 1980, when Bill Evans was acting as chaperon and companion to Miles, he had played the piano a great deal. Evans recalled:

I used to play piano for him all the time at his house. Sometimes we'd spend hours writing tunes, and I'd just be playing piano, piano, piano, and he thought it was real natural, the way I played piano. He liked the way I played keyboards, and he started to get the idea that it would be a unique thing to show people that I could play piano at a high level. Some of the situations were embarrassing. We were playing the Hollywood Bowl, and Joe Zawinul, Chick Corea and George Duke and every major keyboardist of the time were in the front row. And he brings me over, and he counts off the rhythm section (at an extremely fast tempo), one, two, three, four, one, two, three, four, and he drags me over to the keyboard to play for these guys. And I was petrified, and eventually after like a minute, you know, just playing it seemed very humorous to me at the time. I just thought . . . this is hilarious. But he loved that. You know, he loves to create a thing, and it was just an interesting thing during the show that he liked to do. That's all.

At the Savoy, Miles seemed to be in good spirits and full of energy when on stage, but Cheryl McCall was shocked when she went backstage to find 'Miles Davis in a state of collapse, sweating like a prizefighter between rounds and similarly attended by men with towels, drink, encouragement and aid'.[34] Miles explained to her later that it was necessary to relax the tension when out of the public eye, but in fact, his health was precarious throughout this three-month touring stretch. Two things kept him going: his willpower and the commitment of the new band he loved so much. But, in never sparing himself when performing, he put himself continually at risk, and it was only when there were several days' rest between engagements that he could recover his full strength. After the two Savoy concerts, the band played the Warner Theatre at Washington, DC, on 28 July, and then there were a couple of weeks off, before the next concert at Chicago on 14 August.

Cicely Tyson had the use of a cottage at a resort called Gurney's at Montauk, near the eastern tip of Long Island, and she and Miles went there to relax because his New York brownstone house was in the process of being renovated. They invited Cheryl McCall for the weekend – during which she would interview Miles – and the road team, Jim Rose and Chris Murphy, manager Mark Rothbaum, and right-hand man Bill Evans were also invited. Miles wanted to do the interview immediately, and when it was over, everyone relaxed for the rest of the stay. McCall was surprised by his unfailing good spirits and friendliness: 'I had expected to see everyone waiting on him and found the reverse: Miles the host, providing food, beer, conversation and humour; Miles the joker, sparring with everyone who passed, sneaking Bill Evans's ring off his finger, palming my lighter, engaging in conversation with his invisible alter-ego Leroy.' But she also saw beneath the surface, remarking: 'For all the warmth of his presence, and for all his humour . . . there is still an air of inconsolable grief about him, which I think Cicely has finally touched.'[35] McCall's earlier between-rounds boxing image was also apposite. In the photographs taken of him during this whole initial period of his comeback, with his little moustache and a shadowy tuft of beard on the chin, he often has the faraway look in his eyes of a boxer who has taken a terrible beating, but who knows there are a few more rounds yet to go.

The band's concert at Chicago on 14 August was the occasion of a family reunion, and an opportunity for Miles to introduce

Cicely Tyson to his sister Dorothy, his daughter Cheryl and his brother Vernon. McCall, whom he now treated as part of his entourage, also met them and some of his childhood friends from St Louis, who recalled Miles's shyness and loneliness as a youngster. He had experienced shortness of breath during some of the comeback concerts, and in Chicago he had to take oxygen to help him through the performance. McCall also mentions that sometimes his joints were so stiff that he could not bend enough to put on his trousers and the band had to help him. It was, however, at the Chicago concert that the band played, in public for the first time, Miles's appealing little nursery song, 'Jean Pierre'. The motif for this had been in the back of his mind for years, and he had first played it on 9 April 1960 in Holland during Coltrane's last tour with the quintet. Miles's solo on 'Walkin'' on that occasion was quite magnificent and in his sixth chorus, he played the motif of what would become, twenty years later, 'Jean Pierre', named after his first wife Frances's son by a previous marriage. Bill Evans described how it finally came about:

> He'd just get these little ideas, you know, like 'Jean Pierre'. He wrote that a few months before the band even got together and he started taking his trumpet out every now and then. It was great to hear him playing again. He'd just play little lines and comes out with this line – dah dah, da da dah. I thought it was a neat little line that really characterized his style. And when we were playing at Kix, he says, 'Well, what do you feel like playing, Bill? Just name it. Just what do you feel like playing?' And I said, 'I like that little melody.' He said, 'No, I don't want to play that. I don't like that tune.' That was the first day, and on the second and third day I kept on saying, 'Well let's play that little tune.' But he wouldn't . . . and then it turned out to be the tune he would close *every* show with, and that he played for years.

It may be that Miles felt comfortable enough to play it in Chicago, because of the presence at his concert of his sister, brother and daughter, all of whom knew Jean Pierre.

Cheryl McCall noted that the friendliness and warmth of the Montauk weekend continued during the tour:

> He could not have been more affectionate with his band, hugging them, reassuring them, defending them fiercely from bad reviews . . . I've travelled with a lot of bands in my time, but I've never encountered anything like the atmosphere of reciprocity and love that Miles Davis brings with him. Cicely Tyson says he's always been like that and that the toughness is all façade.[36]

Two days after Chicago, the band played Detroit and Miles again had to take oxygen, but the next concert at Denver, Colorado, was not until 4 September, which gave him ample rest. The last leg of this part of the tour finished in September with (19) Ann Arbor, Michigan, (25) Hollywood, California, and (26) Concord, California. After the Ann Arbor concert, Miles contracted pneumonia, but managed to get out of bed to play the Hollywood Bowl – where he had Bill Evans play in front of all those pianists in the front row. But Miles was in shocking health that night, and his concert was given a damning review by Leonard Feather, who said it was musically barren. Later he said to Feather: 'I wasn't bothered by your review of my Hollywood Bowl concert – hell, I was so sick that night I could hardly walk.'[37] Yet the very next day he had to play again at Concord.

Outraged by Feather's dismissive review, Max Roach took up cudgels on Miles's behalf, attacking Feather in a letter to *Jazz Magazine*, but when Miles was later asked about this by the Polish magazine *Jazz Forum*, he said: 'Max is fine. Max is like my brother and anything (negative) that anybody would say about me, Max is going to challenge them to fight or anything. Max declares war on them. Poor Leonard.'[38] In fact, Leonard Feather was musically literate, one of the most knowledgeable and perceptive of critics, and had been, over the years, a good critical friend to Davis –

quick to recognize his unique gifts and to say so in limpid prose, but equally ready, if he felt Miles was falling below his own high standards, to say so in print. Feather had been in tune with Miles's work up to the later 1960s, but had lost touch after that, and it was probably with all this in mind that Miles could, even after a scathing review, still utter the sympathetic words 'Poor Leonard'.

After the Concord concert, Miles and the band flew to Japan to play seven concerts for a fee of $700,000 with all expenses paid. From the 1960s onwards, an almost godlike status had been conferred on him by his Japanese audiences – he was admired and loved by both fans and critics alike, and it seemed that, in their eyes, he could do no wrong. He arrived there on 29 September, and his mini-tour began with three concerts on consecutive nights (2–4 October) at Shinjuku Nishi-Guchi Hiroba, Tokyo. It is possible that three consecutive concerts were simply too much of a drain on his strength, because the recording of the third night (4 October) reveals that his energy and range are somewhat diminished, there are often longer pauses between phrases, there are no forays into the extreme upper register and even his moderately high notes sound slightly sour and out of tune. Also, the Harmon mute is so poorly amplified that instead of its usual breathy resonance in the middle register and shriller high notes, it has a thin, piercing nasal sound like a straight mute in all registers. Yet it was this concert that provided the two pieces that completed *We Want Miles* – a full performance of 'Jean Pierre', which is the opening track, and a short version of it, which concludes the first half of the album.

But if, during that 4 October concert, Miles was in poor health and his playing below par, his spirit informed the music even when he was not playing, and his presence inspired the band, which was now a superb unit – a working band playing magnificently. The concert hall atmosphere was electric with anticipation, and as soon as they walked on stage, the audience erupted with applause, whistles and shrieks, soon drowned by the two massive, slow 'A-men' chords of 'Back Seat Betty'. This piece was given an epic treatment, punctuated by those heavy 'A-men' pauses, with Miles using the straight mute much of the time, and sounding less sure when he removed it to play open. The rhythm section (Miller, Foster and Cinelu) was now a superbly flexible combination of drive and subtlety, Mike Stern's accompanying chords enhanced the sound and atmosphere, and his solos seemed to grow organically, with some dazzling flights of fancy, while Evans – on tenor or soprano – paced himself like a master, moving from spare, lyrical moments to bravura passages replete with freshly minted phrases. That concert also revealed how the band had developed their performance of 'My Man's Gone Now' during the preceding engagements. It was now taken at a much slower tempo, with the band staying longer on the harmonically static rocky section and the ballad area, where Miles, first with straight mute, then open, played his main solo. When he brought in the time-change, the tempo *quadrupled*, with both Stern and Evans playing their solos over the fast, jazz swing feel, and in this way the whole drama of Miles's arrangement was heightened.

'Jean Pierre' tended to be a feature for the band, with Miles playing the motif but leaving most of the soloing to Stern and Evans, so it matters little that his Harmon mute has that thin, nasal sound or that he doesn't solo at length. That is why this was the only track from the concert good enough to complete the album *We Want Miles*. His initial improvisation of the motif, in 1960, had been in the key of F, but 'Jean Pierre' is in A which, while not in favour with many trumpet players, is a comfortable key for guitars, and bass guitars, because the keynote (A) is an open string for both instruments. The hypnotic little theme juxtaposes major and minor thirds, implying the blues, which is, perhaps, why Bill Evans thought it really characterized Miles's style, and each member of the band refers rhythmically and melodically to the motif now and then. The rhythm section gives the slow spacy pulse an ecstatic lift, Stern plays some delicious single-note riffs in the early stages, and Miles and Evans (on soprano) play the theme in unison and harmony. Miles's economical solo has a folky element in it all the way, then Stern plays a solo bristling with ideas, and after the two horns restate the motif, Evans begins by playing with it, until he and the rhythm section, all ears and imagination, take it far out and back in again, with wild climaxes and excellent dynamics. A quiet restatement of the theme is followed by a gigantic chord, after which the audience applauds wildly. As the opening track for *We Want Miles*, this was the perfect choice – just over ten minutes long, highly focused, a tour de force rhythmically, with dynamic solos and with a catchy, recurring, singable motif: essence of Miles.

The second piece on the album, 'Back Street Betty' from the Avery Fisher Hall concert in July, provides a sensational contrast to 'Jean Pierre'. Although still in the key of F, it is no longer a slow piece reminiscent of 'Miles Runs the Voodoo Down', but a powerfully urgent, rocky outing, edited down to just over eight minutes, with Miles as the only soloist – solos by Stern and Evans have been edited out – and the trumpeter is in devastating form here. Miles begins with the Harmon mute, which sounds full and resonant, and his first few notes echoing 'Voodoo' again alternate major and minor thirds, drawing a wild response from the audience. His muted playing is masterly, lyrical and funky, and Stern, Miller, Foster and Cinelu respond intensely. Suddenly, the mute is removed and Miles's huge open trumpet sound stabs out dramatically. He soars to the upper register, hits a majestic high F, and the band is with him all the way, building tension, releasing it, reacting to his flurries, his stabs, his pauses and his complex lines and interval leaps. This is collective music-making of a high order, under the spell of Miles's trumpet. Eventually an 'A-men' chord brings the piece to a close. These two opening pieces and a four-minute version of 'Jean Pierre' from the Tokyo session, plus the three performances from the Boston engagements in June, 'Fast Track', 'My Man's Gone Now' and 'Kix', completed the album *We Want Miles*, which was scheduled for release in the summer of 1982.

Miles and the band had four more concerts to play in Japan, at Nakano Sun Plaza, Tokyo on 6 October, then three concerts moving ever further south west – Nagoya, Osaka and Fukuoka, on 9, 10 and 11 October. Yet again, three concerts on consecutive days would give his failing health no chance to recover, and when he and the band began the long night-and-day flight back to the USA, he already had a touch of pneumonia. They arrived in New York on 14 October and he had only three days to try and gather his health and strength, before appearing on the popular NBC TV show, *Saturday Night Live*. It was not enough time, and he was exhausted and sick during the transmission. In his autobiography, he said:

> I remember Marcus Miller asking me, 'What hurts?' before we did that show, and I told him, 'What *don't* hurt!' I felt so sick that if I had sat down, I didn't believe I could get up again. All through that show I just walked my ass off, while I was playing and even while I wasn't playing; I just walked the whole time.[39]

In the second volume of his biography of Davis, *Milestones II*, Jack Chambers says that the performance of 'Jean Pierre' was taken at too fast a tempo with disastrous results, and that Miles 'limped around the stage, the cameras losing him and finding him again awkwardly, his face taut, his eyes unseeing'.[40] Fortunately, he had two weeks in which to revive himself, before his next concert, on 4 November at Boston, Massachusetts.

In some ways, Miles Davis seemed to be almost sleep-walking through this whole period, ill, distracted, and only half aware of what was going on, except on the occasions when his energy was up and he was playing really well. He seems to have sleep-walked even into marriage with Cicely Tyson. On 27 November, Thanksgiving Day 1981, they were married at comedian Bill Cosby's house in Massachusetts by the Reverend Andrew Young, with Max Roach, Dizzy Gillespie, comedian Dick Gregory and Miles's manager, Mark Rothbaum, present. At the ceremony Miles felt desperately ill. He recalled: 'I had that gray look of almost-death in my face. Cicely saw it. I told her I felt like I could die at any minute.'[41] During the previous summer he had injected some drug into his leg and it had gone gangrenous, which had compounded his health problems. But in his autobiography, he confesses to going to bed with another woman five days after his marriage to Cicely, explaining, 'because I didn't feel that sex thing for Cicely any more. I respected her as a woman and felt like she was a good friend to me, but I also needed that sex thing that I couldn't get from her. So I got it in other places.'[42] It was as if the 'sex thing' was something quite far apart from love and affection in his experience. Yet, only the previous August, he'd told Cheryl McCall: 'I'm happy now. I could have been happy years ago if I had married Cicely. But years ago . . . no. Time takes care of that, time takes care of everything. If I had married Cicely she wouldn't have been a star now.' McCall asked pointedly, 'Wasn't she a star then?' Miles continued: 'Yes, but she was too involved with me to be, you know, to keep her mind and body and work on it. And *I* work. And besides she's very smart. I know a couple of women like that who are very smart and I try to stay out of their way – even if I do love them.'[43] Cicely Tyson had been a rising star before she met Miles and had been featured regularly in the role of secretary in the TV series *East Side West Side* in 1963–4. Then she became a big star with her role in the 1972 film *Sounder*, for which she was nominated for an Oscar as best actress. She also played acclaimed roles in the TV dramas, *Roots* and *The Autobiography of Miss Jane Pittman*. Miles was well aware that Cicely had become a big star since they were last together in the late 1960s, and admitted that she was probably more famous than he was. But he also insisted that her accent in *The Autobiography of Miss Jane Pittman* came from copying his voice and the way he talked, so that his influence had aided her success. He seems to have felt uneasy about her stardom, and in fact, she was just the kind of woman – strong, intelligent, successful – that he described to Cheryl McCall and said he tried to avoid. Tyson was much in demand and away working a great deal, and Miles said, somewhat resignedly, 'Anyway, when she was in town, she would be over to my place.'[44]

Still in fluctuating health, he went back on tour in the USA in December, and after playing Toronto, Canada, on the thirteenth, ended the year with a concert on 31 December at the Beacon Theatre, New York City. Sheer willpower, and the youthful energy and optimism of his group, had pulled him through seven months of public performances, and these had put him back on the map. *The Man with the Horn* had been released in the autumn, and had received, in general, mediocre or bad reviews. Some critics thought he was just a shadow of his former self, but the album sold well and was even voted Best Album of the Year by the readers of *Down Beat*. The previous August, the *Village Voice* had published a detailed and perceptive appraisal of Davis's career by the fine critic, Gary Giddins, who stated clearly one of the central facts about the trumpeter:

> Good musicians, justly proud of the individualism that is at the core of jazz, may invent new sounds and variations, but how many have addressed the fundamental issues of structure, instrumentation and repertoire? Miles Davis does, constantly, and every time he comes up with a new answer, the whole music shifts in its seat ... His popularity probably accounts for the frequent omission of Davis's name from discussions of jazz radicals ... Still, he is a terribly conscientious avant-gardist, continuously remaking jazz in his own image, and often remaking himself in the process.[45]

Giddins was also one of the few critics to point out that Miles was currently reinvestigating his past, which was his usual prelude to discovering new musical visions, and although critical of *The Man with the Horn*, he saw positive things in it, and promise for the future. The readers of *Down Beat* had also voted Miles Jazz Musician of the Year, so at the end of 1981, he was poised on the threshold of a new phase in his career. The only problem was that he was still dicing with death in his private life, smoking three or four packets of cigarettes a day and consuming alcohol and drugs. When a doctor asked him if he wanted to live, he replied in the affirmative, but did not give up these indulgences. He would purge himself of them only after he had had a terrifying shock.

TWENTY

Crisis and Rebirth

'I do like Gil Evans told me to do, years ago, say
"Always keep the tape recorder on." Yeah, I'm never
gonna turn it off. You don't know what you might
stumble upon and you can't – on the gig, you
really can't go back to it because you don't
know what it is.'[1]

Miles Davis

When Miles Davis had returned from his Japanese tour in October
1981, and played the *Saturday Night Live* NBC TV show, he had
felt extremely unwell, yet chose to ignore obvious signs of serious
bodily malfunction. His urine was full of blood, and after the effort
of struggling through the TV show, he began to feel a numbness in
his right hand and fingers, but he simply ignored these warnings.
Then, in January 1982, Cicely Tyson went to Africa to do some
work for the US State Department and Miles, without her
restraining presence, began to over-indulge himself again.
Although he had stopped using cocaine by now, he was still smoking three or four packets of cigarettes a day, and after Cicely left,
he began drinking excessive amounts of beer. Then one night, he
got the fright of his life: after closing his right hand, he found he
was powerless to open it again, and realized he had lost the use
of it. Cicely Tyson had always had a sixth sense about Miles's
condition, and even far away in Africa her intuition told her something was wrong. She telephoned him, and he told her he couldn't
move his hand or his fingers. She said that it sounded like a stroke,

and, cutting short her trip, came straight back to the USA. Hospital tests confirmed that it had been a stroke and there was nothing they could do about it except give him some physiotherapy and hope for the best. But it looked as if Miles might never be able to play the trumpet again, and the huge shock of this realization at last gave him the impetus to stop all his excesses – cigarettes, alcohol, any residual drugs were banished from his life. The doctors had told Cicely that he would never be able to use that arm and hand again, but she kept this information from Miles.

He and the band were booked to do a series of concerts on the West Coast starting in February, but they had to be cancelled. Miles's stroke was a closely guarded secret, and the mysterious cancellations were regarded as yet another manifestation of the famous Davis wilful, unpredictable persona. For over a month there was no sign of movement in the hand and Cicely Tyson told Leonard Feather: 'One of the most difficult things was to convince him that his physician wasn't giving us any answers. I could not sit by and just see Miles there in that condition. Finally I just physically picked him up one Sunday and took him to a Chinese acupuncturist.'[2] The acupuncturist, Dr Chin, also gave him herbs that would clean up his whole system. So after a month or two of acupuncture, herbs, physiotherapy, good food, inhaling only air and drinking only Perrier water, he woke up one night and found he could move and use his hand again. From that moment on, he began swimming regularly to improve his breathing capacity and general health. But during that whole testing period, he had lost most of his hair, which really upset him because, as he admitted later: 'I have always been vain about my appearance.'[3]

Although he was now on the mend, Miles was still very weak, and his energy ebbed and flowed unpredictably. He was also extremely thin, and had only a few strands of hair left, but his recovery from the stroke would prove to be the second fundamental turning point, after the one in 1979. Slowly, his health and strength would return and the last phase of his career would mirror the great creative periods of 1954–60 and 1965–71, because his self-discipline would again be good, his energy high, the whole glory of his playing would return, and again he would find new modes of procedure. But before that happened, he would have to force himself by sheer willpower to play the trumpet when his strength and health were often at a low ebb. The use of his hand and the ability to hold and play the trumpet had returned to him like a miracle; it was a kind of rebirth. He said to Leonard Feather:

> They had some kind of cast on my hand. One night I woke up, picked up the horn and found I could play it. See how strong it is now! Feel this! It's not just back to normal – it's better than normal. And I keep exercising it on the keyboard to keep my circulation good ... I owe it all to Cicely. If it hadn't been for her and that doctor, I don't know where I'd have been. I'll never fear anything, ever again.[4]

Now that the ability to play had returned to him, he wanted to waste no time and planned to start a European tour in April. His band had not played together for three months, and so he called a rehearsal towards the end of March, to see how it sounded and felt. All was well and they warmed up for Europe by playing three concerts in the USA – at the Bradford Hotel, Boston, Massachusetts, on 1 and 2 April, and the University of Massachusetts at Amherst on the third.

It was six or seven years since Miles Davis had played in Europe, and interest there had now reached fever pitch. Fans, critics and musicians had been reading reports about his comeback, were aware of the adverse criticisms (which made them feel that Miles was once again himself), had heard *The Man with the Horn*, and were agog to hear him and his band in person. News of his stroke had not leaked out, and no one was prepared for the wraithlike figure who sometimes felt so weak that he had to sit down in order to play, who had good days when all went well, and bad days when he felt like quitting and going back to America.

The European concerts were, invariably, an early sell-out, and he and the band played in Stockholm on 13 April, Copenhagen on the fourteenth, Hamburg on the sixteenth and Frankfurt am Main on the following day, before flying to London on 19 April for three concerts at Hammersmith Odeon on 20, 21 and 22 April. All three concerts were sold out in advance, and arrangements had been made for an independent production company to film the second concert for London Weekend Television's *South Bank Show*, which had also made a documentary film about Davis's life and career. In the process of researching the documentary the *South Bank Show* had also managed to get hold of a copy of the very rare black-and-white 1959 film *The Sound of Miles Davis*, which featured his quintet with Coltrane playing 'So What', and Miles with the Gil Evans Orchestra playing 'The Duke', 'New Rhumba' and 'Blues for Pablo'. From the point of view of sound and vision, this was, and remains, one of the finest films of jazz ever made, and once LWT had unearthed it, it tended to stay intermittently in view. Miles's concert on 21 April would, of course, be filmed in colour, and its producer Gerry O'Reilly was an avid Miles Davis fan, and very excited about the possibility of filming him. On 19 April, O'Reilly went to London Heathrow Airport to meet Davis's plane, but began to feel very apprehensive when the passengers filed past him and there was no sign of Miles Davis. When it seemed that the last passenger had departed, suddenly a wheelchair appeared with Miles in it, his right arm strapped up, and pushing it was Cicely Tyson, wearing a fur coat. As they passed him, Miles seemed so say something incoherent to O'Reilly, who quickly learnt the bad news: Davis felt very ill and didn't want to play a concert the following day. After registering the shock of Davis's apparent frailty, O'Reilly accompanied Miles and Cicely to their hotel and said he would send a doctor round. Then he asked his father-in-law, Dr Sam Weinstock, who was a psychiatrist as well as a medical practitioner, to visit Miles at the hotel in his capacity as doctor, but to use his psychological skills to get Davis into a frame of mind that would enable him to perform the following day. Weinstock spent several hours in Davis's company that day, and later that evening reported to O'Reilly, 'He *will* play on the first night, but not for very long. He'll play more

on the second night, and on the third night he'll be unstoppable.'
And that is exactly what happened.

On the first night the whole atmosphere at the Hammersmith
Odeon was extraordinary, highly charged with emotion and seething with expectancy. Without announcement, Miles limped on
stage and stood there looking bewildered and lost, but was not at
first recognized by the audience, because his appearance and stance
were so different from what they were expecting. His moustache
was now quite full, he was wearing a cream skull cap and a beige
suit, and it was only after the young band followed him on stage
that a smattering of applause broke out. The audience were still
recovering from the shock of seeing him looking so gaunt and
frail. He had a tiny radio in a leather wallet attached to the left
side of his trumpet with a fine wire running to a tiny microphone
clipped to the bell of the instrument, and in this way his sound
was beamed to the PA speakers and monitors. This arrangement
gave him complete freedom of movement – he could play anywhere
on stage, although he did not walk around much on that first
evening, but played mostly sitting down, his face often expression-
less except when something played by one of his musicians brought
a pleased smile of recognition. He was not in good lip, but for
the audience it was thrilling to hear even a weak Miles playing,
and his group was really excellent in terms of rhythm, dynamics,
flexibility and solo strength. They played the same programme on
each of the three nights – 'Back Seat Betty', 'My Man's Gone
Now' and 'Aida' in the first half, and in the second half, a version
of 'Ife' (first recorded in 1972 and issued on the album *Big Fun*),
'Fat Time' and 'Jean Pierre'. But length and treatment varied
widely on each evening. The first concert was very short, with a
first half of thirty-five minutes and a second half of only twenty-
three, and at the end it was moving to see Miles and the band
come to the front of the stage with their arms around one another
and take a bow. That kind of close comradeship and mutual
support had never before been demonstrated in public by him and
his musicians. The newborn Miles Davis had not yet found his
full strength, but he was audibly himself, and the band knew he

was listening intently to everything they played. He inspired them; they provided the energy and panache whenever he most needed that. On the second night, he was in better shape, although still having some problems in playing, but the third night saw him utterly transformed, his energy and stamina right up, soloing for long stretches, with majestic high notes and flowing ideas. That night however, ironically, the band was not quite as incisive. This pattern of his being below strength one day and in full power the next was to repeat itself during the next part of his tour, which included two concerts in Rome (25 and 26 April), Den Haag (28), Théâtre du Chatelet, Paris (2 and 3 May), Brussels (8) and Toulouse (10). The band then returned to the USA.

Cicely Tyson and one of her friends travelled with the band during that European trip, which was such a crucial time for Miles, grappling as he was with precarious health and the struggle back into music – and the watchful, restraining presence of Cicely was an important factor. She had, after all, for the second time since 1979, taken charge, saved him from himself and put him on the road to recovery, and it was essential that he stayed on that road. But Miles still complained about her, because while he, the five members of his band and the road crew of four each had two luggage bags with them, Cicely and her friend had over eighteen bags, and the road crew were having to handle them. By this time Cicely was a big star, and this seemed to bother Miles, who thought that fame had gone to her head, and complained that she behaved in a very high-handed way with the road crew and other people. In Rome, Miles told her that he needed a rest, and took a separate hotel room, only rejoining her in the double room after the second concert. Then in Paris he had another break from her when he went to visit his one-time girlfriend, Juliette Greco. But Cicely's influence on him was still beneficial and on this tour he began a therapeutic activity she had initiated. In the summer of 1981, Cicely had bought him some sketch pads, which he had hardly used, but now he began drawing regularly on this trip. It kept him occupied when his mind might have turned to nicotine, alcohol or drugs, and this activity, plus painting in water colours and oils, would grow and grow, absorbing and enriching his leisure hours for the rest of his life.

Back in the USA in the middle of May, he had a couple of weeks' rest before he played a Kool Jazz Festival concert on 30 May at the Kennedy Centre, Washington, DC, then apart from one more Kool concert in Atlanta in June, he had the rest of that month off. It was around this time that he and Cicely spent some time at a health farm in New York State, and Miles had a fortuitous meeting with Jack and Lydia DeJohnette. They lived in a town called Kingston in New York State, and on this particular occasion they were standing in a very old broken-down and closed-down shopping mall. Lydia recalled:

I don't even know why we were there, but Jack and I were having a fight – and we never fight. And this was one of those height of our relationship, blow-out fights. And we're shouting at each other standing beside our car, and I said, 'So where do we go from here? Forward or not? Or is it all over?' And we're yelling at each other, and I hear this hoarse voice calling, 'Jack!' And there's Miles, and it was such a surreal scene. Jack's yelling and I turn round and there's this Ferrari and there's Miles. And I say, 'Jack, there's Miles!' And Jack suddenly stops and is dumbfounded. And Miles is standing there laughing at the two of us. Then *we* started laughing, and I said to Miles, 'What are you doing in Kingston, New York?' And he said, 'Is that where I am?' Then he said, 'What are you arguing about? . . . Forget it!' Then he looks at me and says, 'Are you happy to see me?' In fact he was in a health farm with Cicely in New York State, a fasting, cleaning-out place, and I asked him what he was doing in this obscure provincial town, and he said he had a nurse in the car with him and she hadn't heard his music and he was trying to buy her some albums in a local record store. So we went to the record store with him and there was this very sweet scene of him trying to show the nurse who he was. The shop had some of his old, old albums, and he was looking at them in wonderment and saying, 'Wow! I did that?!' He may not have exactly saved our relationship, but I always felt he was in our lives. I never felt this about any of the other bands Jack worked for. Miles affected us on a personal level and beyond music.

This was becoming a good time for Miles, because it was easy to book his band and he could work as much as he wanted to. Not only he did he love his band, but he was also *really* on the mend and could feel his instrumental powers coming back to him with each concert. On 4 July his concert at East Rutherford, New Jersey, began a tour of the United States and Canada that went on, with a few breaks, until the end of the year, finishing in late February 1983, when he played at the Grammy award ceremony in Hollywood. *We Want Miles* was released in the early autumn of 1982 and received a Grammy, which Miles collected at the 1983 ceremony. After the New Jersey concert, the band played Montreal, Canada, on 11 July, Boston, Massachusetts, on the twelfth and Hudson River Pier No. 84, New York City, on the seventeenth. Then with a gap before the next engagement on 28 July at Vancouver, Canada, Miles took some more time off with Cicely, and they flew to Lima, Peru, for a few days, where she was one of the judges at a Miss Universe contest. The hotel had an indoor and outdoor swimming pool, and Miles said: 'All I did for three or four days was swim and lie around the hotel pool and rest and eat good seafood. I was even starting to look like myself again, only my motherfucking hair wouldn't grow back and that was pissing me off.'[5]

After Vancouver, there were four concerts in the USA, then on 11 August Miles and the band went into the recording studio to work on music for the next album, and this time Gil Evans was also present as consultant and arranger. History was again beginning to repeat itself and as Miles worked his way back into music and his abilities blossomed again, so his vision sharpened, and his approach to music-making in the studio began to change radically. The old loose methods with fragmentary motifs, as exemplified by his pieces on *The Man with the Horn*, would be abandoned, and because he was fascinated by the music of Prince and certain white rock groups, he would soon begin painstakingly constructing his music in the studio. Improvisation, however, would still be a key factor in the genesis of ideas. He had told Cheryl McCall in August 1981 that he was following Gil Evans's advice to record all performances and solos, and very soon he would have Evans transcribing solos played even in the recording studio. Gunther Schuller has said that until it died out in the early part of the nineteenth century, improvisation used to be the backbone of all music-making, and of course, real improvisation is composition in motion, and the player can stumble upon all kinds of fresh ideas during it. Joe Zawinul has usually composed by recording his keyboard solos, transcribing them and selecting the best motifs or phrases to develop, and Keith Jarrett has always recorded all his own concerts with this (among other things) in mind.

On this occasion in the studio Miles was beginning work on an album that would be called *Star People*; it showed the beginnings of a transition, from his methods on *The Man with the Horn* and *We Want Miles*, to his future approach to composition. After a concert on 28 August at Jones Beach Theatre, Long Island, he and the band were back in the studio to do more work on the album at the beginning of September, and this time guitarist John Scofield was also there. Recently, Mike Stern had not been in the best of health, and although he was still playing well, he either didn't want to, or couldn't play the intricate melodies that Gil Evans was transcribing from solos. As a result, Miles wanted a second guitarist, and Bill Evans recommended Scofield. At that recording session he played only a little, and was not asked to join the band. On 5 September, Miles was back on tour with a concert in Chicago, followed in October with three more dates in New Jersey (23), Syracuse, New York (29), and Berkeley, California (31), and at that point he told Bill Evans to call John Scofield and ask him to come out and join the band for the next concert, on 4 November in Cleveland, Ohio. Scofield was completely surprised, but came straight out and was present at the Cleveland concert, but didn't play because he was paid to stand at the side of the stage and listen. The same thing happened the next night at Pittsburgh, Pennsylvania, and Scofield commented, 'It was great – easiest money I ever made!' But at the next concert, Yale University, New Haven, Connecticut, on 17 November, he played and became a regular member of the band. Talking of his relationship with Stern, Scofield said:

Mike was a good friend of mine, so I had to go – sort of be the other guitar player. It was my job to play the heads [themes] and Mike was still taking most of the solos and stuff, and I was just brought in to play the written music that Mike didn't want to learn ... not that he didn't want to, it just wasn't, for some reason, happening. But Miles loved Mike and was just really trying to help him, actually. Mike was playing really beautifully then, you know.

When he joined Miles Davis, John Scofield was a few weeks away from his thirty-first birthday, and already a player of consummate grace and inventiveness, who was steeped in the blues and could conjure melodic lines out of thin air. In the later 1970s and early 1980s, he had been a key member of a very fine small group led by Miles Davis's trusted friend Dave Liebman, and he had also played and recorded with other leading musicians, including Gerry Mulligan, Chet Baker, Billy Cobham, Tony Williams and Ron Carter. In other words, Scofield's highly personal style of playing was already in place, and he was not the little-known, inexperienced kind of musician Miles liked to find and shape to his music and his ideas. But Scofield seemed to have a very open mind and an infinite capacity for growth, qualities which were to make his time in the band fruitful for Miles, and invaluable for Scofield himself. Miles actually liked the idea of having two guitarists in his band. He was convinced that the guitar was the key instrument of the day, particularly where younger musicians and fans were concerned, and believed that two such very different-sounding guitarists would create tension that would be good for the music. He also thought that if Stern listened to Scofield, he might learn something about understatement, which would restrain his tendency to overplay.

But change was in the air because, now that Miles's health and strength were improving daily, he was playing longer solos and, with two guitarists, there was less solo space for Bill Evans. Furthermore, along with his burgeoning trumpet powers, Miles's musical vision was also becoming clearer and he was beginning to direct the band with hand signals, shaping the performances that way. Bill Evans explained the dilemma:

When Miles was trying to get his playing together, I was able to play as much as I wanted, every show, with Al and Marcus and Stern, and it was great. But as time went on, he was beginning to change it around where he was playing more, which is totally fine. He was beginning to really get into guitar, and wanted to hear more guitar, so after three years or so, all of a sudden he's really into leaving soloists at the top of their form, so when you're in the middle of your solo, he'll stop the band. And after you've been with the band for a few years, that can really start getting on your nerves.

Two more recording sessions for *Star People* were done on 20 December 1982 and 5 January 1983, and after the second one, Marcus Miller left the band, having recommended a young bass guitarist called Tom Barney. Miller had kept up a working relationship with saxophonist Dave Sanborn, and was in constant demand as a studio musician and as a producer and composer/arranger. He was losing career opportunities and money by playing with Miles, who really understood his dilemma. But his departure was a great blow, because Miles admired Miller's brilliant musicianship, and liked his humour and steady temperament. Their relationship would recommence later in the decade, when he and Miller would make some definitive recordings together.

Star People reflects the changes of emphasis in the band. Bill Evans gets only two short solos on the album, one tenor saxophone chorus on the title track, which is a slow blues in B flat, and a brief soprano solo on the light-hearted and lightweight scrap of melody 'U'n'I'. Miles, in excellent form, gets much of the solo space, and the two guitarists are also strongly featured. 'Come Get It' opens the album and begins with the first two rubato chords of 'Back Seat Betty', of which it is a direct descendant, in the same key (F), but taken at a much faster, rocky tempo, and performed with explosive energy. After a long build-up by the rhythm section, Miles comes in on open trumpet and he's in great shape, his sound singing, and his bristling, passionate phrases sometimes screaming up to trumpet Fs and Gs. He's a little down in the mix, with the rhythm section slightly in the foreground, but this doesn't seem to matter, because they respond to his fiery attack, fanning his blaze. After several minutes at this awesome pace, Miles pauses and the band simmers down to half tempo for an atmospheric and compelling guitar solo by Mike Stern. Eventually an edited-in organ passage played by Miles takes the piece into 'It Gets Better', which has several new features. The tempo is medium slow and the drums play an extraordinarily spare and light swing rhythm, while the bass line consists mostly of three triplet notes on the first beat of each bar, and is silent on the remaining three beats. This skeletal rhythmic continuum has an eerie contemplative atmosphere, and is given a repeated harmonic sequence of nine basic chords, which Miles said he'd borrowed from the old country blues singer and guitarist, Sam 'Lightnin'' Hopkins. The brooding spirit of the blues hangs over this whole performance, and the solo honours are shared more or less equally between Miles and John Scofield, who play alternately throughout. Miles, using the Harmon mute, its pent-up sonorities so appropriate for this highly charged mood, sculpts his phrases beautifully, once or twice refers obliquely to trumpeter Harry 'Sweets' Edison's bluesy phrasing, and even plays an occasional muted scream. Scofield is also in his element here, never wasting a note, his sound airy and eloquent. At one point the rhythm section stops, and Scofield plays rubato chords while Miles meditates in free time. This fine performance is utterly contemporary, but shot through with the blues tradition.

Tom Barney, the bass guitarist replacing Marcus Miller, plays only on the third album track, 'Speak', an up-tempo rock outing that has Miles, with open trumpet in one hand and other hand on the keyboard, punching out simultaneous riffs on both. He even managed this subsequently in live performances, although the trumpet notes were high – a further sign of his ever expanding powers. Miles also plays a quite prominent organ backing from time to time, and there are some riffs by saxophone and guitar, but Scofield is the main featured soloist. The organ also ushers in the fourth piece, 'Star People', which becomes a really basic slow twelve-bar blues with a 12/8 feel. But it has an unusual drum rhythm, with a single bass drum note on the first and third beat, and cymbal beats on the second and fourth. This time Miles, using the Harmon mute, and Stern share the solos, each playing several times. Stern's initial solo is an unabashed, tonally distorted, bluesy affair that digs deep, but later on he also plays airily and lyrically, first rubato with keyboard accompaniment, then with quiet, spare backing from the rhythm section. Bill Evans, on tenor, gets one chorus of the blues and preaches a whole sermon in those twelve bars. The least substantial piece, 'U'n'I', is tucked away penulti-mately on the album, and the final performance is 'Star on Cicely', another up-tempo rocky piece with some transcribed solo lines played by guitar and tenor sax. Once again, the order of pieces is important. It is significant that the opening one, 'Come Get It', harked back to 'Back Seat Betty', which it had already replaced as opener for the live performances, while the final one, 'Star on Cicely', with its transcribed solo lines, looked towards Miles's future methods of working.

Star People was released in the spring of 1983, to be available at the time of Miles's next European and Japanese tours, and its packaging showed two significant changes. All the coloured drawings on the front and reverse covers were by Miles, and on the back there were liner notes by Leonard Feather. This was the first time a current Miles Davis album had had liner notes since the double-album *Miles at Fillmore* and single-album *Jack Johnson*, both recorded in 1970, and the *Johnson* notes had been written by Miles himself. Feather had often explained Miles to the general public in the 1950s and 1960s, and perhaps the uncomprehending adverse criticisms that had currently so upset Davis's young musicians made him decide to ask Feather once again to explain his present musical stance. Leonard Feather was one of the most respected of all music critics, because he wrote with insight and clarity, he was a pianist, musically literate and a friend of many musicians, including Louis Armstrong and Cannonball Adderley, both of whom had played and recorded some of Feather's compositions. Feather had also written the first scholarly analysis of bebop, *Inside Bebop*, published in 1949, and as a critic, he had considerable authority. He had usually been friendly to Miles, and although the latter had said that he wasn't bothered by Feather's total dismissal of his September 1981 Hollywood Bowl concert, he wanted to re-establish cordial relations with the critic. That is why Miles and Cicely Tyson had agreed to a joint interview with Feather in 1982, for *Ebony* magazine, giving him the chance to break the news of Davis's stroke and his recovery from it.

It's not every day that a jazz critic gets such a dramatic scoop. During the interview Miles was on his best behaviour, his conversation free of obscenities, and he was at pains to co-operate with Cicely's attempts at explaining his 'evil genius' image: 'He used that façade to protect his vulnerability. Beneath that false surface you see what a sensitive, beautiful person he is. Nobody could play that without having a great depth of soul.'[6] Feather's liner notes for *Star People* are professional, friendly, but rather non-committal because he quotes Miles frequently and offers no strong opinions of his own.

Bassist Tom Barney's first concert with the band was at Phoenix, Arizona, on 28 January 1983, followed by Denver, Colorado, on the twenty-ninth, and three February dates in Texas: Dallas (1), Houston (3) and Austin (4). Then after Toronto and Ottowa on 15 and 17 February and the Grammy award ceremony on the twenty-third, Miles and the band had a month off before their European tour, which started at Lille, France, on 29 March. After seven concerts in France and one each in Italy and Belgium, they came to London's Hammersmith Odeon for two concerts on 27 and 28 April. The fact that Miles Davis could get seven concerts in France and only two in the UK speaks volumes about the relative states of jazz in those countries at that time. In London, he did a long interview with Richard Williams for the *Sunday Times* and actually wanted to be interviewed on TV by someone. Here was the opportunity for a very rare event, but no British TV stations were interested, and the BBC spokesman, when contacted, had never heard of Miles Davis. At Hammersmith Odeon, when the house lights dimmed, Miles and his band came on stage to enthusiastic applause, which he acknowledged with a flamboyant wave of the hand. He was wearing a flat-topped black Spanish hat with a wide brim, dark glasses with bright, orange-pink rims, a black boiler suit, and reddish-brown high-heeled boots. Although he still limped slightly, the overall impression he gave was of energy, contained and tigerish. From the audience's viewpoint, the band was set up in a semi-circle with Bill Evans positioned at the far left, next to him, but nearer the centre was John Scofield, and more central still was the new bassist Tom Barney. Al Foster and the drums were centre stage rear, in front of them was Miles and his keyboard, and to the right were first Mike Stern and then Mino Cinelu and his percussion.

After a perfunctory arm wave that started the usual two dissonant chords (Stern), Miles shrieked out a high trumpet G above top C and the band went into a fast rock beat and 'Come Get It'. This was an exceptionally dramatic opening, and the dynamism of the performance was almost overwhelming. Miles was in utterly magnificent form, with a gloriously big, singing sound, huge range, and great power and stamina. If anything, he sounded even more majestic than he had done at his other peak in 1969. It was also dramatic, when someone else was soloing, to see him holding the trumpet with one hand, the left hand at the keyboard as he stabbed out electronic chords and high trumpet riffs. From his keyboard at centre stage he controlled the whole performance of the piece, eventually bringing it to an end and introducing 'Star People', the slow blues with a 12/8 gospel kind of feel. This was an utter contrast to the opening piece; now the quiet, empty, brooding rhythm section was electrifying and his playing sent chills up and down the spine. Once the piece was established, Miles left his place in the centre of the band's semi-circle, and walked to the front of the stage, slowly playing occasional phrases all the while. He crouched and played to the photographers in the pit on the right side of the stage, then walked slowly to the centre of the front apron and played to the audience there, then to the left side to repeat the performance.

This was Miles feeling relaxed and confident enough to recognize the existence of the audience and to indulge in some fundamental showmanship. But it never seemed cheap because his playing was so powerful, with marmoreally sculpted phrases, the huge singing sound of his trumpet in the middle and lower registers and the wild screams that also sang at the top end of the trumpet. At one point, during a tenor saxophone solo, Miles walked over to Bill Evans, stopped him in mid-flight and led him over to the electric keyboard. While Evans began creating luminous atmospheric sounds, Miles stood in the shadows beside John Scofield, listening. This was the only time, so far in the concert, that attention was not focused directly on Davis. After some minutes, he went up to Evans, patted him on the cheek and sent him back to his sax. The subtlety of the band's backing was quite magical, with different timbres, textures and little rhythmic interjections, and the dynamics all evening were superbly managed, ranging from a whisper to a roar. Miles was in such playing form that he dominated the whole evening, and there were shorter spots for the other soloists. The programme included all the pieces from *Star People*, plus a new piece, 'Hopscotch', and 'Jean Pierre', which was given a full performance and then, as an encore, a brief reprise. The British critics recognized the enhanced power of Miles and his band and, as they had been a year previously, were perceptive and generous in their appreciation of both.

Cicely Tyson, beaming with happiness, was backstage throughout the concert, and Miles, too, seemed in exceptionally good spirits and health, full of smiles and with a sheen on his skin. Someone said to John Scofield, 'It's a pity you didn't get to play so much yourself tonight.' Scofield replied: 'God! I was listening to Miles. Did you hear how Miles played tonight?!! It's so great to be with someone who can really play! Being with Miles is like being back at school again – I'm learning all the time.' After the second London concert, the band went back to America for about three weeks off before a four-concert tour of Japan. The only negative happening in that triumphant European tour seems to have been the departure from the entourage of roadie Chris Murphy who, according to Miles, left because he'd had enough of Cicely.

It was now becoming clear that Miles Davis's return to playing, which had begun as a kind of giant lap of honour by an ailing man with a glorious past and little apparent future, was turning into something much more dynamic. He was in yet another new phase, and the essential activity in this one was live performance – he seemed to want to be permanently on tour and playing concerts. The recordings would be like blueprints for the live performances, where the music and the magic really happened. In concert, the next few years would see some of the most eloquent and moving playing of his whole career, and some of the most subtle use of dynamics and electronic orchestral colours by his band.

There had been another significant change earlier in the year. After an argument with Mark Rothbaum, Miles fired him, and found two new managers, Lester and Jerry Blank. They had set up the short European tour and the following briefer Japanese tour. But Miles's fortunes under their management slumped, and he complained that they seemed to have great difficulty in getting bookings for his band. It may have been that as he and his music were now regularly available to the public, familiarity was breeding indifference. If so, it was cruelly ironic that just as he was arriving at yet another different artistic peak, with new modes of procedure and new heights of expression, his drawing power should decline. Certainly, he felt the financial pinch during this period, and had to sell his prize possession, the brownstone house on West 77th Street, still in the process of being redecorated, in order to pay off money he owed to the Blank brothers. John Scofield said:

When I joined the band, the money was more than when I left the band. It was one of those strange situations when the money went down. When I joined the band, we were picked up in limousines to go to the airport and we were treated incredibly well ... Anybody in their right mind is not going to over-pay the band, but Miles could sometimes be very generous. After he got new management, then the money went down.

The Japanese tour took in Sendai on 20 May, two concerts at Osaka (25 and 26), and Kanagawa in the Tokyo area (29). The concerts were shared with the Gil Evans Orchestra, with Miles playing the first half and Gil the second, and though the houses were all sold out, it is possible, because of the shared billing, that Miles received lower fees than he had the previous year. The Japanese audiences were as enthusiastic as ever. Back in the USA, the band played St Louis, Missouri, on 7 June, Pittsburg, Pennsylvania (13 June), and three days later they were in the Hit Factory recording studios, in New York which was bassist Tom Barney's last date with Miles. The latter's nephew, Vincent Wilburn, had recommended a Chicago-based replacement called Darryl Jones, who was nineteen years old. Jones had come to New York in May and auditioned at Miles's house. His ability to play a B flat blues at a very slow tempo earned him his place in the Davis band.

No details of the music played or rehearsed at the 16 June recording session are available, but it is almost certain that Miles took that opportunity to start updating the pieces in his repertoire he wanted to retain and adding fresh pieces, using his new methods of procedure in both cases. Scofield said:

When I first started playing with Miles, his method in the studio was to jam [improvise] and record it and find the best spots ... just a constant evolution of really jamming and listening back to the tapes and finding one or more spots. That's when Gil Evans was helping. I mean Gil was probably the most over-qualified transcriber in the world, because Miles would have him transcribing trumpet and guitar solos, and then we would play the transcribed parts of the solos as heads [thematic motifs]. Then we would work on a bass line, or write out a bass line that had been improvised and that would become the bass line to a song. And I was new in the band and fresh, and he liked what I was blowing [improvising] so he used some of my solos, but some of his melodies came from his solos too. My guitar solo on the song 'Speak' on the album *Star People* later became the melody of one of the pieces on side two of the LP *Decoy*.

Miles's next concert was at the Avery Fisher Hall, in New York, on 26 June. This was Jones's first gig and Mike Stern's last with the band, and the next four American concerts were played by the sextet with Scofield as the only guitarist. But that summer and autumn Miles was again in the studio, working on the music for his next album, *Decoy*, and he brought Robert Irving III into the band to play keyboards and synthesizer. Irving had, of course, played an important role in the conception and realization of the two soul/funk pieces on *The Man with the Horn*, and now Miles seemed to want Irving, not just for his excellent musicianship, but also because he was young and in touch with current trends in popular music. Apropos of his Grammy award for *We Want Miles*, Davis had told David Breskin, 'I don't like to record at all, live or studio. I just do it to make money.'[7] With this comment, he may have been just shrugging off his Grammy with a nonchalance that belied the fact that the award had pleased him mightily. But there was perhaps a deeper truth underlying the comment; it was the live concerts that were his *raison d'être*, at this moment in time, and in the studio there was almost a sense of manufacturing the music. John Scofield commented: 'He would be sort of getting the music together for the recording, and we would be recording, and then we'd go out on tour and the music would really blossom.'

Decoy's title track, composed by Irving, is an inoffensive rocking piece with a rolling bass line and a little riff melody. Miles, using the Harmon mute, improvises with fluency and warmth, and the whole thing feels mellow enough to reassure the faintest heart. Branford Marsalis is the soprano player on this track and he and Scofield repeat at intervals the little melody, which is not as angular or convoluted as some of the Miles/Scofield motifs, but rather as disarming as a nursery rhyme. Marsalis solos excellently, as does Scofield, who always seems to find new things to say. He and Marsalis play another more lyrical motif, then the latter solos again briefly as the piece fades out. This is the opening track on the album and it seems designed to court radio play. The second track, 'Robot', is performed by a trio consisting of joint composers Miles and Irving playing synthesizers plus Mino Cinelu on percussion. Irving also plays synthesized bass, and did the electric drum programming. It is very short, without any solos, and has a heavy robotic rhythm and ominous synthesizer sounds. It fades with a tiny touch of trumpet. 'Code MD' is another fairly bland Irving composition, a medium-tempo rocky piece with, at times, an ensemble sound reminiscent of the Mahavishnu Orchestra. At other times a long, slow, moaning synthesizer melody wanders drunkenly across the soundscape, and Miles's open trumpet screams seem an appropriate comment on the proceedings. 'Freaky Deaky' is another strangely atmospheric, but musically slight synthesizer outing for Miles, who is listed as composer, and is aided and abetted by Cinelu, Foster and Jones.

The last three tracks, 'What It Is', 'That's Right' and 'That's What Happened', all attributed to Miles and Scofield, are the most convincing performances of the whole album. According to Jack Chambers,[8] the first and third pieces come from the Davis sextet's concert at Montreal's international jazz festival on 7 July 1983. 'What It Is' has a bustling rock rhythm with exciting boppish riff melodies played by Bill Evans on soprano and Scofield. Evans gets his only solo on *Decoy* in this piece, acquitting himself beautifully, and Miles's trumpet duet with himself is achieved, Chambers says, by overdubbing another solo from the same concert. 'That's Right', is bluesy but not a blues structure. It's based on two roots – C and F – and is a slow, gentle performance with an unhurried triple feel (3/4, or 12/8) with a haunting little melody played by guitar and saxophone once or twice. Marsalis is the saxophonist on this track and shares the solo honours with Scofield and Miles. 'That's What Happened', is simply a short punchy excerpt from the concert, and ends abruptly.

The album *Decoy* seems to be a moment of trial and error and indecision for Miles Davis. It seesaws between the blander soul/rock pieces by Robert Irving III, which imply or require a tighter, more fixed structure, and the short, impressionistic, but insubstantial electronic ensemble pieces without improvised solos, or the performances, which have the looser but more dynamic approach of his working band. He was perhaps seeking some kind of synthesis of these three areas into a coherent new direction.

Decoy was packaged tastefully by CBS. Although a single LP, it was given a gatefold cover with a moody photograph of Miles in dark brown and sepia tints, the full length of the open gatefold, his hat, head and shoulders on one panel with the rest of his torso down to his left arm and hand, which is holding his trumpet, on the other panel. His luminous, unsmiling eyes stare left at the camera, and the indentation from the trumpet mouthpiece is clearly visible on his upper lip. It is a portrait at once sombre and elegant, of a man in control of himself and his life. A couple of his coloured, semi-abstract sketches of faces and bodies decorate the inside surfaces of the gatefold, alongside the track and personnel information and the credits.

Miles liked Branford Marsalis's playing and wanted him to join the band, making it a two-saxophone group, but Branford was committed to playing with his brother Wynton. So Bill Evans, who had had so little solo space on *Star People* and *Decoy*, and was not too happy about the way he was treated during concerts, was still the sole saxophonist in the working group, but would not be there much longer. After a concert at Elizabeth, New Jersey, Miles took his septet to Europe for a six-concert mini-tour, starting on 23 October at the annual Jazz Jamboree in Warsaw, Poland.

This Warsaw concert turned out to be an extraordinary event. Poland was still part of the Eastern bloc, the Iron Curtain was in place, though somewhat eroded, and *glasnost* (openness) and *perestroika* (restructuring) were some years away. It has to be remembered that during World War II, jazz was banned in Germany and Japan, partly for racial reasons – the African and Jewish elements – but also because small-group jazz can be a perfect metaphor for democracy and liberty, as opposed to licence. This occurs when the bandleader is a central authority under whose auspices each member of the group can develop his or her own identity and creativity. The greater each musician's individuality, the more potent the collective identity of the group, and all the qualities necessary for jazz – individuality, spontaneity, autonomous control, trust in one's chosen associates – have always been anathema to totalitarian regimes. During World War II, jazz became an important part of the Resistance in countries all over Europe during the Nazi occupation, and after the war it became a form of resistance and a symbol of the assertion of the individual in the Soviet Union and its Eastern European satellite countries.

Poland's Jazz Jamboree had started modestly in 1958, but gradually developed into one of the most important international jazz festivals in the Eastern bloc. In 1965, the Polish international jazz magazine, *Jazz Forum*, edited by Pawel Brodowski, was launched and, written in English and Polish, soon became the most important such publication in Europe. In 1982, its annual poll voted Miles Davis Musician of the Year and top trumpeter, *We Want Miles* was voted Record of the Year, and the band was third in the small-group poll. His musicians, Mike Stern, John Scofield, saxophonist Bill Evans, and Mino Cinelu, also gained places in their respective instrumental categories. Miles held on to his personal poll positions in 1983, but young lion trumpeter Wynton Marsalis was hot on his heels, and also played with his own group, which included his brother Branford, on the first day (20) of the Polish Jazz Jamboree. Miles Davis had been a legend among Polish jazz enthusiasts for decades, but he had never before played in the country. Tomasz Szachowski noted this in his *Jazz Forum* review of the Marsalis concert: 'The young trumpeter's group is a direct descendant of Miles Davis's last acoustic quintet and plays contemporary jazz worthy of that tradition. The quintet made up for the fact that Warsaw had never hosted either Miles's old group or VSOP' (Davis's 1960s quintet with Freddie Hubbard replacing Miles).[9]

The fact that Miles Davis might at last play in Warsaw triggered a fever of anticipation, made more intense by knowledge of his unpredictability and the possibility that he might simply fail to appear. Also, since 13 December 1981, Poland had been under martial law, which meant that the government had permanent emergency powers, and the 1982 Jazz Jamboree had been cancelled as a protest by the jazz community at this Communist repression. In this atmosphere nothing seemed certain, and the visit, at long last, of Miles Davis seemed almost too good to be true. But when he did arrive at the Polish airport, without Cicely Tyson, but with his six musicians, his three-man sound team, his manager Robert Blank, and his nephew Vincent Wilburn, who was now travelling with him as helper and bodyguard, he was treated like royalty. He did not have to go through customs, but was ushered out via the VIP lounge, where the customs officers were all smiles and had 'We Want Miles' badges in their lapels. Outside the airport was a crowd of foreign journalists and American TV crews, and a Russian-made Chaika limousine, of the sort used to transport the then Russian President, Yuri Andropov, waiting to take Miles to his hotel. Personal messages from Andropov were relayed to Miles . . . the President sent his best wishes, called him 'one of the greatest musicians of all time', and said he wanted to come to the concert but was too ill to do so. The limousine took Miles to Warsaw's most luxurious hotel, the Victoria, where he had a suite with two bedrooms, living room, bathroom and kitchen. One of the riders in Davis's contract stipulated that a swimming pool should be available to him at all times, and the hotel's basement swimming pool had been filled with fresh water for him, though he seemed not to use it during his short stay. He spent all of the following day indoors sketching, drawing and seeing only his closest associates. But his great welcome in Poland had warmed his heart, and uncharacteristically, late in the day, but well before his evening concert was due to take place, the surprising message came to Pawel Brodowski and musician Janusz Szprot that it might be possible to interview Miles. Sure enough, they experienced the most friendly and relaxed interview Miles had given in years. It was published in *Jazz Forum*, and later published in full in Sweden's *Orchester Journalen*.

The concert itself was superlative. In a letter, Pawel Brodowski wrote:

The Miles Davis appearance in Warsaw at Jazz Jamboree 1983 was a great, traumatic experience and can easily be considered the single most important event in the history of jazz in Poland ... The 3,000-seat Sala Kongresowa was filled to over-capacity. According to estimates, there were some 5,000 people in the audience, and their feeling was best described by keyboardist Wojtek Karolak in his review for the Polish edition of *Jazz Forum*: 'When the world's funkiest orchestra started I felt as if I was sitting in a Formula One car taking off. I was knocked deep into into the seat, trying to say something, but I was capable of producing only some inarticulate sounds unknown in any language. The Sala Kongresowa became, for the moment, the most important place on earth. This whole foolish world disappeared suddenly without even apologizing. The super funk radiated from the stage, hypnotizing amazed people. No one ever played in such a way and no one ever listened in such a way in this place before. Something exceptional was happening.'[10]

Miles's musicians were fired up by the whole situation, and played with great urgency and purpose. They began with 'Speak', which had an almost superhuman impetus, and now several attractive riff motifs punctuated the various solos. The rhythm section was superlative throughout their programme, which also included

'Star People', 'What It is', 'It Gets Better', 'Hopscotch' and 'Jean Pierre'. Miles, Scofield and Bill Evans were in peak form, and the whole sound of the band is unlike that of any other group – the performances eternally shifting soundscapes with solos constantly coming and going. The audience response was ecstatic, and Miles played *three* encores, probably for the first time in his career. The audience chanted, '*Sto lat, sto lat, niech zyje, zyje nam!*' (One hundred years, one hundred years, may he live for us – a traditional Polish birthday song, rather like 'For He's a Jolly Good Fellow'). Miles was pleased, and after lifting his trumpet a few times in acknowledgement to the crowd, he eventually took off his hat and bowed, baring his bald head to the public. Thinking of previous Jamborees, and putting this whole occasion into historical perspective, Tomasz Szachowski wrote in *Jazz Forum*:

Each of the Jamborees was unique with its own emotions, experiences, sometimes dramatic ups and downs. But the 25th Warsaw Jazz Jamboree – unlike its distinguished predecessors with their rich history – was dominated by the personality of but one musician, Miles Davis. Moreover, perhaps for the first time, the Jazz Jamboree was a true mirror reflecting the contemporary jazz scene.[11]

After Warsaw, Miles and the band played to enthusiastic audiences in Madrid, then two concerts in Berlin and two in Paris. Paris was Bill Evans's last gig with the Miles Davis band. He was tired of having his solos curtailed:

We were still friends and everything, and I had talked to him about it, and he'd say, 'Well, this is something I hear, you know', but what I heard was completely different, so I knew it was just a matter of time. I wanted to move on. There had been some tension during some of the shows over the last year, where it would even show on stage that I was frustrated, and sometimes he would be, but after the show we'd still hang out and joke around. So when the call came to join

John McLaughlin, it was perfect timing for me to move on, and Miles accepted that completely. I walked into his dressing room in Paris and told him I was going to be joining John McLaughlin in the next month, and that this was probably my last gig. So we sat and talked and it was basically all right. It wasn't a thing where if I got mad, I would say, 'Well, I'm going to quit', and he'd say, 'All right, you're fired.' It was nothing like that because we knew each other too well. We had a relationship, and we still do so, you know.

Back in the USA, George Butler, Columbia's vice-president for jazz, with the aid of Cicely Tyson, had organized a retrospective celebration of Miles's life and work, which took place on 6 November at Radio City Music Hall. It was called 'Miles Ahead: A Tribute to an American Music Legend', and it was co-produced by the Black Music Association, with comedian Bill Cosby as host. It was an elaborate four-hour show, covering Miles's music from the 1940s to the present, and musicians from all areas of his career played a part in the presentation. From the early days, there were J. J. Johnson, Jackie McLean and Philly Joe Jones, Jimmy Heath; from the 1960s, George Benson, Ron Carter, Herbie Hancock, Tony Williams and George Coleman. An all-star band conducted by Quincy Jones played some Slide Hampton versions of Gil Evans arrangements from *Porgy and Bess* and *Sketches of Spain*, after the president of Fisk University presented Miles with an honorary degree in music, he and his group played a half-hour set to wind up the proceedings. At the end of his set, however, Bill Cosby pressed him to make a speech, but all Miles could say was, 'Thank you', which annoyed some people, who thought he was ungrateful for such a lavish evening of tributes. But he insisted in his autobiography, 'I meant it from the bottom of my heart . . . It was a beautiful night, and I was happy that they honoured me the way they did.'[12]

After the celebration, Mino Cinelu left Miles because he had been asked to join Weather Report, and he was replaced by Steve Thornton. On 17 and 18 November, the band, with Thornton on percussion but without a saxophonist, was back in the recording studio, and with Gil Evans working as arranger, they recorded some pop tunes on the first date and some rock tunes on the second. Then Miles was hospitalized once more, because his hip implant had started disintegrating, and he had to have yet another operation. He was expected to recover in time to resume performing six weeks after the operation, but he caught pneumonia in December 1983 and was out of action for two months. Illness, once again, gave him the respite necessary for reflection on his life and music after the intense activity of this extraordinarily dramatic first phase of his comeback. He was not to perform in public again for six months, but from the end of January 1984 until the following May, he was constantly in the recording studio with his band. There would be changes, musical and otherwise, in the immediate future, some coming as a pleasant surprise to him, and some more radical that he himself would initiate.

TWENTY-ONE

Honours, Insults and Changes

'I've got scars all over my body ... they are like
medals to me, badges of honour, the history
of my survival.'[1]

Miles Davis

Miles Davis began 1984 by recuperating from his hip operation
and pneumonia, and although he did not play any public concerts
until June, he spent many hours in the recording studio in the
intervening months. He had said only recently that he didn't like
recording and did it just to make money, which may have been
why, from 26 January to 14 April, he spent eight days in the
recording studio with his band, minus a saxophonist, but with Gil
Evans as consultant/arranger. In early May he was back in the
studio without Gil Evans, but with saxophonist Bob Berg, who
had joined the band two days previously. During this period Miles
recorded about forty AOR (Adult Oriented Rock) songs, including
Cyndi Lauper's 'Time After Time', Tina Turner's 'What's Love
Got to Do with It', Dionne Warwick's 'Deja Vu', and various
pieces by Toto, an American AOR group formed in 1978 by
leading session musicians, including their composition 'Human
Nature', which Michael Jackson had made a hit. In the 1950s
Miles had also included popular songs (without the vocals) in his
repertoire, and had been castigated for it, and now he was once
more looking at popular material with recording and public performance in mind. The next album would be *You're Under Arrest*,
which he would not complete until the first two weeks of 1985,

and he would include only three of the AOR pieces: 'Time After Time', 'Human Nature' and 'Something's on Your Mind', an H. Eaves III/J. Williams lyrical rock/soul composition.

Later in the year, he explained to Howard Mandel:

I've found, like a lot of guys, I guess, that studio music sucks. There ain't nothin' happenin' in the studio; you don't get no feelin'. I just got through recording 'Time After Time', and I don't ever play it but once a night, but we had to sit there and do it over and over. I had to do that on *Porgy and Bess*, and I swore I'd never do it again. It's not the retakes; it's the feelin' you put in it ... I mean you can't say 'I love you' twice. You have to say it when you feel it. And when I play a ballad, more than anything else, it's all *me*.[2]

Miles was well aware, however, that an album is a product or artefact which advertises the existence of the bandleader and the group, shows their current musical stance and is often bought as a memento of a live performance. The blueprint, in other words, has its uses and the finances it does or does not raise can have a crucial impact on a band's fortunes. Fortunately, whether he liked it or not, many of Miles Davis's concerts during this last phase were recorded, documenting the magic and the music, which flowered in live performance.

As in his other vital periods, he had fallen in love with the trumpet all over again, and told Howard Mandel:

I practise every day. Got to do that – you don't practise, you can't play nothin'. Scales, mostly – trumpet stuff. Long tones are best. If I can play a low F sharp, loud and clear, then I know my tone is there. I had to work real hard to get that tone back when I came back; it took me two years to get it right. Now that it's back, I'm gonna keep it ... If you don't have a pleasant sound, you can't play any melody. And my head is full of melodies.[3]

Miles would do some new things during this last phase – find, as always, new ways of saying the same things – and as usual, his band's music had his unique identity stamped on it, but the real glory and *raison d'être* of his comeback was his trumpet playing. Once again, Chico Hamilton's statement rings true: 'Miles Davis is a sound . . . the whole earth singing.'⁴ John Scofield is one of the most perceptive commentators on Miles's comeback:

> Miles almost didn't make it through retirement. He was sick and he realized he had to play in order to live. To me, any-thing he did was OK, because he was just trying to survive. He didn't want to work hard at being an innovator at the very end. He didn't want to say it, but he wanted to play good music and make great money . . . He wanted people to come to his gigs and dig it, you know? He didn't want to be an esoteric jazz legend. Nobody else could do big tours *every* summer and fall and sell out stadiums all over Europe. And these people were not jazz snobs; they just dug Miles. He could make a believer out of a non-jazz person with the beauty of his sound and his rhythm and his notes. That's pretty heavy.⁵

Miles Davis's awareness of his own mortality, and his descrip-tion of the scars all over his body as 'like medals to me, badges of honour, the history of my survival', bring to mind a few lines from W. B. Yeats's magnificent poem, 'Sailing to Byzantium':

> An aged man is but a paltry thing,
> A tattered coat upon a stick, unless
> Soul clap its hands and sing, and louder sing
> For every tatter in its mortal dress.⁶

The extraordinary power and lyricism of Miles's trumpet playing in this period seems to derive from this very source – the rejoicing of his spirit or soul making the trumpet sing for every scar or tatter in his mortal self. Miles and Duke Ellington have much in common with W. B. Yeats – all three were great lyrical poets – Davis and Ellington in music, Yeats in language, and each of the three created some of his most moving work in the last decade of his life.

In June 1984, Miles began again playing concerts with his septet, which now included Bob Berg on tenor and soprano, Robert Irving III on synthesizer and Steve Thornton on percussion, as well as seasoned sidemen Al Foster and John Scofield, plus Darryl Jones on bass. Miles was pleased with Jones and, in an interview with *Jazz Forum*, said: 'I need a bass player with some weight and some kind of style ... Darryl fits where I want. He's also one of the greatest bass players I've ever heard in my life. He has that same approach that Jimmy Blanton used to have with the Duke.'[7] Saxophonist Berg was thirty-three when he joined Davis, and from the same generation as Scofield. In his teens, Berg had been much influenced by the later Coltrane, and had become deeply involved with free jazz, but at the end of the 1960s, he was sick of abstraction and went back to study the 1950s work of Miles and Coltrane. He also studied Charlie Parker's work, and spent the 1970s playing acoustic bop, first with Horace Silver, then with Cedar Walton's quartet. In this manner, he had strangely worked his way *backwards*, from free jazz to bebop, to Miles's current band. Berg said: 'I needed a change, and I always felt I had the ability to do it and not just play straightahead jazz. Playing with Miles is different from being in a fusion band because you don't have to play funk licks.' Berg was developing into one of the most gifted of the post-Coltrane generation of saxophonists, with an excellent technique, great harmonic awareness, a finely poised sense of time and a massive, emotive sound on tenor saxophone.

On the first three days of June, the septet played in three different towns: a concert of over ninety minutes in San Carlos, California, two concerts, each of ninety minutes, at the Beverly Theatre, Hollywood, California, and a concert of over ninety minutes in Niles, Illinois. Berg had not known quite what to expect from Davis when he had joined the band. He had seen the October

1981 *Saturday Night Live* TV show, which Miles had done when he was exhausted and ill, and recalled:

I'll swear, I really thought Miles was dying. He looked awful! He couldn't play, you know. I mean he *really* couldn't play. He just kind of hobbled around. Then I saw him about a year later at Hammersmith Odeon in 1983, because I was playing in London at Ronnie Scott's with Cedar Walton, and I was friendly with Al Foster, Mike Stern and Bill Evans, so they invited me to the concert, and I was really impressed. Miles was playing a lot better. He was great. It was really inspiring. And then when I joined the band, which was the next time I heard him, the first gig we played out in San Carlos, California, I was shocked. I mean, not shocked, but pleasantly surprised at how strong Miles was. And I personally felt that, the whole time I was with the band. His playing was what really stood out among everything, you know, above the music we were playing, above everything, was Miles's playing ... I was with him until early 1987, and generally he was really *on* the whole time. I mean amazingly. He could hit high notes that I had never heard him play before, and he could stay up there sometimes, playing really long lines, and for a guy of his age, the wear and tear that he's been through, you know, I was really wowed by it.

On 22 June, Miles and the band made what seemed to have become their annual appearance at New York's Avery Fisher Hall, playing two concerts that evening, after which the band went straight to Europe for its now annual European tour. The seventeen-concert itinerary began in Paris on 24 June, finished at the Molde Festival in Norway on 27 July and also included dates in Spain, Austria, Italy, Switzerland, Germany, Finland and Holland. Miles was now so familiar with foreign travel that the novelty of it had worn off, and the music was the one great purpose and reward. But he had also become much more interested in painting, and was building up a collection of international works of art, which he bought on his travels and divided between his house in Malibu and his apartment in New York.

In fact, this current European tour had only fourteen dates, but three of them had two concerts in one evening, and his engagement at London's Royal Festival Hall on 17 July was one such double concert. Miles arrived from Holland the day before it, and was staying at the Grosvenor House Hotel on Park Lane. The previous week, the *Guardian* newspaper had arranged for me to go to his hotel and interview him in the late morning of the day of the concert. Miles had received a copy of the first edition of this biography during his three days in London in 1982. After the 1982 London concerts, he and his entourage had flown straight to Italy, where the critic Giacomo Pellicciotti had interviewed Miles and Cicely and shown them, to their great surprise, the Italian edition, which was published in the same year as the English one. I knew Cicely liked the biography, but had no idea what Miles thought of it, and was pleased that the *Guardian* had given me the opportunity to talk to him at some length for the first time ever.

I was met at the hotel reception by Miles's manager, Robert Blank. He was perhaps in his early thirties and wearing a grey suit with an open-necked shirt. He was pleasant, but affected a slight toughness of manner, a slight remoteness, which I felt was assumed, not natural to him. A woman from one of the other newspapers arrived. She was in her late twenties and of the Sloane Ranger type, from which superior perspective some people regard it as a point of honour to be ignorant of many things. A friend of Blank's joined us, then the English tour manager and some other hangers-on, so that the lift to Miles's suite was quite crowded, and on the way up the Sloane Ranger said to me: 'You wrote the book. Can you tell me something about Miles Davis?'

'Not much in a lift between floors,' I replied.

We were all then ushered into the reception room in Miles's suite. This was a long rectangular room, overlooking Park Lane and Hyde Park. One of the windows was open and a powerful roar of traffic flooded into the room. I asked Blank to close the window, which he did. A low table stood along one side of the room with some chairs around it and a sofa against the wall behind it. In the middle of the table was one of Miles's trumpets, the bell pointing towards the centre of the room. It was lacquered black, but all the moveable slides were lacquered bronze. Clearly, Miles would sit on the sofa behind the trumpet when he arrived. The Sloane Ranger and the hangers-on descended like vultures on the chairs and even the sofa. There was nowhere else for me to go except to a chair at the far end of the room near the window Blank had closed.

I sat there glumly. The Sloane Ranger asked if she could go first when Miles arrived because she wanted to do only a short interview. One of the hangers-on asked if this was a press conference. I began to feel angry and, looking at Blank, who was standing near the door, I raised my voice and said that I had not gone there to attend a press conference, and that if I didn't get the opportunity to ask my questions I would be very angry. At that, Blank turned and went out of the room. A few minutes later, he came back in with Miles and a couple of other people, and I stood up when he entered the room. Miles was limping slightly, and he greeted one or two people, before making a beeline across the room to me. I wondered if I was going to get punched, but no, he shook my hand, clasped my arm with his left hand, picked up my chair with his right and propelled me across the room to the low table, making room for my chair beside it. I was so astonished that I just stood there looking at it, and he said in his low, husky voice, 'Why don't you sit down?' And I did so thinking, 'My God! Maybe he really likes the biography.' I switched on my tape recorder and awaited the Sloane Ranger's questions. Miles, meanwhile, had sat himself down on the sofa next to my chair. He was wearing loose-fitting jeans, a loose black cotton jacket, white, basket-woven, casual shoes with no backs and raised heels. He was also wearing a white yachting cap, with a black peak, from under which the lifeless, straight brown remnants of his hair protruded. He picked up a drawing pad and, with a black felt-tipped pen, began sketching, and continued doing so incessantly throughout the conference.

The Sloane Ranger asked him: 'Where's home and what's it like?'

Miles replied evenly without taking his eyes from his sketch pad: 'Home is in New York. It's an apartment at 70 Fifth Avenue, overlooking Central Park, on the East Side.'

She continued: 'How long are you on the road usually during the year?'

Miles looked up: 'What exactly do you want? . . . Ah, you want to see how my lifestyle is.'

She concurred: 'Your lifestyle, what you like doing, where you live, where you like going to eat.' She seemed to be writing down his replies and so there were gaps between her questions.

Miles said: 'I live in California *and* New York, and I'm not on the road that much. I just go out if I make a lot of money, and if I don't, I don't go out . . . Don't you have a tape recorder? Or do I have to wait while you write it all down? I feel funny while you're writing it down. I have to sit here with egg on my face while you write.'

She said: 'OK, I have a tape', she switched it on. 'When you're at home in New York or California, what do you like doing, where do you like going out? What do you like doing for pleasure?'

A shadow of irritation passed over Miles's face, but he seemed to restrain the impulse to explode and with an effort, replied civilly: 'Playing music, that's my pleasure. I go to the shows.'

She pressed him: 'Do you like going yourself to see musicians?'

'No . . . no, I don't like that, it's kind of boring to me because, I don't know why, but when I go out it rubs me the wrong way.'

She tried a more specific question: 'I wondered what you were thinking of the new movements in music in the States . . . things like hip-hop, break-dancing?'

'What I think about it? I don't think about it.'

She persisted: 'Some people say it's a re-emergence of American music and it's an exciting new departure.'

Miles turned to one of his entourage: 'Do you know what she's talking about?' It was explained to him. 'It's all right as long as it has a beat. As long as something has a beat and some kind of motif, like an eight-bar motif with a beat, it's all right, because it makes a lot of people happy doing it.'

She asked: 'Can I ask you something about your drawing?'

'Well, wait till I get through answering one question first! Drawing . . . my father taught me.'

Miles then asked her to come round to the other side of the table and look over his shoulder at his drawings. In fact, he had been drawing a series of male and female heads and the bubbles coming out of their mouths contained a whole series of overtly sexual questions and answers using the most basic vernacular language. Miles asked her to read out the content of the bubbles to us all. This she did, her plummy voice and Sloane vowels rendering the four letter words hilariously innocuous. But her very English sang froid, and her refusal to be fazed were impressive. She would not be put off and one had to admire that.

She continued: 'Do you do it [sketching] just for yourself, or for friends too?'

'Whatever I feel like – sometimes I give it to friends. A gallery wants some of them, to sell them. On my birthday, 26 May, they had a birthday party and they showed some of my canvas things and some drawings – sketches – on a big screen at the Tower Gallery in New York City. They had a big party. TV was there . . . Entertainment till nine. Everybody was there and I liked them.'

She asked, 'Do you sculpt as well?'

'I started one in clay, but I never finished it.'

She: 'I was going to ask about girlfriends . . .'

Miles: 'No, I don't have any girlfriends, I'm married. Married men don't fuck around with girls, do they?'

She did not answer this apparently rhetorical question.

It was now my turn, and I asked him about his health, and he said: 'I had another operation on the same hip last November. It had deteriorated and they had to put a whole new hip in. You know, they expected to do a five-hour operation, but it wound up taking eleven hours. The old hip replacement had completely disintegrated.'

I asked him how he managed to keep himself in shape during

such long tours: 'I just brace myself and do it, then I rest. As long as my mind is geared to a month of concerts, I'll know how much money I'm going to make and I do it and go back to the States. I usually swim every day to keep in shape. But I haven't been swimming on this tour. When my hand was paralysed, these three fingers' (he indicated the index and next two fingers of his right hand – exactly the fingers for pressing the three valves of the trumpet), 'I took acupuncture and the same doctor told me my energy level was low because when I work, I work so hard, and that I shouldn't swim and play, say, two concerts, or make love to a woman and play two concerts.'

I asked him if he rested mostly in New York or in California: 'Well, I like California because of the weather – we live in Malibu, and it's good for my leg. These old bones don't hurt so much in the sun.' By 'we', he was referring to Cicely Tyson, and I asked if she was away working.

'She's speaking today at the Democratic Convention in San Francisco and she's also working with the Olympic athletes.'

I asked him how he managed to keep his music so alive and fresh.

'It goes with your love of music, or any other form of art. Picasso never did stop because he aged. I want to live to be 201 – just imagine what kind of playing I would be thinking of with all these sounds in the air, synthesizers, electric drums . . . and the way people think – especially black people. They usually shorten everything up, compress it, because they only have one chance. You know that! So, I mean, I'd like to live to be about 250! I'd like to have two or three careers.'

Although Miles had reminisced privately a great deal with friends old and new during his retirement and during his comeback, he never seemed keen to do so publicly and had famously said during an interview, 'Yesterday's dead', but I asked him whether he had warm feelings for certain people in his past.

He hesitated momentarily, then said, 'I can't go back and think how I felt when I made different recordings, because the enthusiasm was there or else the record wouldn't sound like it is. During the Birth of the Cool days [1947–50], we all almost lived together. I remember George Russell had to have his teeth fixed, so Gerry [Mulligan] and myself and Gil [Evans] wrote Lionel Hampton an arrangement. He said, "I want African drums and high trumpets." We said OK and wrote this arrangement in about six hours for George to get his teeth fixed, and Gil paid some rent and Gerry and I paid some rent. I think we got $300. That's the way we were. That was a lot of enthusiasm!'

What did Miles think of the neo-bop music of the 1980s?

'You have to start somewhere, but I don't like to hear what we did twenty years ago, nor people saying that they're trying to keep that tradition – that kind of music – alive and save it. It's already on tape, so you don't have to save it. To play it over again, I think, is just being lazy. After Coltrane left the group [Miles's quintet], nobody could replace him, so you just do something else. There's not a sax player today that has a new sound since Coltrane. The Lester Young sound, nobody has that; Sonny Stitt, he had a unique sound, and Coleman Hawkins, Sidney Bechet, Johnny Hodges, Ben Webster – but nobody else today, there's no individual sound today.'

I said that I thought that saxophonist Bill Evans had played Miles's music beautifully. [Miles considered this for a moment and then said: 'He *tried*. . . yeah, but his upper register! . . . and his attitude has a lot to do with it. He's a kind of player who likes competition – he's more of an athlete than a musician, and you can't combine the two. I told him, "You can't work like that." He called me up and said, "I know what you're saying now," because he had trouble (as a bandleader) with one of his drummers. He asked me, "How do you tell a drummer that he's not playing the music right? That's the same thing that you were telling me I wasn't doing to your music." I said, "Now you figure it out."'

Someone else asked him if he'd ever surprised himself.

'No. I know what I can do and I know what my mind is geared to. I don't think like everybody and I know it. So whatever I think of I do. If people like it – that's all right. If they don't – that's all right.'

Asked if he was enjoying what he was doing, he replied: 'Sure. I wouldn't be here if I wasn't enjoying the band I have now. It's a nice band – wait till you hear it tonight – you'll like it.'

That concluded the press conference and, before leaving, Miles drew a head and a trumpet in my hardback copy of the biography and signed it, saying, 'I haven't read it, but my wife has.'

The two concerts at the Festival Hall that evening each lasted about ninety minutes, and each was a continuous event, with the music making seemingly magical transitions from one piece to another. Drummer Al Foster's rapport with Miles was, as usual, a key factor in these transitions; the cues were nearly always musical, and the intensity of the musicians' listening and concentration was another key factor. But that still does not explain the magic, and the distinguished composer and arranger, Michael Gibbs, who was in the first-house audience, exclaimed ruefully, 'I can never work out how he organizes his music!' Both concerts were superb. The band was now a wonderfully cohesive, flexible unit, swinging and rocking ecstatically, with subtle dynamics and textures, and John Scofield was a pillar of strength as accompanist and soloist. But Miles's own performance was, in the full old sense of the word, awesome; in terms of sound, content and duration, his playing seemed almost superhuman that night. He was still using the radio mike attached to his trumpet, which enabled him to walk around when playing, or between phrases, and not only was his Harmon mute sound full and strikingly emotive, but his open trumpet sound was massive and utterly unbrassy – more like a disembodied lyrical voice than perhaps ever before. As he dialogued with himself and with the rhythm section, the sonorities and passionate elegance of his phrasing spoke directly to the hearts of the audience. His stamina and range were superlative, and even when using the Harmon mute he sometimes played way above trumpet top C. It seemed as if he had no need to nurse his physical or his emotional energy, and could give his all without ever fading, and so it continued for two concerts and just under three hours on stage. His spare, brooding Harmon-muted solos on 'Time After Time' and 'Jean Pierre' moved some members of the audience to tears, and in both pieces, he eventually removed the mute, converting his intense inward-looking lyricism to the beatific singing of his open horn. When not playing the trumpet, he played his keyboards, sometimes sustaining a chord or a single note obtrusively throughout Scofield's solos, and I wondered how the guitarist felt about that. Both houses were sold out, Miles's reception when he appeared on stage was rapturous, and at the end of the concerts there were prolonged standing ovations – so much so after the second concert that he and the band played two encores. The first concert was recorded by Capital Radio London, an independent radio station, and broadcast a few days afterwards. It is an astonishing and even shameful fact that BBC Radio and TV did not interview Miles Davis or record and broadcast any of his concert appearances in the UK during his last ten years of active life, when he was most accessible. Although BBC2 had filmed his band in 1969, the tape had been wiped or lost. Yet such film from the 1960s until 1991, the year of his death, is still available in many other European countries. That is because the rest of Europe deemed him worthy of much media coverage recognizing him as a major musician of this century with a benign global influence. Old snobberies and ignorances die hard in Britain, and the initial damage was done by the first Director General of the BBC, John Reith, who praised the Nazis for banning jazz and was only sorry that 'we should be behind in dealing with this filthy product of modernity'.[8]

Miles's last engagement on this European tour was at the Molde Festival in Norway on 27 July, and not only was his concert filmed by Norwegian Television (NRK), but he also did a televised interview discussing a possible new direction in jazz, how he found the musicians for his band and how necessary is the knowledge of jazz history for a musician. On the same day, he was interviewed for Norwegian Radio about playing with younger musicians, his 'drum-oriented' music, and being his own producer.[9]

Both Norway and Denmark had suffered under Nazi occupation

and, as with many other European countries, the experience had helped their inhabitants, and particularly their cultural moguls and politicians, to appreciate the beauty and importance of jazz, which had been an important part of the Resistance movement all over the continent during World War II. After the war, jazz had become an integral part of the culture of all countries that had been occupied, and the two countries which had banned it, Germany and Japan, became perhaps its most ardent champions. It had, incidentally, already been accepted in France on equal terms with all the other arts after the First World War.

During the later 1960s, the great jazz composer George Russell had spent four or five years living in Scandinavia, where he was composer in residence for the Danish Radio Big Band, which recorded all his compositions and commissioned many more. He had also performed in Norway and received commissions from that country, and most of the now internationally known Scandinavian musicians, including Norwegians Jan Garbarek, Jon Christensen and Terje Rypdal, the Swede Palle Danielsson and Danish trumpeter Palle Mikkelborg, had benefited greatly from working with Russell, as he had also benefited from their youthful enthusiam and talent. Now, in 1984, Denmark wanted to give Miles Davis a unique honour.

Earlier in the century, a Danish woman, Leonie Sonning, had bequeathed a large sum of money to be invested, so that the interest on it could finance the Leonie Sonning Music Foundation Music Prize. This was to be a prize for outstanding contributions by classical composers and classical music performers and the recipients had so far included Igor Stravinsky, Olivier Messiaen, Leonard Bernstein and Isaac Stern, among others. In 1984, the Sonning Prize committee decided that the first non-classical musician to get the prize should be Miles Davis, for his monumental contribution over five decades to twentieth-century music. The committee wrote more than once to Davis, inviting him to receive the prize, but he did not reply to their letters, so the committee asked Erik Moseholm, head of the Danish Radio Big Band department and consultant to the committee for this particular project, to go to the USA and talk to Miles. This he did, and when Miles saw the list of earlier prize-winners, among them Stravinsky, he felt it was all right for him to receive the prize. Moseholm had already asked Palle Mikkelborg to compose, for the occasion, a piece in which Miles could play for five minutes, and in New York, he asked Miles if he would like to play in a composition by Mikkelborg, who recalled:

> I'm sure he didn't know very much about either me or Danish musical life at that time, though he later told me that he heard from Gil Evans that Gil liked my music, and of course he knew that I had played with Gil Evans's band a couple of times. So I think he took the risk and said, 'Yes, I will play five minutes in a composition by this man.'

Palle Mikkelborg was the perfect European musician for composing a tribute to Miles Davis. He was and is one of the finest trumpeters, a magnificent acoustic player with a lyrical sound and huge range and also, perhaps, the very finest exponent of electric trumpet, deploying the new sounds and timbres with great artistry. His main influence has always been Miles Davis, but he also admires other trumpeters and one of his main influences as a composer is Miles's alter ego, Gil Evans. Mikkelborg is also steeped in the work of Charles Ives and Olivier Messiaen, and works a great deal as an orchestral conductor.

Mikkelborg devised a composing system for his tribute to Miles Davis's musical aura. He gave each chromatic note a letter from the alphabet, and from that he gave each letter of the name MILES DAVIS a note, and that became the main theme of the composition, which was also related to the prime colours of the spectrum. Mikkelborg also derived a scale from the theme – starting on C an octave above middle C, it descended B, A, G sharp, F sharp, E, D sharp, C – and mainly using the theme and this scale, he composed the piece *Aura*, in several movements and over fifty minutes long. Miles Davis was meant to play only in the final movement.

The presentation of the Sonning Prize was to take place in Copenhagen in December 1984 at the Falconer Centre concert hall. Mikkelborg rehearsed the large Danish Radio Orchestra, and Miles arrived a couple of days beforehand to get to know the music and rehearse. When he arrived, Mikkelborg recalled:

> We were almost well enough rehearsed to receive him and his ideas, and we had the whole band on stage in the Falconer Centre. I had decided that I wanted some coloured lights as well, with colours related to the prime colours in the human being's aura. This was my tribute to Miles's musical aura as I had been seeing it over the years. At that time I had no idea how he was as a person – this was only my reflection on his *musical* aura. He was immediately very positive to me, a bit reserved about the whole thing . . . what was this music going to be like?

Miles had not expected such an enormous band to be waiting on stage for him, and he was also surprised and pleased to see the prime colours of the aura projected on to a screen on stage behind the band, and the whole event looking so good. He sat in the hall while Mikkelborg conducted the musicians through the piece. Nearing the end, at thirty-five or forty minutes, Mikkelborg looked round to see if Miles was still in the hall, but he had left. Mikelborg decided to finish playing the piece, thinking: 'I know I have spent this half year doing the very best I could, and if he doesn't like the music, I at least know I have done my best.' After finishing playing the piece, Mikkelborg went outside and there was Miles, who apologized for having to go to the toilet, and said the piece was 'a motherfucker', to Mikkelborg's relief and joy.

So now they could start full rehearsals, especially on the part where Miles was supposed to play – the last movement, where Mikkelborg chose to use two chords from an organ piece by Olivier Messiaen, whom he thought and still thinks is one of the greatest composers ever. 'So we played that over and over again,' Mikkelborg recalled.

Miles walked around in the hall with his radio microphone on the trumpet, trying to find his way into the piece. And I can tell you from a trumpeter's point of view and from a Miles lover's point of view, it was very, very interesting to hear him trying to find out what he wanted to do with it, because what he did was so weird and so strange when he started to play on these actually very simple and straight-ahead chords. But his way into the music was such a thrill, and his first rehearsals were recorded on a cassette, and slowly but surely he found his way into the music. So he played and gave us some indications of what he would like us to do, and there was a very special atmosphere in those rehearsal days. It was so quiet, because he talks so quietly, and so everyone had to be very silent in order to hear what he had to say. There was an almost church ritual kind of atmosphere during those sessions.

Mikkelborg had also asked John Scofield, whose playing he liked, to come over to Copenhagen and be part of the rhythm section for the concert; Scofield was a member of Miles's band, and it felt natural to include his personality and musical abilities in the proceedings. Miles had played only a few concerts internationally and in the USA that autumn, and had been in the recording studio working on some of the music for his next album, *You're Under Arrest*. The Sonning Prize ceremony took place just before he was due back in the New York studio to carry on with that project. He had arrived in Copenhagen during the second week in December, and on the thirteenth, Danish Radio organized a press conference to interview him about the Sonning award concert. That same day, he first listened to the orchestra, and then rehearsed the last movement, in which he was to play the solo. John Scofield was also present for that rehearsal. There was another rehearsal the following day, 14 December, and that evening the award ceremony took place. Mikkelborg conducted the orchestra through his piece, *Aura*, in eight movements, each named after a colour – 'White', 'Yellow', 'Orange', 'Red', 'Green',

'Blue', 'Indigo', and 'Violet' – and Miles played a solo in the last one. Then the Chairman of the Sonning committee, Boerge Friis, came on stage to make a speech and present him with the Sonning Prize of 100,000 Danish krone (crowns) which sum, in 1984, was probably worth something over ten thousand pounds. Miles Davis looked pleased but a little embarrassed during the speech, and chewed gum throughout. In fact he had been chewing gum constantly during all the rehearsals because some pills he was taking for his ailments, which included diabetes, made his mouth very dry, and chewing gum generated the necessary saliva for playing the trumpet.

Miles and the band went backstage after the presentation, and the full concert hall continued to applaud ecstatically, so he asked Mikkelborg to repeat the last movement, which they did, with Miles playing another long solo. They went backstage again, and still the applause went on, and Miles asked Mikkelborg to repeat the movement yet again, which they did, after which, John Scofield began playing Davis's famous folky piece, 'Jean Pierre', the rhythm section picked it up and Miles played again. Palle Mikkelborg had written a little arrangement of the Cyndi Lauper ballad, 'Time After Time', as a surprise for Miles, who played the ballad with his own band, but Palle had not had time to write the parts out. The rhythm section, however, also knew 'Time After Time' and Miles and Scofield played that too, for the ever receptive audience. So, in this way, the encores went on for another fifty minutes after the performance of *Aura*, and Mikkelborg commented: 'Miles was very sweet and very happy, I think about the things we had done for him. It looked so good and sounded so good. It was such a beautiful band – all those fine soloists.' Miles was also interviewed for Danish TV that same day.

Three days later, he was back in a New York studio on his own for four days (17–20 December) filming a commercial for Van Aquavit (Japan), for which he overdubbed voice and a brief trumpet solo, and was filmed blowing into an Aquavit bottle and fingering the glass for about ten seconds.[10] Then he spent two intensely busy days, 26 and 27 December, at the Record Plant

Studios with his band and various guests recording several pieces for *You're Under Arrest*, including 'Human Nature', 'MD1'/ 'Something on Your Mind'/'MD2', 'One Phone Call'/'Street Scenes', and a medley of 'Jean Pierre', 'You're Under Arrest', and 'Then There Were None'. The first two weeks of January 1985 were also spent in the studio with John McLaughlin, Robert Irving III, Darryl Jones, Vincent Wilburn Jr (drums) and Steve Thornton, working on the recorded material. 'Ms Morrisine' had been recorded the previous September, but Miles re-recorded it during the January sessions and also recorded new pieces, 'Katia Prelude' and 'Katia'.

Miles, however, kept thinking of his experiences in Copenhagen, and of Mikkelborg's musical tribute to him, *Aura*, with the growing feeling that he would like to play in several of the other movements, and one night in January 1985, he telephoned Mikkelborg at 3 a.m., asking how soon they could record the piece. Mikkelborg said he needed a couple of days to see when all the musicians would be available, and in exactly that forty-eight-hour period he had the recording fixed and organized for the last day of January and the first four days of February.

Mikkelborg said:

Miles came over again, and the piece did change a lot. Some of it I wasn't really satisfied with, and I'm happy to say, neither was he. I had over-written a couple of things (i.e. composed more than was necessary), but as Miles wanted to play on almost everything, we had to change a lot of things. There were some sections that he thought were too big band-ish, and I did agree fully with him, and cut them out on his advice. He mainly brought his extraordinary intuition to bear on the music, and I really admire his ability to trust his intuition, which is so strong and comprehensive, and which I now see was his guiding light throughout his whole career. That, among other things, was a great lesson to me. So he produced the piece all over again, with the written material as the basis, and out came this *Aura* much purer, much stronger, much cleaner, and much better recorded than the original concert.

Miles's nephew, Vincent Wilburn, was now the drummer in Davis's group and personal assistant to his uncle, so he, too, had come over to Copenhagen for the recording, and was very helpful, organizing things and smoothing the way for everyone in the studio. The first day's recording involved only Miles and the rhythm section, on the second day they were joined by the oboist and the harpist, and the last three days involved the whole orchestra. On one of the first two days, Miles heard that John McLaughlin was in Copenhagen to play a concert, and he asked someone to telephone McLaughlin's hotel and ask him to come to the studio. Mikkelborg said:

> He came in and we got a guitar and amplifier for him, and Miles wanted him to play on the first movement of the piece ('Intro'), which was unbelievably complicated rhythmically with bars of 3/4, 5/8 and 7/8. Miles said to him, 'Just think of Downtown New York and play, man!' There was a part, but John didn't bother with it too much – he just put his headphones on, listened to the track, and played beautifully and strongly, and it was very nice to see a man who just went for it and did it supremely well.

Mikkelborg was astonished at how quickly Miles could read the temperaments of the musicians in the orchestra, which included stars such as the Danish/American percussionist Marilyn Mazur, the Danish electric bassist Bo Stief and acoustic bassist Niels-Henning Ørsted Pedersen. Miles seemed to be able to make musical suggestions appropriate to each individual. He was really taken by the fine quality of Marilyn Mazur's percussion work, and asked her to join his band, which she eventually did in July that year, as second percussionist. According to Mikkelborg, all the musicians, including Bo Stief, Neils-Henning and Marilyn Mazur, played under the spell that Miles created in the studio. Miles tended to cast a spell when musicians realized he trusted them, and he paid Mikkelborg the highest accolade by asking him to be the producer of this album:

> Miles asked me to produce this album, which was very new for me – such an important album, so long and with so many important musicians. But I jumped at it, and I had this enormous number of solos he had played all over the movements – three, four or five trumpet solos everywhere. And it was very interesting and a very complicated business to find out which was the best solo to use. But he told me he had complete trust in me so that I could do with it what I wanted, but of course, to keep him informed – which I did by sending him cassettes. And I called him in Malibu a couple of times to ask his opinion, and he was very pleased with what I'd done in choosing solos and where to go in and where to go out, and what to cut and what to clean up, because when you're improvising *on the cutting edge*, there are always fluffs and mistakes which I knew he would not be happy about. So it was my job to clean up, and I also took some of the beautiful themes he actually played (improvised) during the sessions and I wanted to orchestrate them afterwards, which I did with my own flugelhorn and a couple of synthesizers. So there was a lot of extra work to be done, and Miles really appreciated it when he heard the results. I think I can speak for all the musicians involved, when I say that this was a week or ten days that will forever be a memory for all of us.

During that week or so, Mikkelborg spent much time with Miles. He would go every night to the hotel room where Miles would sit painting, and they would talk about everything from his latest album to the two Floyd Patterson–Ingemar Johansson fights, one of which they actually watched together one night at the television centre. Miles had never heard of Olivier Messiaen, so Mikkelborg introduced him to Messiaen's music and told him his part of the *Aura* composition was built on the Messiaen chords. Miles soon came really to appeciate the beauty of the French composer's music. Unusually for two musicians who played the same instrument, Miles and Palle never discussed trumpets (nor did Mikkelborg ever ask him about trumpets) except on one occasion:

> There was one day when he asked me to pick up his trumpet and put in the mouthpiece, and then he looked at me and he said, 'Play'. And . . . My God! What should I do? I was quite shocked, so I said, 'What can I play?' So I just played a couple of notes and a couple of phrases, and he walked around looking at me with a beautiful little smile on his face, and he said, 'It looks all right.' And I put the trumpet down.

For the actual *Aura* concert the previous December, Mikkelborg had made a background tape to be played in the hall while the audience was coming in. It was an electronic tape with a girls' choir (all voices overdubbed by vocalist Eva Thaysen), and it was all based on the scale and chord derived from the name Miles Davis. Miles had heard it in the hall and he asked Mikkelborg to put the tape on in the studio. There were only five or six musicians in the studio at that time, and he said, 'Put that tape on. I want to play on top of it.' Mikkelborg also had a little theme for the oboe, and asked the oboist to be ready when he was cued to play it. Miles played two solos on the tape and Mikkelborg used them both in the beginning of the piece called 'White'. Mikkelborg recalled,

> He played on it, and I cued the oboe in, and Marilyn did some bell sounds. Funnily enough, she hit some notes that the oboe already had, and there was some kind of magic going on, and Miles was sitting there in the dark playing, completely taken by this sound, not knowing anything of what the chords or scales were . . . he was just playing exactly what he felt, and played twice, and I used both solos, and that was a magic moment. When we finished, the room was

quietly shaking after this event. Miles looked up at me and he said, 'Did you like my calypso?' But this, to quote Stefan Zweig, was a star moment in my life to hear this music.

On the first, second, fourth and fifth days of recording, a Danish TV team filmed the proceedings in the studio, and Miles and Palle were interviewed together for television and for Danish radio about the whole *Aura* project. The resulting thirty-minute TV programme was called *Days with Miles*, and Mikkelborg said that it showed how happy and relaxed Miles was during that time, and how comfortable he felt with the Scandinavian musicians, who also seemed delighted to be in the company of this remarkable man with a great sense of humour and great insight into the human psyche.

Miles Davis's visits to Copenhagen to receive the Sonning Prize and work with Danish musicians had breathed new life into the Danish music scene, inspiring much writing in the press and many interviews with the musicians involved, both while he was there and afterwards. Palle Mikkelborg said that in many ways it changed his life, and after that occasion he had a number of friendly telephone conversations with Miles. He was also lucky enough to meet him again in Copenhagen when Miles was there with his band:

I played some festivals where he also was, and I had the pleasure of being invited to his room to talk about this and that. And I asked him, 'Why me?' and he said, 'Why not?' I wondered why he liked my company, and I know that he liked European music through his work with Gil Evans, who also loved the impressionists like Debussy and de Falla, and Miles often talked about Saint-Saëns, Ravel, Debussy and many times about Chopin. So therefore I think that my sound, which is very European, mixed with sounds of this world, made it comfortable for him to join this universe and feel that it was new in one way and well-known in another way. I think that mixture was a challenge to him, and perhaps my influences over the years from Gil Evans were part of my orchestration and my use of harps, oboe and those kind of instruments. It was wonderful to see him making suggestions to the harpist in one of the movements when she had a lot of things to do. He suggested things to her, not knowing much about the harp technically, but he had some beautiful ideas about what to do and what sounds to find. After that whole experience, I looked on my composing and musical life with new eyes, and it refreshed me in a way. I'm still trying to live up to the knowledge I got from that experience with Miles, and still benefiting from it.

Back in the USA, Miles found no real enthusiasm at his own record company, Columbia, for the *Aura* project, even though they had financed the recording. One of the problems was that the whole concept and atmosphere of the music did not fit in with any of Columbia's market categories – it was neither simply jazz nor simply classical, but a fusion of both disciplines, with rock and ethnic elements also in evidence. Miles wanted to remix the music digitally, but Columbia refused to pay the $1,400 necessary for that, and the tapes were to lie in Columbia's vaults for another four years, before the album – a double-LP – was eventually released. This whole saga seemed to echo Miles's experience in 1949, when he had gone to play at the Paris Jazz Fair, and been not merely valued there, but fêted and even lionized, only to return to his native country and find himself with no status, no work and no prospects. Now, thirty-six years later, having made monumental contributions to music in the interim, he still had not enough standing with his record company to finish *Aura* to his liking and have it released. History seemed to insist on repeating itself, and this treatment brought all his dissatisfaction with Columbia to a head.

Another problem was that, at the beginning of the decade, Columbia had signed up the rising young trumpet star, Wynton Marsalis, born 18 October 1961, who first came to prominence for his ability to play European classical music, which made him acceptable to the dominant musical establishments in countries all over the world. During the time Miles Davis was out of action (1975–80), no significant new direction in jazz had appeared, and the emphasis seemed to be on up-and-coming musicians who played their instruments well and endeavoured to recycle earlier styles. Wynton Marsalis was the doyen of this school, a superlative technician with an excellent sound and good range. His father, jazz pianist and composer Ellis Marsalis, had encouraged his jazz interest, but Wynton was and is probably the only leading jazz musician whose early thinking was formed by critics. Albert Murray and Stanley Crouch were early mentors, and Crouch has continued in the role of personal guru and liner-note writer for the Marsalis jazz albums. These mentors seemed to have inculcated in him a bizarre idea of jazz orthodoxy – that there is one singular thing called 'real jazz', and that every musician ought to be playing in that vein. Like all great arts, however, jazz is (and ought to be) incorrigibly plural, with a rich variety of strands and strains in its warp and weft. At eighteen Marsalis spent a year or so with Art Blakey and, in 1981, toured with Herbie Hancock, Ron Carter and Tony Williams – Miles Davis's 1960s rhythm section. The clearest discernible early influences on his trumpet style were first Miles Davis, then Freddie Hubbard, Clifford Brown, Woody Shaw and Fats Navarro. His first two recordings for Columbia were a jazz album and a classical one, and the company began marketing him aggressively. All went well until he started laying down the law for other musicians, and in particular attacking Miles Davis and his music. In a *Jazz Times* magazine interview with Hollie I. West, published in July 1983, the twenty-one-year old Marsalis said:

> We gotta drop some bombs here. Indict some motherfuckers. Talk about the music. I don't want to cut Freddie [Hubbard] down. I'd rather cut Miles down than Freddie. He ain't doing nothing. I think Freddie has taken enough heat. He's a great trumpet player. He's a great musician. Miles was never my idol, I resent what he's doing because it gives the whole scene

such a let-down . . . I think Bird would roll over in his grave if he knew what was going on . . . There's that interview with Miles where he said he didn't hear me and he's not interested in hearing me because we're all imitating Fats Navarro. He imitated the shit out of Fats Navarro the first five years, and Clark Terry and Louis Armstrong and Monk and Dizzy. Then he sits up and talks about how he listens to Journey and Frank Sinatra. He's just co-signing white boys, just tomming.[11]

The 'co-signing of white boys' must refer to the white saxophonists and guitarists in Miles's 1980s bands. In his autobiography, Miles said of Marsalis's attacks on him: 'When he started hitting on me in the press, at first it surprised me and then it made me mad.'[12]

It's bad enough when *critics* tell musicians or artists in general what to do, but there is something particularly unseemly about a very young musician attempting to tell one of his great masters what he ought and ought not to be doing. It is difficult to imagine a similarly young painter saying to the ageing Picasso, 'Hey Pablo, you shouldn't be wasting your time on ceramics! You should be doing "real art".' Picasso could do anything he wanted to do – and so could Miles Davis. Even writer and songwriter Gene Lees, however, who was extremely mature, and usually sensible in his attitudes, supported Marsalis in this: 'Some of what he has said has needed to be said. His criticism of the later music of Miles Davis, with its admixture of rock and other pop forms, is well taken. Because of the mystique, Miles got away with a lot of meretricious music.'[13] Of course, Marsalis and Lees are talking or writing from the outside, and have only a partial view of Davis and his music. To get a truer view of Miles we must go to an insider, John Scofield:

I never met anybody who enjoyed talking about jazz so much. People said, 'Well, Miles isn't into jazz any more, he's into Prince.' But when I was playing with him, it seemed like all he thought about was what he did, which was to blow and

improvise and make music. And he loved to talk about his
time with Coltrane and playing with Charlie Parker. Somehow during the period I was with him, he thought about Bird
a lot. Because he was his original idol. So for me, it was so
informative to get that input from one of those guys, from
Miles, who really was a jazz musician, who really was there
in the 1940s. He really lived that and was so in love with
that whole thing, and you could tell in his playing. I don't
care what anybody says about he was playing Michael Jackson tunes or whatever, he was the most 'jazz' musician I
ever met, as far as the intensity of the improvisation and the
communicativeness of his solos. He always improvised in the
moment.[14]

Miles was at first very friendly and fatherly disposed to Wynton
Marsalis, but became critical when the latter attacked him. Miles
said:

What's he doin', messin' with the past? A player of his calibre
should just wise up and realize it's over ... Some people,
whatever is happening now, either they can't handle it or
they don't want to know. They'll be messed up on that bogus
'nostalgia' thing. Nostalgia, shit! That's a pitiful concept.
Because it's dead, it's safe – that's what that shit is about!
Hell, no one wanted to hear us when we were playing jazz.
Those days with Bird, Diz, Trane – some were good, some
were miserable ... People didn't like that stuff then. Hell,
why do you think we was playing clubs? No one wanted us
on prime-time TV. The music wasn't getting across, you dig!
Jazz is dead.[15]

Since the later 1960s, Miles had always bridled at the use of the
word 'jazz' to describe his music. Thinking of Marsalis and the
current generations of musicians working in the vein of Miles's
1960s quintet, he said:

What I used to play, with Tony Williams, Jack DeJohnette, Herbie [Hancock], Chick [Corea], Cannonball [Adderley], Bill Evans [the pianist], all those different modes, and substitute chords, we had the energy then and we liked it. But I have no feel for it any more. Other people still do it, but it doesn't have the same spark. It's more like warmed-over turkey.[16]

George Butler at Columbia was the record producer for both Miles and Wynton Marsalis, and seemed to have difficulty in giving as much attention to Miles's music as he gave to Wynton's. Marsalis was getting much notice in the media because of his excellent classical playing, and he was winning polls in both disciplines – classical and jazz. His attacks on Miles Davis also astonished and outraged many musicians and fans, bringing Marsalis more sensational notoriety, and some people saw the attacks as the shrewd ploy of a 'young pretender' with the message: 'The king is dead; long live the king.' Butler liked classical music and wanted Marsalis to record more of that, and Miles referred to Butler as 'one of those black men who wants to be bourgeois – a pitiful condition to be in'.[17] It is surprising that neither Butler, nor anyone else at Columbia, did anything to defuse this destructive and shabby situation, or at least to caution Marsalis to show more respect for a man who had paid many dues and hugely enlarged the scope and possibilities of this dynamic new music. For Miles, the situation was becoming intolerable, and his irritation was compounded when Columbia showed no interest in *Aura*, which was not at all an essay in nostalgia, but a superbly achieved, totally contemporary orchestral album, containing some of Miles's most adventurous playing. And this snub was followed by the final insult: 'George Butler calls me up. He says to me, "Why don't you call Wynton?" I say, "Why?" He says, "'Cause it's his birthday." That's why I left Columbia.'[18]

You're Under Arrest was the last album Miles Davis recorded for Columbia after some thirty years with the company, and in some ways it was another new departure for him, because it was much more overtly programmatic than any of his previous albums. It opens with 'One Phone Call'/'Street Scenes', which, with its aggressive rhythms, wild guitar and synthesizers, and intermittent speaking voices, gives some impression of police harassment of blacks in the USA. The French policeman's voice is played by the rock star, Sting, because bassist Darryl Jones was recording with him at that time, and had asked Miles if he could bring Sting to the *You're Under Arrest* session. The voices are so confused that identification is hardly possible, and it seems never to have occurred to Miles, that Sting's superior earning power and ability to pay high fees to musicians might lure Jones to his band. Harassment by rock stars had not, so far, been part of the Davis experience. Miles had, of course, been arrested and goaled on several occasions, and even at this stage of his life, was aware that his driving a $60,000 yellow Ferrari and living in a house fronting the Malibu beach were both an irritation to the local police. The penultimate piece and title track, 'You're Under Arrest', continues this theme in a less programmatic, more abstract way. Bob Berg and John Scofield play a long, muscular, beboppish theme over an aggressive rock rhythm, and this is repeated between powerful solos by Miles, Berg and Scofield. The eighth and final track, 'Medley', is another extraordinary piece of pictorial music, this time attempting to depict the destructive effects of greed and ecological vandalism. Miles's folky tune 'Jean Pierre' appears briefly and is deconstructed, then beneath it fragments of the boppish theme from 'You're Under Arrest' are played, and the performance ends with 'And Then There Were None' – synthesized nuclear explosions and rushing winds of smoke and flame, human cries of agony, bells tolling, and through all this confusion Robert Irving plays a perfectly symmetrical and orderly classical-sounding piece on celeste that is clearly audible in the mix.

In general, there is tremendous vitality and passion in the music of *You're Under Arrest*, but there are also two lovely resting points with the ballads 'Human Nature' and 'Time After Time', both of which feature Miles on Harmon mute throughout. The other pieces include 'Something on Your Mind', by Eaves/Williams, a rock-soul outing with Miles first muted and then open, and he and Scofield on devastating form, followed by 'Ms Morrisine' and 'Katia', both featuring guitarist John McLaughlin and Miles on open horn. The cover design of *You're Under Arrest*, however, boldly combines 'camp' with kitsch. Against a red background, a colour reminiscent of the decor of a Toulouse Lautrec brothel, Miles – wearing a black homburg and the black garb of a Spanish dancer – holds an automatic gun in both hands. He is looking up at the camera from under the brim of his hat, so that the whites of his eyes are prominent, and his mouth is closed, his face serious. On the front cover he is facing to his right, and on the rear cover his body is angled to his right, but he is looking straight at the camera. The position of the gun is slightly different in the pictures. In 1981, Miles had told Cheryl McCall: 'I'm an entertainer. I got a certain amount of ham in me . . . I'm doin' what I'm doin' but I know I'm a big ham. It doesn't take away from the music, because I just enjoy what I'm doin' at that particular time.'[19] Miles the ham certainly prevailed on the outer covers of the album. Inside there were some of his large coloured figure drawings, and both sides of the LP sleeve were absolutely covered with his black line drawings of people. The packaging may or may not have helped, but *You're Under Arrest* sold over one hundred thousand copies in a few weeks.

After the early-February recording of the album *Aura*, in Copenhagen, Miles went back to the West Coast of America to spend time with Cicely at her cottage in Malibu, until he bought his own house there with its private beach. The warm weather was better for his hip, and life was much more laid-back there than in New York. In Malibu he drew and painted for several hours a day, and got plenty of rest. An hour or two's work on the trumpet would keep his embouchure in condition. When he and Cicely were in New York, they stayed at her fourteenth-floor apartment on Fifth Avenue, overlooking Central Park. The loss of his house on West 77th Street still grieved him, and around this time he sacked the Blank brothers as his business and tour managers. Cicely had recommended her manager, David Franklin, who was black, and he became Davis's new manager. Franklin negotiated a signing fee of over a million dollars when Miles left Columbia and joined Warner Brothers Records, but gave the company the publishing rights to any new Davis compositions, which did not please him. Miles kept on Peter Shukat as his lawyer, a position the latter had held, with only a brief hiatus in the early 1980s, since 1975.

At the beginning of March, Miles was interviewed at his Malibu home by a Mr Nakayama, of the Japanese jazz magazine, *Swing Journal*, and in late April and most of June he toured in the USA, playing the music of *You're Under Arrest*, as well as some of his other recent repertoire. Then he toured Europe from 5–24 July, followed by one concert in Tokyo. His solitary London date consisted of two concerts at the Royal Festival Hall on 20 July. Again, both houses were sold out, and the air of expectancy before each concert was electrifying. Each concert was well over two hours long, and Miles played long, searching and lyrical solos with seemingly endless physical stamina and powers of invention. For the first time since his 'comeback', he appeared without a hat – bareheaded, revealing his almost totally bald head to the world. In fact his fine head looked even more striking without hair, because it appeared even more marmoreally sculpted. But he looked extremely thin, his clothes flapping around on him as on a scarecrow. He was wearing belted, loose white trousers with pockets capacious enough to house the Harmon mute when he was not using it. He wore two wide-shouldered black jackets – one for each concert – the first one made of leather and the second of some slightly shiny material, and in each concert he removed the jacket to reveal, in the first house, a sleeveless black T-shirt, and in the second, a black T-shirt with a massive coloured motif on the back. On his feet, he wore the high-heeled white sandals identical to the ones he had worn the previous year. Throughout both concerts, he paced restlessly about the stage, playing in all parts of that area, and during the second house even got up on to the drum rostrum and played from behind the drummer, his nephew Vincent Wilburn. He also at various times brought each member of the band individually to the front of the stage and presented them to the audience. It was the first time I had ever seen him do this. The almost superhuman amount of time he spent on stage, playing and directing the band, required an extraordinary act of will. Seen close up backstage between houses, his apparent frailness was quite shocking. It was as if he were showing two fingers to the grim reaper and saying, 'To hell with you! I'm going to play for four and a half hours.'

During both houses there were moments of sheer magic from him, also some longueurs, but even on the odd occasions when nothing much was happening, the beauty of his sound beguiled the audience. There were also some excellent solos from Scofield and Berg, but astonishingly, considering the physical demands of the trumpet, Miles played longer than either of them. He pushed himself, as usual, to the limits, using the extreme high register as well as the lowest one, and he would occasionally break off in mid-solo to wave his arms and his red-lacquered trumpet at the audience, who always responded with applause. It may well have been the realization of how much audiences loved him and his work that made Miles lose much of his shyness and feel able to acknowledge the existence of the audience in these ways.

Backstage at the end of the second-house concert, Miles and the band were huddled at the far end of the waiting chamber. The crowd were demanding an encore and the MC was saying to them, 'If you show your appreciation, Miles will come back and play again.' Miles had already been on stage for over four hours, and the focus of attention for two houses each of three thousand people, but he went back on stage with the group. They immediately broke into a raunchy, almost violent rocky groove, and Miles played a short solo, but with some powerful high notes even at this stage of the proceedings, then he waved his trumpet at the audience and walked – almost stalked – off stage. As soon as he had got down the short flight of stairs and out of the audience's sight, two men were waiting for him, and each grabbed an arm and supported him as he suddenly sagged and almost caved in. It was this moment that revealed the great act of will the long evening had required from him, and it was very moving to see. In fact he

had to work harder at directing the band now that drummer Al
Foster had left. With Foster's rapport, the transitions from one
piece to another had happened like magic. The new drummer,
Vincent Wilburn, could create hypnotically driving rhythms, but
had to be strongly directed by Miles in the transitions from one
piece or area to another. As soon as Miles had left the stage during
the encore, the band went wild, with Bob Berg and John Scofield
facing each other and trading eight- and four-bar exchanges with
phenomenal intensity. It was almost as if after the teacher had
gone, the pupils went berserk.

Four days later, Miles played a concert at the Molde Festival
in Norway, and Marilyn Mazur sat in with the band as second
percussionist to Steve Thornton. By 17 August, she was a regular
member of the group and working with them in the USA. Some
more personnel changes were also in the offing. John Scofield had
told Miles that he would be leaving the band after this foreign
tour, which was to end after two concerts in Tokyo on 28 July
and 7 August. Scofield's three years with Miles had given his guitar
playing greater authority and emotional power than ever, and his
musical vision and integrity had also been crucially important to
Miles, who trusted him as a musician and as a man. But although
Scofield was listed as composer or co-composer of several of the
band's pieces, he was ready now to write his own music for a
group of his own choosing, which he was not able to do while he
was in the Davis band. To lead his own group, Scofield would
need to be available for the summer festivals in Europe, and Miles
was always working during that period. He also felt that Miles
was looking for a different guitar sound:

> I got the feeling he was looking for more of a Van Halen
> [hard rock/heavy metal], real pop rock guitar sound, which
> I wasn't interested in doing . . . not that he ever told me to
> play like that, but he would say, 'Listen to that. That's great.
> Check that out.' And I really learned a lot about rhythm
> guitar in Miles's band, but when you put me next to a real
> great rhythm guitar player (and we're talking rhythm in the

443

sense of 1988, on a R&B record), I mean like Paul Jackson
Junior who plays on Michael Jackson's records – a real
snappy thing. I can't do it nearly that well. And Miles was
always trying to get me to do that sort of thing. Also things
were changing and Miles's albums weren't going to be reflections of the live gigs so much, so I thought it was the right
time to go.

It always seemed that Miles and Scofield were close both musically and as people, but Scofield said that wasn't so:

Miles and I were never really close as people. I don't know
how close you can get to somebody that's in such an exalted
position and rightfully so. He's Miles. But he was very nice
to me, you know. I think he knew I had really checked him
out, and the music that he'd done, and we didn't really even
talk about it. He would always be telling me, 'You sounded
beautiful last night.' So he was very supportive that way,
personally with me.

Scofield also explained how the emotive power of his own playing
was unleashed during his time with Davis:

There was something in me that always wanted to be more
emotional, but having a big respect for a more cerebral kind
of jazz, I'd been putting myself into [musical] situations where
I felt inhibited about really stretching out and really playing
out. And when I joined Miles – he's the inventor of cool
jazz, we could say – I always thought of him as the perfect
combination of intellect and emotion. But when I had Miles
telling me, 'Man, just don't worry about a damned thing.
Just play. Just get into it' . . . not that he even *said* that, but
that was the sort of vibe, the feeling you got. All of a sudden
there, I realized it was OK just to really let it all hang out –
so that definitely happened to me.

I asked Scofield how he had felt when Miles programmed a continuous synthesizer note throughout his solo:

Sometimes it was terribly irritating, I mean it was a drag, but sometimes it'd be great. He had heard some record by some pop group that had one note all the way through it, and he thought that was so great that, for about a year, he did it all the time. So it would have this one note going, and sometimes it would be during a B flat blues and the note would be an A [i.e. a dissonant note]. I remember once at the Berlin Festival he really turned it up loud and I was trying to blow over it, and this note was there – yes, it was hard, yeah [*laughs*]. He did it originally because he liked the idea . . . and every day's a different story with Miles, and I don't know why he does a lot of stuff . . . But sometimes, maybe, just for the hell of it, you know, to bug you. I don't know [*laughs*]. I think he enjoys ambiguity. So you don't really know if he's trying to, one, blow [sabotage] your solo when he puts on this long sustaining tone; number two, create some mood; or number three, just generally piss everybody off. And it's a combination of those three things and you can't really nail it on the head . . . It's fascinating. You get food for thought. I never know what he's doing.

Scofield also had strong feelings about Miles's direction of the band with hand signals, cutting short solos and changing the direction of the music:

It was incredibly nerve-wracking and made you really mad when he cut you off right before an idea. There was this constant feeling. 'Oh hell! Am I playing good enough music for Miles? Is he going to cut me off or not?' And I'm not even sure that was why he cut you off at some points. It was just that he felt like playing, or he was wanting to end the set, or whatever. He's real self-indulgent that way, I mean we're talking about the world of Miles. But at the same time,

I think it's absolutely fascinating the idea of having somebody directing a band like that, where there are no choruses [i.e. set structures], where it's just sort of open, and somebody's sort of sculpting the whole musical thing. And that's what we got into live that wasn't really ever recorded. And that's what happened with the band he had [1973–5] before he retired – it was all on hand cues and stuff. He would cut the rhythm section off, and the soloist would play alone, and then, bam! – the vamp would be back in … and it was all being directed by Miles. It's really like painting a picture. And on a good night it would stretch for a whole hour-and-a-half concert, with the mood changing and I just thought it was great, because it wasn't only the solos – he would bring in ensemble parts, which would be me and the sax with the keyboards playing a written-out improvised line, and he would bring in something else under it, or he'd improvise over it. So it was just a constant, changing, shifting thing, and it never got recorded. It was just fascinating to me … kind of feeling it out for the moment, so the arrangements never really strangled us, like in some bands where you're a slave to the arrangements.

Summarizing his time with Davis, Scofield said:

I had never experienced greatness like that … to play with somebody like that. And it opened my eyes in both ways; I got over being naïve about idol worship and I also got to see how directed somebody can be musically and have integrity and faith in their own ideas. One thing that Miles did was really trust his rhythm sections. He would go with what was going on in the band instead of trying to force it in another way a lot. And that really affected me.

On the way to Japan, where John Scofield was to play his last two concerts with the band, Miles Davis had another health scare. This was due to the tyranny of his sweet tooth, which caused him to eat a lot of sweet French pastry that he had bought before boarding the plane. As a diabetic, he should have avoided such food, but the old compulsive urge took over, and by the time the plane made a stop in Anchorage, Alaska, he was losing consciousness. His road manager, Jim Rose, now always alert to Miles's condition, had him taken off the plane and briefly hospitalized. He was allowed back on the plane only when he was perfectly fit again, and after that experience, he began injecting insulin every day. This brought other minor problems, because the various airport authorities were always suspicious that the syringes and medical equipment were for shooting up illegal drugs. During his ten days in Japan, Miles also took part in a Honda commercial.

Back in the USA, he began a seven-concert American tour on 17 August at the Hudson River Pier, New York City, with guitarist Mike Stern back in the band to replace Scofield, and Marilyn Mazur as second percussionist. During this mini-tour, with its last concert on 22 September, Miles worked briefly as an actor, playing the part of the brothel owner, Ivory Jones, in an episode of *Miami Vice* called 'Junk Love',[20] and he and his band also played two concerts at the University of California, Berkeley, the first one of which, on 1 September, was Darryl Jones's last appearance with the band, and the second concert – on 19 September – was his replacement, electric bassist Angus Thomas's, first one. After recording the album *Dream of the Blue Turtles* and taking part in the film *Bring on the Night* with Sting, Jones had done some gigs with the rock star and then joined his band permanently. His departure really hurt Miles, because he loved the way Jones played, and was kindly disposed towards him – Darryl was also a close friend of Vincent Wilburn, and seemed like part of the family. Despite his anger and distress, however, Miles pulled himself together and Jones parted with his blessing.

Also early in September, Miles Davis was one of a whole host of jazz, rock, soul and pop stars who recorded in New York City for 'Artists United Against Apartheid'. His 1960s rhythm section, Hancock, Carter and Williams, were among the performers, and, according to Jan Lohmann, 'All Davis's parts were done on the same tape in New York with [guitarist] Stanley Jordan plus a log drummer, all in one day.'[21] Fragments of speeches by Nelson Mandela and Bishop Desmond Tutu were used, Miles's trumpet and voice are heard and this whole experience seems to have made a considerable impression on him, because his first album for Warner Bros would be recorded during the first few months of 1986 and and entitled *Tutu*.

During the last week of September 1985, Davis and his band were in recording studios for a couple of days working on unspecified music, and subsequently played two concerts. At the beginning of October, he and Robert Irving III, again according to Jan Lohmann, 'recorded music which was used as the soundtrack in an episode of *Alfred Hitchcock Presents* entitled "The Prisoner"'.[22] Then, from 24 October until 8 November, he and the band toured Europe again, taking in France, Sweden, Denmark (the Falconer Centre in Copenhagen again), Belgium, Germany, Switzerland, Austria and Italy.

Miles, in his autobiography, said that 1985 was the year in which he and Cicely Tyson really began growing apart, and blamed her possessiveness and jealousy. But we are told nothing of her side of the story, and it seems possible that her patience was sorely tried. Even though the relationship was deteriorating, they stayed together for another year or two. Musically, at the end of 1985, Miles Davis was preparing to record his first album for his new record company and this would, once more, break new ground, winning awards and critical acclaim. The phoenix was about to renew himself yet again.

TWENTY-TWO

Tutu

'The only place where I'm not given the respect I get
everywhere else, is in the United States. And this is
because I'm black and I don't compromise, and white
people – especially white men – don't like this in a
black person, especially a black man.'[1]

Miles Davis

In 1985, Miles Davis had once more wiped the slate clean, by
leaving Columbia, his record company of the last thirty years, in
order to join Warner Bros and start afresh. Such a bold, radical
step quickens the pulse rate and gets the adrenaline flowing, and
so he was also looking for new musical visions as well as different
modes of procedure in the recording studio. John Scofield had felt
that Miles's albums were not going to 'reflect the live gigs so
much', but when he left the band, he had no idea how profound
the dichotomy was to become between Davis's function in the
recording studio and in the concert hall. Now he was about to
spend the first three months of 1986 working on the first recording
for his new record company. As his manager, David Franklin, had
yielded the publishing rights of Miles's compositions to Warner
Bros, Miles was reluctant to put any of them on his albums. His
intuition told him to concentrate on featuring his trumpet playing
– but how? and in what context? The answer to these questions
came from one of his most loved ex-sidemen, the bass guitarist
Marcus Miller, who had left the band at the end of December
1982.

Miller had developed into a truly exceptional musician. He was a multi-instrumentalist, a superb composer/arranger and a record producer, and he was much in demand in all these capacities. Before he had joined Miles at the end of 1980, he had been active as a studio musician in New York, working with Bob James, Grover Washington Jr and Roberta Flack, among others, and by the time he heard that Miles had changed from Columbia to Warner Bros, Miller had also produced and written songs for Luther Vandross, Aretha Franklin, David Sanborn and Natalie Cole. Miles had complete trust in Miller's musicality and his personal qualities. Miller phoned Miles's producer at Warner Bros, Tommy LiPuma, and told him that he had some ideas for recording, which he'd like to send to Davis. LiPuma informed Miles, who welcomed the suggestion. Miller recounted:

I finished three demos, 'Tutu', 'Portia' and 'Splatch', and asked Tommy if he wanted me to send them to LA. He said, 'Nah, just come out here and we'll record them.' I went, but I was really nervous because they hadn't heard a note. I was scared they'd put me on the next plane back to New York. Tommy liked them, but the big test was Miles. The first one was 'Tutu'. A friend of mine, Jason Miles, who's a synthesizer programmer, just happened to have a Miles sample, so we used it on that demo. I played the solo on a keyboard, thinking I sounded just like Miles. When I played it for Miles I waited for his reaction. He listened for a while, finally turned to me, and said, 'Who's that on trumpet? Sounds like Nat Adderley.'[2]

And so began one of the most extraordinarily successful collaborations of Miles Davis's career. There would be no band in the studio to record the album *Tutu*, because Miller, with some assistance from studio associates would, by using electronics, synthesizers and drum machines, create on tape orchestral structures with written passages for Miles to play, and areas in which he would improvise. In this way, Marcus Miller took over the role of Gil

Evans, in providing musical contexts that suited the trumpeter perfectly. When necessary, Miller could also play several other instruments that might be required to fill out the orchestral colour. The beauty of this method of working was that by using similarly programmed synthesizers with his own band Miles could achieve something he had long desired – he could get a Gil Evans full orchestral sound cheap, even with a mere sextet or septet.

Although he had played in Miles's comeback band for its first two years, Miller said:

> I didn't really get to know Miles until I started producing him, on *Tutu*. . . I was scared to give him any kind of direction. I was even scared to tell him where to play. Because he's Miles, you know? I'd just turn on the tape and say, 'Do what you want –' But he pulled me aside and said, 'C'mon, man, I don't mind a little bit of direction. You wrote the tunes. Tell me where you want me to play. It helps me out, gives me a framework.'[3]

Miller always tried to have the tapes prepared and the machinery set up ready to go when Miles arrived at the studio, because his first or second takes were usually the most creative, and it would have been counter-productive if some fault in the machinery or in the balance of the tape had rendered those first takes unusable. But even under these austere conditions, Miles could initiate spontaneous happenings:

> He's unpredictable, too. 'Portia' on *Tutu* was a first take. I showed him the melody on a soprano sax I had, so he could relate to another horn, and then we started running tape. I was sitting there while he was playing, and he picked me up by my collar and pushed me up to the microphone to play the melody with him. I'd never played soprano on a record before, and we were both going on to the same track. He was playing so great that I was afraid I was going to make

a mistake and ruin everything Miles played. That was one of the most tense experiences I'd ever had.[4]

Miller quickly grasped the essence of his new role with Miles:

I saw it developing as a conversation between me and Miles. You know how jazz musicians used to do albums with big bands; they'd play the melody, then solo for sixteen bars, then play the melody again. That's how I envisioned these albums. Gil Evans was a big influence; I knew him, and I've really been influenced by him as a person. But I never really checked out *Sketches* [*of Spain*] until a couple of years ago. What I *did* check out, though, was one of my main influences – Herbie Hancock's writing, especially around his *Speak Like a Child* period. He was writing really interesting stuff, using chords he didn't even have names for – they just worked. Then one day I pulled out *Speak Like a Child* and I read on the back that Herbie during that period was inspired by Gil Evans [*laughs*]. So now I understand why people tell me that *Tutu* sounds like *Sketches* for the 1980s.[5]

Miles Davis remembered the beginning of this new and very different relationship with Marcus Miller in a rather different way. The pianist George Duke had sent Miles a tape of some music, and after Miller listened to it, he composed something in the same vein. This process was repeated several times, like a sort of invisible palimpsest of the original George Duke music, until Miller produced something that pleased both him and Miles. The latter also said that although Miller wrote most of the music on *Tutu*, Davis suggested the alternation of ensemble and solo passages. The album was provisionally entitled *Perfect Way* after the happy, catchy Green and Gamson popular song, which Miles wanted to include, but as the recording progressed, there were more profound resonances in the music and he agreed to producer Tommy LiPuma's suggestion to name the album after the South African priest, Desmond Tutu, Anglican Archbishop of Cape Town, one of the leading figures in the struggle against apartheid, and recipient of the 1984 Nobel Peace Prize.

George Duke did, however, arrange some of the music on *Tutu*, and Miller also recruited Jason Miles, a synthesizer programming expert, for the project, and another synthesizer player called Adam Holzman, who had become a regular member of Miles's working band after some sessions in October 1985. Miller would play the bass guitar plus soprano saxophone and bass clarinet passages, and one or two other musicians would be brought in when needed. The musical relationship of Miles Davis and Marcus Miller was deeply symbiotic because Miles had been an important catalyst in the development of Miller, and the latter was now taking over Gil Evans's Svengali role in Davis's reinvention of himself. Miller acknowledged his debt to Davis several times in print, and on one occasion said:

Miles is always good at putting pressure on you. He really made me find my own voice as a bass player. I mean, I had the facility, but ... It's one thing to play like somebody else on a record. If you get criticized you don't really feel responsible. But in Miles's band, there was no one I could copy and sound right. He forced me to play what I felt. And once you put your soul on a record, you have to deal with criticism, because it's criticism of you. Miles taught me how to deal with that, too, because he's always heard it, but you could tell criticism never got beyond that first layer. He'd go, 'Yeah, yeah, I'm gonna do what I do anyway.'[6]

It seems likely that Miles's ever growing passion for drawing and painting led him to this radical change in his whole approach to recording. In painting, artists have complete control of their materials, and if they don't like a colour or shape they can, at will, simply change or remove it; but members of a jazz group in the recording studio bring their own colours to the music, and to change them in any way, the leader/artist has to deal with the whole personality of each musician. In his autobiography, Miles complained about the difficulties of recording when musicians didn't feel good, or felt insecure when asked to play in a particular way, and said: 'That holds things up. Doing it the old way, recording like we used to, is just too much trouble and takes too much time.'[7] And Miles also showed that he was becoming increasingly aware of the difference between a recording and a live concert, when he expressed this in an interview:

> They ought to say on the product that this record is only a *guide* to what you will hear in person . . . you can't use the same tempos live that you do on a record. It's got to be faster live. You've got to get the people *up* when they come to hear you.[8]

Also, the experience of recording *Aura* was still fresh in his mind, and that too had been related to painting, because Palle Mikkelborg had created the whole orchestral structure, which Miles had helped to readjust and edit, and on to which he could put his own colours and imprint. There was even a visual element to the public performance of *Aura*, because Mikkelborg had given each movement the name of a colour, and this was expressed in the lighting of the concert. Mikkelborg was a highly gifted working musician and a superb composer/arranger in whom Miles could put his trust, and the whole project was achieved with a minimum of aggravation and a maximum of good feeling, made possible by all the preparatory work Mikkelborg had put into it and the control he exercised over it.

All these factors help to explain why, in 1986, Miles Davis began to function in the (recording) studio in a way similar to that of the great Flemish painter, Sir Peter Paul Rubens (1577–1640), who had several assistants in his studio to help him with his work. Davis had actually signed with Warner Bros in the late spring or early summer of 1985, and had spent much time in the recording studio that autumn, with his band and sometimes other musicians, searching for new ideas and new modes of procedure. Late in the year, he had even telephoned Paul Buckmaster again, asking him to write and send some pieces, and Paul, using an Apple Mac SE with a sequencing programmer, a mixer and an eight-track machine, had created two or three electronic orchestral tracks, each about eight minutes long, with hypnotic rhythms, polytonal harmonies and a melody on top. But by the time they arrived, it was too late: Miles had discovered his new *modus operandi*. His two main assistants were Marcus Miller and the Warner Bros record producer Tommy Lipuma, both of whom had great knowledge of the electronic sound sources at their disposal in the studio, allied to considerable powers of concentration. Miles liked them both and trusted Miller to create electronic orchestral structures on which he was able to paint his own colours and shapes. He said that he liked Miller because he was 'an unbelievably sweet guy', and added:

Marcus is so hip and into the music that he even *walks* in tempo, ain't never out of tempo in whatever he does. So now I don't mind going into the studio so much, because I know I'm going to be in there with people who know how to take care of business.[9]

But inadvertently, by offloading some responsibility for his music-making on to the shoulders of his assistants in order to concentrate on his trumpet playing, Miles yet again broke new ground and created something of a masterpiece. Marcus Miller said that his friends called *Tutu* the *Sketches* of the 1980s, but it is more closely related to *Miles Ahead*, on which Miles is the only soloist and plays flugelhorn throughout. Apart from a few brief phrases on open trumpet, he features the Harmon mute exclusively throughout *Tutu*, and the focus, the pith and moment of his playing border on the miraculous. His relationship with Miller developed as they worked, and the latter's role became more active. The studio was a big one and Miller explained:

Miles would be at the microphone, and I'd be next to him. And right before the take he'd tell me to play (on soprano saxophone) the melodies that I wanted him to play. I'd play the melodies, he'd play them back and I'd say, 'Yeah, that's cool.' Then we'd record it. And I'd be under him, supporting him, just playing a line under him or giving him something to bounce off. As we got more and more comfortable with the situation, he started saying, 'Look, I want you to just copy my phrases. When I play something, I want you to play the same thing right behind me.' So he's playing, and I'm trying to play it back to him. And I was really at the edge of whatever I had as far as saxophone chops, because I never really practised that thing. It was an instrument I played at the beach for fun, you know? So I had a hard time, but Miles seemed to like what was coming out. I would say to him, 'Miles, you know you got a bad [= good] saxophone player in your band ... Get him in here.' And he would say, 'Not for this stuff. I like the way you play. You don't play like nobody else. And there's something about somebody who's playing something he wrote that's different than somebody who's playing something that somebody told him to play.' So that's the reason I ended up playing saxophone on the date, and it got real comfortable after a while.[10]

The title track 'Tutu' opens the album, and the listener is plunged yet again into a new musical world, a radical but attractive and coherent soundscape. From the explosive introductory chord, the piece breathes beautifully all the way, and Miller's bass playing assists the seductive swing of the mostly programmed rhythm section. The atmosphere is all Miles – haunting, buoyant, but reflective with a touch of melancholy – and the whole piece is a dialogue between him and the orchestral sounds. At times he also plays written orchestral parts in between his solo passages. It is an extremely demanding context, but he always sounds as though he really means everything he plays and sometimes pushes himself to the limits with passionate phrases and screams which are so bottled-in and claustrophobically emotive when played with the Harmon.

'Tomaas' is attributed jointly to Davis and Miller, and has a strange intense feel with multiple rhythmic ingredients, and Miles dialogues with Miller's soprano sax. The perpetually shifting orchestral sounds are subtly organized, Miller also plays some bass clarinet, and Miles's Harmon has been overdubbed so that he momentarily dialogues with himself. 'Portia' is perhaps the most beautiful piece, with the bass used melodically as a lead voice for some orchestral phrases and Miles at his most lyrical. The whole performance soars and sings, before playing out with a repeated orchestral phrase hauntingly harmonized like a kind of prayer with Miles playing his responses over it.

'Splatch', which follows, is also by Miller, and this has a tough, dancey dancey rhythmic feel, a catchy, cheeky theme, and some sardonic and equally tough comments from muted Miles, plus a couple of brief flourishes on open trumpet. The only pieces not composed by Miller are 'Backyard Ritual' by George Duke, which begins and ends mysteriously, and the jolly, upbeat pop song 'Perfect Way'. Two of Miller's pieces bring the album to a close. 'Don't Lose Your Mind' has a moody African atmosphere with, at times, a kind of reggae rhythm, and some electric violin by Michal Urbaniak; and the final track, 'Full Nelson', is dedicated to Nelson Mandela. It has an urgent rocky rhythm and theme, and the organization of sound is superb, with Miles's imperative lyricism in full cry. Like each of the orchestral albums Davis made with Gil Evans – *Miles Ahead*, *Porgy and Bess*, and *Sketches of Spain* – *Tutu* has the unity of a suite, because it is the product of the vision of two men, Miller's understanding of, and rapport with Miles, and the latter's mysterious ability to invest his playing with the most potent and subtle emotional resonances. Miller said later: 'I would say that my bass style solidified on *The Man with the Horn*, and my composing took giant strides beginning with *Tutu*.'[11] The album received good reviews, won over some critics who had been hostile to Miles's recent music, sold well, and in 1987 won a Grammy award. Two years after that, the perceptive critic and commentator, Mike Zwerin, wrote,

The best jazz record of the decade is *Tutu* by Miles Davis.

Absolutely no doubt about it. It is the soundtrack to the movie of our lives in the urban centres of the 1980s, even the suburbs, the perfect accompaniment to the shame and splendour of our cities ... We must also admit that quality of life is becoming more minimal, so *Tutu*, a minimalist masterpiece, fits on the formal level also.[12]

The androgynous pop/rock star, Prince, whose work Miles Davis admired, also recorded for Warner Bros, and people at the record company said that the admiration was mutual, that Prince also loved Davis's music and looked up to him, which pleased Miles greatly. When he and Marcus Miller were working on *Tutu*, Prince wrote a song for the album and sent a tape of it to them, and they in turn sent back a tape of the kind of things they were putting on the album. When he heard them, Prince realized that his piece was not appropriate and withdrew permission to use it. This saved Miles the embarrassment of having to reject it. Such an external contribution would certainly have damaged the unity – the emotional and sonic coherence – of *Tutu*, which emanated from the subtle and delicate rapport of Davis and Miller.

Once *Tutu* was completed, Miles wanted to continue touring and playing concerts, and there were now some personnel changes in, and additions to, his band. In the autumn of 1985, when he had been in the studio exploring ideas for his first Warner Bros album, he had even recruited the help of a member of the original young band Vincent Wilburn had brought to New York for him in 1980: the singer/songwriter, Randy Hall. The latter also brought along someone new, the twenty-eight-year-old rock-oriented keyboardist, Adam Holzman, who had played and done some programming on one of Hall's albums. The original electric bassist with that young band, Felton Crews, would now replace Angus Thomas in Miles's band. However, none of Miles's current band had played on *Tutu*, and so they needed to be rehearsed through the pieces that would become part of the repertoire.

The 1985 autumn studio sessions produced some pieces that were added to the repertoire and Holzman recalled:

When Miles started working on the project that would end up being *Tutu*, he had Randy working on some tunes with him, and Randy brought me in on the sessions. My purpose ostensibly was to break the band in on this tune we had cut that Miles liked a lot. I had written some charts and gotten some sounds together. We ended up working on the tune, and Miles showed up, sat on a couch, and played along. After a while, the band had the tune together, Miles and the road manager left the room, and I was sitting around thinking, 'Well, I got through that in one piece.' Then the road manager came back and said, 'Well everybody, I've got an announcement to make. It looks like we have a new member in the band now.' I was thinking, 'Hmm, did they get a new saxophone player or something?' Then he said, 'Adam, did you bring your passport?' They were leaving for Europe in three days – and I went with them.[13]

It was late October 1985 when Adam Holzman had joined the band, and that happened because Miles was not computer- or synthesizer-literate. He had an Oberheim OB-Xa in the band for his use, but said of it:

I don't get out of it what it can do, because I don't know that much about it. Adam shows me. I hired Adam because I couldn't tell Bobby Irving how to get the sound that Adam got. So I don't know. You'd have to ask Adam. I said, 'Adam, come on. You can go with us.' So he left his truck out at the airport, and he came on. Adam was working in a store, showing people how to work keyboards.[14]

So the band that toured Europe from 24 October to 8 November 1985 was a nonet with two keyboardists and two percussionists.

The same nine-piece line-up now played a six-date US mini-tour from 21 March to 25 April 1986, with one personnel change: Felton Crews on bass guitar. The rest of the band comprised Bob Berg, Mike Stern, Robert Irving III, Adam Holzman, Vincent

Wilburn, Steve Thornton and Marilyn Mazur as second percussionist. Mazur was white, and the first woman Miles had ever
had in his band. After the first two dates, Mike Stern was replaced
by guitarist Robben Ford. The repertoire included some earlier
pieces, plus 'Portia', 'Splatch' and 'Tutu', and some new pieces that
hadn't yet been recorded: 'Maze', 'Wrinkle', 'Burn' and 'Carnival
Time'. Holzman described how improvisation and fluidity were
an integral part of the structure of 'Wrinkle':

> It has five or six variable elements that Miles can bring in
> and out – two really hip bass lines, a rhythm guitar part that
> goes all the way through, and then some melodies that he
> plays with the saxophonist and another which brings in a
> breakdown. So he has all these elements going; it's just a
> matter of whom he points to, what direction he takes it
> in. The song ends quite different each night. He keeps you
> watching him, keeps you on your toes, so you don't just
> become a player in the band, playing a tune. He doesn't want
> you to think you know what's going to happen. Especially
> if you're the drummer. A lot of times Miles will direct the
> drummer to cut the rhythm into half-time in the middle of a
> piece.[15]

It seemed that Miles Davis was overcoming the problem of his
musicians being in demand and therefore not always available to
him, in two ways: first, by developing a pool of players schooled
in his musical practices, from which he could replace absentees;
and second, by being able to record albums without using his
band. The last three dates of this mini-tour were at the Beacon
Theatre, New York City, on 5 and 6 April, and at Saenger Hall,
in New Orleans on 25 April. On the first night at the Beacon
Theatre, the band played two full concerts, and on the second
night only one, because they shared the bill with bluesman B. B.
King. By this time, Miles had had a wig woven into the remains
of his hair, and on the second night, just before his concert, he
and Cicely had a row which so infuriated her that, according to

Miles, she jumped on his back and tore his hair weave right out of his head. Although he felt that this was the last straw, they continued to stay together. After New Orleans, Miles and the band did not play another concert until mid-June, because he was coming up to his sixtieth birthday on 26 May, and there was a rising tide of interest in this.

He went back to his home in Malibu, and at the beginning of May recorded an in-depth interview for radio with Ben Sidran, who included excerpts from *Tutu*. Cicely Tyson softened his heart by organizing a tremendous surprise party on a yacht in Marina del Rey, on Santa Monica Bay, California. The unsuspecting Davis arrived to find a host of celebrities waiting for him, including Quincy Jones, Eddie Murphy, Camille Cosby, Whoopi Goldberg, Herbie Hancock, Herb Alpert, critic Leonard Feather, Sammy Davis's wife, and the mayor of Los Angeles, Tom Bradley, who presented Miles with a citation from the city. Other guests included Miles's sister Dorothy, his brother Vernon, and daughter Cheryl, his manager David Franklin and the Chairman of Warner Bros Records, Mo Ostin. Cicely's birthday present for him was an oil painting of his mother, father and grandfather, which she had commissioned from an artist called Artis Lane. This touched Miles's heart and he said he would always cherish the painting. The party was enjoyed by all the guests, and *Jet* magazine did a four- or five-page spread on it, with many photographs. In fact, Miles's sixtieth birthday, combined with his dramatic change of record company, and his superbly realized album *Tutu*, with its radical new sound and evocative lyricism, sparked off a whole series of national and international in-depth appreciations of him throughout the year. New York's *Village Voice* produced a special jazz supplement in August, entitled 'Miles Davis at 60' and devoted entirely to him, the British glossy style magazine, *The Face*, had a six-and-a-half-page feature on him in its October issue, and there was a long tribute on 15 November in the *Guardian* newspaper, to list only a few of the acknowledgements in English-speaking countries.

It was beginning to dawn on those critics who had been closely following Miles's 1980s career that something exceptional had been happening. The *Village Gate* jazz supplement had essays by different writers on Davis's work covering the 1950s, 1960s and the last quintet, which never made a studio recording – Miles, Wayne Shorter, Chick Corea, Dave Holland and Jack DeJohnette – but the star contribution was Gary Giddins's essay entitled 'Miles Davis Superstar', which reappraised his current work and related it to the rest of his career. Giddins had attended the 1984 North Sea Jazz Festival in Holland, where 6,000 people waited impatiently for Davis's concert, and only then had Giddins fully realized the enormity of the trumpeter's celebrity, the unique identity of his music, and its power to involve an audience of the current generation. Giddins's mind went back to Miles's New York concert at the Lincoln Center in the summer of 1985:

... the kids who crowded the stage at Lincoln Center last summer to press Davis's flesh were responding to the immediacy of the moment. They have no attachments, sentimental or otherwise, to Davis's apprenticeship with Charlie Parker, or his quintets of the 1950s and 1960s, or his work with Gil Evans. What they recognize in Davis is a powerful centre, a force of authority, who continues to produce concert music unlike that of anyone else ... Davis had sustained his musical mystique with florid and compelling concert appearances. He can do what few musicians in history could do: with a few notes on the trumpet, he stills qualms, raises expectations, confuses issues, and mesmerizes the doubtful. It isn't that his sound is unique, though of course it is, but that it touches people in a place where they have to reach for metaphor to explain the effect. No brass player since Louis Armstrong has been able to make such plenary claims on his audience as Davis. From the time he arrived in New York, at eighteen ... Davis demonstrated the determination to speak a language of his own ... In 1960, [Gil] Evans met the musician who inspired him most, Louis Armstrong, who told him he'd bought *Porgy and Bess* and suggested they make an album

462

together. Armstrong joked, 'You're not gonna hand me any of those funny chords,' and in a more serious vein, observed of Davis, 'That boy reminded me of Buddy Bolden. Yes, he reminded me of Buddy Bolden.'[16]

Giddins ended by sketching the landmarks in Miles's illustrious career, and concluding: '. . . the one thread that ties it all together is the stubborn, insinuating drama of his trumpet, a healing blast, steamy yet icy, with which he continues to crest fashion, fame, and the illusory geometry of a stable backbeat.'[17]

In early June 1986, Davis was interviewed for a Public Broadcasting System (PBS) special TV documentary in their series *Great Performances*, called 'Miles Ahead: The Music of Miles Davis'. Extracts from the interview and excerpts from albums and TV performances were interspersed with comments from Dizzy Gillespie, Herbie Hancock, Bill Cosby, Gil Evans, Robben Ford, Tony Williams, Keith Jarrett and others.[18] This was the first American TV documentary about Davis since Robert Herridge's thirty-minute film, *The Sound of Miles Davis*, in 1959, which featured the quintet playing 'So What', and three orchestral pieces with Gil Evans conducting, but neither Miles nor Gil was interviewed on camera for that, because the uniquely high standard of TV sound and visual presentation enabled the remarkable music to speak for itself. The singer/songwriter Oscar Brown was the narrator and link man for the 1986 documentary, which gave a series of glimpses of various stages of Miles's career, and included inserts from the 1959 film with Miles and Coltrane playing 'So What', and excerpts from the orchestral performances. Miles talks at intervals throughout, dressed in loose clothes and sitting, apparently on the floor, in his apartment, looking somewhat frail and worn, with a sparse hair weave. There are good stretches of performance by the 1960s quintet, a glimpse of his 1969 group, some shots of him in action with one or two of his 1970s bands, and three excerpts from the current nine-piece band at the Saenger Theatre, New Orleans, on 25 April. The various interviewees make some illuminating comments, and Gil Evans, his warm and vigorous voice at strange odds with his gaunt appearance, says of Miles, 'I'm sure glad you were born!', calls him a 'sensational singer of songs', and asserts that Miles changed the tone of the trumpet for the first time since Louis Armstrong. The shots of the current Davis band give two views of Miles's now outlandish sartorial garb; at one time he is wearing what looks like a long dressing gown or bath robe with padded shoulders, and in other shots he is wearing a kind of loose blouse and trousers in silver lamé. The hour-long documentary, however, was exclusively about Miles Davis the musician and music-maker; no women were interviewed, and his life – the complexities of his character and personality – was barely touched upon.

The New Orleans concert was Marilyn Mazur's last appearance with the band, and Miles resumed touring, now with an octet, on 13 June at San Diego, California, the first of eight concerts taking in the USA and Canada, before he and the band embarked on their next European tour. The schedule was occasionally punishing, and at the Playboy Jazz Festival in Los Angeles on the fourteenth, the band did not go on stage until 11 p.m., but the next day they had an *early* flight right across the USA to Meadowlands in New Jersey, where they were to play at the Amnesty International concert at Giants Stadium. They were not met at the airport and so had to find their own way to hotels. Several famous rock groups were on the bill, and the whole concert was being broadcast live on television all over the world. The venue had a revolving stage, so that one group could set up while another one was playing its concert, which enabled the smooth transition from one band to another. Ironically, however, the setting up of Miles's band was delayed because it had rained all morning, and gusts of wind blew water down from the stage roof on to their equipment, much of which was electric. In the panic, there was no time for a sound check, but as is often the case, the adrenaline did its work and Miles's twenty-minute spot was warmly received by the audience. After his concert, a number of rock musicians came up to pay their respects to him, including Bono and U2, Sting and the Police, Peter Gabriel and Ruben Blades. Miles, relieved and relaxed because, despite the problems, his concert was successfully over, happily welcomed these friendly overtures.

After the Avery Fisher Hall on 21 June, the Davis band played two consecutive nights at Vancouver, Canada, and the second night on 28 June brought another visitor who was not at all welcome. Wynton Marsalis was due to play a concert at the same festival the following day, but had arrived early. The attempted visitation occurred in the middle of Miles's concert, while he was actually playing. He heard some crowd noises suggesting that something unusual was happening, and became aware of some presence coming on stage . . . Wynton Marsalis carrying his trumpet . . . and now, as Miles continued playing his solo, Marsalis whispering in his ear, 'They told me to come up here.' Davis told him twice to get off stage, and twice Marsalis stayed put, so Miles stopped the band until Marsalis did so. This extraordinary behaviour showed that Marsalis had no real understanding of the man he had pilloried in the press. He had never apologized to Miles. Could it be that he had never actually meant his insulting comments? That he had simply been posturing and attempting to assert himself? And who were the 'they' who had told him to go on stage? Was it the same 'they' who had encouraged him to say disrespectful things about the trumpeter in the first instance? Not anyone, not even Miles Davis's closest friends, would have simply walked on stage with their instruments, without asking first if it were all right to do so. It was simply a question of respect and good manners. Perhaps in Marsalis's case it was a question of hubris. After all, in his mere twenty-four years of life, he'd already had more success, more recognition, more continuous work opportunities than many jazz musicians have in a lifetime. But the kind of indelible mark on the music that Miles had made in his youth and had remade many times since by paying many dues, maintaining constant artistic vigilance and nurturing the profound originality of his vision, had so far eluded the younger man, who had, to coin a phrase, 'risen without a trace'. The music of Miles Davis was a legacy that Marsalis had, willy-nilly, inherited, as had all subsequent jazz musicians.

This leg of the US tour finished on 29 June with a concert at Saratoga, New York, then on 8 July the band began a twelve-concert tour of Europe, taking in Italy, Holland, France, Switzerland and Spain, and returning to the USA on 29 July. Like his great friend, Gil Evans, Miles seemed to be spending more time on tour playing concerts in the last years of his life than ever before. At the Montreux Jazz Festival on 17 July, George Duke was added on keyboard for the performances of 'Tutu' and 'Splatch', and David Sanborn sat in on alto saxophone for the *three* encores, 'Burn', 'Portia' and 'Jean Pierre'. Miles's music now sounds richer, more fully realized than ever, and so full of good pieces that he can even use the exquisite piece 'Portia' as an encore. The band's light and shade, textures and dynamics are deployed with dramatic artistry, the music evolves like a live thing with ever shifting perspectives, and the newer pieces, such as the ferocious 'Maze' and the irresistibly grooving 'Wrinkle', really speak to the Montreux audience, who are utterly involved with the performance, often erupting in excited applause. The ninety-minute-plus concert is very demanding, but Miles is in good lip and never falters, and Bob Berg solos with great power. The *Tutu* pieces take on new dimensions in live performance, also drawing spontaneous and at times almost delirious applause.

Miles Davis's public profile was possibly the highest it had ever been in his whole career in 1986, and this peak of fame happily coincided with some of his most dynamic and intriguing music-making. The one factor that took his fame above its usual levels was the repeated appearance of his Honda commercial on television, which made his image familiar to all American households. Also the episode of *Miami Vice*, in which he'd acted the part of pimp or brothel-owner and dope-peddler, was shown on television that year, which added to his notoriety. After this exposure, complete strangers would recognize him in the street and speak to him. In his autobiography he expressed his outrage that nonentities who appeared regularly on television were more revered than great musicians, writers or painters who did not appear on TV.

Back in the USA after the European tour, starting in early August and finishing at the end of the month, the band played seven concerts and had one ninety-minute rehearsal. After the final concert in Detroit, guitarist Robben Ford left the band because he was getting married and wanted to play his own music, but he had recommended Garth Webber, who took his place. On 8 September, the band played Rio de Janeiro, then flew to Europe for two or three concerts, one of which was in Cologne, Germany, where Miles was also interviewed by Karl Lippergaus about his past career and *Tutu*, from which excerpts were played. He was interviewed again in Cologne, this time by Rolf Klinke, for the West German NDR-TV programme *Kultur Aktuell*, which was making a documentary film called *Die Miles Davis Story*. Excerpts from Miles's Cologne concert were shown, and he was also filmed walking round an art exhibition in the city.[19] This was followed by a concert at Le Zenith in Paris, which was filmed by Canal TV/Europe-1 RB, for yet another documentary, this time in the series *Les Enfants du Rock*, Antenne 2-TV. Davis was interviewed by his old associate and 1940s nine-piece band member, trombonist/journalist Mike Zwerin, and excerpts from the Zenith concert, plus excerpts from the 1959 film of the orchestral music with Gil Evans, Miles's *Decoy* video, his 1971 Paris concert and the feature film *L'Ascenseur pour L'Echafaud*, were edited into the interview.

Davis and the band returned to the USA at the beginning of September, and late in the month were filmed in a Los Angeles studio for the *Dick Cavett Show* on ABC-TV. After a four-minute version of 'Perfect Way', Miles did a fifteen-minute interview, then the band played a four-minute performance of 'Tutu', followed by a brief play-out fragment of 'Carnival Time'. It may have been Miles's exposure with the Honda commercial and the *Miami Vice* episode that made him a candidate for this popular TV show, and his programme was broadcast on 10 October. That same month, he recorded the soundtrack for the movie *Street Smart*, a crime melodrama about a leading journalist who writes a story that gets him involved with pimps and prostitutes, and starring Christopher

Reeve, Morgan Freeman, Kathy Baker and Mimi Rogers. Miles entrusted much of the writing and preparation to Robert Irving and Adam Holzman, who took over the Marcus Miller role, but guitarist Mike Stern and percussionist Steve Thornton were also involved. Irving did most of the composition and Holzman wrote some cues, then they spent much time playing the parts and recording them in the Yamaha QX1 sequencer, using Irving's home studio. Afterwards, in New York's A&R studios and using an ensemble comprising Tom Harrell on trumpet, Bob Berg and Bob Mintzer on reeds, Irving, Stern, Darryl Jones on bass guitar, double bassist Alex Blake, drummer Adam Nussbaum and Thornton, they recorded material from the sequencer, using a click track, and married the live band's music to the tape that had the sequencer material on it. In this way they could decide, when mixing the music, which parts to retain and which to discard. Holzman commented:

> That was the hard work. The magic began, as usual, when Miles came in to overdub his parts. He just nailed one cue after another. It was incredible! We worked with him for about four hours, in one night. Since we had most of the recordings prepared and ready for him to go, we just started rolling them off. Miles was reading music and soloing over it, and he sounded great. We paced it, mixing slow things with fast things. It was almost like a mini-concert; he went through these mood changes right along with us and laid it all down.[20]

Street Smart was released in 1987, and got some good reviews, with occasionally favourable comments on Miles's music, but it was no box office draw and was soon taken out of circulation.

In October, Miles had yet more media exposure in the USA. He was interviewed for *Morning News* CBS-TV, and the interview was broadcast in five-minute instalments over three *Morning News* programmes, covering first clothes, second musical influences, drugs and his art work, and finally his marriage to Cicely Tyson.

Excerpts from his *Tutu* video were also shown. This was followed by some radio exposure, when David Sanborn interviewed Miles Davis, Marcus Miller and Tommy LiPuma about the new album *Tutu*, on *The Jazz Show*, Westwood One Network-RB. LiPuma and Warner Bros were definitely succeeding in orchestrating Miles's publicity agenda with maximum effect – 1986 was becoming one of the busiest years of his entire career, and on 21 October, with his concert at Montpellier in France, he began his *third* European tour that year.

The twelve concerts took in seven countries, including Yugoslavia and Spain, and the tour ended with three concerts in London at Wembley Conference Centre – two on 16 November and the third a day later. Either the year's punishing work schedule had drained Davis, or he may have had health problems, but for the first time he appeared to be struggling with the trumpet, cracking and missing notes. The band, however, was superlative and his direction of it masterful. While in London he was interviewed for the Tyne-Tees TV programme *The Tube* about his paintings, his idea for a *Romeo and Juliet* video, and his *Tutu* video. Excerpts from the latter video, from the 1959 orchestral performance of 'Blues for Pablo', and from his wonderful Montreux concert in July, were edited into the interview.

Once back in the USA, Miles ended this full year with four concerts, the last two of which were at the Universal Amphitheatre, Los Angeles, on 28 and 31 December, and for these he added saxophonist Gary Thomas to the band, which did not please Bob Berg, who already felt that Miles did not give him enough solo space. It would be only a matter of weeks before Berg left the band. But for Miles Davis himself, the year had been something of a triumph on all fronts, with a ground-breaking new album, a much higher profile in America and elsewhere, and a vast itinerary of national and international concerts with a band that consistently reached new peaks of expression.

With the irony of fate, perhaps, 1987 brought some rude social shocks. Cicely Tyson had been invited by President Ronald Reagan and his wife, Nancy, to a party at the Kennedy Center in

Washington, where Ray Charles and some other prominent people were going to be honoured with a Lifetime Achievement Award. Cicely wanted Miles to accompany her there, and because he and Charles had been friends for a long time, and Miles loved his music, he decided to go with her. First they were to have dinner at the White House, but even in the limousine which picked them up at the airport, things began to go wrong. Miles clearly had no idea how ignorant, arrogant and out of touch certain rich people are, and there were some such white men and women travelling in the limousine with him and Cicely. Here he was, an international superstar, a major twentieth-century figure in the new art of jazz, now a global phenomenon, but in the tiny world of this limousine, none of the whites knew anything about him. One of the women said to him, 'Miles, the limo driver says he likes the way you sing and he's got all your records.'[21] This drew no reply, but the atmosphere became highly charged. The two other blacks in the limousine, Billy Dee Williams and Willie Mays, tried to release the tension by talking black slang with Miles, but this only embarrassed Cicely. One of the other white women said, 'Miles, I know your mammy's proud of you coming down to meet the President.' 'Mammy' to blacks was and is a patronizing, pejorative term, and the atmosphere became even more strained as Miles, speaking in a level voice, his eyes holding hers, said that his mother was not a 'mammy' which was a word that people didn't use any more, and that his mother was more elegant than she, and his father was a doctor, and this woman should never again say anything like that to a black person. The woman had the good grace to apologize.

At the White House Miles met the President, whom he found amiable, but he preferred his wife, Nancy's, spontaneous warmth. There were perhaps ten or twenty black people there, including Quincy Jones and Lena Horne. At dinner Miles found himself sitting with one or two people he liked and who seemed better informed, but a politician's wife tried to involve him in a discussion about jazz. He could see that she was not really interested, but was just trying to make polite conversation, which was exactly the kind of stance he loathed. Miles had no small talk, and usually spoke only when he really had something to say. So this time he really said something – home truths about the white man wanting to win everything, but white people being unable to win at jazz and blues because they were created by black people, and how Europeans are quick to recognize the achievements of blacks in jazz, but most white Americans would not admit this. The woman turned red and asked, 'Well what have you done that's so important in your life? Why are you here?' Miles replied, 'Well, I've changed music five or six times, so I guess that's what I've done and I guess I don't believe in playing just white compositions.' Then looking at her coldly, he said, 'Now tell me what have you done of any importance other than be white, and that ain't important to me, so tell me what your claim to fame is?'[22] The woman was so angry that speech failed her, and the tension was so thick that, in Miles's words, 'you could cut it with a knife'.[23] Eventually, he whispered to Cicely, 'Let's get out of here as soon as this shit is over. You can handle this kind of shit, I can't.'[24] This whole experience horrified and depressed Davis, and he resented the fact that the ignorance of the white guests made *him* feel bad. He was also disgusted that although Ray Charles was there to receive a Lifetime Achievement Award, most of the people there had no idea who he was. Miles wished never to experience this kind of thing again, and it had made him realize how incompatible he and Cicely were.

Although Cicely Tyson had known Miles since the mid-1960s and certainly helped to save his life in the 1980s, Lydia DeJohnette pointed out: 'She obviously didn't know him on some deep level. She thought she was going to change him, but she had an illusion about who he was, because he hated all that social stuff she liked. She tried to put him in Society and he would just walk out.' In fact, Miles's non-conformism was so strong that it bordered on the subversive – he was beyond the pale of high society, but an aristocrat in the musical world he had created. He was essentially a maverick in art and life, and this was his strength. Ironically, his father and mother had belonged to the higher echelons of black society, and a middle-class Miles with his educated accent had been sent to the Juilliard College of Music. But once he had decided to devote himself one hundred per cent to jazz, he gradually adopted the colloquial speech of the black street community, and slowly changed his sartorial style and image, until they were antithetical to those of white Society. His parents might well have felt reasonably at ease in the White House, and would certainly have dressed to suit the occasion. Invitations to such events usually indicate the desired dress for men – such as either 'black tie' (dinner jacket etc.) or 'lounge suit'. If there were such instructions on Cicely Tyson's invitation, she may not have shown them to Miles, or he may have disregarded them. It seems that the White House function was a 'black tie' affair, which means that every man looks the same and no one stands out. In the 1950s Miles had worn a dinner jacket and black bow-tie on certain occasions, but for this exalted occasion, he wore something by the Japanese designer Kohshin Satoh – a long black waistcoat with tails and a red snake on the back trimmed in white sequins, over two vests also made by Kohshin, one red and the other white broadcloth with silver chains crossing it, and some shiny black leather trousers. Of course, he stood out among the penguin suits but he was socially naïve enough to feel peeved when the conventionally dressed whites looked askance at him. He was like a fish out of water in that milieu, and though he may have blamed Cicely for taking him there, he could always have refused and stayed at home. However, because of his upbringing, he may have needed that direct personal experience in order to confirm his intuitive aversion to that kind of society and event.

Miles's desire for street credibility with blacks, which made him discard certain of his bourgeois characteristics, also made him yet more like Louis Armstrong who, in contrast, had had a deprived and totally unprivileged upbringing. As a child and adolescent, Armstrong had got his wisdom in the roughest university of life, eking out a living among pimps, prostitutes (one of whom he married at the age of seventeen) and hoodlums, all handy with razors and knives, in an atmosphere of barely contained violence which heightened his sensitivities and awareness – inability to anticipate or 'read' certain situations might result in disfigurement or death. Armstrong had never felt the tug of bourgeois respectability, as Miles had in his childhood and adolescence, but Louis was also a natural aristocrat, lord of the musical world he had created, and he had never sought the company of the wealthy or powerful, black or white. When Howard University wanted to confer an honorary doctorate on him, he brushed the offer aside, saying, 'Where were they forty years ago when I needed them?' And in 1969, when he was invited to the White House by Richard Nixon, he turned it down saying, 'Fuck that shit. Why didn't they do it before? The only reason he would want me to play there now is to make some niggers happy.'[25] This loathing of cant, artificiality and snobbery, and a natural predilection for honesty and plain speaking, were attitudes and qualities common to Armstrong and Davis, and the bedrock of their life and art.

Miles Davis may have felt like a nonentity at the White House, but in 1987 his stock, world-wide, seemed higher than ever before, and he was able to take more time off – the months of April, May and August – and yet do perhaps more touring than ever. Again he went to Europe on three occasions, toured extensively in the USA and played the usual places in Canada. But it was now also financially possible for him to perform isolated concerts in faraway places, and on 2 June he played his first ever concert in Israel, followed by the Berg Isel Stadium at Innsbruck, Austria, on the fifth, then flew back to the USA. The early part of the year, however, saw some important personnel changes. First Miles brought back percussionist Mino Cinelu in place of Steve Thornton, then at the end of January, Bob Berg left the band in order to make his own music, saying later:

> The hardest part of the gig for me to deal with, which in the end, consequently, was the reason I left, was that I didn't feel I had enough room to really stretch out. But sometimes, I did have enough room, and I did really want to do what's best for the music. I know it's not the Bob Berg show, I mean

I know it's the Miles Davis band – and he reminded me of that several times . . . But being around Miles was, I guess, just really inspiring for me; being around that level of creativity, that level of genius, is the thing that stands out most. Before Miles I was much more involved with acoustic jazz, and playing with him got me much more involved in the electric aspects of the music. And I got to play for a much larger audience than I was playing to before that, because then I was basically doing clubs and small venues although I was working a lot at that time and making a lot of records. But somehow, playing with Miles, I feel, put me on another level in a certain way. I'm not saying any better or any worse than what I had been doing, but just different, you know. And just standing next to Miles every night, and hearing him play the trumpet . . . I mean that still stands out as the biggest thing of the whole gig – to hear Miles play.

In February, alto saxophonist Kenny Garrett was brought in alongside tenorist Gary Thomas: the first black reed players Miles had had in his band since his comeback. After four concerts, however, Thomas left the band, and Garrett (born 9 October 1960) would now prove himself to be the perfect saxophonist and flautist for the band, staying with it until Davis's death. Garrett had, immediately after leaving high school, begun a three-year stint with the Mercer Ellington Orchestra, then worked with various other leaders, including trumpeters Freddie Hubbard and Woody Shaw, and Art Blakey's Jazz Messengers. By the time he joined Miles, he was one of the most promising young stars on the American jazz scene.

The hardest task Davis had to do at this time was to fire Vincent Wilburn because, in Miles's own words, he was 'always dropping the time' – in other words, not holding the tempo. Miles loved his nephew and felt very close to him. Vincent was, after all, the son of Miles's sister Dorothy, who had been such a good friend and support over the years, and whose prompt action had not only rescued him from his slow reclusive disintegration, but who, with the assistance of Vincent, had given him emotional and moral support in his halting return to music-making. Miles put off the awful task as long as he could, but eventually told Vincent, who left after the concert on 27 February, at Washington, DC. Needless to say, the sacking caused some bad feeling between Miles and Dorothy and her husband, particularly because Vincent was their only son. Vincent was replaced in March by Ricky Wellman, a young drummer from Washington DC, whom Miles had heard playing on an album by Chuck Brown and the Soul Searchers. When Wellman accepted Miles's invitation to join, he was sent a tape of the repertoire and told to learn it, and on 25 March he played his first concert with the band. Saxophonist Gary Thomas left the band at the end of March, leaving Kenny Garrett as sole saxophonist and flautist. There had been several deputy guitarists at the end of the previous year and in the early days of 1987, so Miles was also looking for a more permanent replacement who would suit the music. Marcus Miller sent him a tape of Joseph Foley McCreary, a young black guitarist from Cincinnati (known to his friends simply as 'Foley') and he, like Kenny Garrett, soon had an excellent musical rapport with Davis and remained in the band until the latter's death. Miles commented: 'Foley . . . playing that funky blues-rock-funk, almost Jimi Hendrix-like . . . I had truly found the guitar player that I had been looking for.'[26] So, in mid-1987, Miles Davis felt he had the perfect band for his present purposes, and he was in good health and high spirits.

In January and March, Miles, working again with Marcus Miller, synthesizer programmer Jason Miles, and one or two other musicians, had recorded the music for the feature film *Siesta*, which was based on a novel by Patrice Chaplin, and starred Ellen Barkin, Jodie Foster, Julian Sands and Martin Sheen. It was set in Spain, where an amnesiac skydiver, visiting her ex-lover, became implicated in a murder. It has been described as a 'pretentious, deliberately obscure movie where there is little reward for working out what is happening',[27] and despite its star cast, it flopped. It seems that the only film worthy of Miles Davis's music was the French director Louis Malle's first effort, in 1957 – *Ascenseur pour*

L'Echafaud, (*Lift to the Scaffold*) – and both the film and the music have stood the test of time. Even though Marcus Miller composed and arranged all the electronic/acoustic music for *Siesta*, the brooding spirit of Miles's and Gil Evans's *Sketches of Spain* underlies this aural palimpsest. *Siesta* is, in fact, a series of sketches, and Miller's methods were much more improvisatory than they had been for the creation of *Tutu*, in which Miles's organic relationship to the structures of the pieces was much more fully realized. Recording the music for *Siesta* was a much simpler and more straightforward affair, according to Miller:

> I'd just roll the video tape, which was SMPTE'd [married] to the multi-track [tape], and play some things that I thought matched the scenes. Then I'd get my bass clarinet and Miles and I would react to that, then go back and see how it worked with the film. The trick was to have Miles play Spanish music and not have it be a carbon copy of *Sketches of Spain*. It may remind you of *Sketches*, but the movie had a lot of eeriness to it, so I got to use darker colours and more space. It really let Miles explore his tones. And he's a master of that. He can imply different keys without playing them; he can imply time without playing time. The more space he gets, the more creative he gets. What you need to do to produce Miles is really get to know him and his music – hang out and listen. A lot of people associate Miles with one kind of music: whatever period of Miles's career they love the most. But you have to combine all the elements of Miles's experience with what's new and exciting today, because that's what Miles is into.[28]

The above last three sentences are a graphic description of Miller's relationship as a producer with Davis, and each new project widens and deepens his understanding of the trumpeter. The detailed plotting of events in *Tutu* was simply not necessary for the *Siesta* music, and Miller's loose, improvisatory approach, and the much freer rein he gave to Miles, worked beautifully in this case. The skeletal structures were achieved with synthesizers and a couple of added musicians – John Scofield on acoustic guitar and drummer Omar Hakim for the January sessions, and guitarist Earl Klugh and flautist James Walker in March. Other instruments were played by Miller, and his extensive use of the bass clarinet helped to darken the colours, heightening the atmosphere and harking back to the ominous, emotional hotbed of *Bitches Brew*. But the whole climate of *Siesta* differs in one fundamental way from that of *Bitches*; far from being hot, it is often cool, sometimes icy. The mood is set up by the brief, remarkable first movement, 'Lost in Madrid Part I', which opens with synthesized winds hissing and howling in some bleak, unspecified landscape of the heart, against which Miles Davis pits his desolate, lonely calls on open trumpet, causing the wind to pause. Miles's trumpet continues during the silence, and a subdued wind returns only to fade away when his calls summon the more humane accompaniment of string synthesizer harmonies and phrases. His sound and his playing in these starkly contrasting settings has an extraordinary evocative power. The economy of means of the composer, Miller, and of the composing player, Miles, borders on the miraculous, and this whole sequence, lasting no longer than one minute forty-seven seconds, speaks volumes. The second movement or sequence, 'Siesta, Kitt's Kiss, Lost in Madrid Part II', features Miles at length on open trumpet, with broken tango drum rhythms, synthesizer backings, and some fine acoustic guitar by John Scofield. Here, Davis is at his most poetic and impassioned, sculpting his phrases and occasionally reaching up to singing high notes. Miller's bass clarinet joins in the backing figures and general dialogue.

The third sequence, 'Theme for Augustin/Wind/Seduction/Kiss', begins with synthesized choral voices and bass clarinet, then Miles enters with a glorious Harmon mute sound, accompanied by acoustic piano, the synth choir backs him, plus bass clarinet and bass, and he soars into the upper register with consummate lyricism. Miller's use of the upper register of the bass clarinet is quite superb. The wind appears again briefly, followed by string synth chords, and a synthesized cello melody without rhythm, plus the bass clarinet, and Miles plays a haunting fragment of theme to bring the sequence to a close. Despite the fact that Davis doesn't play on three short pieces and one long one, his presence seems to dominate the music because he does play at length on four of the five longest pieces, and is also featured on two out of the five short pieces. Thanks to the great rapport between Miller and Davis, there is a tremendous unity of atmosphere throughout this music, but also thankfully, only that first movement expresses such stark desolation. The subsequent sequences, also beautifully conceived and executed, express a kind of tender sorrow and regret for things past – lost love, lost friends and opportunities – which is both touching and seductive.

Just as Miles Davis was riding high in 1987, and taking an even firmer grip on his life and art, he was given a rude reminder of mortality. His good friend, the novelist James Baldwin, died. They had first met in the early 1960s, when Miles had already read some of Baldwin's books, and the latter had a good knowledge of Davis's music, so that the respect and admiration were mutual. Every time Miles went to the south of France to play at the Antibes festival, he would try to spend a day or two at Baldwin's villa in St Paul de Vence, relaxing, swapping stories, and in Davis's phrase, 'lying our asses off'.[29] It was Baldwin who had described Miles as a 'miraculously tough and tender man'. His death shook Davis, who recalled their easy-going friendship, and the beautiful villa, with its fine garden.

Miles made other changes in his organization this year, firing his manager, David Franklin, and persuading his lawyer, Peter Shukat, to take on the role of manager as well. Davis had been unhappy about the way Franklin was handling his finances. Usually, after a concert, the road manager, Jim Rose, would collect the money and give it to Franklin, or if he was not on the tour, to one of his assistants. But, according to Miles, after a particular concert, he asked Rose to give him the money, and when the latter prevaricated, Davis slapped his head and took the money from him. After that, Rose left his job with the band, and Miles had to find another road manager. This was a sorry end to a long and excellent working relationship, and it saddened Miles. Rose had been fiercely loyal to him through bad times and good, for many years. This whole episode seems to have happened because Davis had stretched himself financially by buying a New York apartment on Central Park, and also spending substantial amounts of money on other things. This was probably because his higher profile and successful recordings had increased his earning power. He was also trying to wipe the slate even cleaner by making the final break with Cicely Tyson, and that involved another worry: she could, if she wished, make things difficult and perhaps take him to the cleaners financially.

Meanwhile, he seemed to rejoice in a gruelling tour schedule, playing concerts in the USA, Canada and Europe in June and July, and after that, more of the same through the months from September to November. On 29 June he played a concert at the Royal Festival Hall, London, with the band we now know he liked so much: Kenny Garrett (alto saxophone), Bobby Irving and Adam Holzman (keyboards), Foley McCreary (guitar), Darryl Jones (bass guitar), Ricky Wellman (drums) and Mino Cinelu (percussion), an octet with Miles as the eighth member. He looked fit and well, his long hair (weave) down his neck, and he was wearing a white jacket sparkling with sequins and very loose silver/grey shiny trousers. His obviously young band were excellent but, as had been the case the previous year, he seemed a little lacking in energy, playing only in short bursts, and spending much time using the Harmon mute, the sound of which was sometimes swamped by the band. For several years, the band's sound and balance in concert had been excellent, with Miles always audible and the Harmon coming through full and clear, but for some reason, though the band sounded good on this occasion, the Harmon was sometimes barely audible. Also, Miles played none of those heart-searing high notes which disappeared through the roof. But none of this really mattered, because his open sound was as lustrous as ever, and he worked the band beautifully, creating such good feeling onstage, that the listeners felt they were witnessing a benign, even beatific event. It was clear that the audience adored him and were hanging on his every gesture and every note. He played in more sustained bursts towards the end of the concert, and then an extraordinary event happened. The band played a long encore – the marvellous rhapsodic ballad from *Tutu*, 'Portia', with its wonderfully sonorous harmonies. After a fairly long, lyrical solo from Miles, Kenny Garrett played superbly and, as he did so, members of the audience began leaving their seats and crowding round the stage, trying to touch Miles – just touch his clothes – and he walked along the front apron touching outstretched hands, a couple of minders following and keeping a watchful eye on him. It was an astonishing event, almost religious in its intensity – Miles in his white jacket like a priest, and all the outstretched hands of the supplicants. Even the beautiful final chords of 'Portia', which were repeated over and over again, sounded like a hymn. Miles walked off, waving to the audience. Then the rest of the band, in turn, played a little at the front of the stage, waved to the audience and walked off. The last one to go off was Bobby Irving, anchor man on the multiple keyboard stack, and he merely reprogrammed his synthesizer to carry on repeating the final cadences, then turned, waved to the audience and walked off. Shortly afterwards, a road manager came along and switched off the synthesizer – it needed a *deus ex orchestra* to end that amazingly beatific finale. It seemed like the apotheosis of Miles Davis, and one almost expected a heavenly chariot to descend and carry him off.

Four months later, on 27 October, Miles had a perhaps more mundane experience in Norway, which may well have pleased him as much or more. When he and the band disembarked from the plane in Oslo, someone came up to him and said, 'Excuse me, Mr Davis, but we have a car waiting for you over here. You don't have to go through customs.'[30] And sure enough, there was a long white stretch limousine that whisked him away from the airport sparing him the hassle of customs. The only other time he had had such preferential treatment at an international airport had been in 1983 in Warsaw. In Norway he was told that this kind of favoured treatment was meted out to visiting heads of state, presidents, prime ministers, kings and queens . . . and Miles Davis.

This so pleased him that he recalled, 'how could I help but play my ass off that night?'[31]

Around this time, Davis was becoming almost obsessively interested in the androgynous, multi-talented black pop star Prince, whom he rated very highly as an artist. The admiration was mutual – Prince had said that Miles was one of his heroes, and the knowledge of this may well have helped to fuel Davis's interest. He appreciated Prince's astonishing range of abilities – a superb multi-instrumentalist, a composer and singer who could also dance, produce music in the recording studio, act in films and produce and direct them. But Miles was also besotted with Prince's image and style, his elaborate high camp, gender-bending persona, which he had projected so successfully in his musical performances and videos, that he had become immensely rich. Miles noted Prince's black musical influences – James Brown, Marvin Gaye, Jimi Hendrix, Sly Stone, Little Richard – commenting: 'He's a mixture of all those guys and Duke Ellington.'[32] In that list, Ellington must be the odd man out, and his inclusion seems arbitrary and bizarre, unless the one thing they all have in common with Ellington is that Miles likes them and rates them highly. Davis also heard the influence of the black church in Prince's music, and made the cryptic comment: 'Prince *is* like the church to gay guys.'[33] But what Miles really liked about Prince's music was that it was rooted in the tradition, but new, freshly minted and absolutely of its time. As far as Prince's image is concerned, Miles says it all in one sentence: 'He's got that raunchy thing, almost like a pimp and a bitch all wrapped up in one image, that transvestite thing.'[34]

One thing Miles Davis never mentions in his reasonably honest and remorselessly outspoken autobiography is his own bisexuality. He is very frank about his brother Vernon's total homosexuality, recounting that the women in the family, his mother, sister and grandmother, always treated Vernon like a girl, and his sister Dorothy and her friends would bath Vernon, comb his hair and dress him up in girls' clothes, like a baby doll. Miles thought that this was at least part of the cause of his brother's homosexuality. Miles was older than Vernon and much nearer Dorothy in age, and so she could not play such games with him, and much of his childhood and adolescence was spent in opposition to and argument with his mother, because he resisted her influence. Of course, his bisexuality helps to explain a lot – particularly about his relationships with women, who must have had great difficulty in understanding the situation, and when when they did realize the truth, in coming to terms with it. But it also explains his extraordinary sensitivities and insights, his great intuition, and the wonderful Janus-like power of his music – its arresting strength and the immense subtlety of its more emotional resonances. He was, after all, a Gemini, and duality was part of his essence. Some of Miles's friends believe that some of the critical abuse he has received has been homophobic in origin and, indeed, much of it has been so arbitrary and irrational that that might well be the case. One reason Miles found Prince so fascinating was probably because he saw aspects of his own nature reflected in the younger man, and when, towards the end of 1987, Prince invited Miles to come over to his place in Minneapolis to see in the new year of 1988, and play some music together, the invitation was accepted with delight.

But first, Miles finished off the old year in fine style. Three months of solid touring with his group ended after their concert in Marseille, France, on 28 November. Miles himself remained very active in December, recording 'Oh Patti', with the rock group Scritti Politti, then with Larry Carlton, David Sanborn and Paul Shaffer, and others, he recorded a version of the Christmas carol 'We Three Kings of Orient Are', for the soundtrack of the film *Scrooged*. On 11 December, the same group, billing itself as Miles Davis with Paul Shaffer and the World's Most Dangerous Band, played 'We Three Kings' on the ABC-TV show, *Late Night with David Letterman*. On 20 December, aided and abetted by Foley McCreary, Miles hosted a two-hour video show, *New Visions Disk Jockey Show*, on VH1-TV, commenting on the artists between videos and talking about his sketching and band.[35] He had never, in his entire career, had so much media interest or such varied new work opportunities as in the last two years. He was looking forward to his visit to Prince's establishment to bring in the new year, and was probably wondering if that event would open up more new vistas in his life and work.

TWENTY-THREE

Amandla

'It's always been a gift with me hearing music the way
I do. I don't know where it comes from, it's just there
and I don't question it.'[1]

Miles Davis

Miles Davis and his guitarist, Foley McCreary, arrived at Prince's
Paisley Park Studios in Minneapolis, Wisconsin, on 31 December
1987, and were suitably impressed by its size and lavish facilities.
It covered half a block, and contained apartments to house visitors,
concert halls, and studios for sound recording and filming. At this
point in time, Prince was twenty-nine years old and perhaps the
only act to rival Bruce Springsteen in terms of sales, though in
terms of visual style and musical interest, he was perhaps more
influential than the white rock star. Born on 7 June 1958, to a
father who was a half-Italian black jazz pianist named Prince
Rogers, and a mother who was a singer, the precocious young
Prince taught himself piano, guitar and drums, and was soon
leading bands. While still a teenager, he was signed by Warner
Bros, and began to make a sensational impact with his bizarre
synthesis of religion and sex. At times, sex took over from God,
and his work became even more outrageous with the 1980 album
Dirty Mind, which included songs about oral sex and incest, while
his live performances found him in black lace underwear and
supported by a titillating female backing trio. However, his more
conventional commercial soul tracks had several big hits, and his
1984 album and film, *Purple Rain*, brought him superstardom.

Like him or loathe him, Prince was (and is) a true original, a one-off, a loner, much like Miles.

That New Year's Eve celebration at Prince's Paisley Park Studios took the form of a benefit concert for the homeless people of Minneapolis. People were charged $200 each to get into this hippest of hip parties, and the place was packed. At midnight, Prince sang 'Auld Lang Syne', and then invited Miles and Foley to go on stage and play something with his band, which they did for about four minutes, though the title of the piece is not specified. Miles was charmed by Prince, finding him 'very nice, a shy kind of person, a little genius, too . . . He gets over with everyone because he fulfills everyone's illusions.'[2] In other words, he panders to their fantasies. Davis was, however, astonished and intrigued when Prince suggested that they record an album together and do a joint tour with their groups, though neither project ultimately happened. In January 1988, Miles was interviewed for an English TV documentary about Prince entitled *Prince: Musical Portrait*, during which he commented on some of Prince's concert recordings. Miles's visit to Minneapolis had obviously pleased Prince, and in May the latter returned the compliment by coming to Davis's sixty-second birthday party, which was held at a restaurant in New York. About thirty guests were invited to dinner, including some members of Miles's band, plus Hugh Masekela, Marcus Miller, the rock group Cameo, Miles's lawyer and manager, Peter Shukat, and his road manager Gordon Meltzer.

By 1988, Miles Davis was probably more famous than he had ever been, due to his international and now national exposure on television, his relentless touring schedule, the energetic promotion of his record company, Warner Bros, and all the prestigious honours he was receiving, at first abroad, and now even in his own country. Also, the warm recognition he received from his audiences in the USA and abroad helped to dispel his shyness and make him far more outgoing in public. That is why he was confident enough to be far more visible and accessible at this time; he was not afraid of revealing himself. For years, Cicely Tyson had been urging him to write his autobiography, but he had always demurred, protesting that he could not discuss the women in his life. By 1988, however, his fame made an autobiography a financially feasible idea, and because he had timely things to say in reply to his critics and a desire to put the record straight, he decided to take on this massive task, but needed the assistance of a skilled writer. The leading American publishing firm, Simon & Schuster, were interested in the autobiography, and with this backing, Miles asked poet, journalist and university professor Quincy Troupe to collaborate with him on the project.

Troupe had been a Miles Davis fan since he was thirteen years old, when somebody had played him Davis's recording of "Round Midnight'. 'It just blew me out,' Troupe said, 'and went straight to my heart.'[3] Then in the 1960s, Troupe and a friend of his from St Louis walked into a bar in San Francisco and found Miles sitting there alone. The friend went up to Davis and said jovially, 'Miles Davis! How are you doing, man?' Miles turned and looked expressionlessly from one to the other, but the friend from St Louis was not intimidated and said, equally jovially, 'Hey, you black motherfucker! I'm a home-town boy and if you don't speak to me I'm gonna kick your ass.'[4] This broke the ice and they were asked to sit down and introduce themselves. Troupe met Miles again later in St Louis, and later still, after he had become a professor, and was contributing occasional essays about music to various periodicals, he was asked to write an article about Miles Davis. He contacted Columbia to try and arrange an interview, and by a stroke of good luck found himself talking to one of his ex-students, who was working for the company. She made an appointment for him to talk to Miles for one and a half hours the following day, and Troupe ended up spending ten hours with him, during which time they got to know each other well, and became friends. By the time he began collaborating with Davis, Troupe had won the 1980 American Book Award for poetry, published essays and articles in the *Village Voice*, *Newsday*, *Musician*, and many other publications. He was also the editor of *James Baldwin: The Legacy*, and a professor at the City University of New York, and at Columbia University. In January 1988, Miles began recording a whole series of in-depth interviews with Troupe, and this process continued at intervals throughout the year and into 1989.

In February 1988, Miles's concert tours began again, but this time with shorter 'legs', and frequent commuting back to the USA. This year he had no concert in the UK, but he broke new ground by playing Australia, New Zealand, Hawaii and Turkey, as well as his usual three visits to Europe, and his annual events in the USA and Canada. The previous year, percussionist Rudy Bird had replaced Mino Cinelu, and in April, Bird was himself replaced when Marilyn Mazur rejoined the band. The only other personnel change occurred when Miles fired bassist Darryl Jones, because his experiences with the rock star Sting had inflated his sense of the dramatic and made him a liability rather than an aid to Davis's musical purpose. The new bass guitarist, Benny Rietveld, was from Hawaii. Miles was riding high at this time – he liked his band very much, he was in demand, work was plentiful, his health seemed good and the future looked rosy. There was, however, one tiny shadow on the horizon because, although his trumpet sound retained its unique lustre and his phrases were as sculptured and cloquent as ever, there was a slight but perceptible decline in his physical strength and stamina. The awesome, incandescent power of his playing in 1983, 1984, and 1985, with its repeated ascents into the highest registers of the trumpet, was now very rarely in evidence.

Miles Davis and the world of jazz were given another shocking reminder of mortality when, on 20 March, Gil Evans died. His last illness had not been publicized, and so no one, except perhaps close relatives and Miles himself, had been prepared for Gil's possible demise. Also, Evans's contributions to music were so monumental, and he seemed such a permanent and benign fixture in the world, that his continuing presence was taken for granted. But he was, in fact, so other-worldly that he took little care of himself, either physically or financially, and in his last year of life had lost so much weight that he was wraith-like. The great irony was that, having spent much of his life in dire poverty, it was only in his final decade that he began to get the regular work and earning opportunities he had always so richly deserved. His seventy-fifth birthday was on 13 May 1987, and that was the busiest year of his entire life, with concert tours, writing assignments, and even personal appearances in advertisements. But by then his energy and health were beginning to fail, and he had mentioned to some people – but never to those closest to him – that he was tired and had had enough and wanted to die. In January 1988, at New York University Hospital, he had an operation for prostate cancer, and after it, to escape the bitter New York winter and recuperate, he went to the Mexican town of Cuernavaca, situated a few miles south of Mexico City. There Evans stayed in a place near tenor saxophonist Dexter Gordon, who was suffering from emphysema and had also gone there for the warmer climate, as had Charles Mingus, who died there in 1978. Gil Evans either forgot to take his medication (which included antibiotics) with him to Cuernavaca, or deliberately left it behind, but he did take some music with him in order to prepare for his next concert tour, which was to begin in May. After a visit to a healing hot springs establishment, however, he got an infection and died of peritonitis, and the shocked jazz world mourned his loss. His wife Anita and eldest son, Miles Evans, were determined to keep Gil's now well-established orchestra going, and the tour schedule, starting in May, was fulfilled.

Gil Evans was Miles Davis's closest and oldest friend, and their rapport was almost mystical because each was the other's alter-ego. There was an extraordinary affection and mutual trust between them and, musically, each had brought out the best in the other. Evans's wisdom and musical vision had often helped Miles in the development of his small-group music, and their three orchestral albums stand out like beacons in the music of the twentieth century. Two months before he died, Evans had telephoned Miles and said he was at last ready to do something they had discussed twenty years ago: an orchestral version of excerpts from Puccini's opera *Tosca*, with Miles as 'singer'. It was not something that currently interested Davis, but he might well have tried to do it for Gil's sake. The latter had said to this writer in 1975, 'Don't believe anything you read about Miles; he's a sweet guy.' Davis had helped Evans financially from time to time, and now he grieved for him and the fact that Gil had never had enough money for his own musical projects. Evans's music publisher, Eckart Rahn, had often expressed disgust at the way Gil was not valued in the USA, and had said that he would have been more cherished in a European country. Miles echoed these sentiments in his grief for Evans, saying, 'He should have lived in a place like Copenhagen where he would have been appreciated . . . To me Gil is not dead . . . All my best friends are dead. But I can hear them, I can put myself into their heads, into Gil's head.'[5]

Meanwhile, Miles's concert tours had begun again in February, continuing in April, May and through the summer months. On 29 June, at the Hit Factory, in New York, he overdubbed trumpet and additional vocal on a Chaka Khan track, 'Sticky Wicked', for which Prince had created all the music except for the saxophone, trumpet and vocal parts. Chaka Khan was, of course, the main vocalist, and the session musicians were trumpeter Atlanta Bliss and saxophonist Eric Leeds. That day, Miles was the only trumpeter on a second Khan track, 'I'll Be Around', arranged by Dave Grusin for a group including harp, synthesizer, guitar, drums and Marcus Miller on electric bass.[6]

By now, he had become far more deeply interested in painting, and in his leisure time at home in Malibu, or his apartment in New York, each day would often be divided between painting for five hours or more, practising the trumpet for two hours, and writing and thinking about music. Many musicians of all persuasions had taken up painting in later life as a creative hobby. Composer Arnold Schoenberg, creator of twelve-tone serialism, began painting during his latter years in the USA, and his visual work was much more conventional than his music. George Gershwin also became a talented representational painter, and the maverick jazz clarinettist, Pee Wee Russell, and mainstream drummer, George Wettling, both took up abstract painting, while the great French drummer, Daniel Humair, has been so successful as a painter in recent years that he could easily have relied on that skill alone to earn a comfortable living. The fine jazz guitarist and composer, Volker Kriegel, who is also one of Germany's leading cartoonists and book illustrators, remarked: 'If Picasso had played an instrument as well as Miles Davis paints, he would have recorded an album.' Miles's own paintings were now becoming known nationally and internationally. The previous year he had had two one-man exhibitions in New York, and in this current year 1988, he had several international shows, one in Madrid, two in Japan and some in Germany, one of which, an exhibition of thirty oils and pen-and-ink drawings, opened on Sunday, 10 July at the Mosel and Tschechow Gallery in Munich, to coincide with his concert in that city. The exhibition ran until 12 August, the prices ranged from $750 to $15,000 and the show almost sold out. Miles attended the opening of this exhibition and was filmed and interviewed there for ZDF (South German) TV.

Trombonist Mike Zwerin, one-time Birth of the Cool sideman and now jazz correspondent for the *International Herald Tribune*, interviewed Miles early in July, in New York, about his coming exhibition in Munich and his painting, and described the following scene:

> After looking at colour photographs of more than 100 of his works – signed 'Miles' – and seeing the pile of canvases in various stages of completion spread over the floor of his Central Park South apartment, it is obvious that this is no mere 'celebrity' painter. But there is also an electric piano in a corner, a synthesizer in another, a trumpet on an easy chair, cassettes piled against a wall and the latest Prince record playing on a professional sound reproduction setup.[7]

Zwerin found Miles in relaxed and expansive mood, and when a visitor quoted one of Davis's own statements, that musical training is important in helping to find what rules to break, and asked if that holds true for painting, Miles replied:

The first piano music Art Tatum heard was two boogie-woogie piano players on a cylinder. He didn't know there were two of them. He thought that's the way a piano should sound and he learned how to play like two piano players at the same time. Some guys don't have to know about theory because they have something you can't learn in a book.[8]

This idea of education's potential for undermining or warping natural artistic gifts was a recurring theme with Miles, and on another occasion, he said:

A guy like Jimi Hendrix or Sly [Stone] or Prince, might not do what they have done if they had known all the rest of that technical stuff, because it might have gotten in their way, and they might have done something else [i.e. less original and less powerful] had they known all that other stuff.[9]

Zwerin asked Miles if he approached painting on a canvas like creating a musical composition, with some form in mind:

The color. I get the color first. Then all the rest I improvise. Lines and circles. Maybe I'll want to wiggle the lines, maybe I'll draw a breast and an eye. I work from the subconscious, like music. It has to do something to me. I couldn't write a piece of music that doesn't make me tap my foot or make me feel something inside. Once the form is there, it's like an arrangement with openings for solos. It's a matter of balance. You can't have too much black, black is heavy. Like you can't have too much saxophone. Supposing there's a composition and the saxophone player can't get the style. You have to get another guy to fit in there. Like another color. Don't force it.[10]

Zwerin also discovered that Miles now employed his own art tutor, assistant and adviser, Michael Elam, a young painter who had graduated from New York University, and kept Miles informed about art history and painting techniques. Elam also travelled on tour with Miles, who explained:

> Michael and I go to see what the young artists in a town are up to. We bought some beautiful paintings from a Moroccan in Tours, in France. I think his name was Jamal. I like Europe. The music sounds better in Europe. I say, 'Michael, we'll spend $5,000. Let's go out and buy some paintings.'[11]

Finally, Zwerin asked Miles if musicians start to paint because music no longer satisfies them: 'It doesn't have anything to do with that,' Davis said.

> There's always music in my head. I hear music walking down the street. I hear it talking to you, now. Look, some of these people paint flowers and desks. They copy things. I can't copy, it always ends up being something else. And once I start painting, I can't stop. I have to *make* myself stop a week before a concert or I'd never pick up the trumpet and practise. When I don't paint, I get nervous. But they both turn me on. Why should I have to choose?[12]

But Miles's comment about not being able to copy and how when he tries to do so it always ends up being something else, also brings to mind one of Maurice Ravel's statements: 'When I copy, I innovate.' But this is not to over-estimate the importance of Davis's painting; it has far more subjective importance for Miles than any objective significance. Like his music-making, which was absolutely central to his life, the act of painting was necessary for his health, but an auxiliary occupation that kept him in shape for his main purpose. The *process* of painting was a crucial factor in his life, and it was unnecessary to make great claims for the *product* of his efforts. His paintings are semi-abstract and vividly coloured views of the highly stylized human form and face, interiors, still lifes, sometimes spare and linear, often in denser collage effects. But his best efforts do have a kind of coherence –

a harmony of colour and line – that often projects joyful vitality.

Mike Zwerin asked Larry Rivers, one of America's most amiable and successful pop artists, what he thought of Miles's work. Rivers is also a saxophonist who attended the Juilliard School at the same time as Davis in the 1940s, and still plays regularly. Rivers commented:

> I keep wondering what I would think of the paintings if I didn't know who painted them. They're certainly not bad, they're not ugly. I just have trouble relating to them. When I hear Miles's records, I *see* him. I don't see him in his paintings. This may be a fault or a virtue. But I wonder if I'm only looking at them because they're by Miles.[13]

But there is no need for Rivers or anyone else to agonize over that problem. People notice and buy the paintings because they're by Miles Davis, and this does not mean that they are otherwise worthless. His paintings are often very attractive and are liked by the people who buy them. His Madrid exhibition in 1988 sold out completely, and the various shows in Germany and Japan sold many of his works. People are fascinated by very great artists – musicians, writers, painters – partly because that process of creation is so mysterious, but also because such artists touch on so many aspects of the human condition that strike chords in the hearts of their audiences. That is precisely what Miles Davis has done throughout his long artistic life, and his processes of creation in music are so mysterious that musicians who have worked with him often spend years trying to understand what their daily experience with him meant and why, in his company, they played differently. He was loved not only by musicians, but also by audiences all over the world, who took him to their hearts because his music had touched them. People often want to know everything possible about artists who so move them, and to acquire something of theirs – a letter or a painting – is to own something personal and precious.

Miles was surprised by the success of his painting, and

murmured to himself, 'Just doing this, could I make a living? Maybe so ... Fortunately, I have something to fall back on. I make enough royalties so that I'll be ninety-five before I spend all the money and wear all my clothes.'[14] There would be many more exhibitions and successful sales of his art work, but Miles had absolutely no illusions about his painting talent, and said to Lydia DeJohnette: 'They call me an artist, but I'm not an artist. But that's what they want to call me.'

After playing Munich and attending the opening of his exhibition there, Miles played several other concerts in Europe, concluding that leg of his tour with three in France on 13, 14 and 16 July. He then played a concert in Turkey on the twentieth, and two concerts in Japan on 31 July and 7 August. Back in the USA, he played the University of California at Berkeley, on 13 August; this was a superlative concert. The audience's excitement seemed barely contained and when Miles and his musicians went on stage there was a wild eruption of shouts and whistles. The band was now a magnificent unit, playing with great intensity and flexibility, sustaining ecstatic grooves, whether urgently loud or quietly insistent, for long periods. Miles, in good health and spirits, was on dynamic form, his Harmon sound and open horn as glowing as ever and his 'chops' in great shape. The opener was a raunchy, unstoppable version of 'Perfect Way', with Miles using Harmon mute and then open trumpet all the way. In the second piece, the sparse, slow blues, 'Star People', his first muted notes drew cries of recognition from the audience, and after his solo, Foley played a powerfully bluesy guitar solo that spoke volumes and also inflamed the crowd. 'Human Nature' was a kind of resting point, because muted Miles allowed the quiet theme, which he played, and the sonorous arrangement with its catchy synthesizer arpeggiated riffs, to speak for themselves. It was only when the piece had been fully played that the final chords were continually repeated for first, Miles's solo, followed by a long, brilliantly paced alto saxophone solo by Kenny Garrett. After that, the first few notes of 'Tutu' got a storm of audience applause. Then 'Time After Time', hymn-like, with its quiet organ chords and Miles preaching soulfully first muted, then open, drew occasional ecstatic responses from the audience. The whole occasion revealed the tremendous amount of thought and experience that lay behind Miles Davis's concert programmes. The familiar, and the new or fresh, were juxtaposed all the time, and the music was based always on clear rhythms beautifully performed. There was never a string of solos, but either one soloist (Miles), or at most two on any one piece. The melodies and harmonies also had great clarity and soloists and other members of the group would restate or refer back to the thematic material. The backgrounds would change subtly behind soloists, and often a solo might be punctuated by written passages. In these ways the attention of the audience was continually drawn in several directions, and the clarity and beauty of the contemporary rhythms drew in the listeners, who could virtually inhabit the musical continuum, and so feel like conspirators in the act of music-making. The pace and intensity of the concert were varied constantly by juxtaposing contrasting pieces, and the audience seemed to hang on every note and phrase.

After another concert in California on 22 August and one in New York on the twenty-seventh, Miles had the whole of September off. On 17 October, he was back on tour in Europe, this time with organist (and trumpet player) Joey DeFrancesco on synthesizer, replacing Bobby Irving III, who had left the band. After concerts in Denmark, Norway, Belgium, Poland, Austria and West Germany, he went to Spain to play a concert on 15 November in Madrid. He arrived early in the country, because two days before his concert, he personally had to go to Granada in southern Spain to receive a very prestigious award – to be dubbed a Knight of Malta. The full title of the Order of St John is 'Knights Hospitallers of St John of Jerusalem', the oldest order of Christian chivalry, named after the hospital at Jerusalem founded about 1048 by merchants of Amalfi for pilgrims, whose travel routes the knights defended from the Muslims. The Knights of St John of Jerusalem were a military religious order founded about the time of the first crusade (1096–9) by European crusaders. There are about 8,000 knights (male and female), and the Grand Master is the world's highest-ranking Roman Catholic lay person. When the knights were forced out of Palestine, they went to Cyprus in 1291, then to Rhodes in 1309, until Emperor Charles V granted Malta to them in 1530; they governed it until 1798, when Napoleon conquered it and expelled them. Since then their headquarters have been at Palazzo di Malta, in Rome. On 13 November, at Alhambra Palace, Granada, Miles Davis, along with three African doctors and a Portuguese doctor, was inducted into what he describes as 'The Knights of the Grand Cross in and for the Sovereign Military Hospitaller Order of St John of Jerusalem, of Rhodes, and of Malta'. It was another welcome international recognition of the sustained quality of his work and his benign influence on music and musicians. He was honoured and pleased by it, but his health was beginning to fail again and he had barely enough strength to make it through the ceremony.

His own account of the course of this illness is very unclear, but piecing together the known facts, it seems that the full power of the malady, bronchial pneumonia, did not immediately hit him, because he was able to play the concert in Madrid two days later. Exhaustion may have been the cause of this relapse. Only a month previously, the great Danish bassist, Bo Stief, recalling his time working with Miles and Palle Mikkelborg on the *Aura* music, had insisted that Davis was a workaholic who drove himself on relentlessly, and in an interview a few months later Miles described a visit to his Chinese doctor around this time: 'He takes my arm like this' (gripping the wrist to feel the pulse), 'and he say, "How long you play?" I say two and a half hours. He shakes his head and says, "You [will] have heart attack!" '[15] After the Madrid concert on 15 November he returned to the USA and did no further concerts until 17 and 18 December, both of which were played at Indigo Blues in New York. Each night was a double concert and so Miles must have played at least two and a half hours and perhaps even longer on each occasion. As if that were not enough, he spent the last days of December, and the early days of January 1989, recording the music for his next album, *Amandla*, followed by some recordings for Quincy Jones's album,

Back on the Block. During the sessions, Miles gave an interview on film for a Time Warner video entitled *Listen Up: The Lives of Quincy Jones*. It must have been after this final heavy spate of work that Miles fell victim to the full power of bronchial pneumonia, because he collapsed, spent three weeks in hospital in Santa Monica, California, with 'tubes up my nose and in my arms, needles everywhere. Anyone who came into my room had to wear a mask because there was a danger I could be infected by germs brought in by visitors or even by doctors or nurses.'[16] It was this illness which gave rise to the rumour that he had AIDS, and the baseless nature of this imputation made him very angry.

The illness forced Miles to cancel his early 1989 tour, which, he said, cost him over a million dollars. But he was so weak that when, in March, he went home to Malibu to recuperate, his sister Dorothy, brother Vernon and nephew Vincent all came to take care of him. The rift between Miles and Dorothy over his sacking of Vincent from his band was healed in this way, and family solidarity established once more. Dorothy did the cooking, Miles began taking fresh air and exercise, and slowly his health returned. In late March he rehearsed his band for three days in a New York studio, because there were some personnel changes. Marilyn Mazur had left and was replaced by percussionist Monyungo Jackson, Japanese keyboardist Kei Akagi was the new and permanent replacement for Bobby Irving and, because Adam Holzman was temporarily unavailable, John Beasly took over his synthesizer duties. The nucleus of the band was unchanged – Kenny Garrett, Foley McCreary, Benny Rietveld and Ricky Wellman. Miles was well again, although not yet at full strength, but wanted to commence touring as soon as possible, and a European mini-tour starting on 9 April was, probably hastily, put together. This comprised two concerts in Italy, one in France and three in British provincial cities.

The British concerts showed that Miles had definitely not regained his strength after the serious illness. In the 1950s and 1960s, he had often wandered off stage when his band was playing, largely because he knew that when he was in view, people tended to watch him rather than whoever else was soloing. But after he came back to music in the 1980s, he was always on stage, either playing a solo, or his keyboards, or actively directing his band; he might walk all over the stage, but he rarely walked off. But during his two concerts at the Apollo Theatre, Manchester, on 18 and 19 April, he played much less than usual and went off stage for quite long periods, leaving his band to take care of itself, and when the concerts were over, he disappeared so quickly that the audience were still applauding when he was getting into the car that was to take him back to his hotel. His lack of energy seemed to be giving the audiences a glimpse of the old enigmatic, unpredictable Miles, but in this case it was certainly not wilful, but simply a matter of survival. He and the band played St David's Hall, Cardiff, in Wales on 21 April, in a similarly lacklustre manner. This concert was reviewed in the British magazine *Wire*, by Philip Watson, who praised Kenny Garrett: 'An intelligent and resourceful improviser, he won through a duet with Miles on "Human Nature", by shaping simple, staccato off-beats into a counterpoint of great effect, graduating slowly into an alto solo of sinewy toughness and Sanborn-like rasps.'[17] But Watson also pointed out that Miles played little, seemed much below par, disappeared from the stage for twenty minutes in the middle of the performance, and left the stage never to return twenty minutes before the end. Watson concludes, 'Perhaps the great man is just very ill,'[18] which was very near the truth.

At this very time, when Miles was at a low ebb, he learned during his two days in Manchester that yet another extraordinary honour was about to be given him. In the Swiss city of Zurich there are the offices of a unique magazine entitled *du*, with the explanatory heading, *Die zeitschrift der Kultur*. This is an up-market, highly intellectual monthly magazine dealing with all forms of culture, which first appeared in the late 1960s. It is usually all in German, but sometimes includes other languages, including English and French, and each issue has only one theme or subject, which is explored in detail and depth. In September 1988, for example, issue 9 was entirely devoted to the Colombian author,

Gabriel García Márquez, and in April 1989, the theme of issue 4 was 'Speed' with some consideration of its opposite 'Slowness'. Now, *du* magazine wanted to break new ground by having its entire August issue devoted, for the first time, to a jazz musician: Miles Davis. There were four assistant editors on the magazine, and one of them, Marco Meier, was assigned to the Miles Davis issue. Meier was thirty-four years old, tall and slim, with a thatch of dark hair falling on to his forehead, dark eyes, a thin aquiline nose, a lean jawline, and an honours degree in philosophy. He seemed to be the very epitome of the cultured European intellectual and was extremely knowledgeable about Miles Davis. He found out that Miles would be playing at Manchester in April and went there to try and discuss the project with him. He first approached Miles's road manager, Gordon Meltzer, and showed him an issue of *du*, but Meltzer simply looked at it blankly. Meier, however, managed to smuggle the issue and a note to Miles, who immediately recognized the magazine's quality, and invited Meier to his hotel room. Meier was impressed by Miles's instant appraisal of the magazine, and Davis, at his most courteous and friendly, agreed to co-operate in the project and signed an agreement saying that he would definitely do some drawings for the August issue. In May, Meier flew to the USA with photographer Ralph Quinke and visited Miles in his Malibu beach house, spending three hours with him. He had done many drawings for the August issue of *du*, and he got on so well with Meier that he invited the latter to his sixty-third birthday party the following day. There had been about thirty people at the party, with Quincy Jones and Lionel Richie among the guests. Marco Meier returned to Switzerland well pleased with Miles Davis's enthusiasm for the project.

During the visit to Miles, Ralph Quinke had taken several rolls of film of him inside and outside his house and of scenes at his birthday party, and many of these illustrated a long article by Meier that formed the centrepiece of the magnificent August issue of *du*. The front cover bore a huge close-up of one of the face-and-fingers photographs of Miles from the *Tutu* period, with the caption, 'In a Silent Way. Miles Davis'. Inside there were lavish photographs of Miles, his associates from all eras, his LP covers, and of one or two of his drawings and one of his colourful abstract paintings. There were also many articles by leading European and American jazz writers covering most aspects of his career. The whole production was a graceful and potent testimony to the stature of this remarkable man, who had kept his music alive for so many decades.

Miles played no concerts in that month of May, which was a period of relaxation and fuller recuperation for him. Near the beginning of the month, he gave another interview for his autobiography to Quincy Troupe, and parts of it were broadcast in America Public Radio's (APR) *The Miles Davis Radio Project*. A couple of days later, there was a public discussion by Davis and Troupe at a lecture at the Studio of Harlem, New York, also broadcast in the APR series.[19] Two or three days before Marco Meier's visit in Malibu, Miles's new album, *Amandla*, had been released, and three days after Meier left, British journalist Charles Shaar Murray arrived there to interview Miles, and found him painting with the help of a collaborator, an artist called Jo Gelbard. Miles had first met her in 1986, but they had only recently started collaborating. Recalling their first meeting, Gelbard said:

I was a sculptor at the time and he was painting, and we just started exchanging ideas. He was really getting interested in becoming a better artist and he wasn't sure how to go about it. I think the most important thing I said to him at the time was, 'You can't be an artist if you're afraid of getting dirty.' He used to wear his fancy clothes when he was working. He took that to heart. He loosened up and got sloppier and he realized it was just something you had to really commit yourself to and get into or not. He got freer.[20]

By now, the general price of Miles's canvases had risen, and ranged from $10,000 to $15,000, and Murray was told that Quincy Jones had just bought ten of them, which caused a problem for Miles: 'Lionel Richie was over last night,' he explained, 'and I had a big one like this, only yellow, which I'd promised to Lionel, only Quincy just bought it. So now I got to get it back.'[21]

Again, musing on the subject of painting seemed to make Davis expansive and communicative, with exposition and reminiscence frequently dovetailing:

Music and art? They're one and the same. It's about *composition*. If you can do this you can do *anything*. You just have to know when to start and stop or when to move on to something else. You have to have that instinct. Seems like if you finish somethin', then everybody else knows it's finished. In other words, *you're* no secret to *me*. What we do today, we don't have to do tomorrow. We don't even *think* about tomorrow. I was tellin' somebody that the other day; they say that's *existentialism*. I say, well, they probably copied that off of me. You know I used to go with Juliette Greco? Well in '49 we used to go to a place together with Boris Vian and Jean-Paul Sartre. I couldn't speak French so I didn't know what they were sayin', but we were like *that* together. Can you imagine, someone knockin' on your door that you love and you're in a different country? ... She has different expressions on her face than an American woman; she had the prettiest mouth ... and nose. But the next time I saw her, she'd had her nose cut off. She told me: 'You might not recognize me the next time you see me.' She called me up when she was in New York City. I say: 'Why?' She say: 'I had my nose cut off.' I say: 'Why?' She say: 'Darryl F. Zanuck told me it'd look better when I photograph.' Juliette was the prettiest woman I'd ever seen – since my mother – but when she cut off her nose, her beauty just stopped. *How* can a man tell a woman she's got to have her nose cut off? It's about *going where you want to go* in show business.[22]

Marco Meier's visit may well have triggered this memory of Miles's Parisian experiences in 1949. The August issue of *du* included an account of Miles in Paris, by Noel Simsolo, and illustrated it with a rare photograph from that year, of bassist Tommy Potter, Boris Vian, Kenny Dorham, Juliette Greco, Miles, Michèle Vian (Boris's wife) and Charlie Parker all sitting on chairs and a sofa in someone's house. Vian's May 1949 article on Miles Davis was also republished in the August *du* issue in French. Boris Vian was a mainstream trumpet player, and also a creative writer whose perhaps most famous book, *L'Ecume des Jours*, was a comic fantasy that also poked fun at his friend Jean-Paul Sartre. It was translated into English under the title *Froth on the Daydream*. Vian died of a heart attack in 1959, at the age of thirty-nine, while watching the preview of a film version of one of his novels. Vian's 1949 essay begins with Gallic flights of fancy:

> An examination of his photograph [i.e. of Miles] suggests the conclusion that with this well balanced person the imagination leans a little towards sensuality, which is almost perfectly balanced by intelligence; and I don't know if we should believe all the photographs, but there is one in which he clearly has the ears of a faun, which is good.

But he also has perceptive things to say about Miles's playing, and cites the latter's 1945 solo on 'Now's the Time' as one of the great moments of behop.

During the interview with Charles Shaar Murray, Davis talked about his health, saying that, because of his hip replacements, he couldn't drive his Ferrari for a long time, but he recently went back to New York to see his doctor for a check-up, and was told he could drive again. Back home he called the doctor to ask if he could also ride horses again, and was given the affirmative. He kept some horses in a nearby stable, and when recuperating in March he had gone out riding as well as taking long walks. Also during the interview, Miles's new album was discussed, and he said: '*Amandla*, that means freedom. That's all I can do, to say "freedom" for Africa, for South Africa. *Tutu* was to say, "we know what you people are goin' through", this is to say we know what they got to do now.'[23] *Siesta* had been dedicated to Gil

Evans and now *Amandla* was dedicated to his memory, so it was inevitable that his name would come up in the conversation, and Miles told Murray:

> He was touring in Europe a few years ago, and on Friday all the arrangements for the band were stolen. You know what that means? *Every* part for *every* musician in *every* tune. And you know what Gil did? He locked himself up in a hotel bedroom, and he wrote them all out again. His eyes were poor too; he had to do it like this. [He mimes holding up a piece of paper to his eyes and scribbling on it.] He worked through the weekend, and on Monday they played. That's the kind of guy he was ... But Gil is with me. He's in my mind. I can tune in on him and I know just what he'd say.[24]

It was *Amandla* that initiated the ongoing collaboration of Miles and Jo Gelbard. He said of her:

> I think she's a great artist, I really do. The colours she gets together ... I call 'em crumbs. They just make you want to lick them all over. She gets together so many different colours – blue, black, beige, orange, red, and white. Jo did my portrait for the cover of Amandla ... but I did the little shit that goes with it, the crumbs around the face.[25]

Gelbard commented: 'We seriously started working together when I did the album cover for *Amandla*. That's when we actually started doing whole paintings together, beginning to end. The painting that's on the cover is supposed to look like wood, and then we got the idea [for other paintings] of really using wood.' The portrait of Davis's head on the album cover is a good likeness, but gives him a whiter shade of pale than even Michael Jackson. Miles's own 'crumbs' surrounding the head are colourful and nicely balanced structurally and tonally. A blue and red impression of a trumpet bell seems to abstract itself down left from Miles's invisible neck, and a globe in the lower right corner is a counterbalance to his head, and bears on it an abstract impression of the continent of Africa. The title *Amandla* is handwritten in irregular black capitals, graffito-style, aslant the top of Miles's colourful picture 'frame'.

Amandla was another successful collaboration with Marcus Miller, but this time with a few fundamental changes. Miles is, of course, the star of the album, but Kenny Garrett also has a star part, playing solos and/or dialoguing with Davis on seven out of the eight tracks. Guitarist Foley and drummer Ricky Wellman, from Miles's current band, also play on one or two tracks, but the rest of the personnels include various session musicians, and some old associates such as Al Foster, George Duke and Joey DeFrancesco. The rhythms of the *Amandla* music were another new development. Marcus Miller explained:

> Coincidentally, I had been working with a band called EU from D.C. I wrote a song for them called 'Da Butt', and EU turned me on to go-go rhythms. At the same time, Miles had hired Ricky Wellman, who was the teacher of a lot of the young drummers in the D.C. go-go scene, so it seemed like a natural way to go. Go-go has got a swing to it, and I thought it would be interesting for Miles to superimpose some of the swing phrasing from his earlier days over this beat. The sound is a little like a throwback, yet completely new.[26]

Miles, talking about the gradual way he and his music changed, told Peter Watrous that he liked the new rhythm and commented:

> Last year was go-go music. Now people have added something to it. Those that didn't hear it last year have to listen twice. I love the beat; we got it on the new record. Go-go is like Max [Roach] used to play, the beat swings. I can tell you where it came from. Years ago when Art Blakey and Max and Kenny Clarke, Kenny Klook-a-mop we called him [Davis starts singing rhythms] Salt Peanuts, salt peanuts. See? That's the same thing.[27]

The go-go rhythm has a kind of skipping/shuffle feel that is very catchy, and there are several subtly different varieties of it on the album. Miles uses Harmon mute for the first seven pieces, but on the eighth and last track, 'Mr Pastorius', Marcus Miller's composition in memory of the star bassist who had died in 1987, Miles plays open trumpet all the way with a wonderfully compassionate, non-brassy, 'singing' sound. The piece begins and ends as a ballad, but after the haunting theme statement by Miles, the tempo doubles for his long, loping and lamenting solo. 'Mr Pastorius' was created by just three people: Miles, Marcus Miller (who played synthesizers, bass guitar and bass clarinet), and drummer Al Foster. The memory of Gil Evans is also in Miller's harmonies, textures and colours, and in the burnished lyricism of Miles's phrases. At the end, he plays, unaccompanied, a couple of little ascending trumpet flurries, like a sort of afterthought, or P.S., as if he sensed that he had left many things unsaid in his so eloquent solo.

Marcus Miller composed and arranged six of the eight tracks on *Amandla*, and of the two remaining ones, George Duke composed and arranged 'Cobra', and another of Miles's discoveries, a twenty-three-year-old-black guitarist, John Bigham, composed 'Jilli', which Miller helped him to arrange. The music on *Amandla* begins well with 'Catembe', which has an African flavour to its go-go, and excellent soloing by Miles and Kenny Garrett. Yet the music seems to get even stronger as the album progesses. 'Cobra' is a medium-paced laid-back affair, with an inspired Miles/Garrett dialogue all the way. 'Big Time' has a buoyant, dancey-dancey feel, with strong solos from Miles and Garrett, and a fine bluesy outing by Foley. 'Hannibal' is slow and spare, with a melancholy theme stated by Miles, after which the rhythm becomes jauntier, while Miles plays a sparse, lamenting solo. This fire-and-ice juxtaposition conjures up a similar contrast during Miles's solo on the original 1958 version of 'Milestones'. The title track is magnificently sonorous, with Miles and Garrett really stretching out and soaring, and 'Jilli' has a marvellous rhythmic lift that inspires dancing, and funky phrases from trumpet and alto. The composed music and the improvised music in *Amandla* is immensely pleasing and satisfying because the sense of song and dance is never far way, and this is true of nearly all Miles Davis's music throughout his long and immensely productive career. It was also true of Ellington's music. It is only in the twentieth century that 'dance music' has become a term of abuse, usually in rarefied and ignorant cultural circles. In 1934, Ezra Pound wrote: 'Music begins to atrophy when it gets too far from the dance; poetry begins to atrophy when it gets too far from music.'[28] An English university teacher of composition once said dismissively to a jazz musician, 'Jazz is just a kind of dance music, isn't it?' The musician replied with Johnsonian common sense, 'All music is a kind of dance music, it just depends on what music and what dance.' Yet this received snobbery has percolated into the jazz world. When Miles Davis was interviewed by Peter Watrous in 1989 for *Musician*, Watrous suggested Miles's music had become 'more pop' because it was closer to dance music.

Miles countered with the question: 'For who? All people? Chinese people? Japanese people?'

Watrous replied: 'We're talking about American people. If you play "Kind of Blue" or "'Round Midnight", that's not dance music.'

Miles said: 'It was then' (when he recorded it).

Watrous asked: 'People were dancing in the Blackhawk or at the Vanguard?'

'Not in the Blackhawk, not the Vanguard. But Art Blakey, Kenny Clarke and I would play the Audubon Ballroom and people would dance ... Anyway, I don't think if something is popular it's bad.'

Watrous persisted: 'But people say that, right?'

And that gave Davis the opportunity to show some not uncritical magnanimity towards Wynton Marsalis:

The only person I ever hear say that is Wynton Marsalis, and he doesn't think like that unless he's being interviewed. He wants to be an innovator, and he is, but he doesn't talk like

that. Wynton plays perfect, like Fats and Brownie, he's a hell
of a trumpet player. We're not talking about his mouth,
his vocal cords, we're talking about his musicianship; he's a
motherfucker. Maybe he has to talk to let off steam. I know
some crazy bitches that made the best love . . . You look at
Wynton's mouth. Wynton is a perfect trumpet player. It's just
what he says . . . you have to let people think for themselves a
little bit.[29]

In June, Miles began touring again, playing four concerts and
one TV show in the USA, and starting the second leg of his European tour on 5 July. On 8 June, he was again honoured, this time
in his own country, when, in a ceremony at the Metropolitan
Museum of Art in New York City, the Governor of New York
State, Mario Cuomo, presented him with the 1989 New York
State Governor's Arts Award. Some other people and some organizations were honoured in the same ceremony. Miles was again
proud and pleased; it at least represented more general recognition
at home for his contributions to music. It also pleased him that
Amandla was getting good reviews and sales, and that his old
record company, Columbia, had announced that they were releasing *Aura* in September. Miles said of it: 'I think it's a masterpiece,
I really do.'[30] His divorce from Cicely was also completed in 1989,
another weight off his mind. The negotiations and the property
settlement had not been friendly.

Adam Holzman had returned to Miles's band in June, and the
latter was pleased with the new keyboardist, Kei Akagi, and
recalled:

I just sent out a notice that I was looking for a piano player.
His name came up. He's a hell of a musician. He's so funny.
He never did say anything. I just told him to learn the parts.
I walked up to him one night and said, 'Kei, is there anything
we play that you'd really like to play on?' He's quiet, you
know. The next day he came into rehearsal and said, 'I'd like
to play "Tutu".' He's so good, he just set a whole 'nother

groove. The groove is him. So I ask him again, 'Is there anything else you want to do?' He says, '"Wrinkles".' I know that still waters run deep because I was quiet like that.[31]

Kenny Garrett, however, was not available for the European tour, which stretched from 5 to 21 July, so Miles brought in a young tenor saxophonist, Rick Margitza, who had played in one of the pieces on *Amandla*. During the tour, they played two concerts in England, one in Birmingham on 10 July, and two houses at London's Royal Festival Hall on the eleventh. I saw the first concert from the wings backstage, and the second one from the audience. Here are a few notes I made at the time:

It was a hot summer's day and evening, perfect for a Miles concert. However, he was not in perfect health, and had been taking cod liver oil for his rheumatism, but he'd not taken any for a week and already had some pain in his wrists and shoulders. Also, he complained in the interval between the two concerts that his lips were dry, which was why he was drinking so much water on stage, and why he was cracking so many high notes. But the music was superb tonight – lovely sound colours, dynamics and beautifully organized rhythms. The music was pure Miles, unlike anyone or anything else in music anywhere today.

Also, there was a new aesthetic afoot; the music consists of short solo passages alternating with short composed passages, and a continuing dialogue in the band – all the soloists taking it in turn to converse and/or duet with Miles. The last time I heard Miles with a really strong embouchure was in 1985, when he was on stage for about four and a half hours and played extensively. Tonight, the first concert lasted one hour and the second one for two and a quarter hours.

It was disquieting to learn that Miles's old problem of bursitis in the wrists and shoulders had recurred, and also that the dryness of his lips, presumably still caused by the pills he was taking for

diabetes, was persisting. During his May interview with Charles
Shaar Murray, the latter had commented: 'He treats his frailty as
no more than an irritant.'[32] But these persistant irritants,
undermining his ability to play the trumpet, must have been very
wearing for him. Years later, however, I was given a privately
recorded cassette of his concert in Montreux on 21 July 1989,
with the same band, only ten days after those London concerts,
and Miles was in magnificent form. He featured a lot of open
trumpet, a sure sign he was in good shape, and his muted work
was also powerfully eloquent. The set pieces from the recorded
collaborations with Marcus Miller were opened up and given new
life with solos and all manner of rhythmic, textural and structural
variations. Miles in mid-concert, when he might have been feeling
the strain, played on open trumpet the finely poised, elegiac theme
of 'Mr Pastorius', with its exposed high notes, and after a brief
solo, gave free rein to Kei Akagi's fluent lyrical acoustic-(sounding)
piano solo. The Montreux audience, too, were vociferously and
conspiratorially involved with the music, and a light-hearted bit
of drama occurred when the band performed 'Human Nature'.
After the theme and some solos, the singer Chaka Khan, a good
friend of Miles's, came on stage, sang the lyrics, and proceeded
to swap phrases with Miles's muted trumpet. At one point, he
quoted two or three times the opening phrase of Ella Fitzgerald's
1938 hit with the Chick Webb band, 'A-Tisket A-Tasket', and
Chaka Khan replied by singing it raunchily; this good-humoured
dialogue delighted the audience. The whole concert seemed to
abound in ecstatic rhythms and dynamic solos all round.

After Montreux, Miles went back to the USA, and didn't resume
playing concerts until 24 August, when he had an engagement in
Hawaii, and Kenny Garrett had returned to the band. Garrett's
contribution to the band was important to Miles Davis, because
the saxophonist was one of the most gifted of the current younger
generation of players. He had his own alto saxophone sound, and
had avoided the angular saxophone-exercise kind of phrases that
were everywhere apparent. Instead, his passionate solos seemed
more blues-based and melodic, with a dramatic deployment of

space and timbre. Garrett was profoundly aware of the musical experience and arcane jazz lore to be gleaned from Miles, and told Howard Mandel:

Being with him was a great experience: first of all, I got to hear Miles Davis every day for five years – every day, good or bad, and some days he was just killin'. People would say to me, 'We know you can play – why are you still with Miles?' And I'd say, 'I'm just a sponge.' I'd stay as long as I could and soak up as much music as I could from him. And when he passed away, it was time to move on. But I felt that through Miles I could pick up some Sonny Rollins, some Bird, some Coltrane. Think of the lineage of musicians who played with him . . . Miles didn't want to talk about music, he wanted to talk about other things – cars, stuff like that. When he talked about Bird, he talked mostly of Bird's presence. When Bird walked into a room, he had presence. Miles had the same presence. When he walked into a room it was frightening sometimes, his presence. Not many people have that. He took us into the studio once, in Stuttgart, Germany, just after we'd done a gig. All the stories I'd heard about Miles in the studio, I figured, OK, I'm going to get a chance to witness this, finally. We were doing tunes by Prince, and I remember Miles wanted the drummer to play a certain way, going back to a shuffle. He'd look at me and say, 'Kenny, you understand – explain it to him.' But I'd say, 'Naw, I don't know,' 'cause I wanted to hear him explain it, see what he would do. And Miles just took the music apart, put something in, took something out, and by the time it was finished, the song was completely different. I learned so much from him, from then on, about how he took different things from guys and told them what to play. I played 'Human Nature' with him for five years, but Miles always wanted his musicians to push the envelope. He wanted you to find your own way, but if you couldn't, he'd do it for you – come in and change chords, fix a different rhythm, find a way to make you play differently than you had before. If you played something he'd heard before, it was boring to him, a yawning kind of vibe. He'd push me to think about another way to play the song – that's what he'd done, playing 'Green Dolphin Street' a dozen different ways with different bands. So we did 'Human Nature' a thousand different ways and I had fun, 'cause there was always something happening and I always had to be on my toes.[33]

After four concerts in the USA in late August and early September, Miles appeared on an NBC TV programme early in October, in which the band played 'Tutu' and 'Mr Pastorius', between which Miles was interviewed. There were no other concerts until the end of that month, when the band went back to Europe for two weeks. In September, however, the album *Aura* was at last released and, a little later, *Miles: The Autobiography* was published. So 1989 had been a tremendous year of achievement for Miles Davis. He had made another ground-breaking album, *Amandla*, which pleased the punters as well as the critics, he had played concerts to full houses all over the USA and Europe, and had been interviewed in depth on many occasions. With Quincy Troupe's assistance, he had created and published his autobiography, he had received some prestigious honours – the New York State Governor's Arts Award, and the unique accolade from *du* magazine – and even his hobby, painting, was bringing in substantial sums of money. But perhaps the event that pleased him most of all was the release of *Aura*, four and a half years after it was recorded. Miles Davis was the powerful inspiration behind Palle Mikkelborg's magnificent orchestral writing, and the work was recorded when Miles was at the height of his playing powers – his stamina, range, sound and technique all at their optimum.

Aura is composed for acoustic orchestral instruments and electronic instruments including synthesizers, using European classical methods as well as jazz, rock and ethnic elements, and improvisation. Miles plays on eight of the ten movements, his contribution is all improvised and it is astonishing how well he handles the most diverse musical situations. The first movement, 'Intro', for example, has broken asymmetrical rhythms, violent orchestral punctuations, rather reminiscent of Stravinsky's 'Rite of Spring', yet Miles is undaunted and plays open trumpet with angular comments and soulful high notes. His old friend and associate, guitarist John McLaughlin, is his fellow soloist in this piece and also gets a firm grip on it. The second movement, 'White', has Miles at his most poignant, using the Harmon mute and playing some short, unaccompanied phrases, then quiet electronic harmonies and bell sounds accompany him. When a written slow oboe melody is played, Miles is tacit for a while. This haunting music is without overt rhythm, and in free time. Muted Miles joins in again towards the end with passionately keening phrases.

Miles does not play in the third movement, 'Yellow', an orchestral elegiac piece with harp, oboe, and underpinning bass and tuba drones. There is more movement towards the end with brass and reeds, drums and bells. 'Orange', the fourth movement, has a heavy rock rhythm and some magnificent Davis trumpet, first muted and swinging like mad, then open with wild screams, dynamic phrases and some beautiful low-register playing. The orchestra backing is never over-written or overbearing. Miles's playing is also at a peak in 'Red', the fifth movement, and 'Blue', the seventh, which has a kind of reggae rhythm in 7/4 time, a time signature that Miles had probably not experienced before working with Mikkelborg. This whole album is also a secondary tribute to Gil Evans, with whose orchestra Palle Mikkelborg had played and who was one of the latter's strongest influences, but the very beautiful sixth movement, 'Green', is a primary tribute to Gil. It is all played rubato – in free time – with evocative synthesizer chords, a heavenly synthesized choir, a slow oboe melody and telling contributions, first by Bo Stief on electric bass, then Niels-Henning Ørsted Pedersen on acoustic bass. Miles's Harmon mute, too, adds poignancy to this very moving tribute. The last movement, 'Violet', was the only one in which Miles had played a solo at the actual Sonning Award ceremony in December 1984, and with the encores that night, he had played it five times. For the album performance he is in devastating form, playing muted and open with exultant vitality – clusters, runs, high phrases, great interval leaps and screaming high notes. His final note, a blistering trumpet G sharp above top C, cuts off everything except a long synthesizer after-drone, leaving listeners bathing in the afterglow.

When he finished his European tour in mid-November, Miles played one concert at the Beacon Theatre, New York City, then took off the remainder of the month and the whole of January 1990, for a well-deserved rest.

TWENTY-FOUR

The Final Chapter

'Listen, next year will be perhaps my last year in
music. I'm too ill after the tours. The cold gives me
the sweats. I have a spot on the lung, two hernias
because of my drummers, a pinched nerve here . . .
There are too many things wrong . . . diabetes,
numbness in my feet . . . Yes, next year, next
year, I'll stop playing.'[1]

Miles Davis (June 1991)

'Music is about the spirit and the spiritual, and about
feeling . . . The shit that we played together has to be
somewhere around in the air because we blew it there
and that shit was magical, was spiritual.'[2]

Miles Davis

Miles Davis's comeback years, from 1981 onwards, were like a
gigantic, recurring lap of honour round the concert halls and festivals of the USA, Canada, Europe, Japan, and occasionally taking
in the Middle East, South America and Australia, but they were
also much more than that. He gradually eased himself into new
ways of recording and music-making that were, yet again, unique
to him. Again, he made totally contemporary music and some of
his recordings (*Tutu* in particular) were regarded as the soundtrack
to the era. His trumpet playing, in some years, reached almost
superhuman peaks of expression in terms of content, sound, range
and stamina, and he again drew to his band some key younger

musicians, who flourished in his company. Having been totally invisible during his reclusive years, he suddenly became permanently in view, with yet another dramatic, phoenix-like reinvention of himself. Before his five-year absence, he had been famous, but mainly among the jazz cognoscenti. In 1975, for example, no publisher in the UK or USA was interested in a biography of Miles Davis, and some publishers did not even know who he was. But the regular exposure of his comeback years, the extraordinary international honours he received, and his eventual media coverage in the USA, all brought him superstardom. This naturally rekindled interest in his entire career, and his magnificent body of music on record. He was now so famous that, in 1989, the American publishers, Simon & Schuster, bought the world rights to his autobiography for a million dollars, and in June that year the UK publishing trade magazine, the *Bookseller*, reported:

The hard fight for the autobiography of jazz musician Miles Davis has been won after five rounds by Macmillan and Picador. Agent Jane Gregory, acting on behalf of Simon & Schuster US, orchestrated the auction. Twenty companies were selected to see the manuscript, from a larger number that showed interest. Seven or eight bid; the under bidder was Kate Parkin, making her new presence felt at Collins, but Adam Sisman at Macmillan made the winning offer, which is reported to be £38,000. Simon & Schuster (US) . . . is now selling the book in Europe. Macmillan/Picador have UK and Commonwealth rights, but not serial, which Gregory is yet to sell. Davis, the world's best-selling jazz musician and protégé of Charlie Parker and Dizzy Gillespie, is known for his refusal to give interviews. But he agreed to work with his friend, jazz journalist Quincy Troupe, on the book. Publication is scheduled for next January.[3]

Miles: The Autobiography was based largely on the in-depth interviews with the subject, but also on supplementary interviews Quincy Troupe did with others, but what we hear throughout the book is Miles's voice using his natural conversational style, complete with profanities, obscenities and black vernacular street language – what Miles called 'that black shit that black men talk'.[4] In this argot, the word 'bad' can be used as a word of approval as well as disapproval, and 'shit' can mean anything from the neutral 'stuff' to the pejorative 'rubbish' or 'nonsense', while the word 'motherfucker', also used on occasion by the socially acceptable Wynton Marsalis, can mean anything from the neutral 'guy' to the pejorative 'bastard'. The book was aimed at blacks as well as whites, and no one could expect the hippest man on the planet to change his style, either sartorially or linguistically, to fit in with white ideas of propriety. The style, however, ensured that the majority of the book's readers would be already converted Miles Davis fans or young potential fans. To educated and highly literate people, the style and language of the autobiography might seem unappetizing, offensive, or even impenetrable. This is a pity, because Davis has much wisdom and many insights to impart, and his verbal portraits of his asssociates – most of them major forces in this music – are perceptive, vivid and often very loving.

In his last chapter, he attempts to summarize his views on life and music, and sounds off about women, harassment of blacks by American police, prejudiced whites, and even the problems fame brings:

> I'm a very private person, and it costs a lot of money to maintain privacy when you're as famous a person as I am. It's real, real hard and that's one of the reasons I have to make money; so that I can keep my life private. You have to pay for fame – mentally, spiritually, and in *real* money.[5]

But his autobiography ends on a buoyant, optimistic note:

> But I think right now is the best creative period I have ever gone through, because I'm painting, and writing music and playing on top of what I know ... For me, the urgency to play and create music today is worse than when I started.

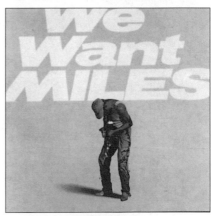

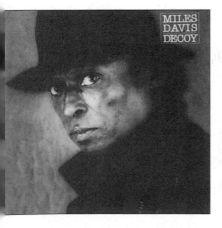

Miles in 1974.

Dave Liebman, 1975.

An ailing Miles Davis with
Marcus Miller at the
Hammersmith Odeon, 1982.

Photo © Allan Titmuss

Miles Davis with John
Scofield, Royal Festival Hall,
London, 1985.

Bill Evans, 1986.

Miles Davis with Bob Berg, Wembley Conference Centre, London, 1986.

Miles Davis with Kenny Garrett, St David's Hall, Cardiff, UK, 1989.

Miles Davis and Herbie Hancock, in
front of a backdrop painted by Miles,
Paris Reunion Concert, 10 July 1991.

Miles Davis with Foley
McCreary, Royal Festival Hall,
London, 19 July 1991.

Miles at the Royal Festival Hall, during his last London concert, 19 July 1991.

It's more intense . . . I'm driven to it – I go to bed thinking about it and wake up thinking about it . . . and I love that it hasn't abandoned me; I feel really blessed . . . I feel the best is yet to come.[6]

Far from refusing to give interviews, Miles, now much in demand by the media all over the world, was very willing to be interviewed during this period. People associated with him were also sought out by the various media, and so new aspects of his past and present life were constantly being discovered. In July 1989, Mike Zwerin, interviewing the founder of Island Records, Chris Blackwell, uncovered an astonishing connection with Miles Davis. In 1959, Blackwell, a white Jamaican, had started modestly by pressing a few hundred copies of Jamaican jazz records and delivering them personally to Kingston stores. On a visit to New York he sought out the Miles Davis Quintet with John Coltrane. Zwerin writes:

He passed only 'maybe six or seven extended occasions' with Davis in New York, but looking back now their importance seems totally out of proportion to the actual time passed. 'It changed my life,' he says. 'The experience is burned into my mind.' Miles was cracking a lot of notes at that time – splitting them, you'd hear half of each . . . and the split notes were more exciting than embarrassing. Were they mistakes or lost chords? The young Blackwell never bought Elvis Presley records. Even Chuck Berry was of marginal importance to him. He considered jazz to be the cutting edge of music and Davis to be the edge of the edge. He could not understand the apparent imperfection amidst the heroics. One day he just up and asked about it. Davis responded: 'I always try for more notes than I'm sure I can hit, so I miss some.' Wow! Blackwell thought. That's the only way to live.[7]

With new resolve and daring, Blackwell went back to Jamaica, then moved to London, soon making Island Records one of the biggest and most influential privately-owned multinational record companies.

Despite the optimistic note on which Miles's autobiography had ended, and his assertion that music-making was as important to him as ever, there had begun, in 1989, a gradual winding down of his concert performances. He was president of his own touring company, Trumpet Productions Incorporated, which grossed three or four million dollars a year in concert fees, and he took good care of his musicians financially. But his touring schedules had been longer, tougher and more unrelenting even than those of young rock musicians. In 1987 and 1988, for example, he had played forty-six and forty-five concerts respectively, with the much heavier burden of double concerts on some dates, and this had been in addition to other demanding projects, such as recording for himself and others. His collapse and illness in 1988 was the direct result of overwork, which had undermined his health and, after his slow recovery, there were no more double concerts. In 1989, he began wearing flat-heeled shoes on stage and played only twenty-six single concerts. The numbness in his feet, of which he complained in the passage quoted at the beginning of this chapter, may have been caused by diabetes, or by the collapse of veins due to his early heroin addiction. In 1990, there were twenty-eight concerts, again with no double events, and he began the year by rehearsing his group in a New York studio for two days in the first week of February.

Keyboardist Adam Holzman had left in October the previous year, and the group was a septet once more with Kenny Garrett, keyboardist Kei Akagi, guitarist Foley McCreary, electric bassist Benny Rietveld, drummer Ricky Wellman and John Bigham on electric percussion. This was the group that had been filmed and recorded on 3 November 1989 at Le Zenith in Paris, and nine of the fourteen performances there were later released on video by Warner Music Vision.[8] Miles played only in short stretches on that occasion, deploying the Harmon mute most of the time with his usual elegance, but making no forays into the extreme upper register. The atmosphere of the whole concert is all his own, but the soloists who really set the music alight are Garrett and Akagi. It may be that Davis was simply exhausted by the continual national and international touring of the previous five months. A cassette recording of his first concert in 1990 on 13 February at Toronto's Massey Hall, Canada, however, shows that his two-month break from touring in December and January had worked wonders. Though he still plays in short bursts, he's in sparkling form, with dynamic ideas and incisive phrases. Again Akagi and Garrett get the lion's share of the solos, and Miles seems to be content to 'play' his band as much as his trumpet. Just as Duke Ellington's band had been his 'instrument', so during this period, in a looser, more improvisatory way, did Miles's bands become his instrument. After playing a second concert the following day at the Massey Hall, Miles and the band attended the Grammy award ceremony a week later at the Shrine Auditorium, Los Angeles, where he received two Grammy awards for *Aura* in the categories Best Instrumental (Solo and Big Band), and a personal Lifetime Achievement Award. He and his band played one piece, 'Hannibal', at the ceremony.

After this event, apart from one further concert on 9 March, the American tour was not resumed until 22 April, because Miles had an acting role in the film *Dingo*, and a playing role on its soundtrack. The perks of his comeback years, and greater fame, brought him many opportunities to have fun doing unaccustomed things and being paid for them. His acting role in the *Miami Vice* episode, and his visual and speaking role in the Japanese commercial for Van Aquavit, were prime examples. Now he was about to renew acquaintance with an old friend and associate, the French musician and composer Michel Legrand. In June 1958, during the period of the great sextet that included Coltrane, Bill Evans and Paul Chambers, Miles had, with those three, been part of an eleven-piece ensemble directed by Legrand, which recorded the latter's arrangements of four jazz standards. Miles had played solos in all four pieces and was the featured soloist in Legrand's arrangement of John Lewis's 'Django'. But since that occasion, he and Legrand had rarely seen each other.

Michel Legrand, born on 24 February 1931, was a child prodigy who entered the Paris Conservatory at the age of eleven and graduated with top honours. In the 1950s, he became a bandleader, singer and songwriter and began composing for films. Five years younger than Miles, in 1958 Legrand had composed the music for just two French films and was less well-known internationally than the trumpeter. But in 1964, his score for the successful film operetta, *Les Parapluies de Cherbourg/The Umbrellas of Cherbourg*, made his international reputation, and from then on, he composed music for the soundtracks of many major French, American and British films. By 1990, Legrand had the music of over sixty films to his credit, and had made his debut as a director with an autobiographical film, *Cinq Jours en Juin/Five Days in June*, about his adolescence during the last stages of World War II and his literal and metaphorical loss of virginity.

Early in March, Legrand stayed at L'Ermitage Hotel in Beverly Hills writing (or perhaps finishing) the score for the Australian film *Dingo*. Miles seems to have been involved as a collaborator as well as a trumpet soloist, because the entire personnel of his current band formed the basis of the huge orchestra of brass, reeds and woodwind that recorded the music in the second week of March at Crystal Studio, Los Angeles. Miles's trumpet represented the character Billy Cross in the film, and Chuck Findley's trumpet represented the character Dingo Anderson. Davis spent the last two weeks of March in Australia filming his role in the movie, and then in early April, he spent a further two weeks in Paris for some additional filming. Reports of the film and Miles's acting were not favourable, but his playing on the soundtrack, though only a minor footnote to his illustrious career, is very focused and to the point. He uses the Harmon mute for most of his contributions, while the excellent trumpeter Findley plays open trumpet for all of his. The music was released on CD by Warner Bros, and two of the pieces featuring Miles, 'Concert on the Runway' and 'Paris Walking II' are taken at very fast tempos, which (using the Harmon) he handles so superbly that they bring to mind his similar playing thirty-three years previously in 'Sur L'Autoroute' on the

Lift to the Scaffold soundtrack. It is as if he is glancing back at his bebop roots. Some of his playing also recalls the brooding atmosphere of his work on *Siesta*.

After the Paris filming, he returned to the USA to play a few more concerts with his band. Electric percussionist John Bigham had left in March, and his place was taken by Miles's son, Erin, who had for some time been living with Davis and travelling with him. Erin's mother was, of course, Marguerite Eskridge. The band played concerts in Los Angeles, Seattle, Washington, and Portland, Oregon, then Miles had yet another individual assignment, playing some trumpet on the soundtrack of a film directed by Dennis Hopper, *The Hot Spot*. *Halliwell's Film Guide* describes it as an 'effective melodrama, much in the manner of a 1940s film noir'[9] and the plot deals with the infidelity of a car dealer's wife, and the results of her casual affair with a drifter and petty crook when he begins working for her husband. So during the period 5–10 May 1990, working in Ocean Way Studio 1, Hollywood, with a small group that included the old bluesman John Lee Hooker and the younger bluesman Taj Mahal both on guitar and singing in alternate pieces, plus Roy Rogers on slide guitar, Tim Drummond on bass and sometimes drummer Earl Palmer, Miles Davis recorded several funky, bluesy performances, again using the Harmon mute throughout. Hooker and Taj Mahal sing the blues always without words on this occasion, with plenty of slurring, sighing and moaning, but Miles is the main 'singer', demonstrating his great affection for this idiom and respect for its practitioners, his round, bottled-in sound the keening 'voice' over the moans and delta swamp rhythms.

Director Dennis Hopper dedicated the soundtrack to Miles saying: 'To Miles Davis, whom I have known since I was seventeen, who punched out the heroin dealer and said he would kill me if I ever did it again. I've wanted him to score every movie I've ever made and we finally got it together, man.'[10] And John Lee Hooker commented:

I been knowing Miles for about twenty-five years. Some

people say how he didn't get along with people too good, but that I don't know about. He always greeted me with a smile and a hug and we talked. Not too long ago we did something together (*The Hot Spot* music). When we got through, he said: 'You the funkiest man alive in the blues. The mud's up to your neck.' That meant a lot to me, coming from Miles Davis. Nobody else played like Miles Davis. *Sketches of Spain* – so deep I didn't understand it. That man could go so far out, you're like in space.[11]

After recording music fot *The Hot Spot*, Miles played a concert in Philadelphia and then took his band to Europe for nine concerts. Electric bassist Benny Rietveld had left Miles and his place was taken by Richard Patterson. The tour began with a concert at London's Hammersmith Odeon on 30 June and after taking in five other countries, the last concert was in Hamburg on 30 July. At the Hammersmith Odeon, Miles played for about two hours, and although the place was nearly full, there were a few empty seats.

My notes at the time were written without the hindsight provided by the cassettes and video I received years later, but here are some impressions of the concert:

Although Miles no longer attempts the extreme upper register of the trumpet, and no longer plays in long stretches, the evening was superbly organized musically and his sound and phrasing are as lyrical as ever. He had put a great deal of thought into the order and nature of musical events during the two-hour time span. There were many subtly different and superbly executed rhythms. There were several long stretches of quiet grooving throughout the evening, which produced much understated and exquisite music. There were glowing vignettes in the duets between Miles and Kenny Garrett, Miles and guitar, Miles and bass guitar, Miles and drums. Everyone in the group was featured, and Miles held up white cardboard strips, each bearing the Christian name of the musician in the spotlight. There were magnificent solos by the Japanese keyboard player (Akagi) and Kenny Garrett on alto. There were pieces from *Tutu* and *Amandla*, and a very lyrical atmosphere predominated, with lovely harmonies and rich orchestral sounds from the electronics. Miles was playing his red-lacquered trumpet, and wore a silver lamé loose suit. Also, for the first time, he was not wearing high heels, but instead, plain beige shoes with a matt finish and low heels. The one anti-climax was the way the evening ended. Miles went off with a wave, the musicians left one by one, leaving the drummer alone on stage. He played an extremely long solo, then came down stage to take a bow and was joined by the other musicians, but not Miles . . . unsatisfactory and somehow incomplete. Maybe that's the impression Miles wanted to leave.

After the European tour, Miles and the band were back in the USA at the beginning of August, and on the thirteenth, at a studio in New York, he played some trumpet in pianist and vocalist Shirley Horn's recording of the song 'You Won't Forget Me'. Then, on 19 August, he rehearsed his band at the Jones Beach Theatre, Long Island in preparation for three concerts in the USA, before returning to Europe.

Meanwhile Miles Davis was becoming ever more deeply involved in his painting, and there was an exhibition of his current work in a New York gallery during the early summer – probably June – which received good reviews and sold well. In 1988, his collaborator, Jo Gelbard, had given him a book on Memphis furniture, because Miles was refurbishing his New York apartment, and the book inspired his enthusiasm for the Memphis design movement founded by the Milan-based Italian designer Ettore Sottsass. This was based on the juxtaposition of bright colours and conflicting shapes, and Miles began creating paintings in this vein, which became so fundamental to his thinking that it led to the gaudy colours of the clothes he wore during his concerts. Jo Gelbard commented:

We used bright colours and zig-zags and dots and things that normally don't go together. He needed a stage design at the time, so we put together a few sketches and ideas. It originally seemed like an extension of the Memphis idea. There was a silk backdrop covered with shapes and amorphous colours – pinks, turquoises, and other typical Memphis stuff. And the platforms that all the musicians stood on were like connecting shapes. It had a lot of cubist influence, too. He was going to Japan, Europe, and Australia, and he needed this kind of stage. Most of the places over here [USA] couldn't accommodate it. He's become more of a superstar over there, and he just wanted to come across as more dynamic and to give his fans more. Unfortunately, we didn't follow through on its building, and it wasn't as effective as we'd intended it to be.[12]

By the time of his 1990s exhibition, however, Davis and Gelbard had exhausted their interest in the Memphis style and were sharing a Manhattan studio lined with tribal masks and images of African art. Their work began to combine Miles's 'totem pole' faces with materials such as 'rope, burlap, copper and nails'. Scott Gutterman wrote: 'The resulting pieces are both sensual and foreboding, angry and resolved; they stake out new territory for both artists. Like African fetish objects, they have about them an aura of mystery and power.'[13] It was these works that were shown in the current exhibition.

It was through Jo Gelbard that Miles became aware of the work of the black artist and painter, Jean-Michel Basquiat, who died in 1988, in his late twenties. He was championed by Andy Warhol, who collaborated with him in some of his paintings, and Basquiat became the darling of the New York art scene, rocketing to fame, fortune and extinction. Jo Gelbard explained: 'I told him [Miles] that his work reminded me of Basquiat. So I got this book of his stuff and showed it to Miles. It turns out Basquiat did a whole series of paintings *based* on Miles, with the word *Miles* in them.'[14] Gelbard also made perceptive comments about Miles and his painting; he was not interested in formal training, but wanted 'to be in a vacuum, listening to his own impulses . . . It's either going to come from within or it's not.'[15]

On 14 October, Miles and the band were back in Europe for six concerts in Germany, one in France, and one at Maastricht in the Netherlands. The tour ended on 11 November, and the band was not to play again until March 1991, when it would yet again be back in Europe. Miles had three months to relax, paint and consider his future. There had been published, in 1990, two lengthy overviews of him and his music, very different in spirit and intention. The first, a seven-page survey by Stanley Crouch, headed 'Miles Davis, the most brilliant sellout in the history of jazz. PLAY THE RIGHT THING', appeared in the 12 February 1990 edition of *the New Republic* and is an extraordinarily schizophrenic affair. Crouch can see nothing of value in the music of Miles Davis's comeback years, and his writing on this subject is loutish, abusive and there is no real attempt at musical analysis. For example, the concluding paragraph of his introduction is as follows:

Beyond the terrible performances and the terrible recordings, Davis has also become the most remarkable licker of moneyed boots in the music business, willing now to pimp himself as he once pimped women when he was a drug addict. He can be seen on television talking about the greatness of Prince, or claiming (in his new autobiography, *Miles*) that the Minneapolis vulgarian and borderline drag queen 'can be the new Duke Ellington of our time if he just keeps at it'. Once nicknamed 'Inky' for his dark complexion, Davis now hides behind the murky fluid of his octopus fear of being old hat, and claims that he is now only doing what he has always done – move ahead, take the music forward, submit to the personal curse that is his need for change, the same need that brought him to New York from St Louis in 1944, in search of Charlie Parker.

This writing is a prime example of criticism as mere self-assertion by the critic; it is simply an ill-tempered rant, giving vent to the bile that has addled his critical faculties. Yet immediately after this, the lout is banished and some critical intelligence appears as Crouch begins discussing areas of Miles's earlier music that he appreciates, from the Charlie Parker years to the latter part of the 1960s. We may not agree with all of his evaluations, but at least there is a discernible critical faculty at work. From 1969 and *In a Silent Way* onwards, however, the loaded language reappears, as Crouch bludgeons his way through what he calls Miles's 'abject surrender to popular trends'. He has nothing intelligent to say about *Silent Way* or *Bitches Brew*, both of which he dismisses as worthless, as he does Miles's recent albums: 'His albums of recent years – *Tutu*, *Siesta*, *Amandla*, and the overblown *Aura* – prove beyond any doubt that he has lost all interest in music of quality.'

The last page and a half of Crouch's article is a demolition job on Davis's autobiography, in which the 'critic' finds virtually no redeeming factor. In general, much of Stanley Crouch's stance, whether loutish or considered, reflects the old clichéd prejudices of the jazz scene. It is puritanical, and regards popular music or any kind of 'commercialism' as of the devil's party. This began during the 1940s with the traditional jazz revival and the birth of bebop. The traditionalists, who were in search of some imaginary lost purity, called the modernists 'Dirty Boppers', and the bebop-pers called the revivalists 'Mouldy Figs'. This puritanism in jazz even goes so far as to insist that financial success is destructive and evil, and that if someone's music is pleasing to the public there must be something wrong with it. Even a catchy melody can be regarded as 'commercial', yet there are few things as blameless as a catchy melody. Jazz has been associated with popular music in one way or another since its inception, and Miles Davis's music – and Gil Evans's – has generally used the popular rhythms of the time. Their music has always had a certain relationship with the dance, as Ellington's also had, and the amazing fact about both Miles Davis and Gil Evans is that they kept their thinking young and virile all their lives. Crouch was born in 1945, but he does not understand the essence of Miles Davis as well as does bassist and collaborator with Miles, Marcus Miller, born in 1959. The understanding and wisdom of Miller's remarks about Davis are exceptional. Miller remembered,

> When I talked to him about the forties or the fifties, I got the impression that there was a direct link between the way people walked down the street, and the popular music, and the bebop that those guys played. The bebop was just an extension of the dance music of the time. So the music was connected with everything in Miles's life, and when you realize that, you begin to see that for a guy like him, music is just a reinterpretation of what's going on ... So for him it didn't make any sense to play in 1983 the same music that he'd played in 1963. I learnt that you should connect your music with your times. The downside being that the music might not last, because there's been plenty of music that was connected to its time and just stayed there. You can only hope that at a certain point, it will also transcend its time. But you can't think about that. You have to concentrate on making your music relevant to what's going on now.[16]

Marcus Miller's wise and perceptive remarks are the most potent answer to the outmoded and jaundiced values of Stanley Crouch. The majority of Miles Davis's vast musical legacy from his time with Parker, to *Amandla*, will stand the test of time. Perhaps it is necessary to point out yet again that Miles Davis cut his musical teeth in the heady excitement of the birth of bebop, but outgrew it, and his music from *The Birth of the Cool* onwards was a critique of bebop, just as his music in the comeback years was a critique of the jazz of the 1980s, which tended to recycle older styles of the music. Crouch is outraged by Miles's non-conformism in terms of bourgeois standards of politeness, language and dress. But Miles himself was outraged by black conformism to white bourgeois standards of behaviour. John Scofield said:

He was the perfect example of going with your gut instinct. If he had an idea it would almost always be the thing that made everybody fresh, spark things off, even if he only brought it up just before you were about to start recording or something. He could be very charming, and he was also one of the angriest people I have ever met – I'm not sure what that came from, but I am sure he had a reason.[17]

It is absolutely certain that Miles Davis's anger was caused by the inhumanity and injustice of racial prejudice. His patrician background gave him a strong sense of his own worth, he was extremely intelligent, very sensitive and aware of nuance – social and otherwise – and had extraordinary gifts for music-making and inspiring musicians. In the case of Mahatma Gandhi, for example, it took just one experience of the inhumanity and injustice of racial prejudice to trigger his entire programme of non-violent opposition to racial discrimination in South Africa, and later to British rule in India. Gandhi, too, had a patrician background and a sense of his own worth. Practising as a lawyer in South Africa, his company booked him into a first-class train carriage, and at one station a white man entered it, saw the colour of his skin and told Gandhi to get out. Gandhi flatly refused, the man called the police and Gandhi was thrown off the train. The sense of inhumanity and injustice, the sheer outrage Gandhi felt, would live with him for ever. In Miles's autobiography he recounts other perhaps more subtle slights to himself and to others, and also, on another occasion, speaking of critics and the USA in general, he said: 'It was a shame the way they ignored Charlie Parker. When he was alive, they hardly gave him the time of day. Stuff like that's got to make you angry.'[18] So far as Crouch is concerned, his name is not mentioned in Davis's autobiography, and it is quite possible that Miles was unaware of his malevolence, or even of his existence.

The second lengthy review of Miles's life and work appeared in the 13 July 1990 issue of the periodical *Goldmine*, and was more balanced and benign. Entitled 'Miles's Styles: An Overview of the Recordings of Miles Davis', it was written by William Ruhlmann and occupied some nine pages, which included a substantial abridged biography of Miles's career, reviews of Columbia's current release of *Pangaea*, Miles's last live recording in 1975, just before his reclusive period, and an approving review of the autobiography. The whole thing concluded with Ruhlmann's 'Selected Miles Davis US Albums Discography', which covered four pages and featured many photographs of the album covers. There were also several photographs from most periods of Miles's career, illustrating the biography.

Miles Davis really needed those three months without touring at the end of the old year and the beginning of 1991, because he had taken on a heavy work schedule for the new year. First, he began by doing something completely new, but which harked back to the street-music atmosphere of *On the Corner*. He wanted to make some music that would get through to the urban black underclass of the USA, the young people who grew up with rap and listened to the radio stations that catered to their tastes. Gordon Meltzer was much more than a mere road manager for Miles; he seemed to supervise the latter's career generally, and was an associate producer of this venture. Miles asked a friend, Russell Simmons, who ran Def Jam records, to find some young producers who could help create the kind of music he was interested in – hip hop – and that was how a young man called Easy Mo Bee became the producer of the album *Doo-Bop*, taking on Marcus Miller's role of creating the musical tracks. But Easy Mo Bee also performed some of the raps himself, and the music contained sampled passages from other people's albums, whereas when Marcus Miller produced for Miles, he used no extraneous sampled music. Miles, however, functioned in this context in his usual way, listening to the completed tracks and, when the spirit took him, overdubbing his trumpet solos on to them. Gordon Meltzer commented:

The plans Miles had for this record were very ambitious: in addition to his collaboration with Easy Mo Bee, there was the ongoing important work-in-progress with Prince. Miles had asked John Bigham to work on material and, in addition, there was another New York producer, Sid Reynolds, with whom Miles had started a collaboration. Then there was the material from the late 1980s that Miles called the RubberBand Session. He wanted to rework and modernize some of the music from that session and use it on this album. At one time, Miles had called Mo Ostin, the chairman of Warner Bros Records, and told him that he had enough material for a double-album.[19]

Miles was to die before these additional projects could be realized, but in January and/or February 1991, he did manage to complete six tracks of the music for *Doo-Bop*, and to record two more unaccompanied trumpet solos, round which Easy Mo Bee later built up natural-sounding musical contexts. So the finished album consisted of eight tracks and a ninth one that was a brief reprise of the opening piece. Miles Davis's *Doo-Bop* is a functional, user-friendly urban or household music, roughly equivalent, perhaps, to Picasso's late work in ceramics. But Miles sounds astonishingly rejuvenated in these performances – his embouchure is strong and there is a terrific buoyancy in the often sustained solos. Except for one track when he plays open trumpet, he uses the Harmon mute throughout, and is frequently just a colour in the performances, because he is at about equal volume in the mix with the other sounds and sometimes quieter even than the percussion. In 'The Doo-Bop Song', the rap is in praise of Miles, and he plays for over four minutes, sounding virile and creative all the way. 'High Speed Chase', one of the posthumously completed tracks, is fast and strongly rhythmic, with him in devastating form, utilizing the attack of the Harmon to punch out a ferocious series of notes, and hitting some very high ones with wild urgency. 'Blow' is a hypnotic dance track with Easy Mo Bee rapping about his collaboration with Miles, who plays all the way to fade. 'Fantasy', the other posthumously completed track, has him on open trumpet, sounding lyrical and strong though down in the mix and still a colour in the soundstream. Easy Mo Bee's rap is overtly sexual doggerel. In general the mood and the method are much the same in these tracks, but amazingly, Miles's enthusiasm and creative energy endure all the way, with many different approaches and a great variety of phrases. The opening and closing tracks of *Doo-Bop* are aptly entitled 'Mystery' and 'Mystery' (reprise). Miles moved in a mysterious way, to realize his musical, missionary and monetary aims, and it is clear that at the time of recording *Doo-Bop*, he had many plans for the future, even though he was bored and exhausted by the international concert tours.

In 1991, he was definitely considering giving up touring and perhaps even public music-making. According to Gordon Meltzer, Miles was by this time financially secure, and even though the divorce settlement with Cicely Tyson had been expensive, he could now *jokingly* introduce the lawyer, Dorothy Weber, who had finalized it, as 'the lady who gave all my money to Cicely'. Meltzer also said that Miles had reached a point in his life where the thrill of music was not sufficient any more. This ought not to be surprising when we consider how he had spent himself over five decades of music-making, fired by his constant vigilance and readiness to change. The more fame and success a musician has, the more courage is needed to plunge yet again into uncharted territory in search of new orders of music. (It is easy to understand why even moderately successful musicians have been loath to take that plunge, and instead, have been content to go on working the same musical vein all their lives.) Retirement from performance would give him more time for his painting, which was now very important to him, and time to relax and enjoy himself. It may have been this kind of thinking which lay behind the two major retrospective concerts he played in 1991 – the performance again of the orchestral music scored by Gil Evans, and a concert reunion with several of his musicians from the 1960s, 1970s and 1980s.

Miles Davis was famous for 'not looking back', but this was always a misreading of him. In actual fact, he looked back a great deal, but only moved forward. 'Life has to be lived forwards, but it can only be understood backwards,' is a statement that neatly describes the way Miles functioned. The past, personal and otherwise, is important to everyone, because it holds the key to identity, and for an artist in particular, the old adage holds true: 'If you don't know where you've come from, you can hardly know where you're going.' Miles had lived through much jazz history and had made great swathes of it himself. He had been friendly with Louis Armstrong and Duke Ellington and many of the other seminal figures, and was very much aware of the whole tradition. Throughout his career, he had usually begun a new phase by playing music that reviewed his own immediate past, and this had happened even in his last phase. His working band in 1981 was functioning in the same loose, improvisatory manner as his groups in the early and middle 1970s, until new modes of procedure emerged. But he had never indulged in the postmodern practice of playing repertory music. Over the decades musicians and others had often asked if he and Gil Evans would perform the orchestral music again, and the idea had certainly crossed their minds, too, but the occasion had never arisen for them to do so. But in 1991, the idea was impressed on Miles by external forces.

For three years, Miles's friend and neighbour in California, composer Quincy Jones, had been co-producer of the Montreux Jazz Festival, with its Swiss founder, Claude Nobs. Miles had often played there since the festival had begun, and 1991 was its twenty-fifth anniversary. Quincy Jones was a great admirer of Miles and Gil Evans, and he had often attempted unsuccessfully to persuade them to perform the music again. Now in 1991, he persuaded Claude Nobs that they should re-create that music at the current festival and also get Miles to play his own part in it. Jones had known Miles since the end of the 1940s, and had become much more friendly with him since Miles moved to Malibu. Jones had also bought several of Davis's paintings, and was a consistent champion of the trumpeter. Quincy Jones, one of the most successful and talented composer/arrangers in popular music, and very much wealthier than Miles, nevertheless always had an awed respect for the latter's mysterious creativity, and crucially, he also had Miles's trust.

To go back and play the music over again went against Miles's inclinations and instincts, and he was reluctant to do it. Over the years he had not thought about it a great deal and he had forgotten much of it, whereas the main participants needed to be steeped in this subtle and complex orchestral music when they performed it. Normally an idea of such magnitude for a major international festival would have been discussed and planned at least a year before the event, and possibly two years before it. But Quincy Jones had suggested it only in the early part of the year of its projected performance. He would conduct the orchestra, but there were several imponderables, the most pressing one being the necessity of getting Miles's agreement to take part. Jones told Leonard Feather:

> At one point Claude [Nobs] came to New York and we sat with Miles and we talked and talked, and finally, he said 'OK.' But he said, 'This stuff's gonna be expensive.' I said, 'What do you mean? The cost of the band can't be that much.' 'It ain't that, man,' he said. 'It's just that this shit is hard to play.'[20]

Miles really did not want to do it because he was not in great shape physically, time was short, and he would have to learn the music all over again, but Gordon Meltzer said that he was offered such a huge sum of money to take part in the project that he accepted. It seemed an ordeal, and in accepting to do it, Miles was reported to have said, 'I must confront this beast!' But once he had decided, he got happy about it, Meltzer said, and remembered how much Gil Evans meant to him, and did it for love of Gil and of the music – as well as for the huge (undisclosed) sum he was paid.

Once Miles agreed to take part, Quincy Jones and Claude Nobs decided to use members of the Gil Evans Orchestra, which still continued posthumously under the supervision of Evans's wife, Anita, and their son Miles Evans, and the George Gruntz Band – in effect, a double orchestra. But the next problem was to locate

Gil Evans's scores of the music for *Miles Ahead*, *Porgy and Bess*, and *Sketches of Spain*, which had been kept in the basement of Miles's brownstone house on West 77th Street, which had been sold. Claude Nobs faxed Anita Evans asking about the scores. Anita said later:

> Initially, nobody could find the music. Gil always told me that the scores were over at Miles's house in New York. But when Cicely [Tyson] sold that house, only she knew where the stuff in the basement went.
>
> Miles said as far as he knew, Cicely had the music. But Quincy called her and she said she didn't. Finally [Gil's sons] Noah and Miles started digging up some of Gil's old stuff that hadn't seen the light of day in thirty years. And what they came up with were rough sketches of the charts, things that Gil had worked on before completing the official score for the record. Most of it was on score paper . . . incredibly precious stuff, like Gil's brain on a piece of paper. So, I sent those to Quincy and he looked them over. At this point, Gil Goldstein became very important to the project in helping Quincy make sense of Gil's charts.[21]

It was only three months before the actual concert that Quincy Jones telephoned Gil Goldstein, whom he had never met, and said, 'Anita Evans says you're the man to put this music together.' Goldstein had been playing keyboards in Gil Evans's band since the early 1980s, and was very much in tune with Evans's thinking and musical practices. So he took on the task of transcribing much of the music and organizing the scores. Goldstein said:

> Finding those rough sketches of Gil's charts was like finding the Dead Sea Scrolls of jazz. It freaked me out when I saw them. No real complete scores, but really historical kinds of sketches on music paper. It was just unbelievably fascinating to see this stuff and have it in your hands. I already had full scores for 'Blues for Pablo' and 'Springsville', which Gil had

given me when I took some quasi-lessons with him when he was still here. So, I had a head start on those two. The rest I had to just fill in the blanks by looking at these sketches and going back and listening to the records. In the end, I had to basically re-orchestrate a lot of it, so what we played is not the actual orchestration that is on the record. I had to make some educated guesses to fill in the blanks, but I was just gratified that it was all sounding like Gil and giving this general impression of those charts.[22]

It seems ridiculous that the scores of some of the twentieth century's most beautiful music should have simply disappeared in that way, and one had visions of them turning up 200 years later and fetching a huge price at auction. The truth is more mundane – and much more satisfactory. Gil Evans's scores were found in 1997, in the locker of a New York storage warehouse where they had been lodged by Miles Davis, presumably after his brownstone house on West 77th Street had been sold. Perhaps he had forgotten about that, or was it that he did not want to facilitate the very testing challenge of playing that music again? Or did he want to make it also a test of the ingenuity and tenacity of the organizers of the project? Now that the scores have been found, there is no need for any more guesswork as to Gil Evans's intentions.

When the reconstituted scores were ready, Gil Goldstein got together a New York band to see how the music sounded. Goldstein wanted Miles Davis to play his part in the rehearsal, to get his opinion on the reconstruction of the scores and also to give him the chance to familiarize himself with the music again. Goldstein said: 'I started to get nervous about Miles being able to play all of this stuff without coming to a rehearsal, because it's a hell of a lot of music. It's like classical music. You have to play it with the orchestra.'[23] He telephoned Miles, who responded with a warm, rasping 'Hi, Gil!' almost as if he were talking to Gil Evans himself. Goldstein asked him to come to the rehearsal, but Miles didn't want to do that. Goldstein pressed him and Miles hung up on him. Goldstein said, 'I called him right back, and asked if I could bring the music round to his house to show it to him, and he said "Yes". I took it round and he was very friendly, looked at it, made some comments and introduced me to his girlfriend.'

But Miles did not attend the initial rehearsal sessions, which were performed by a band not going to Montreux anyway. Instead, he would attend the only two rehearsals with the full double orchestra at Montreux, one on 7 July, and the other in the daytime before the actual concert on the eighth. But there was always some doubt that Miles would turn up at all. Quincy Jones would telephone Goldstein and say he had received a message that Miles had a problem with his lip and couldn't play. Miles would then be contacted and his fee increased, and this happened more than once, until Davis was offered the fee he could not refuse. But even so, there was doubt right up until the time he appeared in Montreux.

But even at Montreux he missed much of the first rehearsal. Goldstein said:

The first rehearsal in Montreux was full of confusion. A million things were still up in the air as far as details of what was really gonna happen. People were uptight about various business issues. It was just a kind of nervous not-knowing-what-was-going-to-happen environment. Quincy showed up at 2 p.m. That was the first time we had actually met face to face. By 11 p.m., Miles showed up. It was unbelievable, just the perfect entry for Miles Davis. We were rehearsing 'Boplicity' [from *Birth of the Cool*] and he just kind of walked in right at the first phrase, sat down, and started taking out his horn.[24]

There may have been a method in Miles's absences, because to be the only soloist in a whole concert of the orchestral music would impose an impossible strain on the creativity and stamina of any trumpet player. The original recordings had been done at the rate of only two or three pieces day. If he did not attend the rehearsals, someone else would play his part in the proceedings, and then later, Miles could pick and choose the parts he wanted to play. Talking of that first rehearsal at Montreux, Goldstein said:

> Miles didn't show up and we needed someone to play his part. At first we were going to have trumpeter Benny Bailey do it, but at the last minute we gave it to Wallace Roney, who was one of the trumpets in George Gruntz's band. So Wallace was up there playing Miles's part when Miles finally walked in during 'Boplicity'. Wallace just kind of stayed up there and started playing unison lines and trading solos with Miles.[25]

Before coming to Montreux Miles Davis had, in March, played two concerts and a recording session in Germany and one concert in Switzerland. After a concert in Philadelphia on 23 June, he and his band had returned to Europe, playing two more concerts in Germany on 28 and 30 June and two in France on 1 and 5 July. Then he and his band had come to Montreux on 7 July. Miles's trusted alto saxophonist, Kenny Garrett, would also help out with the solos in the orchestral music and he was on time for that first full rehearsal on 7 July. The concert was so special that it was billed as 'L'Événement' (the Event), and it had generated so much excitement that some fans managed to get into the auditorium to watch the rehearsal. No one was certain that Miles would participate until he appeared at 11 p.m., some nine or ten hours after everyone else had got there.

Wallace Roney, one of the finest of the Wynton Marsalis generation of trumpet players, recalled his experience of Davis's arrival and of how he actually got to play in the concert:

> I was never supposed to play on this concert, but when they rehearsed the orchestra, they needed somebody to play Miles's part. We rehearsed for a couple of hours and then Miles came in. Kenny Garrett was joking that he knew Miles must be coming in because his horn was shaking. I heard a

voice behind me say, 'Hey, you sound good as a motherfucker on that.' And Miles handed his horn to me. I said, 'No, man, you come up and play it.' He said, 'No, act like I'm not here.' I finished playing – the next thing I know, he and I were playing together. The next day he gave me more stuff to play. By the time it got to the concert, we were sharing everything. If it wasn't for Miles, I would have been just listening to this concert.[26]

At the late-night rehearsal Miles seemed to have great difficulty playing his part. The composer Michael Gibbs was in the audience, and said later:

I'd met him a few times and he scared the hell out of me – you felt he could see through everybody. But at Montreux this year, when he worked with Quincy Jones on the *Sketches of Spain* collaboration with Gil Evans's musicians, it was different. He was painfully thin, but he had these lavish clothes on, which hung off him, and he was surrounded by a heavy entourage which kept people away. There was a noon rehearsal and he arrived at eleven that night, and clearly couldn't get his fingers round the written parts. Next day he was a little better, then they shooed everybody out of the hall and said he wanted to rehearse in peace. I don't know what happened between then and the concert, but it was phenomenal. Wallace Roney was playing his written parts and sounded great, but like the 1960s records. But Miles's solos sounded completely new. It really lifted the hairs on the back of my neck. After Charlie Parker, he had to be the greatest giant in jazz for me.[27]

Miles was obviously helped by the presence of Quincy Jones, his longtime supportive friend, and he also warmed to Gil Goldstein, who not only bore Gil Evans's first name, but also had thick white hair resembling Evans's. Miles also liked Wallace Roney, enjoying his company and his playing, and spent much time with him during the three days at Montreux. Roney said:

> He was telling me everything he could think of about music, like he was trying to cram forty-five years of music into three days. I didn't know he was ill, I didn't think he was going to die, but maybe he did. Things just spilled out; he talked about Bird, Dizzy, Monk, everything you could think of. He knew how much I love him and he said that's cool, because that's the way he loved Dizzy. I'd like to do with Miles's style what he did with Dizzy's style. Take it and make something very personal out of it, that would be my best tribute to him.[28]

Miles Davis was at that time thinking of retirement from music, but was by no means preparing for death. He had many things planned for the future. Given the fact that Davis did die about ten weeks later, however, Roney's assumption was natural enough. Gil Goldstein said of the young trumpeter's contribution to the concert: 'I don't think that anybody could've done it as good as Wallace did in terms of just having real courtesy and respect and still play his ass off. He had to walk a kind of fine line between being a brat and being totally respectful. And, I think he was both.'[29]

Miles was not ill at the time of the concert, but his energy level seemed low; he rarely played as high as an ordinary trumpet top C, he used the Harmon mute most of the time and occasionally his effort to play was clearly evident. The concert was later released on CD and video, and though people who were at the actual event said that the recorded sound of the orchestra was much less full and lustrous than the live sound, it is astonishing that this huge double ensemble played those complex scores so beautifully after so little rehearsal time. Gil Goldstein paid tribute to Quincy Jones's contribution:

> I also thought Quincy was amazing. I just dig the fact that

he can hang with Madonna and Michael Jackson and still be the total fan of this music . . . And he really brought a lot of ideas to the thing. He went through the scores and really refined the stuff with a fine tooth comb. I think as much as the guys were playing for Gil and Miles, they were playing for Quincy, too.[30]

The concert began with the medium-tempo, laid-back feel of Miles's and Gil Evans's joint composition arranged by Evans, 'Boplicity', and this allowed him to ease himself into his role. Using the Harmon mute, he played the theme and a succinct, lyrical solo, and after some excellent open trumpet from Roney, Miles plays a second more intense solo. There must have been sighs of relief and delight all round – Miles was sounding something like himself. Next came a medley from the album *Miles Ahead*, beginning with the fast and tricky 'Springsville' composed by Johnny Carisi. The previous evening Miles had been unable to get his fingers round the lively trumpet introductory phrase, but now he made it, again on Harmon, and even played a daring short solo. Roney, on open trumpet quoted several phrases from Miles's 1957 solo in the original recorded performance. They had stood the test of time very well. 'Maids of Cadiz' had Miles playing the theme, but then removing the Harmon and sounding good on open trumpet. His open horn does not sound so sure in 'The Duke', but his playing, muted and open, in Kurt Weill's ballad, 'My Ship', is measured and very moving. Throughout the performances, Roney often sensitively plays along with the written passages, but never upstages Miles, who leaves the really demanding passages to the younger man. During the *Porgy and Bess* medley, muted Miles is poignant in the tender lament, 'Gone, Gone, Gone', and eloquent in 'Summertime', which also has a magnificent alto solo by Kenny Garrett. The latter also stars in his dialogue with Davis in 'Solea' from *Sketches of Spain*, but Miles is somewhat uneven, at times producing flashes of his earlier self, but never achieving the grandeur of his recent self in 1983, 1984 and 1985. Gil Goldstein recalled:

To me, one of the nicest things of the whole experience happened on the last rehearsal. I kind of walked over to Miles
to give him some [chord] changes I had written out, and he
was just standing there listening to the band rehearse
Sketches, and he said, 'Nobody will ever write like that again.'
It was obvious that he loves Gil's writing, but it was just nice
to hear him say it again.[31]

After the concert, Miles Davis was pleased and happy about
the whole occasion and said to Goldstein, 'That was nice!' He
also wanted to take the whole operation on the road to play six
concerts in capital cities, mentioning Rome and Paris. Quincy
Jones was also very pleased with his first ever working project
with Miles. He said: 'At the performance itself, I saw Miles, after
just one number, smiling the biggest smile I ever saw in my life,
waving his towel to the audience. I'd never seen him that outgoing
in all the years I'd known him.[32] But Quincy Jones had also been
given a glimpse of the old Miles during the concert. When, after a
ballad, Jones had murmured 'Beautiful!' to him, Davis had replied,
'Fuck you!'

Two days later, Miles Davis had a very different retrospective
concert at La Grande Halle, La Villette, in Paris. He opened the
concert with three pieces by his current working band – 'Perfect
Way', 'Star People' and 'Human Nature'. Then the personnels
kept changing as he brought in old friends and associates from
the 1950s to the 1980s. Once again the concert generated a powerful sense of occasion, something Miles had been able to do so
many times during his career. Here the audience were once again
agog, fired up, electric with expectation. This was another unique
event – Miles Davis looking back lovingly in public – and the
occasion seemed to have rejuvenated him. With his own band he
played with extraordinary urgency and power. 'Perfect Way' was
hot and fast with a barely containable rhythmic momentum, the
whole group collectively inspired, and Miles pushed it along with
dazzling muted lines and some strongly emotive high notes. He
retained this vitality all evening, but kept a lower profile when his

guests were featured. Guitarists John McLaughlin and John Scofield plus bassist Darryl Jones replaced members of Miles's own
band to play in 'Katia'. Miles revisited bebop with a sextet comprising altoist Jackie McLean, tenor saxophonist Steve Grossman,
Chick Corea on electric piano, bassist Dave Holland, and Al Foster
on drums. They played a fast, boppish 'Out of the Blue', with the
two saxophonists handling the melody and taking the main solos,
but Miles also added a couple of short, crisp solos, before passing
the baton to Corea for an electrifying keyboard and synthesizer
outing. They followed that with another fast one – Miles's own
1940s composition, 'Donna Lee', based on the chords of 'Indiana'.
Again the two saxes play the theme, but this time Miles takes the
first solo – just one chorus fleetly and effortlessly performed. The
two saxes stretch out in their solos, and Corea's comping is marvellously inventive and full of surprises. Jackie McLean said later
that year:

This summer, before Miles was knighted in France, we played
a concert that I enjoyed very, very much ... That was the
first time I played with Miles in a long, long time, probably
thirty years, and I thought he played great ... He looked
great. I found that he had mellowed so much. He was the
same Miles that I had known from early on but his wisdom
and his whole thing had just developed and mellowed down.
I was really shocked at how great he sounded. He sounded
fresh, just like he had never stopped playing traditional jazz.[33]

The French knighthood of Miles, to which McLean refers,
occurred in August 1991, when he was made a chevalier in the
French Légion d'Honneur. Minister of Culture Jack Lang called
him 'the Picasso of jazz' and said that Davis had 'imposed his law
on the world of show business: aesthetic intransigence'.[34]

Miles, Kenny Garrett and the rhythm section with Al Foster on
drums, were joined by Herbie Hancock and saxophonist Bill Evans
on soprano, for a marvellously buoyant and good-humoured performance of Hancock's classic, 'Watermelon Man'. Hancock pro-

grammed a burry Harmon mute sound on his synthesizer and traded phrases with Miles's actual Harmon mute, and the audience went wild with delight. Garrett's solo dug in deeply. The band's joy was infectious. Miles played a lovely solo on his own classic piece, 'All Blues', which featured Grossman and Evans on tenor and soprano respectively, Chick Corea, Dave Holland and Al Foster. Evans and Corea were star soloists here. Then Miles announced the presence of Joe Zawinul and Wayne Shorter, and the duo played 'In a Silent Way' poetically and passionately. Then the duo, with Miles's band and Al Foster on drums, played Miles's own classic, 'It's About That Time', from *Silent Way*, and when at last the famous bass line appeared, with Shorter's soprano solo and Miles on open trumpet, the audience again went wild with delight. This whole concert was an astonishingly light-hearted affair with Miles Davis, surrounded by musicians who knew him well and loved him, retracing his own and their own, musical footsteps – collective footprints that have blazed trails and inspired subsequent generations of musicians. There was even a reconstitution of his 1969 quintet (but with Al Foster on drums), to play Wayne Shorter's also classic piece, 'Footprints'. This visitation of guests ended with sixteen musicians on stage playing a raunchy version of Miles's contemporary classic, 'Jean Pierre'.

But some of the most striking aspects of the concert were the four performances by Miles's current working band. 'Human Nature', for example, was taken at a cracking pace with Davis in devastating muted form, with incisive phrases and sustained high notes that drew several crowd-bursts of applause. He dialogued with Kenny Garrett, who then took over the solo, playing far-out and far-in with extraordinary passion, great rhythmic ingenuity and momentum, and almost superhuman climaxes. Bill Milkowski, in his *Down Beat* account of the orchestral concert at Montreux, wrote of Garrett on that occasion: 'Garrett responded with his finest solo of the evening [in "Summertime"], blowing more horn than he's ever had a chance to play in the context of Miles's electric band.'[35] That statement is simply untrue; in his five years with Miles Davis, Garrett played many magnificent long solos in which he had to dig deep. That solo in 'Human Nature' in Paris was not only fine, it was awesome.

Four days later, Miles and the band continued their European tour by playing at the North Sea Jazz Festival at Den Haag, Holland. Then on 16 and 17 July they played at the Nice Festival in southern France, before flying to London for their concert at the Royal Festival Hall on 19 July. There can be no doubt that the intense activity of the previous three weeks of Miles's European tour, and the unusual demands of the two special concerts, had taken their toll on him. He looked very healthy and seemed to be in an excellent mood, benign and relaxed, directing the band genially, but although his sound, both open and muted, still glowed, his strength and range seemed much depleted. Occasionally, if he was alone in the middle of the stage, he seemed to lack focus, fluffing some notes, and once even holding his trumpet at arm's length and looking at it perplexedly. Then he would beckon to Foley or one of his other musicians to come closer and shadow him as he played, and his playing would regain its focus. It was very moving to see how this great master of music drew strength from his young musicians. The photographer Allan Titmuss had taken, in 1985, one of Miles's favourite photographs of himself in action, and the latter was in such an expansive mood on this occasion that he allowed Titmuss to position himself on stage behind the band, and take his photographs from that vantage point throughout the concert.

The tour ended with a concert three days later at Chapiteau, Andernos, France, after which Miles and the band returned to the USA. Gordon Meltzer said that Miles took the financial welfare of his musicians seriously and was always aware, for example, that his drummer had a mortgage. Retirement from touring was in the forefront of his mind, but he felt his responsibility to his musicians and was not yet quite ready for that big step. The European tour had been particularly lucrative because of his personal fee at Montreux, and after paying off the band and other tour expenses, Miles bought himself, *for cash*, a brand-new, dark blue 348 TS Ferrari. He was financially secure, he had plans for painting and recording, and he had no fears for the future. Yet, ironically, his next concert, at the Hollywood Bowl in California on 25 August, was to be his last one ever. There was another powerful sense of occasion at that performance, with tremendous audience responses to the music. The band was on superlative form, and Miles, too, was unstoppable, achieving something of the power and grandeur of his 1983–5 period. Someone in his entourage or in the audience must have had a birthday, because, during his solo in 'Hannibal' he played 'Happy Birthday to You'. The whole performance was hot, seething with energy and life, joy and optimism.

Back home at the end of August, he was feeling a little run-down, and heading for yet another bout of pneumonia. George Russell's wife, Alice, told the story of Miles at this time, with a girl on each arm, barging into the reception room of an acupuncturist and saying he needed some treatment. The receptionist produced a form and asked him to fill it in. He rasped, 'I don't fill in forms,' and swept straight out again with his two women. At the beginning of September, according to Gordon Meltzer, 'Miles went in the hospital, "for a tune-up", he said; just routine, nothing major, "I'll be right back." '[36] Miles had gone into St John's Hospital and Health Care Center, Santa Monica, California, and Gordon Meltzer, with Miles's nephew, Vincent Wilburn, went to visit him there. He was in good spirits, but suffering from bronchial pneumonia and the resultant breathing difficulties, which were by now very familiar to him. While Meltzer and Wilburn were there, the doctors arrived to check on Miles's condition. They noted the laborious breathing and said they wanted to put a tube down into Miles's lungs to give him oxygen. He did not want that. The doctors insisted and Miles went purple with anger, had a massive stroke, and went into a coma. He was put on a life-support system and his family were informed. His brother Vernon, sister Dorothy and daughter Cheryl arrived at his bedside. Meltzer said that Cheryl, in particular, fought to have him kept alive in case some new remedy was found. Steve Ross, the chairman of the Time-Warner Corporation, sent the message: 'Put Miles's medical bill on my account, and spare no expense to get him well. Get any doctors, fly anybody in.' The doctors analysed his blood and found that he had so much brain damage from the clotting that they couldn't bring him back to life. On 28 September, his body was allowed to die and his death was announced to a shocked world.

It was a tragic irony that Miles Davis was killed prematurely by his own anger. But although the causes of his death were made known as pneumonia and a stroke, the events which caused his unforeseen anger, which triggered the stroke, were known only to the immediate circle of his relatives and associates. Before he died, the news had slipped out that Miles Davis was in a coma, and then it had appeared in newspapers. To people who did not know the actual facts of the case, it had seemed that Miles's last eighteen months of life had been a process of preparing for death. In some ways the wheel seemed to have come full circle. At the very beginning of his career, he had recorded with an old blues singer, Rubberlegs Williams, and in 1990 Miles recorded with John Lee Hooker, another old bluesman. In the 1950s, Davis had recorded with Michel Legrand and, in 1990, he again recorded with Legrand. It seemed that his performance of the orchestral music at Montreux was another way of closing the book and saying goodbye, and this impression was reinforced two days later by his retrospective concert in Paris with many of his old friends. His death, shortly after this sequence of events, gave them a heightened significance, but he was actually preparing for his ultimate withdrawal from music and an enjoyable retirement; death was not on his menu. The tragic irony consisted in the fact that Miles Davis was, perhaps for the first time in his life, in the right psychological and physical condition to enjoy a relaxed, healthy and carefree retirement, secure in the knowledge that he had given his utmost to music, and created what has been called 'one of the greatest musical legacies of the twentieth century'. In retirement, his new passion, painting, would have been his absorbing pursuit and, with assistants, it was a social activity. It was also physically far less demanding than trumpet playing or playing concerts. But this reward of time to spare and leisure to paint was not to be vouchsafed to him.

Miles Davis had held centre stage in jazz for some five decades, and his music was known and loved by fans, musicians and even critics, so that the shock, the sense of loss and grief at his death were universal. All round the world there were long obituaries in newspapers, and tributes on radio and television. Writer Richard Williams, one of Davis's most sympathetic critics, wrote: 'No more of those moments, walking to the shop or stopped at the traffic lights, when you found yourself humming a few bars of "Milestones" or "On Green Dolphin Street" and wondering what he was up to now. A world without Miles Davis in it. Unthinkable, really.'[37] Musicians who had worked with him had pondered the experience for years afterwards, and his loss provoked a flood of memories in various magazines, usually under the title 'Remembering Miles', or 'Sketches of Miles'.

He was buried at Woodlawn Cemetery in the Bronx, near the Duke Ellington family site. One of his trumpets was buried with him, and the others, plus all his personal effects, including music, scores, tapes and mementos, remained in his family's possession. Shortly afterwards, there was a memorial service at St Peter's Church in Manhattan, and Dave Liebman wrote later:

I recall a thought I had during Miles's memorial service in the fall of 1991. Looking around and seeing many of the musicians who had played with Miles during the last thirty years, I realized that we all had at least two elements in common. He had hired us when we were all young and virtually unformed, and for many of us the style we played with Miles was unique – we would never play that way again. And of course there was the benediction factor meaning you were with the Prince, your career was on the way. But the unspoken and deeper truth was that by example, he taught you a whole bag of things: timing, nuance, subtlety, focusing energy, leading a band, even matters of business.

There were other aspects to observe which were outside

of the music directly, but when discussing Miles Dewey Davis, you have to separate the personal from the music.[38]

Jack DeJohnette, in conversation with Bill Milkowski and John Scofield, said:

I saw the videos of the Montreux concert at the memorial service. He looked good and he sounded great on that Gil [Evans] stuff. Quincy showed that footage after the service, so we heard him playing 'Summertime'. I had tears in my eyes, man. His phrasing just killed me. It was unbelievable.

Milkowski asked if Miles looked really ill at the time, and John Scofield, speaking of the retrospective concert two days after Montreux, said:

No, I thought he looked good. This was a concert where there were something like fifteen different groups that he played with. Many of the people he used to play with came out and played one tune with him. So he made it all the way through the rehearsal and the gig, and it was something like a three-hour concert. But he looked good and he played good. He seemed in really good spirits. And he was funny, man, cracking jokes.[39]

Jack DeJohnette added:

. . . In the later years he got looser somehow and more generous with people, giving encouragement to younger musicians. And he was more communicative with his audience. It wasn't so much a distraction to him as it was in the earlier times when, in order for him to play the way he played, he was detached from the audience . . . But I guess the best thing Miles taught us, not only in music but in life, was that we should learn to accept change, to embrace change rather than fear change.[40]

Keith Jarrett, in an interview with Hank Bordowitz, said:

When he died, I asked myself what does this mean? Miles, while he was alive, was a resonating object. Everyone's playing resonated, somehow, off him. When he's gone, there's no object there. Players are, all of a sudden, alone. I thought that this might be very healthy, because it's going to become very obvious to young musicians who want to use their head a little bit that they are the only ones who can do it. There's no resonating object sending them back a message saying 'Yeah, that's cool, keep going.' I think that's healthy in a way. Everyone dies, but I think Miles was the strongest jazz presence that many people will ever see in their lifetimes, whether anyone thinks he was playing jazz at all in the last twenty years. It doesn't matter. He was still there. You can hear that he was capable of doing that if he wanted to ... When Miles was playing, just before he died, you can hear the man's consciousness behind his sound: that's the message of jazz. That's the history of jazz.[41]

Jarrett's remarks are echoed in the final words of Marcus Miller's reflections on Davis's death:

The first thing I learned from Miles was about being true to yourself. Here was a guy who was acclaimed and criticized, and nothing that was ever said to him made him change what he felt he had to do. That's very important for a musician to learn, because you can be so easily swayed by people who have nothing to do with what you're about. They only know what you've already done; they have no idea of your goals. You've heard people say, when their parents have died, they finally feel like adults? Even if they're in their fifties? That now they're really on their own? Musically, I feel that way about Miles. I'm on my own now. This is it now. Figure out what to do, and do it. Right now, I'm working on an instrumental record of my own.[42]

Still on the subject of criticism, Gil Goldstein proclaimed:

Every style he played became a genre. Even the things everybody hated, that the musicians said were bullshit, now they're all styles. To me, that makes the whole thing about Wynton [Marsalis] and their debate so stupid. How are you going to compare those guys? *Everything* Miles did became a classic.[43]

And Dave Holland also spoke on that theme:

Miles taught me that the more naturally the music develops the more real it is, and he was a master of creating the conditions for something to happen. That's why it was way off line for Wynton Marsalis to have shown disrespect for a man who's made it possible for him to be what he is. Miles did a concert in Vancouver once and Wynton came on stage in the middle of the show, to sit in. Miles just stopped the band. He gestured Wynton over and then said in his ear in that big hoarse whisper, 'Come back tomorrow night.' Miles wasn't going to be there the next night, of course.[44]

But Marsalis himself came up with a graceful, if belated tribute to Davis in the 14 November 1991 issue of *Rolling Stone* magazine:

However controversial the last twenty years of Miles Davis's career might have been, there is no doubt that the lyrical beauty, the poignancy of his sound, his swing, the depth of his feelings and the ability he had to address the fundamentals of jazz will forever be of value to all musicians and all true listeners. He knew how to organize a personal style and he also knew how to organize bands. Few in jazz or in any other music have been as good as he was at his best.[45]

Miles's longstanding and faithful friend, Max Roach, also recalled their relationship:

It has always amazed me with Miles and Charlie Parker and all of us who came up at that time – working conditions weren't the best in those days. It was an uphill battle for all of us. You worked in environments where all kinds of distractions prevailed. It took its toll on a lot of us. The day after he died, I went out to see his family. It was the first time I was in his Malibu home. What knocked me out was that it looked like a painter's pad, not a musician's place. He had his own work – huge, beautiful things all over the walls, in the living room, in the bedroom, in the garage. It always seemed that Miles had that Midas touch artistically and materially.[46]

The above quotes give some idea of the breadth of response to Miles Davis's death, and of how profoundly his life and work had affected other musicians. But there were others – musicians and fans – who had only a tangential relationship to him, or had never even met him, but who yet had a special relationship to him and his work. He had something of the universality of all very great artists, and his music spoke and speaks to people on a multitude of levels.

His will was made public in October 1991, and it was surprising to learn that his estate was worth only £625,000, or about $2,000,000. His two sons by Irene Birth, Gregory and Miles IV, were excluded from the will, but forty per cent of his estate went to Erin, his son by Marguerite Eskridge, and twenty per cent to his daughter Cheryl (by Irene Birth). His nephew, Vincent Wilburn Jr, was left ten per cent and the remaining thirty per cent was divided equally between his brother Vernon and his sister Dorothy. But the major part of his estate is his enormous body of recorded work, his compositions and his paintings.

Miles lives on in his music, and his spirit also imbues the music of musicians he has influenced. Just as Louis Armstrong's music of the 1920s, and Charlie Parker's of the 1940s, can never be superseded, because both were a perpetual invasion of the unknown, breaking new ground, influencing and inspiring other musicians, so Miles Davis's work over several decades will remain a permanent touchstone of creative adventure and excellence over a long and radical artistic life. Max Roach talked of Miles's 'Midas touch', and even his very last, light-hearted rap album *Doo-Bop* won a Grammy award and reached sales of a third of a million by 1993. Warner Bros also released two singles from it, of 'Blow' and 'Doo-Bop Song', both including several different versions of the pieces, and each single lasting longer than the album. Since then there have been releases of several superb box-sets of his work. First came the Sony Japan seven-CD *Complete Live at the Plugged Nickel (1965)*, later released by Sony Columbia. Then came the great orchestral music in a six-CD set, *Miles Davis & Gil Evans: The Complete Columbia Studio Recordings*, and in 1998 a six-CD set of the great *Miles Davis Quintet 1965–68*.

But one of the most interesting events has been the release by Sony Columbia of *Panthalassa* – 'The music of Miles Davis 1969–74, reconstruction and mix translation by Bill Laswell'. Laswell, a bass guitarist and record producer, has been active in music since the 1970s, and loved Miles Davis's electric fusion music – the very music that has been so denigrated by conventionally minded jazz musicians and critics. This was the period when Miles worked rather like the American writer, Thomas Clayton Wolfe, who produced vast stretches of creative writing, some of which was edited posthumously into novels including the famous *You Can't Go Home Again* (1940). In the period 1969–74, Miles recorded vast stretches of music, which Teo Macero often edited into coherent entities for album release. There are possibly hundreds of hours of unreleased material in the record company's vaults, and Laswell remixed and re-edited passages from *In a Silent Way*, *On the Corner*, *Agharta*, and *Get Up with It*, putting them together in a coherent and very attractive suite. Laswell explained:

> I knew Miles personally and had a lot of conversations with him about the records which I've ended up remixing ... I spoke to Miles about a lot of things – about working [with him] on future music, which I think would have had a lot

more in common with the music we've just mixed [*Panthalassa*] than the music he did in the 1980s. He was also convinced that he had made a breakthrough with *On the Corner*. He knew that record was a departure from how people were putting music together and [he] was ultimately disappointed with the response from critics at the time and the total lack of commercial success. He felt he had created a new style, which in fact he had. When *On the Corner* first came out I can remember all those two-star reviews with people saying how terrible it was, yet for me it was the same feeling as when hip-hop first got abstract – going against pitch, against the rhythms. *On the Corner* represents that type of freedom to me. That was the beginning of an emergent form of hip-hop, and I connected to it immediately.

On the Corner is really just two bass lines over a beat, and all just cut up. You hear those little things which are just two minutes long; they're just quick cuts pulled from the longer 15–20-minute beats. I have six reels of outtakes from *On the Corner* which didn't even make the record.[47]

Miles Davis would certainly have approved of this recycling, re-editing and reissuing of aspects of his more discursive music. The fixed masterpieces of his earlier career, however, ought never to be tampered with. It looks as if the potential of some of Miles's later music will continue to be explored and realized long after his death. He always wanted his music to be in a state of becoming, and that can continue to happen even after his death. The general dialogue about Miles Davis and his work will never cease; much of the music falls on the listener like a blessing, and the heights and deeps of his legacy seem endlessly fascinating.

Postscript

Several people have suggested that I should include in this update of my biography of Miles Davis the obituary I wrote, published in the *Independent* on 30 September 1991.

MILES DAVIS

The work of Miles Davis, the jazz trumpeter, composer and band-leader, is a crucial part of twentieth-century music and his extra-ordinary career is documented by a monumental body of recordings. An inspirational figure who lived a long and immensely fruitful artistic life, Davis was a dominant force in the world of jazz from the moment he appeared in 1945.

Duke Ellington once compared him to Picasso in the multiplicity of his genius, and Davis certainly had something of the universality of all great artists. Because he was never content to rest on his laurels, but searched incessantly for new modes of music-making, he confounded critics and his career was dogged by controversy. But this very vitality was part and parcel of his greatness – he was a central figure in virtually every new movement in jazz from the 1940s to the 1990s.

He was the first person since Louis Armstrong to change the sound of the trumpet, and did so by producing a beautifully rounded, non-brassy tone without vibrato that projected a lyricism so profound that Chico Hamilton once said, 'Miles Davis is a sound – the whole earth singing!' This unique sonority was enhanced by a brilliant plasticity of inflection, great rhythmic dynamism, and a deployment of space so audacious that the pauses in a Miles Davis trumpet solo often seemed as marmoreally sculpted as his melodic lines.

Davis was born in 1926 into a wealthy middle-class family. His grandfather had been a landowner in Arkansas, and his father was a successful dentist who owned a ranch. His parents were leading members of the black community in East St Louis, and these patrician origins left an indelible imprint on him, even though in later life he tried to shake them off in order to gain some street credibility with less privileged American blacks. He got his first trumpet at the age of nine or ten, and by the time he was seventeen he was playing with a local rhythm-and-blues band and often rehearsing it when the leader was absent. He was befriended by the trumpeter Clark Terry, who was six years older and already had the epigrammatic melodic flair typical of the East St Louis school of trumpet-playing, and Terry's style strongly influenced his young protégé. Miles also met Dizzy Gillespie and Charlie Parker when they came to St Louis with the Billy Eckstine band.

In 1944 Davis's father sent him to New York to study at the Juilliard School of Music, but he soon dropped out in order to play jazz in the small clubs on 52nd Street. In November 1945, when he was still only nineteen, he made the first fully realized bebop recordings with Charlie Parker. This session included the classic blues performance 'Now's the Time', which established Davis immediately as a master of understatement and an alternative trumpet stylist to Gillespie. Miles Davis had begun his professional career in the very eye of the bebop hurricane, and he was to spend the rest of his artistic life seeking that kind of creative intensity. He was a member of Parker's group during its most dynamic period (1946–48) and played on all of the saxophonist's finest sextet and quintet recordings.

Davis left Parker in late 1948 and began leading his own groups in New York, including a nine-piece band that created a revolutionary new ensemble sound. With the composer/arranger Gil Evans, Miles Davis and the saxophonists Gerry Mulligan and Lee Konitz devised an ensemble that could achieve a full orchestral palette from a minimum number of instruments – French horn, trumpet, trombone, tuba, alto and baritone saxes, piano, bass and drums. The group's urbane sound, the subtle innovatory scoring, and the calm, unhurried solos seemed to be a reaction against the frenetic excesses of bebop and ushered in what came to be called the 'cool school' of jazz.

Evans, Mulligan and Davis did most of the composing and arranging, but it was Davis's unique trumpet sound that gave the group its essential identity, and Gerry Mulligan said later that he could not imagine any other trumpet player leading that ensemble. This band established Davis as a leader and a talent quite separate from Charlie Parker. At twenty-three, he was already an original and influential trumpet stylist, and also leader of a trailblazing orchestral group that included some of the most dynamic young musicians of the day. It was a brilliant beginning.

Then, after appearing as a star soloist at the Paris Jazz Fair in 1949, Davis succumbed to the narcotics addiction so widespread among musicians at that time. His magnificently promising career suddenly lost all impetus and direction, and for four years, (1949–53) he hardly worked at all. As an addict, he diced with death, suffered humiliation and degradation, becoming at times a virtual derelict and experiencing, for the first time in his life, the hopelessness of the black ghetto victim. After several attempts, he managed to kick the habit 'cold turkey', but the whole period of addiction had left its mark on him. His vision was immeasurably deepened, and his father said that the experience had put a hard crust on Miles. From now on, he would always maintain complete control of his circumstances and career – he would never again be the victim. From the mid-1950s onwards the famous Miles Davis persona began to emerge – unpredictable, wilful, mercurial, enigmatic, sardonic . . . keeping everyone guessing and imposing his will on the world.

There now began a six-year period (1954–60) of sustained creativity, which in terms of range, quality and innovation has no parallel in jazz. During this time Davis produced a succession of recorded masterpieces that astonished and delighted musicians and non-musicians alike, which opened up several new avenues of musical development and brought him a huge international audience, many of whom knew little about jazz in general. His artistry was at such a finely honed pitch that the often extremely radical nature of his work was hidden by its beauty and emotional eloquence. Quartet, sextet and quintet recordings of magnificent quality appeared in 1954 as Davis experimented with different line-ups. It also saw his first use in the recording studio of the metal harmon mute (without its stem) played very close to the microphone – a superbly evocative new sound that Miles introduced to jazz and which was then taken up by numerous other trumpeters.

Then in 1955, the first great Miles Davis quintet was formed with John Coltrane, Red Garland, Paul Chambers and Philly Joe Jones – a group so brimful of new ideas that they recorded six influential LPs in one twelve-month period. During one long night in Paris, in December 1957, using three French musicians and Kenny Clarke on drums, Davis improvised the music for Louis Malle's film *Lift to the Scaffold* (*Ascenseur pour l'echafaud*) and made two important discoveries. First, he found that it was possible to create completely satisfying music out of minimal predetermined material, and secondly, in the process of doing this, he became aware, in the words of one French critic, 'of the tragic character of his music'. This deepening of awareness resulted in two superb sextet albums – *Milestones* (1958) and *Kind of Blue* (1959) – both seminal, but the latter probably the most influential (and most loved) LP in jazz history.

With *Kind of Blue* Davis had fully established the beauty and relevance of modal improvisation, which is based on static scales rather than a moving sequence of chords and which soon became part of the jazz language. His group for this recording included John Coltrane and Cannonball Adderley on saxes, Paul Chambers on bass, Jimmy Cobb on drums and, perhaps most significantly, pianist Bill Evans, whose plangent chord voicings complemented the almost unbearable poignancy of Davis's muted work and the melancholy lyricism of his open trumpet. The exquisite playing and the feelings expressed on *Kind of Blue* brought new dimensions of subtlety and sophistication to jazz.

The quintet and sextet recordings of the 1950s would have been enough to establish Miles Davis as one of the jazz immortals, but in the last three years of the decade, in collaboration with Gil Evans, he recorded three albums that rank among the glories of twentieth-century orchestral music: *Miles Ahead* (1957), *Porgy and Bess* (1958) and *Sketches of Spain* (1959–60). Davis is the only soloist in all three mini-concerti, which brought the integration of an improvising player with a large, scored ensemble to a new and sustained peak. In *Miles Ahead* he chose to play only the little-known flugelhorn, and did so with such beautiful expressivity that it became *de rigueur* as a second instrument for trumpeters and was soon ubiquitous. In the other two albums, Davis played trumpet, sometimes using the harmon mute, which brought a new timbre to orchestral music. Deploying brass, reeds, woodwinds, flutes, bass and drums, Gil Evans created combinations of sounds, textures and techniques new not only to jazz, but to all music. Again, Davis's sound and style were absolutely integral to the music and the orchestra seemed to take on all his qualities – the passionate commitment, fluidity and profound feeling. Each of the three albums has its own unique identity, and all three have had a pervasive influence internationally.

By the end of the 1950s, Davis had become the dominant figure in jazz, admired by his peers, revered by musicians all over the world and with a substantial audience for his music. His quintet and sextet were generally recognized as the leading groups of the period and his rhythm sections were regarded as the finest. The myth-making was in full spate – he was dubbed 'Evil Genius of Jazz' and 'Prince of Darkness' – jazz critics strove to find new metaphors to describe his music, and even that doyen of theatre critics Kenneth Tynan wrote a long magazine article describing Davis's charisma and lifestyle. The latter was surviving, even thriving, without subsidy or sinecure in the cut-throat world of laissez-faire economics and yet also making music of the very highest quality – an astonishing achievement.

In the 1960s, Davis formed a new quintet, yet again drawing together some of the most gifted young musicians of the time: Herbie Hancock (piano), Ron Carter (bass), Tony Williams (drums) and Wayne Shorter (saxes). This particular rhythm section was generally considered to be perhaps the greatest time-playing unit in jazz, and its supreme virtuosity can be heard in a series of live albums (1963–4) in which Davis and the group explore conventional structures – standard tunes, ballads, modal pieces and blues – so radically that they are sometimes taken to the verge of disintegration. The greatest of these albums, and one of the finest live recordings in jazz history, is *My Funny Valentine* (1964).

From 1965, Davis and his group began exploring a new way of playing, which came to be called 'time-no-changes'. This was a form of abstraction in that the improvisation occurred in regular time, but without a set harmonic structure; after the theme statement the musicians tended to refer to thematic motifs in their solos, choosing what notes and chords they wished. This approach added yet another dimension to the jazz language, and in the later 1960s, the critic Leonard Feather commented that Davis had taken small-group improvisation to such a pitch of brilliance that he had 'nowhere to look except down'.

Up to this point, virtually all of Davis's small-group music had been based on themes that related clearly to popular song structures, but in 1968 he began to think more in terms of longer pieces, often without written themes. He also began to change the instrumentation of his group, using electric keyboards, electric guitars, multiple percussion and sometimes Indian musicians and instruments (sitar, tabla). The harmonic and linear abstraction remained, but he employed rock rhythms that created a coherent pulse, giving his music a human face. Yet again, some of the most gifted of the current generation were drawn to his band, including pianist Keith Jarrett, drummer Jack DeJohnette, and two Britishers – bassist Dave Holland and guitarist John McLaughlin.

In two years of furious activity (1969–70), Davis recorded enough material for more than ten LPs, focusing and launching the jazz-rock-fusion movement. The key albums that had a global influence were *In a Silent Way* (February 1969) and *Bitches Brew* (August 1969), the former an exquisite expression of Davis's contemplative and lyrical side, and the latter a double-album with a wide emotional range and a dark, brooding atmosphere all its own. As with all of Davis's most creative work, the radically different sound of these two albums came as a shock, resulting in controversy and, this time, the alienation of some of his older fans. He continued exploring this vein until 1975, when illness and physical and creative exhaustion incapacitated him. He was inactive until 1980, when he began to perform again.

In the 1980s he felt his way slowly into a new phase, which was like a summary of his whole career. He steadily regained all his trumpet magnificence – the huge singing sound, the stamina, the use of the entire range from the lowest notes to the extreme upper register, and his lyrical genius. Once more he drew to his band some key people from the current generation, including saxists Bill Evans, Bob Berg and Kenny Garrett, guitarists Mike Stern and John Scofield and bass guitarists Marcus Miller and Darryl Jones, and he returned to using structures related to popular songs. His studio albums such as *Decoy* (1984) and *You're Under Arrest* (1985) were highly organized, with an immense attention to detail and considerable complexity, yet they seemed like blueprints for the looser live performances where the magic and the music really happened. However, the album *Tutu* (1985), which featured Miles on harmon-muted trumpet in an electronic orchestral setting devised by Marcus Miller, had all the resonances of Davis's best work.

During the 1980s, he toured regularly in the US, Europe and Japan, playing to huge and ecstatic crowds. Although he still employed electronics and rock rhythms, the whole of his past seemed to glow in the music, and yet he never coasted or purveyed nostalgia. Some of his most eloquent and moving playing was done on those tours and, as always, he pushed himself to the limit. For his London appearance in 1985, he was on stage for about five hours, playing and directing his band in two superlative performances.

With Louis Armstrong and Dizzy Gillespie, Miles Davis is one of the three most influential trumpet players in jazz, but whereas the first two each introduced basically one stylistic approach, Davis has evolved at least three interrelated trumpet styles: the lyrical minimalist approach (*Kind of Blue*); the voluble brilliance of the live albums (1961–64); the abstraction and chromaticism of the late 1960s and the electric trumpet of the early 1970s. The emotional scope of his work is also greater than that of any other trumpeter, ranging as it does from the painful introspection of some of his ballad playing to the unbridled joy of some middle-tempo performances, or the violent aggression of one or two performances of his 1970s electric bands.

What set Davis apart was his sense of his own development as an artist – he didn't wish to repeat himself and so he would record only when he felt he had something fresh to say. That is why his vast body of recorded work is of such a high standard. His career divides roughly into five-year periods, and each one is dotted with seminal masterpieces that opened up new areas of exploration and set new standards of excellence. This is why he was such an inspiration for successive generations of musicians. Of course, some people tried to copy his phrases and mannerisms, but the real lesson he gave us was how to keep his art alive throughout his life, which he did heroically in an environment that was basically unsympathetic and often openly hostile.

All art, if it is any good, has something to say about the human condition, and Davis's work on record and in performance has always had these wider terms of reference. All true art is also a process of self-discovery for the artist, and Davis travelled further down that road than almost anyone else in jazz. His confidence in his own taste and vision came from this hard-won self-knowledge. Decade after decade, musicians have been able to witness Miles Davis working his way, often painfully and at great physical and psychological cost, into new areas of music. He was human and could falter and make mistakes, but this obvious humanity made his achievements all the greater.

Jazz is a very new music and perhaps Davis's greatest feat was to have imposed his own artistic values on it: unflagging intelligence, great courage, integrity, honesty and a sustained spirit of inquiry always in the pursuit of art – never mere experimentation for its own sake. His artistic life, whatever its faults or failings, was a triumph of vision and will. His serious commitment and superb achievements have enriched and dignified the music and its audience and we musicians have been magnified by his example.

References

All unattributed quotations are from personal interviews with the author.

Chapter 1: Miles Dewey Davis III
1 Leonard Feather, *From Satchmo to Miles*, Stein and Day, 1972, p. 230.
2 Marc Crawford, 'Miles Davis: Evil Genius of Jazz', *Ebony*, January 1961.
3 Ibid.
4 Nat Hentoff, 'Miles Davis – Last Trump', *Esquire*, March 1959.
5 *Melody Maker*, 9 January 1971.
6 Interview, *Playboy*, September 1962.
7 *Down Beat*, 6 March 1958.
8 Ibid.
9 Hentoff, *Esquire*, March 1959.
10 Stephen Davis, 'Miles Davis: An Exclusive Interview', *The Real Paper*, 21 March 1973.
11 *Down Beat*, 6 March 1958.
12 Marc Crawford, *Ebony*, January 1961.
13 *Playboy*, September 1962.
14 *From Satchmo to Miles*, p. 231.
15 Sy Johnson, 'Sparring with Miles Davis', *Changes*, 1974, p. 32.
16 *The Real Paper*, 21 March 1973.
17 *Down Beat*, 2 July 1964.
18 *Down Beat*, 6 March 1958.
19 *The Real Paper*, 21 March 1973.
20 *From Satchmo to Miles*, p. 231.
21 *Encore*, 21/28 July 1975.
22 Don Demichael, *Rolling Stone*, 13 December 1969.
23 *Down Beat*, 2 July 1964.
24 *Down Beat*, 6 March 1958.
25 Ibid.
26 *Melody Maker*, 4 September 1954.
27 *International Musician*, November 1972.

Chapter 2: Bird Land
1 *Down Beat*, 6 March 1958.
2 Ibid.
3 *Changes*, 1974, p. 32.
4 *The Real Paper*, 21 March 1973.
5 *Esquire*, March 1959.
6 *Down Beat*, 6 April 1967.
7 Ibid.
8 *Esquire*, March 1959.
9 Ira Gitler, *Jazz Masters of the 40s*, Macmillan, 1966, p. 208.
10 *Down Beat*, 22 April 1946.
11 Ross Russell, *Bird Lives!* Quartet Books, 1973, pp. 208–9.
12 *Down Beat*, 6 April 1967.
13 *Esquire*, March 1959.
14 *Down Beat*, 13 June 1968.
15 *The Real Paper*, 21 March 1973.
16 *Esquire*, March 1959.
17 Ibid.
18 Ibid.

19 Wilfrid Mellers, *Music in a New Found Land*, Barrie and Rockliff, 1964, p. 341.
20 *Down Beat*, 16 February 1961.
21 *Bird Lives!*, p. 267.
22 *Jazz Masters of the 40s*, p. 34.
23 Gilbert Millsteen, 'Jazz Makes It Up the River', *New York Times Magazine*, 1958.

Chapter 3: The Birth of the Cool
1 *Playboy*, September 1962.
2 *Down Beat*, 2 July 1964.
3 *Music in a New Found Land*, p. 355.
4 Sleeve note.
5 Sleeve note.
6 Nat Hentoff, *The World of Jazz*, Ridge Press Inc., 1976, pp. 103–5.
7 *Down Beat*, 2 July 1964.
8 Ibid.
9 Sleeve note.
10 Mike Zwerin, 'Miles Davis: A Most Curious Friendship', *Down Beat*, 10 March 1966.
11 Sleeve note.
12 *Down Beat*, 2 July 1964.
13 *Down Beat*, 23 March 1951.
14 *Down Beat*, 6 April 1967.

Chapter 4: Cold Turkey
1 Nat Hentoff, *The Jazz Life*, Panther Books, 1964, p. 77.
2 *Down Beat*, 6 March 1958.
3 *Down Beat*, 18 July 1974.
4 *Down Beat*, 23 March 1951.
5 *Melody Maker*, 30 September 1950.
6 Babs Gonzales, *Movin' on Down de Line*, Expubidence Publishing Corp., 1975, pp. 63–4.
7 *Jazz Masters of the 50s*, p. 70.
8 *The Jazz Life*, p. 77.
9 Ibid.
10 *From Satchmo to Miles*, p. 236.
11 *The Jazz Life*, p. 77.

12 *Melody Maker*, 23 February 1952.
13 *Jazz Masters of the 40s*, p. 50.
14 Sleeve note.
15 *Ebony*, January 1961.
16 *Down Beat*, 18 July 1974.
17 *Ebony*, January 1961.
18 Ibid.

Chapter 5: The First Great Quintet
1 *Playboy*, September 1962.
2 *Esquire*, March 1959.
3 Ibid.
4 *Down Beat*, 30 November 1955.
5 Nat Hentoff, 'An Afternoon with Miles Davis', *Jazz Review*, December 1958.
6 Ibid.
7 *Ebony*, January 1961.
8 *Esquire*, March 1959.
9 *Jazz Masters of the 50s*, p. 73.
10 *Down Beat*, 21 September 1955.
11 Ibid.
12 *Esquire*, March 1959.
13 *Down Beat*, 2 July 1964.
14 Sleeve note.
15 *The World of Jazz*, p. 136.
16 *The Jazz Life*, p. 181.

Chapter 6: Miles Ahead
1 *Playboy*, September 1962.
2 *The Jazz Life*, p. 77.
3 *Down Beat*, 29 September 1960.
4 *Jazz Masters of the 50s*, p. 76.
5 *The Jazz Life*, pp. 179–80.
6 *The Jazz Review*, December 1958.
7 Ibid.
8 Sleeve note.
9 Alun Morgan, 'Miles Davis: Miles Ahead', *These Jazzmen of Our Time*, ed. Raymond Horricks, Jazz Book Club, 1960, p. 49.
10 J. C. Thomas, *Chasin' the Trane*, Da Capo, 1975, p. 81.
11 Ibid., p. 69.
12 *Melody Maker*, 16 March 1957.

13 André Malraux, *L'Espoir*, Grove Press, p. 36.
14 *Down Beat*, 2 July 1964.
15 *Down Beat*, 16 February 1961.
16 Quoted by Charles Fox, *These Jazzmen of Our Time*, p. 96.
17 *Jazz Monthly*, February 1960.
18 *New York Times*, 12 January 1958.
19 Ibid.
20 *Jazz Monthly*, February 1960.

Chapter 7: The First Great Sextet
 1 *Ebony*, January 1961.
 2 *Esquire*, March 1959.
 3 *Time*, 20 January 1958.
 4 *Life International*, 11 August 1958.
 5 *Down Beat*, 2 July 1964.
 6 Cannonball Adderley, 'Paying Dues: The Education of a Combo Leader', *Jazz Panorama*, ed. Martin Williams, Cromwell-Collier Press, 1962, pp. 260–61.
 7 Mike Zwerin, 'Miles Davis – A Most Curious Friendship', *Down Beat*, 10 March 1966.
 8 *Jazz Hot*, June 1960.
 9 '30 Ans de Cinema', *Jazz Magazine*, May 1961.
10 *The Jazz Review*, January 1958.
11 *Down Beat*, 29 September 1960.
12 *Jazz Panorama*, pp. 261–2.
13 *Esquire*, March 1959.
14 *The Jazz Life*, p. 181.
15 Ibid., p. 43.
16 Sleeve note.
17 *Playboy*, September 1962.
18 *Ebony*, January 1961.
19 *Music in a New Found Land*, p. 367.

Chapter 8: Porgy and Bess
 1 *Fontana*, June 1959.
 2 *Jazz Review*, December 1958.
 3 *Jazz Panorama*, p. 262.
 4 *Jazz Review*, December 1958.

 5 *Music in a New Found Land*, p. 367.
 6 Sleeve note.
 7 Kenneth Tynan, 'Miles Apart', *Holiday*, February 1963.
 8 *Down Beat*, 10 March 1966.
 9 *Holiday*, February 1963.
10 *Fontana*, June 1959.
11 Ibid.
12 Richard Williams, 'Sketches of Gil', *Melody Maker*, 4 March 1978.

Chapter 9: Is It Jazz?
 1 *Ebony*, January 1961.
 2 *Jazz Review*, December 1958.
 3 Ibid.
 4 Ibid.
 5 Ibid.
 6 Ibid.
 7 Sleeve note.
 8 *San Francisco Sunday Chronicle*, 7 June 1959.
 9 Ibid.
10 Sleeve note.
11 Brian Priestley, 'Cleanhead's Comeback', *Melody Maker*, 3 June 1972.
12 *Down Beat*, 6 March 1968.
13 Jack O'Brien says: 'Bob Herridge Does It Again!' *New York Journal-American*, 22 July 1960.
14 *Melody Maker*, 12 September 1959.
15 *Melody Maker*, 5 September 1959.
16 *Down Beat*, 18 February 1960.
17 *Melody Maker*, 24 October 1959.
18 Nat Hentoff, *Hi Fi Review*, February 1960.
19 Sleeve note.
20 Ibid.
21 *Down Beat*, 27 October 1960.
22 Ibid.
23 Leonard Feather, 'Jazz Beat', *New York Post*, 26 April 1964.
24 *Down Beat*, 27 October 1960.

25 *Jazz News*, 15 October 1960.
26 *New York Times*, 11 September 1960.
27 Barbara J. Gardner, 'The Enigma of Miles Davis', *Down Beat*, 7 January 1960.

Chapter 10: After Coltrane
1 *Ebony*, January 1961.
2 *Playboy*, September 1962.
3 'Jazzmen Not Vaudevillians', *New York Journal-American*, 26 March 1960.
4 'Pourquoi Si Méchant, Miles?', *Jazz Magazine*, October 1960.
5 *The Jazz Life*, p. 196.
6 *Chasin' the Trane*, p. 109.
7 *San Francisco Sunday Chronicle*, 6 March 1960.
8 Quoted by Art Farmer, *Melody Maker*, 25 March 1960.
9 *Chasin' the Trane*, p. 109.
10 Paul Ackerman, 'Davis Sets Vanguard Fans Jumping', *Billboard*, 8 August 1960.
11 Leonard Feather, 'The Real Miles Davis', *Melody Maker*, 17 September 1960.
12 *Jazz Monthly*, December 1960.
13 *New York Post*, 16 October 1960.
14 *Playboy*, September 1962.
15 *Down Beat*, 16 February 1961.
16 Sleeve note.
17 *Playboy*, September 1962.
18 Sleeve note.
19 *Ebony*, January 1961.
20 *New York Times*, 29 May 1961.
21 Bill Coss, *Down Beat*, 6 July 1961.
22 George T. Simon, *New York Herald Tribune*, 20 May 1961.
23 *New York Post*, 21 May 1961.
24 Ibid.
25 Ibid.

Chapter 11: In and Out of the Doldrums
1 *Playboy*, September 1962.
2 *Melody Maker*, 18 March 1961.
3 *Down Beat*, 17 August 1961.
4 Ibid., 20 July 1961.
5 Ibid., 25 April 1963.
6 Ibid., 21 October 1963.
7 Sleeve note.
8 Leonard Feather, 'The Modulated World of Gil Evans', *Down Beat*, 23 February 1967.
9 *Playboy*, September 1962.
10 *Down Beat*, 10 September 1964.
11 *Down Beat*, 14 July 1977.
12 Ibid.
13 Ibid.
14 *Melody Maker*, 1 February 1964.
15 *Down Beat*, 18 June 1964.
16 Ibid.

Chapter 12: Miles in the Sky
1 Hollie I. West, 'Black Tune', *Washington Post*, 13 March 1969.
2 Clive Davis, *Clive: Inside the Record Business*, William Morrow, 1974.
3 *Louisville Times*, 9 December 1967.
4 *Down Beat*, 13 June 1968.
5 Ibid.
6 Ibid., 23 February 1967.
7 Ibid., 13 June 1968.
8 Ibid., 21 October 1965.
9 Ibid., 13 June 1968.
10 *Melody Maker*, 20 April 1968.
11 Sleeve note.
12 *From Satchmo to Miles*, p. 242.
13 *Clive: Inside the Record Business*, p. 260.
14 *Melody Maker*, 20 January 1973.
15 *Jet*, August 1966.
16 *Clive: Inside the Record Business*, p. 260.
17 *Washington Post*, 13 March 1969.

Chapter 13: Play What's *Not* There!
1 *Rolling Stone*, 13 December 1969.
2 *Playboy*, September 1962.
3 *Down Beat*, 18 June 1974.
4 Ibid., 14 November 1968.
5 *Melody Maker*, 4 March 1978.
6 *Washington Post*, 13 March 1969.
7 *New Musical Express*, 1 February 1975.
8 Ibid., 8 February 1975.
9 Ibid., 1 February 1975.
10 *Washington Post*, 13 March 1969.
11 *Time Out, The Times Union*, 28 February 1969.

Chapter 14: Miles Runs the Voodoo Down
1 *Newsweek*, 23 March 1970.
2 *Washington Post*, 13 March 1969.
3 Ibid.
4 *Time Out, The Times Union*, 28 February 1969.
5 *Jazz Review*, December 1958.
6 *Down Beat*, 3 September 1970.
7 *Newsweek*, 23 March 1970.
8 *Village Voice*, 31 July 1969.
9 Ibid.
10 *Time Out, The Times Union*, 28 February 1969.
11 Ibid.
12 *Melody Maker*, 17 January 1970.
13 Larry Kart, *Down Beat*, 7 August 1969.

Chapter 15: Jazz into rock Will Go
1 *Rolling Stone*, 13 December 1969.
2 *Los Angeles Times Calendar*.
3 *From Satchmo to Miles*, pp. 246–7.
4 *ZygoteIIZygote*, 12 August 1970.
5 *Afrostar*, 6 November 1969.
6 *New York Post*, 6 January 1970.

7 *Newsweek*, 23 March 1970.
8 *Down Beat*, 23 July 1970.
9 *From Satchmo to Miles*, p. 240.
10 *Newsweek*, 23 March 1970.
11 Al Aronowitz, 'Go' *Magazine*, June 1970.
12 Ibid.
13 *San Francisco Chronicle*, 13 April 1970.
14 *ZygoteIIZygote*, 12 August 1970.
15 *New York Times*, 18 July 1970.
16 Ibid.
17 Ibid.
18 *Sunday Denver Post*, 14 June 1970.
19 *ZygoteIIZygote*, 12 August 1970.
20 *Down Beat*, 4 March 1971.
21 *New York Times*, 18 July 1970.
22 *ZygoteIIZygote*, 12 August 1970.

Chapter 16: Live-Evil
1 *New York Post*, 3 July 1972.
2 *Melody Maker*, 9 January 1971.
3 *The Real Paper*, 21 March 1973.
4 Interview with Brian Priestley, *Down Beat*, 14 March 1974.
5 *Essence*, March 1971.
6 *Melody Maker*, 9 January 1971.
7 Ibid., 31 July 1971.
8 *New York Post*, 23 July 1971.
9 *Melody Maker*, 31 July 1971.
10 *Stereo – Das Deutsche Hi-Fi und Musik Magazin*, Number 17/75.
11 *Down Beat*, 18 July 1974.
12 *The Herald*, 7 April 1972.
13 *New York Post*, 3 July 1972.
14 *Encore*, 21/28 July 1975.
15 Ibid.
16 *Down Beat*, November 1972.
17 *Melody Maker*, 20 January 1973.
18 *The Real Paper*, 21 March 1973.

Chapter 17: Manhattan Jungle Symphony
1 *Melody Maker*, 20 January 1973.
2 *Sounds*, 19 March 1973.
3 *Down Beat*, op. cit.

4 Eugene Chadbourne, *The Herald*
5 Quoted in Hentoff's *The World of Jazz*, pp. 135–6.
6 *The Real Paper*, 21 March 1973.
7 Ibid.
8 *From Satchmo to Miles*, p. 255.
9 *The Real Paper*, 21 March 1973.
10 *Stereo-Das Deutsche Hi-Fi und Musik Magazin*, Number 17/75.
11 *The Real Paper*, 21 March 1973.
12 *From Satchmo to Miles*, p. 246.
13 *Encore*, 21/28 July 1975.
14 Gary Giddins, *New York Magazine*, 13 September 1974.
15 *Changes*, 1974.
16 Ibid.
17 *Melody Maker*, 7 September 1974.
18 *Rolling Stone*, 11 March 1976.
19 Ibid.
20 Ibid.

Chapter 18: The Silent Years, 1976–80
1 Miles Davis with Quincy Troupe, *Miles: The Autobiography*, Simon and Schuster, New York; Macmillan, London, 1989, p. 336.
2 Conrad Silvert, 'Miles Davis Brews Up a Recovery', *Rolling Stone*, 11 March 1976.
3 Interview with T. M. Stevens, in *Bass Player*, June 1994.
4 *Miles: The Autobiography*, p. 340.
5 Leonard Feather, 'Miles Davis's Miraculous Recovery from Stroke', *Ebony*, December 1982.

Chapter 19: A Tentative New Beginning
1 Cheryl McCall, 'Miles Davis', *Musician, Player and Listener* 41, March 1982.
2 J. B. Leishman (trans.), *Rilke:*

Selected Poems, Penguin Books, 1964, p. 21.
3 Howard Mandel, 'Miles Davis's New Direction is a Family Affair', *Down Beat*, September 1980.
4 Brian Case, 'Full Blown', *20/20 Magazine*, No. 12, March 1990.
5 Jack Chambers, *Milestones II, The Music and Times of Miles Davis Since 1960*, p. 301.
6 Mandel, *Down Beat*, September 1980.
7 *Miles: The Autobiography*, p. 344.
8 Ibid.
9 McCall, *Musician, Player and Listener*, March 1982.
10 Ibid.
11 *Miles: The Autobiography*, p. 345.
12 Ibid.
13 Sam Freedman, 'Marcus Miller: The Thumbslinger–Bassist for Hire', *Down Beat*, April 1983.
14 Nick Coleman, 'A Little Bit of Slap and Tickle', *Independent*, 14 April 1995.
15 Gen Santoro, 'Miles Davis the Enabler Part II', *Down Beat*, November 1988.
16 McCall, *Musician, Player and Listener*, March 1982.
17 *Miles: The Autobiography*, p. 346.
18 Feather, *Ebony*, December 1982.
19 *Miles: The Autobiography*, p. 346.
20 Feather, *Ebony*, December 1982.
21 *Miles: The Autobiography*, p. 347.
22 Richard Williams, 'On Top of All the Beat', *The Times*, 28 April 1983.
23 Ibid.
24 McCall, *Musician, Player and Listener*, March 1982.
25 *Down Beat*, 22 April 1946.

26 McCall, *Musician, Player and Listener*, March 1982.
27 Ibid. p. 42.
28 Sam Freedman, *Down Beat*, April 1983.
29 Ibid.
30 Williams, *The Times*, 28 April 1983.
31 Feather, *Ebony*, December 1982.
32 McCall, *Musician, Player and Listener*, March 1982.
33 Ibid., p. 42.
34 Ibid., p. 38.
35 Ibid., p. 40.
36 Ibid.
37 Feather, *Ebony*, December 1982.
38 Pawel Brodowski and Janusz Szprot, 'Miles Speaks', *Jazz Forum 85*, 1983.
39 *Miles: The Autobiography*, p. 349.
40 *Milestones II*, p. 334.
41 *Miles: The Autobiography*, p. 348.
42 Ibid.
43 McCall, *Musician, Player and Listener*, March 1982.
44 *Miles: The Autobiography*, p. 348.
45 Gary Giddins, 'Miles' Wiles', *Village Voice*, 5–11 August 1981.

Chapter 20: Crisis and Rebirth
1 McCall, *Musician, Player and Listener*, March 1982.
2 Feather, *Ebony*, December 1982.
3 *Miles: The Autobiography*, p. 350.
4 Feather, *Ebony*, December 1982.
5 *Miles: The Autobiography*, p. 353.
6 Feather, *Ebony*, December 1982.
7 David Breskin, 'Searching for Miles: Theme and Variations on the Life of a Trumpeter', *Rolling Stone 405*, 29 September 1983.

8 *Milestones II*, p. 354.
9 Tomasz Szachowski, 'Jazz Jamboree 1983', *Jazz Forum 85*, 1983.
10 Pawel Brodowski, letter to the author, 14 November 1996.
11 *Jazz Forum 85*, 1983.
12 *Miles: The Autobiography*, p. 358.

Chapter 21: Honours, Insults and Changes
1 *Miles: The Autobiography*, p. 364.
2 Howard Mandel, 'Miles Davis', *Down Beat*, December 1984.
3 Ibid.
4 *Ebony*, January 1961.
5 'Sketches of Miles', *Musician*, December 1991, p. 48.
6 W. B. Yeats, *Collected Poems*, Macmillan London, 1958, p. 217.
7 Pawel Brodowski and Janusz Szprot, *Jazz Forum 85*, 1983.
8 Ian Macintyre, *The Expense of Glory: A Life of John Reith*, London: HarperCollins, 1993.
9 Jan Lohmann, *The Sound of Miles Davis: The Discography 1945–1991*, Jazz Media, Copenhagen, Denmark.
10 Ibid.
11 Quoted by Gene Lees in 'Jazz Black and White Part II', *Jazzletter* Vol. 12, No. 11, November 1993.
12 *Miles: The Autobiography*, p. 360.
13 Gene Lees, *Jazzletter*, November 1993.
14 Bill Milkowski, 'Politics and the Miles Factor', *Down Beat*, April 1992.
15 Nick Kent, 'Prince of Darkness', *The Face 78*, October 1986, pp. 21–2.

16 'Miles Davis: A Life in Four Scenes', *Musician*, December 1991, p. 58.
17 Nick Kent, *The Face*, October 1986.
18 *Musician*, December 1991, p. 62.
19 McCall, *Musician, Player and Listener*, March 1982.
20 *The Sound of Miles Davis*.
21 Ibid.
22 Ibid.

Chapter 22: Tutu
1 *Miles: The Autobiography*, p. 383.
2 Ted Drozdowski, 'Doin' the Rat Dance', *Musician* 127, May 1989.
3 Ibid.
4 Ibid.
5 Gene Santoro, 'Miles Davis the Enabler Part II', *Down Beat*, November 1988.
6 *Musician*, May 1989.
7 *Miles: The Autobiography*, p. 371.
8 Charles Shaar Murray, 'Miles Davis: Cat Who Walks by Himself', *Observer in London* 40, 18 June 1989.
9 *Miles: The Autobiography*, p. 372.
10 Bill Milkowski, 'Marcus Miller: Miles's Man in the Studio', *Down Beat*, February 1987.
11 Chris Jisin, 'Marcus Miller', *Bass Player*, October 1992, p. 46.
12 Mike Zwerin, 'Top Records of the Decade', *International Herald Tribune*, 14 November 1989.
13 Mark Dery and Bob Doerschuk, 'Miles Davis: His Keyboards Present', *Keyboard*, October 1987.
14 Bob Doerschuk, 'Miles Davis: The Picasso of Invisible Art', *Keyboard*, October 1987.

15 Dery and Doerschuk, *Keyboard*, October 1987.
16 Gary Giddins, 'Miles Davis Superstar', *Village Voice*, special jazz supplement 'Miles Davis at 60', August 1986.
17 Ibid.
18 *The Sound of Miles Davis*
19 Ibid.
20 Dery and Doerschuk, *Keyboard*, October 1987.
21 *Miles: The Autobiography*, p. 379.
22 Ibid, p. 381.
23 Ibid.
24 Ibid., p. 382.
25 Laurence Bergreen, *Louis Armstrong: An Extravagant Life*, HarperCollins, 1997, p. 487.
26 *Miles: The Autobiography*, p. 384.
27 *Halliwell's Film Guide*, eleventh edition, HarperCollins, 1995.
28 *Musician* 127, May 1989.
29 *Miles: The Autobiography*, p. 281.
30 Ibid., p. 383.
31 Ibid.
32 Ibid., p. 384.
33 Ibid., p. 385.
34 Ibid.
35 *The Sound of Miles Davis*, p. 291.

Chapter 23: Amandla
1 *Miles: The Autobiography*, p. 397.
2 Ibid., p. 385.
3 Quincy Troupe lecture, USA, December 1991.
4 Ibid.
5 *Miles: The Autobiography*, p. 387.
6 *The Sound of Miles Davis*, p. 302.
7 Mike Zwerin, 'Rio Women and

Colorful Squares by Miles Davis the Painter', *International Herald Tribune*, 11 July 1988.

8 Ibid.

9 *Miles: The Autobiography*, p. 389.

10 Zwerin, *International Herald Tribune*, 11 July 1988.

11 Ibid.

12 Ibid.

13 Ibid.

14 Ibid.

15 Murray, *Observer in London* 40, 18 June 1989.

16 *Miles: The Autobiography*, p. 389.

17 Philip Watson, 'Miles Davis, Cardiff St David's Hall', *Wired* 61, June 1989.

18 Ibid.

19 *The Sound of Miles Davis*, p. 315.

20 *The Art of Miles Davis* (Davis and Gutterman), Prentice Hall, 1991, p. 10.

21 Murray, *Observer in London* 40, 18 June 1989.

22 Ibid.

23 Ibid.

24 Ibid.

25 *The Art of Miles Davis* p. 10

26 Ted Drodzowski, 'Doin' the Rat Dance', *Musician* 127, May 1989.

27 Peter Watrous, 'Miles Davis: Rebel without a Pause', *Musician* 127, May 1989.

28 Ezra Pound, *ABC of Reading*, Faber, 1961.

29 Watrous, *Musician* 127, May 1989.

30 *Miles: The Autobiography*, p. 389.

31 Josef Woodward, 'Miles Smiles: The Prince of Darkness Lightens Up and Talks About Life, Music and Painting', *Jazziz*, September 1989.

32 Murray, *Observer in London* 40, 18 June 1989.

33 Howard Mandel, 'Kenny Garrett: Mission Possible', *Down Beat*, September 1997.

Chapter 24: The Final Chapter

1 Francis Mormande, 'Rencontre à New York avec la Trompettiste Americain', *Le Monde*, June 1991, Supplements Arts-Spectacles (author's translation).

2 *Miles: The Autobiography*, p. 411.

3 Nicolette Jones, 'Book News First Report', *Bookseller*, 16 June 1989.

4 *Miles: The Autobiography*, p. 379.

5 Ibid., p. 409.

6 Ibid., p. 412.

7 Mike Zwerin, 'From Jazz to Pop to Reggae to Jazz', *International Herald Tribune*, 11 July 1989.

8 *Miles in Paris*, Warner Music Vision, 9031–71550-3.

9 *Halliwell's Film Guide*, p. 544.

10 'Sketches of Miles', *Guardian*, 3 October 1991.

11 'Remembering Miles', *Rolling Stone*, 14 November 1991.

12 *The Art of Miles Davis*.

13 Ibid.

14 Ibid.

15 Ibid.

16 Richard Williams, *Guardian*, 27 October 1995.

17 'Sketches of Miles', *Guardian*, 3 October 1991.

18 James T. Jones IV, 'Davis Took Jazz to New Frontiers and Miles Beyond', *USA Today*, 30 September 1991.

19 Gordon Meltzer, sleeve note, *Doo-Bop*, Warner Bros 7599–26938-2.

20 Leonard Feather, sleeve note, *Miles Davis & Quincy Jones Live at Montreux*, Warner Bros 9362–45221-2.

21 Bill Milkowski, 'Miles Plays Gil at Montreux', *Down Beat*, October 1991.
22 Ibid.
23 Ibid.
24 Ibid.
25 Ibid.
26 'Sketches of Miles', *Musician*, December 1991.
27 'Sketches of Miles', *Guardian*, 3 October 1991.
28 'Sketches of Miles', *Musician*, December 1991.
29 Milkowski, *Down Beat*, October 1991.
30 Ibid.
31 Ibid.
32 Feather, sleeve note.
33 Bret Primack, 'Remembering Miles', *Jazz Times*, February 1992, Vol. 22/No. 1.
34 *New York Times*, 29 September 1991.
35 Milkowski, *Down Beat*, October 1991.
36 Meltzer, sleeve note.
37 Richard Williams, 'The Man in the Green Shirt', *Independent on Sunday Review*, 6 October 1991.
38 Dave Liebman, liner note, *Dark Magus*, Sony Columbia 1997.
39 Bill Milkowski, 'Politics and the Miles Factor', *Down Beat*, April 1992.
40 Ibid.
41 Hank Bordowitz, 'The Zen of Jazz Moves Keith Jarret', *Jazziz*, April/May 1993.
42 Howard Mandel, 'Sketches of Miles', *Down Beat*, December 1991.
43 Ibid.
44 'Sketches of Miles', *Guardian*, 3 October 1991.
45 'Remembering Miles', *Rolling Stone*, 14 November 1991.
46 Ibid.
47 Bill Laswell talking to Kevin Martin, *TOP* magazine December/January 1997/98.

Bibliography
First Edition

Books

Bogle, Donald *Toms, Coons, Mulattoes, Mammies & Bucks: An Interpretive History of Blacks in American Films*, The Viking Press, New York, 1973

Cleaver, Eldridge *Soul on Ice*, Jonathan Cape, London, 1969

Cole, Bill *Miles Davis: A Musical Biography*, William Morrow, New York, 1974

Davis, Clive *Clive: Inside the Record Business*, William Morrow, New York, 1975

Feather, Leonard *Inside Be-bop*, J. J. Robbins & Sons, New York, 1949

Feather, Leonard *The Book of Jazz*, Arthur Barker, London, 1961

Feather, Leonard *The Encyclopedia of Jazz in the Sixties*, Horizon Press, New York, 1966, Quartet Books, London, 1978

Feather, Leonard *From Satchmo to Miles*, Stein and Day, New York, 1972, Quartet Books, London, 1975

Gitler, Ira *Jazz Masters of the 40s*, Macmillan, New York, 1966

Gleason, Ralph J. *Jam Session*, Peter Davies, London, 1961

Goldberg, Joe *Jazz Masters of the 50s*, Macmillan, New York, 1965

Gonzales, Babs *Movin' On Down De Line*, Expubidence Publishing Corp., New York, 1975

Harrison, Max *A Jazz Retrospect*, David and Charles, Newton Abbot, 1976

Hentoff, Nat *The Jazz Life*, Peter Davies, London, 1962

Hentoff, Nat *The World of Jazz*, Ridge Press, New York, 1976

Hodeir, André *Jazz: Its Evolution and Essence*, Grove Press, New York, 1956

Horricks, Raymond *These Jazzmen of our Time*, Victor Gollancz, London, 1960

James, Michael *Miles Davis*, Cassell, London 1961

Jazz Improvisation: Miles Davis, Vol. I and II, Nichion Publications Inc., Japan

Jones, LeRoi *Blues People*, William Morrow, New York, 1963

Mellers, Wilfred *Music in a New Found Land*, Barrie and Rockliff, London, 1964

Middleton, Richard *Pop Music and the Blues*, Victor Gollancz, 1972

Reisner, Robert *Bird: The Legend of Charlie Parker*, Quartet Books, London, 1974

Russell, Ross *Bird Lives!*, Quartet Books, London, 1973

Schuller, Gunther *Early Jazz: Its Roots and Musical Development*, Oxford University Press, New York, 1968

Stearns, Marshall *The Story of Jazz*, Oxford University Press, New York, 1956
Thomas, J. C. *Chasin' the Trane*, Elm Tree Books, London, 1976
William, Martin (ed.) *Jazz Panorama*, Crowell-Collier Press, 1962
Wilmer, Valeria *Jazz People*, Allison and Busby, London, 1970

Articles

Ackerman, Paul 'Davis Gets Vanguard Fans Jumping', *Billboard*, 8 August 1960
Crawford, Marc 'Miles Davis: Evil Genius of Jazz', *Ebony*, January 1961
Davis, Miles 'Self-Portrait', *Down Beat*, 6 March 1958
Davis, Stephen 'Miles Davis: An Exclusive Interview', *The Real Paper*, 21 March 1973
Demichael, Don 'Miles Davis', *Rolling Stone*, 13 December 1969
Feather, Leonard 'The Real Miles Davis', *Melody Maker*, 17 September 1960
Feather, Leonard 'Jazz Beat', *New York Post*, 26 April 1964
Feather, Leonard 'Miles and the Fifties', *Down Beat*, 2 July 1964
Feather, Leonard, 'The Modulated World of Gil Evans', *Down Beat*, 23 February 1967
Gardner, Barbara J. 'The Enigma of Miles Davis', *Down Beat*, 7 January 1960
Gleason, Ralph J. 'Miles Davis', *Rolling Stone*, 13 December 1969
Gleason, Ralph J. 'Miles Davis: 3 Hours to Unwind', *New York Post*
Grove, Gene 'The New World of Jazz', *New York Post*, 16 November 1960
Hall, Gregg 'Miles: Today's Most Influential Contemporary Musician', *Down Beat*, 18 July 1974
Hentoff, Nat 'An Afternoon with Miles', *Jazz Review*, December 1958
Hentoff, Nat 'Miles Davis – Last Trump', *Esquire*, March 1959
Hentoff, Nat 'Miles Davis', *Hi-Fi Reivew*, February 1960
Hentoff, Nat 'The New York Jazz Scene', *New York Herald Tribune*, 7 April 1963
Hoefer, George 'Early Miles', *Down Beat*, 6 April 1967
Johnson, Sy 'Sparring with Miles', *Changes*, 1974
Kolodin, Irving 'Miles Ahead of Miles' Head', *Saturday Review*, 12 September 1959
Malle, Louis 'Le Problème de la Musique de Film', *Jazz Hot*, June 1960
'Miles Davis' *Playboy*, September 1962
Miller, Manfred, 'Miles Davis', *Stereo – Das Deutsche Hi-Fi und Musik Magazin*, 17 November 1975
Millstein, Gilbert 'Jazz Makes It Up The River', *New York Times Magazine*, 1958
Morgenstern, Dan 'Sippin' at Miles', *Metronome*, May 1961
Murphy, Frederick D. 'Miles Davis: The Monster of Modern Music', *Encore*, 21–28 July 1975
'Pourquoi si Méchant Miles?', *Jazz Magazine*, October 1960
'Pourquoi si Gentil Miles?', *Jazz Magazine*, November 1960
Priestley, Brian 'Cleanhead's Comeback', *Melody Maker*, 3 June 1972
'The Prince of Darkness also brings Light', *Zygotel/Zygote*, 12 August 1970

Tynan, Kenneth 'Miles Apart', *Holiday*, February 1963

Vartan, Eddie 'Miles Davis', *Jazz Magazine*, March 1960

Watts, Michael 'Miles Davis', *Melody Maker*, 20 January 1973

Williams, Richard 'Sketches of Gil', *Melody Maker*, 4 March 1978

Zwerin, Mike 'Miles Davis: A Most Curious Friendship', *Down Beat*, 10 March 1966

Bibliography
Second Edition

Books

Bergreen, Laurence: *Louis Armstrong: An Extravagant Life*, HarperCollins, London, 1997; Broadway Books, USA, 1997

Chambers, Jack: *Milestones I: The Music and Times of Miles Davis to 1960*, University of Toronto Press, Toronto, Buffalo; London, 1983. *Milestones II: The Music and Times of Miles Davis Since 1960*, University of Toronto Press, 1985

Davis, Miles with Quincy Troupe: *Miles: The Autobiography*, Simon and Schuster, New York; Macmillan, London, 1989

Davis, Miles and Gutterman, Scott: *The Art of Miles Davis*, Prentice Hall Editions, New York and London, 1991

Halliwell, Leslie: *Halliwell's Film Guide*, 11th Edition, HarperCollins, London, 1995

Lees, Gene: *Cats of Any Color: Jazz, Black and White*, Oxford University Press, New York, Oxford, Toronto, 1994

Leishman, J. B: *Rilke: Selected Poems*, Penguin Books, London, 1964

Lohmann, Jan: *The Sound of Miles Davis: The Discography* (listing of records and tapes 1945–91), JazzMedia, Copenhagen, Denmark, 1992

Mac Intyre, Ian: *The Expenses of Glory: A Life of John Reith*, HarperCollins, London, 1993

Pound, Ezra: *ABC of Reading*, Faber and Faber, London, 1961

Williams, Richard: *Miles Davis: The Man in the Green Shirt*, Bloomsbury, London, 1993

Yeats, William Butler: *Collected Poems*, Macmillan, London, 1958

Articles

Breskin, David, 'Searching for Miles: Theme and Variations on the Life of a Trumpeter', *Rolling Stone* 405, 29 September 1983

Brodowski, Pawel and Szprot, Janusz, 'Miles Speaks', *Jazz Forum* 85, 1983

Carr, Ian, 'Miles Further Ahead', *Guardian*, 19 July 1984

Case, Brian, 'Full Blown', *20/20 Magazine* 12, March 1990

Coleman, Nick, 'A Little Bit of Slap and Tickle', *Independent*, 14 April 1995

Cook, Richard, 'Miles Runs the Voodoo Down', *New Musical Express*, 13 July 1985

Doerschuk, Bob, 'Miles Davis: The Picasso of Invisible Art', *Keyboard*, October 1987

Doerschuk, Bob and Dery, Mark, 'Miles Davis: His Keyboards Present – Bobby Irving and Adam Holzman', *Keyboard*, October 1987

Drozdowski, Ted, 'Doin' the Rat Dance', *Musician* 127, May 1989

Ephland, John, 'Miles to Go', *Down Beat*, October 1988

Feather, Leonard, 'Miles Davis Recovery from Stroke', *Ebony*, December 1982

Freedman, Sam, 'Marcus Miller: The Thumbslinger – Bassist for Hire', *Down Beat*, April 1983

Giddins, Gary, 'Miles Wiles', *Village Voice*, 11 August 1981

Giddins, Gary, 'Miles Davis Superstar', *Village Voice* NYC, special supplement, 'Miles Davis at 60', August 1986

Jisi, Chris, 'Marcus Miller', *Bass Player*, October 1992

Jones IV, James T. 'Davis Took Jazz to New Frontiers and Miles Beyond', *USA Today*, 30 September 1991

Jones, Max, 'The Return of Miles Davis', *Melody Maker*, 21 June 1980

Jones, Nicolette, 'Book News First Report', *Bookseller*, 16 June 1989

Keepnews, Orrin, 'Miles Davis: Past Keyboardists', *Keyboard*, October 1987

Kent, Nick, 'Prince of Darkness', *The Face* 78, October 1986

Lake, Steve, 'Miles at 50', *Melody Maker*, 29 May 1976

Lake, Steve, 'Miles Smiles', *Guardian*, 15 November 1986

Lees, Gene, 'Jazz Black and White Part II', *Jazzletter* 12 No. 11, November 1993

McCall, Cheryl, 'Miles Davis', *Musician Player and Listener* 41, March 1982

Mandel, Howard, 'Miles's New Direction a Family Affair', *Down Beat*, September 1980

Mandel, Howard, 'Miles Davis', *Down Beat*, December 1984

Mandel, Howard, 'Sketches of Miles', *Down Beat*, December 1991

Mandel, Howard, 'Kenny Garrett: Mission Possible', *Down Beat*, September 1997

Marmande, Francis, 'Rencontre à New York avec la trompettiste Americain', Miles Davis interviewed in *Le Monde*, Supplement Arts – Spectacles, June 1991

Martin, Kevin, Interview with Bill Laswell, *TOP*, Dec/Jan 1997/98

Miles, Jason, 'Programming and Sessions with Miles Davis', *Keyboard*, October 1987

Milkowski, Bill, 'Politics and the Miles Factor', *Down Beat*, April 1992

Milkowski, Bill, 'Marcus Miller: Miles's Man in the Studio', *Down Beat*, February 1987

Milkowski, Bill, 'Miles Plays Gil at Montreux', *Down Beat*, October 1991

Mitchell, Charles, 'Miles Resting on His Laurels', *Down Beat*, September 1980

Murray, Charles Shaar, 'Miles Davis: Cat Who Walks by Himself', *Observer* (in London issue) 40, 18 June 1989

Primark, Bret, 'Remembering Miles', *Jazz Times* 22, No. 1, February 1992

'Remembering Miles', *Rolling Stone*, 14 November 1991

Santoro, Gene, 'Miles Davis the Enabler Part II', *Down Beat*, November 1988

Schachowski, Tomasz, 'Jazz Jamboree 1983', *Jazz Forum 85*, 1983

Silvert, Conrad, 'Miles Brews up a Recovery', *Rolling Stone*, 11 March 1976

'Sketches of Miles', *Guardian*, 3 October 1991

'Sketches of Miles', *Musician*, December 1991

Stevens, T. M., interview in *Bass Player*, June 1994

Sweeting, Adam, 'A Little Loving Goes Miles and Miles', *Guardian*, 30 June 1987

Watrous, Peter, 'Miles Davis: Rebel without a Pause', *Musician* 127, May 1989

Watson, Philip, 'Miles Davis, Cardiff St David's Hall', *Wired* 61, June 1989

Williams, Richard, 'Miles Ahead Again', *The Times*, 21 April 1982

Williams, Richard, 'On Top of All the Beat', *The Times*, 28 April 1983

Williams, Richard, 'The Man in the Green Shirt', *Independent on Sunday* (Sunday Review), 6 October 1991

Williams, Richard, interview with Marcus Miller, *Guardian*, 27 October 1995

Woodward, Josef, 'Miles Smiles', the Prince of Darkness Lightens Up and Talks About Life, Music and Painting', *Jazziz*, September 1989

Zwerin, Mike, 'Rio, Women and Colourful Squares by Miles Davis the Painter', *International Herald Tribune*, 11 July 1988

Zwerin, Mike, 'From Jazz to Pop to Reggae to Jazz', *International Herald Tribune*, 11 July 1989

Zwerin, Mike, 'Top Records of the Decade', *International Herald Tribune*, 14 November 1989

APPENDIX A

Musical Examples

A Note of the Solo Transcriptions

These transcriptions of solos by Miles Davis are only approximations. I have tried to be as accurate as possible, but Western notation is inadequate to codify precisely the subtleties of rhythm and pitch inflextion which characterize jazz. In all cases the reader is urged to go to the recordings and listen to the solos in context.

Figure 1

"Godchild' by George Wallington from *The Birth of the Cool.*

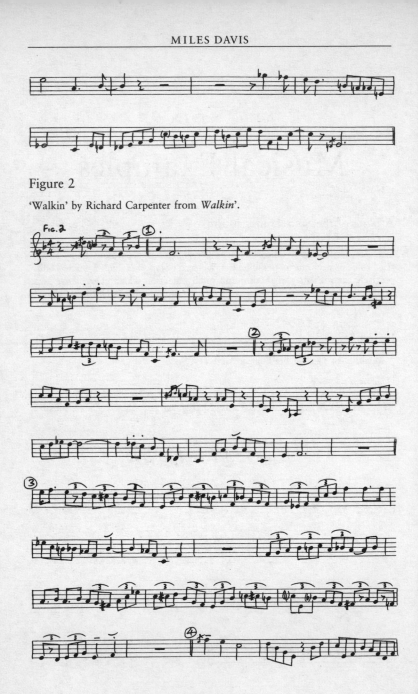

Figure 2

'Walkin' by Richard Carpenter from *Walkin'*.

Figure 3

'Bags' Groove' by Milton Jackson from *Bags' Groove*.

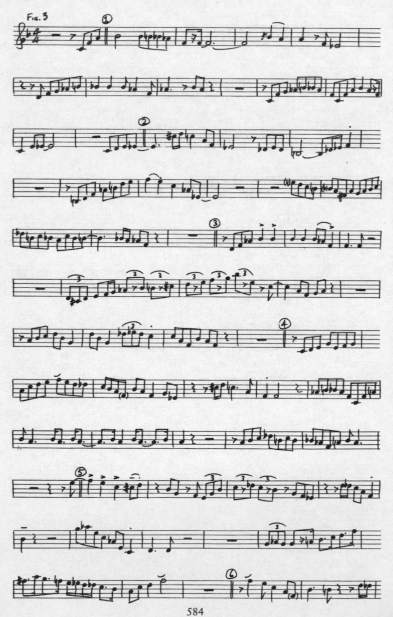

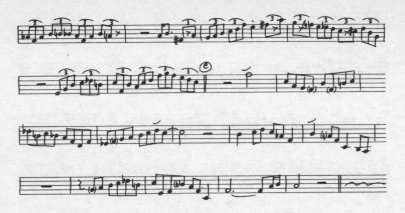

Figure 4

'My Funny Valentine' by Richard Rodgers from *Cookin'*.

Figure 5a

'Florence sur les Champs Élysées' by Miles Davis from *Jazztrack*.

Figure 5b

'Chez le Photographe du Motel' by Miles Davis from *Jazztrack*.

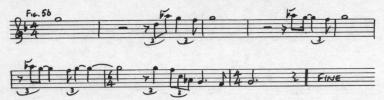

Figure 6

'Sid's Ahead' by Miles Davis from *Milestones*.

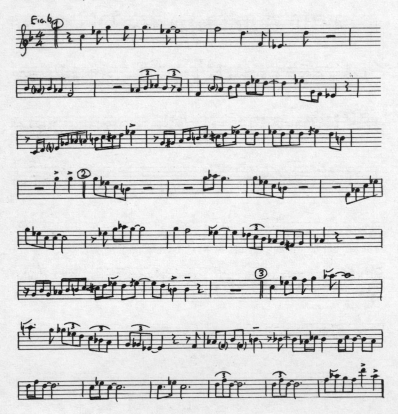

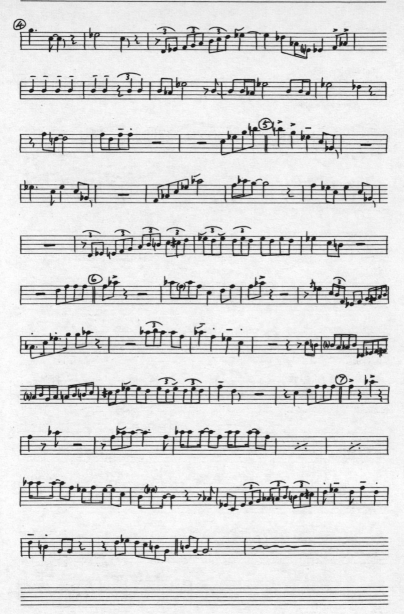

Figure 7

'My Funny Valentine' by Richard Rodgers from *My Funny Valentine*.

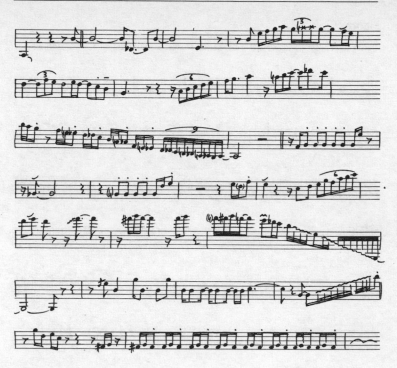

Figure 8

'Country Son' by Miles Davis from *Miles in the Sky*.

Figure 9

'Petits Machins' ('Little Stuff') by Miles Davis from *Filles de Kilimanjaro*.

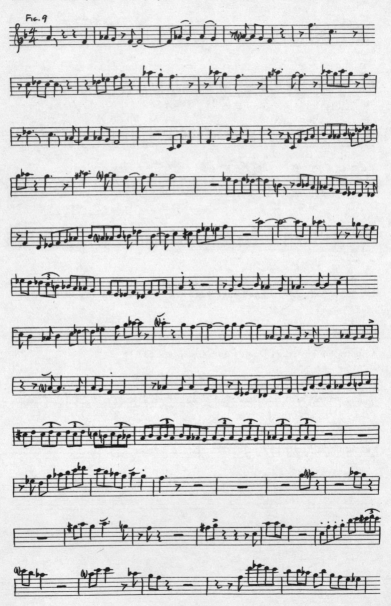

APPENDIX B

Notes on Repertoire

Brian Priestley provided the following list of songs which were recorded by Frank Sinatra and which crept into Miles Davis's repertoire during the 1950s:

Sinatra recorded
    'There's No You' (November 1944)
    'I Fall In Love Too Easily' (December 1944)
    'Stella by Starlight' (March 1947)
    'S'posin'' (October 1947)
    'It Never Entered My Mind' (twice: November 1947 with Bobby Hackett and March 1955)
    'Spring is Here' (twice: March 1949 and May 1958)
    'My Funny Valentine' (October 1953)
    'I Thought About You' (January 1956)

The last two came respectively from the albums, *Songs For Young Lovers* and the even more influential *Songs For Swinging Lovers*.

I am indebted to Trevor Timmers for the following list of comparative recordings by Ahmad Jamal and Miles Davis:

	Jamal	*Davis*
'Surrey with the Fringe on Top'	25 October 1951	11 May 1956
'Will You Still Be Mine'	25 October 1951	7 June 1955
'Ahmad's Blues'	25 October 1951	11 May 1956 (rhythm section)
'Gal in Calico'	25 October 1951	7 June 1955
'But Not For Me'	January 1954	29 June 1954
'New Rhumba'	23 May 1955	23 May 1957
'All of You'	25 May 1955	10 September 1956
'Autumn Leaves'	25 May 1955	9 March 1958 (*Somethin' Else*)
'Love For Sale'	25 May 1955	9 March 1958 (*Somethin' Else*)
'Green Dolphin Street'	27 September and 4 October 1956	26 May 1958

Discography

This lengthy appendix is nevertheless a mere synopsis since, in most cases, only the original catalogue number is listed for each title. The exceptions occur where different versions of the same material, for instance mono and stereo or LPs and 45s (and, in the early fifties, 78s), were released more or less simultaneously, although in practice it has been difficult to draw a line between such instances and 45RPM *reissues*, often some years later and prompted by Miles's increasing popularity.

The fact that some of the Dial items with Charlie Parker have appeared on up to 50 separate issues should be enough to show why a synopsis was thought necessary, but an attempt has also been made to cross-reference with an index of current album numbers from (1) to (80), demonstrating that over 90% of Miles Davis's issued output is available at the time of going to press. As to private recordings and air-shots, everything thus far issued commercially has been listed, plus known unissued material up to and including 1960, after which date the proliferation of private recorders eventually renders this task impossible.

Where location recordings have been issued under incorrect titles, these have been placed in parentheses after the original title, while retitled *studio* items have the issued title first with the title of any subsequent issue (or distinguished by the prefix 'i.e.', the title of other known recordings) shown in parentheses.

Other innovations include the use of asterisks after catalogue numbers to indicate performances which are (*) incomplete on the record or (**) edited on the issue in question; however, these are dropped for album tracks after 1968, since Miles's recording practices render such descriptions applicable to all his later studio work. The more standard legend 'breakdown' refers to a performance which was terminated in mid-stream but was issued complete as it stands, while 'theme' describes a radio signature-tune, often played for no more than a few bars. The following standard abbreviations have also been used:

alt	alternative take
arr	arranger
as	alto saxophone
b	bass
bar-h	baritone-horn
bars	baritone saxophone
bcl	bass clarinet
bgo	bongo

btb	bass trombone
cga	conga
cl	clarinet
cond	conductor
d	drums
dir	director
Du	Dutch
E	English
el	electric
F	French
fl	flute
flh	flugelhorn
fr-h	french-horn
G	German
g	guitar
hca	harmonica
J	Japanese
keyb	keyboards
mc	master of ceremonies
narr	narrator
org	organ
p	piano
perc	percussion
ss	soporano saxophone
synth	synthesizer
tb	trombone
tp	trumpet
ts	tenor saxophone
tu	tuba
tymp	tympani
vcl	vocal
vib	vibraphone
vtb	valve trombone

Brian Priestley

1945:

April 24	RUBBERLEGS WILLIAMS & ORCHESTRA
New York City	FEATURING HERBIE FIELDS

Miles Davis (tp); Herbie Fields (as,ts); Teddy Brannon (p); Leonard Gaskin (b); Eddie Nicholson (d); Rubberlegs Williams (vcl)

S5805	**That's the stuff you got to watch**	Savoy 564
S5806	**Pointless mama blues**	—
S5807	**Deep sea blues**	Savoy 5516
S5808	**Bring it on home**	—

November 26	CHARLEY PARKER'S REE BOPPERS
New York City	

Miles Davis (tp); Charlie Parker (as); 'Hen Gates' (Dizzy Gillespie) (p); Curley Russell (b); Max Roach (d)

S5850-1	**Billie's bounce**	(1)	Savoy MG 12079
S5850-2	**Billie's bounce** (breakdown)	(1)	—
S5850-3	**Billie's bounce**	(1)	—
S5850-4	**Billie's bounce** (breakdown)	(1)	—
S5850-5	**Billie's bounce**	(1)	Savoy 573
S5851-1	**Now's the time** (breakdown)	(1)	Savoy MG 12079
S5851-2	**Now's the time** (breakdown)	(1)	—
S5851-3	**Now's the time**	(1)	—
S5851-4	**Now's the time**	(1)	Savoy 573

Sadik Hakim (p) replaces Gillespie

S5852-1	**Thriving on a riff**	(1)	Savoy MG 12079
S5852-2	**Thriving on a riff** (breakdown)	(1)	—
S5852-3	**Thriving on a riff**	(1)	Savoy 903

Note: Davis and Hakim out on remaining titles from this session

1946:

c.early March	CHARLIE PARKER QUINTET
Finale Club	Miles Davis (tp); Charlie Parker (as); Joe Albany (p);
Los Angeles	Addison Farmer (b); Chuck Thompson (d)

	Anthropology	(2) Queen-Disc Q-017
	Billie's bounce	(2) —
	Blue 'n' boogie	(2) —
	All the things you are	(2) —
	Ornithology	(2) — *

March 28	CHARLIE PARKER SEPTET
Los Angeles	Miles Davis (tp); Charlie Parker (as); Lucky Thompson (ts);
	Dodo Marmarosa (p); Vic McMillan (b); Roy Porter (d)

D 1010-1	**Moose the mooche**	(3) Dial DLP201
D 1010-2	**Moose the mooche**	(3) Dial 1003, 1004
D 1010-3	**Moose the mooche**	(3) Spotlite 105, 101
	Arv Garrison (g) added	
D 1011-1	**Yardbird suite**	(3) Dial DLP201
D 1011-4	**Yardbird suite**	(3) Dial 1003
D 1012-1	**Ornithology**	(3) Dial DLP208
D 1012-3	**Bird lore (Ornithology)**	(3) Dial 1006
D 1012-4	**Ornithology**	(3) Dial 1002
D 1013-1	**Famous alto break**	(3) Dial DLP905 *
D 1013-4	**Night in Tunisia**	(3) Dial DLP201
D 1013-5	**Night in Tunisia**	(3) Dial 1002

Notes: **D1010-2, D1011-4, D1012-4** and **D1013-5** have also been reissued as by MILES DAVIS; **D1012-1** originally issued as by DODO MARMAROSA SEXTET

March 31	**BENNY CARTER**	
Streets of Paris,	Miles Davis (tp); Al Grey (tb); Benny Carter (as); Bumps	
Los Angeles	Myers (ts); Sonny White (p); Jimmy Cannady (g); prob.	
	Tommy Moultrie (b); prob. Percy Brice (d)	
	Just you, just me	Air-shot
	Don't blame me	—
	Sweet Georgia Brown	—

c. May/June	**BENNY CARTER AND HIS ORCHESTRA**	
Los Angeles	As above plus 3 tp, 3 tb, 3 sax – unknown	
	Just you, just me	(4) AFRS Jubilee 186
	Jump call	(4) —
	untitled original	(4) AFRS Jubilee 191

October 5	**BILLY ECKSTINE AND HIS ORCHESTRA**	
Los Angeles	Hobart Dotson, Leonard Hawkins, Miles Davis, King Kolax	
	(tp); Walter Knox, Chips Outcalt, Gerry Valentine (tb);	
	Sonny Stitt, John Cobbs (ts); Gene Ammons, Arthur	
	Sammons (ts); Cecil Payne (bars); Linton Garner (p);	
	Connie Wainwright (g); Tommy Potter (b); Art Blakey (d);	
	Billy Eckstine (vcl-1, vtb-2)	
NSC164	**Oo bop sh'bam** -1,2	(5) National 9125
NSC164(alt.)	**Oo bop sh'bam** -1,2	(5) CBS-Sony (J) SOPL-54
NSC165	**I love the loveliness** -1	(5) National 9030
NSC166	**In the still of the night** -1	(5) National 9037
NSC167	**Jelly jelly** -1,2	(5) National 9021
NSC167(alt.)	**Jelly jelly** -1,2	CBS-Sony (J) SOPL-54

c. Autumn	**EARL COLEMAN/ANN HATHAWAY**	
Los Angeles	Miles Davis (tp); Gene Ammons (ts); Linton Garner (p);	
	Connie Wainwright (g); Tommy Potter (b); Art Blakey (d);	
	Earl Coleman-1, Ann Hathaway-2 (vcl)	
	two unknown titles -1	Sunset unissued
	two unknown titles -2	—

1947:

March	**ILLINOIS JACQUET AND HIS ORCHESTRA**	
New York City	Marion Hazel, Miles Davis, Fats Navarro, Joe Newman (tp);	
	Gus Chappel, Ted Kelly, Eli Robinson, Dickie Wells (tb);	
	Ray Perry, Jimmy Powell (as); Illinois Jacquet, Big Nick	
	Nicholas (ts); Leo Parker (bars); Bill Doggett (p); Al Lucas	
	(b); Shadow Wilson (d); Tadd Dameron-1, Jimmy Mundy	
	(arr)	
94-4	**For Europeans only** -1	Aladdin 180
95-3	**Big dog** -2	—
96-4	**You left me alone**	Aladdin 179
97-2	**Jivin' with Jack the bellboy**	—
	2- Leonard Feather (p) replaces Doggett	

May 8	**CHARLIE PARKER ALL STARS**	
New York City	Miles Davis (tp); Charlie Parker (as); Bud Powell (p);	
	Tommy Potter (b); Max Roach (d)	
S3420-1	**Donna Lee** (breakdown)	(1) Savoy S5J5500
S3420-2	**Donna Lee**	(1) Savoy MG12001
S3420-3	**Donna Lee**	(1) —
S3420-4	**Donna Lee**	(1) Savoy MG12009
S3420-5	**Donna Lee**	(1) Savoy 652
S3421-1	**Chasin' the Bird**	(1) Savoy MG12001
S3421-2	**Chasin' the Bird** (breakdown)	(1) Savoy S5J5500
S3421-3	**Chasin' the Bird**	(1) Savoy MG12009
S3421-4	**Chasin' the Bird**	(1) Savoy 977
S3422-1	**Cheryl** (breakdown)	(1) Savoy MG12001
S3422-2	**Cheryl**	(1) Savoy 952

S3423-1	**Buzzy**	(1) Savoy MG12009
S3423-2	**Buzzy** (breakdown)	(1) Savoy MG12001
S3423-3	**Buzzy**	(1) —
S3423-4	**Buzzy** (breakdown)	(1) Savoy MG12000
S3423-5	**Buzzy**	(1) Savoy 652

Note: **S3421-4** originally issued as by MILES DAVIS ALL STARS

June
New York City

COLEMAN HAWKINS ALL STARS

Miles Davis (tp); Kai Winding (tb); Howard Johnson (as); Coleman Hawkins (ts); Hank Jones (p); prob. Curley Russell or Tommy Potter (b); prob. Max Roach (d)

215	**Bean-a-re-bop**	Aladdin 3006
216	**Isn't it romantic**	Aladdin EP516
217	**The way you look tonight**	Aladdin 3006
218	**Phantomesque**	Aladdin EP516

August 14
New York City

MILES DAVIS ALL STARS

Miles Davis (tp); Charlie Parker (ts); John Lewis (p); Nelson Boyd (b); Max Roach (d)

S3440-1	**Milestones** (breakdown)	(1) Savoy S5J5500
S3440-2	**Milestones**	(1) Savoy 934
S3440-3	**Milestones**	(1) Savoy MG12001
S3441-1	**Little Willie leaps** (breakdown)	(1) —
S3441-2	**Little Willie leaps**	(1) —
S3441-3	**Little Willie leaps (Wailing Willie)**	(1) Savoy 977
S3442-1	**Half Nelson**	(1) Savoy MG12001
S3442-2	**Half Nelson**	(1) Savoy 951
S3443-1	**Sippin' at Bells** (breakdown)	(1) MG12009
S3443-2	**Sippin' at Bells**	(1) Savoy 934
S3443-3	**Sippin' at Bells** (breakdown)	(1) Savoy S5J5500
S3443-4	**Sippin' at Bells**	(1) Savoy MG12001

Note: All issues except 78s as by CHARLIE PARKER

October 28
New York City

CHARLIE PARKER QUINTET

Miles Davis (tp); Charlie Parker (as); Duke Jordan (p); Tommy Potter (b); Max Roach (d)

D1101A	**Dexterity**	(6) Dial DLP203
D1101B	**Dexterity**	(6) Dial 1032
D1101C	**Dexterity**	unissued, presumed lost
D1102A	**Bongo bop (Blues)**	(6) Dial 1024
D1102B	**Bongo bop (Parker's blues)**	(6) Dial 1024
D1103A	**Prezology (Dewey Square)** -1	(6) Dial 1056 *
D1103B	**Dewey Square**	(6) Dial DLP203
D1103C	**Dewey Square**	(6) Dial 1019
D1104A	**The hymn (Superman)**	(6) Dial 1056
D1104B	**Superman**	(6) Dial DLP212
D1105A	**Bird of paradise (All the things you are)**	(6) Dial 1032
D1105B	**Bird of paradise**	(6) Dial 1032
D1105C	**Bird of paradise**	(6) Dial 1032
D1106A	**Embraceable you**	(6) Dial 1024
D1106B	**Embraceable you**	(6) Dial 1024

November 4
New York City

D1111C	**Bird feathers (Schnourphology)**	(7) Dial 1058
D1112A	**Klactoveedsedstene (Klact-oveeseds-tene)**	(7) Dial 1040
D1112B	**Klactoveedsedstene (Klact-oveeseds-tene)**	(7) Dial DLP904
D1113B	**Scrapple from the apple**	(7) Dial DLP203
D1113C	**Scrapple from the apple**	(7) Dial 1021

D1114A	**My old flame**	(7) Dial 1058
D1115A	**Out of nowhere**	(7) Dial DLP207
D1115B	**Out of nowhere**	(7) Dial DLP904
D1115C	**Out of nowhere**	(7) Spotlite 105
D1116A	**Don't blame me**	(7) Dial 1021

1- opening ensemble edited out on most issues
Notes: **D1105C, D1106A, D1113C, D1114A** and **D1115A** have also been reissued as by MILES DAVIS; **D1104B** originally issued as by MILES DAVIS QUINTET

December 17
New York City

CHARLIE PARKER SEXTET
As last plus J.J. Johnson (tb)

D1151B	**Giant swing (Drifting on a reed)**	(8) Dial 1056
D1151D	**Drifting on a reed**	(8) Dial DLP904
D1151E	**Drifting on a reed**	
	(Air conditioning)	(8) Dial 1043
D1152A	**Quasimodo**	(8) Dial DLP203
D1152B	**Quasimodo (Trade winds)**	(8) Dial 1015
D1153B	**Charlie's wig**	(8) Dial DLP905
D1153D	**Bongo bop (Charlie's wig)**	(8) Dial DLP203
D1153E	**Charlie's wig**	(8) Dial 1040
D1154B	**Dexterity (Bird feathers)**	(8) Dial DLP904
D1154C	**Bird feathers (Bongo beep)**	(8) Dial DLP207
D1155ABX	**Crazeology II**	(8) Dial 1034**
D1155C	**Crazeology**	(8) Dial DLP905
D1155D	**Crazeology**	(8) Dial 1034,1055
D1156A	**How deep is the ocean**	(8) Dial 1055
D1156B	**How deep is the ocean**	(8) Dial DLP211

Note: **D1155ABX** is a montage of the opening and the alto solo of take A, the alto solo of take B, and the alto solo and remainder of take C

December 21
Detroit

CHARLIE PARKER ALL STARS
As last except Johnson out

D830-1	**Another hair-do** (breakdown)	(1) Savoy MG12000
D830-2	**Another hair-do** (breakdown)	(1) —
D830-3	**Another hair-do** (breakdown)	(1) Savoy S5J5500
D830-4	**Another hair-do**	(1) Savoy 961
D831-1	**Bluebird**	(1) Savoy MG12000
D831-2	**Bluebird** (breakdown)	(1) Savoy S5J5500
D831-3	**Bluebird**	(1) Savoy 961
D832-1	**Klaunsen's vansan's (Klaunstance)**	(1) Savoy 967
D833-1	**Bird gets the worm**	(1) Savoy MG12000
D833-2	**Bird gets the worm** (breakdown)	(1) Savoy S5J5500
D833-3	**Bird gets the worm**	(1) Savoy 952

1948:

c.January
prob. New Savoy
Ballroom, Chicago

CHARLIE PARKER QUINTET
As last plus Kenny Hagood (vcl-1)

unknown title	Private recording
Drifting on a reed	—

c.March
Three Deuces,
New York City

Dizzy atmosphere	(9) Spotlite SPJ141
My old flame	(9) — *
All the things you are -1	(9) — *
Half Nelson	(9) — *
Drifting on a reed (Big foot)	(9) —
52nd street theme (3 versions)	(9) —

c.Spring
Onyx Club,
New York City

52nd street theme	(10) Jazz Workshop JWS501**
Shaw nuff	(10) — **

Out of nowhere	(10)—	**
Hot house	(10)—	**
This time the dream's on me	(10)—	**
Night in Tunisia	(10)—	*
My old flame	(10)—	**
52nd street theme (2 versions)	(10)—	*
The way you look tonight	(10)—	**
Out of nowhere	(10)—	**
Chasin' the Bird	(10)—	*
This time the dream's on me	(10)—	
Dizzy atmosphere	(10)—	**
How high the moon	(10)—	**

c. Autumn
Three Deuces,
New York City

How high the moon	Private recording
52nd street theme	—

September 4
Broadcast,
Royal Roost,
New York City

MILES DAVIS AND HIS ORCHESTRA
Miles Davis (tp); Mike Zwerin (tb); Junion Collins (fr-h); Bill Barber (tu); Lee Konitz (as); Gerry Mulligan (bars,arr-1), John Lewis (p,arr-2); Al McKibbon (b); Max Roach (d); Gil Evans (arr-3); Kenny Hagood (vcl-4); Symphony Sid (mc)

Move -2		Air-shot
Why do I love you -1,4	(11)	Ozone 2
Godchild -1	(11)	—
S'il vous plait -2	(11)	—
Moon dreams -3	(11)	—
Hallucinations -2	(11)	— *

Same broadcast

CHARLIE PARKER ALL STARS
Miles Davis (tp); Charlie Parker (as); Tadd Dameron (p); Curley Russell (b); Max Roach (d)

52nd street theme	(11a)	Savoy MG12186
Ko-ko	(11a)	Le Jazz Cool LJC101
52nd street theme (theme)		Air-shot

September 18
New York City

As last except John Lewis (p) replaces Dameron

B900-1	**Barbados**	(1)	Savoy MG12000
B900-2	**Barbados** (breakdown)	(1)	Savoy MG12009
B900-3	**Barbados**	(1)	—
B900-4	**Barbados**	(1)	Savoy 936
B901-1	**Ah-leu-cha** (breakdown)	(1)	Savoy MG12000
B901-2	**Ah-leu-cha**	(1)	Savoy 939
B902-1	**Constellation** (breakdown)	(1)	Savoy S5J5500
B902-2	**Constellation**	(1)	Savoy MG12000
B902-3	**Constellation** (breakdown)	(1)	—
B902-4	**Constellation** (breakdown)	(1)	Savoy MG12009
B902-5	**Constellation**	(1)	Savoy 939

Note: Davis out on **Parker's mood** from this session

September 18
Broadcast,
Royal Roost,
New York City

MILES DAVIS AND HIS ORCHESTRA
As for September 4 except poss. Ted Kelly (tb) replaces Zwerin

Darn that dream -1,4	(11)	Alto AL701
Move (Mood) -2	(11)	—
Moon dreams -3	(11)	—
Hallucinations -2	(11)	—

September 24
New York City

CHARLIE PARKER ALL STARS
As for September 18

B908-1	**Perhaps**	(1)	Savoy MG12014
B908-2	**Perhaps** (breakdown)	(1)	Savoy MG12009
B908-3	**Perhaps**	(1)	—
B908-4	**Perhaps** (breakdown)	(1)	Savoy S5J5500

603

B908-5	**Perhaps** (breakdown)	(1) Savoy MG 12000
B908-6	**Perhaps**	(1) —
B908-7	**Perhaps**	(1) Savoy 938
B909-1	**Marmaduke** (breakdown)	(1) Savoy S5J5500
B909-2	**Marmaduke** (breakdown)	(1) Savoy MG 12000
B909-3	**Marmaduke** (breakdown)	(1) Savoy S5J5500
B909-4	**Marmaduke** (breakdown)	(1) —
B909-5	**Marmaduke**	(1) Savoy MG 12000
B909-6	**Marmaduke** (breakdown)	(12) Savoy SJL1129
B909-7	**Marmaduke** (breakdown)	(12) Savoy MG 12001
B909-8	**Marmaduke** (breakdown)	(12) —
B909-9	**Marmaduke**	(12) —
B909-10	**Marmaduke** (breakdown)	(1) Savoy S5J5500
B909-11	**Marmaduke** (breakdown)	(1) Savoy MG 12009
B909-12	**Marmaduke**	(1) Savoy 938
B910-1	**Steeplechase** (breakdown)	(1) Savoy S5J5500
B910-2	**Steeplechase**	(1) Savoy 937
B911-1	**Merry-go-round**	(1) Savoy MG 12000
B911-2	**Merry-go-round**	(1) Savoy 937

September 25 *Broadcast,* *Royal Roost,* *New York City*	MILES DAVIS Miles Davis (tp); Lee Konitz (as); John Lewis (p); Curley Russell (b); Max Roach (d); Kenny Hagood (vcl-1); Symphony Sid (mc)	
	52nd street theme (Broadway theme)	Session Disc 101
	Half Nelson	—
	You go to my head -1	—
	Chasin' the Bird	—

December 11 *Broadcast,* *Royal Roost,* *New York City*	CHARLIE PARKER ALL STARS Miles Davis (tp); Charlie Parker (as,vcl-1); Al Haig (p); Tommy Potter (b); Max Roach (d); Symphony Sid (mc)	
	Jumpin' with Symphony Sid (theme)	Air-shot
	Groovin' high	(13) Le Jazz Cool LJC101*
	Drifting on a reed (Big foot)	(13) Le Jazz Cool LJC102
	Ornithology	(13) Le Jazz Cool LJC101*
	Slow boat to China	(13) ESP ESP-BIRD-1

December 12 *Broadcast,* *Royal Roost,* *New York City*	**Hot house**	Le Jazz Cool LJC101, LJC103
	Salt peanuts -1	Le Jazz Cool LJC102

December 18 *Broadcast,* *Royal Roost,* *New York City*	**Chasin' the Bird**	(14) Meexa 1776
	Out of nowhere	(14) Le Jazz Cool LJC102
	How high the moon	(14) —

1949:

January 3 *New York City*	METRONOME ALL STARS Dizzy Gillespie, Fats Navarro, Miles Davis (tp); J.J. Johnson, Kai Winding (tb); Buddy DeFranco (cl); Charlie Parker (as); Charlie Ventura (ts); Ernie Caceres (bars); Lennie Tristano (p,arr-1); Billy Bauer (g); Eddie Safranski (b); Shelly Manne (d); Pete Rugolo (cond,arr-2)	
D9-VB-0021-1	**Overtime** -2	Victor 20-3361
D9-VB-1000-2	**Overtime** -2	(15) Victor EPBT3046, LPT3046

D9-VB-1001-3 Victory ball -1   (15)   —   —
Note: Davis, Navarro, Johnson and Caceres out on two other
issued takes of **Victory ball**

January 21
New York City
MILES DAVIS AND HIS ORCHESTRA
As for September 4, 1948 except Kai Winding (tb); Al Haig (p);
Joe Shulman (b) replace Zwerin, Lewis and McKibbon

3395-3	**Jeru** -1	(16) Capitol 60005
3396-3	**Move** -2	(16) Capitol 15404
3397-2	**Godchild** -1	(16) Capitol 60005
3398-1	**Budo** (i.e. **Hallucinations**) -2	(16) Capitol 15404

February 19
Broadcast,
Royal Roost,
New York City
TADD DAMERON BIG TEN
Miles Davis (tp); Kai Winding (tb); Sahib Shihab (as); prob.
Benjamin Lundy (ts); Cecil Payne (bars); Tadd Dameron
(p,arr); John Collins (g); Curley Russell (b); Kenny Clarke (d);
Carlos Vidal (bgo); prob. John Lewis (arr-1); Symphony Sid
(mc)

Focus	(17) Jung Cat RBD948
April in Paris	(17) —
Good bait	(17) —
Webb's delight	(17) —

February 26
Broadcast,
Royal Roost,
New York City

Milano (Miles) -1	(17) —
Casbah	(17) —

March 5
Broadcast,
Royal Roost,
New York City

Good bait	Air-shot
The squirrel	—

April 21
New York City
As for February 19 except J.J. Johnson (tb) replaces Winding;
Lundy definite; Kay Penton (vcl-1) added

3760	**John's delight**	Capitol 60015
	What's new -1	Capitol (Du) 5C052. 80852
	Heaven's doors are open wide -1	—
3763	**Focus**	Capitol 60015

April 22
New York City
MILES DAVIS AND HIS ORCHESTRA
Miles Davis (tp); J.J. Johnson (tb); Sandy Siegelstein (fr-h);
Bill Barber (tu); Lee Konitz (as); Gerry Mulligan (bars,arr-1);
John Lewis (p,arr-2); Nelson Boyd (b); Kenny Clarke (d);
Gil Evans-3, John Carisi-4 (arr)

3764	**Venus de Milo** -1	(16) Capitol 1221
3765	**Rouge** -2	(16) Capitol EAP2-459,H459
3766-2	**Boplicity** -3	(16) Capitol 60011
3767-2	**Israel** -4	(16)

May 8
Broadcast,
Salle Pleyel,
Paris
MILES DAVIS – TADD DAMERON QUINTET
Miles Davis (tp); James Moody (ts); Tadd Dameron (p);
Barney Spieler (b); Kenny Clarke (d); Frank Tenot, Maurice
Cullaz (mc)

Rifftide	(18) Columbia JC34804
Good bait	(18) —
Don't blame me -1	(18) —
Lady bird	(18) —

May 9,12,14,15
Broadcasts,
Salle Pleyel,
Paris

Wahoo (Wah hoo)	(18) —
Allen's alley	(18) —
Embraceable you	(18) —
Ornithology	(18) —

All the things you are	(18)	—
The squirrel	(19) Phontastic NOST7602	
Wahoo	Air-shot	
Crazy rhythm	—	
All the things you are	—	

1-Moody out

<table>
<tr><td>

May 15
Broadcast,
Salle Pleyel,
Paris

</td><td>

JAM SESSION
Aime Barelli, Bill Coleman, Miles Davis, Kenny Dorham, Hot
Lips Page (tp); Russell Moore (tb); Hubert Rostaing (cl);
Pierre Braslavsky, Sidney Bechet (ss); Charlie Parker (as);
Don Byas, James Moody (ts); Hazy Osterwald (vib); Al Haig
(p); Toots Thielemans (g); Tommy Potter (b); Max Roach (d)
Blues (Farewell blues)   (20) Bird in Paris CP3*

</td></tr>
</table>

December 24
Broadcast,
Carnegie Hall,
New York City

JAM SESSION
Miles Davis (tp); Bennie Green (tb); Sonny Stitt (as); Serge
Chaloff (bars); Bud Powell (p); Curley Russell (b); Max Roach
(d); Symphony Sid (mc)

Move	(21) VOA JC6
Hot house	(21) IAJRC 20
Ornithology	(21) — *

1949-50
c. Winter
Harlem(?),
New York City

JAM SESSION
Miles Davis (tp); Charlie Parker (as); unknown p, b, d
Drifting on a reed   Private recording

1950:
February 10
Broadcast,
WNYC Studio,
New York City

MILES DAVIS SEXTET
Miles Davis (tp); J.J. Johnson (tb); Stan Getz (ts); Tadd
Dameron (p); Gene Ramey or Tommy Potter (b); Max
Roach (d)

Conception	Ozone 1
Ray's idea	—
Max is making wax	—
Woody'n you	—

Note: Davis and Johnson play final chord only of **That old
black magic** from this session

March 9
New York City

MILES DAVIS AND HIS ORCHESTRA
As for September 4, 1948 except J.J. Johnson (tb); Gunther
Schuller (fr-h) replace Zwerin and Collins

4346	**Deception**	(16) Capitol EAP1-459, H459
4347	**Rocker** -1	(16) Capitol EAP2-459, —
4348	**Moon dreams** -3	(16) Capitol EAP1-459, —
4349	**Darn that dream** -1,4	Capitol 1221

May 18
New York City

SARAH VAUGHAN WITH JIMMY JONES'S BAND
Miles Davis (tp); Bennie Green (tb); Tony Scott (cl); Budd
Johnson (ts); Jimmy Jones (p,arr); Freddie Greene (g); Billy
Taylor (b); J.C. Heard (d); Sarah Vaughan (vcl)

CO43825	**Ain't misbehavin'**	Columbia 38896
CO43826	**Goodnight my love**	Columbia 38897
CO43828	**It might as well be spring** -1	Columbia 38899

May 19
New York City

Mundell Lowe (g) replaces Greene

CO43829	**Mean to me**	Columbia 38899
CO43830	**Come rain or come shine**	Columbia 38898
CO43831	**Nice work if you can get it**	Columbia 38897

1-Johnson and Greene out
Note: Davis out on two remaining titles from these sessions

June 30	**BIRDLAND ALL STARS**	
Birdland,	Miles Davis (tp); J.J., Johnson (tb); Brew Moore (ts); Walter	
New York City	Bishop (p); Curley Russell (b); Art Blakey (d)	
	Eronel (Overturia)	(22,23) Session Disc 102
	52nd street theme	(22) — *
	Conception (Poobah) -1	Alto AL701
	Tadd Dameron (p) replaces Bishop	
	Wee (Rambunctious rambling)	(22) —
	Hot house (Miles's midnight	
	breakaway)	(22,23) Session Disc 101*
	Embraceable you	(22) —
	Brew's blues	Private recording
	For you my love	—

1-Fats Navarro (tp); Charlie Parker (as) join in on last chorus
Note: Davis out on **September in the rain** and **Chubbie's blues**
from this session

1951:

January 17	**CHARLIE PARKER AND HIS ORCHESTRA**	
New York City	Miles Davis (tp); Charlie Parker (as); Walter Bishop (p);	
	Teddy Kotick (b); Max Roach (d)	
C489-2	**Au privave**	(24) Verve MGV8010
C489-3	**Au privave**	Mercury/Clef 11087
C490-3	**She rote**	(24) Verve MGV8010
C490-5	**She rote**	Clef 11101
C491-1	**K.C. blues**	(24) —
C492-2	**Star eyes**	(24) Mercury/Clef 11087

January 17	**MILES DAVIS BAND**	
New York City	Miles Davis (tp); Bennie Green (tb); Sonny Rollins (ts); John	
	Lewis (p,arr-1); Percy Heath (b); Roy Haynes (d)	
128A	**Morpheus** -1	(25) Prestige 734
129B	**Down**	(25) Prestige 742
130B	**Blue room** -2	(25) Prestige PRLP140**
130BB	**Blue room** -3	(25) Prestige 734
131B	**Whispering**	(25) Prestige 742

2-Green out; consists of one take and part of another spliced
together (Davis prob. plays p on second part)
3-Green and Rollins out

Same session	**SONNY ROLLINS QUARTET**	
	As last except Green and Lewis out; Davis plays p	
132	**I know**	(25) Prestige 757

January 24	**METRONOME ALL STARS**	
New York City	Miles Davis (tp); Kai Winding (tb); John LaPorta (cl); Lee	
	Konitz (a (ts); Serge Chaloff (bars); Terry Gibbs	
	(vib); George Shearing (p,arr-1); Billy Bauer (g); Eddie	
	Safranski (b); Max Roach (d); Ralph Burns (arr-2)	
6252	**Early spring** -2	Capitol 1550
6253	**Local 802 blues** -1	—

February 17	**MILES DAVIS ALL STARS**	
Broadcast,	Miles Davis (tb); J.J. Johnson (tb); Sonny Rollins (ts); Kenny	
Birdland,	Drew (p); Tommy Potter (b); Art Blakey (d); Symphony	
New York City	Sid (mc)	
	Evans	Air-shot
	Half Nelson	—
	Tempus fugit	—
	Move	—
	Jumpin' with Symphony Sid	
	(theme)	—

March 8	LEE KONITZ SEXTET	
New York City	Miles Davis (tp); Lee Konitz (as); Sal Mosca (p); Billy Bauer (g); Arnold Fishkin (b); Max Roach (d)	
140B	**Odjenar**	(25) Prestige 753
141B	**Ezz-thetic**	(25) Prestige 843
142B	**Hi Beck**	(25) —
143B	**Yesterdays** -1	(25) Prestige 755
	1-Roach out	
	Note: Davis and Roach also out on further take of **Yesterdays**	

June 2	MILES DAVIS ALL STARS	
Broadcast,	As for February 17	
Birdland,	**Move (Moo)**	(26) Session 102, Ozone 7
New York City	**Half Nelson**	(26) — —
	Down (Mick's blues)	(26) — —
	Jumpin' with Symphony Sid (theme)	—

September 29	Miles Davis (tp); Lockjaw Davis, Big Nick Nicholas (ts); Billy	
Broadcast	Taylor (p); Charles Mingus (b); Art Blakey (d); Symphony	
Birdland,	Sid (mc)	
New York City	**Move (Mod)**	(26) Ozone 7
	The squirrel	(26) —
	Lady bird	(26) —*

October 5	As for February 17 except Jackie McLean (as); Walter Bishop	
New York City	(p) replace Johnson and Drew	
228	**Conception**	(25) Prestige 868, PREP1349,PRLP124
229	**Out of the blue** (i.e. **Evans**) Pts.1 and 2	(25) Prestige 876, PREP1361,PRLP140
230	**Denial**	(25) Prestige PREP1361
231	**Bluing Pts.1,2 and 3**	(25) Prestige 846/868, PREP1355,PRLP140
232	**Dig Pts.1 and 2**	(25) Prestige 777, PREP1339,PRLP124
233	**My old flame Pts.1 and 2** -1	(25) Prestige 766, PREP1339,PRLP124
234	**It's only a paper moon** Pts.1 and 2 -1	(25) Prestige 817, PREP1339,PRLP124
	1-McLean out	

1952:

c.Spring	MILES DAVIS	
Club Barrelhouse,	Miles Davis (tp); Jimmy Forrest (ts); Charles Fox (p); John	
St Louis	Hixon (b); Oscar Oldham (d); unknown bgo-1, vcl-2	
	All the things you are	Jazz Showcase 5004
	Wahoo	—
	Our delight -1	—
	Ow! -2	—*
	Lady bird -1	—
	What's new	Private recording

May 2	Miles Davis (tp); Don Elliott (mellophone-1,vib); Jackie	
Broadcast,	McLean (as); Gil Coggins (p); Connie Henry (b); Connie	
Birdland,	Kay (d)	
New York City	**Evans**	Ozone 8
	Confirmation -1	—

May 3		
Broadcast,	**Wee dot** -1	—
Birdland,	**The chase**	—
New York City	**It could happen to you** -2	—

	Evans (Opmet)	—
	2-McLean out	

Similar period	As for May 2 except Beryl Booker (p); Chuck Wayne (g) replace	
Broadcast	Coggins and McLean	
	The squirrel	(27) Stash ST113
May 9	As for May 2 except J.J. Johnson (tb); Oscar Pettiford (b);	
New York City	Kenny Clarke (d) replace Elliott, Henry and Kay	
BN428	**Dear old Stockholm**	(28) Blue Note 1595,
		BLP5013
BN429	**Chance it** (i.e. **Max is making wax**)	(28) Blue Note 1596,
		BLP5013
BN430	**Donna** (i.e. **Dig**)	(28) Blue Note 1595,
		BLP5013
BN430(alt.)	**Donna**	(28) Blue Note 45-1633
BN431	**Woody'n you**	(28) Blue Note 1596,
		BLP5013
BN431(alt.)	**Woody'n you**	(28) Blue Note BLP1501
BN432	**Yesterdays** -1	(28) Blue Note 1597,
		BLP5013
BN433	**How deep is the ocean** -1	(28) —
	1-Johnson and McLean out	

June	JAZZ INC.	
New York City	At last except Zoot Sims (ts); Milt Jackson (vib,p); Percy Heath	
	(b) replace McLean, Coggins and Pettiford	
	unknown titles	unissued

1953:

January 30	MILES DAVIS	
New York City	Miles Davis (tp); Sonny Rollins, 'Charlie Chan' (Charlie	
	Parker) (ts); Walter Bishop (p); Percy Heath (b); Philly Joe	
	Jones (d)	
450	**Compulsion**	(25) Prestige PRLP7044
451-1	**Serpent's tooth**	(25) —
451-2	**Serpent's tooth**	(25) —
452	**Round midnight**	(25) —
	Well you needn't -1	unissued, presumed lost
	1-Parker (or Rollins?) out	

February 19	Miles Davis (tp); Sonny Truitt (tb); Zoot Sims (ts); Al Cohn	
New York City	(ts,arr); John Lewis (p); Leonard Gaskin (b); Kenny Clarke (d)	
423	**Tasty pudding**	(25) Prestige PRLP154
424	**Willie the weeper**	(25) —
425	**Floppy**	(25) —
426	**For adults only**	(25) —

April 20	Miles Davis (tp); J.J. Johnson (tb,arr-1); Jimmy Heath (ts,	
New York City	arr-2); Gil Coggins (p); Percy Heath (b); Art Blakey (d)	
	Tempus fugit	(28) Blue Note 1618,
		BLP5022
(alt.)	**Tempus fugit**	(28) Blue Note 45-1649
	Enigma -1	(28) Blue Note 1618,
		BLP5022
	Ray's idea	(28) Blue Note 1619,
		BLP5022
(alt.)	**Ray's idea**	(28) Blue Note BLP1502
	I waited for you -3	(28) Blue Note 1619,
		BLP5022
	Kelo -1	(28) Blue Note 1620,
		BLP5022
	C.T.A. -2	(28) Blue Note 1620,
		BLP5022

(alt.)	**C.T.A.** -2	(28) Blue Note BLP1501
	3-Johnson and J. Heath out	

Similar to next	DIZZY GILLESPIE QUINTET	
Broadcast,	Dizzy Gillespie, Miles Davis (tp); Charlie Parker (as); Sahib	
Birdland,	Shihab (bars); Wade Legge (p); Lou Hackney (b); Al Jones	
New York City	(d); Joe Carroll (vcl-1)	
	The bluest blues -1	Klacto MG102

May 16	MILES DAVIS	
Broadcast,	As last except Gillespie and Parker out; Candido Camero	
Birdland,	(cga-2) added	
New York City	**I got rhythm** -1,2	Chakra CH100MD
	Move	Air-shot
	Tenderly	—
	Night in Tunisia -2	—
	Dig -2	—
	Lullaby of Birdland (theme)	—

May 19		
New York City	Miles Davis (tp); John Lewis (p); Percy Heath (b); Max Roach	
	(d)	
479	**When lights are low**	(25) Prestige 902,
		PREP1326,PRLP161
480	**Tune up**	(25) Prestige 884,
		PREP1326,PRLP161
481	**Miles ahead**	(25) Prestige 902,
		PREP1326,PRLP161
482	**Smooch** (i.e. **Weird nightmare**) -1	(25) Prestige 884,
		PREP1326,PRLP161
	1-Charles Mingus (p) replaces Lewis	

1954:

March 6	As last except Horace Silver (p); Art Blakey (d) replace Lewis	
Hackensack, N.J.	and Roach	
	Well you needn't	(28) Blue Note 45-1633,
		BLP5040
	Lazy Susan	(28) Blue Note 45-1649,
		BLP5040
	Weirdo	(28) Blue Note 45-1650,
		BLP5040
	The leap	(28) — —
	Take-off	(28) Blue Note BLP5040
	It never entered my mind	(28) —

March 15		
New York City		
556	**Four**	(25) Prestige 898,
		PREP1360,PRLP161
557	**Old devil moon**	(25) Prestige 898
		PREP1360,PRLP161
558	**Blue haze Pts. 1 and 2**	(25) Prestige 893,
		PREP1360,PRLP161

April 3	Miles Davis (tp); Dave Schildkraut (as); Horace Silver (p);	
Hackensack,N.J.	Percy Heath (b); Kenny Clarke (d)	
559	**Solar**	(25) Prestige PRLP185
560	**You don't know what love is** -1	(25) —
561	**Love me or leave me**	(25) Prestige PRLP7076
562	**I'll remember April**	(25) Prestige PRLP185
	1-Schildkraut out	

April 29	As last except J.J. Johnson (tb); Lucky Thompson (ts,arr-1)		
Hackensack, N.J.	replace Schildkraut		
	unknown titles -1		unissued, presumed lost
568	**Blue 'n' boogie Pts. 1 and 2**	(25)	Prestige PREP1358, PRLP182
569	**Walkin' Pts. 1 and 2**	(25)	Prestige PREP1357, PRLP182

June 29	As last except Sonny Rollins (ts) replaces Johnson and		
Hackensack, N.J.	Thompson		
590	**Airegin**	(25)	Prestige PRLP187
591	**Oleo**	(25)	—
592	**But not for me Pts. 1 and 2**	(25)	Prestige 915, PRLP187
592(alt.)	**But not for me**	(25)	Prestige PRLP7109
593	**Doxy**	(25)	Prestige PRLP187

December 24	As last except Milt Jackson (vib); Thelonious Monk (p) replace		
Hackensack, N.J.	Rollins and Silver		
676	**Bag's groove**	(25)	Prestige PRLP196
676(alt.)	**Bag's groove**	(25)	Prestige PRLP7109
677	**Bemsha swing**	(25)	Prestige PRLP200
678	**Swing spring**	(25)	Prestige PRLP196
679	**The man I love**	(25)	Prestige PRLP200
679(alt.)	**The man I love**	(25)	Prestige PRLP7150

1955:

June 7	Miles Davis (tp); Red Garland (p); Oscar Pettiford (b); Philly		
Hackensack, N.J.	Joe Jones (d)		
745	**I didn't**	(25)	Prestige PRLP7007
746	**Will you still be mine**	(25)	—
747	**Green haze Pts. 1 and 2**	(25)	Prestige 45-103, PRLP7007
748	**I see your face before me**	(25)	—
749	**Night in Tunisia Pts. 1 and 2**	(25)	Prestige 45-114, PRLP7007
750	**A gal in calico**	(25)	—

July 9	Miles Davis (tp); Britt Woodman (tb); Teddy Charles (vib);		
New York City	Charles Mingus (b); Elvin Jones (d)		
	Nature boy	(29)	Debut DEB120
	Alone together	(29)	—
	There's no you	(29)	—
	Easy living	(29)	—

August 5	Miles Davis (tp); Jackie McLean (as-1); Milt Jackson (vib);		
Hackensack, N.J.	Ray Bryant (p); Percy Heath (b); Art Taylor (d)		
781	**Dr. Jackle -1**	(25)	Prestige PRLP7034
782	**Bitty ditty**	(25)	—
783	**Minor march -1**	(25)	—
784	**Blues changes (Changes)**	(25)	—

October 18	MILES DAVIS QUINTET		
Broadcast,	As for June 7 except John Coltrane (ts) added; Paul Chambers		
Basin St. East,	(b) replaces Pettiford		
New York City	**Max is making wax**		Air-shot
	It never entered my mind		—

October 27			
New York City			
CO54130	**Ah-leu-cha**	(30)	Columbia CL949
	Little Melonae	(31a,32)	Columbia KC32025
	Two bass hit	(33)	Columbia KC2 36278
CO54133	**Budo**	(31a)	Columbia CL1020

814	**Stablemates**	(25)	Prestige PRLP7014
815	**How am I to know**	(25)	—
816	**Just squeeze me**	(25)	—
817	**There is no greater love** -1	(25)	—
818	**Miles's theme (The theme)**	(25)	—
819	**S'posin'**	(25)	—

December 8
Broadcast,
Blue Note,   **Tune up**   (34) Teppa 76
Philadelphia   **Walkin' (Royal garden blues)**   (34)   —

1-Coltrane out
Note: The October 27 **Little Melonae** has also been claimed as being a March 1958 recording

1956:
March 16   Miles Davis (tp); Sonny Rollins (ts); Tommy Flanagan (p);
Hackensack,N.J.   Paul Chambers (b); Art Taylor (d)

864	**In your own sweet way**	(25)	Prestige PRLP7044
865	**No line** (breakdown)	(25)	—
866	**Vierd blues** (i.e. **John Paul Jones**)	(25)	—

c.1956
Broadcast,   As for October 18, 1955
unknown location   **Bye bye blackbird**   Air-shot
May 11
Hackensack,N.J.

888	**In your own sweet way**	(25)	Prestige PRLP7166
889	**Diane**	(25)	Prestige PRLP7200
890	**Trane's blues** (i.e. **Vierd blues**)	(25)	Prestige PRLP7166
891	**Something I dreamed last night** -1	(25)	Prestige PRLP7200
892	**It could happen to you**	(25)	Prestige PRLP7129
893	**Woody'n you**	(25)	—
894	**Ahmad's blues** -2	(25)	Prestige PRLP7166
895	**The surrey with the fringe on top**	(25)	Prestige PRLP7200
896	**It never entered my head** **Pts. 1 and 2**	(25)	Prestige 45-165, PRLP7166
897	**When I fall in love Pts. 1 and 2** -1	(25)	Prestige 45-195, PRLP7200
898	**Salt peanuts**	(25)	—
899	**Four**	(25)	Prestige PRLP7166
900	**The theme I**	(25)	—
901	**The theme II**	(25)	—

June 5
New York City

CO56090	**Dear old Stockholm**	(30)	Columbia CL949
CO56091	**Bye bye blackbird**	(30)	—
CO56092	**Tadd's delight** (i.e. **Webb's (Sid's) delight**)	(30)	—

September 10
New York City

CO56584	**All of you**	(30)	Columbia B9491, CL949
CO56585	**Sweet Sue** -3	(31, 31a)	Columbia CL919*
CO56586	**Round midnight**	(30,31)	Columbia B9491, CL949

1-Coltrane out, except for last chord of 896
2-Garland, Chambers and Jones only
3-Teo Macero (arr); end of last chorus faded on original issues

October 20 *New York City*	BRASS ENSEMBLE OF THE JAZZ AND CLASSICAL MUSIC SOCIETY Miles Davis (tp-1,flh-2); Bernie Glow, Art Stratter, Melvin Broiles, Carmine Fornarotto, Joe Wilder, John Ware (tp); J.J. Johnson (tb,arr-3); Urbie Green, John Clark (tb); Jim Buffington, Ray Alonge, Joe Singer, Art Sussman (fr-h); Ron Ricketts, John Swallow (bar-h); Bill Barber (tu); Milt Hinton (b); Osie Johnson (d); Dick Horowitz (tymp,perc); John Lewis (arr-4); Gunther Schuller (cond)

Three little feelings -1,2,4   Columbia CL941

October 23 *New York City*	**Poem for brass** -2,3 — Note: Davis, Hinton and O. Johnson out on **Pharoah** from this session

October 26 *Hackensack, N.J.*	MILES DAVIS QUINTET As for October 18, 1955

995	**If I were a bell Pts. 1 and 2**	(25) Prestige 45-123, PRLP7129
996	**Well you needn't**	(25) Prestige PRLP7200
997	**Round midnight**	(25) Prestige PRLP7150
998	**Half Nelson**	(25) Prestige PRLP7166
999	**You're my everything**	(25) Prestige PRLP7129
1000	**I could write a book**	(25) —
1001	**Oleo**	(25) —
1002	**Airegin**	(25) Prestige PRLP7094
1003	**Tune up**	(25) —
1004	**When lights are low**	(25) —
1005	**Blues by five**	(25) —
1006	**My funny Valentine** -1 1-Coltrane out	(25) —

November 19 *Concert,* *Zurich*	MILES DAVIS Miles Davis (tp); Rene Urtreger (p); Pierre Michelot (b); Christian Garros (d) **unknown titles** Private recording

November *Broadcast,* *Freiburg*	**Tune up**	(35) Unique Jazz UJ14
	What's new	(35) —

Same broadcast	Miles Davis (tp); Lester Young (ts); Milt Jackson (vib); John Lewis (p); Percy Heath (b); Connie Kay (d); unknown big band personnel; Kurt Edelhagen (cond)

Lester leaps in   (35) Unique Jazz UJ14

1957:

May 6 *New York City*	MILES DAVIS WITH ORCHESTRA UNDER THE DIRECTION OF GIL EVANS Miles Davis (flh); Bernie Glow, Ernie Royal, Louis Mucci, Taft Jordan, John Carisi (tp); Frank Rehak, Jimmy Cleveland, Joe Bennett (tb); Tom Mitchell (btb); Willie Ruff, Tony Miranda (fr-h); Bill Barber (tu); Lee Konitz (as); Romeo Penque, Sid Cooper (woodwinds); Danny Bank (bcl); Paul Chambers (b); Art Taylor (d); Gil Evans (arr,cond)

CO57917	**The maids of Cadiz**	(36) Columbia B10412, CL1041
CO57918	**The Duke**	(36) Columbia B10413, CL1041

May 10 *New York City*		
CO57933	**My ship**	(36) Columbia B10411, CL1041

| CO57934 | Miles ahead | (31,36) Columbia B10413, CL1041 |

CO58017	New rhumba	(36) Columbia B10411, CL1041
CO58018	Blues for Pablo	(36) Columbia B10412, CL1041
CO58019	Springsville -1	(36) Columbia B10413, CL1041

May 27
New York City

CO58171	I don't wanna be kissed	(36) Columbia B10412, CL1041
CO58172	The meaning of the blues	(36) Columbia B10413, CL1041
CO58173	Lament	(36) Columbia B10411, CL1041

1-unknown p heard for a few bars
Note: Jim Buffington (fr-h); Eddie Caine (woodwinds) replace Miranda and Cooper for one session each, but it is not known which one(s)

July 13
Broadcast,
Café Bohemia,
New York City

MILES DAVIS QUINTET
Miles Davis (tp); Sonny Rollins (ts); Red Garland (p); Paul Chambers (b); Art Taylor (d)

Four (Four squared) (Roy's romp)	(37) Ozone 18,Chakra CH100MD
Bye bye blackbird	(37) Ozone 18*,Chakra CH100MD*
It never entered my mind -1	(37) — *
Walkin' (Roy's nappin' now)	(37) — *

December 4
Paris

Miles Davis (tp); Barney Wilen (ts-1); Rene Urtreger (p-2); Pierre Michelot (b); Kenny Clarke (d)

Generique -1,2	(38) Fontana(F)460.603ME, 660.213MR
L'assassinat de Carala -2	(38) —
Sur l'autoroute -1	(38) Fontana(F)460.603ME, 660.213MR
Julien dans l'ascenseur -2	(38) —
Florence sur les Champs-Elysées -1,2	(38) Fontana(F)460.603ME, 660.213MR
Diner au motel	(38) —
Evasion de Julien -3	(38) Fontana(F)460.603ME, 660.213MR
Visite du vigile -4	(38) —
Au bar du petit Bac -1,2	(38) Fontana(F)460.603ME, 660.213MR
Chez le photographe du motel -2	(38) —
Blue 'n' boogie -1	unissued (see note)

3-Michelot only
4-Michelot and Clarke only
Note: The riffs from Blue 'n' boogie (actually borrowed from Disorder at the border) used on the 'Ascenseur pour l'echafaud' soundtrack sound like part of the same performance as Diner au motel

1958:
March 9
Hackensack,N.J.

JULIAN 'CANNONBALL' ADDERLEY
Miles Davis (tp); Cannonball Adderley (as); Hank Jones (p); Sam Jones (b); Art Blakey (d)

	Autumn leaves Pts. 1 and 2	(39) Blue Note 45-1737, BLP1595,BST81595
	Love for sale	(39) —
	Somethin' else Pts. 1 and 2	(39) Blue Note 45-1738, BLP1595,BST81595
	One for Daddy-O Pts. 1 and 2	(39) Blue Note 45-1739, BLP1595,BST81595

Note: Davis out on **Dancing in the dark** from this session

April 2
New York City   MILES DAVIS
Miles Davis (tp-1,flh-2); Cannonball Adderley (as); John Coltrane (ts); Red Garland (p); Paul Chambers (b); Philly Joe Jones (d)

CO60199	Two bass hit -1	(40) Columbia CL1193
CO60200	Billy boy -3	(40) —
CO60201	Straight no chaser -1	(40) —
CO60202	Milestones (Miles) -2	(40) Columbia B11931, CL1193

April 3
New York City

CO60203	Dr.Jekyll (i.e. Dr.Jackle) -1	(40) Columbia B11931, CL1193
CO60204	Sid's ahead (i.e. Weirdo) -1,4	(40) —

3-Garland, Chambers and Jones only; has been reissued as by RED GARLAND
4-Garland out; Davis also plays p

prob. May 17
Broadcast,   Bill Evans (p) replaces Garland
Café Bohemia,

	Bye bye blackbird -1,5	(37) Chakra CH100MD
New York City	Walkin' (Rollin' and blowin') -1,5	(37) —
	Four (Four plus one more) -1,5	(37) —

May 26
New York City   Jimmy Cobb (d) replaces Jones

CO61165	One Green Dolphin Street -1	(31,32) Columbia CL1268
CO61166	Fran-dance -1	(32)
CO61167	Stella by starlight -1,5	(31,32)
	Love for sale -1	(31a,32,33) Columbia PG33402

5-Adderley out
Note: This version of **On Green Dolphin Street** not on 4-33059
(see April 1961)

June 25
New York City   MICHEL LEGRAND AND HIS ORCHESTRA
Miles Davis (tp); Phil Woods (as); John Coltrane (ts); Jerome Richardson (bars,cl); Herbie Mann (fl); Eddie Costa (vib); Bill Evans (p); Paul Chambers (b); Kenny Dennis (d); Betty Glamann (harp); Michel Legrand (arr,cond)

CO61067	Wild man blues	Columbia CL1250, CS8079
CO61068	Round midnight	— —
CO61069	Jitterbug waltz	— —
CO61070	Django -1	— —

1-Woods, Coltrane and Richardson out
Note: An earlier Legrand album (CL1139, Paris 1957), often alleged to feature Davis, in fact has Miles-ish trumpet solos played by Fernand Verstraete

July 3
Freebody Park,   MILES DAVIS
Newport, R.I.   As for May 26

CO81844	Ah-leu-cha -1	(41)	Columbia CL2178,
			CS8978
CO81845	Straight no chaser -1	(41)	—
CO81846	Fran-dance -1	(31,41)	—
CO81847	Two bass hit -1	(41)	—
	Bye bye blackbird -1		unissued
	The theme -1		—

July 22
New York City   MILES DAVIS WITH ORCHESTRA UNDER THE
DIRECTION OF GIL EVANS
Miles Davis (tp-1,flh-2); Bernie Glow, Ernie Royal, Louis
Mucci, Johnny Coles (tp); Frank Rehak, Jimmy Cleveland, Joe
Bennett (tb); Dick Hixon (btb); Willie Ruff, Julius Watkins,
Gunther Schuller (fr-h); Bill Barber (tu); Cannonball Adderley
(as); Phil Bodner, Romeo Penque (woodwinds); Danny Bank
(bcl); Paul Chambers (b); Philly Joe Jones (d); Gil Evans
(arr,cond)

CO61300	My man's gone now -2	(42) Columbia B12741,
		CL1274,CS8085
CO61301	Gone, gone, gone -2	(42) Columbia
		CL1274,CS8085
CO61302	Gone -2	(42) Columbia B12741,
		CL1274,CS8055

Note: Jimmy Cobb has claimed that CO61301, which is certainly
spliced from more than one take, includes part of a version from
one of the later sessions on which he is present

July 29
New York City   Jimmy Cobb (d) replaces Jones

CO61359	Here comes de honeyman -1	(42) Columbia CL1274,
		CS8085
CO61360	Bess, you is my woman now -2	(42) – —
CO61361	It ain't necessarily so -2	(42) Columbia JJ1,JS1,
		CL1274,CS8085
CO61362	Fisherman, strawberry and	
	devil crab -2	(42) – —
CO67547	It ain't necessarily so -2 (edited	
	from CO61361)	Columbia 3-42057**,
		4-42057**,3-42069**,
		4-42069**

August 4
New York City   As for July 29 except Jerome Richardson (woodwinds) replaces
Bodner

CO61366	Prayer -2	(42) Columbia CL1274,
		CS8085
CO61367	Bess, oh where's my Bess -2	(42) – —
CO61368	Buzzard song -2	(42) – —

August 18
New York City

CO61421	Summertime -1	(42) Columbia B12471,
		CL1274,CS8085
CO61422	There's a boat that's leaving	
	soon -2	(42) – —
CO61423	I loves you Porgy -1	(42) Columbia 3-42069*,
		4-42069*,CL1274,
		CS8085

September 9
Plaza Hotel,
New York City   MILES DAVIS
As for May 26

	If I were a bell -1,3	(43) Columbia PC32470
	Oleo -1	(43) —
	My funny valentine -1,4	(43) —

	Straight no chaser (Jazz at the Plaza) -1	(43)	—
	3-Adderley out		
	4-Adderley and Coltrane out		

c. Summer
Broadcast,
unknown location

	Walkin' -1	Air-shot
	All of you -1,3	—
	Sid's ahead -1	—
	Round midnight -1	—
	3-Adderley out	

1959:
January
Broadcast,
Jazz Unlimited,
Washington

| **Sid's ahead** -1 | Air-shot |
| **Bye bye blackbird** -1 | — * |

c. early 1959
Broadcast,
Birdland,
New York City

| **Walkin'** -1,3 | Air-shot* |

March 2
New York City

CO62290	**Freddie freeloader** -1,3	(44) Columbia CL1355, CS8163
CO62291	**So what** -1	(44) – —
CO62292	**Blue in green** -1,4	(44) – —
	3-Wynton Kelly (p) replaces Evans	
	4-Adderley out	

April 2
TV recording,
New York City

MILES DAVIS QUINTET
Miles Davis (tp); John Coltrane (ts); Wynton Kelly (p); Paul Chambers (b); Jimmy Cobb (d) WITH GIL EVANS AND HIS ORCHESTRA: Ernie Royal, Louis Mucci, Clyde Reasinger, Johnny Coles, Emmett Berry (tp); Frank Rehak, Jimmy Cleveland, Bill Elton (tb); Rod Levitt (btb); Julius Watkins, Bob Northern (fr-h); Bill Barber (tu); Romeo Penque, Eddie Caine (woodwinds); Danny Bank (bcl); unknown harp; Gil Evans (arr,cond)

So what -1	(23) Ozone 18
The Duke -2	(23) —
Blues for Pablo -2	(23) —
New rhumba -2	(23) —
1-Quintet plus 3 tb only	
2-Coltrane plays as; Kelly out	

April 22
New York City

MILES DAVIS
As for May 26, 1958

CO62293	**Flamenco sketches** -1	(44) Columbia CL1355, CS8163
CO62294	**All blues** -1	(44) – —
CO67548	**All blues** -1	Columbia 3-42057**, 4-42057**

Note: On original European issues, **CO62293** and **CO62294** listed in reverse

November 15
New York City

MILES DAVIS WITH ORCHESTRA ARRANGED AND CONDUCTED BY GIL EVANS
Personnel similar to next

| **Concierto de Aranjuez** | unissued |

November 20

Miles Davis (tp-1,flh-2); Bernie Glow, Ernie Royal, Louis

New York City	Mucci, Taft Jordan (tp); Frank Rehak, Dick Hixon (tb); John Barrows, Jim Buffington, Earl Chapin (fr-h); Jay McAllister (tu); Albert Block, Eddie Caine, Harold Feldman (woodwinds); Danny Bank (bcl); Paul Chambers (b); Jimmy Cobb (d); Elvin Jones (perc); Janet Putnam (harp); Gil Evans (arr,cond)	
CO63791	**Concierto de Aranjuez** -1,2	(45) Columbia CL1480, CS8271

1960:
March 10	Johnny Coles (tp); Joe Singer, Tony Miranda (fr-h); Bill Barber (tu); Romeo Penque (woodwinds); Jack Knitzer (bassoon) replace Mucci, Jordan, Barrows, Chapin, McAllister and Caine	
New York City		
CO64558	**The pan piper** -1	(45) Columbia CL1480, CS8271

March 11		
New York City	Louis Mucci (tp) added	
CO64560	**Solea** -1	(45) Columbia 4-33037*, CL1480,CS8271
CO64561	**Will o' the wisp** -1	(45) Columbia 4-33037, CL1480, CS8271
CO64562	**Saeta** -1	(45) Columbia CL1480, CS8271
	Song of our country -1	(46) Columbia KC2 36472

March 21	MILES DAVIS QUINTET	
Broadcast,	As for April 2, 1959	
Olympia,	**All of you**	Air-shot*
Paris	**Round midnight**	—
	Oleo	—
	The theme	—

March 22		
Broadcast,	**So what**	Air-shot*
Koncerthuset,	**Walkin'**	Bird Notes unnumbered*
Stockholm	**So what**	Air-shot
	Fran-dance	—
	All blues (Somethin' else)	Bird Notes unnumbered**

March 24		
Broadcast,	**So what**	Air-shot
Tivoli,	**On Green Dolphin Street**	—
Kbbenhavn	**All blues**	—*

April 9		
Broadcast,	**On Green Dolphin Street**	(47) Unique Jazz UJ19
Kurhaus,	**So what**	(47) —
Scheveningen	**Round midnight**	(47) —
	Walkin'	(47) —
	The theme	(47) —

October 13		
Broadcast,		
Koncerthuset,	Sonny Stitt (ts-1,as) replaces Coltrane	
Stockholm	**Walkin'** -1	Bird Notes unnumbered*

1961:
March 7		
New York City	Hank Mobley (ts) replaces Stitt	
CO66235	**Drad-dog**	(30) Columbia S7 31379*, GB9*,GS9*, CL1656**,CS8456**
CO66236	**Pfrancing**	(30) Columbia CL1656, CS8456
CO69815/6	**Pfrancing Pts. 1 and 2**	Columbia S7 31378**

March 20
New York City

CO66500	**Some day my prince will come** -1	(30) Columbia S7 31377*, CL1656,CS8456
CO66501	**Old folks**	(30) Columbia S7 31377*, CL1656, CS8456

March 21
New York City

CO66505	**Teo** -1,2	(30) Columbia CL1656, CS8456
CO66506	**I thought about you**	(30) Columbia S7 31379*, CL1656,CS8456
	Blues no. 2 -3	(33) Columbia KC2 36278
CO69817/8	**Teo Pts. 1 and 2** -1,2	Columbia S7 31380**

1-John Coltrane (ts) added
2-Mobley out
3-Philly Joe Jones (d) replaces Cobb

April 21,22
The Black Hawk,
San Francisco

CO67458	**Walkin'**	(48) Columbia C2L20, C2S820,CL1669, CS8469
CO67459	**Bye bye blackbird**	(48) Columbia S7 31381*, C2L20,C2S820, CL1669,CS8469
CO67460	**All of you** -1	(48) Columbia C2L20**, C2S820**,CL1669**, CS8469**
CO67461	**No blues** (i.e. **Pfrancing**)	(48) Columbia C2L20**, C2S820**,CL1669**, CS8469
CO67462	**Bye bye** (i.e. **The theme**)	(48) Columbia C2L20, C2S820,CL1669, CS8469
CO67463	**Love, I've found you** -2	(48) Columbia C2L20, C2S820,CL1669, CS8469
CO67464	**Well you needn't**	(48) Columbia C2L20**, C2S820**,CL1670**, CS8470**
CO67465	**Fran-dance**	(48) Columbia C2L20, C2S820,CL1670, CS8470
CO67466	**So what**	(48) Columbia C2L20, C2S820,CL1670, CS8470
CO67467	**Oleo**	(48) Columbia C2L20, C2S820, CL1670, CS8470
CO67468	**If I were a bell** -1	(48) Columbia S7 31381*, C2L20**,C2S820**, CL1670**,CS8470**
CO67469	**Neo** (i.e. **Teo**)	(48) Columbia C2L20, C2S820,CL1670, CS8470
CO69451	**On Green Dolphin Street**	(31a) Columbia 7-8565**, 4-33059*,CL1765**, CS8565**

Round midnight   (46) CBS-Sony (J)
36AP1409-10
1-Mobley not heard, as a result of editing of these tracks
2-Kelly only
Note: **CO67466** ends with a few bars of an alternative take of **No
blues**

May 19	MILES DAVIS QUINTET	
Carnegie Hall,	Miles Davis (tp); Hank Mobley (ts-1); Wynton Kelly (p-2);	
New York City	Paul Chambers (b); Jimmy Cobb (d) WITH GIL EVANS	

AND HIS ORCHESTRA: Bernie Glow, Ernie Royal, Louis
Mucci, Johnny Coles (tp); Frank Rehak, Dick Hixon, Jimmy
Knepper (tb); Julius Watkins, Paul Ingraham, Bob Swisshelm
(fr-h); Bill Barber (tu); Jerome Richardson, Romeo Penque,
Eddie Caine, Bob Tricario, Danny Bank (reeds,woodwinds);
Bobby Rosengarden (perc); Janet Putnam (harp); Gil Evans
(arr,cond)

CO69842	**So what** -1,2	(49) Columbia CL1812, CS8612
CO69843	**Spring is here** -2	(49) – —
CO69844	**No blues** -1,2,3	(49) – —
CO69845	**Oleo** -1,2,3	(49) Columbia 7-8612*, CL1812*,CS8612*
CO69846	**Some day my prince will come** -2,3	(49) Columbia CL1812, CS8612
CO69847	**The meaning of the blues/Lament/ New rhumba**	(49) Columbia 7-8612, CL1812,CS8612
CO76258	**New rhumba** (excerpt from above)	Columbia 3-42583,4-42583
	I thought about you -1,2,3	unissued
	Concierto de Aranjuez	—
	Saeta	—
	Solea	—

3-orchestra out
Note: The **New rhumba** portion of **CO69847** has been shown as
re-recorded on July 27, 1962, but the album was in fact shipped
before this date

c. December	No personnel details	
New York City	**unknown titles**	Columbia unissued

1962:

July 27	MILES DAVIS WITH ORCHESTRA ARRANGED AND	
New York City	CONDUCTED BY GIL EVANS	

Miles Davis (tp-1,flh-2); unknown big band personnel including
Steve Lacy (ss); Gil Evans (arr,cond)

CO75683	**Corcovado** -1,2	(50) Columbia 4-33059, CL2106,CS8906
CO76257	**Slow samba (Aos pes da cruz)** -2	(50) Columbia 3-42583*, 4-42583*,CL2106, CS8906

Note: **CO75683** (lasting 2'41") consists of 1'18" of **Corcovado**
spliced to 1'23" of an alternative take of **Slow samba**, starting
at the equivalent of 44" from the beginning of **CO76257**

August 13		
New York City	Similar personnel	
CO75678	**Song no.1** -1	(50) Columbia CL2106, CS8906
CO75837	**Wait till you see her** -1	(50) – —

August 21	MILES DAVIS	
New York City	Miles Davis (tp); Frank Rehak (tb); Wayne Shorter (ts); Paul	

Chambers (b); Jimmy Cobb (d); Willie Bobo Correa (cga); Bob
Dorough (vcl-1,arr)

CO75734	**Blue Xmas -1**	(31a) Columbia CL1893, CS8693
CO75735	**Nothing like you -1**	(51) Columbia CL2732, CS9532

August 23
New York City

CO76323	**Devil may care**	(31,31a) Columbia CL1970, CS8770
CO78873	**Devil may care**	Columbia 4-42853**

November 6
New York City

MILES DAVIS WITH ORCHESTRA ARRANGED AND CONDUCTED BY GIL EVANS

Similar to July 27 including Ernie Royal (tp); Frank Rehak (tb); John Barrows, Jim Buffington (fr-h); Jimmy Cobb (d); Elvin Jones (perc); Janet Putnam (harp); Gil Evans (arr,cond)

CO77119	**Once upon a summertime -1**	(50) Columbia CL2106, CS8906
CO77120	**Song No.2 -1**	(50) – —

1963:

April 16
Los Angeles

MILES DAVIS
Miles Davis (tp); Victor Feldman (p); Ron Carter (b); Frank Butler (d)

HCO71337	**I fall in love too easily**	(52) Columbia CL2051, CS8851
HCO71338	**Baby, won't you please come home**	(52) – —
HCO71340	**Basin Street blues**	(52) – —

April 17
Los Angeles

George Coleman (ts) added

	So near, so far	(46) Columbia KC2 36472
HCO71342	**Summer night-1**	(50) Columbia CL2106, CS8906

Same sessions | **Seven steps to heaven** | unissued

May 14
New York City

As last except Herbie Hancock (p); Tony Williams (d) replace Feldman and Butler

CO78342	**Seven steps to heaven**	(52) Columbia CL2051, CS8851
CO78343	**So near, so far**	(52) – —
CO78344	**Joshua**	(52) – —
CO78872	**Seven steps to heaven**	Columbia 4-42853**

June
Jazz Villa,
St. Louis

	All blues	(53) VGM 0003
	I thought about you-1	(53) —
	Seven steps to heaven	(53) —

July 26,27,29
Pinede Gould,
Juan-les-Pins

As last; Andre Francis (mc)

CO81817	**Autumn leaves**	(54) Columbia CL2183, CS8983
CO81818	**Milestones**	(54) – —
CO81819	**Joshua**	(54) – —
CO81820	**All of you**	(54) – —
CO81821	**Walkin'**	(54) – —
	So what	unissued
	If I were a bell	—
	Stella by starlight	—
	My funny valentine	—
	1-Coleman out	

c. Autumn *Los Angeles*	MILES DAVIS WITH GIL EVANS AND HIS ORCHESTRA		

Miles Davis (tp); Dick Leith (btb); Richard Perissi, Bill
Hinshaw, Art Maebe (fr-h); Paul Horn, Buddy Collette (fl);
Gene Cipriano (oboe); Fred Dutton (bassoon); Herbie
Hancock (p); Ron Carter (b); Tony Williams (d); Gil Evans
(arr,cond)

unknown titles (prob.incl. **General
assembly** and **Hotel me**)　　　　Columbia unissued

1964:
February 12
Philharmonic Hall,　MILES DAVIS
New York City　As for May 14, 1963; Mort Fega (mc)

CO81836	**So what**	(55)	Columbia CL2453, CS9253
CO81838	**Walkin'**	(55) –	—
CO81839	**All of you**	(56)	Columbia CL2306, CS9106
CO81840	**Stella by starlight**	(56) –	—
CO81841	**All blues**	(56) –	—
CO81842	**My funny Valentine**	(56) –	—
CO81843	**I thought about you**	(56) –	—
CO88696	**Four**	(55)	Columbia CL2453, CS9253
CO88697	**Seven steps to heaven**	(55) –	—
CO88698	**Joshua/Go-go** (i.e. **The theme**)	(55) –	—
CO88699	**There is no greater love/Go-go**	(55) –	—

July 14
Kohseinenkin,　Sam Rivers (ts) replaces Coleman; Teruo Isono (mc)
Tokyo

	If I were a bell	(57)	CBS-Sony(J) SONX60064-R
	My funny Valentine	(57)	—
	So what	(57)	—
	Walkin'	(57)	—
	All of you	(57)	—
	The theme	(57)	—
	Stella by starlight		unissued

c. September
TV recording,　Wayne Shorter(ts) replaces Rivers
Los Angeles　**No blues**　　　　(34) Teppa 76*
September 25
Philharmonie,　**Milestones**　　　　(58) CBS(G) S62976
Berlin

	Autumn leaves	(58)	—
	So what	(58)	—
	Walkin'	(58)	—
	The theme	(58)	—

1965:
c. January
The Hungry i,
San Francisco　**unknown titles**　　　　Columbia unissued
January 20
Los Angeles

HCO72230	**E.S.P.**	(59)	Columbia CL2350, CS9150
HCO72231	**R.J.**	(59) –	—

January 21
Los Angeles

HCO72232	**Eighty-one**	(59) –	—
HCO72233	**Little one**	(59) –	—

January 22
Los Angeles

HCO72234	**Iris**	(59) –	—
HCO72235	**Agitation**	(59) –	—
HCO72236	**untitled -1**	unissued	
HCO72237	**Mood**	(59) —	
	1-Williams only		

December 22
Plugged Nickel,
Chicago

If I were a bell	Columbia unissued	
Stella by starlight	—	
Walkin'	—	
I fall in love too easily/The theme	—	
My funny Valentine	—	
Four	—	
When I fall in love	—	
Agitation	—	
Round midnight	(60) CBS-Sony(J) 25AP291	
Milestones/The theme	unissued	
All of you	—	
Oleo	—	
I fall in love too easily	—	
No blues	—	
I thought about you/The theme	—	

December 23
Plugged Nickel,
Chicago

If I were a bell	—
Stella by starlight	(60) CBS-Sony(J) 25AP291
Walkin'	(61) CBS-Sony(J) 25AP1
I fall in love too easily/The theme	unissued
All of you	—
Agitation	(61) CBS-Sony(J) 25AP1
My funny Valentine	unissued
On Green Dolphin Street	(61) CBS-Sony(J) 25AP1
So what/The theme	(61) — *
When I fall in love	unissued
Milestones	—
Autumn leaves	—
I fall in love too easily	—
No blues/The theme	—
Stella by starlight	—
All blues	(60) CBS-Sony(J) 25AP291
Yesterdays -1	(60) — **
The theme	(60) — **
1-Shorter not heard, as a result of editing	

1966:
October 24
New York City

CO91173	**Circle**	(62) Columbia CL2601, CS9401	
CO91174	**Orbits**	(62) –	—
CO91175	**Dolores**	(62) –	—
CO91176	**Freedom jazz dance**	(62) –	—

October 25
New York City

CO91177	**Gingerbread boy**	(62) –	—
CO91178	**Footprints**	(62) –	—

1967:
May 9
Hollywood

	Buster Williams (b) replaces Carter	
	Limbo	(46) Columbia KC2 36472

623

May 16
New York City Ron Carter (b) replaces Williams
    CO93122 **Limbo** (51) Columbia CL2732,
                                         CS9532
    CO93123 **Vonetta** (51) –   —
May 17
New York City
    CO92211 **Masqualero** (51) –   —
    CO92212 **The sorcerer** (51) –   —
May 24
New York City
    CO92218 **Prince of darkness** (51) –   —
    CO92219 **Pee wee -1** (51) – ·   —
June 7
New York City
    CO92239 **Nefertiti** (63) Columbia CS9594
June 22
New York City
    CO92250 **Madness** (63)   —
June 23
New York City
    CO92249 **Hand jive** (63)   —
June
New York City **Water babies** (64) Columbia PC34396,
                                         A2S323
                      Capricorn (64)   —
July
New York City **Sweet Pea** (64)   —
July 19
New York City
    CO92289 **Fall** (63) Columbia CS9594
    CO92290 **Pinocchio** (63)   —
    CO92291 **Riot** (63)   —
December 4
New York City **Circle in the round -2,3** (33) Columbia KC2 36278

December 28
New York City **Water on the pond -2** (46) Columbia KC2 36472
                      1-Davis out
                      2-Joe Beck (g) added
                      3-Davis also plays chimes, bells; Hancock plays celeste

1968:
January 11
New York City
                      Fun (46) Columbia KC2 36472
January 16
New York City George Benson (g-1) added
                      Teo's bag (33) Columbia KC2 36278
                      Paraphenalia -1 (65) Columbia CS9628
February 13
New York City **Side car I** (33) Columbia KC2 36278
                      Side car II -1 (33)   —
February 15
New York City **Sanctuary -1** (33)   —

March MILES DAVIS WITH GIL EVANS AND HIS ORCHESTRA
New York City Miles Davis (tp,el-tp); unknown band personnel; Gil Evans
                      arr,cond)
                      unknown titles   Columbia unissued

May 15	MILES DAVIS	
New York City	Miles Davis (tp); Wayne Shorter (ts); Herbie Hancock (p-1, el-p-2); Ron Carter (b-1,el-b-2); Tony Williams (d)	
	Country son -1	(65) Columbia CS9628
May 16		
New York City	**Black comedy** -1	(65) —
May 17		
New York City	**Stuff** -2	(65) —
June 19		
New York City	**Petits machins** -2	(66) Columbia CS9750
June 20		
New York City	**Tout de suite** -2	(66) —
June 21		
New York City	**Filles de Kilimanjaro** -2	(66) —
CO100069	**Filles de Kilimanjaro Pts. 1 and 2** -2	Columbia 4-44652*

September 24	Chick Corea (el-p); Dave Holland (b) replace Hancock and	
New York City	Carter	
	Frelon brun	(66) Columbia CS9750
	Mademoiselle Mabry	(66) —
November	As last plus Herbie Hancock (el-p); Ron Carter (el-b)	
New York City	**Two faced**	(64) Columbia PC34396
	Dual Mr. Tillman Anthony	(64) — **
November 25	As last except Joe Zawinul (p) replaces Carter	
New York City	**Splash**	(33) Columbia KC2 36278

November 27	As last except Jack DeJohnette (d) replaces Williams	
New York City	**Directions I**	(46) Columbia KC2 36472
	Directions II	(46) Columbia KC2 36472
	Ascent	(46) Columbia KC2 36472

1969:

February 18	As for November 25 except Shorter plays ss; Zawinul el-p,org;	
New York City	John McLaughlin (g) added	
	Shhh/Peaceful	(67) Columbia CS9875
	In a silent way/It's about that time (67)	—
CO103511	**In a silent way/It's about that time Pts. 1 and 2**	Columbia AE13*

August 19	Miles Davis (tp); Wayne Shorter (ss); Chick Corea (el-p); Dave	
New York City	Holland (b); Jack DeJohnette (d); Jumma Santos, Charles Don Alias (perc)	
	Sanctuary	(68) Columbia GP26
	As last plus Bennie Maupin (bcl); Joe Zawinul (el-p); John McLaughlin (g); Harvey Brooks (el-b); Lenny White (d)	
	Bitches brew	(68) Columbia GP26

August 20	As last plus Larry Young (el-p)	
New York City	**Spanish key**	(68) Columbia GP26, G30121*
CO107194	**Spanish key**	Columbia 4-45171*
	As last except Zawinul out	
	Miles runs the voodoo down	(68) Columbia GP26
CO107204	**Miles runs the voodoo down**	Columbia 4-45171*

August 21	As last except Davis and Shorter out	
New York City	**John McLaughlin**	(68) Columbia GP26
	As for CO107194	
	Pharaoh's dance	(68) —

Note: Billy Cobham (d) has claimed to be present on one or more of the above three sessions, and the attribution of the keyboard players to each of the last five items may well be unreliable

November 19 *New York City*	Miles Davis (tp); Steve Grossman (ss); Bennie Maupin (bcl); Chick Corea, Herbie Hancock (el-p), John McLaughlin (g); Khalil Balakrishna, Bihari Sharma (el-sitar,tambura,etc.); Ron Carter (b); Harvey Brooks (el-b); Billy Cobham (d); Airto Moreira (perc)		

Great expectations/Mulher laranja
(i.e. **Orange lady**)   (69) Columbia PG32866
     CO103282   **Great expectations**   Columbia 4-45090*,
                                                                          4-46074*

November 28
New York City   As last except Joe Zawinul, Larry Young (el-p) replace Corea;
                 Jack DeJohnette (d) added
     CO103290   **The little blue frog**   Columbia 4-45090
1970:

January 27
New York City   As last except Wayne Shorter (ss); Chick Corea (el-p); Dave
                 Holland (b) replace Grossman, Hancock, Young and Carter;
                 McLaughlin and Sharma out
                 Lonely fire   (69) Columbia PG32866
                 Guinnevere   (33) Columbia KC2 36278

February 6
New York City   As last except John McLaughlin (g) replaces Maupin; Holland
                 plays el-b replacing Brooks
                 Gemini/Double image   (70) Columbia KC30954
                 Note: Shorter and Balakrishna not heard on issued excerpt
                 (though listed)

February 17
New York City   Miles Davis (tp); Wayne Shorter (ss); Bennie Maupin (bcl);
                 John McLaughlin (g); Dave Holland (el-b), Billy Cobham (d)
                 Duran   (46) Columbia KC2 36472

February 18
New York City   As last except Sonny Sharrock (g); Jack DeJohnette (d) replace
                 Shorter and Cobham
                 Yesternow 'Pt.3'   (71) Columbia KC30455

February 27
New York City   As last except Steve Grossman (ss) replaces Maupin; Sharrock
                 out
                 Willie Nelson   (46) Columbia KC2 36472

March 30
New York City   **Go ahead John**   (69) Columbia PG32866
     CO103283   **Go ahead John**   Columbia 4-46074*

April 7
New York City   Miles Davis (tp); Steve Grossman (ss); Herbie Hancock (org);
                 John McLaughlin (g); Mike Henderson (el-b); Billy Cobham (d)
                 Right off 'Pt.1'   (71) Columbia KC30455
                 Right off 'Pt.3'   (71)   —
                 Right off 'Pt.4' -1   (71)   —
                 Yesternow 'Pt.1' -2   (71)   —
     CO109409   **Right off Pt.1** (excerpt from
                    'Pt.1' above)   Columbia 4-45350
     CO109410   **Right off Pt.2** (excerpt from
                    'Pts.1 & 3' above)   —

Same period
New York City   As last plus Keith Jarrett (keyb); Airto Moreira (perc)
     CO103883   **Honky tonk**   (74) Columbia KG33236
                 1-Davis out
                 2-unknown second el-b (Dave Holland?) added on this segment
                 Note: The segments of **Right off** and **Yesternow**, delineating
                 them from the session below, obscure the fact that **Right off**
                 'Pts.4,1 & 3' are (in that order) probably from a single take

Similar period
New York City   Miles Davis (tp) accompanied by pre-recorded backgrounds:
                 1-synth; 2-excerpt from **Shhh/Peaceful** rec. February 18, 1969;
                 3-unknown brass, b, d; 4-Brock Peters (narr); Teo Macero (arr)

	Right off 'Pt.2' -1	(71) Columbia KC30455,
		Teo Macero 99045-1A
	Yesternow 'Pt.2' -2	(71) —
	Yesternow 'Pt.4' -3,4	(71) —
	Yesternow 'Pt.4' -3	Teo Macero 99045-1A

Note: Davis's solo on these three segments is identical; the two segments on the Teo Macero LP are edited together as one piece titled **Jack Johnson**

April 10
Fillmore East,
San Francisco

Miles Davis (tp); Steve Grossman (ss); Chick Corea (el-p); Dave Holland (el-b); Jack DeJohnette (d); Airto Moreira (perc)

Black beauty Pts.1,2,3 and 4   (72) CBS-Sony (J)
SOPJ39-40

May 21
New York City

Miles Davis (tp); Keith Jarrett (el-p); John McLaughlin (el-g); Airto Moreira (perc)

Konda   (46) Columbia KC2 36472

June 3
New York City

Miles Davis (tp); Steve Grossman (ss); Hermeto Pascoal (el-p-1, vcl-2,whistling-3); Chick Corea, Keith Jarrett, Herbie Hancock (keyb); Ron Carter (el-b); Jack DeJohnette (d); Airto Moreira (perc)

Nem um talvez -2   (70) Columbia KC30954
Selim -2,4   (70) —

June 7
New York City

As last plus John McLaughlin (g); Dave Holland (el-b) replaces Carter

Little church -1,3   (70) Columbia KC30954
4-Moreira out

Note: **Nem um talvez** and **Selim** are alternative takes of the same piece

June 17
Fillmore East,
New York City

As for April 10 plus Keith Jarrett (org)
Wednesday Miles   (73) Columbia KG30038

June 18
Fillmore East,
New York City

Thursday Miles   (73) —

June 19
Fillmore East,
New York City

Friday Miles   (73) —

CO109337   **Friday Miles**   Columbia 4-45327*

June 20
Fillmore East,
New York City

Saturday Miles   (73) Columbia KG30038

CO109336   **Saturday Miles**   Columbia 4-45327*

August 29
Isle of Wight

Miles Davis (tp); Gary Bartz (ss-1,as-2,fl-3); Keith Jarrett, Chick Corea (keyb); Dave Holland (el-b); Jack DeJohnette (d); Airto Moreira (perc)

Call it anythin' -1   Columbia G3X30805**

December 18
The Cellar Door
Washington

John McLaughlin (g); Mike Henderson (el-b) replace Corea and Holland

Sivad   (70) Columbia KC30954
What I say -1,3   (70) —
Funky tonk -1   (70) —
Inamorata -2,4   (70) —

4-Conrad Roberts (narr) added on issued version

Note: **Funky tonk** and **Inamorata** may in fact be Pts.1 and 2 of the same performance

1971:

November 26
Philharmonic Hall,

Don Alias, James M'tume Foreman (perc) replace McLaughlin and Moreira

627

| New York City | Bwongo -1 | Session Disc 123 |
| | Ananka -1,2 | — |

1972:

June 1	Miles Davis (tp); Dave Liebman (ss); Bennie Maupin (bcl);
New York City	Herbie Hancock, Chick Corea, Harold Williams (keyb); John
	McLaughlin (g); Colin Walcott (sitar); Mike Henderson (el-b);
	Jack DeJohnette (d); Billy hart (d,perc); Don Alias, M'tume
	(perc); Badal Roy (tabla)

On the corner/New York girl/
Thinkin' one thing and doin'

	another/Vote for Miles	(75) Columbia KC31906
CO113952/3	**Vote for Miles Pts.1 and 2**	Columbia 4-45822*
June 6	Carlos Garnett (ss,ts) replaces Liebman
New York City	**Black satin**	(75) Columbia KC31906
	One and one	(75) —
	Helen Butte	(75) —
	Mr. Freedom X	(75) —

June 12	Sonny Fortune (ss,fl) added; Lonnie Liston Smith (keyb); Al
New York City	Foster (d) replace Hancock, Corea and DeJohnette; Williams
	plays keyb and sitar; McLaughlin, Walcott and Alias out
	Ife	(69) Columbia PG32866

July 7	
New York City	Personnel similar to last or next session
CO112691/2	**Molester Pts.1 and 2**	Columbia 4-45709

September 6(?)	Miles Davis (tp-1,org-2); Carlos Garnet (ss); Cedric Lawson
New York City	(keyb); Reggie Lucas (g); Khalil Balakrishna (el-sitar); Mike
	Henderson (el-b); Al Foster (d); Mtume (perc); Badal Roy
	(tabla)
CO112591	**Rated X** -2,3	(74) Columbia KG33236
CO112994	**Billy Preston** 1,3	(74) —

September 29	**20.45** -1	(76) Columbia KG32092
Philharmonic Hall,	**25.23** -1	(76) —
New York City	**18.12** -1	(76) —
	20.21 -1	(76) —
	3-Garnett not heard on issued excerpts of these tracks

1973:

poss.January	Miles Davis (tp) accompanied by (prob.pre-recorded) unknown
New York City	brass (poss.incl.Joe Newman (tp)); Wally Chambers (hca);
	Cornell Dupree (g); Mike Henderson (el-b); Al Foster, Bernard
	Purdie (d); Mtume (perc); Wade Marcus, Billy Jackson (arr)
	Red China blues	(74) Columbia KG33236
CO118934	**Red China blues**	Columbia 3-10110*

February 13	Prob. as for September 29, 1972 except Dave Liebman (ss)
New York City	replaces Garnett
	unknown titles	Columbia unissued

September	
New York City	Similar to next
CO117260	**Big fun**	Columbia 4-45946
CO117261	**Holly-wuud**	—

Similar period	
	Miles Davis (tp-1,org-2); Dave Liebman (fl); John Stubblefield
New York City	(ss); Reggie Lucas, Pete Cosey (g); Mike Henderson (el-b); Al
	Foster (d); Mtume (perc)
CO117296	**Calypso Frelimo** -1,2	(74) Columbia KG33236

1974:

March 30
Carnegie Hall,
New York City

Liebman plays ts,ss; Azar Lawrence (ts) replaces Stubblefield; Dominique Gaumont (g) added

Dark Magus-Moja -1   (77) CBS-Sony (J)
                                             40AP741-742

Dark Magus-Wili -1,2   (77) —
Dark Magus-Tatu 1,2   (77) —
Dark Magus-Nne 1,2   (77) —

late May
New York City
   CO118537

Liebman plays fl; Lawrence out
He loved him madly 1,2   (74) Columbia KG33236

June 19
New York City
   CO121653
June 20(?)
New York City
   CO121652

Sonny Fortune (fl) replaces Liebman
Maiysha -1,2   (74)   —
Maiysha   Columbia 3-10110*

Gaumont out
Mtume-1,2   (74) Columbia KG33236
Note: Fortune not heard on issued excerpt

1975:

February 1
Festival Hall
Osaka

As last except Fortune plays ss-3, as-4, fl-5; Cosey plays g. synth, perc

Prelude Pts.1 and 2 1,2,3,4   (78) CBS-Sony(J)
                                         SOPJ92-93

Maiysha 1,2,5   (78) —

   CO123133   **Maiysha** -1,2,3,5   Columbia AS214**
Theme from Jack Jackson -1,2,4,5 (78) CBS-Sony(J)
                                         SOPJ92-93

   CO123144   **Theme from Jack Johnson** -1,2   Columbia AS214*
Interlude -1,2,5   (78) CBS-Sony(J)
                                         SOPJ92-93

Zimbabwe Pts.1 and 2 -1,2,3,4   (79) CBS-Sony(J)
                                         SOPZ96-97

Gondwana Pts.1 and 2 -1,2,5   (79) —
Note: **Theme from Jack Johnson** and **Interlude** reversed on labels of all album issues, hence **CO123144** is actually an excerpt from **Interlude**; **CO123133** contains excerpts from both **Prelude Pt.2** and **Maiysha**

c. 1975
New York City

BETTY DAVIS
Fred Mills (keyb); Carlos Morales (g); Larry Jackson (el-b); Nicky Neal (d); unknown brass; Gil Evans (brass,arr,cond); Miles Davis (dir); Betty Davis (vcl)
You and I   Island ILPS9329
Note: Neither Evans nor M. Davis is implicated in other tracks on this album

1978:

c. February
New York City

MILES DAVIS
Miles Davis (org); Masabumi Kikuchi, George Pavlis (keyb); Larry Coryell (g); T.M. Stevens (el-b); Al Foster (d); unknown brass; Bobby Scott (brass arr)
unknown titles   Columbia unissued

1980:

c. May-July
New York City

Miles Davis (tp,el-p); Bill Evans (saxes,woodwinds); Robert Irving (keyb); Randy Hall (g,vcl); Felton Crews (el-b); Vince Wilburn (d); Sammy Figueroa (perc); unknown vcl group
Spider's web   Columbia unissued

Solar energy

Space	–	
Burn	–	
I'm blue	–	
Mrs. Slurpey	–	
Thanksgiving	–	
1980s	–	
The man with the horn	(80) Columbia FC36790	
Shout	–	

1981:

c. March New York City	Miles Davis (tp), Bill Evans (ss), Barry Finnerty (g), Marcus Miller (el-b), Al Foster (d), Sammy Figueroa (perc).	
	Ursula	(80) Columbia FC36790
	Aida	—
	Back seat Bertha	—
	Mike Stern (g) replaces Finnerty	
	Fat time	—
June 27 Kix Boston	Miles Davis (tp); Bill Evans (ss); Mike Stern (g); Marcus Miller (el-b); Al Foster (d); Mino Cinelu, (perc).	
July 5 Avery Fisher Hall New York	Jean-Pierre	CBS. 88579
	Back Seat Betty	
	Fast Track	
	Jean-Pierre	
October 4 Tokyo	My Man's gone now	
	Kix	

Acknowledgments: As well as previous Davis discographers Jørgen Jepsen, Jan Lohmann and Michel Ruppli, I should like to thank Hugh Attwooll (CBS), Johs Bergh, Brian Davis, Mike Doyle, Charles Fox, Graham Griffiths (Mole Jazz), Ian Kendall, Michel Legrand, Alun Morgan and David Yates (RCA) for assistance at various stages in the compilation of this listing.   B.P.

Index to Discography

Miles Davis
Additional Discography

After Brian Priestley's discography (pp. 595–629) from the original edition of this biography, the author lists some details of recordings during Miles Davis's last ten years, and of some key re-releases and box-sets of music from his earlier career now on CD. Sony acquired Columbia/CBS Records during the 1990s, and so the entire Columbia Miles Davis catalogue is now on Sony Jazz.

Album

STAR PEOPLE
(CD 25395)   Miles Davis (tp, keyb); Mino Cinelu (perc); Bill Evans (ts, ss);
1982–1983   Al Foster (d); Marcus Miller (el-b); John Scofield (g); Mike
Sept–Jan   Stern (g); Gil Evans (arr-1)
New York City   Come get it   Columbia FC38657
                  It gets better – 1   –
                  Speak – 2   –
                  Star People   –
                  U'n'I   –
                  Star on Cicely – 1   –
              2 – Tom Barney (el-b) replaces Miller.

DECOY
(468702 2)   As above, but Stern out, and Barney is replaced by Darryl
1983   'The Munch' Jones.
July
International   What it is   Columbia FC38991
Jazz Festival   That's what happened   –
Montreal
1984   Personnel as above, but Branford Marsalis (ss), replaces Bill
              Evans and Robert Irving (synth, arr-1) is added.
                  Decoy – 1   Columbia FC38991
                  Robot 415 – 1   –
                  Code M.D. – 1   –
                  Freaky Deaky   –
                  That's right   –

YOU'RE UNDER ARREST

(468703 2)
1984–5
Sept–Jan
NYC

Bob Berg (ts, ss) and Steve Thornton (perc), replace Marsalis and Cinelu.

One phone call/street scenes – 3	Columbia FC40023
Time after time	–
You're under arrest	–
Medley: Jean Pierre/You're under arrest/Then there were none	–

Vince Wilburn (d) replaces Foster, Berg out.

Human nature	–
MD1/Something's on your mind/MD2	–
Ms Morrisine – 4	–
Katia prelude – 4	–
Katia – 4	–

3 – Davis, Thornton, Marek Olko, James Prindiville, 'Sting' (narr) added on this track, 4 – John McLaughlin (g) replaces Scofield.

AURA

(463351 2)
1985
Jan–Feb
Copenhagen
Denmark

Miles Davis (tp); Vincent Wilburn (simmon's d); John McLaughlin (g); the Danish Radio Big Band conducted by Palle Mikkelborg (tp, flh, arr, comp)

Intro	CBS (A) 463351
White	–
Yellow	–
Orange	–
Red	–
Green	–
Blue	–
Electric Red	–
Indigo	–
Violet	–

In 1985, Miles Davis left Columbia Records and signed with Warner Bros.

TUTU

(9254902)
1986
6–13 Feb
Capitol Records
Studio Los Angeles,
California.

Miles Davis (tp); Marcus Miller (el-b); Paulinho da Costa (perc); George Duke (other instruments)

Backyard Ritual	WB25490

George Duke out; Adam Holzman (synth) and Steve Reid (perc) added. Marcus Miller (comp, arr, other inst)

Splatch	WB25490

Holzman and Reid out.

Tutu	–
Portia	–

12–25 March
Clinton
Recording
Studio NYC

Miles Davis (tp); Michal Urbaniak (v-1); Bernard Wright (synth-2) Omar Hakim (d, perc-3), Marcus Miller (other inst).

Tomaas (2,3)	WB25490
Perfect Way	–
Don't Lose Your Mind (1, 2)	–
Full Nelson	–

SIESTA
(7599-25655-2)
1987

January
Sigma Sound
Studios NYC

Miles Davis (tp); John Scofield (g-1); Omar Hakim (d-1); Jason Miles (synth programming); Marcus Miller (other inst)

Siesta (1)/Kitt's Kiss*/Lost	WB25655
In Madrid Part II*	
Theme For Augustine/	–
wind*/Seduction*/Kiss	
*= Davis out	

March
Amigos Studios
North Hollywood,
California.

Miles Davis (tp); Earl Klugh (g-1); James Walker (fl-2); Jason Miles (synth programming); Marcus Miller (other inst)

Lost In Madrid Part I	WB25655
Lost In Madrid Parts I &	–
IV/Rat Race*/The Call*	
Claire (1)/Lost In Madrid	–
Part V	
Los Feliz (2)*	
*= Davis out	

NB. There are three other short pieces in which Davis does not play: Submission; Lost In Madrid III and Afterglow.

AMANDLA
(9258732)
1988–1989
Dec–Jan
Clinton Recording
Studio NYC

Miles Davis (tp); Kenny Garrett (as); Marcus Miller (el-b, keyb, d, g, bscl, ss); Don Alias and Mino Cinelu (perc).

Catémbe	WB25873

Cinelu out; add Joe 'Foley' McCreary, Jean-Paul Bourelly (g); Ricky Wellman (d).

Big Time	WB25873

Omar Hakim (d) and Paulinho da Costa (perc), replace Wellman and Alias. Bourelly out.

Hannibal	WB25873

Miles Davis (tp); Kenny Garrett (as); Rick Margitza (ts); Jean-
Paul Bourelly (g); Marcus Miller (el-b, keyb); Paulinho da
Costa (perc)

Jo-Jo	WB25873

Davis, Garrett, Miller with Joe Sample (p); Omar Hakim (d);
Don Alias and Bashiri Johnson (perc).

Amandla	WB25873

Right Track
Studio NYC

Davis, Garrett, Miller, McCreary, Wellman, with Billy
'Spaceman' Patterson (g); John Bigham (d programming, g,
keyb).

Jilli	WB25873

Davis; Miller; Al Foster (d); Jason Miles (synth programming)

Mr Pastorius	WB25873

Davis; Garrett (ss); Miller; George Duke (keyb, synclavier);
Joey DeFrancesco (keyb); Michael Landau (g).

Cobra	WB25873

MILES IN PARIS
WB Video
(9031 71550-3)
1989
3 March
Le Zenith
Paris, France

Miles Davis (tp, keyb); Kenny Garrett (as, fl 1); Kei Akagi
(synth); Joe 'Foley' McCreary (g); Benny Rietveld (el-b); Ricky
Wellman (d); John Bigham (el. perc).

Human Nature (+1)	WB38186(video)
Jilli	–
Hannibal	–
Don't Stop Me Now	–
Amandla	–
Tutu	–
Wrinkle	–
New Blues	–
Mr Pastorius	–

Miles Davis and Michel Legrand
DINGO
(7599-26438-2)
1990
March
Crystal Studio
Los Angeles,
California.

Miles Davis septet personnel as above, with the Michel Legrand orchestra and Chuck Findley (tp).

The Arrival	WB26438
Concert On The Runway	–
The Departure	–
Trumpet Cleaning	–
The Dream	–

	Paris Walking II	–
	The Music Room	–
	The Jam Session	–
	Going Home	–

DOO-BOP
(7599-26938)   Miles Davis (tp), with Easy Mo Bee and other rappers.
1991
Jan or Feb   Mystery   WB26938
NYC   The Doo-Bop Song   –
                 Chocolate Chip   –
                 High Speed Chase   –
                 Blow   –
                 Sonya   –
                 Fantasy   –
                 Duke Booty   –
                 Mystery (reprise)   –

MILES DAVIS AND QUINCY JONES
LIVE AT MONTREUX
(9362-45221-2)   Miles Davis and Wallace Roney (tp), Kenny Garrett (as), with
1991   the Gil Evans orchestra and the George Gruntz Concert Band
8 July   together conducted by Quincy Jones.
Casino
Montreux,   Boplicity   WB45221
Switzerland   Springsville   –
                 Maids of Cadiz   –
                 The Duke   –
                 My Ship   –
                 Miles Ahead   –
                 Blues For Pablo
                 Orgone   –
                 Gone, Gone, Gone   –
                 Summertime   –
                 Here Come De Honey Man –
                 The Pan Piper   –
                 Solea   –

BLACK DEVIL
(Bootleg CD)
Beech Marten Records (Italy)
(BM 043-2)
Miles Davis and friends:
                 Miles Davis (tp, keyb); Kenny Garrett (as); Deron Johnson
1991   (keyb); Joe 'Foley' McCreary (g); Richard Patterson (el-b);
10 July   Ricky Wellman (d).

La Grande Halle	Perfect Way	WB unissued
La Vilette,	Star People	–
Paris, France	Human Nature	–

Miles Davis (tp, keyb); Steve Grossman (ts), Bill Evans (ss); Chick Corea (elp); Dave Holland (bass); Al Foster (d).
    All Blues   WB unissued

Davis (tp); Wayne Shorter (ss); Bill Evans (ss); Kenny Garrett (as); Joe Zawinul (keyb); Richard Patterson (elb); Al Foster (d).
    In A Silent Way   WB unissued
    It's About That Time   –

Davis (tp); Deron Johnson (keyb); John McLaughlin (g); John Scofield (elg); Darryl Jones (elb); Ricky Wellman (d).
    Katia   WB unissued

Davis (tp); Jackie McLean (as); Steve Grossman (ts); Chick Corea (elp); Dave Holland (b); Al Foster (d).
    Out Of The Blue   WB unissued
    Donna Lee   –

Davis (tp); Bill Evans (ss); Kenny Garrett (as); Herbie Hancock, Deron Johnson (keyb); Joe 'Foley' McCreary (g); Richard Patterson (elb); Al Foster (d).
    Watermelon Man   WB unissued

Davis (tp, keyb); Garrett (as); Johnson (keyb); McCreary (g); Patterson (elb); Ricky Wellman (d).
    Penetration   WB unissued

As for Penetration, but Darryl Jones (elb) replaces Patterson.
    Wrinkle   –

Davis (tp); Wayne Shorter (ss); Chick Corea (elp); Dave Holland (b); Al Foster (d).
    Footprints   –

Miles Davis (tp, keyb); Bill Evans (ss); Jackie McLean, Kenny Garrett (as); Wayne Shorter, Steve Grossman (ts); Chick Corea (elp); Deron Johnson (keyb); John Scofield, John McLaughlin, Joe 'Foley' McCreary (elg); Dave Holland (b); Darryl Jones, Richard Patterson (elb); Al Foster, Ricky Wellman (d).
    Jean Pierre   WB unissued

Miles Davis's last concert was at the Hollywood Bowl, California, on 25 August 1991 and he died a month later on 28 September. Many bootleg recordings exist of live sessions from various periods of his career. It is likely that the bulk of his official musical legacy will remain perennially available. Below is a list of some of his earlier recordings re-released on CD and currently available.

WALKIN' Miles Davis All-Stars
Prestige (LP 7076) OJCCD-213-2. Rec. 3 April and 29 April 1954

BAGS' GROOVE
Prestige (P 7109) OJCCD-245-2. Rec. 29 June and 24 December 1954

MILES DAVIS AND THE MODERN JAZZ GIANTS
Prestige (7150) OJCCD-347-2. Rec. 24 December 1954

COOKIN'/RELAXIN' The Miles Davis Quintet
Prestige (7094/7129) CDJZD 003. From sessions 11 May and 26 October 1956

The following are all on SONY JAZZ:

THE MILES DAVIS TADD DAMERON QUINTET
Paris Festival International de Jazz
(485257 2) live rec. May 1949

'ROUND ABOUT MIDNIGHT
(460605 2) The Miles Davis quintet. Rec. 1955–56

MILES AHEAD
(CK 65121) Miles Davis and Gil Evans. Rec. 1957

MILESTONES
(460827 2) Miles Davis sextet. Rec. 1958

PORGY & BESS
(CK 65141) Miles Davis and Gil Evans. Rec. 1958

JAZZ AT THE PLAZA Vol 1
(471510 2) Miles Davis sextet. Rec. 1958

KIND OF BLUE
(CK 64935) Miles Davis sextet. Rec. 1959

SKETCHES OF SPAIN
(CK 65142) Miles Davis and Gil Evans. Rec. 1959–60

SOMEDAY MY PRINCE WILL COME
(466312 2) Miles Davis quintet. Rec. March 1961

FRIDAY NIGHT AT THE BLACKHAWK
(463334 2) Miles Davis quintet. Rec. April 1961

SATURDAY NIGHT AT THE BLACKHAWK
(465191 2) Miles Davis quintet. Rec. April 1961

MILES DAVIS AT CARNEGIE HALL
(2CD) (472357 2) Miles Davis Quintet & Miles Davis with Gil Evans orchestra.
Live rec. 19 May 1961

QUIET NIGHTS
(CK 65293) Miles Davis with Gil Evans orch. Rec. July and November 1962

SEVEN STEPS TO HEAVEN
(466970 2) Miles Davis quintet. Rec. April Los Angeles and May New York
1963

MILES IN ANTIBES
(462960 2) Miles Davis quintet. Rec. July 1963

THE COMPLETE CONCERT 1964
(2CD) (471246 2) Miles Davis quintet, My Funny Valentine & Four & More.
Rec. 12 February 1964 at Philharmonic Hall NYC

MILES IN BERLIN
(CD62976) Miles Davis quintet. Rec. 25 September 1964 Philharmonie, Berlin

MILES DAVIS/E.S.P.
(467899 2) Miles Davis quintet. Rec. January 1965

MILES SMILES
(471004 2) Miles Davis quintet. Rec. October 1966

SORCERER
(474369 2) Miles Davis quintet. Rec. May 1967

NEFERTITI
(467089 2) Miles Davis quintet. Rec. June 1967

MILES IN THE SKY
(472209 2) Miles Davis quintet. Rec. January and May 1968

FILLES DE KILIMANJARO
(467088 2) Miles Davis quintet. Rec. June and September 1968

IN A SILENT WAY
(450982) Miles Davis group. Rec. February 1969

BITCHES BREW
(2CD) (460602 2) Miles Davis ensemble. Rec. August 1969

A TRIBUTE TO JACK JOHNSON
(471003) Miles Davis sextet. Rec. April 1970

BLACK BEAUTY
(2CD) (C2K 65138) Miles Davis sextet. Rec. 10 April 1970, Fillmore West San
Francisco

MILES DAVIS AT FILLMORE
(2CD) (C2K 65139) Miles Davis septet. Rec. 17–20 June 1970, Fillmore East
NYC

LIVE-EVIL
(2CD) (C2K 65135) Miles Davis Various ensembles. Rec. studio NYC June 1970
and live at Cellar Door, Washington, 18 December 1970

ON THE CORNER
(474371 2) Rec. studio NYC June 1972

IN CONCERT
(2CD) (C2K 65140) Rec. live, 29 September 1972, at Philharmonic Hall NYC

DARK MAGUS
(2CD) (C2K 65137) Rec. live, 30 March 1974 at Carnegie Hall NYC

GET UP WITH IT
(2CD) (485256 2) Studio recordings 1970–74

AGHARTA
(2CD) (467897 2) Rec. live February 1975 in Osaka, Japan

PANGAEA
(2CD) (467087 2) Rec. live February 1975, Osaka Japan

THE MAN WITH THE HORN
(468701 2) Rec. 1980–81

WE WANT MILES
(469402) Rec. live 1981, New York City, Boston, Tokyo

CIRCLE IN THE ROUND
(2CD) (467898 2) This contains previously unreleased studio tracks from
1955–70

MILES & JOHN COLTRANE
(460824 2) The Miles Davis sextet live at Newport on 4 July 1958, and two quintet studio tracks from 1955

Sony Jazz have also released some magnificent box-sets including the following:

MILES DAVIS AND GIL EVANS/The Complete Columbia Studio Recordings (6CD) (CXK 67397) this charts the creation of some of the most beautiful orchestral music of the century.

THE COMPLETE LIVE AT THE PLUGGED NICKEL 1965
(8CD) (CXK 66955) Miles with his second great quintet at the Plugged Nickel in Chicago on 22 and 23 December 1965.

THE COMPLETE QUINTET RECORDINGS
(6CD) (CXK 67398) Documents the Columbia studio recordings of Miles's second quintet from January 1965 to June 1968.

PANTHALASSA
(CK 67909) Is a very effective suite Bill Laswell has created by remixing and reconstructing some of the music from Davis's more discursive period, 1969–1974.

Miles Davis's recorded output, which has rightly been called 'one of the greatest musical legacies of the twentieth century', is so vast that this biography could not accommodate a fully comprehensive discography. People interested in the complete discography should acquire Jan Lohmann's magnificent, 400-page book, *The Sound of MILES DAVIS: The Discography 1945–1991*, published (1992) by JazzMedia ApS, Dorheavej 39, DK-2400, Copenhagen NV, Denmark. Lohmann's book is a meticulously organized act of love.

Ian Carr

Index